Tahiti &
French Polynesia
a Lonely Planet travel survival kit

Tony Wheeler
Jean-Bernard Carillet

Tahiti & French Polynesia

4th edition

Published by
Lonely Planet Publications
Head Office: PO Box 617, Hawthorn, Vic 3122, Australia
Branches: 155 Filbert St, Suite 251, Oakland, CA 94607, USA
10 Barley Mow Passage, Chiswick, London W4 4PH, UK
71 bis rue du Cardinal Lemoine, 75005 Paris, France

Printed by
Pac-Rim Kwartanusa Printing
Printed in Indonesia

Photographs by
Tony Wheeler
Jean-Bernard Carillet
Lionel Pizzoli
Tahiti Tourism Board

Front cover: Hand-painted pareu, Maharepa village, Moorea (Tony Wheeler)
Title page: Rurutu ancestor god A'a

First Published
October 1985

This Edition
January 1997

National Library of Australia Cataloguing in Publication Data

Wheeler, Tony, 1946-.
Tahiti & French Polynesia

4th ed.
Includes index.
ISBN 0 86442 287 3

1. French Polynesia - Guidebooks
I. Carillet, Jean-Bernard. II Kay, Robert F., 1953-.
Tahiti and French Polynesia. III. Title. (Series: Lonely Planet travel survival kit).

919.6204

text & maps © Lonely Planet 1997
photos © photographers as indicated 1997
climate chart for the Tuamotus compiled from information supplied by Patrick J Tyson, © Patrick J Tyson, 1997

Tony Wheeler

Tony was born in England but grew up in Pakistan, the Bahamas and the USA. He returned to England to do a degree in engineering at Warwick University, worked as an automotive design engineer, returned to London Business School to complete an MBA, then set out on an Asian overland trip with his wife, Maureen. That trip led to Tony and Maureen founding Lonely Planet Publications in Australia in 1973, and they've been travelling, writing and publishing guidebooks ever since. In 1996 they moved to Paris, with their children Tashi and Kieran, for a one-year stay.

Jean-Bernard Carillet

Having obtained master's degrees in translation from the Sorbonne-Nouvelle (Paris) and in international relations (Metz), Jean-Bernard was planning to go on a trip around the world with one-month-old Eva strapped to his back. This was delayed, however, due to a traineeship at Lonely Planet's Paris office, where his consummate skills in the art of tea-making quickly rendered him indispensable. Adopted by one and all, he is currently working at LP France as an editor. Diving instructor and incorrigible traveller, Jean-Bernard dons his walking shoes (and flippers) at the slightest opportunity to travel round the world from Europe to the South Pacific, Africa and the Americas.

From the Authors

Tony Wheeler Thanks to Julia and Jean-Christophe Scolari on Maupiti, without whom I would never have found the top of Teurafaatui, and for all the coconuts we drank on the way up and down; to Philippe Lavaux of Air France and Paris for keeping me on the right side of the road while driving around Raiatea; to Marie-France Philip of the Marie-France Pension for advice, information and a bicycle; to Christoph Muller and Isabel Duvoibin for the invitation to dinner on Tubuai; and to Heidi Lemaire of Blue Pacific Diving Adventures for her information on Huahine.

Jean-Bernard Carillet I would like to express my deepest gratitude to my friend Yan Peirsegaele, a translator and talented dancer, and to his family, for their warm welcome and the sumptuous *maa tahiti* dishes prepared by Yan's mother and grandmother. (You can enjoy a sample too – see their recipe for raw fish in coconut milk in the Facts for the Visitor chapter.) I'm grateful to Yan for having acquainted me with the mysteries of the Tahitian language.

Many thanks to the Majerus-Polidor family (Luce, François and Cathy), who share my passion for the Marquesas and who travelled with me part of the way in Nuku Hiva. I saved lots of time thanks to their invaluable tips.

I'm equally indebted to Yvette Tabah (for flight bookings), Olivier Cirendini (who lent me photographic equipment), Moearii Darius (Air Tahiti), Yann Beugnet, Jacques Dordillon,

Pierro Ottino Jean-Pierre Duponchel, Tiare Sanford, Didier Vogel, Christel Masini, Ludovic Berne, Jean-Pierre Moreau and Michel Carrade for all their help.

Many apologies to Christine and Eva for all the times I wasn't there.

This Edition

The first three editions of *Tahiti & French Polynesia* were written by Robert Kay. This edition was completely rewritten by Tony Wheeler and Jean-Bernard Carillet. Jean-Bernard covered the Tuamotus and Marquesas, contributed much of the diving information for the Society Islands and also much of the walking and mountain climbing information. Tony covered the Society Islands and the Australs. Both authors had visited French Polynesia before, Jean-Bernard spending two months in the Society Islands and Rangiora with his partner and their daughter.

From the Publisher

This book was edited in Lonely Planet's Melbourne office by Rowan McKinnon with help from Suzi Petkovski, Liz Filleul and Janet Austin. Lou Callan prepared the language section, Kerrie Williams produced the index and Adrienne Costanzo proofed the book. Jane Hart coordinated the mapping, drew the illustrations and designed the book and colour wraps. Other cartographers who contributed were Maliza Kruh, Matt King, Andrew Tudor and Jenny Jones. The cover was designed by David Kemp and Michael Signal. The French parts of the book were translated by Anne Richardson, Véronique Lyttle and Adrienne Costanzo. Special thanks to Jane Hart for great work and good coffee, Adrienne Costanzo for a mighty effort and help assembling a jigsaw puzzle, and French-edition editor Isabelle Mueller for trans-hemispheric help.

Thanks to the many travellers who wrote with comments:

Cornelio G Ancheta, Hanne & Casper Andersen, Ina Anderson, Maria Arlidge, Sophie Aruanitopoulos, Nikki & Ray Barber, RJ Basra, Tracy Benson, Sylvia Bergman, Donna Bolton & Ed Blair, Joy Bloom, David Bulgci, Mario Dorg, Mrs P Drennan, Paddy Browne, Harold Bruce, Rowland Burley, Lawrence Calder, Jennifer Carioto, Glen Chabot, BT Cousins, Chris Crumley, Baron CR von der Decuen, Graham Dowden, Mari Fagin, La Petite Ferme, Deborah Girasek, Vera Graaf, Hermione Grinston, Jackie & Casey Halter, Laurence Hirschhorn, Boudry Hjalmar, Karen Landstad, Earle Layser, Pamela Osgood & Steve Leeds, Andy Leitner, Edward Lister, Werner Loher, Ian Mackersey, Isabelle Main, Marian G Maksimowicz, Stephanie Malach, Eriko de la Mare, Pat Mathews, Albrizio Mauro, Michael Monsour, Stephen Mortimer, Lee Nevchell, Seth Norman, Bill & Laura O'Connor, T O'Grady, Pamela Osgood, Ross C Palm, Joe Parkhurst, Veronica Proud, Chad Reed, Ralph Reed, Suzanne Reider, James & Pamela Russ, Samantha Sams, Sandi Fisher Schmidt, M & C Seaton, Jim & Sharey Shafer, Don Lee & Mary Simmons, Janice Simpson, Vincent & Virgini Soustrot, Urs Steiger, Jay J Stemmer, Richard Tack, Peter Taylor, JE Taylor, Vicki Thiele, Mr Thomas, Jay Trimble, Armin Uhlig, Mark A Varnau, Ellen Wagner, Rich & Alison Wald, Espin Walderhang, Mr & Mrs Alan Watkins, Marguerite Watkins, Birgit Wijsmans, Dave Williams, Kathleen Yasuda & Alberto Cioni

Warning & Request

Things change – prices go up, schedules change, good places go bad and bad places go bankrupt – nothing stays the same. So, if you find things better or worse, recently opened or long since closed, please tell us and help make the next edition even more accurate and useful.

We value the feedback we receive from travellers. Julie Young coordinates a small team who read and acknowledge every letter, postcard and email, and ensure that every morsel of information finds its way to the appropriate authors, editors and publishers.

Everyone who writes to us will find their name in the next edition of the appropriate guide and will also receive a free subscription to our quarterly newsletter, *Planet Talk*. The very best contributions will be rewarded with a free Lonely Planet guide.

Excerpts from your correspondence may appear in updates (which we add to the end pages of reprints); new editions of this guide; in our newsletter, *Planet Talk*; or in the Postcards section of our Web site – so please let us know if you don't want your letter published or your name acknowledged.

Contents

Map Legend

BOUNDARIES

............International Boundary
............Regional Boundary

ROUTES

............Freeway
............Highway
............Major Road
............Unsealed Road or Track
............City Road
............City Street
............Railway
............Underground Railway
............Tram
............Walking Track
............Walking Tour
............Ferry Route
............Cable Car or Chairlift

AREA FEATURES

............Parks
............Built-Up Area
............Pedestrian Mall
............Market
............Cemetery
............Reef
............Beach or Desert
............Rocks

HYDROGRAPHIC FEATURES

............Coastline
............River, Creek
............Intermittent River or Creek
............Rapids, Waterfalls
............Lake, Intermittent Lake
............Canal
............Swamp

SYMBOLS

✪ CAPITAL	............National Capital	............Embassy, Petrol Station
◉ Capital	............Regional Capital	............Airport, Airfield
⬤ CITY	............Major City	............Swimming Pool, Dive Sites
● City	............City	............Shopping Centre, Zoo
● Town	............Town	............Winery or Vineyard, Picnic Site
● Village	............Village	............One Way Street, Distance Marker
■ ▼	............Place to Stay, Place to Eat	............Stately Home, Monument
☎ ▼	............Cafe, Pub or Bar	............Castle, Tomb
✉ ☎	............Post Office, Telephone	............Cave, Hut or Chalet
❶ ⑤	............Tourist Information, Bank	............Mountain or Hill, Lookout
◉ Ⓟ	............Transport, Parking	............Lighthouse, Shipwreck
�🏛 ⌂	............Museum, Youth Hostel	............Pass, Spring
⚷ ⚑	............Caravan Park, Camping Ground	............Beach, Surf Beach
✝ ✚	............Church, Cathedral	............Archaeological Site or Ruins
☪ ✡	............Mosque, Synagogue	............Ancient or City Wall
⚑ ✿	............Temple, Gardens	............Cliff or Escarpment, Tunnel
✛ ★	............Hospital, Police Station	............Railway Station

Note: not all symbols displayed above appear in this book

Introduction

From the time the first European explorers returned from Tahiti with their reports of a paradise on earth, the islands of Polynesia have exerted a magnetic attraction. Of course much of it was fantasy and Louis-Antoine de Bougainville, the aristrocratic French explorer who narrowly missed the honour of being the first European arrival, started the game by musing about 'noble savages' and dubbing the island 'New Cytheria', after the legendary birthplace of Aphrodite, goddess of love.

There was no shortage of followers as succeeding visits brought back vivid descriptions of exotic temples where human sacrifices and other strange rites were practised, chieftains with fleets of magnificent outrigger canoes and, far from least important to European interests, beautiful women and erotic dances. Soon Tahiti became a popular haven for passing explorers and then a retreat for whaling ships, a profitable port for Pacific traders and a treasure trove of lost souls for missionaries to convert. The effect on the unfortunate Polynesians was disastrous. Within a generation their native culture had been all but obliterated. Besieged with new weapons which turned their partly ceremonial wars into deadly clashes, new poisons like alcohol and new diseases to which they had no natural immunity, their population was soon in free fall. As a final indignity the islands became pawns on the European colonial chessboard.

Yet the myth persisted and attracted writers like Herman Melville and Robert Louis Stevenson and artists like Paul Gauguin. The reasons why are incredibly

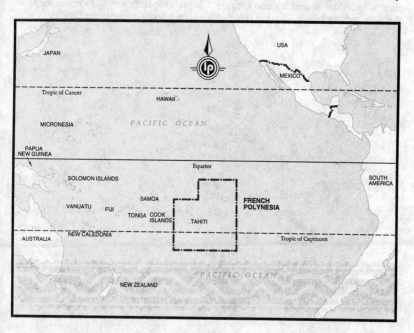

What's in a Name?

Ask where French Polynesia is or what it consists of and many people would have some difficulty in giving you an answer. Ask about Tahiti, however, and a vision of a beautiful tropical island rising from a deep-blue sea immediately materialises on the map. The reality is that Tahiti is just one island in one of the five island groups which make up French Polynesia. It's the largest island, the best known and the most historically interesting, but for visitors it's just one corner of a larger picture. In turn, French Polynesia is only part of the whole Polynesian or 'many islands' region of the South Pacific. The Cook Islands are the other major Polynesian island group, but the Maoris of New Zealand, the native Hawaiians and the people of Easter Island are also Polynesians. ■

simple and one glance out of your aircraft window as it spirals down over the lagoon to an island like Bora Bora tells it all, this is a place of incredible beauty. It's also a region of wildly varying beauty from the postcard greens and blues of the mountainous Society Islands to the transparent lagoons edged by white-sand *motus* in the low-lying atolls of the Tuamotus. Further north and east are the savage and mysterious Marquesas while to the south lie the remote and rarely visited Australs and Gambier Islands.

For visitors the natural beauty is a large part of the picture, mixed with a liberal dose of sophisticated restaurants and luxurious resort hotels. The back page of a colourful brochure adds that, unfortunately, you may find the price tag rather painful but, as ever, brochures are only part of the picture. Yes, there are fancy hotels and pricey restaurants, but there are also economical backpacker havens and friendly family pensions. There are cheap snack bars under the palm trees and a small fleet of ships waiting to carry adventurous travellers from island to island. Certainly you can laze on the beaches, but you can also climb mountains, embark on 4WD expeditions, ride bicycles or dive beneath the surface to find some of the most exciting scuba diving in the Pacific.

Facts about the Islands

HISTORY

The Society Islands of Tahiti came into existence sometime between one to three million years ago, the product of huge volcanic eruptions under the sea. Human settlement came much later as the islands of Polynesia and New Zealand were the last places on earth to be settled by humans.

Polynesian Migration

Archaeologists, linguists and anthropologists have argued for years about where the ancestors of today's Polynesians came from and even why they came to the islands of the Pacific. Was it all just a mistake, some great voyage that went astray? Or was it a carefully planned movement, perhaps an escape from land pressures and overpopulation? Because the settlement of the Pacific was, comparatively speaking, so recent, the area holds great interest for academics.

Despite Thor Heyerdahl and his *Kon-Tiki* theories of a South American source, it's generally agreed that the Polynesian people started from South-East Asia and began to move westwards about 3000 to 4000 years ago. The first waves of migration took them to the islands scattered off the north coast of the island of New Guinea (modern Irian Jaya and Papua New Guinea). From there they moved on to the islands of Fiji and Tonga around 1500 BC and then to Samoa around 1000 BC. And there they stopped, becoming the people we know today as Melanesians, who are darker skinned than modern Polynesians.

About 1000 years passed before the next great migration wave, which moved west from around the start of the Christian era to 300 AD. This wave of voyages overshot the Society Islands and the Tuamotus of modern-day French Polynesia and reached the remote Marquesas. Again there was a long pause, perhaps over 500 years, before the next migratory movement. This time the voyages took place in all directions, carrying settlers north to the Hawaiian Islands, south-east to Easter Island and south-west to the Society Islands, all of which were reached by around 850 AD. A final push carried the Polynesian people via Rarotonga in the Cook Islands down to New Zealand around 1000 AD. Thus the Polynesian people of French Polynesia, the native Hawaiians and the Maoris of New Zealand all come from common Marquesan ancestors and all speak a basically similar language, known collectively as Maohi.

These long voyages were phenomenal feats of navigation and endurance. The coconuts, breadfruit, taro and sugar cane, along with dogs, pigs and chickens, carried on the great canoes were all originally brought from South-East Asia.

European Exploration

The idea that a place did not exist until discovered, and preferably named, by a European visitor has been thoroughly discredited in recent decades. Nevertheless the story of the early European explorers and their daring visits to the Pacific is a fascinating one. Finding islands in the Pacific was a needle-in-a-haystack operation, and the primitive navigational instruments were such that, having chanced upon an island, it was equally problematic to locate the same island on a return trip.

Magellan Vasco Núñez de Balboa was the first European to set eyes on the Pacific, but just seven years later, in 1520, Ferdinand Magellan was the first European to actually sail across the vast island-dotted ocean. Sprinkled with islands the Pacific may be, but Magellan managed to miss nearly all of them. The Philippines was his main find and he also came across Guam, but his one sighting in Polynesia was remote Pukapuka, the furthest north-east of the Tuamotus.

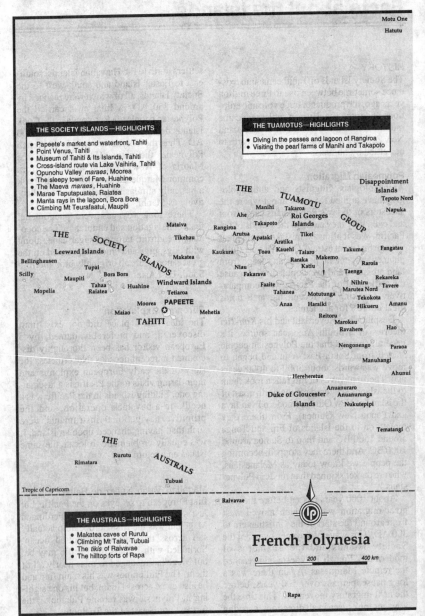

THE SOCIETY ISLANDS—HIGHLIGHTS

- Papeete's market and waterfront, Tahiti
- Point Venus, Tahiti
- Museum of Tahiti & Its Islands, Tahiti
- Cross-island route via Lake Vaihiria, Tahiti
- Opunohu Valley *maraes*, Moorea
- The sleepy town of Fare, Huahine
- The Maeva *maraes*, Huahine
- Marae Taputapuatea, Raiatea
- Manta rays in the lagoon, Bora Bora
- Climbing Mt Teurafaatui, Maupiti

THE TUAMOTUS—HIGHLIGHTS

- Diving in the passes and lagoon of Rangiroa
- Visiting the pearl farms of Manihi and Takapoto

THE TUAMOTU GROUP

Disappointment Islands

Tepoto Nord

Napuka

Manihi Takaroa

Ahe Roi Georges Islands

Mataiva Takapoto

Rangiroa Tikei

Tikehau Arutua Apataki Takume Fangatau

Aratika

Makatea Kaukura Toau Kauehi Taiaro Raroia

Raraka Makemo Taenga

Niau Katiu Rekareka

Fakarava Nihiru Tavere

Faaite Marutea Nord

Tahanea Motutunga Tekokota Amanu

Anaa Haraiki Hikueru

Reitoru

Marokau

Ravahere Hao

Nengonengo Paraoa

Manuhangi

Ahunui

Hereheretue

Anuanuraro

Duke of Gloucester Anuanurunga

Islands Nukutepipi

Tematangi

THE SOCIETY ISLANDS

Leeward Islands

Bellinghausen

Scilly Tupai

Maupiti Bora Bora

Mopelia Tahaa Huahine

Raiatea Tetiaroa

Windward Islands

Maiao Moorea PAPEETE

Mehetia

TAHITI

Motu One

Hatutu

THE AUSTRALS

Rimatara Rurutu

Tubuai

Tropic of Capricorn

Raivavae

French Polynesia

0   200   400 km

THE AUSTRALS—HIGHLIGHTS

- Makatea caves of Rurutu
- Climbing Mt Taita, Tubuai
- The *tikis* of Raivavae
- The hilltop forts of Rapa

Rapa

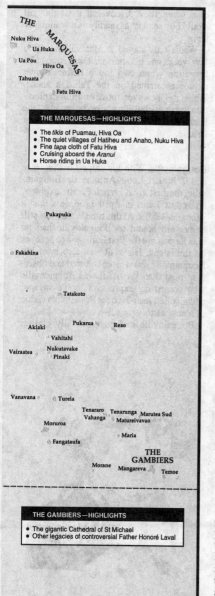

THE MARQUESAS

Nuku Hiva
Ua Huka
Ua Pou
Hiva Oa
Tahuata
Fatu Hiva

THE MARQUESAS—HIGHLIGHTS

- The *tikis* of Puamau, Hiva Oa
- The quiet villages of Hatiheu and Anaho, Nuku Hiva
- Fine *tapa* cloth of Fatu Hiva
- Cruising aboard the *Aranui*
- Horse riding in Ua Huka

Pukapuka

Fakahina

Tatakoto

Akiaki Pukarua Reao
Vahitahi
Vairaatea Nukutavake
Pinaki

Vanavana Tureia

Tenararo Tenarunga Marutea Sud
Vahanga Matureivavao
Moruroa
Maria
Fangataufa

THE
GAMBIERS
Morane Mangareva Temoe

THE GAMBIERS—HIGHLIGHTS

- The gigantic Cathedral of St Michael
- Other legacies of controversial Father Honoré Laval

Mendaña & Quirós Magellan was Portuguese, but in the service of the Spanish, and it was once again Spanish expeditions which made the next major forays into the Pacific. From Acapulco, their Mexican Pacific coast port, the Spanish established trade with Manila. In 1567, Alvaro de Mendaña de Neira set out from Acapulco to search for the great southern continent which was to be the holy grail of European exploration for the next two centuries. He came across the Solomons on that first voyage and in 1595 set out on a return trip. This time he was not able to locate them again, but en route he came upon the Marquesas, the furthest north-east of the Polynesian island groups, which he named Las Marquesas de Mendoza after his patron, the Viceroy of Peru. His visit was a bloody affair as Mendaña was of the 'shoot first and ask questions later' school when it came to encounters with 'savages'.

His chief pilot, Quirós, followed with his own expedition in 1606 and he discovered a number of the Tuamotu Islands before continuing to the Cook Islands and other island groups of the Pacific. This, however, was the end of serious Spanish exploration in the Pacific.

Le Maire & Roggeveen The Dutch, already firmly established in the Dutch East Indies (modern Indonesia), took up the banner and in 1615-16 Jacques Le Maire sailed through the Tuamotus on his way west. Other Dutch explorers started to trace in the boundaries of Australia, New Zealand and other islands of the western Pacific, but it was not until 1722 that the first of the Society Islands, the most important group of modern French Polynesia, was sighted. Jacob Roggeveen came to Easter Island during Easter of that year and continued west through the Tuamotus, passing the island of Makatea on his way to the Society Islands, where he came across Maupiti, the most westerly of the high islands in the group. Since other islands of the group are clearly visible from Maupiti and the natives of Maupiti were well aware of their existence, it's a mystery why

Roggeveen did not 'discover' other islands as well.

Byron, Carteret & Wallis The Dutch were in turn followed by the British, led in 1765 by John Byron, the English admiral and grandfather of the poet. Byron found more of the Tuamotus. He was followed in 1767 by the expedition of Philip Cartaret, in command of HMS *Swallow*, and Samuel Wallis, in HMS *Dolphin*. As they rounded Cape Horn, they lost contact so the small fleet became two separate expeditions both searching for that mythical great southern continent. Cartaret found Pitcairn Island, later to be the refuge of the *Bounty* mutineers, and went on to rediscover Mendaña's long lost Solomons. But Wallis was to carry the real prize home when he became the first European to visit Tahiti.

The *Dolphin* anchored in Tahiti's lagoon, Matavai Bay, in late June, but a quarter of the crew were down with scurvy and poor Wallis was incapacitated below decks during most of his visit. Initially their arrival was greeted with fascination as up to 500 canoes with 4000 men on board, not to mention many canoes each carrying 'a fair young girl... who played a great many droll wanton tricks,' surrounded the ship. Then fascination turned to fear and an attack was launched on the *Dolphin*. Stones rained down upon the ship's crew and when an attempt was made to board the ship the *Dolphin's* cannons, loaded with deadly grapeshot, were turned upon the Tahitians. Two days later the havoc was followed by a further fusillade, on this occasion unprovoked, and a British raiding party went ashore and destroyed 80 canoes.

Surprisingly, this violent show of force did not turn the Tahitians against the explorers and from then on a friendly trade was carried on each day. The crew were desperate for fresh supplies and the Tahitians, who had not yet discovered metals, were delighted to receive knives, hatchets and nails in exchange. At this point the *Dolphin's* crew also took the first steps towards creating the long lasting image of Tahiti as a sexual paradise when they discovered a single nail would buy sex just as readily as it would buy a pig.

Wallis only stayed in Matavai Bay for a few weeks and his short visit was soon to be forgotten when two much better known explorers arrived on the Tahitian scene. Wallis did, however, move on from exploration to empire building when he renamed the island King George's Land and claimed it for Britain.

Bougainville With his ships *La Boudeuse* and *L'Etoile*, Louis-Antoine de Bougainville, the first great French Pacific explorer, arrived at Tahiti in April 1768, less than a year after Wallis. At this time Wallis was still homeward bound so Bougainville had no idea he was not the first European to set eyes on the island. His visit was also brief but Bougainville was a more cultured and observant man than Wallis. It was Bougainville who coined the expression 'noble savage' and inspired Jean-Jacques Rousseau's vision of a new earthly paradise.

Bougainville had no unfriendly clashes

Louis-Antoine de Bougainville (1729-1811)

Two Visitors

Bougainville took a Tahitian named Aotourou back with him to Paris where the explorer was widely fêted but never much at home. It's said that Aotourou was unable to learn more than a dozen words of French and although Bougainville attempted to send him home with a ship bound for the Pacific, he died en route.

Bougainville's crew also brought an unexpected visitor to Tahiti. The ship's naturalist, Dr Philibert Commerçon, had a young valet named Jean Baret (or Baré). On his first visit ashore, the Tahitians immediately took a great interest in him, crowded around him and stripped his clothes off, to reveal that Baret was actually a woman! Commerçon was extremely embarrassed but Baret became not only the first European woman to visit Tahiti but also the first woman to circumnavigate the world. ■

with the Tahitians, in fact quite the reverse. Perhaps it was Bougainville's cultured outlook on life, but he did not complain of 'droll wanton tricks' by half-naked nymphs. In fact, he wryly noted, the Tahitians 'pressed us to choose a woman and come on shore with her; and their gestures, which were not ambiguous, denoted in what manner we should form an acquaintance with her'. When he returned to Europe his reports of Venus-like women with 'the celestial form of that goddess' and of the Tahitians' uninhibited attitude towards matters sexual swept through Paris like wildfire.

Bougainville also discovered a less attractive side to the Tahitian character: they were expert thieves. A year later Cook's expedition was also to suffer from these skilful pickpockets, who quickly carried off anything not closely watched. In part, this proclivity to theft was simply a different attitude towards private property, but equally, it may have been due to the fact that one of the most enduring figures of the Polynesian religion was Hiro, the god of thieves.

Anchorage problems at Bougainville's landing place, well east of Matavai Bay where Wallis, and later Cook and Bligh, all anchored, cut short his visit. Unaware that the Union Jack had already flown over the island, Bougainville also took time out to claim Tahiti for France but, like Wallis, he was soon to be overshadowed when the greatest Pacific explorer of them all arrived on the scene.

Cook In three great expeditions between 1769 and 1779, Cook filled out the map of the Pacific so comprehensively that future expeditions were reduced to completing the fine details. Cook had been sent to the Pacific with two great tasks. One was for the Royal Society, to observe the transit of Venus as it passed across the face of the sun. By timing the transit from three very distant places it was hoped that the distance from the earth to the sun could be calculated. Tahiti, news of which had just reached England from the Wallis expedition, was selected as one of the three measuring points (the other two were in Norway and Canada). Cook's second objective was to hunt for the elusive great continent of the south.

The instruments of the time proved to be insufficiently accurate to achieve Cook's first objective and, of course, the great southern continent was never to be found, but

Omai

The Bougainville expedition brought Autourou back to Paris, but he died on the return trip, while Cook's first expedition took back two Tahitians, Tupai and Tayeto, both of whom died during the *Endeavour's* disastrous layover in Batavia. During Cook's second expedition, two Tahitians, Odiddy and Omai, joined the two ships for their long loop south to New Zealand and towards the Antarctic. After the return to Tahiti, Omai continued with the second ship, the *Discovery*, back to England. He stayed in England for 11 months and met King George III. 'How do, King Tosh,' he is reputed to have declared. Cook took him back to Tahiti on his third expedition but his return was not altogether a happy one. The Tahitian nobility were clearly unenthusiastic about welcoming a rich commoner into their midst and Cook eventually had to leave him in Huahine. ■

The Island of Love

The first European visitors to Tahiti brought back descriptions of beautiful islands populated by a handsome people who were superb navigators, but the part of the tale which really intrigued London and Paris was simple: sex. The *Dolphin's* official report was matter-of-fact and dull, but already the below-decks gossip was constructing the great Tahitian dream: an island of beautiful women and handsome men where love was unconstrained.

If Wallis was uncommunicative, Bougainville compensated with his tales of a New Cytheria and Dr Commerçon's gushing avowals that the Tahitians knew 'no other god than love'. Cook was much more matter-of-fact but his prosaic reports simply confirmed suspicions about Tahiti, where young girls would 'dance a very indecent dance' while 'singing most indecent songs' all the while 'keeping time to a great nicety'. Furthermore they enjoyed recounting 'the most indecent ideas in conversation without the least emotion.'

Sex, 1t would appear, was simply part of everyday Tahitian life, to be enjoyed just like a good meal. However, visiting sailors began exchanging sex for nails (coveted by the locals for making fish hooks), thereby jumping the gap to prostitution and contributing to the rapid decline of the Polynesian culture. ■

otherwise Cook's arrival in Tahiti was the start of one of the most impressive scientific expeditions of all time. Cook was the perfect man for the task, an expert seaman, a brilliant navigator, a keen observer, an inspiring leader and an indefatigable explorer. Furthermore he was ably supported by endlessly enthusiastic and inquisitive associates, most notably the wealthy young Joseph Banks. As a result Cook's expedition brought the wonders of not only Tahiti but also New Zealand and Australia home to an appreciative European audience.

Cook arrived in Tahiti on board the *Endeavour* in April 1769 and stayed for three months before sailing south to New Zealand and Australia. His comprehensive survey of the Australian east coast ended in a disastrous encounter with the Great Barrier Reef. After emergency repairs, the *Endeavour* limped into Batavia, the capital of the Dutch East Indies (present-day Jakarta). The enforced stop for repairs in the desperately unhealthy city was a disaster as dysentery and malaria killed seven of the crew during the three-month stop and 23 more died on the way home. Nevertheless the voyage was considered a resounding success and Cook returned to Tahiti during a second expedition in 1772-75 and a third in 1776-80. Cook was killed during a clash with Hawaiians in early 1779.

Boenechea The history of Tahiti's European discovery and early contact is so redolent with familiar British and French names that it's easy to forget there was also an early Spanish visitor. The Spanish, firmly established in South America, looked upon the Pacific as their backyard and were less than happy to hear of the visits to Tahiti by other European navigators. Accordingly, in 1772 the *Aguilla*, under Don Domingo de Boenechea, was despatched from Peru, anchored in the lagoon off Tautira on Tahiti Iti and, for the third time, claimed the island on behalf of a European nation. Boenechea took four Tahitians back with him to Lima for a short indoctrination course, but while he was away Cook returned on his 1774 visit and this time also paused off Tautira. Boenechea came back later in the year with two of the four Tahitians. (Of the other two, one had died in Lima and one opted to remain there.) Boenenchea established Tautira as the first long-term European settlement on the island with two missionaries and two military men. He died on Tahiti during the course of his second visit.

Twelve months later, in 1775, the *Aguilla* was back from Peru again. The Spanish missionaries, who had been spectacularly unsuccessful at converting the heathen, were more than happy to scuttle back to Peru. Thus ended the Spanish role in Tahiti, but

Cook had the last word. He was back at Tautira again in 1777 where he found the Spanish cross in front of the abandoned mission house, carved with the 1774 year of its establishment. On the back of the cross Cook added the far more impressive list of Tahitian visits by his own and Wallis' expeditions.

The Mutiny on the Bounty

Wallis made his brief visit to Tahiti in 1767, Bougainville paid his compliments to the earthly paradise in 1768, Cook made his three definitive visits between 1769 and 1779, punctuated by the Spanish forays from Peru, but after that there was a pause of nearly 10 years. It was an important break because it marked the transition from exploration to the first phase of exploitation. Perhaps the first whaling ship turned up at this time but the next recorded visit to Tahiti took place in 1788, when the *Lady Penryhn*, part of Australia's First Fleet carting convicts to Botany Bay, dropped in to Tahiti on its way home. Quite why it stopped there is a mystery – the entire crew was in the final throes of scurvy but perhaps they were simply the first tourists? They didn't stay long and no sooner had they sailed off than a boat which was to be much more famous turned up.

European involvement in Tahiti's history has had some colourful chapters but none more so than the *Bounty* incident. It made HMS *Bounty* one of the most famous ships in history, made William Bligh's name a byword for bad-tempered cruelty and was certainly the most famous naval mutiny in history. It also inspired three Hollywood extravaganzas, almost the sum total of cinematic interest in Tahiti.

Separating myth and reality when it comes to the *Bounty* and Bligh is nearly impossible. The facts are fairly simple. Food was needed to sustain the African slaves working the profitable plantations of the Caribbean. Someone had the bright idea that the breadfruit of Polynesia would make a fine

---

The Great Problems – Navigation & Scurvy

Early European exploration of the Pacific was bedevilled by two great problems: knowing where they were and avoiding illness. Today, when pocket-calculator-size GPS navigation systems have consigned sextants to the world's maritime museums, it's hard to envisage what a huge problem navigation was to these pioneering sailors. By taking sights on the elevation of the sun above the horizon they could work out their latitude, the distance north or south of the equator, with reasonable accuracy. But calculating longitude, the position east or west around the world, was almost impossible. So when an early explorer chanced upon some undiscovered island, marking its location for a return trip was far from simple.

Not only were the crews uncertain of their position, but on long ocean crossings they were often desperately ill. Without methods of preserving fresh food, the diet on board soon became abominably distasteful and unhealthy and expeditions were frequently plagued by the dreaded sailor's disease: scurvy. The crew's limbs and gums would swell, teeth would loosen, depression and lassitude would set in and death often resulted. The cure was a simple one – fresh food – but where to find it on the endless ocean crossings?

The Wallis and Cook expedition came at a time of major onslaughts on these twin problems. The invention of the sextant, replacing the primitive astrolabe, allowed latitude to be calculated with much greater accuracy. Furthermore, by calculating the angle between the moon and certain stars and relating it to the local time, the longitude could also be calculated using tables known as Lunars. Of course the only way of telling the time was by pinpointing noon, when the sun was directly overhead, but nevertheless Wallis was able to record the position of Tahiti with some accuracy. Cook's second expedition took another major step forward when the ship was equipped with a chronometer and a reliable and accurate clock. Time was always related to England.

Wallis, Bougainville and Cook also pioneered new attacks on the problem of scurvy. On the *Dolphin* a quarter of the crew were suffering its effects when they anchored at Tahiti but at least nobody had died. Soon after, Bougainville and then Cook arrived with substantially healthy crews, in part because of the miraculous benefits of a regular diet of pickled vegetables in the form of sauerkraut. ■

New Names
The early European explorers' passion for laying claim to any piece of land they chanced upon, irrespective of the claims for prior possession by any current inhabitants, and at the same time renaming it, was certainly applied to Tahiti. Wallis no sooner dropped anchor in 1767 than he claimed the island for Britain and renamed it King George's Land. Neighbouring Moorea was tagged the Duke of York's Island. A year later Bougainville claimed the island for France and dubbed it New Cytheria, after the legendary birthplace of Aphrodite, the goddess of love. Cook, of course, fell in with Wallis but fortunately he also recorded the locals' own appellation Otaheite, which in pronunciation is probably even closer to reality than 'Tahiti'. The O is simply 'It is'.

Cook asked, 'What island is this?'

And the Tahitians replied, 'O Taheite'. It is Tahiti.

A third European name was applied in 1772 when the Spanish explorer Boenechea popped by, claimed the island for Spain and decided Isla de Amat sounded good. Tahiti definitely sounds better than any of the European suggestions but some explorers' names have stuck: Point Venus, for example, and the Society Islands. ■

substitute for bread, rice, bananas or any other starch food you care to mention. Sir Joseph Banks, botanist on Cook's first expedition and then Britain's number one man of science, agreed that breadfruit was the ideal plant, and Bligh was sent off to convey them from Tahiti to the Caribbean. He was perfectly qualified for the job, an expert navigator who had learnt his trade under Cook and had already visited Tahiti once.

His expedition started late in 1787, found it impossible to round stormy Cape Horn and had to double back and sail right around the world eastbound to Tahiti. As a result the *Bounty* arrived in Tahiti, after an arduous 10-month voyage, at a time when the breadfruit-tree saplings could not be immediately transplanted. This meant they had to remain in Tahiti for six long, languorous months. Eventually, with the breadfruit trees loaded on board, the *Bounty* set sail, westbound, for the Caribbean. Three weeks later, on 28 April

1789, when passing by the Tonga islands, the crew, led by the mate, Fletcher Christian, mutinied and took over the ship.

Bligh was pushed on to the *Bounty's* launch with 18 faithful crew members and set adrift. That might have been the end of Bligh, but whatever the controversy about his management style nobody has ever denied that he was a champion navigator and sailor. With consummate skill he sailed his overloaded little boat across the Pacific, past islands inhabited by hostile cannibals, threaded it through the dangerous complexities of the Great Barrier Reef and through Torres Strait, rounded the north-east coast of Australia and eventually made landfall in Dutch-controlled Timor after a 41-day, 5823-km voyage which was promptly written into the record books.

By early 1790 Bligh was back in England; an inquiry quickly cleared him of negligence and a ship was despatched to carry British naval vengeance to Tahiti. Christian and his mutineers had not all meekly waited for justice to catch up. After dumping Bligh in late April, the *Bounty* returned to Tahiti and hung around for less than a month before sailing off to find a more remote hideaway. Two attempts were made to settle on Tubuai in the Austral Islands (see the *Bounty* section in the Australs chapter for more details of the saga). After the second Tubuai interlude had ended without success, Christian returned briefly to Tahiti, where the mutineers split into two groups, a larger group remaining there while a smaller group left with Christian and the *Bounty* in late September and simply disappeared.

So what happened to the two bands of mutineers? Well, the 16 who remained in Tahiti met exactly the fate Christian had predicted. Vengeance arrived in 1791 in the shape of HMS *Pandora*. Captain Edward Edwards, who made Bligh look like a thoroughly nice guy, quickly rounded up the 14 surviving mutineers (two had already been killed in disputes), told their new Tahitian wives they were going back to Britain to get their just desserts and stuffed the lot into a cage on deck to travel home in considerable discomfort. Arriving at the Great Barrier Reef, Edwards proved to be nowhere near the navigational equal of Bligh and sent his ship to the bottom on Pandora's Reef. Four of the mutineers went with it as the key to 'Pandora's Box' was only 'found' at the last moment. Back in Britain the surviving 10 mutineers were put on trial. Six of them were eventually sentenced to death but three were reprieved. Some of these 'mutineers' probably had no part in the mutiny since Bligh's overloaded getaway boat was close to foundering with 19 men aboard, and there were probably other crew who would have followed their captain had there been room.

As for Christian's mob, eight or nine British seamen, together with six male and 12 female Tahitians, sailed all the way to uninhabited Pitcairn Island, where many years later reports trickled back of a strange little English-Tahitian colony, where half the residents bore the surname Christian. Today, thanks to Fletcher Christian's mutiny, Pitcairn Island is one of the last vestiges of the British Empire.

Bligh himself was back in Tahiti in 1792, this time in command of HMS *Providence* and with 19 marines to make sure there was no possibility of similar problems second time round. Bligh duly picked up his breadfruit saplings and transported them back to the Caribbean in record time where, of course, the ungrateful slaves never developed a taste for them. Surprisingly, given all the trouble spent on trying to take breadfruit to a new home, Bligh's voyages did manage to successfully transfer two other plants to a much more appreciative audience. On his first voyage he picked up pineapples in Rio de Janiero and introduced them to Tahiti where they remain popular to this day. On his second voyage he brought the apple to Tasmania, and even today the island is known as Australia's 'Apple Isle'.

The Mutineers & the Pomares

The effects on Tahiti of the *Bounty* mutiny lasted long after the mutineers had been rounded up and carted back to England. Prior to the arrival of Europeans, Polynesian power had essentially been a local affair. Certainly the war-like rulers of Bora Bora, propelled by their lack of arable land, frequently sailed off to wreak havoc on neighbouring Raiatea, but essentially no ruler was strong enough to extend control very far. Tahiti was in fact divided into a number of squabbling groups, who, when they tired of fighting with each other, sailed off to take on Moorea. European arms would soon change all this.

The Tahitians had quickly realised the importance of European weaponry and had pressed the early explorers to take sides in local conflicts. Cook and the other early visitors had strenuously resisted this, but with the *Bounty* mutineers it was a different proposition. They offered themselves as mercenaries to the highest bidder and the highest bidders were the Pomares. The first of the Pomare dynasty, Pomare I, was Tu, the nephew of Obarea, the 'fat, bouncing, good looking dame' who befriended both Wallis and Cook and whom the early explorers thought was the 'queen' of Tahiti. Before the arrival of the *Bounty*, the Pomares were simply one of a number of important family power centres, but they were by no means the most important and certainly not the most prestigious. The mutineers and their weapons were the first step towards one group controlling all of Tahiti and the Pomares were destined to become the most important rulers of the islands. Pomare I already controlled most of Tahiti when he died in 1803 and then his son, Pomare II, took over.

Missionaries, Whalers, Traders & Depopulation

The early explorers were portents of the dangers to come and the mutineers were a murderous, but brief, revelation of the impact of European technology. But the real disaster arrived in the early 19th century in the form of missionaries and traders. The double-pronged attack was insidious and for the Polynesians utterly disastrous. Within a few decades their culture had been virtually

Mutiny Theories

Exactly why the mutiny on the *Bounty* took place is one of those questions that is never going to be answered, but there are two equally colourful theories. The 'Bligh the monster' theory posits that he was an unbearably cruel and despotic captain who made his men's life a living hell and only got what he deserved. That was certainly the portrait of Bligh painted in the first two Hollywood efforts where Bligh was busily flogging his crew even before he'd sailed from England. In fact the records show that nobody got flogged until nearly three months into the trip and although Bligh would certainly have been a tough captain, as they all were, he was by no means unusually brutal.

The alternative theory puts it all down to sex and the fact that Tahiti was seen as some sort of earthly paradise. The cinematic *Bounty* I and II certainly hint at that side of the story but the *Bounty* III film, with lots of female nudity and some quite breathtakingly lush scenery, makes Tahiti look like some sort of fantasy. The truth probably lies somewhere between the alternative theories. On the other hand, fantasy or not, life on beautiful Tahiti must have had some real charm compared to cold and miserable Britain and the tough life of a seaman.

Whether Bligh provoked the mutiny or not it's certainly fact that there were two more mutinies during his dramatic career. In 1797 he suffered another naval mutiny and in 1808, as governor of the colony of New South Wales in Australia, he was on the wrong side of a mutiny by the notorious Rum Corps. In both cases Bligh came out of the subsequent enquiries smelling of roses. ■

---

destroyed and their population was in a freefall that, for a time, looked like destroying them as well.

Descriptions of Tahiti and its people had European intellectuals speculating on theories of the noble savage, but before long devout church-goers were planning to do something about the savages, noble or not. Heathen religion, infanticide and human sacrifices could all be stamped out, nudity could be covered up and sex could be put in its proper place – behind closed doors. To put these goals into action 30 members of the London Missionary Society (LMS) set out on the *Duff* to bring Christianity to the Pacific. In March 1797, 25 of them landed at Point Venus and set to work, their eventual success can be measured by the Protestant churches dotting islands throughout the Society group, the Tuamotus and the Australs.

Success, however, was not immediate and within a few years most of the original missionaries had drifted off. Pomare II fell from power in 1808 and the remaining Tahitian missionaries, too closely associated with him, also had to flee the island. Pomare II took refuge in Moorea but when he returned to power in Tahiti in 1815 Christianity came too. The missionaries may have had the best

intentions but their effects were often disastrous and their new beliefs killed off the old ones. Soon dancing was forbidden, singing indecent songs was certainly out, tattoos and even wearing flowers in the hair were banned, cover-all clothing was decreed, silence on Sunday was enforced and, most important, indiscriminate sex was outlawed. A century later, the English writer Robert Keable, who had been a vicar with the Church of England, commented about the pioneering missionary William Ellis that 'it was a thousand pities that the Tahitians did not convert Mr Ellis'.

Whalers started to appear in Polynesian waters in the 1790s, even before the first missionaries arrived. Sailing from England, and later from the New England region of the newly independent USA, and crewed by uncompromisingly tough men, they hunted whales in southern waters during the summer months, then retreated to islands like Tahiti during the winter, buying supplies and spreading diseases. Traders also started to appear from the convict colonies of Australia, trading weapons for food supplies, encouraging prostitution and establishing stills to produce alcohol.

Listless, disinterested and plagued by diseases against which they had no natural immunity, the population began to plummet. Cook had estimated the population of Tahiti at 200,000, although it's felt that 40,000 was probably a more accurate figure. In 1800 another estimate put the population at less than 20,000 and by the 1820s it was certainly down to around 6000. In the Marquesas the situation was even worse – it has been estimated the population dropped from 80,000 to only 2000 in one century.

The Pomares & the Missionaries

After 1815 the Pomares ruled Tahiti but the English Protestant missionaries were the power behind the throne, advising on government and laws and doing their best to keep unsavoury influences, like whalers and Australian traders, at arm's length. Pomare II had adopted Christianity more as a conve-

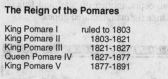

The Reign of the Pomares

King Pomare I	ruled to 1803
King Pomare II	1803-1821
King Pomare III	1821-1827
Queen Pomare IV	1827-1877
King Pomare V	1877-1891

Queen Pomare IV

nience than a real belief and probably drank himself to death in 1821. His son Pomare III was also gone in 1827 and was succeeded by the young Queen Pomare IV.

The new queen's missionary advisers saw her only as an interim ruler until the next king and as a result they turned a blind eye to some of her youthful excesses. The new queen was not averse to a little singing and dancing of the old premissionary days and even visiting passing ships was not unknown. But Queen Pomare was not a passing fancy; she ruled over Tahiti for 50 years, extended her control to other islands in the Austral groups and forged strategic alliances with other islands in the Society group. Unhappily, she also lived to see her islands fall into the hands of the French.

Perhaps it was Tahiti's very isolation which was the problem. Spain's era as a colonial power had ended and the British had their hands full with Australia, New Zealand and assorted other islands in the Pacific. Places like Tahiti were simply in a vacuum, waiting to suck in some would-be colonial power. The missionaries were effectively the colonial power and the LMS missions reigned supreme in the Societies, the Australs and the Tuamotus, while in the Marquesas and the Gambier Archipelago it was French Catholic missionaries who were in control.

In 1836 Honoré Laval and François Caret, French missionaries from the Gambier Archipelago, were quietly dropped off near Tautira at the eastern extremity of Tahiti Iti (see the Gambiers chapter for more on their extraordinary activities). The reason for this clandestine landing at a remote backwater was very simple: they knew the last thing the English Protestants wanted on Tahiti was French Catholics. Sure enough when they arrived in Papeete they were arrested and deported.

The French Takeover

France was already effectively in control of the Marquesas and the enforced departure of the two French missionaries from Tahiti was treated as a national insult. Demands, claims, counterclaims, payments and apologies shuttled back and forth until 1842, when Admiral Dupetit-Thouars turned up in the ship *La Reine Blanche*, pointed his guns at Papeete and took over. The unhappy queen was forced to yield to the French, and soldiers and Catholic missionaries were promptly landed.

The French, now in control, moved quickly and George Pritchard, the British missionary, consul and unofficial chief adviser to the queen, was arrested and forced to leave the islands. The queen, still hoping for British intervention, fled to Raiatea in 1844 and a guerrilla rebellion broke out in Tahiti and on other islands. French forts around Tahiti confirm that it was a fierce struggle but eventually the rebels were subdued, and by 1846 France had control over Tahiti and Moorea. In 1847 the queen was persuaded to return to Tahiti, but she was now merely a figurehead – the French were in control.

Queen Pomare died in 1877 and she was succeeded by her son, Pomare V. He had little interest in the position, effectively abdicating power in 1881, and drank himself to death in 1891. French power, did not initially include all the Society Islands, which remained with local rulers and their mission advisers. Most of them came under French control in 1888, although rebellions rumbled on in Raiatea until almost the end of the century. Perhaps the Protestant missionaries had the last laugh, as Catholicism has never made serious inroads on the islands originally converted by the Protestants.

20th Century

The foundations of the colonial system, laid during the course of the 19th century, were consolidated at the turn of the 20th century. At the outbreak of WWI, the economy was flourishing. The Établissements français d'Océanie (French Pacific Settlements, or EFO) exported local products (vanilla, cotton, copra, mother-of-pearl and fruit) in exchange for manufactured goods.

French Nuclear Testing

French nuclear testing, undertaken to provide the basis of France's independent *Force de Frappe* (strike force), commenced in the Sahara desert, but Algerian independence forced France to look elsewhere for a testing site. In 1963, General de Gaulle announced that Moruroa and Fangataufa, atolls in the Tuamotus, were to be the lucky sites and testing commenced with atmospheric nuclear explosions in 1966. The Centre d'expérimentations du Pacifique, the euphemistic name for the nuclear-testing programme, soon became a major component of the French Polynesian economy.

In 1963 the USA, USSR and Britain agreed to stop patently unsafe atmospheric testing, although they continued testing underground, but in 1973 France refused a World Court request to halt above-ground testing. In that year the New Zealand government sent a naval ship to Moruroa in protest, the first Greenpeace protest vessels were boarded by French forces and Peru broke off diplomatic relations with France. By 1974, 39 atmospheric tests had been conducted at Moruroa and a further five at Fangataufa. In the face of continuing international opposition to any form of testing, the French then moved their testing underground and from 1981, possibly because of severe damage to the outer slopes of the atoll, drilled the bomb shafts under the central lagoon rather than on motus around the reef edge. Today over 150 tests have been conducted, ranging up to 200 kilotons, more than 10 times as large as the bomb which destroyed Hiroshima. One would have hoped that by this time any competent bomb manufacturer would have been pretty certain the damned things worked.

Despite French protestations that their testing procedures have been perfectly safe, the evidence is far from conclusive. In 1966, an above-ground test for the benefit of de Gaulle was conducted in unsuitable weather conditions because the impatient general would not wait for winds to shift to the desired direction. As a result, fallout was spread across inhabited islands to the west of the Tuamotus. In 1979, a bomb jammed halfway down its 800-metre shaft and since it could not be freed the decision was made to explode it at that depth. It is believed the explosion caused fissures in the outer slopes of the atoll. Tight restrictions on visits to the Gambier Islands, south of the Tuamotus, may be because of French fears that fallout has affected these islands.

This rapid economic and commercial expansion increasingly required a larger work force than was locally available. Colonists, the majority of them French, settled in Polynesia. In 1911, there were about 3500 Europeans in the EFO. Chinese immigration, which began in 1864 with the production of cotton at Atimaona, continued, and the foundations of a multiethnic society were in place.

Although removed from the main theatres of operation, Polynesia was directly involved in both world wars. In WWI, almost 1000 Tahitian soldiers fought Germany in Europe. On 22 September 1914, two German cruisers patrolling the Pacific bombed the Papeete market.

The EFO distinguished themselves again in WWII. With the entry of the US into the war in December 1941, Polynesia acquired strategic significance. To thwart the Japanese advance in the Pacific, the Americans used Bora Bora as a supplies base, in agreement with the Free French authorities. Five thousand soldiers set foot on the island in February 1942. At the same time, young Tahitian and half-Tahitian (mixed race) volunteers in the Pacific Battalion fought from April 1941 side by side with the forces of the Free French.

After the war, the beginnings of a desire for emancipation from metropolitan France gradually took shape. A political party, the RDPT (Democratic Assembly of Tahitian Populations), founded in 1949 by nationalist Pouvanaa a Oopa, took centre stage on the political scene for about 10 years.

The 1960s were a real turning point. On 22 July 1957, the EFO officially became French Polynesia. In the referendum held in September 1958, 65% of Polynesians demonstrated their wish to remain linked to France. Three events in quick succession had a considerable impact on Polynesian society. In 1961, the construction of Faaa international airport helped to make Polynesia less of an enclave. Shortly after, the filming of the superproduction *Mutiny on the Bounty*

Some observers believe that the Moruroa atoll's substructure, riddled with faults from over 100 underground explosions, could fracture and allow contamination to escape into the ocean. International observers have consistently been denied access to large parts of Moruroa, so French assertions that the tests have presented no danger remain unverified.

International and local opposition to nuclear testing in the Pacific has grown stronger and stronger over the years. In 1985 French commandos, in what can only be called a terrorist operation, sank the Greenpeace ship *Rainbow Warrior* in Auckland harbour, New Zealand, killing a Portuguese photographer on board. Dominique Prieur and Alain Mafart, two of the terrorists, were captured, tried and sentenced to 10 years imprisonment on reduced charges of manslaughter rather than murder. The French government pressured New Zealand to allow Prieur and Mafart to be transferred to serve reduced sentences on the island of Hao in the Tuamotus. To no-one's surprise France soon reneged on the agreement, their Club Med-style of prison sentence was ended and they were returned to France, to be rewarded for their parts in the fiasco.

In 1995, recently elected French president Chirac announced that a new series of underground tests would be conducted and a storm of protests broke out worldwide. Pacific nations and countries around the Pacific rim uniformly condemned the announcement and Greenpeace vessels were once again sent into the fray. In Australia the French consulate in Perth was burnt down by protesters and a joke quickly raced around the country that the culprits, if caught, would be rewarded with a resort holiday on the Barrier Reef and a medal. When the first test was conducted in September another round of protests followed around the world and Chile and New Zealand recalled their ambassadors from Paris. Most tellingly, severe rioting broke out in Papeete – buildings were set alight, hundreds of cars were turned over and the Faaa International Airport terminal was badly damaged. In Europe, far from the strong antinuclear sentiment in the Pacific and around the Pacific rim, the French government appears to have no awareness of the strong opposition to its policies. The tests were finally concluded in early 1996 and the French government has announced there will be no further Pacific testing. ■

with Marlon Brando called on thousands of extras and poured millions of dollars into the island's booming economy. In 1963, with the establishment of the Pacific Experimentation Centre (CEP) at Moruroa and Fangataufa, Polynesia came straight into the nuclear age. In addition to the international controversy raised by these 'experiments', the CEP totally overturned the socioeconomic structures of Polynesia, thrusting it straight into a market economy. The signing of a Progress Pact between the State and the Territory in 1993, whereby France has undertaken to continue its aid until 2005, and the final stop to nuclear testing in February 1996, have sounded the death knell for the artificial prosperity of the last 30 years.

Throughout this period, the institutional development of the Territory continued. In July 1977, by virtue of a new statute, Polynesia was granted administrative autonomy, then, in September 1984, domestic autonomy which was consolidated in 1990 and extended in 1996.

GEOGRAPHY

French Polynesia is 6000 km west of Chile, 5200 km east of Australia, 6200 km south-west of the Californian coast and 15,700 km from Paris, to the east of the international date line.

The Territory is extremely fragmented. Its 118 islands, only six of which are larger than 100 sq km, are scattered between 8° and 28° south and 134° and 155° west. Hatutu, the northernmost island, is more than 2000 km from Rapa, the southernmost.

Polynesia consists of five archipelagos. The Society archipelago, the furthest west, comprises the Windward and Leeward islands and is home to over three-quarters of the population. The administrative capital of Polynesia, Papeete is on Tahiti (1043 sq km), which also has the Territory's highest point, Mt Orohena (2241 metres).

The Austral archipelago straddles the Tropic of Capricorn. It consists of five high islands and an atoll, each a great distance from the others and lying between 575 and 1275 km south of Tahiti.

Between Tahiti and the Marquesas, the Tuamotu archipelago consisting of 77 atolls, stretches more than 1500 km north-west to south-east and more than 500 km east to west.

The tiny Gambier Archipelago, 1600 km from Tahiti, is an appendage to the south-east continuation of the Tuamotus.

The Marquesas archipelago, 1400 km north-east of Tahiti and not far from the equator, comprises about 15 islands and islets, six of which are inhabited.

The total surface area above water is barely 3500 sq km (not even half that of Corsica).

High Islands

These are mainly found in the Society, Austral and Marquesas archipelagos. They are shaped like mountains placed on the surface of the ocean, surrounded by a coral ring which forms the barrier reef, except on the Marquesas. Between the barrier reef and the island proper is the lagoon, a sort of shallow buffer zone with a gentle aquatic environment where the calm turquoise waters contrast with the lapis lazuli of the ocean.

Atolls

Atolls are the chronological continuation of high islands (see the Volcanic Activity & Formation of Islands aside) and are particularly common in the Tuamotus. Varying in shape and size, they are ring-shaped coral reefs emerging above the surface of the water and surrounding a lagoon.

The strip of land they form, made of coral debris and calcareous substance, can reach a height of three to six metres. Its width can vary from a few dozen to several hundred metres. The ring is generally broken by openings called channels or smaller, shallower passages called *hoa*, which connect the lagoon and the ocean at each tide.

CLIMATE

Seasons & Temperatures

French Polynesia has a tropical climate with two distinct seasons. The wet season (south-

Volcanic Activity & the Formation of Islands

The Polynesian islands were all created by volcanic eruptions. From a fixed point in the asthenosphere, called a hot spot, a rising column of magma produces an oceanic volcano or, if the eruption is sufficiently violent to rise above the surface of the ocean, a seamount (an underwater mountain). In accordance with plate tectonics, the newly formed island drifts westwards at an average rate of 10 cm a year. The stationary hot spot meanwhile continues to erupt periodically and another island is formed and in turn moves westwards and so on. The result is a string of islands positioned on the same axis and stretching from south-east to north-west.

As the island drifts to the north-west, it sinks about one cm a year (subsidence). Other geological processes are also at work. As soon as the volcano is extinct, the vent through which the magma was expelled is no longer fed and therefore empties. Under the weight of the lava accumulated on top, it collapses and fills in, giving rise to a huge basin (caldera) which may be several km in diameter. Erosion continues to shape its relief. Water courses cut into the caldera and form valleys.

The clear, warm waters cause coral constructions to form (from a depth of 70 m). The coral grows on the rocky substrate of the underwater sides of the island and gradually builds up a fringing reef, immediately adjoining the island. As the island breaks down, the coral continues to grow, seeking to stay at the surface of the water to catch the light it needs to live. It then forms a circular crust above the volcano, known as a barrier reef. Between the fringing reef and the barrier reef is a channel of variable width, the lagoon. Finally, the original volcano disappears completely under the water. Only the coral ring remains, encircling the lagoon, a sort of inner sea. The atoll has been created.

Under the combined effect of these geological factors, the island passes gradually from the high volcanic island stage to the atoll stage over several million years. The Society archipelago perfectly illustrates these different stages of development: Mehetia, near the hot spot, is a young island with no coral reef, Moorea is a high island with a coral reef, Bora Bora is nearly an atoll with a barrier reef and Scilly is an atoll.

In time, the atoll continues to break up. If the coral's rate of growth cannot compensate this sinking, the atoll gradually disappears and dies. ∎

ern summer) is from November to April. Temperatures are highest in February and March (between 27 and 30°C in March in Tahiti) and lead to considerable evaporation over the ocean. The air is very humid, there is plenty of cloud cover and the atmosphere is heavy and muggy. Three-quarters of the annual rainfall occurs during this period, generally in the form of brief, violent storms.

The dry season (southern winter) lasts from May to October. This is the ideal season as a vast anticylcone is positioned over the South Pacific. Rain is rare, the air is dry and temperatures are slightly cooler (24.5 to 28°C in August in Tahiti).

Average relative humidity ranges from 75 to 85% from one archipelago to another and from year to year. Average annual rainfall is 1800 mm at Papeete. Sunshine varies from 2500 to 2900 hours a year. The temperature range between day and night is limited (about 5 to 8°C), the ocean acting as a thermal regulator. The water temperature is relatively constant throughout the year (between 26 and 29°C).

The Marquesas, although close to the Equator, is the driest archipelago in Polynesia. Rain is mainly concentrated between June and August. In the Tuamotus, the trade winds are more noticeable due to the low-lying relief. The Australs, the southernmost archipelago, have a high annual rainfall of about 2500 mm a year. Winter is cool: the mercury can drop to 10°C.

Prevailing Winds

French Polynesia is subject to trade winds which blow from the north-east sector to the south-east with a force of 40 to 60 km/h in all seasons. The *maraamu* (south-east trade wind) is common throughout the dry season. The *toerau* (north-north-east wind) blows occasionally during the wet season. In the high islands, a pleasant morning breeze known as the *hupe* relieves the suffocating heat of the plain.

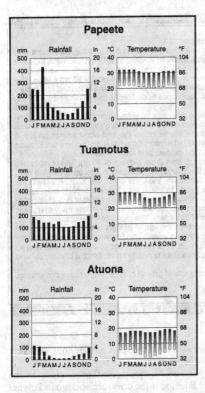

Papeete

mm Rainfall in | °C Temperature °F

Tuamotus

mm Rainfall in | °C Temperature °F

Atuona

mm Rainfall in | °C Temperature °F

Cyclone Risk

Polynesia has suffered a litany of disastrous cyclones in the 20th century, the most recent in the 1982-83 season.

In the Pacific, they generally originate in an area stretching from Samoa to the southeast edge of Polynesia. As a rule, they move from the north-west to the south-east and should normally spare almost all of Polynesia. However, it is assumed that each cyclone which has affected the region formed more to the north-east and that currents and air masses caused it to follow an unusual path.

For weather forecasts, phone ☎ 36 65 09.

FLORA & FAUNA

It is thought that the Pacific flora and fauna originated in Austronesia and spread towards

Polynesia, becoming somewhat impoverished. Numerous plant and animal species have been introduced by humans at different times.

Flora

In the course of their migrations to the east, Polynesian navigators brought plants and fruits which easily became acclimatised. In the 19th century, missionaries and settlers imported other plants of commercial value.

Vegetation varies significantly from one archipelago to another. On the atolls, bushy vegetation and coconut palms predominate. On the high islands, plant cover is more diverse and varies according to altitude. The plants most often found are the following:

Ahi (sandalwood) – A species essentially indigenous to the Marquesas, it was systematically plundered last century by westerners. The sawdust from its wood, renowned for its subtle fragrance, is mixed with coconut oil to make *pani*, Marquesan monoi.

Auti or *ti* (*Cordyline fructicosa*) – This member of the Lilieaceae family used to have a sacred function and was planted near traditional religious buildings. Its foliage opens in a V shape and its colour ranges from yellow to green or purplish red.

Banana (*Musa sapientum*, meia) – Its leaves are used in traditional Tahitian ovens to wrap food for cooking. One variety is the *fei*, similar in appearance to the plantain, the fruit of which grows upwards and can only be eaten when cooked.

Banyan (*Ficus prolixa*, ora) – This Indian fig tree has numerous aerial roots which form a dense tangle. A sacred tree, its ghostly silhouette is often seen near traditional religious buildings.

Breadfruit tree (*Artocarpus altilis*, uru or maiore) – This impressive grey-trunked tree, of which there are several dozen varieties in Polynesia, has a large grainy fruit which forms the basis of local cuisine. Its whitish fibrous flesh is rich in starch and can be eaten cooked or in the form of a fermented paste. The bark was used to make tapa.

Coconut palm (*cocos nucifera*, tumu haari) – Found everywhere, this is Polynesia's fortune tree. It is thought to have been introduced by the first Polynesians then cultivated by the missionaries last century. Its uses are many (see the Coconut aside).

Flamboyant (*Delonix regia*) – This majestic tree which forms an umbrella shape originated in Madagascar and has vivid crimson flowers at the beginning of the wet season.

Frangipani (*Plumeria acuminata*, tipanie) – This bush has very strongly scented white flowers with yellow centres.

Hibiscus (*Hibiscus rosinensis*, aute) – Very widespread, this plant has strongly scented flowers of varying colours, generally orangey-yellow.

Hotu (*Barringtonia asiatica*) – This tree can be recognised by its pear-shaped fruit with protruding ridges. The grated kernel of the fruit mixed with *hora* root and shaken underwater near coral formations has the property of paralysing the fish which can then be caught by hand.

Ironwood tree (*Casuarina equisetifolia*, aito or toa) – This tree, which grows on the seashore or in the mountains, can reach a height of 20 m and looks like a pine. Its wood, which is very solid, was used to manufacture weapons (clubs, spears), tools and canoe parts.

Mango tree (*Mangifera indica*) – Widely cultivated in Polynesia where several varieties are found, this tree is smothered in delicious fragrant fruit with a fibrous orange flesh. The trunk is used to make canoes.

Mape (*Inocarpus fagiferus*) – This white-wood tree, often grouped together in plantations, used to be found near traditional religious buildings. Its roots form buttresses around the base of the trunk. It produces an edible fruit, a sort of chestnut.

Miconia calvescens – Introduced in the 1930s, this plant proliferates spectacularly and is now a threat to Tahitian flora which is in danger of being smothered. Eradication programmes are being studied.

Miki miki (*Pemphis acidula*) – Typical of the flora of the atolls, this bush grows to three to five metres and is found mainly on the oceanside where it forms scrub.

Myrobalan (*Terminalia cattapa*, auteraa) – Quite widespread near beaches or at the mouth of valleys, the branches of this tree have a characteristic widened appearance. The leaves acquire a red or yellow tinge before falling. The kernel of the fruit is edible.

Nono or *noni* (*Morinda citrifolia*) – The yellowish fruit of this tree looks like a bloated soft potato. It is edible but its nauseating goat's cheese smell and acidic taste are not very appealing. It has medicinal properties.

Pandanus (fara) – This tree, with a span of five to seven metres, is easily recognised by its aerial roots which grow obliquely from the trunk and look like arches. The strong leaves are dried to make traditional roofing, wickerwork and woven articles. The flower is called *hinano*. It is found on the atolls and on the high islands up to an altitude of 800 m.

Purau (*Hibiscus tiliaceus*) – Extremely widespread, it sometimes forms tangled clusters due to its contorted branches. The wide heart-shaped leaves are used in the Tahitian oven. The bark, cut in strips, is used to attach fish by the gills. It is also used to make *more* (purau fibre skirts), worn in traditional women's dances.

Rosewood (*Thespesia populnea*, miro) – This is often used in craftwork and carving.

Tamanu or *ati* (*Calophyllum inophyllum*) – The reddish-brown wood of this tree is very strong and rot-resistant. It was used to make canoes and for carving.

Taro (*Colocasia esculenta*) – The purplish-red rhizome of this plant is commonly eaten in Polynesia.

Tiare (*Gardenia tahitiensis*) – Its flower is the emblem of Polynesia. Snowy-white in colour, it gives off a subtle fragrance. They are used to make garlands or are woven into the hair.

Tou (*Cordia subcordata*) – Extremely common on the Marquesas, this medium-sized tree with heart-shaped leaves gives a dark, hard, grained wood which is greatly valued by sculptors.

Vanilla (*Vanilla tahitiensis*, vanira) – This epiphytic orchid produces a pod 20 cm long. It is cultivated particularly on Tahaa, Huahine and Raiatea.

Among the fruit trees, you are bound to find soursop (the surface of the fruit is covered with soft spines), pineapple plantations (on Moorea), guava, avocado, tamarind (the light-brown pod contains sweet acidic flesh), lemon, lime (on the Marquesas), grapefruit, pacayer (with green pods), cashew, papaya and custard apple. Melons and watermelons are also grown. *Mati* (the berries of which provide a red colouring), acacias and kapok trees are fairly common.

At higher altitudes, in addition to *puarata* (which has red flowers), you will note several types of fern (*maire*). The *Albizia falcata* has recently been introduced to counteract the effects of erosion, particularly on the Marquesas.

Ylang-ylang (*motoi*), with strongly scented flowers, also grows in Polynesia, as does jasmine (*pitate*) and bougainvillea.

Fauna

Like the flora, the fauna is rather poor compared to regions in the west of the Pacific, due to the distance from the great continents.

Land Fauna At the time of the great migrations, the first Polynesians brought pigs and dogs in their canoes. The rat arrived on the westerners' ships. Reptiles include the harmless, insectivorous gecko, a sort of small lizard with a translucent colour. There are no snakes in Polynesia.

There is little variety of insect species. You are certain to meet with wasps, cockroaches and their predators, centipedes. The latter can be up to 20 cm in length and the spikes at the front of the head inject a venom which causes inflammation. Mosquitoes are there in profusion and can transmit dengue fever and filariasis. The nono (black or white) is a minute midge which is a particular problem on the Marquesan coast where eradication campaigns are being carried out. It is not a disease carrier, but its bite causes itching and inflammation.

Horses, which originated in Chile, were introduced on Tahuata by Dupetit-Thouars in 1842 and have bred on the Marquesas. They are between a pony and a thoroughbred in size. Goats are also a familiar part of the landscape on this archipelago where they roam around in semifreedom. Sheep were introduced for rearing, notably on Tahiti, the Australs and the Marquesas.

The waterways are home to eels and shrimps.

Bird Life There are about 100 species of birds (*manu*) in Polynesia. On the low islands, many nest on the ground or in the bushes. The feathers of certain birds were once much sought after for costume accessories (eg head-dresses, chieftains' belts).

Sea birds include terns, petrels, noddies, frigatebirds, boobies and the superb tropicbirds (phaethons) with long red or white feathers in their tails. All of them live on fish. The sheltered Tetiaroa atoll is home to several species. On Ua Huka, the number of sooty terns (*kaveka*) nesting on two islets is estimated at nearly one million. In the Tuamotus there are numerous 'bird islands'.

There are also migratory land-based birds such as the sooty rail or the curlew which winter in Polynesia.

The pigeon and the buzzard were intro-

duced by humans, as was the chicken, brought at the time of the first migrations and now partly reverted back to its wild state.

Lagoon, Reef & Ocean Fauna The coral constructions of the high islands and atolls are favoured environments where a diverse fauna can be found.

Crustaceans – Greatly prized for their flesh, the squilla and lobster live on the outer slope of the reef (on the Tuamotus) or carpet the bottom of caves in the cliffs (in the Marquesas). Hermit crabs, which are common on reefs, wedge their abdomens inside the empty shells of gastropods.

The place teems with crabs. In the Tuamotus, the coconut crab (*kaveu*), which can reach an impressive size, feeds at night. Its flesh is highly prized. The land crab (*tupa*) infests the coconut plantations where it digs a network of tunnels.

Echinoderms – Sea urchins hide in the cracks in the reef. The two most common species are the black sea urchin with long spines (*vana*) and the pencil urchin (*fetue*) with long cylindrical spines. Their gonads, eaten raw, are greatly prized.

Long and cylindrical, the sea cucumber (*rori*) looks like a fat black or grey sausage. It sucks in the sand and filters it to feed on micro-organisms.

Molluscs – Shells, which were once used as decorative or ceremonial jewellery, are now used to make ornaments. Most shellfish are edible.

They have a diverse habitat: reef crevices, coral pinnacles or the sandy bottom of lagoons. The most numerous are gastropods and bivalves, including the symbol of the Tuamotus, mother-of-pearl (pearl oyster) and the giant clam (*pahua*). Pearl shells were once used to make fish hooks, lures, utensils, tools and during the last century, buttons. Giant clams are recognised by their brightly coloured, velvety-looking mantle, which they draw in when threatened. The outer edges of the shells are crinkled.

Fish – Among the ocean fish that come to hunt near the reef are sharks. Very common in the Tuamotus, the grey shark (*Carcharhinus amblyrhinchos*, raira), powerful and streamlined and about two metres in length, is found in abundance near channels or shelves. The lemon shark (*Negaprion acutidens*, arava) has a slightly yellowish skin and can reach three metres in length. It swims around near the bottom, including in lagoons, and can be aggressive. The white-finned reef shark (*Carcharhinus albimarginatus*, tapete), can be recognised by the white mark at the tip of its dorsal fin. It frequents the shelves around the Tuamotus at greater depths than the grey shark but may come up if enticed by food. It can reach more than three metres in length. The black-finned reef shark (*Carcharhinus melanopterus*, mauri) and the white-finned lagoon shark (*Trianodon obesus*, mamaru) are small, harmless and found primarily in the lagoons and channels. The tiger shark, hammerhead shark and sleeper shark can occasionally be seen. Barracuda (*ono*), alone or in shoals, are also predators and swim close to the channels.

Three types of ray (*fafa piti*) are found in Polynesian waters: manta rays, easily recognised by the horns on either side of the mouth, can be as much as four metres across; leopard rays are smaller and have dark spots; and whip-tailed stingrays live on the sandy bottom where they partially bury themselves.

Among the hundreds of species of smaller fish, the moray eel is the most impressive. Hidden in the coral crevices of the shelf, only its half-open mouth, edged with sharp fangs, can be seen. The good-natured napoleon wrasse (*mara*), with its blue-green livery, thick-lipped mouth and bump on its forehead, is often more than one metre in length. The loach and grouper (*roi*) family is well represented, as are the surgeonfish (*maito*), especially the black surgeonfish and the convict surgeonfish.

Clownfish and damselfish have a symbiotic relationship with the anemones. The duckbills and trumpetfish are very streamlined. Scad (*uruti*) often move around in shoals. Parrotfish have a beak which they use to graze the coral. Unicornfish (*ume*) are recognised by their rostrum, which projects above the mouth. Mullet, soldierfish and squirrelfish, with an orange-red skin, shelter in the faults in the reef.

The perch family includes several species, among them the blue-striped perch. The filefish family is diverse and includes the picasso fish among others. The chaetodons are devoted to a diet of coral paste. The most attractive specimens are the whipfish, emperorfish and butterflyfish. The stonefish, which is difficult to see because of its camouflage, can give a dangerous sting, as can the scorpionfish. The porcupinefish and the aptly named pufferfish puff themselves up like a balloon when in danger.

Dolphin fish (*mahi mahi*), bonito, *thazards* and tuna, greatly appreciated for their meat, are only found in the open sea. It is not unusual to see dolphins near the reef. Turtles (*honu*), which are strictly speaking reptiles, are an endangered species.

Protection of the Environment

Several factors pose a threat to Polynesian flora and fauna. Pollution due to waste dis-

charged by purification plants, run-off water or rubbish dumped near the shore damage the fragile ecological balance of the lagoons. On the atolls, waste disposal is a real problem that has yet to be resolved.

Travellers must exercise a little common sense. It is preferable to refrain from collecting shellfish which suffer from being gathered in too great a number. Divers and swimmers should take care to avoid untimely fin movements which damage the fragile coral. Yachties at moorage should ensure that the anchor does not drag the on madreporian coral banks. In the early 1990s, a natural phenomenon caused by warming of the water led to bleaching of the coral, which resulted in the death of whole banks. The process appears to have stopped.

Although turtles are highly protected, they continue to be poached for their flesh and their shells, which are used as ornaments. Do not encourage this practice in any way. The island of Scilly has been classified as a reserve where they can lay their eggs in complete safety.

GOVERNMENT & POLITICS

French Polynesia is a French overseas territory, which has had autonomous status since April 1996. It comprises the Windward, Leeward, Tuamotu, Gambier, Marquesas and Austral islands and also the surrounding areas of sea.

The French State remains in control of the following areas: Territorial defence and law and order, foreign affairs, nationality and immigration, justice, higher education and research, audiovisual communications and currency.

The land administered by the Territory includes the soil and subsoil of inland waterways, including lagoons, as well as those of Territorial waters. The Territory regulates exploration and development rights relating to the resources of these maritime areas. It is also responsible for Territorial administration, education (primary and secondary), taxation, prices and foreign trade.

The Territory's institutions are the government of French Polynesia, the assembly of French Polynesia and the economic, social and cultural council (CES).

The Republic of France is represented in the Territory by a high commissioner, appointed by the government of the republic. He or she can submit a matter to the administrative court.

The president of the government of French Polynesia, head of the Territorial administration, is elected by the Polynesian assembly from among the 41 territorial council members. He or she then appoints a council of ministers. He can represent the authorities of the republic before regional Pacific organisations and negotiate and sign agreements with the Pacific States within the areas for which the Territory has responsibility.

The Territorial council members are elected by direct universal suffrage every five years by 125,388 electors (1996). The assembly sits in Papeete, the Territory's capital.

The elections in May 1996 elected 22 council members from Tahoeraa Huiraatira (the local RPR, or Union for the Republic), Gaston Flosse's party, which thus obtained an absolute majority in the assembly. Gaston Flosse has been president of the territorial government since 1991.

The opposition consists mainly of pro-independence parties which obtained 11 seats in the 1996 election. At their head is Oscar Temaru's party, Tavini Huiraatira.

ECONOMY
Economic Indicators
The GDP was established at about 1.6 million CFP per head of population in 1993, a level comparable to that of Australia. According to 1988 figures, unemployment affects 9.7% of the active population, especially women and unqualified young people.

The main trading partners are metropolitan France (45% of imports and 33% of exports), the USA, Japan (46% of exports) and New Zealand.

Cost of Living
The cost of living in Polynesia is among the highest on the planet. Some prices will dampen the enthusiasm of even the wealthiest travellers: 1200 CFP (US$13) for a load of laundry (washing and drying), and 2700 CFP (US$29) to develop a 24-exposure film.

The enemy is taxation. The taxation system is totally unbalanced in favour of indirect taxes, particularly import taxes. All goods entering the Territory are weighed down with import duty which varies according to the type of product and can be as much as 200% of the product's value. Added to this are customs duties, except on goods from the European Union (EU). Bearing in mind the Territory's extreme dependence on imports, it is easier to understand why the cost of living is exorbitant. Locally manufactured goods do not escape this implacable logic as they include imported products.

There is no VAT however, nor any personal income tax (in its strictest sense), wealth tax or inheritance tax. Tax reform is still in progress.

Travellers on a limited budget, while penalised, nevertheless benefit from the opportunities to live at lower cost. Hiring a bicycle to get around, using the schooners for inter-island transport, staying at guesthouses and eating snacks or plates of fish in coconut milk significantly reduce the bill. ■

The Polynesian economy is extremely reliant on imports and the French State has considerable influence.

The Pacific Experimentation Centre

The CEP & Its Effects From the time of establishment of the CEP (Centre d'expérimentation du Pacifique) in 1963, the flood of finance into the Territory has reached colossal proportions. Army expenses rapidly accounted for three-quarters of French Polynesia's GDP. The import duties alone on equipment imported by the CEP amounted to six thousand million CFP in 1994, which went straight into the Territory's coffers. Despite the lack of official data, in 1992 the ORSTOM (Overseas Scientific & Technical Research Office) estimated that there were 7750 people directly employed by the CEP, 3350 of whom were civilians and 4400 military personnel.

Thanks to the CEP, the standard of living in French Polynesia has risen considerably, causing a socioeconomic upheaval. Many Polynesians have abandoned traditional activities and emigrated en masse to Papeete which has been urbanised with desperate eagerness (1943 there were 13,800 inhabitants on Tahiti, in 1983 there were 93,300). The service sector has experienced an unprecedented boom. The territorial public service, the main beneficiary of this growth which it takes for granted, has hypertrophied, employing more than a third of the active population. This money-for-nothing situation has led indirectly to social splits: alongside a comfortably-off class benefiting from the advantages of the CEP, a dispossessed proletariat has developed in the working-class districts of Papeete where frustrations simmer. The pro-independence parties obtain a growing response from these rejected individuals. Faced with an identity crisis, cultural renaissance movements, which are in some cases vindictive, are appearing and advocating a return to *maohi* (Tahitian Polynesian) roots.

With the end of CEP activities, the quest for economic autonomy has become the Territory's priority.

Progress Pact The French State has undertaken to compensate the loss of financial resources linked to the cessation of CEP activities. A 'Progress Pact' between the Territory and the State was signed in January 1993, leading, in February 1994, to the adoption of a 10-year adjustment law and five-year 'development contracts'. The State provides assistance in the fields of education, training, research, health and transport infrastructure, agriculture, tourism and housing. Financial transfers from the State to the Territory will amount to 990 million francs (US$193 million) per annum until 31 December 2005.

Traditional Activity Sectors

Agriculture The spectacular boom in the services sector and the public service has been achieved at the expense of agriculture. Between 1956 and 1988, the proportion of agricultural workers dropped from 50% to 9% of the active population. A marked rural exodus has been the result.

Copra production is the main source of income for more than 10,000 people, particularly on the Tuamotus (50% of production) and the Marquesas. Aware of the social issues at stake, the Territory guarantees a price per kg which is considerably higher than that on world markets. Market gardening is particularly concentrated on the Leeward Islands and the Australs. Of all the fruit produced, only pineapples from Moorea are exported. Although it's still very reliant on costly lamb imports from New Zealand and Australia, Polynesia has begun to promote stock rearing and now supplies three-quarters of its own demand for pork.

Certain constraints inhibit the development of the agricultural sector, notably the practice of joint property ownership.

Fishing Polynesia is endowed with a huge marine area and yet makes little use of its fishing resources. Deep-sea industrial fishing is carried out by Korean boats in exchange for substantial dues to the Territory. The latter is encouraging the development of a small semi-industrial

The Coconut

Postcard symbol, economic backbone and staff of life, the coconut is truly the tree of Polynesia. On the great migration voyages which brought the Polynesian navigators to their new islands, coconuts would have been a staple food and drink. On atolls, where water supplies are often unreliable, the coconut is an important source of liquid in times of drought.

The coconut tree has countless uses. As it starts to sprout the young coconut palm is the basis of palm heart salad. When the coconut is young the water makes a refreshingly cool drink and some varieties contain up to a litre of coconut water. Coconut water is also completely sterile and can be used medicinally. The coconut milk squeezed from the immature coconut flesh is the real basis of Polynesian cooking. As the coconut matures the flesh can be eaten or grated for use as a cooking ingredient. Fully mature coconut flesh can be dried out to produce copra, from which coconut oil is extracted. For many years copra production was the mainstay of island economies and, although it has declined in importance of late, copra remains an important economic factor. You'll often see the metal racks of coconut meat drying out while awaiting a copra ship. Scented with tiare flowers, the monoi cosmetics of Tahiti use coconut oil as their basis.

Apart from food and oil from the nut, the rest of the tree has many other uses. Once the meat has been extracted the nut can be used to make cups, bowls or other vessels. The sweet tree sap is the principal ingredient in palm wine or it can be boiled down to make a natural candy. The tough fibres that encase the nut can be plaited into ropes that are used in traditional house and canoe construction. On Bora Bora they even burn the discarded coconut husks to generate electricity. The green palm leaves are woven into bags, baskets or matting (*peue*) while the dried leaves are used for roofing. The trunks are used for construction but, until recently, the exceptional density of coconut wood limited its use in normal carpentry. With modern saws coconut wood can be cut into boards. Beyond all those uses the coconut tree simply looks right, they're easy on the eye and the perfect match for an atoll beach. They sound right as well – is any noise more seductive than the rustle of the wind through coconut trees?

A coconut tree produces its first coconuts at about six years of age and during its prime, from around 10 to 70 years of age, a full-size tree will produce about 60 coconuts a year. If the nuts are not cut down they eventually fall, which is why it is not a good idea to take a nap under a coconut tree. They're one of the real dangers of the Pacific and every year falling coconuts cause deaths. The resounding thwack when a coconut falls on the tin roof of a building beneath a tree will bring that message noisily home. ■

---

fishing fleet. Small-scale fishing by fishers on a self-employed basis is still very widespread. Four large aquicultural farms produce prawns and shrimps.

Pearl Culture Pillar of the economy, pearls are the Territory's second-largest source of income. Between 1990 and 1994, exports boomed. Japan buys up 84.6% of production.

The apparent buoyancy of this sector should not, however, conceal certain structural weaknesses and, despite scientific support, production remains dependent on natural risks. Furthermore, despite the existence of trade unions, the unauthorised sale at low prices of poor-quality pearls has been instrumental in undermining the market (the average price per gram fell by a third between 1990 and 1994) and tarnishing the image of this product. Lastly, the dependence on Japan makes it essential to diversify markets.

Tourism At 20% of the GDP, this is the main source of income. After a slack period between 1986 and 1991, in 1994 it took off and exceeded 166,000 visitors, mostly Americans, French and Japanese. This improvement is partly due to the reduction in airfares and partly to promotion efforts. In 1995 it suffered from the boycott linked to the resumption of nuclear testing, but the situation augurs well for the period 1996-2000. It is still geared to the 'top end of the market' (cruises, nautical activities, honeymoons).

Industry & Mining The lack of local primary resources and the high duty on imported raw

LIONEL POZZOLI

LIONEL POZZOLI

LIONEL POZZOLI

LIONEL POZZOLI

Top:	Feeding a lemon shark, Moorea, Society Islands
Middle:	A manta ray, Rangiroa, Tuamotus
Bottom:	A morey eel, Rangiroa, Tuamotus
Right:	Swarm of lagoon fish and sharks, Moorea, Society Islands

JEAN-BERNARD CARILLET

JEAN-BERNARD CARILLET

JEAN-BERNARD CARILLET

JEAN-BERNARD CARILLET

A: Corossol   D: Coconuts
B: Kapokier   E: Taro
C: Starfruit

Vanilla

The harvesting of *Vanilla tahitiensis*, which is grown on Tahaa, Huahine, Raiatea and Nuku Hiva (Marquesas), where it was introduced last century, has declined alarmingly from 3000 tonnes in 1949 to two tonnes in 1980. The use of synthetic vanilla and the availability of regular paid employment generated by the CEP partly explain this slump.

An equally plausible reason is the unattractive nature of this demanding crop, which requires constant care and attention. Since there are no pollinating insects, fertilisation, which consists of bringing the pistil and the pollen into contact when the corolla of the flower is ready, is performed manually. The resulting fruit, the pod, grows to about 20 cm in a few months. Initially green, it gradually turns yellow. The pods are harvested after nine months and put to dry. They shrivel and turn brown and it is then that they give off their powerful and unmistakeable aroma.

A 'vanilla plan' designed to revive production was inaugurated in 1983, but it has not achieved the desired objectives. As part of the Progress Pact, a new programme has been launched in an attempt to increase production by 20 tonnes a year.

The high hopes of reviving the cultivation of this orchid on a large scale have not borne fruit. ∎

Vanilla pods

materials weigh heavily on the expansion of this sector (10% of GDP). Phosphates have been found to exist on the Tuamotus, but, for the time being, the project is confronted by hostility from the inhabitants.

POPULATION & PEOPLE

The total population of French Polynesia is now estimated at about 216,000 inhabitants, 47% of whom are under the age of 20.

The average density is 50 inhabitants per sq km of land above water (ie an area of 3675 sq km). However, 86% of Polynesians live in the Society archipelago (103 inhabitants per sq km) whereas only 4% live on the Marquesas Islands, 3.5% on the Australs and 6.5% on the Tuamotu-Gambiers.

The average number of children per woman is 3.1. The average annual growth rate is 2.21%. The birth rate (24.8%) and the death rate (4.9%) have decreased slightly in the last few years. Life expectancy is 68 years for men and 72 years for women.

While Europeans brought with them various diseases (measles, smallpox, influenza, tuberculosis, dysentery etc) which devastated the population in previous centu-

ries, the standard of health is now equivalent to that in industrialised countries: $US240 a year per inhabitant is spent on health, which represents 9% of the GDP. While there is an average of 1.7 doctors to 1000 inhabitants most of the doctors, pharmacists, dentists and hospital beds are on Tahiti. This compensated by a good system of medical evacuation.

Although traditionally scattered, Polynesian settlement has changed: as a result of the establishment of European religious missions, military bases and colonists, the population has deserted the mountains and gathered near the coast.

Ethnicity

Four ethnic groups make up the population of French Polynesia: Polynesians, those of Polynesian-European or Polynesian-Chinese mixed race, Europeans and Chinese – or French of Chinese origin.

Polynesians and assimilated races predominate as they account for 82.8% of the total population, whereas Europeans account for 11.9% and Asians for 4.7%.

The first Chinese landed in the mid-19th

century to work in the cotton plantations. Today, they own grocery stores and businesses and are perfectly integrated in to Polynesian life. Despite the descriptions of a paradise on earth given by travellers, the metropolitan French and other Europeans have never settled long term in large numbers in French Polynesia.

EDUCATION

The basic education structures are identical to those of metropolitan France. School is compulsory between the ages of five and 16. Teaching is in French only; a few hours a week of Tahitian are provided in primary and secondary schools.

In 1994, there were 278 primary schools (19 of which were private) and 38 secondary schools (10 private). The geographical fragmentation of the Territory complicates the organisation of education, notably on the Tuamotus and Marquesas, where teenagers have to go to boarding school in order to continue their studies.

The French university of the Pacific (UFP) was created in May 1987. It has two centres: one in French Polynesia (campus at Utumaoro, near punaauia) and the other in Noumea (New Caledonia). The qualifications awarded – diplomas, bachelor's and master's degrees – are nationally recognised.

ARTS

The pioneering missionaries made a strong attempt at wiping out Polynesian art and culture. They destroyed temples and carvings, banned tattoos and dancing, and generally took a lot of the joy out of Polynesian life. Fortunately, some of it managed to survive and in recent years there has been a real revival of Polynesian culture, particularly in music and dance. See the Things to Buy section in the Facts for the Visitor chapter for information on crafts, including woven pandanus, pareus and tattoos.

Music

Although traditional musical instruments have been largely supplanted by western imports traditional music is still played, particularly as an accompaniment to dances. Traditional instruments included the drums known as *pahu*, which were covered with shark or dog skin and beaten with sticks or the hands. In the Marquesas, where the drums tended to be larger, slit drums known as *toere* were also found. Conch shells became the wind instrument known as the *p*, but the most unique Polynesian wind instrument was the nose flute, or *vivo*.

Early this century the ukuleles and guitars started to arrive in Polynesia, and popular music today is a unique local version of country & western, complete with the same tales of lost love but in an island and lagoon setting. *Himenes*, full-throated renditions of Polynesian hymns, are another example of the local love of music.

Dance

Early explorers all commented on the excitement and erotic explicitness of Polynesian dancing so, not unnaturally, it was one of the first things the missionaries banned. It continued clandestinely and eventually made a low-key return to life, although with female dancers wearing the all enveloping 'Mother Hubbards' which the missionaries had prescribed as more appropriate dress. Between the wars dancing became more active, but it was not until the 1950s that Polynesian dancing once again became really energetic. Today there are dance troupes performing at tourist hotels, at important festivals and in international contests with other Polynesian centres.

The Polynesian dances which really left the missionaries open-mouthed with shock were the maiden's dance known as the *timorodee* and, even worse, the couple's dance known as the *upaupa*. In the neighbouring Cook Islands the pioneer missionary William Wyatt Gill reported that: 'respecting the morality of their dances, the less said the better, but the *upaupa* dance is obscene indeed'.

Traditional dances which have survived include the war-like *otea* dance step, the comedy routines of *aparima* and the group dancing of *hivinau*. *Tamure* is the all-purpose term for Polynesian dancing, similar to the way *hula* now encompasses all Hawaiian dancing.

Tapa

The ancient technique of tapa making, prac- tised throughout the Pacific, consisted of making nonwoven fabric from the bark of breadfruit, banyan or paper mulberry (*aute*) trees.

The bark of young trunks or branches is slit and removed from the wood using a sharpened stick. It is then soaked in water to soften. The outer layer is scraped away with a shell, leaving just the sapwood. The sheets of bark, about 15 cm wide, are spread out on a flat, elongated stone anvil positioned in front of the operator who sits cross-legged. Using a square-shaped *aito* (ironwood) beater with parallel slots, she pounds it repeatedly for several hours, during which the bark becomes thinner and gradually stretches. When the piece is finished, it is put to dry then dyed with the sap of various plants or decorated with traditional designs.

Collecting the bark was the men's job while the preparation of the tapa fell to the women.

Nowadays, this craft is almost disappear- ing, as it's fast being replaced by woven fabrics. Only the women on Fatuiva (Marquesas) still practise this ancestral tech- nique.

Architecture

The *fare* (house) is the traditional dwelling. It is constructed entirely from plant materials and is built directly on the ground, without foundations. The framework is made of coconut wood and the roof of woven coconut palms or pandanus leaves, which are water- proof.

On the Marquesas, housing was different. The house was made of plant material but was placed on a stone terrace (*pae pae*), made of blocks of basalt placed side by side and piled up. The *tohua*, a vast paved space, was the communal area, the public place where the tribe's important secular events –

mainly festive gatherings – took place, com- parable to the Roman forum.

Nowadays, fares are made of plywood or cement with corrugated iron roofs to better withstand cyclones. In tourist spots, bunga- lows imitate the traditional style.

SOCIETY & CONDUCT

French Polynesia is generally very easy going and there are few pitfalls for the unwary visitor. Remember the standards of conduct today are often a blend of Polyne- sian and French customs – you'll see Polynesian friends greeting with a kiss on both cheeks, just as if they were in Paris.

Dress standards are generally relaxed, and coats and ties are not necessary even at the fanciest Papeete restaurants. On the beach nudity is only generally permissible on iso- lated motus, although Papeete's pricey hotels have their own private floating motus moored a discreet distance offshore. Unlike Fiji and other more straight-laced Pacific islands, bikini tops are not required in French Polynesia.

If visiting a Polynesian home the first rule, as in Japan, is to take your shoes off at the front door. Your hosts may insist that it's unnecessary but you'll win friends if you refuse their entreaties and insist that you would be more comfortable shoeless. At the table simple politeness and watching what others do will usually work. Offer to fill other glasses before your own, for example. Some Tahitian foods are eaten with fingers, so don't always expect utensils.

Polynesians are serious about their reli- gion. Attending church on a Sunday can be an interesting insight into their lives but always dress and behave politely.

The Family System

In Polynesia the family is not seen as just the parents and children, but as an extended system including uncles, aunts, cousins, distant cousins, grandparents etc. The members of this extended family are the *fetii*.

The Polynesian family unit should not be

regarded as a rigid administrative and possessive structure as in the west. It is more open. In addition to natural children, there are *faaamu* (adopted) children. It is also common for children to be entrusted to other relatives or to a childless woman.

Role of the Vahine

Polynesians practised sexual equality well before the 20th century. In ancient times, power was passed to either women (*vahine*) or men without distinction. Queen Pomare on Tahiti or the Marquesan female chieftains (such as Vaekehu on Nuku Hiva) are a perfect example of this. Polyandry was common on the Marquesas. Fishing was the only activity that was restricted to men only.

Nowadays, women are very well represented in the tertiary sector, which predominates in Polynesia, and they fill up to 80% of posts, particularly in commerce, hotels, health, insurance and social services. Arts and crafts are also their stronghold (except on the Marquesas where the sculptors are mostly male).

In the private domain, women generally take charge of children's schooling, domestic chores, administrative tasks or social and cultural responsibilities. What is more, they are often the land-holders.

RELIGION

The religious history of French Polynesia can be neatly divided into two periods – premissionary and postmissionary.

Premissionary Beliefs

The missionaries attempted to obliterate the pre-European religion of Polynesia, destroying *tikis* and other religious figures, demolishing buildings and constructing their own churches on the foundations of the most important *maraes*. Archaeologists have done their best to study the ancient religion from what the missionaries left and the Polynesians managed to hide.

The Polynesians worshipped a supreme god along with a panoply of lesser gods. When the first Europeans arrived, the supreme god Taaroa was in the process of being supplanted by a new supreme god, Oro, the God of War. The gods were worshipped in open-air temples known as maraes, with festivals, ceremonies, dances and music, and sacrifices, including, occasionally, human sacrifices.

In the Society Islands religious activities were led by a priestly caste known as the Arioi who travelled among the islands performing rites and ceremonies. Early European accounts of the Arioi remarked that their ceremonies seemed to include a great deal of sexual activity, but any resulting offspring were killed at birth, to prevent the ranks of the Arioi from becoming overcrowded.

Maraes There are remains of maraes, in various states of decay or reconstruction, on many islands throughout French Polynesia. Today it's difficult to envisage what a marae would have been like because only the stone or coral marae platforms remain; the associated wooden fares have all disappeared. Maraes vary in design and construction from island to island but generally follow the same basic pattern of a rectangular platform with an *ahu*, a construction somewhat like an altar, at one end of the rectangle.

In the Society Islands, the Windward Island maraes were generally enclosed by walls, whereas in the Leeward Island maraes the platform was open. The Windward Island ahus were often constructed like a stepped pyramid while the Leeward Island ahus were longer and made of two rows of large vertical slabs with the space in between filled with smaller stones and pebbles. In the Tuamotus, however, the ahus were made of slabs piled up on one another.

Vertical stones and carved and painted poles or planks known as *unu* stood around the ahu. The marae would usually have a treasure house where the important religious symbols and figures were kept. The *fare atua* was a chest-like statue with a compartment to store the most important figures. Tikis were human-like figures used to represent supernatural beings and were found at maraes but also on canoes. Some of the finest tikis were found in the Austral Islands and most particularly in the Marquesas. In the Society Islands tikis were known as *ti'i*.

The most common maraes were family or group maraes, although the marae of an important ruler or noble could be a large and imposing structure. Obarea (or Purea), the 'queen' who befriended Wallis, Cook and other early visitors, had the huge Marae Mahaiatea on Tahiti's west coast. The largest and most important maraes, however, were usually community or national maraes. There were also differences in style between the coastal maraes, often built right on the lagoon edge, and the inland maraes.

Meaes On the Marquesas, archaeologists have uncovered distinctive religious structures built from basalt blocks placed side by side and piled up. These are not called maraes but *meaes*. Generally in the valleys and away from secular places, the meae is the sacred precinct par excellence. A place of worship, burial and offerings, the meae was strictly *tapu* (prohibited). Access was restricted to a few initiated individuals endowed with *mana* (supernatural force), such as the *taua* (priest) or the *hakaiki* (chieftain). Cannibalistic rites, restricted to chieftains, priests and warriors, also took place there when human sacrifices were made. The meae was generally built near a banyan, the sacred tree.

Tikis In the overlap between art and religion, tikis (ti'i in the Society Islands) are anthropomorphic statues carved from blocks of basalt or volcanic tuff (*keetu*) or from wood. Their characteristic shape gives them a hieratic, enigmatic appearance. They nearly all conform to the same model: the legs are short and bent and the elbows are held close to the sides. In some cases however, the upper and lower limbs are hardly discernible. The head

is a direct extension of the trunk. The mouth and eyes are the most striking features. The disproportionate mouth is represented by an extremely long but narrow rectangle while the eyes are large concentric circles.

Generally erected on or near a marae or meae, tikis are believed to have had a religious and symbolic function, representing deified ancestors or protective power. Sculpted in the form of statues, they can also be carved in bas-relief, on weapons (clubs), paddles, canoes or utensils (pestles). The most significant remains are found on the Marquesas.

Petroglyphs Petroglyphs are designs carved on stones, the significance of which has not yet been established. The pictures feature octopuses, tortoises, canoes, suns, geometric designs, anthropomorphic figures or extremely schematic features. The best known are those at Tahiti Iti and on the Marquesas.

Postmissionary Beliefs
The arrival of the first European explorer's ships may have heralded the changes to come, but the arrival of the first LMS missionaries in 1797 was the major event. Spanish missionaries had come more than 20 years earlier but their stay was spectacularly unsuccessful. The two frightened men of God hardly dared to venture out of their fortified mission station. The first LMS missionaries were scarcely more successful and within a few years had either drifted off to Australia or been converted to a more liberal outlook on life by the Polynesians.

Nevertheless, these pioneering Protestant missionaries were definitely here to stay and once Pomare II had taken their side the writing was on the wall for the old Polynesian religion. Catholicism did not arrive until much later, first in the Gambier Archipelago and in the Marquesas, and then on the other islands with the French takeover. Despite having the French government firmly behind it, Catholicism has never made a serious dent in the Protestant strength in the Society Islands, the Australs and Tuamotus. Today, Protestants account for 55% of the population and Catholics 30%. The Mormons have recently made serious inroads, as they have elsewhere in the Pacific, and have a major following on many islands. They constitute 6% of the population followed by Seventh-Day Adventists (2%) and, among the Chinese community, Buddhists and Confucianists (2%).

LANGUAGE

Tahitian and French are the official languages of French Polynesia although Tahitian is spoken much more than it is written. Much of the tourist industry uses English but, if you venture to the more remote and less touristy islands where the Tahitian dialects are spoken, it's definitely useful to know some French. Fortunately, bad French is readily accepted in French Polynesia – you won't be ignored just because your accent is poor!

Tahitian, known as Maohi, belongs to the linguistic group of Polynesian languages which includes Samoan, Maori, Hawaiian, Rarotongan and Tongan. It has only been a written language since the 19th century, when the missionaries set about translating the Bible. There are many dialects of Tahitian, including the Tuamotan or Paumotan dialect of the Tuamotus, the Marquesan dialect of the Marquesas and the Mangarevan dialect of the Gambier archipelago. It was the spread of Christianity through French Polynesia that helped to make Tahitian, the dialect spoken on Tahiti, the most widespread dialect.

Few Tahitian words have managed to make their way into English or any other languages. The two familiar exceptions are 'tattoo' from the Tahitian *tatau* and 'taboo' from the Tahitian *tapu* (or *tabu*). There are, however, a number of Tahitian words which are regularly used by local residents speaking other languages, even though they have not made the leap to international usage.

One of the most common is *fiu*, a word expressing a peculiarly Polynesian blend of boredom, despair, exhaustion and ennui. You can be *fiu* with somebody or you can simply feel *fiu*. Some of Gauguin's models, lying there with faraway thoughts, are definitely in the grip of *fiu*. Another everyday word is *popa'a* (written in this book as *popaa*), an all-encompassing word used to refer to any non-Polynesians. You may hear of a nightclub or bar popular with Tahitians and popaa or a place where the popaa are definitely tapu. Like Australians, the Polynesians have a 'No problems' or 'She'll be right' attitude towards life, summed up in the expression *aita e peapea*.

An interesting characteristic of Tahitian is the formation of words by agglutination. For 'helicopter', you say *manu tautau na te reva*, literally 'bird suspended in space'; 'television' is *afata teata*, literally 'theatre box', while 'refrigerator' is *afata fa'ato'eto'eraa ma'a* or 'box for cooling food'.

Tahitian

The same word in Tahitian can be a verb, adjective and noun. Thus, *inu* means 'to drink', 'a drink' or 'drinkable', according to the context. There are no declensions, conjugations, auxiliaries or genders in Tahitian, and plural forms are solely denoted by the article. The definite article ('the') is *te* in the singular and *te mau* in the plural. The notions of past, present and future are expressed by using prefixes or suffixes with the verb.

Pronouncing words in Tahitian is fairly simple. Tahitian only has eight consonants: f, h (aspirate), m, n, p, r (rolled), t and v. The five vowels are:

a	like the *u* in 'hut'
e	like the French *é* (as in café)
i	as in 'hit'
o	as in 'hot'
u	as in 'cook'

These vowels also have a long sound, indicated in this language section by a macron (a line over the vowel). Imagine that the macron is stretching the sound out. (Note that macrons have not been used elsewhere in this book.)

a	like the *a* in 'father'
e	sounds like 'air'
i	as in 'feet'
o	as in 'coat'
u	as in 'cook' but longer

There are some combinations of vowels where the vowels are not pronounced separately. Each one of the following diphthongs (vowel combinations) denotes a single vowel sound:

ai	as in 'height'
ae	as in 'pay'
oi	as in 'boy'
ao	as in 'cow'
au	run the sounds of *a* and *u* together

Tahitian also uses a glottal stop, called *'eta*. To pronounce it correctly, you must block off the air in the glottis before pronouncing the following vowel. If you were to say 'a apple' rather than 'an apple', you would be performing a glottal stop. In Marquesan, this stop is commonly replaced with a 'k', eg *vaka* ('canoe') and *tiki* instead of *va'a* and *ti'i*. The glottal stop is indicated in this language section by an apostrophe, although Tahitian words in the rest of this book are rendered without glottal stops. The exceptions are names of particular hotels, restaurants or other businesses which always feature the glottal stop in their advertising. Thus Tahiti's international airport is shown as Faaa airport but in Tahiti you may also see it as Faa'a airport.

French

All French nouns are either masculine or feminine and adjectives change their form to agree with the noun. In the following list of words and phrases, just the masculine singular version of nouns and adjectives are given.

Basic vowels are pronounced as they are in Tahitian, but there are a few peculiarities of French pronunciation you should remember:

ai	like the *e* in 'pet'. Any single consonant following this sound is usually silent.
eau/au	like the *au* in 'caught' but shorter
ll	pronounced as *y*, eg *billet* is pronounced 'bee-yeh'
ch	always pronounced as *sh*
qu	pronounced as *k*
r	halfway between a rolled *r* and an *l*

There is a distinction between *u* (as in *tu*) and *ou* (as in *tout*). For both sounds, the lips are rounded and pushed forward, but for the *u* sound try to say the sound 'ee' while keeping the lips pursed. The *ou* sound is pronounced as in 'cook'.

For nasal vowels the breath escapes partly through the nose. They occur where a syllable ends in a single *n* or *m*; the *n* or *m* is silent but indicates the nasalisation of the preceding vowel.

Diving You'll find that most dive centres are used to dealing with English speakers but the following French terms may be useful.

a dive
une plongée
dive centre
un centre de plongée
diving licence
un brevet de plongée
drift dive
une plongée à la dérive
air tanks
des bouteilles de plongée
flippers
des palmes
mask
un masque
regulator
un détendeur
snorkel
un tuba
wetsuit
une combinaison de plongée
weight belt
une ceinture de plomb

Some Useful Phrases

English	French	Tahitian
Hello/Good morning.	Bonjour.	Ia ora na, nana.
Goodbye.	Au revoir.	Pārahi, nana.
Welcome.	Bienvenue.	Maeva, mānava.
How are you?	Ça va?	E aha te huru?
My name is ...	Je m'appelle ...	To'u i'oa 'o ...
Thank you.	Merci.	Māuruuru roa
Pardon?	Comment?	E aha?
Excuse me/Sorry.	Pardon.	E'e, aue ho'i e.
No problem/Don't worry.	Pas de problème.	Aita pe'ape'a
No.	Non.	Aita
Yes.	Oui.	E, 'oia
Good luck!	Bon courage!	Fa'aitoito!
I don't understand.	Je ne comprends pas.	Aita i ta'a ia'u.
How much?	Combien?	E hia moni?
How many?	Combien?	E hia?
Where is ...?	Où est ...?	Tei hea ...?
When?	Quand?	Afea?
What time is it?	Quelle heure est-il?	E aha te hora i teie nei?
Cheers! (for drinking)	Santé!	Manuia!
I am ill.	Je suis malade.	E ma'i to'u.

Some Useful words

address	l'adresse	i'oa fa'aeara'a
bank	la banque	fare moni
bathroom	la salle de bain	piha pape
beach	la plage	tahatai
bed	le lit	ro'i
beer	la bière	pia
bicycle	le vélo	pereo'o tāta'ahi
boat	le bateau	poti
breakfast	le petit déjeuner	tafe poipoi
bus	l'autobus	pereo'o mata'eina'a
car	la voiture	pereo'o uira
chemist/pharmacy	la pharmacie	fare ra'au
coffee	le café	taofe
country	le pays	'ai'a
day	le jour	ao
embassy	l'ambassade	fare tonitera rahi
film (camera)	la pellicule	firimu
food	la nourriture	ma'a
map	le plan	hoho'a fenua
menu	la carte	tāpura mā'a
money	l'argent	moni
now	maintenant	i teinei
parents (extended family)	les parents	fēti'i

English	French	Tahitian
plantation	*la plantation*	*fa'a'apu*
police station	*le commissariat*	*fare mūto'i*
restaurant	*le restaurant*	*fare tāmā'ara'a*
room	*la chambre*	*piha*
shop	*le magasin*	*fare toa*
telephone	*le téléphone*	*niuniu paraparau*
that	*cela*	*terā*
today	*aujourd'hui*	*j teie nei mahana*
tomorrow	*demain*	*ānānahi*
tonight	*ce soir*	*i teie pō*
water	*l'eau*	*pape*

Numbers

1	*un*	*hō'ē/tahi*
2	*deux*	*piti*
3	*trois*	*toru*
4	*quatre*	*māha*
5	*cinq*	*pae*
6	*six*	*ono*
7	*sept*	*hitu*
8	*huit*	*va'u*
9	*neuf*	*iva*
10	*dix*	*hō'ē 'ahuru*
20	*vingt*	*piti 'ahuru*
100	*cent*	*hō'ē hānere*
500	*cinq cents*	*pae hanere*
1000	*mille*	*hō'ē tauatini*
5000	*cinq mille*	*pae tauatini*
10,000	*dix mille*	*hō'ē 'ahuru tauatini*
1,000,000	*un million*	*hō'ē mirioni*

Facts for the Visitor

VISAS & EMBASSIES

Except for French citizens anyone visiting French Polynesia needs a passport, and the regulations are much the same as for France itself: if you need a visa to visit France then you'll need one to visit Tahiti. Anyone from an European Union (EU) country can stay for up to three months without a visa. So can citizens of a number of other European countries including Switzerland.

Citizens of Canada, Japan, New Zealand, Singapore, the USA and some other European countries can stay for up to one month without a visa. All other nationalities, including Australians, need a visa which can be applied for at French diplomatic missions. In Australia a five-day visa to Tahiti costs A$5.40 and for longer stays (up to one month) a visa costs A$16.20.

Apart from permanent residents and French citizens, any visitor to French Polynesia must have an onward or return ticket, although this rule will probably soon be relaxed for EU citizens. Visitors from Fiji or from Pago Pago in American Samoa must have their baggage fumigated upon arrival. Visa regulations for French Polynesia can change at short notice so visitors should check with a French diplomatic office or their travel agent shortly before travelling.

For details of foreign consulates in Tahiti see the Information section in Papeete.

Visa Extensions & Exemptions

Travellers who must have a visa, or those who have a one-month exemption and wish to extend their stay beyond that month, should contact the DICILEC (air and border police) office at Faaa airport, open Monday to Friday from 8 am to noon and from 2 to 5 pm, at least one week before the visa or exemption expires. The extension granted is a maximum of two months. These travellers will have to pay a tax of 3000 CFP.

Travellers with a three-month visa exemption (essentially those from the EU and Switzerland) and all other foreign travellers who wish to extend their stay beyond three months must complete a form at the Direction de la Réglementation et du Contrôle de la Légalité (DRCL; Blvd Pomare, ☎ 54-27-00), which is the only authority that can deal with stays of over three months by foreign visitors. You must apply with plenty of time to spare, during the second month of your stay in the Territory, and extensions are not given automatically. One to three additional months may be granted. If you are successful, a tax of 3000 CFP is payable.

Stays by foreign visitors may not exceed six months. For longer periods, you must apply to the French consular authorities in your own country for a residence permit.

French Embassies

Addresses include the following (note that BP means 'post office box'):

Australia
  Embassy: 6 Perth Ave, Yarralumla, ACT 2600 (☎ (06) 270 5111, fax (06) 273 3193)
  Consulates: Level 4, 492 St Kilda Rd, Melbourne, Vic 3004 (☎ (03) 9820 0944, 9820 0921; fax (03) 9820 9363)
  20th floor, 31 Market St, Sydney, NSW 2000 (☎ (02) 9261 5931, 9261 5779; fax (02) 9267 2467
Belgium
  14 Place de Louvain, 1000 Brussels 23 (☎ (02) 229 8500, fax (02) 229 8510).
Canada
  Embassy: 42 Sussex Drive, Ottowa, Ontario K1M 2C9 (☎ (613) 789 1795, fax (613) 789 0279)
  Consulate: 130 Bloor St West, Suite 400, Toronto, Ontario M5S 1N5 (☎ (416) 925 8041, fax (416) 925 3076)
Chile
  65 Avenida Condell, Provindencia, Santiago (☎ (2) 225 10 30)
Fiji
  Dominion House, Thomson St, Suva (☎ (679) 300 991)
Germany
  Consulates: Kurfrstendamm 211, D-10719 Berlin (☎ (030) 885 90243, fax (030) 882 5295)

Johannisstrasse 2, D-66111 Saarbrücken (☎ (0681) 936 750, fax (0681) 31028)
Richard Wagner Strasse 53, D-70184 Stuttgart (☎ (0711) 23 74 70, fax (0711) 23 60 537)

Hong Kong
26th floor, Admiralty Centre, Tower Two, 18 Harcourt Rd, Admiralty (☎ 2529 4351, fax 2866 9693

Ireland
36 Ailesbury Rd, Ballsbridge, Dublin 4 (☎ (01) 260 1666, fax (01) 283 0178)

Israel
Consulate: Migdalor Building, 1/3 Ben Yehuda St (11th floor), 63801 Tel Aviv (☎ (03) 510 1415/6/7, fax (03) 510-4370/4)

Italy
Embassy: Via Giulia 251, 00186 Rome (☎ (06) 6880 6437, fax (06) 6860 1260)
Consulate: Corso Venezia 42, 20121 Milan (☎ (02) 6559 141, fax (02) 6559 1344)

Japan
11-44 4-chome, Minami Azabu, Minato-ku, Tokyo 106 (☎ (03) 5420 8800, fax (03) 5420 8847)

New Zealand
Robert Jones House, 1-3 Willeston St, Wellington (☎ (04) 472 0200, fax (04) 472 5887); postal address: PO Box 1695, Wellington

Netherlands
Vijzelgracht 2, Postbus 20018, 1000 HA Amsterdam (☎ (020) 624 83 46, fax (020) 626 0841)

Singapore
5 Gallop Rd, Singapore 1025 (☎ 466 4866, fax 469 0907)

South Africa
1009 Main Tower, Cape Town Center, Heerengracht, 8001 Cape Town (☎ (021) 21 2050, fax (021) 26 1996)
807 George Ave, Arcadia, 0083 Pretoria (☎ (012) 43 5564, fax (012) 43 3481)

Spain
Consulates: Calle Marques de la Enseada 10, 28004 Madrid (☎ (91) 319 7188, fax (91) 308 6273)
11 Paseo de Gracia, 08007 Barcelona (☎ (93) 317 8150, fax (93) 412 4282)

Switzerland
Embassy: Schosshaldenstrasse 46, BP 3000, 3006 Berne (☎ (031) 351 2424-9, fax (031) 352 0526)
Consulate: 11 Rue Imbert Galloix, 1205 Geneva (☎ (022) 311 34 41, fax (022) 310 83 39)

UK
Embassy: 58 Knightsbridge, London SW1X 7JT (☎ (0171) 201 1000)
Consulate: 21 Cromwell Rd, London SW7 2DQ (☎ (0171) 838 2000, fax (0171) 838 2001). The visa section is at 6A Cromwell Place, London SW7 2EW (☎ (0171) 838 2051). Dial ☎ (0891)

887733 for general information on visa requirements.

USA
Embassy: 4104 Reservoir Rd NW, Washington DC 20007 (☎ (202) 944 6195, fax (202) 944 6148)
Consulates: 934 Fifth Ave, New York, NY 10021 (☎ (212) 606 3688/9, fax (202) 606 3620)
540 Bush St, San Francisco, CA 94108 (☎ (415) 397 4330, fax (415) 433 8357)
Other consulates: Atlanta, Boston, Chicago, Honolulu, Houston, Los Angeles, Miami, New Orleans and San Juan (Puerto Rico).

Formalities for Pleasure Boats

In addition to presenting the certificate of ownership of the vessel, sailors are subject to the same passport and visa requirements as those arriving by air (see earlier in this section). Unless you have a return air ticket, you must pay a repatriation bond of 118,200 CFP for non-EU Europeans, 89,000 CFP for Canadians and Americans and 79,000 CFP for those from the Pacific region. For citizens of EU countries, the need for a bond or return ticket was about to be reviewed at the time of writing.

Yachties must advise the air and border police at Papeete of their final departure and the police will then issue a release from the bond. This release document must be presented to the police on the last island at which they call (generally Bora Bora). Yachties may then have their bond refunded. It should be noted that each crew member must pay the bond.

It is compulsory that the first port of call be one of those with a police station, namely Papeete, Afareaitu, Uturoa, Fare, Vaitape (Society Islands), Taiohae, Hakahau, Atuona (Marquesas), Mataura, Moerai, Raima (Australs) or Tiputa (Tuamotu). The police must be advised of each arrival and departure. Any change of crew must also be notified.

With regard to customs, the boat and equipment on board are considered exempt of tax for six months, which can be extended for a further six months on application to the director of customs. Note that if the skipper works anywhere other than on the boat, he or she is no longer entitled to this exemption and must pay import duty on the boat.

Before arriving at the port of Papeete, notify your arrival on channel 12. Two anchorages are provided: the quay or the beach. There are no reserved places. Report to the harbour master's office to complete an arrival declaration. You will have to pay several taxes, payable in one lump sum when you leave Papeete (you will then be issued with a departure permit): a single entrance tax (2200 to 3700 CFP according to the size of vessel), a daily quay tax (939 CFP at the quay with water and electricity, 367 CFP at the beach with no water or electricity for a 12-metre yacht). In addition to the port of Papeete, the anchorage points are the Yacht Club at Arue and Maeva Beach. It is forbidden to anchor in Taaone Bay. Advise the harbour master's office of all your movements. Notify on channel 12 if passing close to the airport.

In Papeete, the offices of the air and border police are open Monday to Friday from 7.30 to 11 am and from 1.30 to 3.30 pm; customs are open Monday to Friday from 7.30 to 11.30 am and from 2.30 to 5 pm; and the harbour master is open Monday to Thursday from 7 to 11.30 am and from 1 to 4 pm and Friday to 3 pm. They are all in the same building on the seafront, 50 metres from the tourist office. Be aware of the opening hours, especially if you intend leaving Papeete on the weekend. In this case, report to these offices on Thursday to complete your departure formalities.

On the other islands, the police are the relevant authority, but in Papeete you must report to the three offices mentioned.

Sailing in the atolls of the Anaa quadrant is subject to authorisation. At the time of writing, the right of way through the territorial waters surrounding Fangataufa and Moruroa atolls was suspended. Request information.

DOCUMENTS
See the Visas & Embassies section for passport regulations. Certification of cholera, yellow fever or plague vaccination is required if you arrive from an infected area. You will need your driving licence if you plan to rent a car and your scuba-certification card if you plan to do any scuba diving.

CUSTOMS
The usual alcohol and tobacco limitations apply to visitors to French Polynesia. Note that people arriving from Fiji or Pago Pago in American Samoa will have their baggage fumigated upon arrival at the airport. No live animals can be imported and certification is required for plants.

MONEY
The unit of currency in French Polynesia is the Cour de Franc Pacifique (or CFP). There are coins of 1, 2, 5, 10, 20, 50 and 100 CFP and notes of 500, 1000, 5000 and 10,000 CFP. The CFP is at a fixed rate to the French franc and therefore varies against other currencies with the franc.

Exchange Rates

France	1FF	=	18 CFP
USA	US$1	=	93 CFP
Australia	A$1	=	73 CFP
United Kingdom	UK£1	=	145 CFP
Canada	C$1	=	68 CFP
New Zealand	NZ$1	=	64 CFP
Germany	DM1	=	64 CFP
Japan	¥100	=	84 CFP

Banks
There are four major banks operating widely in French Polynesia. Banque Socredo is the one you find most often; if there's only one bank on an island it will probably be a branch of Banque Socredo. The other three banks are Banque de Polynésie, Banque de Tahiti and the Australian bank Westpac. Of course there are branches of all four banks in Papeete and other centres on Tahiti and in other busier centres – Vaitape in Bora Bora or Uturoa in Raiatea for example.

Banking hours vary slightly from branch to branch but they're typically from 8 am to noon and 1 to 4 pm. Some branches in Papeete do not close for the traditional Polynesian lunchbreak and a handful of Tahiti branches open on Saturday morning. There

. are banking facilities open at Papeete's Faaa airport for flight arrivals.

Changing Money

There are hefty bank charges for changing money or travellers' cheques in French Polynesia. For each transaction Banque Socredo charges 350 CFP, Banque de Polynésie and Banque de Tahiti charge 400 CFP and Westpac charges 450 CFP. This means on a simple US$100 exchange you lose around 5%. The answer, of course, is to spread the cost over a larger transaction and, given the high cost of living, the money is soon going to disappear in any case! The exchange rates vary from one bank to another so check first before assuming the lower fixed charge at one bank automatically makes it a better deal.

ATMs

Automated teller machines will give you cash advances on your Visa or MasterCard or, if linked to the international Cirrus or Maestro networks, they will let you withdraw money straight from your home bank account. The exchange rate on these transactions is usually better than you get with travellers' cheques and, since the banks have a hefty fixed rate on all exchange transactions, the charge your own bank makes on these withdrawals (typically about US$3 to US$5) doesn't hurt.

ATMs can be found at numerous locations on Tahiti but they're less common on other islands. Moorea, Huahine, Raiatea and Bora Bora currently have ATMs although there may only be one or two on the whole island.

Tipping

Officially, tipping is not compatible with the Polynesian outlook on life and the tourist office supposedly discourages it. In practice tipping is becoming more prevalent in tourist-oriented outlets, at least on Tahiti. On the outer islands it's still rare.

Bargaining

The Pacific is not like Asia: nowhere in the Pacific is bargaining the norm and the price listed is the price you're expected to pay. Throughout French Polynesia virtually the

---

An Expensive Place?

Tahiti has a reputation for being horribly expensive, rather snobbish and not as much fun as it should be. Well it is pretty pricey, but if you can push thoughts of ticking meters to the back of your mind it can be an enormously enjoyable place to visit. The big international hotels are costly, a high-class meal for two with a bottle of French wine will often set you back US$100, and anything imported, from sunscreen to film, will make you wish you'd stocked up before you left.

However, some of those five-star over-water bungalows are truly superb, and the islands can still be deservedly popular with backpackers. You can rent bicycles or motor scooters to get around, there's a selection of small family-run pensions on almost every inhabited island and, so long as you've got plenty of time, there are also lots of inter-island boats to shuttle you from one island to another. It's no wonder backpacks are a common sight in the dockside bustle of Papeete.

Nor is everything in French Polynesia priced through the ceiling. Two great bargains are public transport in Tahiti and sandwiches just about anywhere. Le truck, as the truck-like local bus service is known, is definitely the way to get around the Papeete area. It's cheap (120 CFP or about US$1.30 along the hotel strip of the coast), very frequent and easy to use. And we may wish the French had left their nuclear bombs at home, but any visitor will be glad they brought their bread with them. Tahiti's terrific French-bread sandwiches (casse-croûte) have to be the best food bargain in the Pacific.

Why are things so expensive? First of all, because it's a colonial economy with a heavy layer of French-style bureaucracy run not just at metropolitan-French costs but at that level of costs plus an overseas loading! French Polynesia is weighed down with French civil servants pulling down huge salaries. In turn, many other pay scales are related to this inflated baseline. Secondly, there is only minimal income tax but there are heavy import duties on many products. Finally, a great many products are shipped all the way around the world from France rather than being bought from neighbouring Pacific nations. ■

only exception is for black pearls or similar expensive jewellery where some discounting can always be expected.

WHEN TO GO

June through October is drier and cooler, and visibility for scuba diving is likely to be better. November through May tends to be warmer and more humid. In June, July and into August the *maraamu* tradewinds can bring blustery weather and rain from the south. During that period it's often better on the more sheltered northern sides of the high islands.

The month of activities in July, combining the local Heiva festivities with the French Bastille Day celebrations on 14 July, draws in big crowds. There's dance, music, all sorts of sporting and cultural events, beauty contests and big crowds. It's not only popular locally but it's also one of the most popular times of year for international visitors to French Polynesia, so plan ahead. March is a popular holiday month in the outer islands including the Australs, Marquesas and Tuamotus.

French Polynesia may be south of the equator but school holidays still fall in line with France, and they can add to crowds at resorts and make flights more difficult to get. This means that from Christmas to the beginning of January, the end of February or beginning of March, the Easter period, the beginning of May, the longer northern-summer holiday in July-August and the beginning of October are likely to be busier.

WHAT TO BRING

The climate is mild and dress rules are relaxed so you don't need to bring much with you. Coats and ties are not required except on the most formal business occasions and it would take a cold day in the Australs, the most southerly islands of the group, to need more than a short-sleeved shirt or blouse. Shorts, swimsuits and lightweight cotton clothes are the order of the day.

This is the tropics and visitors should be prepared for the intense sun (bring sunscreen, sunglasses and a hat) while not forgetting the sun can disappear to be replaced by heavy (but usually short) downpours. The temperatures will remain high, however, so an umbrella is probably wiser than a raincoat. Insect repellent can be near vital, particularly if you have any sensitivity to mosquito bites, and a small first aid kit (see the Health section) is always wise. Plastic shoes or an old pair of sneakers are a good idea for avoiding cuts when walking on coral.

Imported goods are always expensive in French Polynesia so bring sunscreen, film, toiletries and any other consumables. If, however, you find you need a swimsuit or a new T-shirt there's lots on sale, often at not too excessive prices. Such items are imported from Europe, the USA and Asia.

If you're backpacking or travelling to the more remote islands, you'll need to pack some essentials which are unnecessary for those staying at the big hotels. Small family-run *pensions* (guesthouses) may not supply towels or soap so bring both. Although overseas visitors are given some leeway, the official baggage weight limit on Air Tahiti flights is just 10 kg, so pack light. You can always leave things behind in Papeete but bring something to pack the leftovers in. If you're going to be travelling extensively, jumping on and off inter-island boats, riding *le trucks* and so on, then a soft bag, either a backpack or a travel pack, will be easy to travel with.

TOURIST OFFICES
Local Tourist Offices

There is a major tourist office on the quayside in Papeete and counter at Faaa airport which may or may not be operating. For information contact GIE Tahiti Tourisme (☎ (689) 50-57-00, fax (689) 43-66-19), BP 65, Papeete, Tahiti.

The more touristed of the other islands will often have some sort of tourist office or counter but they vary widely in usefulness and dependability. These local tourist offices are generally run by local government or local businesses, and even finding them open is a hit-and-miss affair.

Tourist Offices Overseas

Overseas addresses of the Tahiti Tourist Board include:

Australia
Tahiti Tourism Promotion Board, Suite 301, 620 St Kilda Rd, Melbourne 3004 (☎ (03) 9521 3877, fax (03) 9521 3867)

Chile
Tahiti Tourism Board, Ave 11 de Septiembre 2214, OF 116, Box 16057, Stgo 9, Santiago (☎ (2) 261 28 26, fax (2) 261 28 26)

France
Office du Tourisme de Tahiti et ses Îles, 28 Blvd Saint-Germain, 75005 Paris (☎ 01 46 34 50 59, fax 01 43 25 41 65)

Germany
Tahiti Tourisme, Haingasse 22, D-61348 Bad Hamburg VDH (☎ 6172 21021, fax 6172 690 488)

Hong Kong
Tahiti Tourist Promotion Board, c/o Pacific Leisure, Room 902, Tung Ming Bldg, 40 Des Voeux Rd, Hong Kong Central (☎ 2 524 1361, fax 2525 3290)

Indonesia
Tahiti Tourist Promotion Board, c/o PT Aviamas Megabuana, Wisma Metropolitan II, Jendral Suderman Kav 29-31, Jakarta 12920 (☎ (021) 570 1666, fax (021) 522 6317)

Japan
Tahiti Tourist Promotion Board, Sankyo Building (No 20), Room 802, 3-11-5 Iidabashi, Chiyoda-Ku, Tokyo 102 (☎ (03) 3265 0468, fax (03) 3265 0581)

Korea
Tahiti Tourist Promotion Board, Daerim Apt 6-802, Ogum-dong 2, Songpa-Ku, Seoul (☎ (02) 448 5644, fax (02) 448 5645)

Malaysia
Tahiti Tourist Promotion Board, c/o Pacific Leisure, 2.5 – 2.6 Angkasa Raya Building, Jalan Ampang, 50 450 Kuala Lumpur (☎ (03) 24 13 070, fax (03) 24 21 129)

New Zealand
Tahiti Tourist Promotion Board, Level 1, Southpac tower, 45 Queen St, Auckland (☎ (09) 373 2649, fax (09) 373 2415)

Singapore
Tahiti Tourist Promotion Board, 72 Amoy St, Singapore 0106 (☎ 223 0144, fax 227 8500)

Taiwan
Tahiti Tourist Promotion Board, c/o Travelswift Ltd, 98 Nanking East Rd, Section 2, 5th floor, Taipei (☎ (02) 511 4484, fax (02) 563 7425)
Tahiti Tourist Promotion Board, c/o Pacific Leisure, 8th floor Maneeya Centre Bldg, 518/5 Ploenchit Rd, Bangkok 10 330 (☎ (02) 2511 393, fax (02) 2556 839)

USA
Tahiti Tourist Promotion Board, 300 N Continental Blvd, Suite 180, El Segundo, CA 90245 (☎ (310) 414 8484, fax (310) 414 8490)
Tahiti Tourist Promotion Board, 444 Madison Ave, 16th floor, New York, NY 10020 (☎ (212) 838 7800, fax (212) 838 7855)

USEFUL ORGANISATIONS

The Territorial Cultural Action Office (OTAC; ☎ 42-88-50636, Blvd Pomare, BP 1709, Papeete) is devoted to promoting all cultural events. In addition to the traditional Heiva, it organises concerts and craft exhibitions and stages plays in French and Tahitian. Cultural weeks or gatherings are held there regularly. Tahitian language courses at beginners and more advanced levels are also available. It's open Monday to Friday from 8 am to noon and 1 to 5 pm (4 pm on Friday).

BUSINESS HOURS

Normal business hours are Monday to Friday, from around 8 and 10 am to 5 pm. There are frequent exceptions particularly with larger stores, which may stay open later, or small food stores, which may stay open very late. A long and leisurely lunchbreak is the norm, even for banks outside Tahiti. On weekends shops are usually open on Saturday morning but most close in the afternoon and on Sunday everything is closed.

HOLIDAYS & SPECIAL EVENTS

Public holidays, when businesses and government offices shut down, are: 1 January (New Year's Day), 5 March (Arrival of the First Missionaries), Good Friday, Easter, Easter Monday, 1 May (May Day), 8 May (V-E Day), last Thursday in May (Ascension), first Sunday and Monday in June (Pentecost and Pentecost Monday), 29 June (Internal Autonomy Day), 14 July (Bastille Day), 15 August (Assumption), 1 November (All Saints' Day), 11 November (Armistice Day) and 25 December (Christmas Day).

Popular holidays and festivals include:

New Year's Day
New Year's Eve and New Year's Day are cele-brated with friends, family, singing and dancing.

Chinese New Year
Usually falling between late January and mid-February, the new year is ushered in with dancing, martial arts displays and fireworks.

International Marathon
The Moorea Marathon takes place in late Febru-ary for anyone keen to run around most of the island.

Arrival of the First Missionaries
The arrival of the first LMS missionaries on board the *Duff* is commemorated on 5 March each year. The landing is re-enacted at Point Venus and there are celebrations at Protestant churches on Tahiti and Moorea and in the stadiums in Tipaerui on Tahiti and Afareaitu on Moorea. Actually, the missionaries arrived on 4 March but they did not know about the International Date Line.

Beauty Contests
The Tahitians love beauty contests and there are lots of them held in April and May leading up to the Miss Tahiti and Miss Heiva i Tahiti contests in June. Just to show there is no sexism involved Mr Tahiti contests are also held.

Tahiti International Golf Open
The four-day championship takes place at the Olivier Breaud Golf Course on Tahiti in late June to early July.

Hawaiki Nui Canoe Race

In French Polynesia the big event – the sporting spectacular that has the entire nation glued to its TV sets and talking passionately about favourites and challengers – is a canoe race. The three-day, four-island, 116-km Hawaiki Nui Va'a race pits 60-odd of the islands' best six-man pirogues against each other and against any paddlers brave enough to turn up from overseas.

The first day of the race, held in early to mid-November, starts on day one on the island of Huahine and goes out of the lagoon and across 44.5 km of open sea to Raiatea. The canoes are a superb sight, dramatically televised live for the four-hour crossing. The brawny paddlers, often sporting vivid Tahitian tattoos, paddle three on each side for about 10 strokes then switch sides with precise timing and lightning speed.

Day two takes the canoes on a 20-km sprint within the lagoon between the twin islands of Raiatea and Tahaa. Plan on completing this leg in under 1½ hours if you want to remain in contention.

Day three, finishing on a Saturday, is the big one: a 52-km crossing of open sea to Bora Bora. Starting around 6.30 am the leading canoe arrives at the finish line at Matira Beach about four hours later. It's a fantastic sight with thousands of cheering spectators lining the beach and wading out to greet the arriving canoes. Drummers pound out an encouraging rhythm from a float by the finishing line, TV camera crews wade out into the water to film the excitement, and happy supporters wait with flower *leis* to garland their teams.

In 1995 the big question was could Faaa do it again? The supermen from the airport suburb of Papeete were trying for a third victory but they had lost in 1994 and, even worse, they'd been beaten at the Molokai outrigger race in Hawaii (after two consecutive victories there) by, gasp, a team of Hawaiians! Could it happen on home ground? Could the Hawaiian Lanikai Canoe Club beat Tahiti's best?

Sixty four canoes started the race, two from Hawaii, half of the rest from the Tahiti island itself. Leg one was not good for Faaa, they finished 5th, well behind the popular favourites, the Fare Ara canoe of Huahine island. The fastest Hawaiians were way back in 29th place, partly because their escort boat got lost! Day two, however, saw the men from Faaa show their stuff, storming off to victory. On day three the canoes divided into two major groups, setting off in different directions on the longest and toughest paddle. The Faaa canoe led one group while the challengers from Huahine led the other.

A third canoe, from the Pirae district of Tahiti, took a unique route and in the final race to the finish looked like it might have made a wise choice, but once again it was Faaa that came through to victory. Second place went to the underdog Huahine paddlers. The Hawaiians finished the Bora Bora leg 7th, to loud cheers, and 15th overall. Hawaiians have not been the only overseas challengers. In 1994 a team of German Olympic kayakers entered the Hawaiki Nui – their best finish was 18th on the first leg.

For the first time there was also a women's pirogue race, the Vaa Hine, a pun on *vaa*, Tahitian for canoe, and *vahine*, Tahitian for 'woman'. The one-day 40-km race made a circuit of the island of Tahaa. The Rautere team from Tahiti won, with Hawaiian teams taking 5th and 9th place. The race was such a success that there is talk of using the same four-island route as the men's race next year, but permitting the women's teams to substitute paddlers along the way. ■

Heiva i Tahiti

The month-long Tahiti Festival (*heiva* means 'festival') features dancing, singing, sporting competitions, arts and crafts displays and beauty contests. The sporting events include a host of local specialities including surfing events, canoe races, stone-lifting contests, javelin-throwing contests and fruit-carrying races. The major French holiday on Bastille Day, 14 July, falls in the middle of the Heiva Festivities and is a highlight of the month.

Annual Flower Show

This kicks off in September in the Bougainville Park in Papeete.

Surfing Contest

In September there is a major surfing competition at Punaauia on Tahiti.

Stone-Fishing Contest

Traditional stone-fishing celebrations take place in Bora Bora during the first half of the month. There are also stone-fishing festivities on other islands.

Hawaiki Nui Canoe Race

French Polynesia's major sporting event of the year is the three-day *pirogue* (outrigger canoe) race from Huahine to Raiatea, Tahaa and Bora Bora.

All Saints' Day

Graves are cleaned and decorated and families sing hymns in the candle-lit cemeteries on 1 November.

Tiare Tahiti Days

The national flower is celebrated on 1 and 2 December. The Festival des Îles Marquises in December is a major arts festival at Ua Pou with the accent on the Marquesan identity.

Christmas

Christmas Day on 25 December is celebrated with enthusiasm.

POST & TELECOMMUNICATIONS

Post

Mail to Europe, the USA or Australia takes about a week and the postal system is generally quite efficient. There are modern post offices on all the main islands. French Polynesian stamps are often beautiful but even more often they're massive, so put stamps on your postcard first so you know how much space is left to squeeze the address in. If you're lucky there may still be room for your message.

Post offices are generally open Monday to Friday, usually from 7 am to around 3 pm. In Tahiti the main post office in Papeete has longer opening hours and a post office is open at Faaa airport in the evenings even on weekends. Aerograms cost 76 CFP. Other postal rates include:

Destination	letters up to 20 g	small post cards
France	51 CFP	51 CFP
elsewhere in Europe	110 CFP	100 CFP
North America	110 CFP	92 CFP
Australia & New Zealand	102 CFP	88 CFP
Hawaii & Pacific Islands	94 CFP	84 CFP
Asia	102 CFP	88 CFP

Sending & Receiving Mail There is no door-to-door mail delivery in French Polynesia, so mail is usually addressed to a BP (*boîte postale* – post office box) number. If you want to receive mail ask for it to be addressed to you at poste restante at the appropriate post office, eg:

John Doe
Poste Restante
Vaitape
Bora Bora
French Polynesia

American Express card or travellers' cheque holders can have mail addressed to them care of the American Express agent in French Polynesia: Tahiti Tours, BP 627, Papeete, Tahiti, French Polynesia.

Telephone

The telephone system is modern, easy to use, widespread and, when it comes to international calls, rather expensive. Public phone boxes are found even in surprisingly remote locations but most of them require phonecards rather than coins. Phonecards can be bought from post offices or from many retail shops. They're even available from vending machines at Faaa airport. Phonecards are available in 1000, 2000 and 5000 CFP denominations. A 5000 CFP card will give you a 15-minute phone call from a public phone box to a US number.

Local Calls There are no area codes in Tahiti although the first two digits of the local number indicate its location. Tahiti numbers start in the 40s, 50s, or 80s; Moorea is 56,

Raiatea 66, Bora Bora and Maupiti 67, Huahine 68, Marquesas 92, Rurutu 94, Tubuai 95, Tuamotus 96 or 97, and Gambier Archipelago 97. Local phone calls cost 50 CFP.

International Calls To call a number in French Polynesia from overseas dial the international access number, then 689 (Tahiti's country code), then the local number.

To call overseas from French Polynesia dial 00, then your country code, area code (dropping any leading 0) and the local number. Country codes include 1 for the USA and Canada, 31 for the Netherlands, 33 for France, 39 for Italy, 41 for Switzerland, 44 for the UK, 45 for Denmark, 46 for Spain, 47 for Norway, 49 for Germany, 56 for Chile, 61 for Australia, 63 for New Zealand, 353 for Ireland, 358 for Finland, 682 for the Cook Islands, 852 for Hong Kong and 972 for Israel. It is generally not possible to make reverse-charge calls or calls billed to a credit card or overseas phonecard from a phone box. Information cards in the phone boxes explain, in French and English, how to make overseas calls but the suggestion that you dial 19 to get the operator only gets you a message that you cannot dial 19 from a phone box. Try dialling 12. If the operator does not speak English, request a reverse-charge call by asking for a call 'payable à l'arrivée'.

International phone calls from Tahiti are expensive but they're certainly much cheaper than they used to be. A regular series of price cuts brought the cost of a standard one-minute call down to the following levels as of early 1996:

Australia & New Zealand	220 CFP
Hawaii & Fiji	250 CFP
France	300 CFP
USA, Canada & Japan	330 CFP
EU Countries, Switzerland, Singapore,	
Hong Kong & Chile	380 CFP
other South American nations	450 CFP

If international phone calls from Tahiti are expensive to start with, from hotels they are

simply amazing. From a public phone a call to the USA is 330 CFP or about US$4 a minute. Calling Tahiti from a US public phone would be about the same, although call rates from a private or business phone in the US to Tahiti can be less than 50c a minute. Dial a US number on your room phone in a friendly Polynesian Sofitel, however, and the bill will mount up at a positively stratospheric 2300 CFP (US$26) a minute, or over US$130 for a five-minute call. Talk about the *force de frappe*! Do not phone overseas from your hotel room without making absolutely certain what it is going to cost you. Sofitel also charges 1500 CFP a minute to France, 2000 CFP elsewhere in Europe and 2300 CFP to Japan.

TIME

French Polynesia is 10 hours behind GMT, and is just two hours east of the International Date Line. When it is noon in Tahiti it is 2 pm on the US West Coast, 5 pm on the US East Coast, 10 pm in London, 11 pm in Paris, 8 am the next day on the Australian east coast or 10 am the next day in New Zealand. The Marquesas are a half hour ahead of the rest of French Polynesia (noon in Tahiti is 12.30 pm in the Marquesas) but check flight schedules carefully: Air Tahiti departures and arrivals in the Marquesas may run to Tahiti time.

ELECTRICITY

Electric current is generally 220 v, 60 MHz, as in most of the western world apart from Japan and North America. Sockets are generally the French-style outlets requiring a plug with two round pins. Some deluxe hotels may have 110-v supply for electric shavers.

WEIGHTS & MEASURES

French Polynesia uses the metric system; see the inside back cover for a conversion chart.

LAUNDRY

Laundry can be a real problem in French Polynesia. Big hotels will, of course, wash clothes at prices which make it feasible to simply throw things away and buy new ones. Otherwise laundrettes are just about unknown outside of Papeete and even there the prices are amazing. Can you picture US$8 to run a load of washing through the machine? And the same again to dry it? On the other hand you'll certainly need to wash some clothes if you're doing anything other than lazing back in air-conditioned comfort. A day's bike riding or mountain walking will work up a sweat that can cause your clothes to develop alien life forms within 24 hours if they're not washed.

BOOKS

There is a surprisingly wide range of literature on French Polynesia and a number of excellent bookshops in Papeete. Some of the most interesting titles are only readily available in French Polynesia and there are some very interesting books which are only available in French. Although the suggestions that follow are predominantly for books available in English, there are a few suggestions for French titles which may be of interest even if your French is poor (or nonexistent). See the relevant island chapters for information on bookshops. But it's Papeete that has the best bookshops in French Polynesia.

The European Arrival

For a concise, succinct and highly readable account of the collision between Europe and Polynesia, David Howarth's *Tahiti: a Paradise Lost* (1984, Viking) is hard to beat. European explorers encountered the beauty of Tahiti with a mixture of bewilderment and delight, but in a remarkably short period of time private property (an alien concept to late 18th-century Tahiti), alcohol and prostitution had virtually destroyed all the qualities the first visitors found so attractive. The contrast between the early explorers' accounts and the disillusionment of writers like Herman Melville and Robert Louis Stevenson just a century later is a measure of the Tahitian tragedy.

The Fatal Impact, by Alan Moorehead (1966, possibly available in Penguin paperback) traces the three voyages of Captain Cook and the impact they had upon the untouched cultures of the Pacific and Australia. Cook, a man of high ideals and insight, had some concern for the dramatic changes which were to irrevocably change the Pacific, so long isolated from the rest of the world.

Cook's logbooks of his voyages are the prime accounts of his pioneering visits to Polynesia. Originally they were published in a heavily edited version taking considerable liberties with his own observations. Professor JC Beaglehole's four volume, 3000-page edition of Cook's logbook, published progressively between 1955 and 1967, is the most thorough version of the original logs: *The Voyages of the Endeavour, 1768-1771*, by Captain James Cook. A briefer introduction to these fascinating accounts is *The Explorations of Captain James Cook in the Pacific* (1971, Dover, New York). These annotated extracts from his logs are fascinating but they really only give you a taste of the real thing.

Professor Beaglehole, the renowned expert on the Cook expeditions, also edited Sir Joseph Bank's account in *The 'Endeavour' Journal of Joseph Banks* in two volumes. Many other early visitors from Wallis to Morrison, the boatswain's mate on the *Bounty* wrote their accounts of Tahiti, but you would have to use a major library to track them down. One of the few accounts of pre-European Tahiti from the Polynesian side is Teuira Henry's account of her investigations into the ancient religion of the islands in *Ancient Tahiti*, published in 1928.

The American duo of Nordhoff & Hall wrote three books on the *Bounty* mutiny and its aftermath, published in 1934. *Mutiny on the Bounty* recounts the famous mutiny and provided the plotline for the first two cinematic versions of the story. *Men against the Sea* follows Bligh's epic open-boat voyage while *Pitcairn Island*, with much more imagination because so little is known about the Pitcairn story, follows Fletcher Christian and his band of mutineers and Tahitians to their Pitcairn hideaway.

Travel Literature

A remarkable number of renowned writers have written books either using Polynesia as a setting or describing their own visits. Herman Melville, Pierre Loti, Robert Louis Stevenson, Jack London and Somerset Maugham all paid visits.

Melville was the first of the important visitors, deserting whalers in the Marquesas and then in Tahiti. His experiences in the 'cannibal' valley, where he made his Marquesan escape, became his first novel, *Typee* (1846). Seductively subtitled in the British edition a 'Narrative of a Four Months' Residence among the Natives of a Valley of the Marquesas Islands: or, a Peep at Polynesian Life', it was an instant success. He followed it up with *Omoo* (1847), based on his further adventures on another whaling hell-ship, an attempted mutiny, his arrest by the French (who were in the process of taking over Tahiti), imprisonment in Papeete and then a spell on Moorea.

French literature's primary contribution to the Tahiti bookshelves was Pierre Loti's 1876 novel *The Marriage of Loti*, which made its own contribution to the romantic Tahitian myth and also gave the author his pen name.

Robert Louis Stevenson cruised through Polynesia with visits to the Marquesas, the Tuamotus and Tahiti which resulted in the book *In the South Seas*, published in 1900. This was the visit that inspired him to settle in Samoa but, although he was clearly falling in love with the region, the book is far from Stevenson at his best. Tahiti, where he made a protracted stay in Tautira on Tahiti Iti, doesn't even feature in the account. Jack London also cruised the Pacific but, again, *South Sea Tales* (1911) is not the writer at his best. The greedy pearl buyer portrayed in 'The House of Mapuhi' successfully took London to court.

W Somerset Maugham managed rather better with Tahiti, which he visited to research his 1919 novel *The Moon & Sixpence*. Rather loosely based on Gauguin's life, the tortured artist in the novel, Charles Strickland, is English rather than French,

visits Tahiti only once and dies there, whereas Gauguin made three separate visits to Polynesia and died on Hiva Oa in the Marquesas. Strickland is also a resolutely single-minded individual, totally uninterested in what any other artist was doing, whereas Gauguin was clearly very interested in other artists' work and only developed his own style after a great deal of experimentation and imitation.

Art & Culture

The Art of Tahiti, by Terence Barrow (1979, Thames & Hudson, London), gives a succinct and colourfully illustrated introduction to the art of the Society, the Austral and Cook islands. Unfortunately, it does not extend to the Marquesas. Although the pioneering missionaries did such a thorough job in suppressing the pre-European culture and destroying the native art, they did thoughtfully save a few prime pieces, now on display in Europe's finest museums.

There are countless books on Gauguin and his works, while *Noa Noa* is his own illustrated autobiographical account of his life in Tahiti.

Tatau – Maohi Tattoo, by Dominique Morvan, with photographs by Claude Corault and Marie-Hélène Villierme (1993, Tupuna Productions) is a fascinating account of the resurgence of traditional tattooing in French Polynesia.

Hiva Oa – Glimpses of an Oceanic Memory, by Pierre Ottino and Marie-Noëlle de Bergh-Ottino (1991, Département Archéologie, Papeete), is a locally produced book on the archaeology and art of the Marquesan island of Hiva Oa.

Natural History

The Tahiti Handbook, by Jean-Louis Saquet (1993, Éditions Avant et Aprés, Tahiti), has interesting information on Tahiti's history and culture as well as the natural environment including the geography, flora and fauna. It's also available in French.

A variety of smalls books are available on the flora and fauna of Polynesia. Two worth looking at are *Birds of Tahiti*, by Jean-Claude

Thibault & Claude Rivers (1988, Les Éditions du Pacifique), and *Sharks of Polynesia*, by RH Johnson (1990, Les Éditions du Pacifique).

Modern Accounts

More recently, James Michener launched his prodigious output of writing with *Tales of the South Pacific* in 1947, stories drawn from his experiences in the region during WWII. The most famous of those tales created the myth of Bali Hai, which was of course Bora Bora, although it had migrated many miles before becoming the stage play and film *South Pacific*. Michener returned to this happy hunting ground with *Return to Paradise* (1951) and *Rascals in Paradise* (1957), the latter offering an interesting study of Bligh and his mutinies.

The congenitally acerbic Paul Theroux was at his sourest when he visited *The Happy Isles of Oceania* (1992). Crossing the whole South Pacific from Australia and New Zealand to Hawaii, he didn't find much of it, apart from Hawaii, very happy, but the insights are up to his usual high standards. In French Polynesia he visits Tahiti and Moorea but saves most of his energy for a trip on the *Aranui* to the Marquesas. As usual, his fellow passengers are prodded unmercifully with his sharpest pen and the beautiful but gloomy, historic but tragic, isolated yet spoilt Marquesas are the perfect site for a Theroux visit. The French don't come out of it very well but nor do the Polynesians, eagerly embracing their own decline.

Much more upbeat is Gavin Bell's *In Search of Tusitala* (1994) which won the 1995 Thomas Cook/Daily Telegraph Travel Book Award and is also available in paperback. The author traces the Pacific wanderings of Robert Louis Stevenson a century earlier with visits to the Marquesas, Fakarava in the Tuamotus, and Tahiti. He also stops off in Rangiroa, which Stevenson did not visit, for a little communing with the sharks. Like a number of other writers, Bell finds the Marquesas fascinating, beautiful and deeply, almost frighteningly, depressing. He also finds the blackflies unbearable and

that it rains nonstop. 'How long has it been raining?' Bell asks the first Marquesan he meets, after a terrifying five-approach landing. 'About one year,' comes the reply.

Guidebooks

Nouvelles Éditions Latines in Paris and the Société des Océanistes produce a number of small guidebooks to French Polynesia, most of them available in French and English. Published in the 1960s and '70s they're unfortunately all rather old and often outdated. They even tend to look old, clearly having spent many tropical years on bookshop shelves. Nevertheless, a number of them have interesting material. They include the booklets *Moorea*, *Huahine*, *Wings over Tahiti* (the history of aviation in French Polynesia), *Sacred Stones & Rites* (about Polynesian temples), *Pomare – Queen of Tahiti* and *Bougainville in Tahiti*.

If you're doing the coast-road circuit of Tahiti, Bengt Danielsson's *Tahiti – Circle Island Tour Guide* (1987, Les Éditions du Pacifique) makes a good companion. Danielsson first arrived in Tahiti in 1947 with Thor Heyerdahl's *Kon Tiki* expedition and has lived in French Polynesia permanently since 1971. He has specialised in annoying the government over its nuclear-testing programme. First written in 1971, his book has been periodically updated, but there have been significant changes on the islands in the past 10 years so not everything will be as it suggests. Danielsson is the author of a number of other interesting books on Tahiti and Polynesia.

Diving in Tahiti – a Divers' Guide to French Polynesia, by Thierry Zysman (1991, Les Éditions du Pacifique, Singapore), has general diving information for French Polynesia plus the specifics on facilities and dive sites on the main islands in the Society group and Rangiroa and Manihi in the Tuamotus. It's also available in French.

Even if they can't understand French, keen walkers may find a copy of *Randonnées en Montagne – Tahiti – Moorea* by Paule Laudon (1995, Les Éditions du Pacifique,

Tahiti Literati

Tahiti has clearly had a magnetic effect on writers who have flocked to the islands like bees to honey, gaining inspiration to launch careers, produce masterpieces or simply sit back and enjoy the scenery. Writers who have come to Tahiti include the following:

Herman Melville Melville (1819-1891) was only a would-be writer when he turned up in French Polynesia in 1842, but he arrived at a critical time, when Tahiti was about to lose its independence and the French were in the process of taking over. He deserted the whaler *Acushnet*, a real hell-ship which became the *Dolly* in his novel, and escaped into an almost-forgotten valley on the island of Nuku Hiva. His adventures there provided the material for *Typee*, his first literary success.

Herman Melville

Joining another whaleboat, the Australian *Lucy Ann*, which became the American *Julia* in his second book, *Omoo*, Melville sailed on to Tahiti, where he was accused of attempting a mutiny. He managed to arrive just as the French admiral Dupetit-Thouars was threatening Papeete. Melville was promptly arrested and imprisoned, at first on the French warship and then in the Calaboose Beretanee, the British prison in Papeete. It was a comparatively benign form of imprisonment and, with the government collapsing in the face of the French threats, Melville simply wandered off and continued to Moorea, where he briefly worked on a plantation, enjoyed a last look at the delights of Tahitian dancing and sailed off, thoroughly disheartened by the French and the missionaries.

Victor Segalen A doctor in the French navy, Segalen (1878-1919) sailed round the world on the *Durance* and spent a year in Polynesia. He wrote a magnificent narrative about it, *Les Immémoriaux*, which appeared in 1907 under a local pseudonym and is a vibrant homage to Polynesian civilisation. He also published the *Journal des îles*, which grew out of his day-to-day impressions.

Following in the steps of Paul Gauguin whom he passionately admired, Segalen examined the painter's attachment to the Polynesians but also used the sensitivity expressed in the artist's painting and writing to gain a better grasp of the cultural complexity of the country.

Robert Louis Stevenson Stevenson (1850-1894) came to the Pacific not seeking inspiration but good health. Chronically unhealthy from childhood, Stevenson nevertheless became one of the world's most successful authors and, in 1888, he chartered the 74-ton *Casco* for a prolonged Pacific voyage from San Francisco. They paused first at Nuku Hiva in the Marquesas, an island which had suffered a catastrophic population decline since Melville's stay 40 years earlier. From it they moved on to Hiva Oa and then to Fakarava in the Tuamotus.

Finally, they stopped in Papeete, which Stevenson did not like, but then continued on to a prolonged and delightful stop at Tautira on Tahiti Iti, the remote eastern part of the island. In fact, Stevenson enjoyed himself so much at Tautira that writing was pushed very much to one side and his account of the voyage is not Stevenson at his best. The trip did inspire him to settle in the Pacific and he spent the rest of his life in Samoa.

Robert Louis Stevenson

Jack London A larger than life character, London (1876-1916) was born in San Francisco, grew up across the bay in Oakland and was working on his legend while still a teenager. Poaching oysters on San Francisco Bay, riding trains across the USA and joining the Klondike Gold Rush were all part of the story. The fortune he made from his many successful books never caught up with the even greater fortune he spent. His 1907-08 Pacific voyage was recounted in his 1911 book *Cruise of the Snark* and provided the background for *South Sea Tales* in the same year.

Pierre Loti Despite his statue at Loti's Pool, on the outskirts of central Papeete, there was no Pierre Loti. That is just the pen name of Louis-Marie-Julian Viaud (1850-1923), the French naval officer whose life often imitated his art. Pierre Loti was the main character in *The Marriage of Loti*, based on the writer's experiences in Tahiti during a pause there in 1872.

Rupert Brooke A brief meteorite, Rupert Brooke (1887-1915) was the patriotic soldier-poet of the beginning of WWI, before the supreme idiocy of the war had really sunk in. His sonnets *1914*, with the lines about foreign fields which are forever England, are still remembered. He came to Tahiti in 1914, almost as a spur-of-the-moment sidetrip from the US west coast. His brief two-month stay was highlighted by a passionate love affair with the beautiful Mamua, as he called his Tahitian lover, the inspiration for his poem *Tiare Tahiti*. Brooke was soon back in the USA but died a year later of food poisoning on a hospital ship in the Mediterranean while en route to the madness in the Dardanelles.

Pierre Loti

Robert Keable Nobody much remembers Keable (1888-1928) whose religious novels *Simon Called Peter* and *Recompense* enjoyed huge sales early this century and have since been completely forgotten. He came to Tahiti in the 1920s hoping to find a cure for his ill-health, as he was suffering from tuberculosis, but he only lived another five years. He did, however, write about Tahiti in two books, *Tahiti, Isle of Dreams* and *Numerous Treasures*, and he was far from impressed by the efforts of the missionaries in Tahiti, despite his religious background.

W Somerset Maugham Novelist, short-story writer and playwright, Maugham (1874-1965) not only did well with his Gauguin-inspired novel *The Moon & Sixpence* but he also managed to find one of Gauguin's works, something which had eluded other visitors who had trekked out to Tahiti intent on finding forgotten masterpieces. During his 1916 sojourn on the island, Maugham lived in Papeete and in Mataiea, Gauguin's old haunt between 1891 and 1893, and tracked down a glass-panelled door Gauguin had painted for his local landlord. Maugham bought it for 200 francs, and later installed it in his villa in the French Riviera. Shortly before he died in 1965 it sold for £13,000.

W Somerset Maugham

Nordhoff & Hall James Norman Hall (1887-1951) and Charles Nordhoff (1887-1947) were a two-man act who came to Tahiti after WWI and eventually settled there, turning out a variety of articles, books and other works either separately or as a team. Their big inspiration was to take the records of the *Bounty* mutiny and turn it into a three-part historic novel, based on the facts but somewhat embroidered. They used Bligh's log, the British court-martial proceedings, the account of James Morrison (the *Bounty's* boatswain's mate) and subsequent accounts of the discovery of the mutineers' descendants to write three books, first published in 1934.

James Michener The American novelist (1907-), whose name goes hand-in-hand with the word 'epic', was a foundling, adopted and brought up as a Quaker. He commenced his love affair with the Pacific as a WWII naval historian from 1944 to 1946. His first book, *Tales of the South Pacific*, was based on his experiences around the Pacific and was an instant success, winning the Pulitzer Prize and appearing on Broadway as *South Pacific* a year later. Michener followed his initial success with two more South Pacific books and has continued to write massive, fact-filled tomes based on vast amounts of research and lots of travel. ■

Singapore) invaluable. It grades by difficulty all the best walks on Tahiti and Moorea.

Visiting yachties will probably carry a copy of *Landfalls of Paradise*, subtitled 'A Cruising Guide to the Pacific Islands', by Earl R Hinz (1993, University of Hawaii Press, Honolulu). It gives a thorough coverage of Pacific cruising, including a number of islands in French Polynesia.

Coffee-Table Books

The European impact on the human culture of the islands may have been dramatic, but French Polynesia remains a region of amazing natural beauty, so it's hardly surprising that there are some excellent collections of high-quality photos.

Tahiti from the Air, by Erwin Christian and Emmanuel Vigneron (1985, Les Éditions du Pacifique, Singapore), has wonderful aerial photographs of French Polynesia. However, the construction of new hotels has already made some of the shots look out of date.

Islands of Tahiti by Raymond Bagnis with photographs by Erwin Christian (1991, Kea Editions) is a big coffee-table book on French Polynesia with good photographs and some interesting text. Equally weighty, and now out of print, James Siers' *Tahiti – Romance & Reality* (1982, Millwood Press, New Zealand) has some very interesting long excerpts from early visitors' journals.

MAPS

Tahiti Archipel de la Société (map No IGN 3615) is a good-quality 1:100,000 scale map of Tahiti and the other Society Islands, published by the IGN (Institut Géographique National). The map is widely available in Papeete or overseas from good map shops. Nautical charts and other larger-scale maps are available in Papeete from Polygraph.

MEDIA
Newspapers & Magazines

Le Kiosque in the Vaima Centre in downtown Papeete has a wide selection of international newspapers and magazines. There are other well-equipped newsstands in Papeete, but elsewhere around the islands local TV is probably the best way of keeping up to date with world events. Even finding current editions of the two French-language Tahitian dailies, *Les Nouvelles* and *La Dépêche de Tahiti*, is not easy away from Tahiti and Moorea.

Tahiti Beach Press is a free English-language weekly tourist paper with some local news coverage. Published in Fiji *Pacific Islands Monthly*, also known as *PIM*, is the news magazine of the ex-English and Australian colonies of the Pacific. It's published in Fiji, which does raise some problems of political bias when it comes to reporting in that area.

Radio & TV

There are about 15 independent radio stations broadcasting mainly musical programmes, a few interviews, news flashes in French and Tahitian and advertising. Broadcasting is mainly from Tahiti and Moorea with some on the Leeward Islands. Among the best known are Radio Tiare, the pioneer, Radio Tahiti Api, Radio Bleue, Radio Maohi, Te Reo o Tefana (proindependent), Radio 1, NRJ and RFO Radio. Radio Marquises is based on Nuku Hiva. RFO Radio is received everywhere and broadcasts many local programmes in Tahitian as well as the news from France Inter live every hour.

Radio France Outremer has two channels, RFO Canal 1 and RFO Canal 2. The first channel broadcasts from 6 am to midnight and the second from 9 am to midnight. The programmes consist of a selection of the main films and broadcasts from the three national channels, particularly the TF1 news (live) and France 2 news (delayed broadcast). The local news (Vea Tahiti) is in Tahitian at 6.45 pm and in French at 7.15 pm. In addition to these, on Tahiti only, are Canal 20+ (since December 1994) and Télé-fenua, a cable package including, among others, CNN, Canal J, Planète, Eurosport and Ciné Cinéma. The Australs, Tuamotus and Marquesas have to make do with RFO Canal 1 for the moment.

Mutiny in the Cinema

Three times in 50 years the story of the famous uprising aboard the *Bounty* has been borrowed and embellished by big-budget film makers.

Mutiny on the Bounty The original and most Hollywood-like of the Bounty epics was made in 1935. It was directed by Frank Lloyd and starred Charles Laughton as Bligh at his worst. Fletcher Christian was played by Clark Gable at his clean-shaven (this was the last film he made prior to the appearance of his trademark moustache), all-American best. Although critics insist that this is the classic *Bounty* film, it certainly played fast and loose with history. Bligh is an absolute ogre, flogging, keel hauling, lying and cheating his way through the entire length of the film. Life on the ship is unbearable and Fletcher Christian is a charming, brave, purposeful, rather American aristocrat. Furthermore, in this film version, quite unlike the facts, it's Bligh himself who comes storming back to Tahiti to round up the mutineers and Bligh who sends the *Pandora* and its boxful of mutineers to the bottom of the sea after running onto the Great Barrier Reef. Christian and company even hang around in Tahiti waiting for British naval justice to turn up, when in reality they abandoned the island as quickly as possible. Very little of the film was made in Tahiti.

Mutiny on the Bounty The lavish 1962 remake was directed by Lewis Milestone and takes almost three hours to unfold, with Trevor Howard as Bligh and Marlon Brando as Fletcher Christian. The second *Bounty* film is a much lusher and bigger budget affair than the B&W original. Filmed in Tahiti and Bora Bora, it makes the islands look just like the Polynesian myth, but Bligh remains a monster and Brando's Fletcher Christian is a very strange creation – a sort of simpering fop who clearly would have driven any captain nuts. Brando's lease of Tetiaroa Island resulted from his protracted visit. Making this film in Tahiti had a great effect on the local economy.

The Bounty The third film drops the mutiny from the title, and although much less known than the two earlier versions it's a surprisingly respectable film. Moorea, where most of the location filming was done, looks quite mouth-wateringly beautiful. Bligh is not quite the unrequited villain of the first two films, Christian is a much more tortured soul and 1980s cinematic freedom meant that Polynesian nudity, those goddess-like 'celestial forms' which Bougainville had so enthusiastically described, finally made it on to the screen.

Produced by Dino de Laurentis, directed by Roger Donaldson and released in 1984, Anthony Hopkins is the not-quite-so-bad-and-mad Bligh and Mel Gibson is the more-handsome-than-ever Fletcher Christian. The scenery on Moorea looks fantastic, but better on the big screen than on video. This production abandoned the standard Nordhoff-Hall text and was based on *Captain Bligh & Mr Christian: The Men and the Mutiny* by Richard Hough, and thus seems to paint a somewhat more realistic portrait of Bligh: more driven, stubborn and uncompromising than simply cruel and vindictive. It's not a bad film at all. If you want to re-enact your own *Bounty* adventure, the ship built for this version now operates cruises on Sydney Harbour in Australia. ■

CINEMA

Tahiti would seem to offer lots of cinematic possibilities but nobody has made a movie about Wallis, Bougainville or Cook, the big names in early Polynesian exploration. James Michener's *South Pacific* may have been about Polynesia but it certainly wasn't filmed there. The great Polynesian migration voyages have also been ignored, as has French colonialism and the world wars in the Pacific (there's been no interest in Count Felix von Luckner and the *Seeadler* for example). In fact, Tahiti's role as a movie backdrop is almost exclusively tied up with the *Bounty*. Three times Hollywood has despatched Bligh, Christian and the *Bounty* back to Tahiti to relive the mutiny.

Tabou is the only quality film shot in Polynesia that has nothing to do with the HMS *Bounty*. In 1931, American Robert Flaherty and German Friedrich Murnau filmed this 80-minute work of fiction, showing the inhabitants of Bora Bora in their natural environment. Reri, a young woman, becomes a priestess and, as such, is *tapu* (taboo) to men. Her lover, Matahi, takes her away. Their unfortunate liaison finishes with the death of the young man who has broken the law. Friedrich Murnau's accidental death just after filming was completed in March 1931 was a shock to the whole film crew, and some even thought that it may have been linked to the fact that he included certain taboo parts of the island in the film.

A 1979 big-budget remake of a 1937 classic (the original wasn't filmed in Tahiti), *Hurricane* was based on another Nordhoff & Hall novel. It was filmed in Bora Bora and was a major flop despite an all-star cast which included Mia Farrow, Max von Sydow, Timothy Bottoms, Jason Robards, Jan Troell and former William Bligh, Trevor Howard. For TV it was retitled *Forbidden Paradise*. Produced by Dino de Laurentis, it clearly didn't kill his passion for Tahiti, as he came back to make the third *Bounty* epic.

FILM & PHOTOGRAPHY

The tropical light is intense in French Polynesia, so it's better to take photographs in the early morning or late afternoon. Take slow film (100 or 50 ISO) and more sensitive film (200 or 400 ISO) and a flash for archaeological sites hidden in the vegetation, particularly on the Marquesas. A 28-80 mm lense, or even a 35-80 mm lense will meet most of your needs, and don't forget a polarising filter or a sunshade.

The sand, heat, salinity and air humidity are very tough on camera equipment. Take a waterproof bag or even a bin liner, and clean your lenses regularly.

No restrictions apply to photography. As a courtesy, always ask permission of any people you wish to photograph.

Underwater Photography

The lack of plankton guarantees maximum water clarity. For beginners, a disposable camera will basically do, but these are waterproof only to three or four metres.

Divers with high-performance equipment should check that the charger and pins are compatible before plugging in the flash.

Manta rays can be seen at Rangiroa or Tikehau between July and December and hammerhead sharks come from November to February. Groupers or marbled loaches come to Manihi and Fakarava in July. Ask the dive centres for information.

HEALTH

French Polynesia is generally a healthy place for locals and visitors alike. Food and water are good, fresh, clean and readily available, there are few endemic diseases, and the most serious health problem that visitors are likely to experience is sunburn. Nevertheless, it never hurts to know some basic travel-health rules, anytime you travel.

Travel health depends on your predeparture preparations, your day-to-day health care while travelling and how you handle any medical problem or emergency that develops. If you do need medical care, the facilities in French Polynesia are generally of a high standard, although on the outer islands the number of medical practitioners may be limited. However, there will be hospitals or dispensaries even out there.

Travel-Health Guides

There are a number of books on travel health.

Staying Healthy in Asia, Africa & Latin America by Volunteers in Asia (Moon Publications) is reasonably compact but very detailed and well organised.
Travellers' Health, by Dr Richard Dawood (Oxford University Press), is comprehensive, easy to read, authoritative and also highly recommended, although it's rather large to lug around.
Where There is No Doctor, by David Werner (Hesperian Foundation), is a very detailed guide intended for someone, like a Peace Corps worker, going to work in a developing country, rather than for the average traveller.
Travel with Children, by Maureen Wheeler (Lonely Planet), includes basic advice on travel health for younger children and pregnant women.

Predeparture Preparations

Health Insurance A travel insurance policy to cover theft, loss and medical problems is a good idea. There is a wide variety of policies and your travel agent will have recommendations. The international student-travel policies handled by STA or other student-travel organisations are usually good value. Some policies offer lower and higher medical-expenses options, but the higher one is chiefly for countries like the USA which have extremely high medical costs. Check the small print.

Some policies specifically exclude 'dangerous activities' which can include scuba diving, motorcycling, even trekking. If such activities are on your agenda you don't want that sort of policy.

You may prefer a policy which pays doctors or hospitals direct rather than you having to pay on the spot and claim later. If you have to claim later make sure you keep all documentation. Some policies ask you to call back (reverse charges) to a centre in your home country where an immediate assessment of your problem is made.

Check if the policy covers ambulances or an emergency flight home. If you have to stretch out you will need two seats and somebody has to pay for them!

Medical Kit A small, straightforward medical kit is a good thing to carry. It could include:

- Aspirin, Disprin or Panadol – for pain or fever
- Antihistamine (such as Benadryl) – useful as a decongestant for colds and allergies, to ease the itch from insect bites or stings, and to help prevent motion sickness
- Antibiotics – useful if you're travelling well off the beaten track, but they must be prescribed and you should carry the prescription with you. If you have an allergy to a commonly prescribed antibiotic, make sure you have the information with you.
- Kaolin preparation (Pepto-Bismol), Imodium or Lomotil – for stomach upsets
- Rehydration mixture – for treatment of severe diarrhoea. This is particularly important if you're travelling with children.
- Antiseptic, Mercurochrome and antibiotic powder or similar 'dry' spray – for cuts and grazes. This is important in tropical climates where small cuts or scratches can easily become infected if not treated.
- Calamine lotion – to ease irritation from bites or stings
- Bandages and Band-aids – for minor injuries
- Scissors, tweezers and a thermometer (note that mercury thermometers are prohibited by airlines)
- Insect repellent, sunscreen, suntan lotion, chap stick and water-purification tablets

Ideally, antibiotics should be administered only under medical supervision and should never be taken indiscriminately. Overuse of antibiotics can weaken your body's ability to deal with infections naturally and can reduce the drug's efficacy on a future occasion. Take only the recommended dose at the prescribed intervals and continue using the antibiotic for the prescribed period, even if the illness seems to be cured earlier. Antibiotics are quite specific to the infections they are prescribed for. Stop taking them immediately if there are any serious reactions and don't use one at all if you are unsure that you have the correct one.

Health Preparations Make sure you're healthy before you start travelling. If you are embarking on a long trip, make sure your teeth are OK; there are lots of places where a visit to the dentist would be the last thing you'd want. If you wear glasses take a spare pair and your prescription. Losing your glasses can be a real problem, although you can often get new spectacles made up quickly and competently.

If you require a particular medication, take an adequate supply, as it may not be available locally. Take the prescription, with the generic name rather than the brand name (which may not be locally available), as it will make replacements easier to get. It's a good idea to have a legible prescription with you to show you legally use the medication – it's surprising how often over-the-counter drugs from one country are illegal without a prescription or even banned in another.

Immunisations No vaccinations are required for entry to French Polynesia unless you are arriving from an infected area. You may need to have a yellow fever immunisation if you are coming from or proceeding to Easter Island and Chile. It's always a good idea to keep your tetanus shot up to date, no matter where you are – a booster is required every 10 years.

Basic Health Rules
Care in what you eat and drink is the most

important health rule; stomach upsets are the most common travel-health problem, but the majority of these upsets will be relatively minor and are not usual in French Polynesia. But trying the local food is part of the travel experience.

Water Tap water is usually safe to drink on the high islands but it can be unpalatable on the atolls. In some places rainwater is collected and stored separately from well water which can be tainted by sea water. Bottled spring water or mineral water is readily available in French Polynesia. If you are very concerned about water purity, boil it for five minutes. Iodine water purification will also work but this is unlikely to be necessary in French Polynesia.

In hot climates you should always make sure you drink enough – don't rely on feeling thirsty to indicate when you should drink. Not needing to urinate or very dark yellow urine is a danger sign. Excessive sweating is another problem and can lead to loss of salt and therefore to muscle cramping.

Nutrition Good food is readily available in French Polynesia so enjoying a balanced diet presents no problems.

Everyday Health A normal body temperature is 37°C (or 98.6°F); more than 2°C (3.6°F) higher is a 'high' fever. A normal adult pulse rate is 60 to 80 beats per minute (children 80 to 100, babies 100 to 140). You should know how to take a temperature and a pulse rate. As a general rule the pulse increases about 20 beats per minute for each °C rise in fever.

Respiration (breathing) rate is also an indicator of illness. Count the number of breaths per minute: between 12 and 20 is normal for adults and older children (up to 30 for younger children, 40 for babies). People with a high fever or serious respiratory illness (like pneumonia) breathe more quickly than normal. More than 40 shallow breaths a minute usually means pneumonia.

Many health problems can be avoided by simply taking a little care. Wash your hands

frequently, as it's quite easy to contaminate your own food. Avoid climatic extremes: keep out of the sun when it's hot, dress warmly when it's cold. Dress sensibly: you can get coral cuts by walking over coral without shoes, for example. Avoid insect bites by covering bare skin when insects are around, by screening windows or beds or by using insect repellents. Seek local advice: if you're told the water is unsafe due to currents, jellyfish or for any other reason, don't go in. In situations where there is no information, discretion is the better part of valour.

Medical Problems & Treatment

Potential medical problems can be broken down into several areas. First there are the climatic and geographical considerations – problems caused by extremes of temperature or motion. Then there are diseases and illnesses caused by insanitation, insect bites or stings, and animal or human contact. Simple cuts, bites or scratches can also cause problems.

Self-diagnosis and treatment can be risky, so whenever possible seek qualified help. Although we do give treatment dosages in this section, they are for emergency use only. Medical advice should be sought whenever possible before administering any drugs.

French Polynesia has modern clinics and hospitals in Tahiti and on many other islands, including all the Society high islands, Rangiroa and the main islands of the Marquesas. There will usually be at least a clinic or pharmacy on islands without a hospital. Your hotel will almost always be able to recommend a doctor or medical assistance.

Climatic & Geographical Considerations

Although the northern islands in French Polynesia can get much hotter and more humid than the islands to the south, the climate does not suffer from major extremes.

Sunburn You can get sunburnt surprisingly quickly in the tropics, even through cloud. Use a sunscreen and take extra care to cover areas which don't normally see the sun, such as your feet. A hat provides added protection and you can also use zinc cream or some other barrier cream for your nose and lips. Take special care in situations where a cool breeze may disguise the power of the sun, such as when riding around in an open 4WD vehicle or travelling in an open boat. Calamine lotion is good for mild sunburn.

Prickly Heat Prickly heat is an itchy rash caused by excessive perspiration trapped under the skin. It usually strikes people who have just arrived in a hot climate and whose pores have not yet opened sufficiently to cope with greater sweating. Keeping cool and bathing often, using a mild talcum powder or even resorting to air-conditioning may help until you acclimatise.

Heat Exhaustion Dehydration or salt deficiency can cause heat exhaustion. Take time to acclimatise to high temperatures and make sure you drink sufficient liquids. Salt deficiency is characterised by fatigue, lethargy, headaches, giddiness and muscle cramps, and in this case salt tablets may help. Vomiting or diarrhoea can deplete your liquid and salt levels. Anhydrotic heat exhaustion, caused by an inability to sweat, is quite rare. Unlike the other forms of heat exhaustion, it is likely to strike people who have been in a hot climate for some time, rather than newcomers.

Heatstroke This serious, sometimes fatal, condition can occur if the body's heat-regulating mechanism breaks down and the body temperature rises to dangerous levels. Long, continuous periods of exposure to high temperatures can leave you vulnerable to heatstroke. You should avoid excessive alcohol or strenuous activity when you first arrive in a hot climate.

The symptoms are feeling unwell, not sweating very much or at all and a high body temperature ($39°C$ to $41°C$). Where sweating has ceased, the skin becomes flushed and red. Severe, throbbing headaches and lack of coordination will also occur, and the sufferer may be confused or aggressive. Eventually the victim will become delirious or convulse. Hospitalisation is essential, but meanwhile get victims out of the sun, remove their clothing, cover them with a wet sheet or towel and then fan them continuously.

Fungal Infections Hot-weather fungal infections are most likely to occur on the scalp, between the toes or fingers (athlete's foot), in the groin (jock itch or crotch rot) and on the body (ringworm). You get ringworm (which is a fungal infection, not a worm) from infected animals or by walking on damp areas, like shower floors.

To prevent fungal infections wear loose, comfortable clothes, avoid artificial fibres, wash frequently and dry carefully. If you do get an infection, wash the infected area daily with a disinfectant or medicated soap and water, and rinse and dry well. Apply an antifungal powder like the widely available Tinaderm. Try to expose the infected area to air or sunlight as much as possible, wash all towels and underwear in hot water and change them frequently.

Motion Sickness Eating lightly before and during a trip will reduce the chances of motion sickness. If you are prone to motion sickness try to find a place that minimises disturbance – near the wing on aircraft, close to midships on boats, near the centre on buses. Fresh air and looking off into the distance or at the horizon usually helps; stale air, cigarette smoke or reading will make it worse. Commercial antimotion-sickness preparations, which can cause drowsiness, have to be taken before the trip commences; when you're feeling sick it's too late. Dramamine, sold over the counter at pharmacies, is the usually preferred medication. Sea Legs tablets or the Scopamine patch worn behind the ear, are also good. Ginger is a natural preventative and is available in capsule form. Lots of people get seasick on the inter-island ships in French Polynesia, so if you think you are a likely victim a few precautions can help prevent a miserable experience.

Diseases of Insanitation

Diarrhoea A change of water, food or climate can all cause the 'runs'; diarrhoea caused by contaminated food or water is more serious. Despite all your precautions you may still have a bout of mild travellers' diarrhoea, but a few rushed toilet trips with no other symptoms is not indicative of a serious problem. Moderate diarrhoea, involving half-a-dozen loose movements in a day, is more of a nuisance. Dehydration is the main danger with diarrhoea, particularly for children where dehydration can occur quite quickly. Fluid replenishment is the number-one treatment. Weak black tea with a little sugar, soda water, or soft drinks allowed to go flat and diluted with 50% water are all good. With severe diarrhoea a rehydrating solution is necessary to replace minerals and salts. You should stick to a bland diet as you recover.

Lomotil or Imodium can bring relief from the symptoms, although they do not cure the problem. Only use these drugs if absolutely necessary – if you *must* travel, for example. For children, Imodium is preferable, but do not use these drugs if the person has a high fever or is severely dehydrated.

Antibiotics can be very useful in treating severe diarrhoea, especially if it is accompanied by nausea, vomiting, stomach cramps or mild fever. Ampicillin, a broad-spectrum penicillin, is usually recommended. Two capsules of 250 mg each, taken four times a day, is the recommended dose for an adult. Children aged between eight and 12 years should have half the adult dose; younger children should have half a capsule four times a day. Note that if the patient is allergic to penicillin, ampicillin should not be administered. Three days of treatment should be sufficient and an improvement should occur within 24 hours.

Although French Polynesia is generally a safe and healthy place, some urban areas and small settlements may have very rudimentary sanitation facilities. Avoid swimming or walking barefoot on beaches which may not be clean and be very suspicious about seafood caught near such communities.

Diseases Spread by People & Animals

Tetanus This potentially fatal disease is found in undeveloped tropical areas. It is difficult to treat but is preventable with immunisation. Tetanus is no more of a problem in French Polynesia than in any other part of the world, but it's still a good idea to keep your tetanus immunisation up to date.

Tetanus occurs when a wound becomes infected by a germ which lives in the faeces of animals or people – so clean all cuts, punctures and animal bites. Tetanus is also known as lockjaw, and the first symptom may be discomfort in swallowing, or a stiffening of the jaw and neck; this is followed by painful convulsions of the jaw and the whole body.

Sexually Transmitted Diseases Sexual contact with an infected partner spreads these diseases. While abstinence is the only 100% preventative, using condoms is also effective. Gonorrhoea and syphilis are the most common of these diseases; sores, blisters or rashes around the genitals, discharges or pain when urinating are common symptoms. These may be less marked or not observed at all in women. Syphilis symptoms eventually disappear completely but the disease continues and can cause severe problems in later years. Gonorrhoea and syphilis are treated with antibiotics. There are many other sexually transmitted diseases, and while most can be treated effectively there is no cure for herpes and there is also currently no cure for AIDS.

HIV/AIDS AIDS, or SIDA as it is known in French, has been reported in French Polynesia but there are few documented statistics. Particularly in Papeete, which has an international mix of tourists, prostitution and a local bisexual population, it would be surprising if HIV and AIDS were not a problem at some level. Using condoms is extremely wise for those engaging in sexual relations with anyone other than a regular partner.

AIDS can be spread through contact with the body fluids of another person, primarily blood and semen, and can be spread through infected blood transfusions as well as by sexual contact. It can also be spread by dirty needles – vaccinations, acupuncture, body piercing and tattooing can potentially be as dangerous as intravenous drug use if the equipment is not properly clean.

Insect-Borne Diseases

Malaria does not exist in French Polynesia but an antifilariasis campaign is in operation and there have been occasional outbreaks of dengue fever. Filariasis affects the lymphatic system and is spread by mosquitoes and flies.

Dengue fever is also spread by mosquitoes and there is no prophylactic available; the main preventative measure is to avoid mosquito bites. A sudden onset of fever, headaches and severe joint and muscle pains are the first signs before a rash starts on the trunk of the body and spreads to the limbs and face. After a few more days, the fever will subside and recovery will begin. Serious complications are not common.

Cuts, Bites & Stings

Cuts & Scratches Any puncture of the skin can easily become infected in the tropics and may be difficult to heal. Treat any cut with an antiseptic solution and Mercurochrome or other protective antiseptic cream. Where possible avoid bandages and Band-aids, which can keep wounds wet; if you have to keep a bandage on during the day to protect the wound from dirt or flies, take it off at night while you sleep to let it get air.

Coral cuts are notoriously problematic – they seem to be particularly susceptible to infection, can take a long time to heal and can be quite painful. If you do get cut by coral, be sure to clean the wound thoroughly, get all the coral out and keep the wound clean and disinfected until it heals. You can treat it with Mercurochrome or other protective antiseptic cream or try the local cure – fresh lime juice. Avoid coral cuts by wearing shoes when walking on reefs and try not to touch coral when swimming.

Since any cut or puncture to the skin can turn septic in this climate, don't hesitate to

visit a doctor if you notice any sign of infection.

Bites & Stings French Polynesia's mosquitoes can be bad but they have absolutely nothing on the blackflies or *nonos* of the Marquesas which, at their worst, make life a misery. Unfortunately, nonos are found on beaches as well. In his book *In Search of Tusitala*, Gavin Bell succinctly describes the problem with these creatures for while mosquitoes are 'like flying hypodermic needles, inserting suckers and withdrawing blood with surgical precision, the latter chew and tear at flesh to drink the blood, leaving ragged wounds susceptible to infection'. Scratching at the itch only makes the problem worse.

There are a number of ways to fight insect problems. First of all, wear an insect repellent; the most effective will have 100% DEET. Carry it with you if you go walking or if you visit maraes. Insect repellents are readily available in French Polynesia. Second, avoid using perfumes or after-shave when the insects are a problem. Wearing light-coloured clothing and covering as much skin as possible by wearing long-sleeve shirts or blouses and long trousers will also reduce the problem. Burning mosquito coils, readily available throughout French Polynesia, will also help. If a mosquito net is available, use it. They're usually provided because mosquitoes are a local problem. Check that window screens are insect proof. Mosquitoes are usually worse during the wet season from November to March.

Other insect stings are usually painful rather than dangerous. Take care on some walking routes where wasp nests sometimes overhang the path. Large centipedes can give a painful or irritating bite but it's no more dangerous than a bee or wasp sting, despite the strange dread Polynesians have of these creatures.

Finally, if you are bitten, using calamine lotion, ammonia, antihistamine skin cream or ice packs to reduce the pain, swelling or itching will help. Or you can try the local remedy: pick a frangipani leaf and rub the white liquid that oozes from the stem onto the bite. If you are allergic to bee or wasp stings, be sure to carry your medication with you.

Snakes There are no land snakes in French Polynesia and sea snakes are rarely a problem.

Jellyfish & Other Sea Creatures Jellyfish are not a big problem in French Polynesia because people mostly swim in protected lagoons and jellyfish are rarely washed in from the open sea. Stings from most jellyfish are simply rather painful. Dousing in vinegar will deactivate any stingers which have not 'fired'. Ammonia is also effective, but the folk remedy, used all over the world, is to apply fresh urine to the stings as soon as possible. This also neutralises the venom. Calamine lotion, antihistamines and analgesics may reduce the reaction and relieve the pain.

Poisonous stonefish are rare but extremely painful for those unfortunate enough to step on one. These ugly and well-disguised creatures lurk on the sea floor and stepping on one forces poison up spines in the dorsal fin and into the victim's foot. Heeding local advice about areas which may harbour stonefish and wearing shoes or thongs (flip-flops) when walking in the lagoon is the best protection. If you do step on a stonefish, seek medical attention because there is an antidote available. Stingrays should also not be stepped upon, as their sharp tail can lash up causing a nasty cut which is difficult to heal. Usually rays zip away as they sense your approach. Sea urchins are another bad thing to step upon. The spines break off in your foot and can be difficult to remove and become easily infected.

You'll sometimes encounter stinging coral and the simple solution is to avoid touching it. If you are stung, it's bothersome rather than dangerous and can be treated like a jellyfish sting. Some coral shells can fire a dangerous, potentially fatal, dart if picked up. Treat any cone shell with caution.

Shark bites are a very unlikely occurrence and other sharp-teethed creatures, like moray eels, are feared more than they deserve.

Ciguatera
Ciguatera is a rather mysterious form of food poisoning that comes from eating infected reef fish. Outbreaks of ciguatera have been reported in French Polynesia as well as many other centres in the Pacific. Reefs that have been disturbed, such as by urban development, are particularly prone to develop the micro-organism which becomes present in fish and passes up the food chain until a human eats it. Diarrhoea, muscle and joint aches and pains, numbness and tingling around the mouth, hands and feet, nausea, vomiting, chills, headaches, sweating and dizziness can all be symptoms of ciguatera. Seek medical attention if you experience any of these after eating fish. It's always wise to seek local advice before eating reef fish as any ciguatera outbreak will be well known. It's also wise to avoid eating fish heads or organs. See the Ciguatera aside in the Tuamotus chapter.

Women's Health
Gynaecological Problems Poor diet, lowered resistance through the use of antibiotics for stomach upsets and even contraceptive pills can lead to vaginal infections when travelling in hot climates. Maintaining good personal hygiene, and wearing skirts or loose-fitting trousers and cotton underwear will help to prevent infections.

Yeast infections, characterised by a rash, itch and discharge, can be treated with a vinegar or even lemon-juice douche or with yoghurt. Nystatin suppositories are the usual medical prescription.

Trichomonas is a more serious infection; symptoms are a discharge and a burning sensation when urinating. Male sexual partners must also be treated, and if a vinegar-water douche is not effective medical attention should be sought. Metronidazole (Flagyl) is the prescribed drug.

Flowers

Getting around French Polynesia

Pregnancy Most miscarriages occur during the first three months of pregnancy, so this is the riskiest time to travel. The last three months should also be spent within reasonable distance of good medical care as quite serious problems can develop at this time. Pregnant women should avoid all unnecessary medication, but vaccinations should still be obtained where necessary. Additional care should be taken to prevent illness and particular attention should be paid to diet and nutrition.

Women travellers often find that their periods become irregular or even cease while they're on the road. A missed period doesn't necessarily indicate pregnancy.

WOMEN TRAVELLERS

French Polynesia is a relatively safe place for solo women travellers, although in the rougher quarters of Papeete, particularly late at night, care should be exercised. The majority of complaints received from women visitors are about cheaper hotels where some male staff have taken an unhealthy interest in the female guests. Peeping toms are also not unknown, so take

---

The Mahus

Don't be surprised when riding le truck into Papeete on a weekend night if some exceptionally tall and glamorous Tahitian women board the bus – except these aren't women, they're *mahus* or *rae rae*, Tahitian transvestites. Some of the earliest European visitors to the islands commented on the presence of mahus and their position in Tahitian society, noting that they were completely accepted and certainly nothing to be ashamed of.

Today the mahus have changed from being part of the village scene to being part of Papeete's raucous nightlife zone, and hormone treatment has changed the practice to something more than mere cross-dressing. Few Polynesian transvestites can afford complete sex-change operations, which would probably require a trip to Europe. The rae rae also dominate prostitution in Papeete, which is officially illegal but accepted for transvestites. ■

---

special care in establishments which look run down and would seem to offer opportunities for spying on guests, particularly in the showers.

GAY & LESBIAN TRAVELLERS

French laws concerning homosexuality are in effect in French Polynesia and there is no legal discrimination against homosexual activity. Homophobia in French Polynesia is uncommon. The mahu and rae rae, traditional Polynesian forms of transsexuality, are well integrated into contemporary society and play an important and visible role, particularly in the restaurant and hotel businesses. Tahiti is said to have more transsexuals per head of population than anywhere else in the world!

DISABLED TRAVELLERS

Travellers with restricted mobility will unfortunately find very little in the way of infrastructure designed to make it easier for them to get around. With narrow flights of steps on boats, high steps on le trucks and difficult boarding on Air Tahiti aircraft, the disabled traveller's itinerary in French Polynesia resembles an obstacle course as special equipment is sadly lacking. What is more, hotels and guesthouses are not used to receiving disabled guests, and nautical and open-air activities are geared for the 'able-bodied'.

Those who are not put off by these obstacles can contact the Handicap Service (☎ 42-37-48), or ask for Madame Jazat, who chairs the union of associations for the disabled, and she can be contacted on ☎ 42-93-70 during business hours in Papeete. They can provide assistance with travel on Tahiti and Moorea.

TRAVEL WITH CHILDREN

The climate, natural setting, aquatic games and lack of poisonous creatures make Polynesia a paradise for children.

You should, however, ensure that vaccinations are up to date and take health records. Take a baby carrier, light clothes which cover the whole body and total-block sunscreen.

Do not leave your child unsupervised near beaches or reefs. Buy bottled mineral water and make your children drink frequently. Nappies (diapers) are very expensive, even in the Papeete supermarkets.

In the event of an emergency, you should be aware that there are medical facilities everywhere in Polynesia. Mamao hospital has a modern paediatric department. Make sure that your repatriation insurance also covers your child.

You will have priority when boarding Air Tahiti aircraft. A family card (*carte famille*), which costs 2000 CFP and requires two photos and three to five days' notice to obtain, entitles you to significant reductions on some flights. At hotels and guesthouses, children under 12 generally pay only 50% of the adult rate. Lastly, the Tahiti Dive Centre takes children aged eight and over on dives.

DANGERS & ANNOYANCES
See the preceding Health section for warnings about heat exhaustion and sunburn, the dangers of coral cuts and tropical ulcers, the importance of avoiding stepping on stonefish or sea urchins and warnings about things which bite or sting. The most unhappy encounters with wildlife in French Polynesia are likely to be with mosquitoes and nonos rather than with sharks, and this problem is also covered in the Health section.

Swimming
Swimming in French Polynesia usually means staying within the protected waters of a lagoon, but swimmers should still be aware of tides and currents, and particularly of the swift movement of water out of a lagoon and through a pass into the open sea. Around Papeete beware of the dangers of untreated sewage contaminating the water.

Mosquitoes
French Polynesia does not have malaria but the mosquitoes can still be an intolerable nuisance. They're usually not a problem around the coast where sea breezes keep them away, but inland they can be a pest and for some reason maraes seem to attract them

in swarms. Standing to read an explanatory noticeboard at a historic marae site can be a real test of any visitor's enthusiasm for scholarship!

Theft & Violence
Although the early explorers all complained about the Polynesian propensity for theft, it is not a big problem in French Polynesia today. Which is not to say that your camera won't disappear if you leave it lying around on the beach. And of course there are occasional robberies and pickpocketings, but compared to cities in the US or Europe, even busy Papeete is very safe.

Take care in cheaper hotel rooms – leaving something on a table close to an open window is no different from leaving it on the beach. If you have real valuables such as jewellery and are staying in a more expensive hotel, it's probably wise to use the hotel safe or other security provisions.

Violence is also rarely a problem in French Polynesia, although the size of the bouncers outside Papeete's nightclubs indicates that it's a good idea to keep well clear of unfriendly drunks. The bars that are most likely to be trouble spots are the ones frequented by French army personnel.

Yacht Security
Yacht crews should take care in popular yachting centres like Bora Bora or in the Marquesas, where theft from yachts has been a problem. See the Yachting section in the Getting Around chapter for more advice.

WORK
French citizens are not required to complete any formalities. By virtue of dispensatory provisions applicable to the French overseas territories, citizens of the EU must follow the procedure described below.

With the exception of those with very special skills, it is difficult for non-French citizens to work in French Polynesia. Authorisation to take up paid employment in

French Polynesia is subject to the granting of two permits: a temporary-residence permit, issued by the French State, and a work permit, issued by the Territory.

The first condition is to have an employer willing to employ you and draw up a work contract. Attach a copy of it to your temporary-residence permit application, which you must lodge with the French consular authorities in your own country (you cannot apply for a residence permit from within French Polynesia). After about one month, the French Consulate will let you know whether the permit has been granted or refused. The temporary-residence permit is generally granted for one year (renewable) or five years for citizens of the EU.

To obtain a work permit, the employer (or you) must send the Agence pour l'emploi et la formation professionnelle (AEFP; Employment & Professional Training Agency, ☎ 54-31-31) the draft employment contract, photocopies of your qualifications, a letter applying for a work permit written by you and addressed to the 'Président du Gouvernement de la Polynésie française' and two passport-size photos. Furthermore, the employer is obliged to advertise the position at the AEFP for four weeks. If equally well qualified French Polynesians apply for it during that time, they will be given preference. The work permit is granted for one year, but it's renewable.

The Territory has clamped down on foreigners working in French Polynesia. Unless you are a Japanese pearl grafter, Chinese chef or banking executive, you stand very little chance of success.

ACTIVITIES

There are lots of sporting facilities in Tahiti and you'll often see basketball, soccer, tennis and athletics sessions underway. Running, bicycle races and the great Polynesian passion, outrigger-canoe races, are also popular. There's an annual South Pacific Games in which French Polynesia participates. See the individual island chapters for more specific details.

Diving & Snorkelling

Scuba diving (*plongée* in French) is enormously popular in French Polynesia and is covered in detail in the individual island chapters with information on dive operators and popular dive sites. For absolute underwater beginners, most beach resorts and hotels will have snorkelling equipment available as well as dive courses for both French CMAS qualifications and PADI certification. Not all dive operators who offer dive courses do PADI instruction, so if you plan to learn to dive in French Polynesia and want the PADI certification check first. If you are already a qualified diver, don't forget to bring your certification card with you.

Although most visitors treat Tahiti mainly as a transit point to the other islands, there are some good dive sites and a surprising number of dive operators. Moorea has some very popular dive sites and a number of dive operators and is the centre in French Polynesia for shark feeding. If you want to see sharks close up, come here. Raiatea-Tahaa and Huahine are both lower-key centres with fewer divers and dive operators, although Raiatea in particular has some excellent dive sites. Bora Bora's two dive operators keep very busy between diving in the large lagoon, where diving with the manta rays is a speciality, and outside the reef.

The atolls of the Tuamotus offer some of French Polynesia's most exciting dives, particularly on Rangiroa, where the daily rush of water in and out of the island's twin passes produces one of the most exciting dives in the Pacific with enough sharks to satisfy even the most hardened adrenalin junkie.

The Austral islands undoubtedly have some good dive sites but there are no regular dive operators.

As of 1996 Manihi, Tikehau and Fakarava have dive centres. On the Marquesas, due to the lack of lagoons, you will see no reef fauna. There's a centre at Taiohae (Nuku Hiva), and it has recently established a secondary base at Atuona (Hiva Oa).

Surfing

Polynesia was the birthplace of surfing so

many international surfers like to try the waves in such a historic spot. In recent years there has been a major resurgence in local interest and Tahiti in particular has surf shops, board shapers and a local surfing scene. Although the waves may not be the best in the world, there are certainly some good breaks to ride usually at the edges of passes (the openings into the lagoon through the reef). In some places this may mean a long paddle out to the break. Like surfers in many other places in the world the Polynesians can be very possessive about *their* waves. If you want to enjoy the surf, observe all the usual surfing etiquette and give way to local surfers.

There are two surfing seasons in Tahiti. The October-to-March season brings strong swells from the north, while in the April-to-September period the winds blow from the south, New Zealand and the Antarctic, bringing big swells which produce very powerful and hollow waves. There are a number of good breaks around Tahiti. Moorea also has some good breaks, while relaxed and low-key Huahine has become something of a surf centre in French Polynesia.

Other Aquatic Activities
Windsurfing has a wide following and many of the resorts offer instruction and use of equipment. Unfortunately, jet-skis, those noisy and antisocial devices, are also popular on some islands. You can rent small boats with outboards for exploring the lagoons on

a number of islands. Further afield, game-fishing boats are available for charter as are a variety of cruising yachts and catamarans.

Walking & Cycling
The high islands of French Polynesia offer some superb walks on tracks that are sometimes hard to follow. Tahiti has some great walks, some of them requiring overnight camping. On Moorea there are some wonderful shorter walks, ideal for a morning or afternoon excursion. On Hauhine, Raiatea and Tahaa there has been little investigation of the walking possibilities but keen walkers can climb Mt Pahia on Bora Bora. Even tiny Maupiti has a walking track up to its impressive central peak.

Although you can rent bicycles on many islands the rough-and-ready backroads on some of the islands are ideal for mountain biking. See the Getting Around chapter for more information.

Other Sports
There are squash courts and tennis courts in Tahiti and the tourist office can provide more information. On other islands tennis courts can be found at the larger hotels. Tahiti has the only golf course in French Polynesia and there's even a bowling alley in Arue. Tahiti has several equestrian clubs but, for visitors, Moorea, Raiatea and Huahine are more popular centres with long and short horse-riding forays on offer.

Keen horse riders will be pleased to find that on the Marquesas horses are a familiar part of the landscape. Ua Huka is nicknamed 'horse island'. Opportunities for hiring horses, with or without the services of a guide, exist throughout the archipelago.

Tahiti's soaring mountains promise interesting opportunities for hang-gliding and sure enough there are facilities for this sport. The Marquesas also have a hang-gliding centre at Taiohae.

COURSES
The Tahitian language can be studied among other places at the ASFOP (☎ 41-33-89), Immeuble Fara, Rue Nansouty, Papeete,

Tahiti, or at the Chamber of Commerce (☎ 42-03-44) Rue du Dr Cassiau, BP 118, Papeete, Tahiti.

HIGHLIGHTS

Visitors planning on seeing a lot of French Polynesia in a short time should bear in mind that the islands are scattered across a vast amount of ocean. Going from one side of the region to the other is much like crossing all of Europe. Listed here are some possible itineraries.

Four days

If you're making a brief stopover on a trans-Pacific trip your pause in French Polynesia could include a day to de-jetlag and explore Papeete and its market. On day two, make a trip round the island and visit the Gauguin Museum and the Tahiti Museum. Day three and four could be spent on Moorea or Bora Bora enjoying the beaches, the underwater life and a 4WD trip into the interior.

One week

A one-week stay could include Tahiti, Moorea and Bora Bora or you could venture further afield to spend a couple of days on an atoll like Rangiroa. The direct Bora Bora-Rangiroa flights make a Tahiti-Bora Bora-Rangiroa-Tahiti circuit eminently feasible in one week.

Three weeks

With a longer stay it would be possible to explore all the main islands of the Society group by air or by sea and also include a visit to the Tuamotus by air. With appropriate timing even the Marquesas would be within reach, and a short inter-island voyage on the *Aranui* could be slotted in if your timing was impeccable.

ACCOMMODATION

Accommodation in French Polynesia is always expensive and can be of poor quality, particularly for the prices charged. There are lower priced places, so visiting Tahiti is feasible for backpackers. If, on the other hand, price is no object, there are some truly beautiful resorts. The problem is often in the middle where a lot of money may not buy you very much.

There are hostel-style dormitory beds available in Papeete and on most of the Society Islands. A bed might cost around US$20 a night. Tahiti is not very good for

camping, but Moorea and Bora Bora both have good camping facilities and it is also possible to camp on Raiatea. Family-style pension accommodation is available on many islands typically at about US$60 for a room. On the more remote islands there may be no real hotels and this style of accommodation will be all that is available.

In the middle bracket there are many smaller hotels and bungalow-style resorts with costs ranging from around US$60 to US200 with lots of places around US$100 to US$150 a night. Standards are quite variable in this category – some places are beautiful, some of them rather spartan and straightforward, but still charging relatively high prices. Apart from one hotel in Raiatea, it is only in Papeete that there any business-style hotels, anonymous places typically with rooms in the US$100 to US$150 bracket.

Finally, there are the luxury resorts, the sort of places you find on the best brochures. Don't count on finding much under US$300 a night in this range and prices over US$500 are not rare, but some of these places will make island fantasies come true.

Many of the bottom bracket and a surprising number of mid-range places in more remote locations do not take credit cards. This can be a nuisance in places where it is also difficult to change money. Prices for places in the mid-range and top end are generally subject to an 8% government tax. Many bottom-end and even some lower mid-range places do not supply towels and soap, and this is particularly true on remote islands. Even some of the most expensive hotels in Tahiti may not have air-conditioning but this is generally a pleasure rather than a discomfort. Even at the hottest times of year a cool breeze seems to blow at night and a fan is all that's needed.

FOOD

Cuisine is multiethnic in French Polynesia. Traditional Polynesian specialities happily coexist with French, Chinese and Italian cuisine; from the typical pizza to a snack, including chow mein and *mahi mahi*, or dolphin fish (which is a fish, not a dolphin), in coconut milk, the repertoire is varied. It is nevertheless a fact that westernisation of eating habits (cans, steak and chips and soda water) is increasingly noticeable.

Prices quoted are an indication only and apply to Papeete. The price of products distributed on the other islands is increased by the cost of transport.

Sandwiches can be great value in Tahiti. They usually cost 100 to 150 CFP in 'snacks' or takeaways, 200 to 300 CFP in places where you can sit down to eat them. The excellent bread and low prices make a *casse-croûte*, as one of these French-bread sandwiches is known, the best food bargain in Tahiti. Snack bars – small food shops-cum-eating places usually with a handful of stools at a bar – are all around the island. Sometimes they may be more like a restaurant but they're always simple and cheap.

The supermarkets, particularly on Tahiti and Moorea, are well stocked with an international range of products, so if you're restocking a yacht or preparing your own food in a place which has kitchen facilities you will have no trouble. But prices are high.

Despite all the sea around French Polynesia, the seafood on offer is limited compared to the variety in cooler climates. For this reason there are no restaurants specialising only in seafood. The usual fish found on menus are tuna, mahi mahi or dolphin fish, *tazar* (wahoo in English) and parrotfish. The salmon and trout have probably been imported from Australia or New Zealand, and lobsters and prawns may also be imported. However, the freshwater shrimps (*chevrettes* rather than *crevettes*) are local.

Poisson cru is the local dish found most frequently on the menu – chunks of raw fish marinated in lime juice or vinegar and salt, and spiced. It's delicious!

Tahitian fruits include watermelon, grown on the motus of Maupiti and Huahine in particular; *pamplemousse*, which here is the South-East Asian variety rather than the grapefruit familiar in Europe or North America; and pineapples, which are cultivated in Moorea, are excellent. The rambutan is another South-East Asian intro-

duction, a red spiny-skinned close cousin to the lychee. Mangoes are so common they fall off the trees and rot on the ground.

Some local market gardening produces European-style vegetables that are also grown on the cooler Austral Islands to the south.

The local starch staples are breadfruit, taro, manioc (cassava), yams and the South American sweet potato. It's something of a mystery how the sweet potato found its way to Polynesia. To western tastes, taro and other local staples can be rather bland and tasteless. They are usually boiled but additional flavouring can make them more palatable. *Poi* is a dessert made from taro flavoured with honey, bananas or papayas, and usually served warm with coconut milk.

Places to Eat

Most restaurants are concentrated in the Papeete area and on the most touristy islands. Prices vary considerably according to specialities and the type of restaurant. Allow between 2000 and 7000 CFP for a meal without drinks.

Hotel restaurants are a possibility worth exploring. Guesthouses, particularly on the Tuamotus, Marquesas and Australs, also accept nonstaying customers if they book.

Small snack bars can be found almost everywhere and offer simple food at reasonable prices (from 600 to 900 CFP for a plate of raw fish in coconut milk).

The markets are full of vegetables, fruit, meat and fish. Papeete market, open from 5 am, is regularly supplied with fresh produce from all the archipelagos. Pirae market is also worth a visit.

The food shops are expensive but well stocked, especially on Tahiti and Moorea. The other archipelagos are reliant on the frequency of visiting schooners. The best stocked supermarkets are the Continent hypermarket (in Arue and Punaauia), Tropic Import in Papeete and the Cash & Carry at Faaa. Avoid imported products from Europe if possible as they are heavily taxed (950 CFP for Camembert stamped 'par avion'!)

Most islands have at least one bakery. A

French baguette costs less than 50 CFP and a *pain au chocolat* costs about 120 CFP.

Small food stalls along the street, particularly on Tahiti, sell fruit and vegetables.

Polynesian Cuisine

The traditional cuisine, based on fresh produce, is called *maaa tahiti* in the Society Islands and Tuamotus, and *kaikai enana* on the Marquesas. Maaa tahiti is traditionally eaten with the fingers.

Fish & Seafood Dishes Open-sea fish (tuna, bonito, thazard, scad and mahi mahi) and lagoon fish (parrotfish, unicornfish, perch and mullet) feature prominently in traditional cuisine. Raw fish in coconut milk is the most eaten local dish. It is also eaten grilled or cooked (poached or wrapped in buttered paper) accompanied by lime or coconut milk. *Fafaru*, raw fish soaked in seawater, is renowned for its particularly strong smell. *Inaa* (young fish), mixed with fried dough, is enjoyed in various ways.

Lobsters, sea urchins and freshwater shrimps are highly prized.

Recipe for Raw Fish in Coconut Milk

This dish appears on almost every menu. For four people, use one kg of red tuna, garlic, limes, two carrots, grated coconut (or failing this, packaged coconut milk), two tomatoes, one capsicum and some green onions.

Cut the fish into small cubes. Rinse it with sea water (or salt water), then leave it to soak for half an hour in salt water with crushed garlic, in the refrigerator.

Grate the carrots, cut up the tomatoes and capsicum and chop the green onions. Drain the pieces of fish and place them in a salad bowl. Squeeze the limes into the bowl and leave the fish to stand in the natural acidity of the lime (at least four to five minutes). Then remove the diced fish.

Put the grated coconut in a cloth and wring it to extract the coconut milk (or open the packaged coconut milk). Add a dash of red-wine vinegar, some salt, pepper and Tabasco sauce. Pour this dressing over the fish, mix, add the vegetables and sprinkle with onions. You can also add crushed hard-boiled eggs and parsley. ■

Fruit & Vegetables Most tropical fruit can be found in French Polynesia, including mangoes, grapefruit, watermelons, pineapples, breadfruit, melons and bananas. Baked papaya is a succulent dish, as is *poe*: small pieces of crushed fruit (papaya or banana) mixed with starch, wrapped in a banana leaf and baked in the oven with a vanilla pod split down the middle. The whole thing is then sprinkled with coconut milk.

Vegetables are eaten together with meat or fish. *Uru* or *maiore*, the breadfruit, is quite unpleasant raw and is eaten cooked. On the Marquesas, the basic dish is *popoi*, a sweet-and-sour dish which looks like a yellow paste. It consists of cooked uru, crushed in a pestle, mixed with uru pulp and left to ferment; coconut milk is added. The whole thing is covered with a *purau* leaf. *Fei*, a sort of plantain banana, is only eaten cooked and has a bittersweet taste. Taro root is eaten cooked, as are sweet potato and manioc. Taro leaves (*fafa*) are often served with chicken.

Meat Suckling pig (*pua*) is the preferred meat for *ahimaa* (see *Ahimaa & Tamaaraa* below). New Zealand beef also often features in dishes, as does chicken. On the Marquesas, goat meat takes pride of place. Dog is still eaten on the remote atolls of the Tuamotus.

Although protected, turtle is still eaten. Categorically refuse to eat it to avoid supporting this practice.

The most common accompaniments are coconut milk (not to be confused with coconut juice), which is obtained by grating the white flesh inside the nut and wringing it in a cloth; *miti hue*, a fermented sauce based on coconut flesh mixed with shrimp-head juice and salt water; and *taiore*, another variety of fermented sauce.

Pastries Coconut bread (*faraoa coco*) is a tasty cake. *Firifiri*, sweet fritters, are generally shaped like a figure 8 or a plait. *Ipo* is Tuamotu bread and has a heavy consistency. The flour is mixed with coconut juice, sugar and grated coconut. *Pai* are turnovers filled with coconut or banana.

Breadfruit

Ahimaa & Tamaaraa Ahimaa is the Polynesian oven in which food is baked. On the most touristy islands, it tends to be replaced by the barbecue. Branches and stones are arranged at the bottom of a hole dug in the ground. The branches are kindled and heat the stones. A layer of banana leaves is then placed on top and the food is placed on this (often a suckling pig, fish and vegetables). The whole thing is covered with leaves and canvas bags and then sand to make it perfectly airtight. Cooking takes several hours. When the oven is opened, the *tamaaraa* (meal or banquet) commences. It is common at family parties and religious festivals.

Other Cuisines
Among the Chinese specialities, *maa tinito* consists of a mixture of pieces of pork and red beans. *Chaomen*, or chow mein, is a mixture of rice, noodles, red beans, vermi-

celli, vegetables and fried pork. Rice is found in everything.

French cuisine is especially common on Tahiti and on the touristy islands. French bread, croissants and snacks (from 100 to 300 CFP) are available everywhere.

DRINKS
Nonalcoholic Drinks
Fruit Juice Several delicious fruit juices are produced locally, notably the Rotui brand of pineapple juice produced on Moorea, grapefruit juice and guava juice. Lime juice added to mineral water is very thirst quenching.

The big international brands of carbonised drinks are distributed in Polynesia.

Coconut Juice *Pape haari* is the healthiest, most natural, cheapest and most thirst-quenching drink. It is totally free of microbes and bacteria. After removing the fibre surrounding the coconut, the top of the nut is taken off with a machete. You cab drink directly from the nut or with a straw. The juice has a slightly bitter taste.

Mineral Water Several brands are available, the main ones being French (Volvic, Vittel). The cheapest is the local spring water, Eau Royale (75 CFP at Papeete supermarkets). With the exception of Papeete, it is not advisable to drink the tap water.

Coffee In most cases this is instant Nescafé. Allow 200 to 300 CFP for a coffee in a Papeete bar.

Alcoholic Drinks
Beer The local Hinano brand of beer (*pia*), sold everywhere, is available in glass 500-ml bottles, 330 and 500-ml cans, and on tap. Foreign beers are also available. Allow at least 350 CFP in a bar or restaurant.

Wines & Spirits The Papeete supermarket shelves have plenty of red and white French wines. The cheapest bottles cost around 800 CFP. Restaurants enjoy a tax reduction on alcohol sold at 'agreed prices', which makes

it affordable (allow between 1500 and 3000 CFP for a bottle).

You must try the *maitai*, a local speciality. This is a cocktail like a punch, made with brown and white rum, pineapple, grenadine and lime juices, coconut liqueur and, in some cases, Grand Marnier or Cointreau.

ENTERTAINMENT

See the relevant island chapters for details of cultural performances, island night dance performances and nightlife ranging from bars to nightclubs and discos. Papeete is the only place in French Polynesia with a really active nightlife and a visit to a local bar can be an interesting way to spend an evening. On other islands things get quiet very early.

Papeete's gay nightlife is centred around the Rue des Écoles. Dance-bars such as the Lido and Club Cinq attract a mainly gay and rae rae crowd. On weekend nights entry may include a drink and a midnight cabaret featuring a rae rae strip show.

THINGS TO BUY

There are plenty of souvenir shops and craft outlets waiting to lure you in. Beware of local souvenirs which aren't local at all – the colourful wood carvings, even with Bora Bora neatly painted on them, probably come from Bali or Colombia. Nevertheless, French Polynesia does have some excellent local crafts and many of them can be found in Tahiti, especially in the Papeete market. When shopping for craftwork remember that bargaining is not the norm anywhere in the Pacific.

There are duty-free shopping facilities in Papeete and at Faaa airport with the usual liquor, tobacco and perfume discounts, but the prices are not very exciting by international standards. Stamp collectors will find some interesting and very colourful stamps on sale. The Papeete post office has a section for philatelists.

Woven Pandanus

Coconut palm leaves are used for the more rough-and-ready woven work, such as the woven walls of a *fare*, but for finer hats, bags and mats pandanus leaves are used and this is one of the best examples of a true local craft. Pandanus are the spindly trees with multiple aerial roots that are often found near the water's edge. Some of the finest work comes from Rurutu in the Austral Islands where the common lagoonside pandanus is not generally used; a hillside pandanus is used for this higher-quality work.

Tapa

Prior to the European arrival there was no woven materials in Polynesia and, since there were few land mammals, hides were not an alternative. The warm climate did not require much clothing, but tapa, produced by beating tree bark until it was paper thin, was used. Tapa could be produced from the bark of breadfruit, hibiscus, banyan or paper mulberry trees. Men gathered the materials but it was the women who stripped the bark from the branches, scraped it thin, soaked it, beat it even thinner and finally decorated it. Tapa clothing was generally in the form of *pareus* (see following entry) or the poncho-like *tiputa*. Tapa rapidly disappeared when European cloth became available but it is still produced, particularly in the Marquesas, for ceremonial use and for collectors.

Pareu

Like the Asian sarong, the pareu is a cool, comfortable, all-purpose piece of attire, directly descended from that made from pre-European tapa cloth. A modern pareu is 180 cm by 90 cm (about six feet by three feet) and is often imported from Asia, although brightly decorated Polynesian pareus are becoming more common. Hibiscus flowers and breadfruit-tree leaves are the most popular Polynesian designs but motifs vary from island to island. For men the pareu is usually worn like a wrap-around skirt for casual wear or around the house. Tucked up like shorts it becomes workwear. Women have a variety of ways of wearing a pareu. It can be worn as a wrap-around skirt with a blouse, halter top or bikini top. Alternatively it can be worn tied above the breasts or with two corners tied behind the neck.

Tifaifai

Brilliantly coloured *tifaifai* are appliquéd or patchwork blankets produced on a number of islands including Rurutu. The craft was introduced by the missionaries and a tifaifai blanket now has several important uses. Wrapping someone in a tifaifai is a sign of welcome. Traditionally, it's an important wedding gift and a tifaifai may also be used to cover a coffin. Flowers or fruit are often used in tifaifai patterns and production can be a very sociable community activity.

Wood Carving

Wood carving was probably never of great importance in the Society Islands but it was an important art in the Australs and the Marquesas, before the missionaries stamped it out. Some wood carving still continues, particularly in the Marquesas, where fierce looking *tikis* are produced. Fine examples of ceremonial canoe paddles and prows and intricately carved handles for fly-switches and fans can be seen in museums. Copies are still sometimes produced.

Monoi

Monoi is a blend of coconut oil perfumed with the fragrance of the tiare flower. It's widely available as a moisturising cream, soap, shampoo, sunscreen and perfume, and is used in a variety of other forms.

Music

Polynesian song has become a sort of island form of country & western music – down home tales of lost love and day-to-day life to the accompaniment of guitar and ukelele. It's easy on the ear and very popular locally. More traditional dance music has strong rhythms and lots of drumming. Both forms can be easily found on tapes and CDs in Papeete and other major centres.

Painting

A number of interesting European and Polynesian artists work in French Polynesia and their work is on display in galleries on Tahiti and Moorea. Originals and high-quality prints and posters are available.

Tattoos

Traditional Polynesian tattooing has enjoyed a major resurgence in recent years and like that pioneering collector, Sir Joseph Banks in 1769, you could come back with your very own example of Tahitian art. There are a number of government-approved tattooists on Tahiti and Moorea. Or you could just buy a sheet of Polynesian tattoo transfers!

Black Pearls

Black pearls, cultivated in the Tuamotus, have become a major factor in the French Polynesian economy. There are jewellery shops and black-pearl specialists in Papeete and on other islands. In Papeete, allow 5000 to 200,000 CFP and more for a pearl. See the Black Pearl aside in the Tuamotus chapter for more on the production process of these beautiful pearls. A good number of farms in the Tuamotus sell directly at prices of about 30% less. However, the most beautiful pearls are rapidly sent to the Papeete jeweller shops.

Getting There & Away

Occasionally a cruise ship calls in to Tahiti and there's a steady but thin trickle of cruising yachts crossing the Pacific, but visitors to French Polynesia generally arrive by air. Tahiti is a long way from anywhere: 6500 km south-west of the Californian coast, 5500 km north-east of Australia, 8000 km west of South America, 9500 km south-east of Japan and 18,000 km from Europe. It's pretty much on the opposite side of the world from almost everywhere.

AIR

There are serious plans for a US$46.5 million project to extend the runway on Nuku Hiva in the Marquesas and to open up these remote islands to international tourism. Meanwhile Faaa airport on the outskirts of Papeete on the island of Tahiti is the sole arrival point on French Polynesia. There are runways on Hao and Moruroa in the Tuamotus but these are purely for French military use, in connection with their nuclear-testing programme.

A problem that has considerably reduced the number of options for getting to Tahiti in recent years, and a problem that's also faced by other Pacific islands, has been the increasing use of long-range aircraft. Most air traffic across the South Pacific flies between North America and Australia or New Zealand. Not so many years ago that long flight required a refuelling stop somewhere along the way, but the advent of the 400 series Boeing 747 changed all that. Los Angeles-Sydney or Los Angeles-Auckland flights have become nonstop affairs and nobody wants to stop in Tahiti in the middle of the night for no good reason. As a result there are now fewer trans-Pacific flights stopping in Tahiti.

Visitors to Tahiti come from a number of directions and on airlines that currently include Air Calédonie International, Air France, Air New Zealand, AOM French Airlines, Corsair, Hawaiian Airlines, Lan Chile and Qantas. Airline schedules are always

prone to change so the details that follow are given as an indication of flight frequencies and the fares available. If you want to organise your travels around French Polynesia and at the same time decipher the complexities of Air Tahiti ticketing it would be wise to contact a good general travel agent rather than one of the low-price specialists recommended here.

To/From Other Pacific Islands

There is remarkably little air traffic between the island nations of the Pacific. In fact, none of the airlines of independent Pacific island nations operates flights to Tahiti. The only flights by the airline of another Pacific island come from France's other Pacific colony: Air Calédonie International has two weekly flights from Noumea in New Caledonia, one via Auckland in New Zealand and the other via Wallis and Futuna. Air New Zealand's three weekly flights through Tahiti include one via Rarotonga and one via Rarotonga and Fiji. See the To/From Australia & New Zealand section for more details on these island-hopping flights. Connections to other Pacific islands such as Tonga or the Samoas will require a change at one of these other islands.

To/From the USA & Canada

Fares to Tahiti from the USA are seasonal, and the end of December to mid-June is the low season. Direct flights from the US mainland to Tahiti are principally under the control of the French, the Australians and the New Zealanders who all fly a Los Angeles-Papeete route. There are no American airlines operating directly on this route. It takes about 7½ hours to fly from Los Angeles to Papeete.

Hawaiian Air does fly Honolulu-Tahiti but only once a week. The flight takes about five hours, about the same time as Los Angeles-Honolulu. Hawaiian Air has connections from major West Coast centres. Honolulu-

Papeete-Honolulu fares cost from US$642 in the low season, which is very similar to the fares from the West Coast.

Otherwise, it comes down to the three Air France, three AOM, two Air New Zealand, two Qantas Los Angeles-Tahiti connections and Corsair's two connections, one with Los Angeles and one with Oakland. AOM can be contacted on ☎ (800) 892 9136, Corsair can be contacted on ☎ (800) 677 0720. Typical AOM and Corsair economy-class fares for Los Angeles-Papeete-Los Angeles for a 14-day advance-purchase ticket with a seven-day minimum-stay requirement is around US$700. With Qantas or Air New Zealand, return fares from Los Angeles to Australia or New Zealand with a Papeete stopover with similar advance-purchase and minimum-stay requirements typically cost from US$1055 in the low season.

Sunday travel sections of major newspapers like the *New York Times, Los Angeles Times, San Francisco Examiner-Chronicle* or the *Chicago Tribune* are good sources for advertisements of competitively priced air fares. Council Travel and STA Travel have very competitive air fares and have offices across the country.

There is no direct connection between Tahiti and Canada so connections are made

---

Air Travel Glossary

Apex Apex, or Advance Purchase Excursion, is a discounted ticket which must be paid for in advance. There are penalties if you wish to change it.

Baggage Allowance This will be written on your ticket: usually one 20-kg item to go in the hold, plus one item of hand luggage.

Bucket Shop An unbonded travel agency specialising in discounted airline tickets.

Bumped Just because you have a confirmed seat doesn't mean you're going to get on the plane (see Overbooking).

Cancellation Penalties If you have to cancel or change an Apex ticket, there are often heavy penalties involved. Insurance can sometimes be taken out against these penalties. Some airlines impose penalties on regular tickets as well, particularly against 'no-show' passengers (see No-Shows).

Check In Airlines ask you to check in a certain time ahead of the flight departure (usually 1½ hours on international flights). If you fail to check in on time, and the flight is overbooked, the airline can cancel your booking and give your seat to somebody else.

Confirmation Having a ticket written out with the flight and date you want doesn't mean you have a seat until the agent has checked with the airline that your status is confirmed. Meanwhile you could just be 'on request'.

Discounted Tickets There are two types of discounted fares – officially discounted (see Promotional Fares) and unofficially discounted. The lowest prices often impose drawbacks like flying with unpopular airlines, inconvenient schedules or unpleasant routes and connections. A discounted ticket can save you things other than money – you may be able to pay Apex prices without the associated Apex advance booking and other requirements. Discounted tickets only exist where there is fierce competition.

Full Fares Airlines traditionally offer first-class (coded F), business-class (coded J) and economy-class (coded Y) tickets. These days there are so many promotional and discounted fares available from the regular economy class that few passengers pay full economy fare.

Lost Tickets If you lose your airline ticket an airline will usually treat it like a travellers' cheque and, after enquiries, issue you with another one. Legally, however, an airline is entitled to treat it like cash – if you lose it then it's gone forever. So take good care of your tickets.

No-Shows No-shows are passengers who fail to show up for their flight, sometimes because of unexpected delays or disasters, sometimes because they simply forget and sometimes because they made more than one booking and didn't bother to cancel the one they didn't want. Full-fare passengers who fail to turn up are sometimes entitled to travel on a later flight, but the rest are penalised (see Cancellation Penalties).

On Request An unconfirmed booking for a flight (see Confirmation).

Open Jaws A return ticket where you fly out to one place but return from another. If available, this can save you backtracking to your arrival point.

either in Honolulu or Los Angeles. As in the USA, Sunday newspaper travel sections will have a wide range of travel agents' advertisements offering interesting fares. Travel Cuts is the Canadian student-travel network with offices around the country offering competitively priced tickets.

To/From Australia & New Zealand

Air New Zealand and Qantas both fly Los Angeles-Papeete-Auckland twice a week, with the Qantas service continuing on to Sydney. Auckland-Papeete takes about five hours. Air New Zealand also has a third Auckland-Papeete and Papeete-Auckland flight each week which does not continue on to Los Angeles. Their three weekly connections go direct via Rarotonga and via Rarotonga and Fiji.

STA Travel and Flight Centres International are major specialists in low-priced air fares out of Australia and New Zealand. Weekend travel sections in major newspapers, such as the *Age*, the *Australian* and the *Sydney Morning Herald*, also carry advertisements from agents specialising in lower priced air fares.

Typical fares from Australia to Tahiti (departing from Sydney or Melbourne) cost around A$1100 one way and A$1600 return.

Overbooking Airlines hate to fly with empty seats and since every flight has some passengers who fail to show up (see No-Shows) airlines often book more passengers than they have seats. Usually the excess passengers balance those who fail to show up but occasionally somebody gets bumped. If this happens guess who it is most likely to happen to? The passengers who check in late.

Promotional Fares Officially discounted fares like Apex fares which are available from travel agents or direct from the airline.

Reconfirmation At least 72 hours prior to departure time of an onward or return flight, you must contact the airline and 'reconfirm' that you intend to be on the flight. If you don't do this the airline can delete your name from the passenger list and you could lose your seat. You don't have to reconfirm the first flight on your itinerary or if your stopover is less than 72 hours. It doesn't hurt to reconfirm more than once.

Restrictions Discounted tickets often have various restrictions on them – advance purchase is the most usual one (see Apex). Others are restrictions on the minimum and maximum period you must be away, such as a minimum of 14 days or a maximum of one year (see Cancellation Penalties).

Standby A discounted ticket where you only fly if there is a seat free at the last moment. Standby fares are usually only available on domestic routes.

Tickets Out An entry requirement for many countries is that you have an onward or return ticket, in other words, a ticket out of the country. If you're not sure what you intend to do next, the easiest solution is to buy the cheapest onward ticket to a neighbouring country, or a ticket from a reliable airline which can later be refunded if you do not use it.

Transferred Tickets Airline tickets cannot be transferred from one person to another. Travellers sometimes try to sell the return half of their ticket, but officials can ask you to prove that you are the person named on the ticket. This is unlikely to happen on domestic flights, but on an international flight tickets may be compared with passports.

Travel Agencies Travel agencies vary widely and you should ensure that you use one that suits your needs. Some simply handle tours while full-service agencies handle everything from tours and tickets to car rental and hotel bookings. A good one will do all these things and can save you a lot of money. But if what you want is a ticket at the lowest possible price, then you really need an agency specialising in discounted tickets. A discounted ticket agency, however, may not be useful for other things, like hotel bookings.

Travel Periods Some officially discounted fares, Apex fares in particular, vary with the time of year. There is often a low (off-peak) season and a high (peak) season. Sometimes there's an intermediate or shoulder season as well. At peak times, when everyone wants to fly, not only will the officially discounted fares be higher but so will unofficially discounted fares, or there may simply be no discounted tickets available. Usually the fare depends on your outward flight – if you depart in the high season and return in the low season, you pay the high-season fare. ■

Round-the-world (RTW) fares from Australia cost between A$1700 and A$2700, depending on the airline and the departure date (mid-January to the end of March and October to mid-November are the cheapest times). There is a Philippine Airlines and Air New Zealand RTW combination that flies to London via Manila and Bangkok, and returns via Los Angeles, Hawaii, Cook Islands, Tahiti, Fiji, Apia (Western Samoa) and Auckland. This starts at around $1700 in the low season.

Return fares to Papeete from Auckland start at around NZ$870 in the low season and NZ$1370 in the high season.

To/From South America

There are remarkably few connections across the South Pacific between Australia or New Zealand and South America, so the Lan Chile connection between Tahiti and Chile is an interesting one. The only other operator in the region is Aerolíneas Argentina, which has an Auckland-Buenos Aires connection that goes far south towards Antarctica.

Lan Chile's thrice-weekly flight goes via Easter Island en route to Santiago, so it's popular not just as a route between South America and Australasia but also as a means of getting to Easter Island. From North America it can be better value to take a Circle Pacific fare looping through the Pacific and South America rather than buying a North America-Chile return ticket and then tagging on a Santiago-Easter Island return ticket, as it allows you to take in more destinations.

Flying from Australia via Tahiti and Easter Island to Santiago and return starts at around A$2200. From the USA, a Santiago return ticket will cost from around US$1000 plus another US$800 for an Easter Island return ticket, versus around US$2090 for an Air New Zealand-Lan Chile combination Circle Pacific fare flying a Los Angeles-Sydney (or Melbourne or Auckland)-Papeete-Easter Island-Los Angeles route.

To/From Japan & Asia

The only direct connection with Tahiti from Asia are the twice-weekly Air France flights. Otherwise, the simplest connections will probably be via Australia or New Zealand, and the Circle Pacific fares put together by combinations of an Asian airline with Qantas or Air New Zealand will probably be the cheapest way of getting to Tahiti. A possible route could be from Bangkok, Singapore or Hong Kong to Sydney-Tahiti-Los Angeles, and from there back to the starting point.

Flying with Air Nauru via Nauru, which has connections to Asia and the Pacific, and then continuing via Fiji might be an unusual alternative.

To/From Europe

There are two types of connections to Tahiti from Europe and they can be summarised as French and British.

The French Connection Three airlines operate between Papeete and Paris and have competed fiercely since the route has been opened up to competition: Corsair (Nouvelles Frontières), AOM and Air France. Travel agencies also offer flights with Air New Zealand with reasonably priced connecting flights to London from where they depart (and with possibilities for extending trips as far as New Zealand). The lowest fares are quite similar. Take advantage of competition for the little 'extras' (type of aircraft, frequency, stopovers, discounts for children, ticket validity, alteration or cancellation fees, baggage allowance etc). All airlines stop briefly at Los Angeles (and/or San Francisco for Corsair). Reckon on about a 20-hour flight to Papeete.

Basically, the low season is from early January to the end of June and September to mid-December. The high season (July-August and the Christmas period) is divided into two fare categories according to departure dates. Get information directly from the airlines or your travel agent.

The airlines have agencies or representatives in Switzerland and Belgium offering connecting flights to Paris at reduced fares.

Corsair has a twice-weekly Paris-Papeete service by Boeing 747 on Friday (via San

Francisco) and Sunday (via Los Angeles), returning on Saturday and Monday. The low-season fare is 5950FF return. The high season is divided into three periods and fares range from 6625FF (green period) to 8200FF (red period). A stopover at Los Angeles or San Francisco is possible on payment of a supplement. Note that for two people travelling together on certain dates in the low season, Corsair charges 5950FF for the first ticket and only half the fare for the second. Contact your nearest Nouvelles Frontières travel agency.

AOM offers three or four DC10 flights a week between Paris and Papeete via Los Angeles. There are three fare categories depending on the season, ranging from 5950FF (low season) to 9600FF (high season) return. A stopover at Los Angeles is possible with certain conditions. Contact AOM (☎ 01-49-79-12-34 in Paris) or your travel agent. For connecting flights to Paris from Belgium or Switzerland, contact the AOM representative in Brussels (☎ (32) 2 646 66 33) or Zürich (☎ (41) 01 212 12 24).

Air France has Boeing 747 flights from Paris to Papeete three times a week on Friday, Saturday and Sunday, returning on Saturday, Sunday and Monday. It will cost you between 5950 and 9980FF return depending on the season. The ticket is valid for 45 days but stopovers in Los Angeles are not permitted. Contact Air France (☎ 01-44-08-24-24 in Paris) or your travel agent.

Air New Zealand (☎ 01-53-77-13-13 in Paris) has a connecting-flight agreement with British Airways departing Paris, Lyon, Nice, Toulouse and Marseille to London. You then fly Paris (or provincial France)-London-Los Angeles-Papeete, changing aircraft in London and Los Angeles. This service operates weekly on Friday. Depending on the season, allow 6165 to 8290FF return departing from Paris. The stopover in Los Angeles is free and the ticket is valid for six months. Belgian or Swiss travellers may depart from Frankfurt. The Frankfurt-Los Angeles-Papeete return flight costs 5190 to 7290FF.

The British Connection The British connection usually means visiting Tahiti en route to Australasia, and the flight through Tahiti will normally be with Qantas or Air New Zealand either as a London-Los

---

Flying to Tahiti

Until the American forces built their air base on Bora Bora during WWII, nobody flew to French Polynesia. True, the French military had stationed a few small seaplanes on Tahiti prior to the war but there were no airports nor, for that matter, were there many aircraft capable of the long ocean crossings.

After the war some test flights were made across the Pacific via French Polynesia. In 1950 a French DC-4 island-hopped across the Pacific from Noumea via Vanuatu (the New Hebrides in those days), Fiji and Aitutaki in the Cook Islands to Bora Bora. In 1951 an Australian Catalina amphibious aircraft flew from Sydney via Papeete and the Gambier Islands to Chile.

TRAPAS (Transports Aériens du Pacifique Sud), a locally established airline using war-surplus Catalinas started a once-monthly Noumea-Tahiti service in 1947 which continued until 1950. Re-invented as Air Tahiti it began a service to Aitutaki, but in 1951 TEAL (Tasman Empire Airways Ltd), the predecessor of Air New Zealand, started a monthly and then twice-monthly Auckland-Suva (Fiji)-Apia (Western Samoa)-Aitutaki-Papeete service using a DC-6 on the first leg, then a four-engined Solent flying boat the rest of the way. With an overnight stop at Western Samoa the trip took at least two days. The Aitutaki stop was purely for refuelling and passengers could have a swim in the lagoon during the two-hour stop. The service continued until 1960.

The wartime airfield at Bora Bora was neglected after the war but it was still in good enough repair for Pan Am to fly to Bora Bora from the USA in 1951. In the late 1950s, a French connection was established using land aircraft (Constellations and then DC-4s) to fly Noumea-Fiji-Bora Bora with an amphibious connection to Papeete. Finally, in 1960 the first stage of Faaa airport was opened on reclaimed land in the lagoon near Papeete and Tahiti entered the jet age. ■

Angeles-Papeete-Auckland return flight or as part of a round-the-world routing.

Multistop fares flying London-Auckland-London with Air New Zealand are available from around £750 to £1200 depending on the time of year. A possible itinerary might be London-Los Angeles-Honolulu-Fiji-Auckland-Tahiti-Los Angeles-London. A similar route with Qantas or British Airways allowing just two stopovers en route to Australia would also allow you to stop in Tahiti with fares from £750 to £1250.

Round-the-world routings offer very varied combinations of airlines and stopovers. A Cathay Pacific or Thai International and Air New Zealand combination will take you round the world with multiple stopover possibilities, including Tahiti from around £850 to £1200, depending on the airline combination and the time of year. Virgin Atlantic and Qantas can be put together for similar routings.

In the UK travel agents offering competitive air fares can be tracked down through the travel pages of the Sunday newspapers, magazines like *Time Out* or in a host of giveaway papers in London. Good travel agents for low-priced air fares include STA Travel, Council Travel and Trailfinders.

SEA
Freighter Travel
There are no regular passenger shipping services to French Polynesia and cruise ships which stop in at Papeete are few and far between. Travel on freighter ships is, however, making a steady comeback on the occasional ships that do call in to Papeete. This is not, however, like deciding which day of the week you want to fly. Getting there by freight ship will mean contacting shipping companies and seeing which month something *might* be going by. In his book *In Search of Tusitala* (see the Books section in the Facts for the Visitor chapter) Gavin Bell manages to get to Tahiti by freighter but it isn't exactly easy.

Yachts
Travelling to French Polynesia by yacht is eminently feasible, even if you don't own one! Cruising yachts heading across the Pacific from the North American or Australia/New Zealand side are often looking for crew and, if you're in the right place at the right time and have the right attitude, it's often possible to pick up a ride. But having some sailing experience does help.

On the eastern side of the Pacific try the yacht clubs in San Diego, Los Angeles, San Francisco or Honolulu. On the western side, Auckland, Sydney and Cairns will be good places to try. Look for notices pinned to bulletin boards in yacht clubs and yachting-equipment shops, and post your own notice offering to crew. Simply asking around the yachts can often turn up possibilities.

The sooner you make contact the better, as it's better to do some sailing with the boat before you really set off. A month from the next landfall is not the time to find you don't get on with the crew (or vice versa) or that your immunity to seasickness was just wishful thinking. Sailing experience will definitely score extra points but so will the ability to cook soup when the boat's heeled over and waves are crashing through the hatch. Simply being an easy-going person who can put up with anything and being always ready to lend a hand will count for a lot.

It takes about a month to sail west from the US West Coast to Hawaii and another month south from there to the Marquesas. With stops a further month takes you west again to Tahiti and the Society Islands and then it's another long leg south and west to Australia or New Zealand. There are distinct seasons for sailing across the Pacific since yachties like to be out of the tropics during the cyclone season. Late September through October and January through to March are the usual departure times from the USA. From Australia or New Zealand yachts tend to set off after the cyclone season, around March and April. It's also possible to pick up crewing positions in Tahiti.

TOURS
There's a variety of tour packages available

from travel agents in all western countries. If you want more than just a straightforward cheap fare, a good general travel agent can be an excellent first stop. A good travel agent can negotiate better prices at the larger hotels and can handle Air Tahiti bookings and have your schedule finalised before you arrive. See the Getting Around chapter for more details.

In France, in addition to the traditional travel operators, there are agencies specialising in diving tours. Their packages typically include flights, accommodation, diving fees and diving tours on the main islands. Some of these agents include:

Ultramarina
    4 place Dumoustier, 44000 Nantes (☎ 02-40-89-34-44) and 70 Rue Pernety, 75014 Paris (☎ 01-05-04-06-63)
Aquarev
    52 Blvd de Sébastopol, 75003 Paris (☎ 01-48-87-55-78)
Fun & Fly
    55 Blvd de l'Embouchure, 31200 Toulouse (☎ 05-61-13-39-28)
Subexplor
    50 Passage des Panoramas, 75002 Paris (☎ 01-40-39-99-33)
Blue Lagoon
    9 Rue de Maubeuge, 75009 Paris (☎ 01-42-82-95-40); also represented in Lyon (☎ 04-78-39-34-66), Marseille (☎ 04-91-55-08-69) and Mulhouse (☎ 03-89-66-23-23)
Aéromarine
    22 Rue Royer-Collard, 75005 Paris (☎ 01-43-29-30-22)
Nouvelles Frontières
    Diving is now an integral part of the products offered by this generalist ('Séjours' brochure). Contact your Nouvelles Frontières travel agency.
Force 4
    20 Rue des Pyramides, 75001 Paris (☎ 01-42-61-66-77)

To book cruises with or without crew from Europe, contact the following specialist travel agencies (some with offices in French Polynesia; see the Getting Around chapter):

Voile Voyage
    6 Rue Jean-Goujon, 75008 Paris (☎ 01-45-61-03-09)
Locamarine
    ZA de Creach Gwenn, 29000 Quimper (☎ 02-98-53-14-00)

Bambou Yachting
    9-11 Rue Benoit-Malon, Suresnes (☎ 01-46-97-77-66)
Tahiti Yacht Charter
    Paris contact: ☎ 01-44-15-90-50.
Alemar Yachts
    32 Rue du Temple, 75004 Paris (☎ 01-42-74-55-90)
Objectif Mer and *Archipels Croisières*
    36 Rue de Dombasle, 75015 Paris (☎ 01-45-32-07-88 and ☎ 01-48-28-38-31 respectively)
Moorings
    20 Rue des Pyramides, 75001 Paris (☎ 01-42-61-66-77); Quai Amiral-Infernet, 06300 Nice (☎ 04-92-00-42-22) and also in Brussels (☎ (32) 02 644 13 10)
Vent Portant
    Hôtel des Entreprises, Avenue Marcillac, 17000 La Rochelle (☎ toll-free 05-10-86-26)
Itinéa
    56 Rue Saint-Jean, 50400 Granville (☎ 02-33-50-52-02)
International Yacht Charter
    14 Rue Pasteur, 06400 Cannes (☎ 04-92-99-39-93/04-93-39-29-77)
Comptoir de la croisière/Stardust Marine
    20bis Ave Mac-Mahon, 75017 Paris (☎ 01-40-68-68-68)
Alcyon
    10 Rue Saint-Marc, 75002 Paris (☎ 01-40-39-93-79)
Bodrum Yachting
    24 Rue de la Rochefoucauld, 75009 Paris (☎ 01-48-78-40-27)
Teos Croisières
    1 Rue Bleue, 75009 Paris (☎ 01-47-70-08-08)
VPM
    ☎ 01-47-83-73-84; represented by Nouvelles Frontières agencies

WARNING

The information in this chapter is vulnerable to change: prices for international travel are volatile, routes are introduced and cancelled, schedules change, special deals come and go, and rules and visa requirements are amended. Check directly with the airline or a travel agent to make sure you understand how a fare works. Get quotes and advice from as many airlines and travel agents as possible before you part with your hard-earned cash. The details given in this chapter should be regarded as pointers and are not a substitute for your own careful, up-to-date research.

Getting Around

Getting from island to island in French Polynesia involves flights or boats, and, thanks to a great deal of French government financial support, travel to the larger and more densely populated islands is relatively easy and fairly reasonably priced. Getting to the remote islands can be time consuming or even difficult but never boring. On some islands there are paved roads, local *le truck* bus services and ranks of rental cars; on others there's just rough dirt tracks and very little local transport.

Island to Island

AIR

There are some charter operators with small aircraft and helicopters, but essentially flying within French Polynesia means Air Tahiti and its associate, Air Moorea. Air Tahiti operates a modern fleet of twin-turbo-prop aircraft. The fleet comprises the 19-seat Dornier 228, the 46-seat ATR 42 and the 66-seat ATR 72. All three are high-winged aircraft so all the window seats offer great views – perfect for flying over the beautiful islands. Air Moorea is the secondary airline operating smaller Islander aircraft on the 10-minute hop between Tahiti and neighbouring Moorea, and also to Tetiaroa, Marlon Brando's island north of Tahiti. Air Moorea also has one larger Twin Otter and a Dornier 228.

Air Tahiti flies to 37 islands in all five of the major island groups in French Polynesia. Air fares are heavily subsidised, but since distances to the more remote islands are great it's inevitable that some fares will be quite costly. The best bargains for travel in French Polynesia are the air passes which allow you to visit a number of islands for one fare. Note that Papeete is very much the centre for flights within French Polynesia and, apart from flights between the Tuamotus and Marquesas or Tuamotus and Gambier Archipelago, you will generally have to pass through Papeete between island groups.

Reservation Problems

If your travel agent tells you that Air Tahiti flights are fully booked, do not despair. Polynesians are in the habit of reserving seats and changing their minds at the last moment. Seats may therefore become available right up to the last minute. Reapply frequently, even on the spot.

It is possible that after battling for weeks to get a seat, you will find that the aircraft is half empty, (especially flights to the Marquesas). Don't get angry: the number of passengers admitted on each flight depends on the weight of the freight.

Frequencies & Flight Times

Flight frequencies vary between the high and low seasons and the frequency indications that follow are generally a minimum. In July and August in particular extra flights are laid on. Although Air Tahiti is pretty reliable, it's still not a good idea to leave your return to Papeete for a departing international flight until the last moment: get back with a day or more in hand.

Society Islands In the Society Islands there are flights every half hour or so between Tahiti and Moorea, and every day between Tahiti and the other major islands except for Maupiti, where connections are less frequent. Between the Society Islands (other than Tahiti) there are daily connections on most routes apart from flights to or from Raiatea and Maupiti. On some routes, like the busy Papeete-Bora Bora, there may be up to half a dozen flights a day. The Society Islands are quite close together, and the longest nonstop flight is 45 minutes between Tahiti and Bora Bora. Other flights may be as short as 10 minutes, or even less between Papeete and Moorea. Apart from the Air

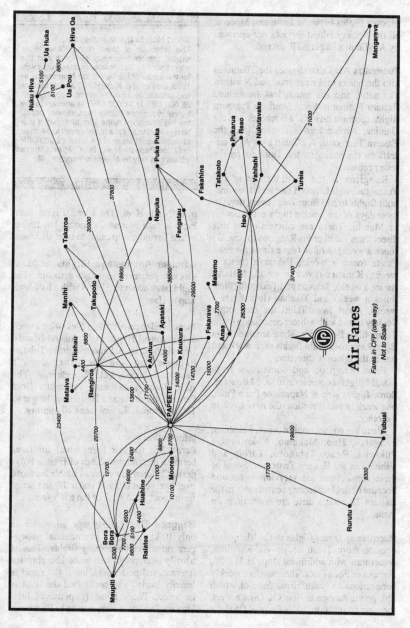

Air Fares

Fares in CFP (one way)
Not to Scale

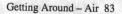

Moorea flights between Tahiti and Moorea, all the Society Island services are operated by Air Tahiti's larger ATR aircraft.

Tuamotus Air Tahiti divides the Tuamotus into the busier and more touristed Northern Tuamotu and the much less frequented Eastern Tuamotu. Some Northern Tuamotu flights continue on to the Marquesas, and the Gambier Archipelago is reached from the Eastern Tuamotus. Air Tahiti uses ATR aircraft on the busier routes, Dorniers on the lesser routes.

Rangiroa is the main centre in the Tuamotus, with between one and three one-hour flights to and from Tahiti every day. On most days of the week a flight continues on to Manihi. There are connections either direct from Tahiti or via Rangiroa to Apataki (once a week), Arutua (three times a week), Faaite (once a week), Fakarava (twice a week), Kaukura (twice a week), Mataiva (twice a week), Takaroa and Takapoto (three times a week) and Tikehau (four times a week). Apart from Tahiti the only other Society island with a direct connection to the Tuamotus is Bora Bora. There are three Bora Bora-Rangiro-Manihi flights each week and one in the opposite direction.

From Rangiroa and sometimes from Manihi flights continue on to the Marquesas. Some flights stop at Napuka or Puka Puka, one week in one direction, the next week in the other.

There are connections to Anaa, Fakahina, Fangatau, Hao, Makemo, Nukutavake, Pukarua, Reao, Tatakoto, Tureia and Vahitahi in the Eastern Tuamotus. Some of these connections are very infrequent and because of nuclear-testing sensitivities in the Eastern Tuamotus there are restrictions on visits.

Marquesas Direct flights to the Marquesas operate from Tahiti or go via Rangiroa, sometimes with additional stops at Manihi, Napuka or Puka Puka. There are five weekly connections to Nuku Hiva, three of which also go via Atuona in Hiva Oa. Once a week there are connections to Ua Pou and Ua Huka

---

Short Hop to the Marquesas
The extension of Nuku Ataha (Nuku Hiva) airport, greater frequency of flights and the alteration of Air Tahiti's fare structure augur well for the future of tourism in the Marquesas. In 1996, the Papeete-Nuku Hiva-Papeete full fare was reduced by a token amount, dropping from 75,600 CFP to 71,800 CFP. In addition to the typical reductions (family card, seniors' pass), the big innovation is the introduction of a discovery fare, valid for a trip of seven to 14 days at certain quiet times of the year: 49,900 CFP only for Papeete-Nuku Hiva return. These tickets can only be bought in Papeete. ∎

---

from Nuku Hiva. The direct flights from Papeete take around 3½ hours but flights with a Tuamotu stop can take over six hours.

Gambier Archipelago Flights to Mangareva operate three times a month. The flight takes about five hours with a half-hour stop at Hao.

Austral Islands Air Tahiti flies twice a week to Rurutu and Tubuai in the Austral Islands. One flight does a Papeete-Rurutu-Tubuai-Papeete run and the other does a Papeete-Tubuai-Rurutu-Papeete run. The ATR flight takes about 1½ hours from Papeete to Rurutu and 10 minutes longer to Tubuai; Rurutu-Tubuai takes 40 minutes.

Information
Fares See the Air Fares chart for fares between the various islands of French Polynesia. Children's fares are available for those over two years old and under 12 and range from about 50 to 60% of the adult fare.

Baggage The free-baggage allowance is only 10 kg except for international passengers on direct connecting flights. This is usually interpreted with some liberality for international passengers, but if the flight is heavily loaded you could find the limit is imposed. There is an (expensive) left-luggage facility at Faaa airport in Papeete.

Reconfirmations You are not officially required to reconfirm Air Tahiti flights, but like many places in the world it's wise to do so, particularly on infrequent services such as the connections to the Marquesas. Note that if you fail to fly on a confirmed flight all your subsequent reservations may be cancelled. So if you decide to get from one island to another by some different means, make sure you reconfirm the rest of your flights. If you haven't told Air Tahiti where you are staying then it is also a good idea to reconfirm.

Other Information All Air Tahiti flights are nonsmoking. See the relevant islands for Air Tahiti phone numbers or contact the head office in Tahiti on ☎ 86-42-42 or fax 86-40-69. Air Tahiti publishes a very useful flight schedule booklet which is essential reading for anyone planning a complex trip around the islands. You can write to Air Tahiti at BP 314, Papeete, Tahiti.

Air Passes

Six different island-hopping air passes are available, and child fares are offered for children between two and 12 years of age. Travel must commence in Papeete and there are restrictions on the number of transits through Papeete before the end of the pass. You are only allowed one stopover on each island but, except for Papeete, you can transit an island so long as the flight number does not change. If you stop at the island to change flights that counts as a stopover. The tickets are valid for a maximum of 28 days and all flights (except Papeete-Moorea or Moorea-Papeete) must be booked at the beginning, although reservations can subsequently be changed for a 1000 CFP fee. You can use either Air Tahiti or Air Moorea on the Papeete-Moorea sector. If the routing is also changed and this changes the pass classification, you will also have to pay the higher fare. Once you have taken the first flight on the pass the fare is non-refundable.

Society Islands Pass YD 215 costs 30,500 CFP for adults and 16,200 CFP for children.

This pass lets you visit all six of the major islands in the Society group: Tahiti, Moorea, Huahine, Raiatea, Bora Bora and Maupiti. Note that this is the only pass which includes Maupiti.

Society Islands & Tuamotus Pass YD 213 costs 45,500 CFP for adults, and 23,700 CFP for children. This pass combines visits from Tahiti to Moorea, Huahine, Raiatea and Bora Bora in the Society group with Rangiroa, Manihi and Tikehau in the Tuamotus. Since you cannot transit Papeete within the pass, you must use the Bora Bora-Rangiroa or Bora Bora-Manihi flight which operates three times a week from Bora Bora to the Tuamotus but only once a week from the Tuamotus to Bora Bora. For this reason you have more flexibility if you visit the Tuamotus after the Society Islands rather than before.

Pass YD 212 costs 50,500 CFP for adults and 26,200 CFP for children. This pass covers exactly the same islands as the cheaper YD 213 pass but allows you to transit Papeete between the Society Islands and the Tuamotus. You are not restricted to the three eastbound and one westbound flight between Bora Bora and the Tuamotus.

Society Islands & Australs Pass YD 214 costs 50,500 CFP for adults and 26,200 CFP for children. This pass combines the Society Islands (Tahiti, Moorea, Huahine, Raiatea and Bora Bora) with the Austral Islands (Rurutu and Tubuai). You are allowed to transit Papeete between the Society and Austral groups.

Moorea & Tuamotus Pass YD 220 costs 35,000 CFP for adults and 18,400 CFP for children. This pass combines Moorea with visits to Rangiroa, Manihi and Tikehau, with one transit through Papeete between Moorea and the Tuamotus.

Society Islands, Tuamotus & Marquesas Pass YD 217 costs 87,000 CFP for adults, 44,400 CFP for children. This pass combines Tahiti, Moorea, Huahine, Raiatea and Bora

Flying with Air Tahiti

Air Tahiti is a nice easy-going little airline that flies modern and well-kept aircraft and generally seems to keep to its schedules. In fact it often seems to run ahead of schedule. If the plane is there and the passengers are ready, Air Tahiti flights are often in the air before their scheduled departure time. On a short flight from Raiatea to Huahine (which is scheduled to take 15 minutes but takes more like 10 minutes) we left 15 minutes early, which meant we arrived in Huahine before we were supposed to have left Raiatea!

Flying from Bora Bora to Raiatea on one occasion I (Tony) discovered, after checking in, that I'd managed to book myself on a flight via Maupiti, which meant I was going to arrive in Raiatea five minutes later than a direct flight which departed 35 minutes later. But obviously five minutes was neither here nor there – it was going to come down to which one left a few minutes earlier or later, or which flight was turned around quicker. Sure enough, my flight turned around in Maupiti in double quick time, and as we headed back towards Bora Bora I could see the later flight heading towards Raiatea ahead of us. But it was still climbing whereas we were already as high as we would get and about to start descending. On the downhill run we slipped ahead and I was already at the rental-car desk when the direct flight pulled in a couple of minutes behind us.

Most of the flights are pleasantly short, the views are often terrific and even the prices, if you get a multi-island air pass, aren't too bad. Not a bad little airline. ■

Bora in the Society Islands; Rangiroa and Manihi in the Tuamotus; and Atuona (Hiva Oa) and Nuku Hiva in the Marquesas. There are three different route variations on this pass. The first goes from Papeete to the other Society Islands, then transits Papeete en route to the Tuamotus and the Marquesas or vice versa. The second uses the Bora Bora-Tuamotus flight to link the Society Islands and Tuamotus without returning to Papeete. The Marquesas are a separate out-and-back trip from Papeete either before or after the Society Islands-Tuamotus circuit. The third simply combines the three groups as one continuous loop without a transit through Papeete.

Charter Operators & Helicopters

See the Tahiti chapter for more details on charter operators and helicopter services including Air Oceania Tahiti, Air Alizé, Tahiti Conquest Airlines, Wan Air and Heli-Pacific. Air Alizé (☎ 66-10-10, fax 66-10-01) operates out of Raiatea and has a nine-passenger aircraft for charter operations.

INTER-ISLAND SHIPS

The huge, multiengine catamarans that shuttle back and forth between Tahiti and

Moorea and the ultra-quick *Ono-Ono*, which operates to other islands in the Society group, have brought aircraft-style schedules and almost aircraft-style speed to travel between those islands. The schedule to other islands and on slower boats is neatly summarised by a note on the Chez Guynette noticeboard in Fare, Huahine:

The boats arrive when they are here and leave when they are ready...

It's worth keeping this in mind if you're travelling off the beaten track as services are very likely to be infrequent, uncertain and undependable. Despite modern competition, it's still possible to travel in traditional fashion, on board ships where freight is the major consideration and passengers are just a sideline. The freighters are still often referred to as schooners.

Tahiti-Moorea services and the regular *Ono-Ono* and *Raromatai Ferry* routes through the Society Islands can be booked at offices right on the docks at most locations. For other ships, booking your passage may mean tracking down the office or local representative or simply waiting for the ship to dock and enquiring on board. In Papeete the tourist office can provide some information on routes and schedules, but for remote locations a stroll down to the inter-island dock area, past the naval station area on Fare Ute, is usually necessary.

The *Ono-Ono* has aircraft-style seating, the *Raromatai Ferry* has seating and cabins and some other ships may have cabins available, but on many freighters the only option is to travel deck class, which means just what it says: you unroll your sleeping bag on a piece of deck. You may have the option of buying meals on the ship or bringing your own supplies with you. Lazily island hopping across the Pacific may have a romantic ring, but on freight ships the reality is that you're likely to get wet and dirty and suffering bouts of seasickness. Come prepared.

Society Islands

Tahiti-Moorea It takes less than half an hour to travel between the two islands on the latest catamarans. Slower car ferries also operate on this route but motorcycles and bicycles can only be taken on the catamarans. See the Moorea chapter for more information.

Ono-Ono The high-speed *Ono-Ono* has quickly become a very popular method of getting around the Society Islands. The Australian-built boat entered service in 1994, carries up to 450 passengers and reaches speeds of 35 knots (65 km/h).

The *Ono-Ono* runs a daily schedule connecting various combinations of Tahiti,

Huahine, Raiatea, Tahaa and Bora Bora. Turnaround times in port are more akin to aircraft than the regular ships – the *Ono-Ono* is usually in port for just 10 to 15 minutes. Leaving Tahiti at 9 am you can reach Bora Bora at 4.15 pm that afternoon. It's just 3½ hours from Papeete to Huahine, less than one hour from Raiatea to Tahaa and one hour from Tahaa to Bora Bora. The weekly schedule is as follows:

Monday & Wednesday

Depart		Arrive	
Papeete	0900	Huahine	1230
Huahine	1245	Raiatea	1330
Raiatea	1345	Tahaa	1430
Tahaa	1440	Bora Bora	1615

Tuesday, Thursday & Sunday

Depart		Arrive	
Bora Bora	1200	Tahaa	1300
Tahaa	1315	Raiatea	1415
Raiatea	1430	Huahine	1530
Huahine	1545	Papeete	1915

Friday

Depart		Arrive	
Papeete	1630	Huahine	1945
Huahine	2000	Raiatea	2100
Raiatea	2115	Bora Bora	2300

Saturday

Depart		Arrive	
Bora Bora	0800	Tahaa	0900
Tahaa	0915	Raiatea	1015
Raiatea	1030	Huahine	1130
Huahine	1500	Raiatea	1600
Raiatea	1615	Tahaa	1700
Tahaa	1710	Bora Bora	1815

One-way fares on the *Ono-Ono* are as follows:

From:	To:				
	Huahine	Raiatea	Tahaa	Bora Bora	Papeete
Papeete	4300 CFP	4800 CFP	5300 CFP	5800 CFP	–
Huahine	–	1600 CFP	1900 CFP	2800 CFP	4300 CFP
Raiatea	1600 CFP	–	600 CFP	1600 CFP	4800 CFP
Tahaa	1900 CFP	600 CFP	–	1200 CFP	5300 CFP
Bora Bora	2800 CFP	1600 CFP	1200 CFP	–	5800 CFP

Children between the ages of two and 12 pay half fare.

Passengers have a 30-kg baggage allowance and the *Ono-Ono* will also take bicycles (1000 CFP to or from Tahiti, 600 CFP between the other islands), small motorcycles and scooters (2500 CFP, 1250 CFP), larger motorcycles (3500 CFP, 1750 CFP), surfboards (600 CFP) and freight. Snacks, drinks and meals are available on board, at rather stiff prices, but meals must be ordered in advance.

In Papeete, bookings on the *Ono-Ono* (☎ 45-35-35, fax 43-83-45) can be made at the office on the Quai d'Honneur in the centre of town. Write to BP 16, Papeete, Tahiti, for more information.

Raromatai Ferry Prior to the *Ono-Ono*, the *Raromatai Ferry* was the fastest and most regular service through the Society Islands, and it's still one of the most popular ships. There are bench seats outside or seating in an air-conditioned lounge for a total of 362 passengers and 18 cabins for two or four passengers. It takes about eight hours to ply between Papeete and Huahine, two hours for Huahine-Raiatea, one hour for Raiatea-Tahaa and two hours for Tahaa-Bora Bora. The *Raromatai Ferry* operates the following schedule: Papeete-Huahine-Raiatea-Tahaa-Bora Bora and back each week.

Depart			Arrive		
Papeete	Mon	1600	Huahine	Tues	0000
Huahine	Tues	0100	Raiatea	Tues	0300
Raiatea	Tues	0400	Tahaa	Tues	0500
Tahaa	Tues	0530	Bora Bora	Tues	0730
Bora Bora	Tues	0900	Tahaa	Tues	1100
Tahaa	Tues	1130	Raiatea	Tues	1230

Depart			Arrive		
Raiatea	Tues	1300	Huahine	Tues	1500
Huahine	Tues	1530	Papeete	Wed	0000
Papeete	Wed	1600	Huahine	Thurs	0000
Huahine	Thurs	0100	Raiatea	Thurs	0300
Raiatea	Thurs	0400	Tahaa	Thurs	0500
Tahaa	Thurs	0530	Bora Bora	Thurs	0730
Bora Bora	Thurs	0900	Tahaa	Thurs	1100
Tahaa	Thurs	1130	Raiatea	Thurs	1230
Raiatea	Thurs	1300	Huahine	Thurs	1500
Huahine	Thurs	1530	Papeete	Fri	0000
Papeete	Fri	1600	Huahine	Sat	0000
Huahine	Sat	0100	Raiatea	Sat	0300
Raiatea	Sat	0400	Tahaa	Sat	0500
Tahaa	Sat	0530	Bora Bora	Sat	0730
Bora Bora	Sun	1430	Tahaa	Sun	1630
Tahaa	Sun	1700	Raiatea	Sun	1800
Raiatea	Sun	1830	Huahine	Sun	2030
Huahine	Sun	2100	Papeete	Mon	0530

A cabin for four costs 6000 CFP per person, a cabin for two is 8500 CFP per person. The *Raromatai* will also carry bicycles, motorcycles and cars between the islands. Bookings (☎ 43-19-88, fax 43-19-99) can be made by writing to BP 9012, Papeete, Tahiti.

Other Ships Since the *Ono-Ono* started operations it has grabbed a large slice of the Society Islands traffic, and people are obviously happy to pay more for the fast and reliable service. The *Raromatai Ferry* continues to attract passengers but other ship operators have cut back on their passenger-carrying operations and are concentrating on freight.

Other predominantly cargo ships operating in the Society Islands include the 13-cabin *Veanu* (☎ 41-25-35, fax 41-24-34), which can be contacted at the Société Ihitai

One-way fares with a seat (*fauteuil*) but without meals on the *Raromatai Ferry* are:

From:	To:				
	Huahine	Raiatea	Tahaa	Bora Bora	Papeete
Papeete	1000 CFP	2000 CFP	3000 CFP	3800 CFP	
Huahine	–	1000 CFP	2000 CFP	3000 CFP	1000 CFP
Raiatea	1000 CFP	–	1000 CFP	2000 CFP	2000 CFP
Tahaa	2000 CFP	1000 CFP	–	1000 CFP	3000 CFP
Bora Bora	3000 CFP	2000 CFP	1000 CFP	–	3800 CFP

Nui, BP 9062, Motu Uta, Tahiti. The *Taporo VI* (☎ 42-63-93 or 43-79-72, fax 42-06-17) takes 12 deck-class passengers and has one four-berth cabin. Write to CFMT, BP 368, Papeete, Tahiti, for information. Travel times are very similar to the *Raromatai Ferry*.

Because the pass into Maupiti's lagoon can only handle small ships, none of the regular services to other Society Islands continue to the last of the Leeward high islands. The small ships which do operate to Maupiti include the *Te Aratai* and the *Maupiti To'u Aia* from Raiatea; the latter sometimes continues on to Mopelia. The *Meherio III* is supposed to have one of the most regular services. Contact the Service de l'équipement, (☎ 42-44-92, 43-32-69 or 43-32-70) for more details.

Tuamotus

The small cargo vessels which serve the Tuamotus are known as schooners or tramps. They are true lifelines between Tahiti and the atolls of the archipelago and their main purpose is to transport freight. They can take passengers, but the standard of comfort is generally basic.

The routes and fares mentioned are purely an indication and are subject to change. Obtain information directly from the shipowners. Their offices are in the Motu Uta port area in Papeete (take le truck No 3 at the town hall) and are generally open from 7.30 to 11 am and from 1.30 to 5 pm Monday to Friday. Some also open on Saturday morning. For inter-island hops, contact the ship's master direct.

Dory This vessel does the Papeete-Tikehau-Rangiroa-Arutua-Kaukura-Papeete route. It departs Papeete on Monday and returns on Thursday. There are no berths on board and no meal service is provided for passengers. A single trip costs 2500 CFP. The office (☎ 42-30-55) is in the same building as that of the *Taporo IV* and the *Aranui*, on the quay at the entrance to Motu Uta port area.

Cobia II Departing from Papeete, this vessel serves Kaukura, Arutua, Apataki, Aratika

and Toau. It belongs to the same company as the *Dory*. The conditions are identical and information is available from the same office.

Kauaora Nui This ship does a Papeete-Faaite-Katiu-Makemo-Papeete circuit, departing on Monday and returning on Friday. The fare for the full trip is 10,600 CFP. No meals are served on board and there are no berths. The office (☎ 41-07-11) is on the quay, at the entrance to Motu Uta port area.

Saint Xavier Maris Stella This vessel does a Papeete, Tikehau, Mataiva, Rangiroa, Ahe, Manihi, Takaroa, Takapoto, Aratika, Kauehi, Raraka, Fakarava, Toau, Apataki, Arutua, Kaukura, Niau circuit twice a month. Departing from Papeete, allow 5000 CFP for Rangiroa, 7000 CFP for Manihi and 21,000 CFP for the complete trip (10 days) on the deck, meals included. To get to the office (☎ 42-23-58), which is in the warehouses, follow the road that goes along the tramp quay and, at the bend, take the right fork.

Manava 2 Twice a month, the *Manava 2* follows the Papeete, Makatea, Tikehau, Rangiroa, Ahe, Manihi, Arutua, Apataki, Takaroa, Takapoto, Aratika, Raraka, Kauehi, Fakarava, Toau, Niau, Kaukura, Mataiva, Papeete route. Allow 4000 CFP for a part trip, 8000 CFP for the full trip (11-12 days) on the rear deck, and add 1800 CFP a day for meals. To get to the office (☎ 43-83-84 or 42-25-53), take the same road as for the *Saint Xavier Maris Stella* office.

Vai-Aito This vessel provides a Papeete, Mataiva, Tikehau, Rangiroa, Manihi, Ahe, Kauehi, Raraka, Fakarava, Faaite, Toau, Aratika, Apataki, Kaukura, Papeete service three times a month. Allow 3681 CFP for a part trip, 7362 CFP for the complete trip (six to eight days) on the rear deck and 2500 CFP a day for food. The office (☎ 43-99-96) is 200 metres from that of the *Dory* and the *Aranui*, at the end of the quay.

Auura'Nui 3 Once a month this ship services 19 remote atolls of the central and east Tuamotus, including Anaa, Hao and Fakarava (Tetamanu). Prices range from 3000 to 7000 CFP on deck and 6000 to 12,000 CFP in a berth, depending on the distance of the atoll, and 2200 CFP a day for food. The complete circuit takes 18 days. To get to the office (☎ 43-92-40) take the same road as for the *Saint Xavier Maris Stella* office.

Kura Ora Once a month this ship visits 18 remote atolls of the central and east Tuamotus, including Anaa and Hao. Prices range from 6350 to 13,650 CFP for a single trip on the rear deck according to distance, plus 1600 CFP a day for food. The complete trip takes 12 to 13 days. To get to the office (☎ 45-55-45), take the same road as for the *Saint Xavier Maris Stella* office.

Rairoa Nui This vessel does a Papeete-Tikehau-Rangiroa-Papeete circuit once a week. It only takes passengers in the Tikehau/Rangiroa-Papeete direction. The passage to Papeete (one day) costs 3000 CFP (no meals). Contact the ship's master direct. In Papeete, telephone ☎ 42-91-69.

Other Ships The *Tamarii Tuamotu*, *Taporo IV* and *Aranui* all also serve certain atolls in the Tuamotus en route to the Marquesas (see the next section). For the *Manava III*, refer to the paragraph on the *Gambiers*.

See the Tuamotus chapter for more details.

Marquesas

Taking a ship to the Marquesas usually means a voyage on the *Aranui*, the passenger and cargo ship which operates a regular schedule between Tahiti and the Marquesas. Although it is essentially a freighter, and a vitally important one for the local economy, the *Aranui* is several steps up from the rock bottom, unroll-your-sleeping-bag-on-the-deck style of inter-island travel. For cabin-class passengers there's even a swimming pool, and because the more expensive tickets include excursions and transport

ashore (costly propositions on the Marquesas) it's worth opting to travel in greater luxury. Paul Theroux's *The Happy Isles of Oceania* has a good description of travelling on the *Aranui*. This is the one ship in French Polynesia which is really worth booking before you arrive. Other services are either too frequent and reliable to make bookings necessary, or too unreliable to make them useful. See the Marquesas chapter for more details.

Aranui A real darling of the tourists, this 104-metre cargo-and-passenger vessel does 15 annual trips departing from Papeete. In order, it goes to Takapoto, the six inhabited islands of the Marquesas (some of them twice) and Rangiroa in 16 days, 10 of which are spent in the Marquesas. The cruise costs 180,000 CFP on the covered rear deck (bunks, sheets and towels provided, shared toilets); 294,580 CFP for a B cabin (air-con cabin with two beds, shared toilets); 339,900 CFP for an A cabin (air-con twin-bed cabin with porthole, private shower and toilet); and 403,760 CFP for a deluxe A cabin (large air-con cabin with porthole, double bed and bath). All fares are per person and include full-board, meals at restaurants ashore and programme of guided visits to the main tourist sites included. A special fare is charged for children. The vessel takes 62 passengers in cabins and about 18 on the rear deck.

Some optional excursions ashore cost extra (diving, horse riding etc). A laundry/drying service is organised twice a week free of charge for all passengers. Depending on space, it is possible to do only part of the trip (in the Marquesas for example) at a pro-rata price calculated on the number of days spent aboard.

There is also a covered 'local deck' intended for local inhabitants who get on or off along the route. Officially, tourists are dissuaded from travelling here, but you may apply directly to the supercargo or the stewards when the vessel puts into port. Allow 2000 CFP for a passage between two islands in the Marquesas. In this case, meals, which are included, are not served in the tourists' dining room and excursions are obviously not included. Only a mattress is provided (take a sleeping bag).

The ship has a bar, small library, shop, restaurant, video lounge, mini-swimming pool and a sickbay. Entertainment is provided some evenings. Credit cards and travellers' cheques are accepted and there are currency-exchange facilities on board.

The company (Compagnie polynésienne de transport maritime, ☎ 42-62-40 or 43-76-60, fax 43-48-89, BP 220, Papeete) has an office at the entrance to Motu Uta port area. It is open from 7.30 to 11.30 am and 1.30 to 5 pm Monday to Friday. Bookings are essential.

In France, contact Quotidien Voyages (☎ 01-47-47-11-16; 119, Ave du Général Charles de Gaulle, 92526 Neuilly Cedex); in the US contact CPTM (☎ (415) 5410674, fax (415) 5410766; 595 Market St, Suite 2880, San Francisco, CA 94105).

Taporo IV This 75-metre cargo vessel follows the following route every two weeks (departing Thursday): Papeete-Takapoto-Fatuiva-Tahuata-Hiva Oa-Ua Huka-Nuku Hiva-Ua Pou-Papeete (11 days). Allow 9000/13,000 CFP on deck/cabin for Takapoto and 20,000/30,000 CFP on deck/cabin for the Marquesas, meals included. The shipowner, Compagnie française maritime de Tahiti, has an office at Fare Ute (☎ 42-63-93) and on the tramp quay at the entrance to Motu Uta port area (☎ 43-89-66).

Tamarii Tuamotu Every five weeks this vessel does a trip lasting about one month and serves several atolls in the Tuamotus (including Takaroa and Takapoto) as well as the six inhabited islands of the Marquesas. Considered the least reliable of the cargo ships, Marquesans have nicknamed it the 'ghost ship'. At the time of our visit, it had been waiting for a new engine for six months. Information is available from the shipowner (☎ 42-95-07; 43 Rue du Prince-Hinoi, Papeete).

Kahoa Nui This small ferry, normally based at Taiohae, travels round the archipelago only on certain occasions (school transport, sports events, religious festivals etc). Information is available at Taiohae town hall.

Australs

Local demand can vary the schedule but the 60-metre *Tuhaa Pae II* operates from Tahiti down the Rimatara-Rurutu-Tubuai-Raivavae chain about twice a month and continues to Rapa once every two months. Very occasionally a pause is made at the Maria Islands. This ship is not particularly comfortable and the schedule is often very unreliable. See the Austral Islands chapter for more details.

Gambier Archipelago

The *Manava II* does a monthly 20-day voyage through some of the more remote islands of the Tuamotus, en route to Mangareva. See the Gambiers chapter for more details.

CRUISES

There are two cruise operations in the Society Islands, both of which use large motorised sail cruise ships – the luxurious *Wind Song* and the larger *Club Med 2*. The *Club Med 2* also visits Rangiroa in the Tuamotus. These boats are a long way from the leaky copra boats of traditional inter-island travel.

Wind Song

The four-mast 134-metre *Wind Song* has 76 cabins, a swimming pool, restaurants, a small casino, nightclub, shops, sauna, scuba-diving equipment, sailboards, a small library and, if you get bored with the scenery or the on-board activities, there are also TVs and VCRs. There are regular weekly cruises from Tahiti to other islands in the Society group. They usually arrive in the early afternoon giving passengers the afternoon ashore, an overnight stay at dock or at anchor and depart at dawn the next day. Papeete-Huahine-Raiatea-Bora Bora-Moorea-Papeete is a typical itinerary.

Seven-day cruises start from around US$2700 per person plus US$130 for port charges. In the USA bookings can be made through Windstar Cruises (☎ (800) 258-7245, fax (206) 281-0627), 300 Elliott Ave W, Seattle, WA 98119. Local reservations can be made by calling ☎ 54-02-25.

Club Med 2

Part of the Club Med empire, the *Club Med 2* is a much larger ship. It weighs 14,000 tonnes, is 187 metres in length and has 196 cabins including five suites. All up she can carry 400 passengers and a crew of 200. There are two swimming pools, four bars, two restaurants, a nightclub, boutiques, and a sauna and a full range of activities on offer including scuba diving, windsurfing and water skiing.

The *Club Med 2's* usual one-week cruise takes it on a Papeete-Moorea-Huahine-Raiatea-Tahaa-Bora Bora-Rangiroa-Papeete circuit. Usually passengers will have booked passage on the ship as part of a Club Med vacation but it is sometimes possible to book cruises in Tahiti, even for just part of the total itinerary. Examples include two days on a Papeete-Moorea-Huahine trip for 52,250 CFP; three days from Papeete to Moorea and Bora Bora for 71,400 CFP or three days from Bora Bora to Rangiroa and Papeete for 71,400 CFP.

Club Med (☎ 42-96-99, fax 42-16-83) has an office in the Vaima Centre in Papeete, Tahiti, and bookings can be made by writing to BP 575, Papeete, Tahiti. Alternatively, write to Translink Polynésie, BP 596 Papeete, Tahiti.

Archipels Croisières

Operating four large 18-metre sailing catamarans, this Moorea-based company does a variety of interesting trips in the different island groups of French Polynesia. A seven-day trip through the Society Islands visits Bora Bora, Tahaa, Raiatea and Huahine for 160,000 CFP per person. An eight-day trip through the Marquesas visiting Nuku Hiva, Ua Huka, Hiva Oa, Tahuata and Fatu Hiva costs 215,000 CFP, including a return flight

from Papeete. A three-day trip around the Rangiroa lagoon costs 60,300 CFP; a four-day version is 81,000 CFP. Eight-day diving trips with the Raie Manta Club cost 200,000 CFP and depart from either Fakarava, visiting Fakarava, Toau and Kauei, or Rangiroa visiting Rangiroa and Tikehau.

Archipels Croisières (☎ 56-36-39) can be contacted through BP 1160, Papetoai, Moorea. In France, Archipels Croisières (☎ 01-42-46-70-13) is at 36 Rue Dombasle, 75015 Paris.

The Aranui

See the previous Marquesas section and the Marquesas chapter for more on the *Aranui* and its service to and around the islands.

YACHTING

French Polynesia is an enormously popular yachting destination, as the international line-up of yachts along the Papeete waterfront testifies. The Marquesas are the first landfall for westbound yachts after Hawaii. (See the Getting There & Away chapter for more information about sailing to French Polynesia. See also Formalities for Pleasure Boats in the Facts for the Visitor chapter for those details.)

Yacht crews should take precautions against theft at popular tourist centres like Bora Bora and in the Marquesas where it can be a problem. Never leave vitally important things like cash, travellers' cheques, passports or other documents on board. Always lock the boat up when you go ashore and take special care of any outboards and tenders. A runabout tied up beside a yacht at night can quite easily sail away before dawn.

Crewing Positions

It's often possible to pick up crewing positions on yachts, particularly if you have had some relevant sailing experience. Check noticeboards in popular restaurants and at the yacht clubs in Tahiti, Bora Bora, Raiatea and other popular yachting stops. Yacht owners have to put up with some complex paperwork when making crew changes so make sure your own papers are in order. The

A Beginner's Guide to Yacht Hire

Before casting off, you should know how to unravel the confusion surrounding the four hire options generally offered by agencies or hirers:

Bareboat Hire You hire a yacht without crew or skipper and you do everything yourself: manoeuvring, navigating and providing your own supplies. This option is for experienced yachties in a group of four to eight people. You set your own itinerary, and a deposit is required.

Hire with Skipper You hire the boat plus the services of a skipper. This is a great way to go if you're not sure of your own capabilities or if you have limited knowledge of the islands. You can also hire the services of a host.

Charter This option is favoured by those in search of maximum comfort and hotel-style service. You charter a boat with crew (one or two hosts and a skipper). They take care of all daily chores, manoeuvres and lead the cruise. The boat, generally a 17-metre catamaran, is a real floating palace. The price includes full board and a programme of excursions ashore.

Cabin Charter This option includes the same services as a standard charter but you only charter one cabin, sharing the boat with other passengers. This suits those who do not have a large enough group to book a whole yacht. The boats generally depart on fixed dates and follow a set itinerary.

But the burning question is: how much does it cost? The prices below, which are merely an indication, were calculated on the basis of information provided by agencies for one week's hire in the high season:

Cabin charter to the Leeward Islands aboard a 17-metre catamaran for eight people costs 15,840 CFP per person, all-inclusive.
   Hire of a 12.60-metre (eight-berth) catamaran costs 529,200 CFP and a deposit of 180,000 CFP is required. Add a flat rate of 14,400 CFP a day for the services of a skipper and 12,600 CFP for those of a host. Allow 2700 CFP a day per person for food and additional expenses. Thus, on the basis of six people hiring the boat, it costs 138,600 CFP per person, excursions not included.

The fact remains that it is difficult to get together six hirers, whereas for the cabin charter departures are generally guaranteed for two or more people. Furthermore, the catamarans available for charter are more luxuriously appointed than the boats offered for hire. Do your sums carefully. ∎

yacht owner will want to vet potential crew members but it's equally important to check the boat and crew you are considering joining. Make sure the boat is safe and the crew are compatible. Readers have suggested that the Marquesas are probably not the ideal place to join a boat. As the first arrival point for yachts from North America it makes little sense for a member of crew to leave his or her boat here – unless there was something seriously wrong with it!

Bareboat Charters

French Polynesia also offers terrific opportunities for bareboat charters, where qualified sailors can rent a fully equipped yacht and set off around the islands. Raiatea, centrally positioned in the Leeward Islands and with a fine lagoon, has become the centre for yacht charters with major operations at

The Moorings & Stardust Marine. See the Raiatea & Tahaa chapter for full details.

Around the Islands

Coast roads trace much of the outlines of each of the major islands of the Society group. Tahiti (where there is even a stretch of freeway), Moorea and Bora Bora have paved and well-maintained highways. On Raiatea and Huahine the coast roads are partly paved, partly formed of ground coral, but generally in good condition. On Tahaa and Maupiti there are only limited stretches of paved or sealed road. On all these islands the roads leading inland into the mountains are often rough-and-ready tracks requiring a 4WD vehicle. Tahiti has an exciting 4WD

BPs & PKs

Most mail in French Polynesia is delivered to post boxes (BP or *boîte postale*) so there is rarely any need for a street address. Since most buildings are found around the narrow coastal strip and most islands have a single coast road running right around the island, locations on high islands are often referred to as 'coast, lagoon or ocean side' or 'mountain side'. In French this would be *côté mer* or *côté montagne*. This doesn't mean a mountainside house is halfway up a mountain, it simply means that it's on the inland side of the road.

On many islands there is also a *pointe kilométrique* or PK system of distance markers around the coast road. These usually start in the main town and run around the island in both directions. On Moorea, for example, the PK markers start at the airport and run anticlockwise to PK 35 and clockwise to PK 24, meeting at Haapiti, the major village on the west side of the island. On other islands locations may be referred to on a PK basis even though there are no PK-marker stones.

Finally, locations may also be referred to by their district name rather than a village name. A hotel in the popular tourist enclave of Hauru Point on Moorea, for example, may fall in the Haapiti district. So a location may be referred to as PK 30, coast side, Haapiti, even though it's some distance from the village of Haapiti. ■

track traversing the rugged centre of the island between the north and south coasts.

On the Austral Islands a sealed road encircles Tubuai and there are reasonable stretches of sealed road on Rurutu. Otherwise, roads on the Australs are fairly limited and little transport is available. There are far more boats than wheeled transport on the Tuamotus, although there is a ground-coral road running the length of the major island in Rangiroa.

Except in towns, there are no sealed roads on the Marquesas. Tracks, suitable for 4WD vehicles only, connect the villages.

LE TRUCK

Le truck is the public bus service of French Polynesia. Le truck is just what the name indicates: a truck. Down each side of the back is a bench seat for the passengers.

Riding le truck is something every visitor in French Polynesia should do. You'll enjoy natural air-conditioning (the breeze blows straight through) and convivial fellow passengers. Unfortunately, only Tahiti has a reasonably comprehensive and regular le truck service. See the Tahiti chapter for more details on using le trucks on that island. Note that you pay at the end of the trip and for many routes there is a set fare, irrespective of distance.

On some other islands there is a more limited service. Moorea has a fairly regular le truck route around the island plus services for ferry arrivals and departures. Bora Bora also has le trucks connecting the major hotel enclave and boat and flight arrivals and departures. On other Society Islands the services are sparse, Raiatea and Huahine will have just a couple of services a day between outlying villages and the main town. Tahaa and Maupiti have no regular le truck service although there are le trucks on both islands, usually for school transport.

There is virtually no public transport in the Austral Islands. Apart from the road running the length of the main island on Rangiroa, there isn't even much road in the Tuamotus.

On the Marquesas, the only le trucks in Taiohae (Nuku Hiva) and Atuona (Hiva Oa) are reserved for school transport.

TAXI

Tahiti has metered taxis, while Moorea, Huahine, Raiatea and Bora Bora also have taxi services. Unfortunately, all these taxis have one thing in common: they are very expensive. The US$20 to US$30 taxi fare for the six-km trip between Faaa Airport and downtown Papeete is a pretty clear indicator of the problem. In many cases it is cheaper to rent a car for a day than it is to take a taxi. Hotels from cheap backpacker hostels through to expensive luxury resorts will generally collect prebooked guests from the airport or ferry quay, and this is a service well worth taking advantage of.

On other islands taxis do not exist as such, but if there's a car and a customer arrangements can usually be made.

There are no taxis on the Marquesas. You have to hire a 4WD vehicle with the services of a driver to get around.

CAR

If you want to explore the larger islands of the Society group on your own, it's generally worth renting a car. Taxi fares are exorbitant and, apart from locations that are reasonably close to Papeete, public transport is too infrequent or inconvenient. A small car, which is all you need for the short distances involved, typically costs US$60 to US$80 per day, including insurance and unlimited km. Fuel costs extra and at about US$5 a gallon it is decidedly pricey. Fortunately, the small cars available are pretty economical and you won't cover too many km no matter how hard you try.

On Tahiti you will find the major international car-rental names like Avis, Budget and Hertz, but they're only second-string operators in French Polynesia, where the big names are Europcar or Pacificar. You'll find one or both of them on Tahiti, Moorea, Huahine, Raiatea and Bora Bora. Tahiti has a number of other smaller operators, and the odd small company can also be found on Bora Bora and Moorea.

There are a handful of rental cars to be found on Tahaa in the Societies and in the Austral Islands on Tubuai. Otherwise there are no regular rental cars available in the Australs or Tuamotus.

On the Marquesas, rental vehicles are mainly 4WD with a driver. Rental without a driver is possible only at Atuona (Hiva Oa) and Taiohae (Nuku Hiva).

Driving standards are not too bad in French Polynesia and traffic is light almost everywhere apart from the busy coastal strip around Papeete in Tahiti. Beware of drunk drivers at night and pedestrians and children who may not be used to traffic, particularly in more remote locations.

SCOOTERS

Pacificar and Europcar, the two major car-rental organisations, also rent scooters on a number of islands.

BICYCLES

French Polynesia is an ideal region to explore by bicycle. Apart from on Tahiti, traffic is rarely a problem and on most islands the distances are relatively short. You can ride a complete circuit of many of the islands in a morning or afternoon. Bicycles can be rented on many of the islands – Moorea, Huahine, Raiatea and Bora Bora in the Society group all have bicycle-rental facilities, with rental costs typically around 1000 to 1500 CFP per day. Unfortunately, the bicycles are generally not ideal for local riding conditions – they vary from single-speed French-village bicycles through to American-style cruisers (ideal for weighty Polynesians) or often badly maintained cheap mountain bikes.

The more remote islands, or the more remote parts of even the major islands, cry out for a good mountain bike. Off the beaten track you may encounter bumpy, pot-holed coastal roads or challenging tracks if you head inland. Furthermore, on the more remote islands bicycles may not even be available. So if you're planning a longer-term visit, or if French Polynesia is part of a more extensive Pacific itinerary, bringing your own mountain bike can be a smart idea. International airlines are generally quite efficient at transporting bicycles so bringing your bike to the region should be simple. Within French Polynesia it probably will not be possible to take your bike on Air Tahiti flights because of the strict baggage-weight limits, but bikes can be taken on all the inter-island ships including the high-speed-catamaran services between Tahiti and Moorea and on the *Ono-Ono* to other islands in the Society group.

HITCHING

Hitching is never entirely safe in any country in the world, and we don't recommend it. Travellers who decide to hitch should understand that they are taking a small but potentially serious risk. However, many people do choose to hitch, and the advice that follows should help to make their journeys as fast and safe as possible.

On the less touristed islands and islands where public transport is limited, hitching is a widely accepted way of getting around. In fact, you may not even need to put your thumb out – just walking along an island road you may well find the occasional car or truck pulling up to offer a ride. On tourist-saturated Tahiti, Moorea and Bora Bora the situation may not be quite so straightforward, although in more remote locations it may still be worth trying. French Polynesia is generally a safe location but the usual worldwide rules for hitchhiking still apply.

LOCAL BOATS
In several places it's possible to rent small outboard-powered boats, but anywhere in French Polynesia if you need to get from somewhere to somewhere else across the lagoon there will be somebody available with the appropriate boat. Just ask.

TOURS ON LAND & SEA
Many of the more touristed islands have regularly scheduled tours. There are straight-forward round-the-island minibus tours on Tahiti, Moorea and other islands, or increasingly popular 4WD trips across the centre of Tahiti and into the highlands of Moorea, Bora Bora and other islands in the Society group. Mountain-bike and hiking trips are also growing in popularity. Boat trips can range from simple sunset cruises to longer round-the-lagoon expeditions with motu picnics or a spot of shark feeding thrown in. See the island chapters for full details.

The Society Islands

The Society Islands

The Society Islands are the main group of islands of French Polynesia. They include the largest islands and are home to the vast majority of the population. Most of the group are 'high islands', as opposed to the low-lying coral atolls of the Tuamotus.

The Society Islands are subdivided into two groups, the eastward Windward Islands (or Îles du Vent) and the westward Leeward Islands (or Îles sous le Vent). The Windward group comprises two major islands: Tahiti and its close neighbour, Moorea. Tahiti is the largest and best known island in French Polynesia, site of the capital, Papeete, and of the only international airport. Moorea is smaller and quieter but it is also visually spectacular and very popular with visitors. Apart from Tahiti and Moorea, The Windward group includes three smaller islands, one of which is unpopulated.

The Leeward group includes five very varied high islands. From east to west the first island is Huahine, popular for its relaxed atmosphere and with the most extensive pre-European *marae* (temple) site in French Polynesia. Next are the twin islands of Raiatea and Tahaa, sharing a common lagoon. Raiatea is the 'sacred island' of Polynesia, a site of legends and with the most important ancient marae on the islands. Further west again is Bora Bora, one of the most beautiful islands on earth and with a steady flow of visitors keen to pay homage to that beauty! Finally, there's remote Maupiti, also beautiful but smaller and far less developed for tourism. The Leeward group also includes four smaller islands, all of them atolls and three of them far to the west.

The Society name was dreamed up by Captain Cook in 1769. Almost every early European visitor took the opportunity to rename Tahiti and any other island they chanced upon. Wallis, the first European visitor to Tahiti in 1767, renamed it King George's Land and Moorea the Duke of York's Island. Fortunately, neither of those names stuck. Cook originally attached the Society tag solely to the Leeward group because they were close to each other, in 'close society'. The name was later applied to the Windward group as well.

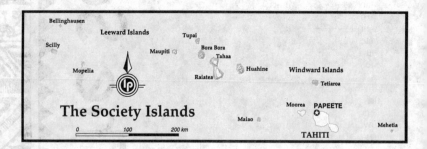

98

Tahiti

Population: 130,000
Land Area: 1045 sq km
Passes: 33
Highest Point: 2241 metres

Tahiti and French Polynesia are used almost synonymously. It's common to speak of Tahiti as if it were the whole colony, when in fact it is merely the largest island and site of the capital, Papeete. Tahiti also has the only international airport in French Polynesia and is therefore the arrival and departure point for the overwhelming majority of visitors to French Polynesia.

Despite the alluring name and the even more alluring image, for most visitors Tahiti is not the high point of a visit to French Polynesia. The beautiful beaches on postcards are on *motus* on other islands, the glamorous over-water bungalows on brochures are at hotels on Bora Bora, the underwater glimpses of sharks cruising past colourful reefs are in the Tuamotus. Even the paintings by Gauguin are probably of the Marquesas, not Tahiti.

Spending too long in Tahiti can be a big mistake and most visitors soon head to the other islands. Nevertheless, Tahiti does have plenty to offer and it's an equally big mistake to ignore it.

Papeete, despite its negative image, can be a vibrant and interesting town, particularly along the waterfront at night. There are good beaches around the island and some fine scuba-diving opportunities. There is history with the remains of ancient *maraes* and reminders that it was here where Cook and Bougainville first anchored and from here that they carried back the first enticing reports of Polynesia's exotic wonders. Least known and appreciated by visitors is Tahiti's virtually untouched interior: rugged, mountainous, barely populated and offering exciting walking, climbing and 4WD expeditions.

HISTORY

Like other islands in the Society group, Tahiti is the creation of volcanic eruptions. The larger circle of Tahiti Nui probably came into existence around 2½ to three million years ago, while smaller Tahiti Iti was created less than two million, perhaps less than a million years ago.

Tahiti was not the first island of the Society group to be populated in the great Polynesian migrations. Legends relate that the first settlers came from Raiatea to Tahiti and even their landing place, on the southeast coast of Tahiti Nui, is painstakingly pinpointed. Despite its size Tahiti was not the most important of the Society Islands – that honour generally went to 'sacred' Raiatea. At the time of its European discovery Tahiti was not even the most powerful of the islands, although European arms would soon upset the delicate balance between the many kingdoms.

Tahiti's rise to central importance started in 1767 when Samuel Wallis made the European 'discovery' of the island. He was soon followed by Bougainville and Cook, who made Tahiti the favoured base for European visitors. It was this European presence that led to Tahiti's rise to power. Prior to European arrival no kingdom exercised more than local power; it was a considerable feat even to control a whole island. European arms, and for a time European mercenaries, soon changed that equation and the Pomare dynasty eventually controlled not only all Tahiti but also various other islands of the Society and Austral islands. It was a fleeting moment for soon Tahiti became a minor pawn in the European colonial quest, and it was only a generation from Tahiti's takeover by Pomare II in 1815 to its annexation by France in 1842.

Wallis followed the time-honoured tradition of claiming possession of Tahiti for Britain and renaming it King George's Land. Within a few years the island was also

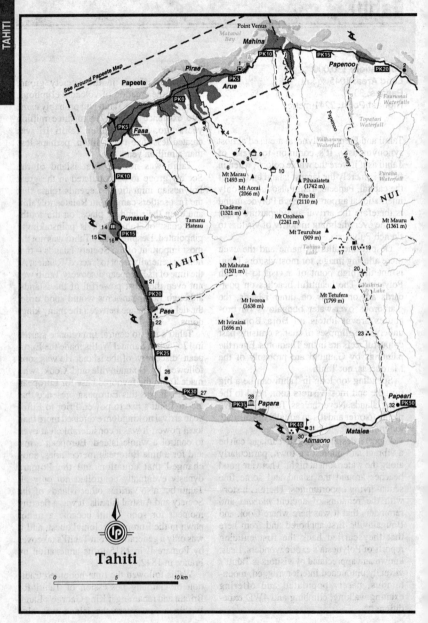

Tahiti

0   5   10 km

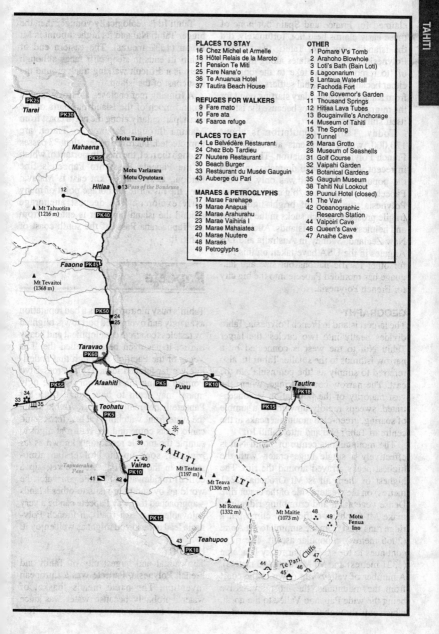

PLACES TO STAY
16 Chez Michel et Armelle
18 Hôtel Relais de la Maroto
21 Pension Te Miti
25 Fare Nana'o
36 Te Anuanua Hotel
37 Tautira Beach House

REFUGES FOR WALKERS
9 Fare mato
10 Fare ata
45 Faaroa refuge

PLACES TO EAT
4 Le Belvédère Restaurant
24 Chez Bob Tardieu
27 Nuutere Restaurant
30 Beach Burger
33 Restaurant du Musée Gauguin
43 Auberge du Pari

MARAES & PETROGLYPHS
17 Marae Farehape
19 Marae Anapua
22 Marae Arahurahu
23 Marae Vaihiria I
29 Marae Mahaiatea
40 Marae Nuutere
48 Maraes
49 Petroglyphs

OTHER
1 Pomare V's Tomb
2 Arahoho Blowhole
3 Loti's Bath (Bain Loti)
5 Lagoonarium
6 Lantaua Waterfall
7 Fachoda Fort
8 The Governor's Garden
11 Thousand Springs
12 Hitiaa Lava Tubes
13 Bougainville's Anchorage
14 Museum of Tahiti
15 The Spring
20 Tunnel
26 Maraa Grotto
28 Museum of Seashells
31 Golf Course
32 Vaipahi Garden
34 Botanical Gardens
35 Gauguin Museum
38 Tahiti Nui Lookout
39 Puunui Hotel (closed)
41 The Vavi
42 Oceanographic
Research Station
44 Vaipoiri Cave
46 Queen's Cave
47 Anaihe Cave

Tiarei
PK25
PK30
Mahaena
Motu Taaupiri
PK35
Motu Variararu
Motu Oputotara
Hitiaa
13 *Pass of the Boudeuse*
12
▲ Mt Tahuotira
(1216 m)
PK40
Faaone PK45
▲
Mt Tevaitoi
(1368 m)
PK50
24
25
Taravao
PK60
PK55
Afaahiti
34
33 35
Teohatu
PK5
Pueu
PK5
36 PK10
Tautira
37 PK18
PK15
38
39
T A H I T I
40
Vairao
PK10
Tapuaeraha Pass
41
42
Mt Teatara
(1197 m)
Mt Teava
(1306 m)
I T I
Mt Ronui
(1332 m)
Mt Maitie
(1073 m)
48
49
Motu Fenua Ino
PK15
43
Teahupoo
PK18
44
45
46 47
Te Pari Cliffs
Aiurua River
Tiraho River
Vaitepiha River
Vaiote River

TAHITI

claimed for France and Spain but none of those early claims held nor, fortunately, did the island's new title. Tahiti, the original Polynesian name, translates along the lines of 'to remove' or 'to take to the border', either because the original settlers came here from Raiatea, the legendary starting point for the migration to Tahiti, or because the island itself shifted here.

Today, Tahiti's population is about 120,000, which represents about 70% of French Polynesia's population. The growth in recent years has been dramatic: in 1956 the population of Tahiti was only 37,000. Papeete has become the 'big city' of French Polynesia, the place of bright lights and fragile prospects which sucks in the hopeful and helpless from other islands. Auckland in New Zealand, Sydney in Australia and Los Angeles in the USA have taken on this role for other Pacific nations but size and language has moulded Papeete into the big city for French Polynesia.

GEOGRAPHY

The largest island in French Polynesia, Tahiti divides neatly into two circles: the larger Tahiti Nui to the west is connected by a narrow isthmus to the smaller Tahiti Iti, also referred to simply as 'the peninsula', to the east. The narrow coastal fringe, where the vast majority of the population is concentrated, sweeps rapidly upwards to a jumble of soaring, green-clad mountain peaks in the centre of Tahiti Nui and into Tahiti Iti.

The mountainous centre of Tahiti Nui is effectively a single huge crater, with the highest peaks arrayed around the rim. The highest of them all is Mt Orohena (2241 metres) on the western side of the crater rim. Dense vegetation and crumbling ridgelines make Mt Orohena difficult to climb but a ridge runs west from the summit to Mt Aorai (2066 metres), a popular ascent. The ridge continues to the spectacular rocky Diadème (1321 metres) and Mt Marau (1493 metres). A number of valleys run down to the coast from the mountains, the most impressive being the wide Papenoo Valley to the north, which cuts through the ancient crater rim.

Tahiti Iti is geologically younger than the bigger Tahiti Nui and its highest point is Mt Ronui (1332 metres). The eastern end of Tahiti Iti ends in steep cliff faces although there is a difficult walking track around the east coast of the island.

A fringing reef encloses a narrow lagoon around much of the island but parts of the coast, particularly along the north coast from Mahina through Papenoo to Tiarei, are unprotected. There are no less than 33 passes through the reef, the most important of which is the Papeete Pass into Papeete's fine harbour. Less than 10 km east is Matavai Bay, the favourite anchorage point of many early explorers. The deepest anchorage around the island however is entered from the Tapuaeraha Pass off the south coast of Tahiti Iti.

Papeete

Tahiti's busy metropolis has a bad reputation as an ugly and overpriced port town, blighted by tasteless concrete development and heavy traffic. It has even been labelled the 'Las Vegas of the Pacific', although that is definitely a far-fetched idea. Try to cross Blvd Pomare during the rush hour and the ugly image may seem to have some truth but Papeete is not really that bad. Amble along the waterfront watching yachts, ferries and cargo boats come and go, return at night to sample the mobile restaurants known as *les roulottes*, soak up the Polynesian atmosphere in the busy Papeete Market, sip a coffee in a sidewalk café while you watch the world go by and plan visits to other islands – approached that way Papeete can be a very enjoyable town. All roads in French Polynesia lead here so you might as well enjoy it.

HISTORY

The capital and largest city of Tahiti and French Polynesia, Papeete was a European invention. The name means 'basket of water', probably because water was once collected from the springs between the Territorial Assembly Building and the High Commissioner's Residence, in what were once the grounds of the Pomare palace.

In 1769, when Cook anchored 10 km west in Matavai Bay, there was no settlement in Papeete. Towards the end of the century European visitors realised the value of its sheltered bay and easy access through the reef. The first LMS (London Missionary Society) missionaries arrived at Papeete in 1824 and the young Queen Pomare became a regular visitor to the growing town. An earlier unsuccessful LMS group were in Tahiti for a few years from 1797.

Visiting whaling ships made Papeete an increasingly important port and Governor Bruat selected the town as the administrative headquarters for the new French protectorate in 1843. By 1860 the town had already taken its present form with a straggling European settlement between the waterfront and the street, then known as 'the Broom' and now as Rue du Commandant Destremau, Rue du Général de Gaulle and Rue du Maréchal Foch. Already development was extending back from the narrow coastal strip into the Sainte Amélie Valley and the district known as the Mission.

Chinese merchants and shopkeepers started to trickle in to Papeete, but at the beginning of the 20th century the population was still less than 5000.

A disastrous cyclone in 1906 and a German naval bombardment in 1914, which destroyed the central market, took their toll, but during WWII the population reached 10,000 and by the early 1960s it was past 20,000.

The curious combination of tourism and nuclear testing, together with the Pacific-wide movement from remote islands to larger centres, led to a population explosion from the early 1960s. Today Papeete has a population of about 100,000 and sprawls 30 km along the coast from Punaauia, past the airport in the west, to Mahina, at Point Venus in the east. Unfortunately, this rapid expansion has certainly had its costs and the almost total destruction of the charming old colonial heart of Papeete is one of them.

ORIENTATION

Papeete curves around an almost enclosed bay on the north coast of Tahiti. The downtown district is a compact area, easily covered on foot. Blvd Pomare follows the waterfront, and most of the central businesses, banks, hotels and restaurants are concentrated along this busy street or in the few blocks back from the water's edge.

Residential suburbs sprawl along the coast in both directions from Papeete and inland, where the altitude increases rapidly. The westward sprawl of Papeete extends beyond the airport in the suburb of Faaa (yes it is three consecutive vowels although it is also spelt Fa'aa). The coast road westwards is complemented by the RDO (Route de Dégagement Ouest), French Polynesia's *autoroute* (freeway) which runs slightly inland, starting on the western edge of central Papeete and extending to just beyond Faaa airport before rejoining the coastal road.

On the other side of Papeete two roads, Ave du Prince Hinoi and Ave Georges Clémenceau, run east through the suburb of Pirae before joining at Arue. The CEP, Centre d'expérimentation du Pacifique, is based on this side of Papeete – an innocent acronym disguising the centre's business of nuclear weapons testing.

INFORMATION

Papeete is a 9 to 5 business city and a busy dining and entertainment spot in the evening but on Sunday it's dead. Once the church services are over the town dies. It's even hard to find a restaurant open on Sunday. Go somewhere else.

Tourist Office

The Tahiti Tourist Board, or GIE, has its tourist office (☎ 50-57-00) in Fare Manihini on the waterfront side of Blvd Pomare, right across from Rue Paul Gauguin in the centre of Papeete. The office has a large collection of information sheets detailing cheaper accommodation, island by island, and also distributes brochures and leaflets from a host

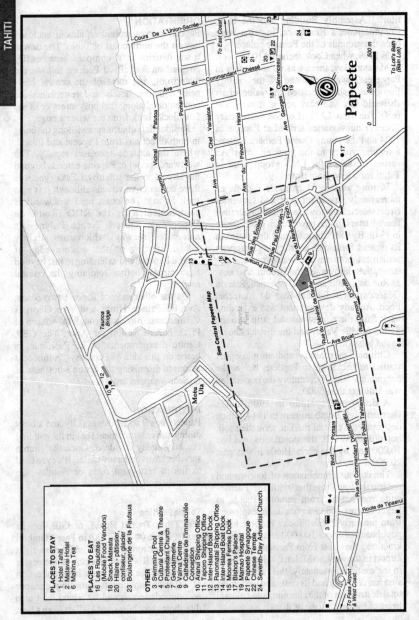

PLACES TO STAY

1 Hotel Tahiti
2 Matavai Hotel
6 Mahina Tea

PLACES TO EAT

16 Les Roulottes
    (Mobile Food Vendors)
18 Snack Mateata
20 Hilaire - pâtissier,
    confiseur, glacier
23 Boulangerie de la Fautaua

OTHER

3 Swimming Pool
4 Cultural Centre & Theatre
5 Protestant Church
7 Gendarmerie
8 Vaima Centre
9 Cathédrale de l'Immaculée
    Conception
10 Aranui Shipping Office
11 Taporo Shipping Office
12 Inter-Island Boat Dock
13 Raromatai Shipping Office
14 Inter-Island Boat Dock
15 Moorea Ferries Dock
17 Bishop's Palace
19 Mamao Hospital
21 Papeete Synagogue
22 Chinese Temple
24 Seventh-Day Adventist Church

of tourist operators. The staff are usually friendly and well informed.

A floating office called Mers et Loisirs (which translates as sea and leisure activities; ☎ 43-97-99) is slightly west of the main office, across Blvd Pomare from the post office. It handles tours, excursions and all sorts of boat trips but not the inter-island ferries. There is an information desk at the airport but it's often unstaffed.

Money

The four major banks represented in French Polynesia – Banque Socredo, Banque de Tahiti, Banque de Polynésie and Westpac – are all found in Papeete. See the Getting Around section in this chapter for information on airport branches and the Money section of the Facts for the Visitor chapter for general information on banks and changing money. ATMs which accept Visa and MasterCards for cash advances are easy to find in Papeete.

Banking hours vary slightly from branch to branch but they're typically around 8 am to noon and 1 to 4 pm. Some branches in Papeete do not close for the traditional Polynesian lunch break and a handful of branches open on Saturday morning. Try the Banque de Tahiti branches at Pirae, Vaima and Faaa or the Banque de Polynésie branches at Ave Bruat in Papeete, at the Continent Shopping Centre just beyond Faaa airport, and at Pirae.

Post & Telecommunications

Papeete's main post office fronts on to the waterfront Blvd Pomare, next to Bougainville Park. For general postal services and postage stamps go upstairs from the Blvd Pomare entrance. Poste restante (general delivery) service is downstairs. The post office, which stretches back the whole block to Rue du Général de Gaulle, also offers phone, fax and telegram services. Opening hours are Monday to Thursday from 7 am to 6 pm; Saturday 8 am to 11 am; Sunday 8 am to 10 am. There are post office branches in Papeete suburbs, at Faaa airport and other centres around the island. Hours are more restricted at other branches but the Faaa

airport office is open in the evening, even on weekends.

Tahiti Tours (☎ 54-02-50) is the American Express agent and will hold clients' mail. Their office is at 15 Rue Jeanne d'Arc, next to the Vaima Centre, and their postal address is BP 627, Papeete, Tahiti.

Foreign Consulates

Many foreign countries are represented in Papeete by honorary consuls rather than fully fledged offices. Amazingly, considering the number of tourists they dispatch to French Polynesia each year, there is no Canadian, Japanese or US diplomatic representation in French Polynesia. If you need a US visa or if you're American and you lose your passport, Suva in Fiji is the place to go! Some of the foreign consulates include:

Australia
  Vaima Centre, Papeete (postal address: BP 1695, Papeete; ☎ 43-88-38, fax 41-05-19)
Austria (also represents Switzerland and Leichtenstein)
  Rue de la Cannonière Zélée, Papeete (postal address: BP 4560, Papeete; ☎ 43-91-14, fax 43-21-22)
Belgium
  Rue Paul Gauguin, Papeete (postal address: BP 1602, Papeete; ☎ 41-70-00 or 53-27-20, fax 42-33-76)
Chile
  Rue du Général de Gaulle, Papeete (postal address: BP 952, Papeete; ☎ 43-89-19, 42-62-40 or 42-90-23, fax 43-48-89)
Denmark
  Te Matai Building, Blvd Pomare, Papeete (postal address: BP 548, Papeete; ☎ 42-04-60 or 54-04-54, fax 41-06-94)
Finland
  Paofai (postal address: BP 2870, Papeete; ☎ 42-97-39, fax 43-42-63)
Germany
  Rue Gadiot, Pirae (postal address: BP 452, Papeete; ☎ 42-99-94 or 42-80-84, fax 42-96-89)
Italy
  c/- Tikichimic, Punaauia, Punaruu Valley (postal address: BP 420, Papeete; ☎ 58-20-29, fax 43-91-70)
New Zealand
  c/- Air New Zealand, Vaima Centre, Papeete (postal address: BP 73, Papeete; ☎ 43-01-70, fax 42-45-44)

Netherlands
   Mobil Building, Fare Ute, Papeete (postal address: BP 2804, Papeete; ☎ 42-49-37 or 43-06-86, fax 43-56-92)
Sweden
   Fare Tony, Blvd Pomare (postal address: BP 2, Papeete; ☎ 43-73-93 or 42-47-60, fax 43-49-03)
UK
   c/- Avis Rent-a-Car, Rue Charles Vienot, Papeete (postal address: BP 1064, Papeete; ☎ 42-84-57 or 42-43-55, fax 41-08-47)

Bookshops & Newsagencies

Archipels (☎ 42-47-30), at 68 Rue des Remparts, is one of the best bookshops in town, with a wide range of books in French, including an excellent section devoted to Tahiti, French Polynesia and the Pacific in general. There are also quite reasonable English-language sections, particularly on travel and French Polynesia.

In the Vaima Centre the Vaima Librairie (☎ 45-57-44) has a good travel section and a separate shop devoted purely to French Polynesia and the Pacific. This separate section may, however, be a temporary feature. Le Kiosque in the Vaima Centre is the best newspaper and magazine stand in town.

Polygraph (☎ 42-80-47) on Ave Bruat

PLACES TO STAY
11 Shogun Hotel
25 Tiare Tahiti Hotel
44 Tahiti Budget Lodge
45 Teamo Pension
65 Hotel Le Mandarin
72 Hotel Prince Hinoi
80 Royal Papeete
84 Kon Tiki Pacific

PLACES TO EAT
1 Snack Paofai
4 La Corbeille d'Eau
7 L'Api'zzeria
8 El Bryanos Tex-Mex Restaurant
10 Moana Iti
13 New Port
16 Le Manava Restaurant
29 Blue Pacifique Café
31 Vaima Centre Restaurants - Le Rétro, L'Oasis, Le Motu, Morrison's Café, La Malaussane, Les Alizés
35 L'O à la Bouche
36 La Squadra
37 Lou Pescadou
39 Chez Roger
41 Snack Malibu

46 Snack Aloha
47 Pitate Mamao
50 Restaurant Tehoa
51 Restaurant Cathay
57 Acajou Café
58 Polyself Cafeteria
60 Waikiki Restaurant
61 Le Dragon d'Or
66 Le Mandarin Restaurant
71 Les Roulottes
76 Restaurant Saïgonnaise

BARS & CLUBS
9 Le Club 106
14 Le Mayana
27 Café de la Gare
32 Vaima Centre Bars & Clubs - Le Rétro, La Malaussane, Le Rolls Club
43 Galaxy Nightclub
67 Piano Bar
68 Lido Club
69 Le Club 5
73 Café des Sports
74 Royal Kikiriri
78 L'Auberge
79 Bar Taina
81 La Cave

83 Le Paradise
85 Le Calypso

LE TRUCK STOPS, TAXI STANDS & FERRY QUAYS
34 Taxi Stand
52 West Coast Le Truck Stop
53 Taxi Stand
55 North Coast Le Truck Stop
62 East Coast Le Truck Stop
77 East Coast & Tahiti Iti Le Truck Stop
82 Moorea Ferry Terminus

OTHER
2 Hospital - Clinique Paofai
3 Intermarket Supermarket
5 Paofai Protestant Church
6 Pearl Museum
12 Government Offices
15 Polygraph Bookstore
17 Air France
18 Government Offices
19 High Commissioner's Office
20 War Memorial
21 High Commissioner's Residence
22 Post Office
23 Pouvanaa a Oopa Memorial

24 Territorial Assembly
26 Fare Tony Centre - Air Tahiti Office
28 Mers et Loisirs (Tour Booking Office)
30 Reva Art Gallery
33 Vaima Centre Shops & Offices - Le Kiosque Newstand, Vaima Librairie Bookshop, Air New Zealand, Lan Chile & Qantas Offices, Club Med Office
38 Cathédrale de l'Immaculée Conception
40 Manuia Curios
42 Hospital - Clinique Cardella
48 Pacificar Rent-a-Car
49 Lavomatic Laundrette
54 Papeete Market - Marché du Papeete
56 Tahiti Tourist Board
59 Matamua Art Gallery
63 Mairie (Town Hall)
64 Archipels Bookshop
70 Customs, Police de l'Air et des Frontieres & Capitainerie
75 Europcar Rent-a-Car

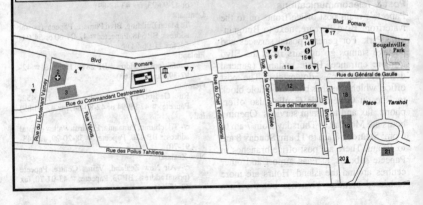

doesn't have such a wide range of books, although their Polynesia section may turn up something you won't find elsewhere, but it does have the best selection of large-scale maps and nautical charts you'll find in Tahiti. There's also a large stationery and magazines section.

Medical Services

For the hospital or a doctor in an emergency phone ☎ 15. You can call SOS Médecins on ☎ 42-34-56. For emergency treatment, the Clinique Cardella (☎ 42-81-90) on Rue

Anne-Marie Javouhey, behind the cathedral, is open 24 hours a day. Clinique Paofai (☎ 43-02-02) is on Blvd Pomare and Rue du Lieutenant Varney. As usual your hotel desk can recommend a doctor or other medical assistance. There are a number of pharmacies open on Sunday morning as well as all week.

Other Services

There are lots of photo-developing centres around Papeete but the costs are fairly astronomical. See the Film & Photography

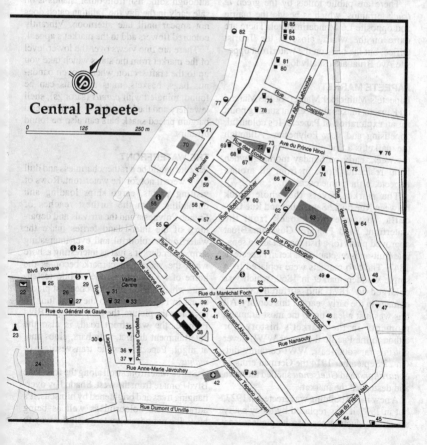

Central Papeete

0   125   250 m

section in the Facts for the Visitor chapter for more information. And then take your undeveloped films home with you!

Getting clothes washed in French Polynesia can be ridiculously expensive. Some of the deluxe hotels (the Beachcomber Parkroyal Hotel for example) have laundry facilities for their guests. The Tahiti Budget Lodge has a washer and drier but at the same sky-high prices as the handful of laundrettes. In Papeete, at the Lavomatic on Rue Paul Gauguin, right across from the *mairie* (town hall), a load of washing costs 550 CFP, drying is 750 CFP.

There are public toilets by the green *le truck* terminus, which is beside the mairie and opposite Le Mandarin Hotel. There are more on the wharf, close to the Tourist Office, but the ones on the waterfront opposite Ave Bruat are usually locked.

PAPEETE MARKET

Papeete's Municipal Market, or the Marché du Papeete, makes an excellent starting point for an exploration of Papeete. It's colourful, appetising and very Polynesian. Although the market is a fine place to visit any day of the week, early on Sunday morning, when local residents flock in from all around Papeete, is the prime occasion.

The market covers the whole block between Rue du 22 Septembre and Rue Cardella, just one block back from the waterfront Blvd Pomare. Governor Bruat approved plans for a fish market and a separate fruit-and-vegetable market in Papeete in 1847. The two markets were replaced by a single wooden market in 1860, which was enlarged in 1871 and suffered cyclone damage in the early years of this century. All this was just a lead up to the most dramatic moments in the market's history, for although the Pacific theatre of WWII never got this far south-east, WWI certainly did. On 22 September 1914 the German cruisers *Scharnhorst* and *Gneisenau* shelled the town and destroyed the market.

A new metal building was erected in 1927, but in 1987 it was replaced by today's airy structure. Much larger than its predecessor, the market covers two floors with fruit, vegetables, meat and fish downstairs, while clothes, materials and tourist crafts can be found upstairs. It's a wonderful place to wander through and see traditional Polynesian produce including taro, breadfruit, coconuts, pineapples from Moorea, watermelons from Maupiti, papayas and rambutans. Chinese market gardens produce carrots, beans, cabbages and other vegetables, which are also shipped in from the cooler climate of the Austral Islands. The seafood section will have lobster, *mahi mahi*, tuna and a variety of smaller fish, but although some fish from other islands is on sale early in the day the Tahitian catch does not appear until late afternoon. Vibrantly coloured flowers add to the market's appeal.

There are fine views over the lower level of the market from the stairs which take you up to the craft section where woven pandanus bags, baskets, mats and hats can be found, mingled with *pareus* (sarongs), shell jewellery and the inevitable T-shirts. Several bargain priced snack bars can also be found upstairs.

THE WATERFRONT

Papeete would be a rather charmless and dull town were it not for the waterfront. Rows of visiting yachts, cargo ships loading and unloading from the furthest reaches of French Polynesia and the arrivals and departures of the inter-island ferries make the waterfront a colourful and ever-interesting strip. After dark it's just as interesting ashore when the waterfront carpark becomes the home of *les roulottes*, the mobile restaurants which are not only the cheapest places to eat in Papeete but also the most fun. To complete the picture, the eastern end of Blvd Pomare, the waterfront road, is also the entertainment district, with bars, clubs and, at night, Papeete's exotic transvestites, or *mahus*.

Start a waterfront stroll along the four-lane Blvd Pomare from the west. Shaded by overhanging trees and brightened by hibiscus, it's attractive and colourful as well as being busy. It's not necessary to go all the way to the end of Blvd Pomare – the imposing Protestant church makes a good starting point. This is also Papeete's starting place, as the first Protestant church, built on this site in 1818, effectively signalled the birth of the town. On the opposite corner of Rue du Temple and Blvd Pomare, a giant black pearl announces the presence of the Pearl Museum, a combination black pearl shop and museum explaining the production process of this Polynesian speciality. It's open Monday to Friday from 8 am to noon and 2 to 5.30 pm; Saturday 9 am to noon; and Sunday 2 to 5.30 pm.

Across the road from the church is a memorial to the great double-canoe *Hokule'a*, which emulated the feats of the legendary Polynesian navigators by sailing from Hawaii to Tahiti in 1967. As you walk east there are racing pirogues, the outrigger canoes which Tahitians paddle with a vengeance, stacked up under trees on the quayside. Seeing a fleet of these speedy craft surging through the water is an experience never to be forgotten. Local teams can be seen practising some afternoons and every Saturday morning. Past Ave Bruat, cruising yachts from both sides of the Pacific as well as local boats give Papeete an international flavour. On the inland side of the road is Bougainville Park and the adjacent post office. The featureless modern post office has replaced the earlier colonial-style wooden post office – another of the retrograde architectural replacements of recent years.

Next up on the island side is the glossy Vaima Centre, with shops, restaurants and airline offices. On the harbour side Fare Manihini is the home of the Tahiti Tourist Board, perched on the Quai d'Honneur. There's usually something interesting tied up at this quay whether it's a visiting cruise ship, the two tall ships which work Tahitian waters, the *Wind Song* and *Club Med II*, or something more unusual like a visiting US oceanographic research ship or a French navy vessel on a duty call.

Late in the afternoon local fishing boats land the day's catch at the quay and at night les roulottes line up in the carpark from here to the Moorea Ferry Terminal. This is the busy shipping centre of the port with powerful high-speed catamarans and more sedate car ferries regularly arriving from and departing for Moorea. On the inland side of Blvd Pomare the sometimes seedy but always noisy and energetic entertainment district starts just south of Ave du Prince Hinoi and extends north past Ave du Chef Vairaatoa.

Tourism and entertainment fades out further along the waterfront as the road continues through the naval yard and Fare Ute. This is the sweaty working part of the harbour where the copra boats unload their cargoes from the islands and the sweetish smell of coconuts hangs in the air. Pallets of everything from building materials to crates of Hinano beer, drums of fuel to shiny new Taiwanese bicycles are loaded on the ships to transport to the outer islands. The road continues across the bridge to Motu Uta, enlarged and extended over the years to become the dry dock and container shipping centre for French Polynesia. It bears little resemblance to the pretty little motu which once stood here. These days the port of Papeete handles over half a million tonnes of overseas freight each year and another quarter million tonnes of inter-island freight.

CHURCHES & TEMPLES
Cathédrale de l'Immaculée Conception
Also known as the Cathedral of Notre Dame and dominating the centre of town, the cathedral's story started in 1856 with plans for it to be built of stone imported from Australia and with a doorway carved out of granite from Mangareva in the Gambier Archipelago. It was a controversial project at the time, deemed far too grand for a tiny port like Papeete, but construction got underway using stonemasons from Mangareva, trained by that island's Catholic missionaries. They had, no doubt, learned their trade building Mangareva's huge St Michael's Cathedral. Money ran out just a year later and the original edifice was demolished in 1867 and a new, smaller cathedral was commenced in

1869 and completed in 1875. It has been restored in two phases, in 1967 and 1987.

From the cathedral Ave Monseigneur Tepano Jaussen leads into the Mission district, originally known as Tepapa Valley and still the site of Catholic colleges and Protestant schools. Jaussen was the Catholic bishop of Tahiti from 1848 who acquired the mission lands in 1855 and turned them into a local botanical garden. He is buried in the mission's cemetery, beside Father Honoré Laval, the controversial apostle of the Gambier Archipelago. The road from the cathedral crosses the Papeava River on a small stone bridge and leads into the gardens of the fine bishop's palace (1875). The gardens also contain a pretty little Gothic-style chapel.

Paofai Church

Although the Catholic cathedral stands squarely in the town centre, Tahiti remains predominantly Protestant, an enduring reminder of the lasting effects of the pioneer LMS missionaries. The bayside Paofai Church on Blvd Pomare is the most important Protestant church and makes a colourful scene at Sunday services with a congregation arriving and departing beneath a flotilla of wide-brimmed white hats and belting out rousing *himenes* (hymns) in the interim. The church was built on the site of Papeete's first Protestant church, which was erected here in wood in 1818, replaced with a stone church in 1824 and then by a predecessor of the current church in 1907.

Other Churches & Temples

Papeete's principal Chinese temple, the 1987 Kanti de Mamao, is on Ave Georges Clémenceau and Ave du Commandant Chessé. It replaced a century-old Chinese temple. There's a Jewish synagogue just off Ave du Prince Hinoi and an imposing Seventh-Day Adventist church just south of Ave Georges Clémenceau, on the Route du Fautaua, the road leading to Loti's Pool.

BOUGAINVILLE PARK

Next to the post office Bougainville Park stretches from Blvd Pomare to Rue du Général de Gaulle and is fronted, on the waterfront side, by a 1909 bust of the great French navigator. Two naval guns flank the plinth. On the east side is a cannon salvaged from Count Felix von Luckner's WWI raider the *Seeadler* (Sea Eagle), which was wrecked on Mopelia in 1917 (see the Other Leeward Islands chapter for more details). On the west side is a gun from the French vessel *La Zélée*, sunk at the harbour mouth during the German raid in September 1914.

TERRITORIAL ASSEMBLY

Named Place Tarahoi after Marae Tarahoi, the royal marae of the Pomare family, the Territorial Assembly and other government buildings occupy the former site of the Pomare palace. The termite-riddled 1883 palace was razed in 1960, but you can get an idea of what it looked like from the modern mairie, which is built in a similar style. On Rue du Général de Gaulle the assembly building is fronted by a statue of Pouvanaa a Oopa, a Tahitian patriot and WWI volunteer. Elected deputy of the Tahitian assembly three times in the 1940s and '50s, his espousement of Tahitian nationalism earned him a prison sentence after riots shook Papeete in 1958. He remains a potent symbol of Tahitian aspirations.

The High Commissioner's Residence stands to one side of the assembly building and, like the assembly building, it also replaces an earlier construction. Termites were also the reason for demolishing the 1843 Palace of the Governor. The earlier building arrived in Tahiti in pieces and was intended to be assembled in Nuku-Hiva in the Marquesas but was sidetracked to become the governor's residence! Behind and between the two buildings is the freshwater spring whose gushing waters gave Papeete its name. The pool is still known as the 'queen's bathing place', as the young Queen Pomare used to visit the spring. The gardens of Place Tarahoi are a centre for activities during the colourful Heiva Festival in July each year.

THE MAIRIE

Papeete's mairie, or Hôtel de Ville or town hall, is two blocks back from the waterfront Blvd Pomare and a block north of Papeete Market. It was completed in 1990, in vague imitation of the old Queen's Palace which was replaced by the modern Territorial Assembly building. The mairie's predecessor was a wooden colonial-style building of the 1880s, demolished in 1988 to make way for the new building.

LOTI'S BATH

From east of the centre, the Route de Fautaua runs inland through lower-income dormitory suburbs to the Bain Loti, Loti's Bath or Pool, 2.5 km inland. It was here in Pierre Loti's 1880 novel *The Marriage of Loti* that the beautiful Rarahu met the novel's hero. This pool on the Fautaua River once supplied the town with drinking water, but, now, led through a concrete channel and surrounded by development, it's no longer the pleasantly rural scene Pierre Loti enjoyed. Nevertheless, it remains a favourite meeting place and swimming hole for local youngsters and a bust of Pierre Loti still overlooks the scene.

From the Bain Loti a walking path leads inland to the Fautaua River waterfalls, the Fachoda Fort and the Garden of the Governor. To go on this walk you'll need to ask permission from the Service de l'Hydraulique (see the Activities section for more information).

PIRAE & THE CEP

Just 1.5 km east of central Papeete is the Centre d'expérimentation du Pacifique (CEP), the euphemism for France's Pacific nuclear-testing project. French president Jacques Chirac's decision in 1995 to conduct a final series of tests at Moruroa and Fangataufa atolls was the grand finale for a project which had always been controversial. The project has been especially divisive in Tahiti, where, on the one hand, many French Polynesians object to the testing just as strongly as the people from other Pacific nations. On the other hand everybody realises that the money France has poured into

French Polynesia to manage and conduct the tests has been a mainstay of the local economy. The sheer number of people working at the establishment here in Papeete, quite apart from the large base on Mururoa, is visible evidence of the investment.

With Chirac's announcement in January 1996 that there will be no further testing, the question of what will happen to the base and what will replace the gap it leaves in the French Polynesian economy remains to be answered.

MT MARAU

Directly across from the Faaa airport terminal, a road signposted as Saint-Hilaire runs inland, under the autoroute and up towards the summit of Mt Marau (1493 metres). It's possible to drive up as far as the TV relay station at 1441, metres although the rough road really requires a 4WD for the 10-km climb. The winding road passes through varied vegetation before emerging among the damp ferns above 800 metres. The road reaches a belvédère (lookout) at 1241 metres.

From the end of the road it is only a half-hour walk to the top of Mt Marau, from where there are superb views. You'll see the high peaks around Tahiti Nui's central crater, the Tamanu Plateau immediately to the south and the ridgeline running east from Mt Marau to the Diadème (1321 metres), Mt Aorai (2066 metres) and Mt Orohena (2241 metres). The Fautaua River and its waterfalls, reached by the walk from Loti's Bath, can be seen to the north. There are also walking paths up Mt Marau from Punaauia that take about 3½ hours.

You can descend from Mt Marau in three hours via the Pic Vert (1159 metres) and the Pic Rouge. The track down starts from just before the TV-transmitter site and there are good views over the upper Fautaua Valley.

BEACHES NEAR PAPEETE

The splendid Polynesian beaches of tourist brochures are not on Tahiti, but if you just want to get into the water there are a few places within reasonable distance of Papeete.

Eight km west of the centre, just beyond Faaa airport, there's a bit of beach by the Sofitel Maeva Beach Hotel. The Outumaoro Le Truck terminus is just across the main road from the hotel, so getting here is very easy. Paul Theroux's *The Happy Isles of Oceania* has an amusing piece on the author's visit by kayak to the pontoon handily moored off the Beachcomber Parkroyal Hotel for sunbathing nudists.

On the other side of town, three km east in the suburb of Pirae, there's a stretch of black-sand beach by the Royal Tahitien Hotel. It's not the most inspiring beach, but things get better if you continue east to the fine black-sand stretch at PK 7 that leads up to the point topped by the Hyatt Hotel. Further along again there's a popular beach at Point Venus at PK 10. Unhappily, beaches within Papeete's urban sprawl, which today means the 30-km stretch from Punaauia in the west to Mahina in the east, can be subject to the same problems as city beaches in many modern countries: pollution from badly treated or even untreated sewage and industrial waste.

PLACES TO STAY

Papeete's places to stay can be neatly divided into two zones: the places in the central city area and the places on the edge of town. They're covered in the following Papeete and Around Papeete sections. In addition a handful of places are found further afield and they're covered in the Around Tahiti Nui, Around Tahiti Iti and Across Tahiti Nui sections.

Central Papeete has the most popular low-priced backpacker establishments, mid-range business hotels and some long-in-the-tooth tourist hotels which have been superseded by more modern establishments. Tahiti's three luxury beach hotels are on the outskirts of Papeete, either to the west of town just beyond the airport or to the east. Be warned that the white-sand beaches, over-water bungalows and translucent lagoons of tourist-brochure Tahiti are not to be found anywhere on Tahiti. Those places are all on other islands.

The prices quoted are generally high-season 'rack rates', which is what anybody will get if they just walk in from the street. If you book through a travel agent you can probably obtain much lower prices at Tahiti's popular tourist resorts. Like anywhere else in the world there can be certain times of year when rooms are hard to find, and in Tahiti the month of July, when the Heiva Festival takes place, is the most likely occasion to find rooms have suddenly become scarce.

At the more expensive places an 8% government tax will be added to your bill. At some of the cheapest places although bedding will be supplied you may have to provide your own towel.

Papeete

Bottom End Papeete's bottom rung category includes two traditional backpacker-style hostels and a spartan but adequate motel/hotel. They emphasise the city's transient nature but are not the sort of places where you would particularly want to hang around. The two backpacker hostels will pick you up from the airport if you contact them in advance.

Although it wouldn't compete with a good backpacker hostel in Australia or New Zealand that costs half the price, the *Tahiti Budget Lodge* (☎ 42-66-82, fax 43-06-79) is the best kept and best run of Papeete's backpacker centres. It's on Rue du Frère Alain, about a 10-minute walk back from the waterfront and town centre, close enough to be convenient but far enough away to be pleasantly quiet. There's a snack-bar area, kitchen facilities and a reasonable amount of open space including a garden. There's even a laundry although it's at the usual pricey French Polynesian level of 700 CFP for washing, 800 CFP for drying. Baggage can be left for 1000 CFP per week.

There are 11 rooms in total, including dorm facilities at 1800 CFP for a bed on night one, coming down to 1500 CFP on subsequent nights. The private rooms for one or two people start at 3800 CFP, or 4800 CFP with attached toilet and shower. The rooms are adequately clean but the communal shower and bathroom facilities feature all the usual little penny-pinching irritations, such as nowhere to hang a towel or put the soap when you're having a shower. Despite these annoyances, the Budget Lodge is conveniently close to the centre, has all the facilities you need and by Tahitian standards it's cheap. Bookings can be made through BP 237, Papeete, Tahiti, and credit cards are accepted. If you have made a reservation free transport is provided from the airport.

Only a couple of minutes' walk from the Tahiti Budget Lodge, and equally conveniently located for central Papeete, *Teamo Pension* (☎ 42-00-35 or 42-47-26, fax 43-56-95) is on a small side street and is a reasonable, inexpensive alternative. There are six rooms in total, including two standards of dormitory. You can choose the grotty dorm (it really is) at 1200 CFP for a bed or the better dorm at 1500 CFP per bed. The other rooms also share communal bathrooms and have a double and a single bed or a double and two single beds. They cost 3500 to 4000 CFP for one or two people. Hot water is available from 6 to 9 am. Bookings can be made through BP 2407, Papeete, Tahiti, and credit cards are accepted.

The *Mahina Tea* (☎ 42-00-97) is more like a cheaper hotel or motel than the two backpacker favourites. To get there turn away from the waterfront up Ave Bruat and from the gendarmerie take the road on the right-hand side, the Route de Sainte Amélie. It's only 10 or 15 minutes' walk from the centre and in a quiet location, although Old McDonald's entire farm seems to break into song around dawn.

There are 16 very plain and spartan rooms with bare concrete walls and tiled bathrooms. They are quite clean, some just have a single bed, some have a double bed and some have kitchen facilities. Prices for a straightforward single or double start at 4000 CFP and drop to 3400/3700 CFP for stays of three days or longer. Other rooms are in the 3500 to 4500 CFP bracket while the studio apartments with kitchen facilities are 10,000 CFP. Longer-term rates are also available, from 60,000 to 80,000 CFP per month. Bookings can be made through BP 17, Papeete, Tahiti, but credit cards are not accepted.

The even more basic *Shogun Hotel* (☎ 43-13-93, fax 43-27-28) is on Rue du Commandant Destremeau just before the Ave Bruat junction. The hotel has dormitory facilities and seven rooms with attached bathroom, five with a double bed and two with a double and a single bed. The nightly cost is 1500 CFP in the dormitory while the rooms cost 5000 or 6000 CFP for one or two people. Bookings can be made through BP 2880, Papeete, Tahiti, and credit cards are accepted.

Half a km inland from the large Matavai Hotel, *Chez Myrna* (☎ 42-64-11) has family-style *pension* accommodation with two rooms at 3500/4500 CFP for a single/double including breakfast. There's a two-night minimum and longer-term rates are available but credit cards are not accepted. The house is in the Tipaerui Valley but there is no sign so it's necessary to phone ahead. Bookings can be made through BP 790, Papeete, Tahiti.

Middle Papeete's mid-range hotels are essentially city business hotels or second string tourist hotels, in some cases very second string. Prices at all these establishments are subject to the 8% government hotel tax and the prices quoted are before this tax is added. All the mid-range hotels accept credit cards.

Hôtel Le Mandarin (☎ 42-16-33, fax 42-16-32) is probably the best of the mid-range downtown business hotels. The location is as central as it comes, on Rue Colette, right beside the mairie and only a short stroll from Papeete Market. The 37 rooms are air-conditioned, with attached bathrooms and TV and cost 11,000 to 12,000 CFP. It's relatively modern, clean, unpretentious and well run with a good little coffee bar for a 700 CFP breakfast and an adjacent Chinese restaurant. Bookings can be made through BP 302, Papeete, Tahiti.

Three other mid-range hotels are along the quayside Blvd Pomare in the centre of town.

Overlooking the Moorea ferry wharf from Blvd Pomare, the *Kon Tiki Pacific* (☎ 43-72-82, fax 42-11-66) has a colourful setting and terrific views over the busy wharf area from the rooms at the front. At 8000/9500 CFP for singles/doubles, the 44 rooms in this unremarkable business-style hotel are not too bad value. Bookings can be made through BP 111, Papeete, Tahiti.

Slightly closer to the centre, along Blvd Pomare, the *Royal Papeete* (☎ 42-01-29, fax 43-79-09), is an old tourist hotel past its use by date. Once upon a time, it's clear to see, it had real South Pacific charm. Now the tourists have moved out of town and the Royal Papeete simply looks tired and a bit worn around the edges, although it still has one of the town's busiest nightclubs. Singles/doubles cost 9000/10,500 CFP, while deluxe rooms are 10,500/12,000 CFP. Breakfast costs 800 CFP and bookings can be made through BP 919, Papeete, Tahiti.

Continue towards the centre and the *Hotel Prince Hinoi* (☎ 42-32-77, fax 42-33-66) is at the junction of Blvd Pomare and Ave du Prince Hinoi, right in the heart of the nightlife quarter. This modern business hotel is featureless but efficient and reasonable value for Papeete. The 72 rooms are all air-conditioned, have private bathrooms and cost 9500 CFP single or double. Bookings can be made through BP 4545, Papeete, Tahiti. The Prince Hinoi puts on a popular buffet lunch. Further along Blvd Pomare, beside the post office, the *Tiare Tahiti Hotel* is a new mid-range hotel which should open in 1996.

Only 1.5 km west of the centre towards the airport, the *Hotel Tahiti* (☎ 82-95-50 or 82-61-55, fax 81-31-51) was clearly a hot tourist spot once upon a time. Now it looks a little faded but still very pink. The waterfront location is fine and it's close enough to town to be convenient but far enough away to avoid the traffic and noise. The 70 rooms have attached bathrooms, verandahs, air-conditioning and a curling-at-the-edges tropical ambience. They cost from 8000 CFP. There are also some larger waterfront bungalows. There's a pool, restaurant, bar and other facilities. Bookings can be made through BP 416, Papeete, Tahiti.

Also on the airport side of the town centre, although a couple of hundred metres back from the coast on the Route de Tipaerui, the *Mataiva Hotel* (☎ 42-67-67, fax 42-36-90) is a nondescript, modernish 140-room hotel. After the post-nuclear-testing riots in 1995 it was taken over by the military as a barracks and looks very shabby and worn; recovery may take some time. There is a restaurant, bar and swimming pool, and singles/doubles cost 12,000/16,000 CFP with longer-term discounts available. Bookings can be made through BP 32, Papeete, Tahiti.

The final mid-range city hotel is the *Royal Tahitien Hotel* (☎ 42-81-13, fax 41-05-35), about three km east of the centre in the suburb of Pirae. Nicely situated on a reasonable stretch of black-sand beach this modern hotel has 40 rooms, very motel-like in character, and a pleasantly grassy garden setting. There's a waterfront restaurant with a wide deck looking out over the beach. The nightly cost is 15,000 CFP and bookings can be made through BP 5001, Pirae, Tahiti. Le truck stops less than 100 metres from the hotel.

Top End There is no top end in Papeete. Although Papeete's mid-range hotels charge decidedly top-end prices, none of the island's three real top-end places is in town. Two of them (the Beachcomber Parkroyal Hotel and the Sofitel Maeva Beach) are just beyond the airport to the west of the town, while the third (the Hyatt Regency Hotel) is to the east of town, two-thirds of the way to Point Venus.

Around Papeete

There are a number of places east and west of Papeete but still within the urban sprawl, including all three of Tahiti's luxury hotels. In addition there are a number of low-priced pensions slightly further to the west of Papeete in the suburbs of Punaauia and Papae. Although only 15 to 20 km from downtown Papeete, these places are covered in the Around Tahiti Nui section of this chapter.

Bottom End There is one backpacker locale to the east of Papeete, just past Point Venus. At one time the *Hiti Mahana Beach Club* (☎ 48-16-13) was a Tahiti budget bargain, ideal for those wanting cheap accommodation and happy to be out of the downtown hustle. Unfortunately, today it looks rather neglected and the grotty stretch of nearby beach is certainly no attraction, although there is a small motu just off-shore. If you just want a place to pitch a tent, a basic dorm bed or a cheap room it may be OK, but neither the area nor the beach club are particularly safe for single women.

The Hiti Mahana turn-off is at PK 10.5 just beyond Point Venus. It's about a km off the road down to the beach – turn right as you get close to the water. From Papeete le truck will cost 160 CFP to the turn-off. You can camp here for 800 CFP; a bed in the 12-bed dorm is 1000 CFP or there are two small rooms at 2500/3500 CFP and a larger one at 5000/6000 CFP. Bookings can be made through BP 11580, Mahina, Tahiti.

On the other side of town, close to the airport, there are two lower priced possibilities. The *Heitiare Inn* (☎ 83-33-52 or 82-77-53) is at PK 4.3, just a km or so from the airport towards Papeete. Free transfers are provided from the airport or you can walk there in 15 minutes, but this is a somewhat noisy and not particularly attractive area. The inn looks superficially neat and clean, despite the empty pool, but this is basically a place to stay when the situation is desperate. It doubles as a small snack bar frequented in the evening by the soldiers of the neighbouring RIMAP. Sleep is difficult when the night echoes with their shouts and bawdy jokes. At the end of the week you have the ungratifying sight in the early hours of young men collapsing over their beer at the bar. If you don't mind this sort of ambience, there are rooms at 4500/5000 CFP for a single/double with shared bathroom or 6000 CFP with attached bathroom. Some of the rooms are air-conditioned and there are communal kitchen facilities. Bookings can be made through BP 6830, Papeete, Tahiti. Credit cards are not accepted.

Chez Sorensen (☎ 82-63-30), also known as 'Chez Fifi', is at PK 5.5 in Faaa. It's right across the road from the airport terminal, take the small road beside the Mea Ma laundry. There's a signpost and it's the second house on the left, 150 metres up the hill. The proprietor, Joséphine Dahl, is known as Fifi, and is very friendly and speaks English. There are three dorm beds at 2000 CFP; it's not really a dormitory in the strict sense but two bunk beds and a single bed installed in a covered terrace. Two rooms with shared bathroom facilities are available as singles/doubles for 3500/6000 CFP, while an upstairs apartment rents for 50,000 CFP a month. Breakfast costs 300 CFP, and lunch or dinner costs 1000 CFP or 1500 CFP if prawns or crab are on the menu. Credit cards are not accepted.

If there is no room you can stay with her daughter (☎ 81-93-25), who lives just 50 metres away and has singles/doubles with shared bathrooms for 3500/5500 CFP, breakfast included, or 5000 CFP a night for three or more nights. In either case, the throb of jet engines may disturb your sleep. After a few nights the schedules of the different airlines will be familiar knowledge!

Middle West of the airport, just beyond the Beachcomber Parkroyal Hotel but up Punaauia Hill, away from the water, the *Tahiti Country Club* (☎ 42-60-40 or 43-08-29, fax 41-09-28) offers a more reasonably priced alternative to the two nearby top-end places. The 40 air-con rooms are straightforward in the extreme, lined up in reasonably modern, two-storey motel-style blocks. This is simply somewhere for an unmemorable night at the beginning or the end of a holiday. There is a swimming pool and tennis courts and rooms for one or two cost 14,400 CFP. The Tahiti Country Club is about six km from the centre of Papeete and can be booked through BP 576, Papeete, Tahiti.

Down at the waterfront below the Country Club is the derelict Te Puna Bel Air, awaiting redevelopment. Meanwhile its very stagnant swimming pool is growing some world-class algae.

Top End There are three 'top-end' hotels around Papeete, two to the west just past the airport and one slightly further out to the east. These hotels have swimming pools, tennis courts, restaurants, bars, boutiques, transport and tour desks: in short all the amenities you'd expect. Naturally these establishments accept every credit card you'd care to think of and the 8% hotel tax is additional to the costs quoted.

The *Tahiti Beachcomber Parkroyal Hotel* (☎ 86-51-10, fax 86-51-30) is eight km from the centre of Papeete, just two km from the airport terminal and only a stone's throw from the end of Faaa airport's runway. Right on the waterfront are 179 regular hotel rooms and 32 over-water bungalows plus restaurants, bars, two swimming pools (one with a sand beach and a swim-up bar) and even a nice little slice of artificial, but quite authentic looking, beach. Other facilities include a gymnasium, two tennis courts and even washing machines and driers for guests' use. Standard singles/doubles run from 24,500/28,500 CFP to 27,500/31,500 CFP. Motu over-water bungalows cost 36,500 CFP while the lagoon ones are 44,000 CFP.

A continental/American breakfast costs 1650 CFP/1950 CFP. *Demi-pension* (breakfast and dinner) is available for 6300 CFP per person. The three restaurants are the poolside *Lotus Restaurant*, the relaxed *Tiare Restaurant* and the more intimate *Hibiscus Restaurant*. There are also three bars and regular island dance performances at night. Bookings can be made through BP 6014, Faaa, Tahiti.

Continue less than a km past the Beachcomber Parkroyal Hotel to the roundabout where the autoroute from Papeete meets the coast road. Immediately beyond the roundabout is the *Sofitel Maeva Beach Hotel* (☎ 42-80-42, fax 43-84-70), on the lagoon side of the road; the Outumaoro Le Truck terminus is on the other. The hotel is right on Maeva Beach, one of the best beaches close to Papeete.

This slightly older and more traditionally hotel-like establishment doesn't have over-water bungalows and other more recent innovations, but it does have 224 comfortable rooms. The garden-view rooms are 18,500 CFP for a single or double; the lagoon-view rooms are 21,500 CFP. There are also some rooms with panoramic views for 25,000 CFP! Breakfast costs 1500 CFP and demi-pension is available for 5000 CFP. There is a Japanese restaurant and the excellent *Restaurant Gauguin*. Bookings can be made through BP 6008, Faaa, Tahiti.

The third top-end hotel is the *Hyatt Regency Tahiti Hotel* (☎ 46-12-34, fax 48-25-44) at PK 8, to the east of Papeete. Dramatically perched on the edge of Taharaa Point, the hotel steps down the hill towards the water, so from reception guests go down to their rooms, rather than up. The hotel overlooks a magnificent sweep of black-sand beach towards Papeete while in the other direction it overlooks Matavai Bay, Captain Cook's famous anchorage. Taharaa Point was dubbed 'One Tree Hill' by Cook.

For setting alone the Hyatt is hard to beat, but the 190 rooms themselves are not very impressive and even feel slightly cramped. They do have large balconies with sweeping views and nightly costs are 27,000 CFP. The restaurants, including the French-Tahitian *Mahana Restaurant* and the Japanese (and weekends only) *Shiosai Teppanyaki*, also enjoy superb views. There's also a spectacular pool with the adjacent *Vaimato* snack bar. Steps lead down from the hotel to the black-sand beach below. Bookings can be made through BP 14700, Arue, Tahati.

PLACES TO EAT

French and Tahitian cooking and ingredients blend to provide some fine dining opportunities in Papeete but the prices are almost always high and some places do manage to show that even the French are not totally insulated from bad cooking. Apart from the French and Tahitian influences, there are also a number of good Italian restaurants and pizzerias and a host of Chinese and Vietnamese specialists. Although you can, with care, eat reasonably cheaply in Papeete, you're far more likely to find yourself spending

US$100 or more for a modest meal for two in a simple bistro.

Papeete dining presents two other problems. If you're planning to pay with a credit card, check that it will be accepted first. And plan ahead for Sunday when many restaurants shut down. Le Rétro and Lou Pescadou are two useful exceptions to the Sunday closing dilemma.

Les Roulottes

Good food, good fun and the best prices in town, that's *les roulottes*, quayside in downtown Papeete every day and most of the night. A roulotte is a van turned into a mobile diner. Flaps lowered on each side become the counters, stools are set up for the customers and the staff inside the van prepare the food. They're arrayed all around the carpark area by the waterfront and people come here to eat, to grab some nightclub sustenance or to kick on after the clubs close. They're a colourful Polynesian institution and something every visitor should try.

What do the roulottes turn out? Well pretty much everything you'll find at regular restaurants around town but at lower prices, although that still doesn't make them cheap by the standards of other countries. Steak and chips at 700 CFP may be a Papeete bargain, but it's still not a cheap meal. Typically, a roulotte meal will be in the 700 to 1000 CFP bracket.

Roulottes' names tell what they're all about; the cast may change from night to night but you may come across mobile pizzerias (would you believe a wood-fired pizza oven on wheels?) like *Vesuvio Pizza*, *Pizza Napoli* and even the *Pizza Hut* (should that be *Pizza Van?*). There's steak and chips at *Chez Roger* or steak and pizza at *Le Romain*, complete with Roman columns to support the van's side flaps and a cut-out figure of a centurion. Of course there are plenty of Chinese roulottes (*spécialités chinoises*) like *Chez Michou*, *Chez Lili*, *Pacifique Sud Roulotte* or *Hong Kong* (a specialist in chao men).

You can finish up with a crêpe or a gaufre (waffle) for 200 to 600 CFP at mobile

crêperies like *Crêperie du Port*, *Moby Dick Crêperie*, *Crêpes et Gaufres à Gogo*, *Chez Patrick* (for crêpes and ice creams) or *Suzy Gaufre*. A fresh fruit roulotte would be a nice idea but otherwise the only thing the roulottes can't provide is alcohol. But the Blvd Pomare bars are just across the road.

Snacks & Light Meals

In the Centre Right in the middle of town the Vaima Centre has a number of excellent cheap-eats possibilities as well as more expensive restaurants. The popular *Le Rétro* (☎ 42-86-83) in the Vaiama Centre can be the right address any time of day. Looking out on busy Blvd Pomare, this open-air bar and restaurant is good for anything from a breakfast coffee and croissant to a light lunch, a sunset beer or even a late-night coffee. Le Rétro is open every day, which is worth knowing on Sunday when many places are shut. You can get sandwiches, complete meals or an excellent ice cream. Main courses cost 1500 to 2000 CFP, salads 600 to 1000 CFP.

On Rue du Général de Gaulle, on the opposite corner of the Vaima Centre to Le Rétro, is *L'Oasis* (☎ 45-45-01). This popular breakfast-and-lunch spot has excellent croissants and pain aux raisins to start the day and terrific French-bread sandwiches come lunchtime. Tahiti's major meal-time bargain is a French-bread sandwich or casse-croûte and the Vaima Centre's third inexpensive eating opportunity is *Le Motu*, which has a great selection. Le Motu is also on the Rue du Général de Gaulle side of the centre, on the corner of Rue Lagarde.

Across Rue Lagarde from Le Motu, the *Big Burger* (☎ 43-01-98) was a popular café offering far more than just burgers. It was damaged in the September 1995 nuclear-testing riots and in early '96 had still not reopened. A few doors further along on Rue du Général de Gaulle, *Café de la Gare* (☎ 42-75-95) looks authentically Parisian and has fairly pricey light meals. A salade niçoise is 1200 CFP, other salads are up to 1600 CFP and pastas are 1200 to 1500 CFP. See the

Bars & Cold Beers section under Entertainment for more information.

If the Vaima Centre is the glossy international market place of Papeete, then Papeete Market is the down-to-earth Polynesian equivalent. There are several good places for a cheap meal upstairs in the market, including the *Cafétéria du Marché*. There are a number of good snack bars around the town centre, many of them catering to city office workers. The *Acajou Café* (☎ 43-19-27), close to Papeete Market on Rue Cardella, is a good example. A block over is the popular self-service *Polyself Cafeteria* (☎ 43-75-32) at 8 Rue Paul Gauguin. *Waikiki* (☎ 42-95-27) on Rue Albert Leboucher is a bargain-priced Chinese establishment. The *Mandarin Coffee Shop* (☎ 42-16-33) is a pleasant little café in Le Mandarin Hotel on Rue Colette.

The prices on the straightforward menu at *Snack Aloha*, on the corner of Rue Nansouty and Rue Charles Viénot, are very competitive. Poisson cru in coconut milk is just 500 CFP, maa tinito (Tahitian for 'Chinese dish', which usually means red beans with meat) is 600 CFP and chow mein is 750 CFP. Soft drinks are 120 CFP or less. It's open Monday to Friday from 6 am to 4.30 pm.

Chez Roger (☎ 58-45-20) is a small snack bar right beside the cathedral. Near the cathedral on Rue Édouard-Ahnne, the American cinema-influenced décor at *Snack Malibu* doesn't have anything from Hollywood but there are photos of popular American actors on the wall. It's difficult to pass up house cocktails like a Marilyn (fruit juice, Grenadine and tonic water) for 400 CFP or a very sensible Tom Cruise (banana, lemon juice and crème de menthe) for 400 CFP, or you can detonate an Eddie Murphy (pineapple and orange juice, Grand Marnier and vodka) for 800 CFP. The menu is varied: salads from 800 CFP or burgers from 900 CFP are followed by fish dishes from 950 CFP and grilled dishes, like chicken or red meat, from 900 CFP. Desserts and ice creams at 400 to 650 CFP complete the meal. There's a 1200 CFP fixed-price menu including a fruit juice, a main course and a dessert. Breakfasts, continental at 500 CFP, American or Polynesian at 900 CFP, are also served. Snack Malibu is open Monday to Friday from 6 am to 3 pm and credit cards are accepted.

East & West of the Centre *Hilaire – pâtissier, confisseur, glacier* (☎ 43-65-85) is a salon de thé on the corner of Ave du Commandant Chessé and Ave Georges Clémenceau, not far from the Mamao Hospital and next to the Chinese temple. It's frequented by many people who work locally because you can get a hot chocolate for 250 CFP, an almond croissant for 200 CFP or a chocolate croissant for 120 CFP. A cheese omelette costs 600 CFP, fruit juices (pineapple, grapefruit or watermelon) are 500 CFP and ice cream is 400 CFP a scoop. The pâtisseries are excellent but sadly the characterless décor is not so special. It's open Monday to Saturday, 5 am to 6 pm and Sunday from 5 to 10.30 am.

Those who love bread and French pâtisserie will find their wishes granted at the *Boulangerie de la Fautaua*, two streets further away on the corner of Ave Georges Clémenceau and Cours de l'Union-Sacrée. Quick snacks include doughnuts, chocolate croissants at 120 CFP and sandwiches at 200 CFP. It's open Monday to Saturday from 2 am to 7 pm, Sunday 2 am to noon.

Across from the Mamao Hospital on Ave Georges Clémenceau, *Snack Mateata* is a good place for a quick meal. Employees of the CPS, the nearby social security office, and hospital personnel often eat here. The poisson cru costs 650 CFP, sashimi is 900 CFP or grilled mahi mahi with chips or rice is 900 CFP. The terrace is pleasant even though it is by the road. They don't sell alcohol, apart from beer. Breakfast is available from 5.30 am and it's open until 4 pm.

Towards the west side of the town, *Le Snack Paofai* (☎ 42-95-76) is close to the Paofai medical clinic, on the corner of Rue du Commandant Destremeau and Rue du Lieutenant Varney.

Restaurants
Cheaper Restaurants On the terrace of the Vaima Centre, throw yourself into *Les Alizés*

(☎ 43-54-63). The pleasant name means a cool breeze and it specialises in French-Polynesian dishes. There is a vast range of salads from 1200 CFP and variety of lovingly prepared dishes. You can try grilled tuna fillets in a rougaille sauce for 1300 CFP or medallions of mahi mahi with vegetable tagliatelle at 1600 CFP. The set meal at 2100 CFP, which includes a salad and a plat du jour (daily special), is a good compromise. Desserts are 400 to 750 CFP. It's open Monday to Friday for lunch and dinner and Saturday for lunch. Credit cards are accepted and the menu is in both French and English.

Also in the Vaima Centre, *La Malaussane* (☎ 42-50-58) is more bar than restaurant but it's a good place for a filling and straightforward meal from the small menu. The plats du jour are popular. La Malaussane is closed Saturday lunchtime and all day Sunday. On Blvd Pomare, just across from the Vaima Centre, the pleasant *Blue Pacifique Café* replaced the Acajou Restaurant in 1995, one of the longest running and most popular restaurants in Papeete. The Acajou Café near the market is still in business.

On the corner of Blvd Pomare and Ave Bruat, the long-running *Bistrot du Port* (☎ 42-76-52) has recently been renamed the *New Port* but still turns out the same mix of local dishes and French cuisine and still has outdoor tables under the trees. The Friday lunchtime special of veal, chips, a drink and coffee is 1350 CFP. It's closed on Sunday. Nearby the *El Bryanos Tex-Mex Restaurant* (☎ 43-49-16) is a recent Blvd Pomare addition.

Italian Restaurants & Pizzerias

Lou Pescadou (☎ 43-74-26) on Rue Anne-Marie Javouhey is a real Papeete institution. It's a block back from Rue du Général de Gaulle, near the cathedral. In this cheerful and noisy restaurant pizzas are 700 to 850 CFP while specials are 1500 to 2000 CFP. Lou Pescadou is open until late at night, seven days a week but credit cards are not accepted.

The apostrophes seem to have gone walkabout at *L'Api'zzeria* (☎ 42-98-30) which you can approach from either Rue du Com-

mandant Destremeau or from Blvd Pomare. This is Papeete's other popular pizzeria with a pleasant open-air dining area just across the road from the waterfront. Pizzas start at 400 to 680 CFP for minis or 680 to 1250 CFP for regular size. There are also pasta dishes at 700 to 1900 CFP or meat and fish main courses at 1200 to 2200 CFP. La Pizzeria, if you cared to remove the apostrophes, is closed on Sunday.

There are other Italian restaurants around among which, right behind Lou Pescadou on Passage Cardella, is *La Squadra* (☎ 41-32-14), where standard Italian dishes such as pasta cost from 900 to 1200 CFP and main courses are 1600 to 2500 CFP including regular Roman mainstays like scaloppine alla Romana at 1600 CFP. La Squadra is closed Monday but other days of the week it's even open for breakfast and it does accept credit cards.

Chinese & Vietnamese Restaurants

Papeete has a number of excellent Chinese and Vietnamese restaurants and although the Chinese seemed to be singled out for special attention in the nuclear-testing riots of 1995 most of them are back in action, sometimes in rather anonymous circumstances. Disorientation is guaranteed as soon as you cross the doorway of *Le Mandarin* (☎ 42-99-03) on Rue des Écoles, just round the corner from the hotel of the same name. It's open for lunch and dinner every day. Wood panelling, hanging tapestries and lacquerwork lend a Far Eastern air to this venerable institution which has hardly acquired a wrinkle, well very few, since its opening in 1964. The chef comes from Hong Kong and manages all the flavours of China in nearly 180 different dishes. Dish No 171, kai lip teo fou, is steamed tofu with pork, chicken and mushrooms for 1900 CFP. Vegetarians are not forgotten, with many vegetable dishes between 550 and 1900 CFP.

Beyond the impressive menu there are three types of set meals, at 2500 CFP, 2100 CFP (two-person minimum) and 2950 CFP (also a two-person minimum). The extensive winelist includes a fine selection of

Bordeaux wines from 1605 CFP. You could even try a bottle of Château Pétrus '88 for a mere 144,910 CFP! Unfortunately, the music is not always so well adapted to the surroundings. Le Mandarin is open every day at lunchtime and in the evenings. There's live music on Friday and Saturday evenings. Credit cards are accepted and there's an English menu.

Next to Le Mandarin Hotel, across from the mairie on Rue Colette is *Le Dragon d'Or* (☎ 42-96-12), with some of the best Chinese food in town. It's closed on Monday. The *Restaurant Cathay* (☎ 42-99-67) and the *Restaurant Tehoa* (☎ 42-99-27), almost side by side on Rue du Maréchal Foch near the market, turn out straightforward and low-priced Chinese dishes. Neither takes credit cards. For Vietnamese food try the *Restaurant Saïgonnaise* (☎ 42-05-35) on Ave du Prince Hinoi. It's closed on Sunday.

The *Pitate Mamao* (☎ 42-86-94) is on the right, at the start of Ave Georges Clémenceau, just after the Pont de l'Est, the bridge over the Papeava River. The Hong Kong chef prepares an eclectic, predominantly Chinese menu but with French and Polynesian specialities, like mahi mahi meunière at 1400 CFP or pork with taro at 950 CFP. The winelist, although it features excellent reds, notably the Bordeaux, has steep prices – count on at least 3000 CFP for a bottle. The desserts are rather disappointing. It's open Monday to Saturday, for lunch and dinner. Credit cards are accepted and the menu is also in English.

More Expensive Restaurants Right in the centre of town, on Passage Cardella, *L'O à la Bouche* (☎ 45-29-76) is a real surprise – very stylish (and very yellow and very blue) and not exceptionally expensive. The menu has a very French flavour with starters at 950 to 1300 CFP, including gazpacho soup. The main courses include a good selection of fish dishes at 1600 to 2000 CFP. Mahi mahi caramelised with honey and parrot fish fillets with a hollandaise sauce are 1700 CFP. The winelist includes a wide selection of bottles at 2400 to 3000 CFP and some half bottles at

1600 to 1800 CFP. It's closed Saturday lunchtime and Sunday evening.

On top of the Vaima Centre, *Morrison's Café* (☎ 42-78-61) takes its name from Jim (not Van) as is abundantly clear as soon as you step inside the restaurant to be met by rock & roll posters, the Doors featuring prominently, and MTV on the video monitors. Once you're in the know you won't come in the main entrance – you'll arrive by the glass elevator that starts from outdoors, right beside L'Oasis downstairs. Featuring rooftop and open-air sections, Morrison's also has a swimming pool right in the middle of the restaurant. The anonymous entrance and discreet signs all go to prove it's one of Papeete's trendier spots with a slightly exclusive feel. Although it has a reputation for being one of the city's pricier establishments, the prices aren't really that bad. There's a daily menu featuring a plat du jour, drink and coffee for 1600 CFP or a Tex-Mex special offering lots of meat for 2600 CFP. The regular seafood menu has dishes like mahi mahi with ginger sauce at 1500 CFP and thazar with mustard sauce at 1400 CFP. Morrison's is closed Saturday lunchtime and all day Sunday but the other nights it's open very late, which means after 10 pm in Papeete!

East of the town centre in the suburb of Pirae, *Le Lion d'Or* (☎ 42-66-50) is by the post office, just back from Ave du Prince Hinoi at the junction with Rue Bernière. Its relatively isolated location makes this strictly a restaurant for people with wheels but it serves excellent French seafood. It's closed on Sunday.

Around Ave Bruat, west of the town centre, there are two more expensive and very French-influenced restaurants aimed at business expense accounts and officials from the nearby government offices. *Le Manava Restaurant* (☎ 42-02-91) is on Ave Bruat on the corner of Rue du Commandant Destremeau and is closed on Saturday and Sunday nights. On Blvd Pomare, just west of Ave Bruat, the *Moana Iti Restaurant* (☎ 42-65-24) is a long-term survivor and is also closed on Sunday.

A little further west *La Corbeille d'Eau* (☎ 43-77-14) is a small, anonymous and modern restaurant on the waterfront Blvd Pomare. It regularly wins accolades as the home of fine French dining in Papeete. Starters run from 1600 to 2800 CFP while main courses are 2200 to 3200 CFP. To complete the extravaganza, le chariot des desserts will wheel by at 1300 CFP, although there is a dessert of the day for 900 CFP. Add a bottle of wine and coffee afterwards and the bill for two will easily top 7000 or 8000 CFP. La Corbeille d'Eau is open Monday to Friday for lunch and dinner, Saturday for dinner only. The restaurant's name translates as 'the basket of water', which is what Papeete means in Tahitian.

Finally, from fine food at sea level ascend to not-so-fine food at high altitude. *Le Belvédère* (☎ 42-73-44) is perched 600 metres above the city, at the start of the walking track to the top of Mt Aroi. The views over Papeete are fantastic, particularly at sunset, but unfortunately the food doesn't attain the same heights. Spending 10,000 CFP to prove that even the French can cook badly is disappointing; come up here for a sunset drink, eat down in the town. Le Belvédère provides free transport from Papeete restaurants. If you drive yourself take the first right turn after the Hamuta Total fuel station. The seven-km road to the restaurant is steep, winding and, towards the top, rather rugged.

ENTERTAINMENT
Bars & Cold Beers
On a balmy tropical evening the first question is where to go for a cold Hinano. *Le Rétro* (☎ 42-86-83) fits the bill for most things and it'll do for a watch-the-world-go-by cold beer as well. Le Rétro is on the waterfront side of the Vaima Centre and a beer will set you back 400 CFP, the perfect combination with a Tahitian sunset.

If you want your beer indoors then head upstairs to *La Malaussane* (☎ 42-50-58), a very popular pub-style establishment with a pool table and a convivial atmosphere A Hinano *pression* (French for on tap rather

than bottled) costs 350 CFP and there's a small variety of other beers and wine by the glass. For a real French-bar experience go back a block from the waterfront to *Café de la Gare* (☎ 42-75-95) on Rue du Général de Gaulle. It looks like it was beamed down here straight from the centre of Paris, complete with a full contingent of chain Gauloise smokers if you're unlucky. There's beer at 380 CFP and a range of sandwiches and light meals at fairly steep prices.

Several places along the busy and noisy nightlife strip of Blvd Pomare are also good spots for a contemplative beer at any time. *L'Auberge* (☎ 42-22-13) is a good example. This restaurant-cum-bar can be a nice place to sit and watch the waterfront activity, while listening to the gentle strumming of Tahitian music.

Of course all the big luxury hotels have wonderful bars, and they are great places to enjoy the ocean breezes and nibble the free peanuts. The *Hyatt Regency Hotel*, *Beachcomber Parkroyal Hotel* and *Sofitel Maeva Beach Hotel* all have a variety of bars.

Island Dance Performances
Island night dance performances are put on regularly at several locations around Papeete. These are real tourist shows, reducing Tahitian culture to variety-show level, but they are colourful and energetic and the dancers are often very good. Just west of Faaa airport the *Beachcomber Parkroyal Hotel* (☎ 86-51-10) puts on one of the best at 8 pm on Sunday. It costs 4850 CFP including a buffet dinner but you can watch the show for the price of a drink at the bar.

Not to be outdone, the *Sofitel Maeva Beach Hotel* (☎ 42-80-42) has a Polynesian spectacle on Friday and Saturday nights at 8 pm. Further along the coast the *Captain Bligh Restaurant* (☎ 43-62-90) at the Lagoonarium at Punaauia at PK 11 also has an island night performance on Friday and Saturday nights. On the other side of Papeete, the *Hyatt Regency Hotel* (☎ 42-12-34) has performances in the Mahana Restaurant.

TAHITI

Clubs, Dance Halls & Discos

Papeete's nightlife is raucous and colourful but most of it is concentrated in a pretty compact zone. There are a few places back from the waterfront but stick to Blvd Pomare and you'll find most things. The Vaima Centre marks the upmarket starting point for the nightlife zone while the Hotel Prince Hinoi marks the most crowded and colourful central zone. The nuclear-testing riots in late 1995 seemed to have spelt the end for a number of Papeete nightlife centres and if the French military structure in Papeete is wound back, changes can be expected.

Papeete is certainly the place where nightlife lovers will be happiest, so long as they are not mistaken about the ambience or the music. During the week the discos are often deserted or closed. In contrast, on weekends you may need to use your elbows to force your way in. Entry charges can be in the 1000 to 1500 CFP range at some establishments, plus you may be required to buy at least one drink. Sometimes entry charges apply only to men and sometimes a foreign passport will get you in for free, so it's worth asking.

Towards the Rue du Général de Gaulle and Rue Lagarde corner of the Vaima Centre *Le Rolls Club* (☎ 43-41-42) or the *Rolls Discotheque* is more conventional and more stylish than the local establishments. Its special evenings are very popular although the attraction seems to be beauty contests and parades. The clientele is predominantly *popaa* (foreigners) and the disco music offers no surprises. You can try your luck with a TGV (tequila-gin-vodka) for 1800 CFP. It's open Wednesday to Saturday from 10 pm to 3 am; on Sunday local music is featured from 6 pm to midnight. Entry is 1500 CFP for men on Friday and Saturday, including a drink. This is probably Papeete's glossiest disco and it attracts the town's wealthiest young people.

Also in the Vaima Centre *Le Rétro* disco, associated with the popular café, was a nuclear-testing-riot victim but reopened in early 1996. Back from the cathedral on Ave Monseigneur Tepano Jaussen, both the Galaxy and the New Orleans had gone into hibernation in early 1996. They may or may not reopen.

Le Club 5 (☎ 42-97-85), on the corner of Rue des Écoles and Blvd Pomare, plays multiple roles and even seems to have a confusing mix of multiple names to go with them. There's a bar at street level, pool tables upstairs and a separate upstairs club with cabaret and show, which means performers taking their clothes off, of course. Downstairs the Jasmin Palace is popular for a beer when the military is on a binge. Special shows are organised regularly and have a reputation for being real sagas. The organisers have lots of imagination, putting on events such as a western evening (with a lasso and rodeo contest) and a beer-drinking contest during an evening dedicated to Alsace (a region of France noted for its beer). At the entry you might find a sign informing you that you will find 'lively lunacy all night'. You have been warned. A whisky and coke costs 800 CFP, cocktails are 1500 CFP. Entry, including a drink, costs 1000 CFP on Friday and Saturday for men and accompanied women but, at the discretion of the owner, 'you don't have to pay if you're in a group and buy a bottle'. The special shows are more expensive. Le Club 5 is open every day from 10 pm to 3 am.

A few steps back from the waterfront along Rue des Écoles brings you to the *Piano Bar* (☎ 42-88-24), one of Papeete's most famous institutions and a centre for *mahus*. It's kind of amusing that this popular nightlife street should be called Rue des Écoles, (Street of the Schools) because it's certainly a place to get an education. At night any woman along Rue des Écoles who looks like far too much of a woman to really be one probably isn't and the Piano Bar certainly isn't a place for prudes. Although the *rae rae* officiate in this quarter and it's popular with gays, the clientele ranges from lovelorn sailors to passing tourists – the whole world seems to come and go from the Piano Bar. Don't miss the annual election of Miss Rae Rae, a favourite subject of the local press. The rae rae put on a cabaret show each night at 1.30 am. The Piano Bar is open every day from 3 pm to 3 am and entry is 1500 CFP on the weekends. Between Le Club 5 and the Piano Bar is the *Lido Club* (☎ 42-95-84), which is not such a mahu hangout but is still right in the centre of things.

Continue along Rue des Écoles and cross the street to *Café des Sports* on the corner of Rue Albert Leboucher. This is a very different sort of establishment – a pure and simple local bar where people come to drink, dance and listen to local music and nobody pretends to be something they aren't. It's crowded, noisy, cheerful and mostly frequented by locals.

Back on the main drag *L'Auberge* (☎ 42-22-13) also has music with a Tahitian flavour. Things start to get noisy beyond this point. *Bar Taina's* (☎ 42-64-40) play list varies from local music to loud rock. It's equally loud at the *Zizou Bar* (☎ 42-07-55).

Le Paradise (☎ 42-73-05), next to the Hotel Pacific and facing the Moorea ferry quay, is the centre for traditional and tropical dancing. The Tahitian-style waltz, fox trot, zouk, reggae, Caribbean-African soukouss and the twist are what's done here. It attracts a slightly older crowd, predominantly popaa but there are also Tahitians, *demis* (mixed-blood Tahitian-Europeans) and Chinese. Fruit juices are 1000 CFP, beers are 1200 CFP, a glass of whisky is 1500 CFP and cocktails are 2000 CFP. It's open every day from 10 pm to 3 am and entry is free.

Nearby, *Le Calypso* (☎ 42-17-53) concentrates on disco and dance music with special evenings which are often rather lacking in originality, like 'Cutty (Cutty Sark whisky) evenings' or 'Heineken evenings'. Drinks cost from 1000 CFP and entry for men is 1500 CFP, with a drink, on Friday and Saturday nights. It's also open from 10 pm to 3 am.

La Cave (☎ 42-01-29), beside the Royal Papeete Hotel, is definitely a Papeete institution and very much in vogue with young Tahitians. The attraction is the music – a band plays an exclusively local repertoire. After several hours the hypnotic rhythms of Maruia, the Royal Band or Te Ava Piti will

all be familiar. There is a fine ambience after midnight and the décor is sober, straightforward and makes it clear to tourists that this is a place exclusively dedicated to the pleasure of dancing. Before inviting one of the *vahines* (Polynesian women) who catches their eye, men should know how to dance the waltz or fox trot, or risk being promptly rejected. The women are lucky, as the Tahitians take pleasure in initiating the popaa into the rhythms of the lascivious *kaina* music. Entry is 1000 CFP with a drink, after which drinks cost from 600 CFP. It's open Friday and Saturday from 10 pm to 4 am.

In the same bar-and-dancing vein as La Cave is the *Royal Kikiriri* (☎ 43-58-64) on Rue Colette, between Rue des Écoles and Ave du Prince Hinoi. Two counters with subdued lighting give this place a more intimate feeling than La Cave. Hinano beers are 600 CFP and good strong maitais are 1200 CFP. The Trio Royal Kikiriri, usually hidden behind the colonnades and the plants, plays from 10 pm. The restaurant has a good reputation and is on the upper level. The Royal Kikiriri is open Wednesday to Sunday from 6 pm to 3 am and Friday from 11 am to 3 pm. Happy hour on Friday is from 5 to 9 pm, entry is free.

Le Mayana on Ave Bruat, next to the New Port restaurant, is a good place. In a spacious room you can dance to local songs, disco or zouk, performed by a live band. A beer costs 700 CFP and the cocktail list, 17 of them from 1500 CFP, reads like a poem. It's open Thursday from 8 pm to midnight; Friday from 3.30 pm to 3 am (happy hour from 5 to 6 pm) and Saturday from 7 pm to 3 am. Entry is 1500 CFP but only men are charged; one drink is included.

Le Club 106 (☎ 42-72-92) is on the waterfront to the west of the town centre, a little after Ave Bruat. It usually features a mix of musical styles from disco to rock via the beguine and techno which usually satisfies the tastes of the clientele which is about 80% popaa between the age of 30 and 40. Theme evenings are sometimes organised, along the lines of an Antilles (West Indian) evening or a pareu evening. You can quench your thirst for the modest sum of 1000 CFP (fruit juice), 1400 CFP for alcoholic drinks and 1800 CFP for cocktails. It's open Tuesday to Saturday from 10 pm to 3 am and entry is free.

Cinemas

Papeete has a number of cinemas where films are shown either dubbed in French or with subtitles. The letters VO (version originale) indicate that if the film started life in English it will still be in English, with subtitles rather than dubbed audio. Admission is usually 700 CFP. The *Concorde* (☎ 42-63-60), on Rue du Général de Gaulle in the Vaima Centre, and the *Hollywood* (☎ 42-65-79) at the Fare Tony Centre on Rue Lagarde are two-screen cinemas. The *Liberty* (☎ 42-08-20) on Rue du Maréchal Foch has three while the *Mamao Palace* (☎ 42-54-69) on Ave du Commandant Chessé has four.

THINGS TO BUY

Although Tahiti is not the centre for any particular crafts you can buy products from all over French Polynesia. Pearls are produced in the Tuamotus, wood carvings are made in the Marquesas, and hats and baskets are woven in the Australs, but it's all on sale here.

Handicrafts

The Territorial Cultural Centre, right down at the western end of Blvd Pomare, encourages local craftwork with displays and demonstrations of traditional Polynesian crafts. The centre also has a library and a theatre. A wide variety of handicrafts is on sale at stands in Papeete Market, particularly upstairs. Pareus, the colourful, sarong-like, all-purpose Tahitian clothing, are sold in the market and in a variety of shops in Papeete but also on many other islands. Beautiful hats and baskets are produced on a number of islands, in particular Rurutu in the Australs.

There are a great many craft and souvenir shops along Blvd Pomare and Rue du Général de Gaulle and in the Vaima Centre and Fare Tony Centre. Manuia Curios (☎ 42-04-94) is at Place Notre Dame, right beside the cathedral. Ganesha (☎ 43-04-18) in the Vaima Centre has craftwork from French Polynesia and from other Pacific centres. Paintings and other artwork can be found at the Matamua Art Gallery (☎ 41-34-95) on Blvd Pomare and at the Reva Art Gallery (☎ 43-32-67) at 36 Rue Lagarde. The Reva Gallery specialises in work by resident artists.

Music

If you develop a taste for the guitars, ukuleles and banjos which have become synonymous with Polynesian music you can take it back on cassette tape or CD. The five musicians in the Royal Band perform regularly in Papeete night spots and you can even get them recorded live at the Royal Papeete. Manuiti is a local record label which produces a variety of Tahitian tapes and CDs.

Pearls

French Polynesia's famous black pearls are produced in the Tuamotus, and you can find out all about them at the Pearl Museum on Blvd Pomare. Black pearl specialists in Papeete include My Pearls (☎ 43-24-69) at 1 Ave du Prince Hinoi or Sibani Pearls (☎ 42-44-55) at various locations including several outlets in the Vaima Centre. Smaller pearl specialists and jewellery shops can be found along Blvd Pomare. See the Black Pearls, Jewel of the Tuamotus aside in the Tuamotus chapter for more information on these beautiful cultured pearls.

Supermarkets

Papeete has a good collection of supermarkets with the widest range of goods and lowest prices in French Polynesia. Just west of the Sofitel Maeva Beach Hotel, past Faaa airport, there's a modern shopping centre with a huge Continent Supermarket which wouldn't be out of place in Australia or the USA. If you're restocking a yacht for the next leg of a Pacific cruise, this is the place to go.

Duty-Free Shopping

There is a duty-free shop at Faaa airport in

the departure lounge but the prices are not particularly exciting.

GETTING THERE & AWAY

The overwhelming majority of visitors to French Polynesia will arrive at Papeete on the island of Tahiti. The rare exceptions are likely to be yachties making their first landfall at one of the outer islands. Papeete is not only the flight centre but also the shipping centre: domestic flights fan out from Faaa airport and inter-island shipping services arrive and depart from the port of Papeete.

Air

Faaa airport is the aviation centre for all of French Polynesia and flight information can be obtained by calling ☎ 82-60-61. International flights all come here and most of the Air Tahiti domestic flights fan out from Faaa. Inter-island flights in each group hop from one island to the next but many connections between island groups will be made via Papeete.

For international flights to and from Tahiti see the Getting There & Away chapter. For general information about air travel within French Polynesia see the Getting Around chapter, but for connections to and from an island group or an individual island see the relevant chapter or section. There is no departure tax from Tahiti.

In Papeete the main Air Tahiti office (☎ 86-40-00, 86-42-42, or on weekends 86-41-84) is upstairs in the Fare Tony Centre, which extends between Blvd Pomare and Rue du Général de Gaulle. It's open Monday to Friday from 7.30 am to noon and 1 to 4.30 pm. Qantas, Air New Zealand, Lan Chile and Hawaiian Airlines all have their offices in the Vaima Centre in central Papeete. Airline offices in Papeete include:

Air Calédonie International
(☎ 85-09-04) Faaa airport
Air France
(☎ 42-40-96 or 43-63-63) Blvd Pomare
Air New Zealand
(☎ 43-87-00) Vaima Centre, Blvd Pomare
Air Outre-Mer (AOM)
(☎ 43-25-25) Rue des Remparts

Air Moorea
(☎ 86-41-41) Faaa airport
Air Tahiti
(☎ 86-40-00, 86-42-42 or on weekends 86-41-84) Fare Tony Centre, Blvd Pomare
Hawaiian Airlines
(☎ 42-15-00) Vaima Centre, Blvd Pomare
Lan Chile
(☎ 42-64-55 or 82-64-57) Vaima Centre, Blvd Pomare
Qantas
(☎ 43-06-65 or 83-90-90) Vaima Centre, Blvd Pomare

Charter operators and helicopter services in French Polynesia include:

Air Oceania Tahiti
(☎ 82-10-47) Faaa airport
Air Alizé
(☎ 66-10-00) Raiatea
Tahiti Conquest Airlines
(☎ 85-55-54) Faaa airport
Wan Air
(☎ 83-57-36) Faaa airport
Heli-Pacific
(☎ 85-68-00) Faaa airport

Sea

Papeete is the shipping centre for all of French Polynesia. Whether it's one of the numerous daily high-speed catamarans to Moorea, the several-times-a-week shipping services to the Leeward Islands, the every-few-weeks services to the other island groups or the unscheduled copra and cargo boats, Papeete is where they arrive and depart. See the Getting Around chapter for general information on inter-island shipping and the individual island chapters or sections for specific information on travel to and from those destinations.

GETTING AROUND
To/From the Airport

Faaa airport is less than six km west of the centre of Papeete but a taxi between the airport and the city will be a clear indicator of how expensive things can be in French Polynesia. There is no airport bus service and le truck, the public transport alternative, is easy to use and very economical but unfortunately does not run in the middle of the night, when most international flights arrive and depart from Papeete.

Le Truck Any le truck going towards town from the airport, that is, east bound, or to your left as you emerge from the airport terminal, will take you straight into the centre of Papeete in about 15 minutes for a flat fare of 120 CFP during the day or 200 CFP at night. Unfortunately, le trucks tend to disappear after 10 pm and, although you should be able to find one until about 1 am, catching one in the early hours will not be easy.

At more reasonable times of the day simply emerge from the airport terminal, walk straight across the open carpark, up the steps to street level and across the road to hail a city-bound le truck.

From Papeete you want a le truck heading for Outumaoro – the destination will be clearly posted on the front.

Taxi Taxis are expensive almost anywhere in French Polynesia and Faaa airport is no exception. If your hotel offers to collect you from the airport jump at the chance. Otherwise the short drive to downtown Papeete, less than six km, will set you back 1600 CFP during the day or 2500 CFP at night. That's US$20 to US$30!

Other fares include the short run west (away from town) to the Beachcomber or Sofitel for 1000 CFP (1500 CFP at night), to the Hotel Tahiti and other places on the way into town for 1300 CFP (2300 CFP at night), or beyond Papeete, further to the east to the Hyatt for 2800 CFP (3900 CFP at night) or right up to the Bélvèdere Restaurant for 4800 CFP (6500 CFP at night). You can rent a car for a day for less than that one-way fare!

The fares are all set by the government and are posted inside the airport terminal near the taxi stand. The taxi drivers are generally quite straightforward, so there is no need to be concerned about being overcharged and they do not expect to be tipped. Taxi fares are more expensive at night from 8 pm to 6 am. Naturally, most international flights to Tahiti arrive in the middle of the night.

Airport Facilities
Money Faaa airport has a Banque Socredo office with an ATM and a Westpac office, both open Monday to Friday but closed for lunch. There's also a Westpac exchange counter in the international arrivals area where you can change money while you wait for your bags to arrive.

Post A post office counter is open Monday to Friday from 5 to 9 am and 6 to 10 pm and Saturday and Sunday 6 to 10 am. Nearby is a vending machine dispensing phonecards. The main post office in Faaa is only 250 metres from the airport and is open during the day when the airport counter is closed.

Shops & Other Facilities There's a pleasant outdoor snack bar, a shop, a number of rent-a-car and tour desks, a tourist office counter and some other low-key facilities. The airport duty-free shop is in the departure lounge.

Left Luggage Officially, Air Tahiti passengers are only allowed 10 kg of luggage. In practice tourists are usually given some leeway but if a flight was heavily loaded you could be asked to leave some of your baggage behind, or pay excess charges. There is a left-luggage office at the airport, just south of the domestic end of the terminal. It's open Monday to Friday from 6 am to 6 pm, Saturday and Sunday 6 am to noon and 2 to 6 pm, plus two hours before any international flight. The daily charges are steep: 180 CFP for a small bag, 360 CFP for a suitcase, 540 CFP for a bike or trunk, 600 CFP for a surfboard, 1000 CFP for a sailboard or malibu board. If you can it will probably be cheaper to leave stuff at your hotel. Big hotels will probably hold baggage free while the popular Tahiti Budget Lodge charges 1000 CFP a week.

Le Truck
Le truck is the standard public transport not only of Tahiti but for all of French Polynesia. It's only in Tahiti, however, that the service

is so comprehensive and well organised. Not only is le truck cheap and convenient it's also very much a part of the Polynesian experience.

Le truck is just what the name says; it's a truck with a bench seat down each side in the back. Passengers get on and get off le truck just behind the driver and pay at the end of the trip. For most routes there will be a standard fare irrespective of distance. Le trucks are privately owned and often very much a family affair, it's not uncommon for a driver's girlfriend or wife to ride along with him and collect the fares, or for the children to be lined up on the front seat, out for the ride.

Tahiti le trucks have their route number and the final destination posted on the front. From Papeete to Faaa airport, for example, you want an Outumaoro le truck, heading for a terminus just beyond Faaa. Although there are official le truck stops, complete with blue 'Le Truck' signs and sometimes with canopies and seats, le trucks will generally stop for anybody who hails them anywhere. In Papeete there are several le truck stations for the various directions.

On weekdays le truck operates from dawn until about 10 pm. On weekends the morning start is likely to be a bit later and there will be more services in the evening, as they ferry entertainment seekers to and from the bright lights of Papeete. Even on Sunday services during the day can be reasonably frequent.

Fares for the shortest trips, from Papeete to a little beyond the airport for example, start from 120 CFP, or 60 CFP for children. Out to about 20 km from Papeete the fare will go up in stages to around 200 CFP while getting to the other side of the island might cost 400 CFP.

Papeete Le Truck Stands Although you can simply hail a le truck heading out of town in the appropriate direction, there are also four colour-coded le truck terminals for the various destinations from Papeete. For le trucks heading west towards Faaa airport, the stop is in front of Papeete Market. The stands have a sign listing the services with their route numbers and destinations. The le truck stands are as follows:

Arrêt Central du Marché – red stop On Rue du Général de Gaulle the red-coded stand outside Papeete Market covers Faaa airport and the dormitory suburbs to the west, including Faaa, Punaauia and Paea, plus destinations further out like Papara and Taravao. The very popular Outumaoro le truck goes to Faaa airport and to the west coast hotels just beyond the airport. Le truck numbers from Papeete Market include 30 Outumaoro, 31 Punaauia/Punaruu, 32 Punaauia/Taapuna, 33 Pamatai, 34 Puurai/Oremu, 35 Taravao, 36 St Hilaire, 37 Teroma/Heiri, 38 Paea/Maraa and 39 Papara.

Arrêt Central du Front de Mer – blue stop On the waterfront Blvd Pomare, opposite the Tahiti Tourist Board in Fare Manihini, the blue-coded stop covers the north coast as far as Papenoo, about 17 km west of Papeete. Le truck numbers from the seafront terminus include 60 Mahina, 61 Arue, 62 Erima, 63 Papenoo, 64 Tenaho, 65 Nahoata, 66 Hamuta, 67 Princesse Heiata and 68 CPI.

Embarquements Longues Distances – yellow stop Also on Blvd Pomare, but further along opposite the Moorea Ferry Terminal, is the yellow-coded stop for le trucks heading further east along the north coast and to Tahiti Iti, the smaller loop of Tahiti's figure-eight shape. Le truck numbers from this long-distance stop include 40 Tevaiuta, 41 Teahupoo, 42 Tautira and 70 Hitiaa/Mahaena.

Gare de l'Hôtel de Ville – green stop On one side of the imposing mairie is the green-coded stop which handles le trucks heading out along the east coast as well as commuter routes to a variety of Papeete dormitory suburbs. The route most likely to be used by overseas visitors is the No 7, which heads east to the tomb of Pomare V. Le truck numbers from the Town Hall stop include 1 Titioro, 2 Mission, 3 Motu Uta, 4 Tipaerui, 5 CPS/Mamao, 6 Vairaatoa, 7 Pomare V, 8 Taupeahotu, 9 Culina and 10 Manganui.

Taxi

Taxis are expensive. From the airport to most hotels there are official government-established flat fares, but for other locations the taxis are metered. The flag fall is 800 CFP (1200 CFP at night) plus 120 CFP (240 CFP at night) per km, and additional charges for baggage. That's a pretty clear indication of the scale of taxi fares – nearly US$10 just to turn the meter on! Any trip of a reasonable length will approximate a day's car rental, so if you want wheels you may as well rent them – it's expensive but cheaper than taking a taxi.

Within the city of Papeete a fare shouldn't be over 1000 CFP. Taxi drivers are taxi drivers anywhere in the world and although problems are rare in Tahiti (with the level of fares it's hardly necessary to cheat you) any complaints should be brought to the Tahiti Tourist Board.

To phone for a taxi call the nearest taxi rank:

Faaa airport (☎ 83-30-07)
Vaima Centre, Papeete (☎ 42-33-60)
Papeete Market, Papeete (☎ 43-19-62)
Jasmin Station, Hotel Prince Hinoi, Papeete
  (☎ 42-35-98)
Le Royal Tahitien Hotel, Pirae (☎ 42-11-83)

Car

If you're intending to explore Tahiti it's worth renting a car since taxis are very expensive and le truck services rapidly fade out as you get further from Papeete. Services to the other end of the island the service is likely to be very infrequent.

Driving in Tahiti is quite straightforward and, although the accident statistics are not encouraging, the traffic is fairly light once you get away from Papeete. Apart from the autoroute, the RDO, out of Papeete to the west, the traffic doesn't go too fast. Beware of children on the road and for a sometimes casual attitude towards overtaking.

The big international names, Avis, Budget and Hertz, are found on Tahiti but they're more expensive. There are a host of local operators but the big names in the rent-a-car business in French Polynesia are Europcar and Pacificar. They often have the best rates, the widest range of cars and are the only companies you will find operating widely through French Polynesia.

While the rates are not cheap by American or even Australian standards, compared to taxi fares they soon start to look very attractive! Distances in Tahiti are not great so for most people a small car will be quite sufficient. With Pacificar and Europcar small cars

(Fiat Panda, Citroën AX, Fiat Uno, Peugeot 106, Renault Clio, Renault Twingo) are typically 1200 to 1800 CFP a day, plus 28 to 35 CFP per km, and 800 to 1200 CFP a day for collision-damage waiver.

Unlimited-km rentals on Tahiti are usually only available for two or more days and cost from 4500 to 6000 CFP per day including insurance. A 4WD Suzuki Samurai will be around 2500 CFP a day plus 40 CFP per km or from 8000 CFP a day with unlimited km. Discounts are often available but you have to ask for them. Your airline-ticket folder, coupons in tourist magazines, deals with your accommodation or even leaflets picked up straight from the rent-a-car company desk all might offer you a 10% discount off the published rates. Fuel costs around 110 CFP a litre, or about US$5 for a US gallon. Check the car over carefully when you rent it, Tahiti car-rental operators are inclined to do the same when you return it and suggest that you may have added to the usual collection of scratches and dents.

At the airport there are car-rental desks for Avis, Daniel, Europcar, Hertz, Pacificar and Tahiti Rent-a-Car. Company desks are also found at many hotels and there are offices in Papeete and at the Moorea Ferry Terminal.

Car-rental companies in Tahiti include:

Avis
  Rue Charles Vienot, Papeete (☎ 42-96-49), Beachcomber Parkroyal Hotel (☎ 82-84-00), Sofitel Maeva Beach Hotel (☎ 42-09-26), Hyatt Regency Hotel (☎ 48-12-07) and Faaa airport (☎ 82-44-23)
Budget
  Mobil Building, Fare Ute, Papeete (☎ 43-80-79)
Daniel Rent-a-Car
  Faaa airport (☎ 82-30-04)
Europcar
  on the corner of Ave Prince Hinoi and Rue des Remparts (☎ 45-24-24), Sofitel Maeva Beach Hotel (☎ 42-80-42), Tahiti Country Club (☎ 42-60-40) and Faaa airport (☎ 86-60-61)
Hertz
  Tipaerui, Papeete (☎ 42-04-71), Beachcomber Parkroyal Hotel (☎ 86-51-10), Royal Papeete (☎ 42-01-29), Tahiti Country Club (☎ 42-60-40), Hyatt Regency Hotel (☎ 48-11-22) and Faaa airport (☎ 82-55-86)

TONY WHEELER

JEAN-BERNARD CARILLET

TONY WHEELER

Top Left: Playing boules, Moerai, Rurutu, Australs
Top Right: Fishing in the lagoon, Mataiva, Gambiers
Bottom: Hawaiki Nui canoe race, Matira Beach, Bora Bora, Society Islands

JEAN-BERNARD CARILLET

JEAN-BERNARD CARILLET

TAHITI TOURISM BOARD

Top Left: Pearl farmer, Takaroa, Tuamotus
Top Right: Grafting, Takaroa, Tuamotus
Bottom: Black pearls

Pacificar
    on the corner of Rue des Ramparts and Ave
    Georges Clémenceau, Papeete (☎ 41-93-93),
    Quai des Ferries, Papeete (☎ 43-88-99), Taravao
    (☎ 57-70-70) and Faaa airport (☎ 85-02-84)
Robert Rent-a-Car
    opposite Vaima Hospital, Rue du Général de
    Gaulle (☎ 42-97-20)
Tahiti Rent-a-Car
    Chez Pierrot et Jacqueline, Fare Ute, Papeete
    (☎ 42-74-49) and Faaa airport (☎ 81-94-00)

Scooter & Bicycle

It's not as easy to rent motorscooters or bicycles on Tahiti as on a number of other islands.
Europcar rents 50 cc motorscooters from an
all-inclusive 2500 CFP for one day. Pacificar
has them in both 50 cc (2400 CFP per day)
and 80 cc (3000 CFP per day) versions.

For sales or repairs Garage Bambou
Despoir (☎ 42-80-09) in Mamao, near the
CPSA office, is a specialist in Peugeot bicycles. On Ave Georges Clémenceau in
Mamao the Tahiti Bike Center (☎ 42-53-52)
deals in a number of international brands of
mountain bikes. The Pacific Bike Shop
(☎ 42-49-00) is on the same road.

Hitching

Hitchhiking is not as easy as it used to be in
Tahiti but it's still possible, particularly when
you get to the far end of the island from
Papeete, where le truck services are infrequent. The worldwide rules for hitching
apply: it's not the safest means of travel,
women should never hitch alone and we
don't recommend it.

Around Tahiti Nui

The island coast road runs right around the
coast of Tahiti Nui, the larger of Tahiti's
double circles. The 114-km circuit is marked
by PK (*pointe kilométrique*) markers which
start at 0 in Papeete and increase in both a
clockwise and anticlockwise direction. They
meet at Taravao, the town and military base
at the narrow isthmus which connects Tahiti
Nui with Tahiti Iti. Taravao is 54 km from
Papeete clockwise (via the north coast) and
60 km anticlockwise (via the south coast).

It's relatively easy to make an island
circuit in one day by car although the trip
could easily be extended to last longer. There
are a handful, but only a handful, of places
to stay around the island. Tahiti's accommodation possibilities are predominantly
concentrated close to Papeete. If you wanted
to make the circuit by bicycle, you should
definitely allow several days. For a cyclist
the traffic can be pretty horrible up to 20 km
west of Papeete and 10 km east, but the rest
of the way around the island is fine. On a
one-day circuit not only is Taravao the PK
marker change point and approximate halfway mark but it's also the best place to stop
for a meal, as it has a variety of small restaurants.

Tahiti is not noted for its superb beaches
and along the north coast they're principally
black sand. Point Venus at PK 10 is one of
the most popular beaches close to the city
and there are short stretches of black-sand

4WDs in Tahiti

If you want to explore central Tahiti you will
need a 4WD, but some caution is required
when renting these vehicles. Europcar has
small Suzuki jeeps and Pacificar has Jeep
Wranglers and these are quite capable of tack-
ling most roads you will encounter in Tahiti.
Where you might have problems is in crossing
the rivers on the cross-island route from the
north coast to the Relais de la Maroto in the
centre of the island. If the rivers are running
deep and fast after rains, the small, petrol-
engined Suzukis may be a questionable
proposition. A larger diesel-engined 4WD may
be necessary.

Insurance compounds the problem – get
your Suzuki jeep stuck mid-river and the car-
rental company is likely to say 'sort it out
yourself'. Get it washed away and you may find
yourself buying the thing! Furthermore, the
fabric-roofed jeeps offer very poor security, so
do not leave anything inside the car and leave
the glovebox open so would-be-thieves can
see it is empty.

For a straightforward round-the-island trip a
normal car is quite suitable, and will be a better
and safer proposition than a small 4WD. ∎

beach further along, such as the small bay just past the Arahoho Blowhole at PK 22. On the opposite side from Papeete, or almost all the way around if you're making a complete circuit, there are white-sand beaches between PK 10 and PK 15 at Punaauia. Getting to the water can be tricky, but the beaches are all public property irrespective of whose property fronts on to them.

The circuit that follows goes around Tahiti Nui from Papeete in a clockwise direction and lists the appropriate PK marker numbers followed by the distance from the starting point. See the Tahiti Iti section for excursions beyond Taravao on to the smaller part of Tahiti.

THE COAST ROAD
Tomb of Pomare V (PK 4.7, 4.7 km)
On Point Outuaiai in Arue, on the water's edge, signposted and just a short detour off the coast road, is the tomb of the last of the Pomare family. Prior to the Pomares, power in Tahiti had been predominantly local, but when Pomare I enlisted *Bounty* mutineers as mercenaries the picture soon changed. Pomare II was forced to flee to Moorea in 1808 but he returned to reconquer Tahiti in

1815, bringing Christianity with him as a result of his time with the missionaries at Papetoai.

He demonstrated his new enthusiasm by constructing a gigantic church at this point, on the site of an equally large marae to the god Oro. His Royal Mission Chapel was over 200 metres long, held up by 30 or so great tree-trunk columns, with 30-odd doors and 130 windows. Up to 6000 worshippers could crowd inside but it soon decayed after Pomare II's death in 1821 and a more durable and more modestly proportioned wooden building replaced the original. In turn it gave way to a 12-sided chapel around the turn of the century and today's building is a slightly larger 1978 version.

The Tomb of Pomare V looks like a stubby lighthouse made of coral boulders. It was actually built in 1879 for Queen Pomare who died in 1877 after 50 years in power. Pomare V, her ungrateful son, had her remains evicted a few years later, and when he died in 1891 it became his tomb. It's said that he drank himself to death and that the Grecian urn replica atop the structure should be a liquor bottle. Gauguin witnessed the funeral and described it in his book *Noa-Noa*.

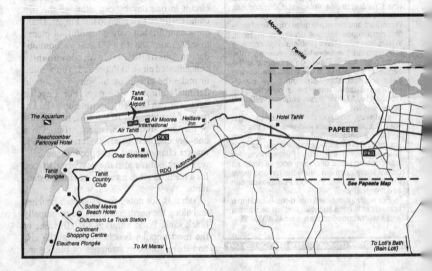

Other Pomares are buried (or may be buried – their tombs are unmarked) in the Cimetière Pomare opposite the artisanat building at PK 5.4. There's a board at the cemetery indicating where Pomare I, II, III and IV are supposed to be interred.

On the mountain side of the road at PK 5.4, just past the turn-off to the Pomare Tomb, is the former home of James Norman Hall, coauthor of the *Bounty* saga which the first two Hollywood films were based on. Hall died in 1951 and is buried nearby but the house is not open to the public so there is nothing to see.

Taharaa Point & One Tree Hill (PK 8.1, 8.1 km)

Taharaa Point is the western boundary of Matavai Bay, the favourite locale of early European explorers who seemed enormously keen on renaming the point. Samuel Wallis, the European discoverer of Tahiti in 1767, had a preliminary tangle with the Tahitians at this point and after demonstrating the destructive power of his cannons he renamed the point 'Skirmish Hill'. When Cook came along two years later he noted a solitary *atae* tree on the point and renamed it 'One Tree Hill'.

There are fine views back towards Papeete from the viewpoint just at the entrance to the Hyatt Regency Hotel. Don't look straight down towards the beach – the viewpoint is also an unofficial garbage dump. The Hyatt Regency is an interesting piece of architecture, stepping down the hill towards the black-sand beach. It was originally opened in 1968 as the Taharaa Hotel, taking the Tahitian name for the point.

Point Venus & Matavai Bay (PK 10, 10 km)

Mahina marks the eastern end of Papeete's coastal sprawl and the site of Tahiti's first real contact with Europe. Wallis and Bougainville had come to Tahiti two years earlier and Wallis had actually anchored in Matavai Bay, but their visits had been fleeting affairs; Cook's three-month sojourn in 1769 was a different story. Cook is remembered as a fearless explorer and skilled navigator but on his first visit to Tahiti his mission was foremost a scientific one, to record the transit of Venus across the face of the sun in an attempt

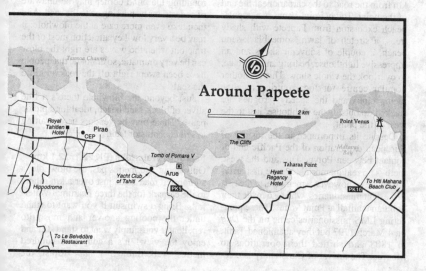

to calculate how far the sun was from the earth.

Point Venus, the promontory which marks the eastern end of Matavai Bay, was the site of Cook's observatory and it was to Matavai Bay which Cook returned on his two subsequent expeditions. Until Papeete began to develop around the 1820s, Matavai remained the principal anchorage for visiting European ships. Bligh too was to make a lengthy stay here during his disastrous visit in 1788-79 although he later shifted anchorages to the west of the point where Pomare V's tomb is located.

Of course there is no trace left today of those early visits. No memorial survives from that time and the Cook expedition's fortifications, erected to protect the surveying equipment from the Tahitians' expertise in theft, have long disappeared. Nevertheless Point Venus retains a historic resonance, a reminder that this was the site of one of history's most daring expeditionary adventures. Some more recent memorials add to the interest.

There is no sign to Point Venus from the main road, just turn off when you see shops and activity at the PK-10 point. It's about a km from the road to the carpark near the end of the point. Today Point Venus is a popular beach excursion from Papeete with shady trees, a stretch of lawn, some black-sand beach, a couple of souvenir shops and an impressive lighthouse, bearing an 1867 date, to overlook the whole show. This is another popular centre for local outrigger canoe racing clubs and the speedy pirogues are stacked up outside the clubhouse, just to the west of the point.

Despite its importance in the history of European exploration of the Pacific and of contact between Polynesians and the west, there is no real memorial to those first arrivals. There is, however, a memorial to the first Protestant missionaries, who also made their Tahitian landfall at Point Venus. These pioneering LMS missionaries came on the *Duff* on 4 March 1797 but they abandoned Tahiti in 1808 and shifted their operations to Moorea. The arrival of Christianity is cele-

brated at Point Venus each year. They were not the first missionaries to visit Tahiti as two Spanish padres had been landed further east at Tautira on Tahiti Iti back in 1774, but their short stay was spectacularly unsuccessful.

Papenoo (PK 17, 17 km)

There's a popular surfing break just before the headland which signals the start of the small village of Papenoo. A long bridge crosses the Papenoo River at the far end of the village and the 4WD route up the Papenoo Valley to the Relais de la Maroto starts up the west side of the river. It crosses the river numerous times on its way right into the centre of the island, following this valley which cuts through the ancient crater rim. See the Across Tahiti Nui section for more information about this interesting route.

Arahoho Blowhole (PK 22, 22 km)

Appropriate swell conditions produce a geyser-like fountain of water from the blowhole (*le trou du souffleur*) by the road just before Tiarei. The blowhole is right on the corner and there's a carpark just beyond, if you're coming from Papeete. Take care walking back to the blowhole, as traffic rounding the blind corner may be unaware of pedestrians wandering on to the road. And then take even more care at the blowhole: it may be a very low-key attraction most of the time but when the waves are right the blow can be very dramatic, so dramatic that people have been swept right off the rock and into the sea!

Just beyond the blowhole there's a fine sliver of black-sand beach, ideal for a picnic pause. There may be vendors here, waiting to sell coconuts or fruit.

Faarumai Waterfalls (PK 22.1, 22.1 km)

Only about 100 metres past the blowhole, a signposted road leads just over a km inland to the carpark for the three Faarumai Waterfalls. Bring a swimsuit if you want to stand under the cooling shower and mosquito repellent if you simply want to stand still and enjoy the view! It's a couple of hundred metres' walk through a *mape* forest, the native chestnut trees, to Vaimahutu, the first of the waterfalls. Another 20-minute stroll leads to the other two falls, the Haamarere Iti and Haamarere Rahi, which stand almost side by side.

Through Tiarei & Mahaena

At PK 25 there's a picture-postcard **copra plantation** beside the road with neat rows of coconut palms aligned across a uniform green lawn. Producing copra, the dried coconut meat, is hard work, and although it remains an important contributor to the French Polynesian economy its relevance has declined and copra production is now predominantly an outer island activity.

The French takeover of Tahiti in 1843 was not accepted happily by the Tahitians and in 1844 a pitched battle took place at Mahaena (PK 32.5). There is nothing to see of the **battle site** and the struggle ended disastrously for the Tahitian defenders. Although they had dug extensive trenches, they were overwhelmed by the sheer firepower of the French onslaught. This was the first and last outright battle between Tahitian and French forces. After this the Tahitians resorted to guerrilla strikes until their final defeat in 1846.

If the weather had been cloudy over Point Venus at the critical moment on 3 June 1769, Captain Cook's long voyage to Tahiti to observe the transit of Venus would have been in vain. So he established a second observation post on tiny **Motu Taaupiri**, a km off the shore around PK 34. As further insurance a third post, commanded by Joseph Banks, was set up on a motu close to Hauru Point on Moorea.

Hitiaa & Bougainville's Anchorage (PK 38, 38 km)

A plaque on the river bridge at the village of Hitiaa commemorates the visit to Tahiti in April 1768 by the French explorer Louis-Antoine de Bougainville. The two ships under his command, *La Boudeuse* and *L'Étoile*, entered the lagoon through the Tapora Pass, also known as the Pass of the Boudeuse, and turned north to anchor near the tiny motus of Variararu and Oputotara. It was not a good anchorage and during their brief nine-day pause no less than six anchors were lost. Future visitors anchored in Matavai Bay, where Wallis had stopped the previous year and where Cook would stay the year after.

Although Bougainville's visit to Tahiti was so short, his glowing accounts of Tahiti as a paradise of stunning beauty and amazing sexual freedom inspired a mythical vision of the islands which has survived to this day. Bougainville, a gentleman and scholar, dubbed the island New Cythera, comparing it to the original Greek island birthplace of Aphrodite, the goddess of love.

The small village of Hitiaa has a new church and a charming but abandoned and fast-decaying, old one, topped by a tower made of coral blocks.

Taravao (PK 54, 54 km)

Strategically situated at the narrow isthmus connecting big Tahiti Nui with small Tahiti Iti, the town of Taravao has been a military base on and off since 1844 when the first French fort was established. The original fort was intended to forestall Tahitian guerrilla forces, opposed to the French takeover, from mounting operations on to Tahiti Nui from Tahiti Iti.

From Taravao roads run along the north and south coasts of Tahiti Iti. The central road into the Tahiti Iti highlands commences a short distance along the north-coast road. Although there is little of interest in the town, it does have shops, banks, fuel stations and a number of small restaurants so this is a good place for a lunch stop on a round-the-island circuit.

Arrival Point of the First Tahitians (PK 52, 62 km)

Tahitian legends relate that the great migration canoes which carried their ancestors across the Pacific made their Tahitian landfall at this point. As a result the chiefs of this district were much more important than those from other parts of the island. Tales of the great migrations, phenomenal feats of ocean navigation, are treated with enormous respect in Polynesia. Their departure and arrival points are pinpointed with equal exactitude on Rarotonga in the Cook Islands and at Taipa on the far north of New Zealand.

Botanical Gardens & Gauguin Museum (PK 51.2, 62.8 km)

Tahiti's fine Botanical Gardens and the interesting Gauguin Museum share an entrance road and carpark. There is a café at the entrance building to the gardens; although it is cheaper than the Restaurant du Musée Gauguin, which is half a km further west, it is definitely not a place for an economical snack. It is possible to get to the gardens and museum from Papeete by le truck but the last return trip usually departs early in the afternoon. Check the departure times or risk being stranded. Mosquitoes in the gardens can be fierce.

Botanical Gardens The gardens are open daily from 9 am to 5 pm and entry is 400 CFP. Interestingly, the gardens concentrate more on exotic vegetation than on Tahiti's own lush plant life. Walking paths wend through the 137-hectare garden past ponds, palms and a superb thicket of bamboo. Look for the huge Galapagos tortoise, the survivor of several of these massive and slow-moving reptiles which were brought to Tahiti in the 1930s for the children of writer Charles Nodhoff, coauthor with James Norman Hall of the *Bounty* sagas.

The Botanical Gardens were founded in 1919 by Harrison Smith, an MIT (Massachusetts Institute of Technology) professor who retired at the age of 37 and devoted the rest of his life to developing these gardens. He introduced many plants to Tahiti including the large, thick-skinned South-East Asian citrus fruit known in Tahiti as *pamplemousse*, the French word for grapefruit, although it is rather different and known in other locales as the *pomelo*. Unfortunately, Smith also introduced one or two botanical disasters which Tahiti could well have done without. He died in 1947 and the garden eventually became public property.

Gauguin Museum The museum is open daily from 9 am to 5 pm and entry is 500 CFP. Only minor works by Gauguin remain in Tahiti so this is a museum of his life rather than a gallery of his work. The Musée d'Orsay in Paris has lent one of its panels from Gauguin's *Maison du Jouir* (The House of Pleasure) in Hiva Oa in the Marquesas to the museum but normally all five are in Paris. Four of them were acquired in 1903 and the last one in the 1980s with the Segalen collection.

The museum is entered through a gift shop with books, cards and a small collection of island crafts. A series of buildings in the beautiful museum gardens lead you step by step through Gauguin's troubled and uncomfortable life. There are exhibits on his earlier painting in Europe and the Caribbean, the family he abandoned, his clashes with French bureaucracy in French Polynesia and his work in Tahiti and the Marquesas. There are reproductions of many of his works but they are not of any quality – the museum is far more interesting as an introduction to his life. One display makes interesting comparisons between his work and Japanese paintings and ascribes to these the inspiration for some of his work.

A gallery within the complex shows temporary exhibits and works by local artists and Europeans who have worked in Polynesia. These interesting works include paintings by the English painter Constance Gibbon Cummings, whose short visit to the islands in 1877 was amazingly productive, the Dutch painter Adrian Hermann Gouwe, who visited the Society Islands in 1827, and Charles Alfred Le Moine, who worked in Tahiti and the Marquesas.

The Gauguin Museum gardens are home to three superb *tikis* from Raivavie in the Austral Islands. The tikis were brought to Tahiti by the yacht *La Denise* in 1933 and had museum homes in Papeete and Mamao before being transferred to the Gauguin Museum in 1965. Tikis do not like to be moved so it's probable that these three shifts have stored up a lot of trouble for some foolish individuals. The huge figure beside the walkway stands 2.2 metres high and weighs in at 900 kg. It's a baby compared to the figure towards the waterfront, which stands 2.7 metres high and weighs 2110 kg. A third, smaller figure stands beside the giant. Although the museum is often dimly lit and wastes the opportunity to bring Gauguin's work vividly to life in its natural setting, it is still definitely worth a visit.

Vaipahi Garden & Vaima Pool (PK 49, 65 km)

Beyond the Botanical Gardens there are more well-tended gardens along the mountain side of the road. Just past these gardens is the Bain de Vaima or Vaima Pool. The Vaipahi Waterfall is a few minutes' walk inland, dropping from pool to pool through a stand of stately mape trees. There are great views from a small plateau beyond the falls and there are a number of short walks you can take from here. A one-hour walk brings you back to the road at PK 50.2.

Mataiea

At PK 47.5 is the turn-off for the rough track up to Vaihiria Lake, the Relais de la Maroto and on across the island to the north coast. See the Across Tahiti Nui section of this chapter for more details.

During his first visit to Tahiti Gauguin lived in Mataiea, near PK 46, between 1891 and 1893. Although he was sick and impoverished, this was a happy period in his so often depressed life and he produced works which include *Two Women on the Beach, Woman with a Mango* and *Ia orana Maria – Hail Mary*. The church of St John the Baptist, dating from 1857, is just outside the town. The curious Protestant chapel by the road in the village looks vaguely like a Hindu temple.

The Mataiea district ends with the golf course at Atimaono at PK 42, the site of the abortive Terre Eugénie cotton plantation in the 1860s. For a brief period during the American Civil War cotton growing made economic sense but the end of the war in 1865 brought Tahiti's cotton growing days to an abrupt end. Descendants of some of the Chinese workers, imported to supplant the unwilling Polynesian labour force, are still

Gauguin Museum

TAHITI

around. The cotton plantation, and other land devoted to coffee and sugar production, played an enormously important role in the Tahitian economy for some years and James Stewart, the Scotsman who ran the operation, was a very rich man while it prospered.

Marae Mahaiatea (PK 39.2, 74.8 km)

Just east of the village of Papara the Marae Mahaiatea was the most magnificent marae in Tahiti at the time of Cook's first visit. The great navigator measured it at 80 metres by 27 metres at its base, rising in 11 great steps to a height of 13 metres. Banks was equally impressed and marvelled at the sheer amount of labour which must have gone into its construction. At the time of their visit in 1769 the marae was probably only a few years old and was said to have been built in only two years. It was the marae of Obarea, the 'queen' of Tahiti who befriended both Wallis and Cook and was an ancestor of the Pomare dynasty.

With the decline of the Polynesian religion, the splendid structure soon decayed, a process speeded along by natural causes and its use as a convenient quarry site for local projects. Today the crumbling remains of the marae are still impressive for their sheer size but it's initially hard to conceive that this was actually an artificial construction. Only as you clamber up the tree-covered 'hill' does it become clear that this is no natural feature. Restoring it would clearly be a mammoth task.

Coming from Papeete take the first turn towards the sea past the 39 km sign. The turn is between the roadside Beach Burger restaurant and the PK 39 sign if you're heading towards Papeete. Follow the road all the way towards the coast, about half a km. In the middle of the carpark area what looks like a densely vegetated hill is, on closer inspection, the massive remains of the stone marae.

Museum of Seashells (PK 36, 78 km, Papara)

In the village of Papara the Musée du Coquillage is open daily from 8 am to 5 pm and admission is 300/200 CFP for adults/chil-

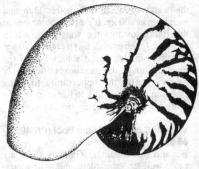

Nautilus shell

dren. The associated shop sells shells, something which doesn't sit well when their rarity and importance is emphasised in the museum.

Maraa Grotto (PK 28.5, 85.5 km, Paea)

Alongside the road a manicured path runs through a garden past a series of overhung caverns, with crystal-clear pools and ferny grottoes. It's a popular stop on round the island circuits.

Paea Maraes

In the Paea district the **Marae Arahurahu** at PK 22.5 is the best looking marae on the island although it was in fact only a secondary marae, of no great significance. Not only has it been restored, however, but it has also been embellished with impressive tikis and a variety of bamboo and cane huts, all of which make it an interesting site, perhaps approximating what a marae might have looked like in its prime. The lushly photogenic site is used for performances, particularly during the July Heiva festivities.

Marae Tataa at PK 19 may have been much more important, but it's on private land and hard to get to; although it was restored in 1973. The village is centred around the **Orofero River** at PK 20, a popular surfing site. This was also the spot where, in 1815, Pomare II fought the battle which brought him back to power over Tahiti and also ensured the ascendancy of Christianity.

Museum of Tahiti & Its Islands (PK 15.1, 98.9 km)

Only 15 km from Papeete in the anticlockwise direction, the Musée de Tahiti et des Îles is in Punaauia and has one of the best collections in the Pacific. The museum is right on the coast, several hundred metres' walk from the coast road after the Punaruu bridge. From Papeete a Punaauia le truck will drop you at the road junction for 160 CFP. In the afternoon check the time of the last return trip, which is generally about 4.30 pm.

The museum is open Tuesday to Sunday from 9.30 am to 5.30 pm and entry (via a bookshop) is 500 CFP. It's in a large garden and if you get tired of history, culture and art you can wander out to the water's edge to watch the surfers at one of Tahiti's most popular breaks.

The museum is divided into four distinct sections – geography and natural history, pre-European culture, the European era and outdoor exhibits. The museum's highlights include:

The Polynesian Environment The geography of Polynesia is shown with some fascinating views of the picture below the water as well as above. Volcanoes, reefs and the formation of atolls are explained and theories on the great Pacific migration voyages are detailed.

Agriculture, Animal Husbandry & Hunting When the first Europeans arrived the Polynesian economy was predominantly a subsistence one, although fertile soil and the abundant waters around the island meant that survival was easy. Horticulture consisted chiefly of growing taro in swampy places and irrigated terraces, and growing sweet potatoes on small sunny terraces where the plants were covered with humus. Digging sticks were virtually the only farming implements although in the Tuamotus shovels of pearl or turtle shell were used. Growing breadfruit was no problem at all and animal husbandry consisted of letting the pigs, dogs and chickens (the only domesticated animals prior to

Cook's arrival) run free. Birds were the only wildlife hunted, both for their flesh and feathers. The *Journal of James Morrison* reported that 'they catch birds by putting breadfruit sap on lengths of bamboo on which the birds alight'.

Polynesian Culture The exhibits on pre-European Polynesian culture feature a wonderful display of tikis and petroglyphs, many of them from the Australs and Marquesas. They include a huge wooden tiki and a very expressive large stone one, both from the Marquesas.

Displays about Polynesian games and sports include archery equipment, surfboards (surfing originated in the Society Islands and was carried from there to Hawaii before being discovered by the west) and even some of the enormously heavy stones used in stone-lifting contests. Also on display are drums, split drums and the xylophones that were once used in the Marquesas.

Warfare & Weapons Until Europeans arrived, bringing with them more sophisticated weapons, no rulers exercised more than purely local power. The exhibits include clubs, daggers and spears. Weapons were often used in an unusual fashion: spears, for instance, were mainly used as a hitting weapon rather than to throw or pierce. Archery was almost only used in ceremonial or sporting events. Only in Mangareva were bows and arrows used in warfare.

European Exploration The early explorers – Wallis, Bougainville, Cook and the rest – are all featured. The displays relating to early European contact also include cannons off the *Mathilda*, an English whaling ship (but French built) which was wrecked on Moruroa Atoll in 1792. They were recovered by divers from the nuclear-testing operations on the atoll in 1968.

The Nobility & Priests Symbols of the power of chiefs and the nobility include the belts of red feathers which were worn only for a single day at the time of investiture of a future great chief. Plaited fans with carved handles were another symbol of power, and the collection of chiefs' wooden stools, including the one Omai carried to Europe with him when he was taken to Britain on Cook's second voyage, are also featured. This is the same stool Omai was holding when his portrait was painted by Nathaniel Dance in 1775. It recently came up for auction in London and was returned to Tahiti. There are some fine headdresses and necklaces of dolphins' teeth.

Religion Pre-European religious exhibits include funeral house posts and wooden figures of gods. The explorers were a passing wave but the European missionaries had a lasting effect on the islands. The missionary exhibits include an interesting panel on the first abortive Mormon missions between 1844 and 1852. They were back in action later in the century and are probably the most active current missionaries. John Williams, the pioneering LMS missionary, is featured, as is Father Laval, whose work in Mangareva still raises so many questions.

Colonial Polynesia The museum features exhibits on the Tahitian royal family, the Pomares, who briefly extended their control further than any previous Polynesian rulers. They were then subsumed by the growing European power. There's an interesting photo collection on turn-of-the-century Tahiti and some fascinating displays about the Chinese community who first turned up to work on Tahiti's short-lived cotton plantations and later as shopkeepers and merchants. Of course the numerous writers who sought inspiration in Tahiti are also well covered.

Tourism's influence on modern Tahiti is so widespread it's enlightening to realise that there was indeed a pretourism Tahitian economy in which copra and fishing played an important part. For a time the mainstay of the French Polynesian economy was, however, the phosphate deposits on the tiny island of Makatea.

Outside the Museum The displays conclude outside with canoes, pirogues and tikis. The museum gardens extend right to the lagoon side where you can watch Tahitian and visiting surfers on the nearby break.

Punaauia

The Museum of Tahiti is in the Papeete urban strip and there are good beaches between PK 15 and PK 10 through Punaauia. The most expensive homes in Tahiti are found along this stretch of coast, often high above the coast where they enjoy fresh breezes and fine views across the strait to Moorea.

On the hillside above the bridge at PK 14.8 in Punaruu Valley is the site of a French fortification, from the 1842-46 conflict when France took control of Tahiti. It's now used as a TV relay station. A walking trail leads further up the valley to the Tamanu Plateau at around 600 metres, an area known for its wild orange trees, escapees from the citrus plantations which once grew here.

Site of Gauguin's Home (PK 12.6,101.4 km)

Gauguin lived here in 1897-98 during his second Tahitian visit, but there is no trace of his wooden colonial-style home, built by a river on the lagoon side. During his unhappy stay – he was in debt and ill, his daughter Aline had died and he tried to commit suicide by taking arsenic – he still managed to paint 60-odd pictures, including some of his masterpieces: *Nevermore, The White Horse* and the evocatively named *Where Do We Come From? What Are We? Where Are We Going?* Of this picture Gauguin wrote: 'Before dying, I painted this with such a painful passion, in horrible circumstances, and with a bright vision, without any corrections, that the hurry vanishes and life arises'.

His house stood just south of the 2+2 = 4 Primary School at PK 12.5. The school was named by the landowner who donated the site. Dubious about the usefulness of the French school system in the tropics, he reasoned that at least the children would learn to add!

Lagoonarium (PK 11 km, 103 km)

In Punaauia, well into the Papeete urban sprawl, the Lagoonarium is a pleasant little tourist trap, a meshed-in area of lagoon with an underwater viewing room you reach by climbing down steps through a giant concrete shark's mouth. If you haven't had an opportunity to do some snorkelling or diving you may find it interesting to watch the small sharks and other creatures at their own level. The Lagoonarium is open daily from 9 am to 6 pm and entry is 500 CFP, and 300 CFP for children. The entrance to the Lagoonarium is part of the Captain Bligh Restaurant, a popular stop for tourist trips. Diners can visit the Lagoonarium without charge.

ORGANISED TOURS

Any hotel tour desk or the waterfront Mers et Loisirs office (☎ 43-97-99) will sign up visitors for all-day bus tours around the island. These trips typically cost around 3000 to 4500 CFP, but check if entry charges and lunch are included or not. Places they may visit include Point Venus, the Arahoho Blowhole, the Faarumai Waterfalls, the Taravao Plateau lookout point on Tahiti Iti, the Botanical Gardens, the Gauguin Museum, the Maraa Grotto, the Museum of Tahiti and the Lagoonarium. Tahiti Ata Mou'a (☎ 41-99-00) and Paradise Tours (☎ 42-49-36 or 42-55-86) are only two of the many operators.

Trips into the interior of the island require more than just a bus. Tahiti Ata Mou'a (☎ 85-55-71), Tefaarahi Adventure Tours (☎ 56-41-24) and Adventure Eagle Tours (☎ 41-37-63) use 4WD vehicles to make half-day trips up to Mt Marau (1200 metres) and round to the Arahoho Blowhole and Faarumai Waterfalls for 5000 CFP per person. The Mt Marau tour or the waterfall and blowhole tour can be done separately for 3000 CFP. Ron's Services (☎ 46-60-80) does similar tours as does Tahiti Safari Expeditions (☎ 42-14-15), which also conducts hiking trips.

Hourly tours of Papeete harbour are made every day for 1200 CFP (1000 CFP for children) and depart from in front of the post office. Check with your hotel or Tahiti Nui Travel (☎ 54-02-00) in the Vaima Centre. Walking tours of Papeete are made from Papeete Market – look for the walking tour kiosk in the market. At the other extreme, Heli-Pacific (☎ 85-68-00) does helicopter tours over the lagoon or the central mountains. The two-day walk across the centre of Tahiti can be condensed to just 35 minutes!

PLACES TO STAY

There are remarkably few places to stay on Tahiti once you've left Papeete. On the north coast to Taravao there is only one small hotel beyond the large Hyatt Regency Hotel, although there are a couple of places on Tahiti Iti, just a few km past Taravao.

On the south coast there are a number of small pensions through Punaaiau and Papae, just beyond Faaa airport and 10 to 20 km from the centre of Papeete, but this is so close to Papeete it's still within the town's urban sprawl.

The North Coast

Fare Nana'o (☎ 57-18-14, fax 57-76-10) is right on the water's edge on the north coast at PK 52, only a few km before Taravao near the isthmus between Tahiti Nui and Tahiti Iti. This imaginative little place has seven individualistic bungalows ranging from a tree house to a Polynesian-style over-water bungalow. Several of them have kitchen facilities and prices for two people range from 5000 CFP for the tree house to 7500 CFP. Some of the rooms have their own separate bathroom facilities but only one of them has an attached bathroom. Additional people, in the rooms that accommodate three or four, are 1000 CFP. Although Fare Nana'o is a pleasant change from the featureless boxes which characterise so much lower-priced Polynesian accommodation, this type of natural construction – wood, stone, pandanus – requires constant upkeep in a tropical climate and can easily get run down.

Transfers from the airport can be arranged and bookings can be made through BP 7193, Taravao, Tahiti. Credit cards are not accepted.

The South Coast

If anything the south coast is even worse for accommodation options than the north. There are a number of low-priced pensions between 15 and 20 km from Papeete in Punaauia and Paea but these are really suburbs of Papeete; further along the coast there is nowhere to stay.

Very few of the Punaauia and Paea pensions have any signs or identification so you should telephone ahead to make arrangements to stay. This is quite a pleasant location, close enough to Papeete for easy connections on le truck, convenient for the airport, close to the museum and other tourist attractions, and along one of the island's best stretches of beach.

Just beyond the Tahiti Museum, *Chez Michel et Armelle* (☎ 58-42-43) is on the lagoon side of the road at PK 15.5 in Punaauia. The house has three rooms with double beds, a living room, kitchen and bathroom. Including breakfast the cost for a single/double in this friendly beachside place is 5000/6000 CFP per day. There is a sign on the road, bookings can be made through BP 13291, Papeete, Tahiti, and credit cards are not accepted.

Pension Te Miti (☎ 58-46-61) is on the mountain side of the main road at PK 18.5 in Paea, only about 200 metres from the shore. There is a sign on the main road. This friendly and well-run place has small dormitories with four beds at 1500 CFP per person and three rooms at 3000 to 4000 CFP. Breakfast is included and other meals are available. Camping is also possible.

Other Punaauia and Papae places are generally less accessible or aimed at the longer-term visitor. *Chez Va'a* (☎ 42-94-32) is at PK 8, but well back up the mountain side. There's just one room at 3500/6000 CFP as a single/double including breakfast. There is a swimming pool and airport transfers are provided. Bookings can be made through BP 828, Papeete, Tahiti. *Le Bellevue* (☎ 58-47-04) at PK 16 also has just one room which costs 15,000 CFP for the first two nights, single or double. There's a kitchenette but this is principally a longer-term

place. Bookings can be made through BP 13451, Punaauia, Tahiti, and airport transfers are provided.

On the lagoon side of the road at PK 17.5 *Chez Tea* (☎ 58-29-27) has two bungalows each with two rooms. It's close to the beach and the rooms cost 5000 CFP as a single or double. Bookings can be made through BP 13069, Punaauia, Tahiti. Again this is generally a longer-term proposition although the owner also has a room in a house further west at PK 29. *Les Bougainvilliers* (☎ 53-28-02), at PK 22 in Paea, has eight apartments from 12,000 CFP per day for two people. Bookings can be made through BP 63, Papeete, Tahiti.

In Paea the *Hiti Moana Villa* (☎ 57-93-33, fax 57-94-44) has three bungalows by the lagoon and a swimming pool. Nightly costs range from 8000 CFP for two people and bookings can be made through BP 10865, Paea, Tahiti. In Papara at PK 39.5, near the golf course at Atimaono and the beach at Mataiea, *Fare Ratere* (☎ 57-48-29) has two bungalows with a kitchen and living room. This is a more expensive place with daily prices up towards 20,000 CFP.

PLACES TO EAT

Finding a place to eat around the island is much simpler than finding a place to stay. There are small shops, some of them selling sandwiches, dotted round the coast. Tourist-style restaurants are found along the south coast including the *Captain Bligh Restaurant* at PK 11.4 and the *Restaurant du Musée Gauguin* at PK 50.5. Other restaurants, like the popular *Chez Bob Tardieu*, are dotted round the coast and there a number of small restaurants at Taravao, the mid-point on the island circuit.

The North Coast

Once you've left the Papeete urban sprawl, east of Mahina, there are not many places to eat before Taravao, at the crossover point of Tahiti's figure eight. Small snack bars are fairly common, like *Snack Terehau*, opposite the Papenoo surfing break and just before the village which is at PK 17. *Snack Tiarei* is at

PK 28, a little beyond the Arahoho Blowhole and Faarumai Waterfalls, and it makes good French bread sandwiches.

At PK 51.8, just before Taravao, *Chez Bob Tardieu* (☎ 57-14-14) has a very pleasant waterfront setting and seafood specialities at 1900 to 3000 CFP. Despite the price levels it's a popular lunch spot and is also open for dinner except on Sunday and Monday.

Taravao

Taravao, at PK 54 in the clockwise direction or PK 60 anticlockwise, is about halfway round Tahiti Nui and is also the crossover point to Tahiti Iti and has quite a collection of snack bars and restaurants. Each seems to have its own opening and closing pattern which also seems to vary from year to year.

First up on the north side is *Snack Restaurant Chez Myriam* (☎ 57-71-01) with an indoor restaurant section, outdoor tables, light meals at 850 to 1300 CFP, snacks and ice cream. Next is the more expensive *Snack Restaurant Maeva Terrasse* (☎ 57-12-60), with a blend of French and Tahitian dishes. Chez Guilloux (☎ 57-12-91) is a small and straightforward place while *Ahki Vairua* (☎ 57-20-38) has Chinese food. *L'Escale Restaurant* (☎ 57-07-16) has fine French cuisine in this rather remote location. It's closed on Sunday and Monday nights.

The South Coast

Continuing on from Taravao there is a rather larger choice of restaurants along the south coast. *Jardin Snack* is at the Botanical Garden, right by the lagoon edge. Unfortunately, this simple little café is not cheap, since most dishes are around 1800 CFP, and credit cards are not accepted.

Just half a km beyond the Botanical Gardens and Gauguin Museum, the *Restaurant du Musée Gauguin* (☎ 57-13-80) is at PK 50.5. It's principally aimed at group tours and shows little interest in individual visitors. Lunch is served from noon to 2 pm and an individual is likely to find the door firmly shut at 1.59 pm.

The *Atimaono Golf Club House* (☎ 57-40-32) at PK 40.2 does lunch, dinner and snacks.

Beach Burger (☎ 57-41-03) is a bright and breezy restaurant on the beach side of the road at PK 39.3, about 100 metres before the turn-off to Marae Mahaiatea if you're heading towards Papeete. At PK 32.5 in Papara the *Nuutere Restaurant* (☎ 57-41-15) serves French food with a Tahitian flavour for lunch and dinner daily.

Punaauia is on the western edge of the Papeete coastal strip and there are quite a few dining possibilities for both tourists and local residents in the fashionable suburbs along this strip of coast. They include the beachfront *Coco's Restaurant* (☎ 58-21-08) at PK 13, with a very French menu and a 5 pm champagne happy hour. It's closed on Sunday. Along this same strip is *Pacific Burger*, a bright-looking open-air place on the coast side of the road. The *Captain Bligh Restaurant* (☎ 43-62-90), at the Lagoonarium at PK 11.4, is a very tourist-oriented restaurant with a Tahitian show on Friday and Saturday evenings. It's closed on Monday. The lagoonside *Auberge du Pacifique* (☎ 43-98-30) is at PK 11.2 and features another French-Polynesian menu. It's closed on Tuesday. There are several other places in Punaauia.

Around Tahiti Iti

The smaller loop of Tahiti's figure eight is Tahiti Iti, little Tahiti as opposed to the larger loop, which is Tahiti Nui or big Tahiti. There are three roads into Tahiti Iti: a road 18 km along the north coast to Tautira, another 18 km along the south coast to Teahupoo and a third up the centre to a lookout. The PK markers start at 0 at Taravao for both the north and south coast roads. The north and south roads do not meet and, although walking trails extend around the coast from both road ends, the sheer Te Pari cliff faces cut the trails off so walking right around the coast is very difficult. There are, however, some superb walks on Tahiti Iti including a fine walk from Tautira to a series of maraes and petroglyphs in the Vaiote River valley.

Despite the cliffs, walking trips are made right around the peninsula (see the Activities section later in this chapter for more details).

NORTH ROAD TO TAUTIRA

The coast road from Taravao runs through Pueu, past steep hills with numerous waterfalls, to Tautira. This stretch of coast has the highest rainfall in Tahiti. It's easy to walk beyond Tautira for a further 12 km.

Tautira & Vaitepiha Bay (PK 18)

The north coast of Tahiti Iti has had some interesting European visitors. In 1772 the Spanish captain Boenechea anchored his ship *Aguilla* off the Aiurua River, about 10 km beyond Tautira, and then closer to the village. He was followed by Cook, on his second expedition in 1774. Later the same year the *Aguilla* was back and, although Boenechea died during this stay, a Spanish mission was briefly established at Tautira. The *Aguilla* was back again, this time with a new commander, a year later when the extremely unsuccessful mission was abandoned. The two Spanish priests had been afraid to venture out of their stockade. Cook was also back for another visit to Tautira in 1777. See the History section in the Facts about the Islands chapter for more about this interesting series of European visitors.

More missionaries followed in 1836, when the *Eliza* dropped two French Catholic workers near Tautira. They arrived in Tahiti at this remote point because they were well aware of the strong antipathy the Protestant missionaries held against Catholicism making any inroads into their territory. The two missionaries walked to Papeete where they were soon arrested and deported. This was ultimately to prove a very bad decision on the Protestants' part for it eventually led to the French takeover of Tahiti and the end of the Protestant monopoly. One of the missionaries was Honoré Laval, whose time in the Gambier Archipelago was so controversial.

Fifty years later Tautira was honoured with another European visitor when the unhealthy, but very successful, Robert Louis Stevenson came by in 1888 in his ship the *Casco*. Stevenson and his party stayed in the village for nearly two months. See the Tahiti Literati aside in the Facts for the Visitor chapter for more details.

West of Tautira

The sealed road ends at Tautira but you can bump along the lagoonside for another km or two before the road finally becomes impassable to vehicles. A good walking track leads round the coast for another 12 or so km before reaching the Te Pari Cliffs beyond the Vaiote River which make walking all the way to Teahupoo on the south coast of Tahiti Iti so difficult.

Boenechea anchored for a time off the Aiurua River, about 10 km around the coast from Tautira. Two km further along is the Vaiote River, with some noted petroglyphs inscribed on boulders near the coast and a series of maraes inland in the valley. See the Activities section of this chapter for information about walking to the Vaiote Valley.

Offshore at this point are two motus; Fenua Ino is the larger of the two and is a popular picnic spot.

CENTRAL ROAD TO THE LOOKOUT

From Taravao two routes climb to a lookout less than 10 km east. Both routes start from the north coast road and can be combined to make a loop. In Afaahiti, at PK 0.6, the first turn is signposted shortly before a school. The seven-km road climbs through green fields, some complete with most un-Tahitian looking herds of cows, to the carpark just before the lookout. The alternative route turns off the north coast road at PK 2.5 and is rather rougher and more potholed. It meets the first route just before the carpark. From the carpark it's a short walk to the viewpoint with superb vistas across the isthmus of Taravao to the towering bulk of Tahiti Nui. It's possible to walk for about an hour towards Mt Teatara (1197 metres).

SOUTH ROAD TO VAIRAO & TEAHUPOO

The south coast road runs by beaches and

bays to Vairao and the small settlement of Teahupoo before abruptly stopping at the Tirahi River at PK 18. From here it is possible to walk about another 10 km before the steep Te Pari Cliffs cut off the path.

Hotel Puunui (PK 6 turn-off)

At PK 6 a road turns inland and climbs to the Hotel Puunui, a military complex briefly turned into a hotel by the Tahitian government but currently not open. Like a small-scale version of the Hyatt Regency Hotel near Papeete, the hotel is draped down the hill and entered from the top. Also like the Hyatt, it offers superb views, in this case down the sweep of land to the narrow Taravao isthmus and up across the eastern end of Tahiti Nui.

Tapuaeraha Harbour & Marae Nuutere (PK 7 to 10)

Author of American westerns, Zane Grey, was a keen fisherman who spent time in Tahiti and New Zealand chasing big fish. During his longest Tahitian sojourn in 1929 he was based at about PK 7.3. He recounts the visit in *Tales of Tahitian Waters*. The Tapuaeraha Pass through the reef is the widest and deepest around Tahiti, suitable for ships that are too large to enter Papeete's harbour. Due to its remote position it's rarely used although French naval aircraft carriers did use the harbour in the late 1960s, during the first round of Moruroa nuclear testing. In the early 1970s the huge ocean liner *France* visited Tahiti on two occasions and anchored here each time.

A turn-off at PK 9.5 leads a short distance inland to **Marae Nuutere**, restored in 1994. The name of this large marae translates as 'armies on the move' and it belonged to the female chief of the district, who was married to a member of the royal family of Huahine. There are three paved yards (*tahua*) with places for the gods (*ahu*) at the end of them and large seats (*turui*) for priests, chiefs or kings (*ari*).

At PK 10.4 there's an **Oceanographic Research Station** operated by CNEXO (Centre national pour l'exploitation des océans).

Teahupoo & Vaipoiri Cave

The south coast road ends very decisively at Teahupoo, where the Tirahi River is crossed only by a footbridge. From here it is an easy 2½-hour walk to Vaipoiri Cave. See the Teahupoo to Vaipoiri Cave walk in the Activities section.

PLACES TO STAY

Fare Nana'o is only a couple of km north of Taravao, so it's another alternative if you want to explore Tahiti Iti.

Along the north coast the *Te Anuanua Hotel* (☎ 57-12-54, fax 45-14-39) at PK 9.8 has charmless little motel-like boxes arrayed around a pleasant garden by the lagoon. The rooms have attached bathrooms and cost 5000, 6000 or 7000 CFP as you leave the road and approach the water. The rooms, most with a double and a single bed, are nothing special but the location is fine and the restaurant (see Places to Eat) is excellent. In the past the hotel has, idiosyncratically, been closed on Monday and Tuesday but at present it seems to be open all week. Credit cards are not accepted but bookings can be made through BP 1553, Papeete, Tahiti.

The *Tautira Beach House* (no telephone) is a new addition to the village right at the end of the north coast road. You can camp for 750 CFP or pay 1000 CFP for a bed in the four-bedroom house near the beach. Three meals, with the emphasis on seafood, cost an additional 2500 CFP a day. Emile and Hinatea Flores, the friendly Polynesian couple who run the beach house, meet backpackers at the airport or you can simply head out to Tautira and ask for the Flores.

On the south coast the turn-off to the *Punuui Hotel* is at PK 6.5 from where it's a four-km uphill climb to the hotel. Unfortunately, it's currently closed but, should it reopen, there's a great pool and tennis courts and the views are superb.

Further along the coast is the small *Pension de Famille Meherio* (☎ 57-74-31) with four rooms at 3000, 3500 or 4000 CFP.

It's signposted on the lagoon side of the road and bookings can be made through BP 3695, Papeete, Tahiti. Credit cards are not accepted.

PLACES TO EAT
The collection of restaurants and snack bars in Taravao is easily reached from the north or south coasts of Tahiti Iti. On the north coast the *Te Anuanua Hotel* (☎ 57-12-54) at PK 9.8 is more popular as a restaurant than a hotel. The lagoonside setting is terrific and the food has a good reputation. The Sunday lunchtime Tahitian buffet is popular.

On the south coast the *Auberge du Pari* (☎ 57-13-44), also known as Chez Jacques & Davy, is in Teahupoo, right at the end of the road and right beside the beach. There are meat and fish main courses from 1600 to 2800 CFP and desserts from 450 to 800 CFP. It's open for lunch Monday to Saturday.

Across Tahiti Nui

Although roads and tracks climb some distance into the central highlands of Tahiti at several points around the island, there is only one route which extends right across the island from one side to the other and it's a wonderful, but quite rugged, trip. The 39-km route from Papenoo in the north to Mahaiatea in the south, via the Relais de la Maroto and Vaihiria Lake in the middle of the island, combines superb scenery with some ancient maraes and other reminders of the island's history.

Although unpopulated today, these central valleys once sheltered a dense population, and it was here that the *Bounty* mutineers took refuge. Their attempts to escape British naval wrath were futile. In 1791 Captain Edwards, sent to Tahiti in command of HMS *Pandora* to round up the mutineers, sent a party under Robert Corner to march across Tahiti from the north coast and take them by surprise. When the missionary influence began to spread along the coastal regions the Papenoo Valley became a last refuge of the ancient Polynesian religion and it was also a shelter for the Tahitian rebel forces that opposed the French takeover until 1846. Archaeologist Kenneth Emory made the first systematic study of the valley's historic sites from 1925.

With a sturdy 4WD vehicle and a competent driver this route can be a real adventure. To make it more interesting there's a fine hotel and restaurant, the Relais de la Maroto, right in the middle of the island. Driving up to this hostelry and overnighting there has become a popular weekend excursion for Papeete residents, and numerous interesting walking tracks fan out from the hotel. The route is equally interesting as a couple of days' walk.

PAPENOO TO THE RELAIS DE LA MAROTO
The 18-km route from Papenoo on the north coast to the Relais de la Maroto in the centre of Tahiti follows the wide Papenoo Valley, the only valley to cut right through the ancient crater. This is the largest river in Tahiti and the route crosses the river 10 times. It's wise to check conditions before starting out, because if there has been heavy rain and the river is too high it may not be possible to make some of the crossings, particularly in a smaller 4WD vehicle.

The turn-off is just past PK 17 in Papenoo and after passing an ugly garbage dump and signs warning you about the dangers of the track, the first crossing is encountered after just 1.5 km. At five km the Topatari Waterfall cascades down to the river. River crossings three to six follow in close proximity over the next two km, with the Vaiharuru Waterfall coming down from the west side and the Puraha Waterfall from the east. The last river crossing is at 12.5 km. At PK 16 the track passes the Bassin Vaituoru (Vaituoru Pool) and reaches the Relais de la Maroto just past PK 18. Remarkably, the climb up the Papenoo Valley only reaches 230 metres at the Relais de la Maroto. From the south side of the island the climb is much steeper, reaching 770 metres at the tunnel through the crater rim and then descending steeply to the Relais de la Maroto.

OTIAROA TO THE RELAIS DE LA MAROTO

Coming from Papeete the turn-off on the south coast is at PK 47.5, just beyond the Seventh-Day Adventist church and just before the Tahiria River bridge and a settlement of modern, prefab-like buildings. At one time this road was officially closed open to private vehicles, but now it has become a popular route for daily cross-island tours, for weekend escapes by Papeete residents and for any visitors enthusiastic enough to rent a 4WD vehicle. Or, of course, for walkers. Close to the ancient crater rim the rough track goes through a tunnel to emerge inside the crater.

From the turn-off the road runs straight inland, about 200 metres before taking a signposted sharp-left turn. From there it follows the Tahiria River upstream to a small catchment lake (6.7 km, 145 metres) and **Marae Vaihiria I** (7.5 km). The extensive remains of the marae stretch up the hillside, on both sides of a small stream which runs down and under the road to the Tahiria River. The marae was in use from the 16th to the 19th century and there are several informative noticeboards by the roadside and up the hill. The remains even include an artificial canal which carried water through the site. Another marae is being restored further down the valley, about four km from the start of the cross-island road.

Continuing uphill there is a second small catchment lake (10 km, 270 metres) before the road makes a very steep and winding, but paved, climb to the major Vaihiria Lake (11.3 km, 450 metres), the 200-metre-long tunnel (14.9 km, 770 metres), a road junction (17 km) and finally the Relais de la Maroto (20.7 km). The 4WD track runs up the west side of Vaihiria Lake to the tunnel, but there is a walking track which runs around the east shore of the lake and then climbs up to meet the vehicle track at the tunnel, just below the Col Urufau (Urufau Pass).

AROUND THE RELAIS DE LA MAROTO

The Relais de la Maroto was originally built as accommodation quarters for workers on the hydroelectricity project. Exploitation of the island's hydropower potential commenced in 1980 and now supplies 40% of the island's electricity. It is intended to increase that to 50% by the year 2000. One major dam on the Tahinu River and three smaller barrages on the Vaitamanu, Vaitapaa and Vainavenave rivers supply water to the turbines. Marama Nui, the power company, claims to have been as environmentally conscious as possible during the construction. Power cables and water conduits have been routed underground and the project workers have also been involved in the restoration of maraes around the project.

From the Relais de la Maroto tracks fan out to the various hydropower dams. From the Barrage Vainavenave track a walking path leads up to the Anapua Grottoes and Marae. The Farehape Marae is close to the Barrage Tahinu route, where a walking path diverts off to the Maroto Waterfall. From the barrage a walking track runs round the edge of the lake to the Tahinu archaeological site.

ORGANISED TOURS

There are some great cross-island tours on offer, typically costing around 6500 to 8000 CFP, including lunch at the Relais de la Maroto. As with other tours the Mers & Loisirs (☎ 43-97-99) office on the waterfront will make bookings. Adventure Eagle Tours (☎ 41-37-63), Ron's Services (☎ 46-60-80), Tahiti Ata Mou'a (☎ 41-99-00), Tahiti Safari Expeditions (☎ 42-14-15), Tahiti Safari Excursion Parapente (☎ 58-26-12) and Tefaarahi Adventure Tours (☎ 56-41-24) all make trips across the island.

PLACES TO STAY & EAT

The *Relais de la Maroto* (☎ 43-97-99, fax 57-90-30) is smack in the middle of the island. It was originally built as quarters for construction workers on the hydropower project but its growing popularity has resulted in considerable upgrading and expansion. There are 25 comfortable rooms

TAHITI

for up to three people, with attached bathroom. For one or two people the rooms are 12,000 CFP. Dinner in the pleasant restaurant costs 3200 to 3800 CFP and there is a bar, lounge and other facilities.

GETTING THERE & AWAY
Organised day trips traverse the island or you can walk across in a couple of days. It would also make an interesting and challenging mountain-bike expedition or you can rent a 4WD vehicle and drive yourself. Driving up from the south coast to the Relais de la Maroto is no problem for any moderately competent 4WD driver, but the northern route from Papenoo requires 10 river crossings and can be tricky in a small petrol-engined 4WD. Don't try it unless you know what you are doing and have ensured that the river is not too high.

Activities

WALKING & CLIMBING
One glance at Tahiti's green, jagged and relatively unpopulated centre is enough to hint that there may be some fine walking in the interior. It's not always very accessible and the heat and humidity can make the walks hard work, but for the fit and energetic Tahiti can provide magnificent walks from short strolls to multiday expeditions.

Tahitian walking routes, like those on other high islands, can become rapidly overgrown and hard to follow. Heavy rain can make the trails slippery, dangerous or even impassable. For some trails a local guide is virtually indispensable.

Some of the best walks on the island include the ascent of Mt Aorai, the cross-island walk from Papenoo to Mataiea, the visit to the lava tubes and the walk around the eastern coast of Tahiti Iti, either just to the maraes and petroglyphs of the Vaiote River valley or on past the Te Pari Cliffs. See the Books section in the Facts for the Visitor chapter for information about the useful guidebook *Randonnées en Montagne* by Paule Landon (1995, Les Éditions du Pacifique, Singapore).

Equipment
If you're planning some serious walking then come equipped with a backpack, tent, cooking equipment and other gear. Wherever you are walking in Tahiti you will need good walking shoes, plastic sandals for crossing rivers and a water bottle. The tropical sun can be fierce, so wear good-quality sunglasses and a hat and bring some sunscreen. Tahiti's insects can also be fierce, so bring mosquito repellent, particularly for longer walks. For day walks in Tahiti you should carry a daypack, rain protection and food. For longer walks bring a backpack, change of clothes, sleeping bag, cold weather gear (the temperature can drop to less than 5°C on Tahitian mountain tops) and a wash kit.

Walking Clubs & Guided Walks
There are a number of organisations which offer walking and 4WD trips into the interior. Don't hesitate to ask for details of their trips and make a comparison of their services. The well-established companies employ guides who don't take chances with safety, and in general they speak English. Remember that most of these walks depend upon favourable weather conditions and a minimum number of participants may be required. If you phone in advance it may be possible to join other individuals or a group which has already been formed. Children under 12 years of age are usually charged a lower rate. Te Ora Naho is a local environmental protection group with which many of the organisations are associated.

Le Circuit Vert The Green Circuit (☎ 57-22-67, BP 7426, Taravao, Tahiti) leads two and three-day walks around the Tahiti Iti peninsula and to the Te Pari Cliffs, with visits to the archaeological sites and nights under canvas for 11,000 CFP per person including meals. Zena Angelien is very well known among walkers in Tahiti.

Presqu'île Loisirs These tours (☎ 57-00-57, BP 7509, Taravao, Tahiti) are led by Mata, a friendly Polynesian from Tautira who knows the Tahiti Iti peninsula like the back of his hand. The Te Pari Cliffs, the valleys and their legends are no secret to him. His 10,000 CFP Te Pari trip includes the boat trip, visits to the archaeological and historic sites and food. A two-day trip, starting near Vaipoiri Cave and including an overnight stop at the refuge at Faaroa Bay, is just 12,500 CFP per person, all-inclusive. There is no minimum number of participants.

Safari Tahiti Expeditions This company (☎ 42-14-15, BP 14445, Arue, Tahiti) prides itself on having produced a well-known French TV documentary about the lava tubes in 1993. It does lava-tube trips for 6000 CFP per person and two-day ascents of Mt Aorai for 8000 CFP as well as 4WD trips up Mt Marau for 3000 CFP and trips across the island for 6000 CFP.

Tahiti Special Excursions This operator (☎ 58-22-88, BP 5323, Pirae, Tahiti) does trips on weekends and during school holidays. Pierre Florentin leads a variety of walks into the interior, including mountain ascents, the cross-island walk, visits to the lava tubes on Tahiti Nui and Tahiti Iti trips. The standard prices for a group of up to eight people, not including food, are 30,000 CFP to climb Mt Aorai, 45,000 CFP for the ascent of Mt Orohena, 16,000 CFP for a visit to the Papenoo Plateau, 15,000 CFP for a trip to the Thousand Springs plateau and 30,000 CFP for the trans-island hike. Other trips can be arranged for 16,000 CFP per day.

Tahiti Trekking Adventures About 20 different walking trips, ranging from family walks to really athletic outings, are organised by this company (☎ 43-65-66 or 48-25-60, BP 20446, Papeete, Tahiti). The trips are run on weekends and holidays to a set calendar. Their major speciality is lava-tube trips of two different types: one for first timers at 7000 CFP and a more arduous trip for 8000 CFP. Other trips include the easy half-day circuit

to the Thousand Springs for 4500 CFP. A one-day traverse from Mt Marau via the Diadème and down Fautaua Valley costs 8500 CFP. A two-day walk right across Tahiti Nui or the two-day walk around the Te Pari Cliffs at the eastern end of the Tahiti Iti peninsula costs 15,000 CFP. The two-day ascent of Mt Orohena for experienced walkers costs 18,000 CFP. The prices are per person and include the loan of any necessary equipment, hot drinks and 4WD transfers from Papeete to and from the walk. Bring your own picnic supplies.

Te Fetia O Te Mau Mato Association This group (☎ 43-04-64, 81-09-19 or 42-53-12, BP 9304, Papeete, Tahiti) leads walks every couple of weeks. They include mountain ascents, walks into Papenoo Valley and visits to the Taravao Plateau on Tahiti Iti. Pierre Wrobel is the contact.

Te Ro O Nui O Te Pari I Honoura Association Trips by boat and on foot from Tautira round to the marae sites at the end of Tahiti Iti are operated by this group (☎ 42-80-19 and ask for Odette or 57-19-56, BP 50155, Pirae, Tahiti). Visits are made to the caves and the petroglyphs of Vaiote Valley. Trips are made only on the weekend when a one-day trip costs 8000 CFP or a two-day-and-one-night trip costs 13,000 CFP, including food and transfers between Tehaupoo and Tautira.

The Fautaua Valley from Loti's Bath
It's only 2.5 km from the centre of Papeete to Loti's Bath (or Bain Loti), featured in the 1880 novel *The Marriage of Loti*. From here a three or four-hour walk climbs up the river valley towards the spiky profile of the Diadème.

Shortly beyond the pool is the gateway of the Service de l'Hydralique (☎ 43-02-15). Permission must be obtained either here or from the Service des régies des recettes in the mairie to walk further up the valley. It takes about an hour for the easy four-km walk to the Fachoda Bridge, also known as the Tearape Bridge. Another hour's walk leads to the first waterfall on Fautaua River. Another hour takes walkers past the belvédère (lookout) to Fort Fachoda where in 1846 French soldiers climbed ropes up a cliff face to overpower a Tahitian position. The Governor's Garden is a little beyond the fort.

Mt Aorai

Mt Aorai, at 2066 metres, is the third-highest peak on the island, and only about a dozen km as the crow flies from Papeete. The ascent is one of Tahiti's classic climbs. The path, regularly maintained by soldiers from the Centre d'Instruction Militaire (CIM) who use this area for training, is clearly visible so a guide is quite superfluous. There are signposts at trail junctions to prevent confusion. Count on at least 4½ hours of steady walking to reach the top.

Two refuges break up the route. They can accommodate about 20 walkers, have electricity and are equipped with aluminium containers which are usually filled with drinkable rainwater. The climb is feasible for anyone in good physical condition who has had experience of walking in the mountains. There are, however, several difficult sections at about the mid-point and near the summit, so people who suffer from vertigo should stop at the first refuge. Hardier walkers can make the return trip in a day, but it's necessary to start at dawn because the summit tends to be covered in cloud after 11 am. All in all it makes more sense to allow a day and a half. By spending a night in the second shelter you are able to be on the summit for dawn, when the view across the neighbouring valleys is unobstructed.

Before starting an assault on Aorai, it's wise to take the safety precautions necessary for mountain walking in this climate and environment. You need warm clothing and a change of clothes, at least two litres of water (in the dry season it is possible that the water cisterns may be empty) and good walking shoes. Never go alone.

The starting point is at Le Belvédère Restaurant, at 600 metres altitude and accessible by car. From central Papeete take Ave Georges Clémenceau and turn right at the corner 200 metres after the Total petrol station. Turn right again 300 metres further along at a sign for Le Belvédère. The route is in a rather pitiful state but is drivable as far as Le Belvédère, seven km from the coast road. Park your car in front of the restaurant or in the field below the CIM. It's imperative to fill in the safety book held by the CIM.

Count on an hour's walk to get to Hamuta Pass (900 metres), the easiest part of the walk. From the CIM you reach the ridge along a reasonably wide track which winds up the flank of the vegetated mountain. From the pass you can see all the Fautaua Valley, the ghostly and disjointed silhouette of the Diadème, Mt Marau (preceded by its TV-transmission aerial to the south), and the walls of the ravines of the Pic Vert massif to the west.

From there count on 1¼ hours' walk to the first refuge, Fare mato, perched on a rocky promontory at 1400 metres. The route this far does not present any particular difficulties except for a steep section before arriving at the refuge. To the north-west, the high profile of Moorea stands on the horizon, while to the east the Pirae Valley forms a veritable breach in the mountainous massif.

The path continues to the crest and about 10 minutes later reaches a difficult passage, the Devil's Rock (Mato Mati), which is probably the toughest part of the climb. The path passes along a flank of the crest and it is necessary to keep a tight grip on the cables and cords judiciously placed here by the walking clubs and the soldiers of the CIM. Count on about an hour's climb to reach the second refuge, which can be distinguished high up on the crest.

At 1800 metres, Fare ata, the second refuge, has two units. An open-sided *fare potee* on the promontory has four columns holding up the roof and functions as the open-air 'dining room'. The water in the cistern here is not drinkable, but there are two cisterns of drinking water outside the actual refuge which is 50 metres away and slightly below, sheltered from the wind.

From the promontory it is possible to see the first refuge, small as a pinhead and far below.

The summit is less than an hour from here. The path continues along a jagged ridge, like a flight of steps, very narrow on this section and bearing off to the south. The vegetation is more sparse as this is the upper limit for the *puarata* bushes. The view from the top is worth a hundred times all the effort: to the east is Orohena, Pito Hiti and the Pirae Valley, streaked with waterfalls. To the north-west lies the indented profile of Moorea, while to the north is the sprawling city of Papeete and beyond that the line of the reef.

Don't relax on the way down since the stone blocks can easily crumble, and don't forget to sign off in the safety book at the CIM.

One Thousand Springs
At around PK 11 at Mahina two roads turn off inland and climb for about three km. At that point the two roads meet and continue for about another km from where the walking track commences. This easy 1½-hour walk continues up the east side of the Tuauru Valley to an altitude of 650 metres from where there are superb views. This is the starting point of the difficult Mt Orohena climb. The walk goes through a water-catchment area and officially you must seek permission from Sotagri (☎ 48-11-84) before setting out.

A more difficult three-hour walk starts from PK 10.2 and follows the Tuauru River up to the waterfall where the Faufiru River meets the Tuauru.

Mt Orohena
The ascent of Mt Orohena (2241 metres) is a tough two-day mission plagued by dense undergrowth, a crumbling ridgeline and often fierce winds. This is a walk which definitely requires the assistance of local experts. Despite numerous earlier attempts the first European ascent of the mountain did not take place until 1953. The ascent starts by taking the Thousand Springs route. From the Thousand Springs the route climbs up to

the ridgeline at Moto Fefe (1142 metres) in about 1½ hours and follows the ridge from there all the way to the summit. It's a further 1½ hours to Pihaaiateta (1742 metres), two hours more to Pito Iti (2110 metres) and another two hours to the summit. There are some extremely narrow ridgelines on the ascent although fixed cables on certain tricky sections make the climb a little easier.

Papenoo-Mataiea Cross-Island Route
Despite the increasing popularity of this 39-km trip as a 4WD route, it can still make an interesting two-day walk across the island. Accommodation is available at the Relais de la Maroto at the halfway point and there are many interesting walks from here, smack in the middle of Tahiti's ancient volcano crater. See the Across Tahiti Nui section for more information on the route up the Papenoo Valley and down the other side past Lake Vaihiria.

The Hitiaa Lava Tubes
The Arahoho Blowhole, at PK 22, is a small lava tube that incoming waves can rush through to produce a dramatic waterspout. It's possible to walk through the much larger Hitiaa Lava Tubes, but this fascinating walk can only be attempted when there is no danger of a sudden downpour. The tubes have been created by lava flows that have cooled and hardened more rapidly on the surface; as the lava below solidified it contracted and left the tube-like space between the two layers.

From the turn-off at PK 39.9 a 4WD track runs six km inland past a dam at 500 metres' altitude and up to another one, at the start of the walk at 630 metres. The first two tubes are pretty straightforward but the third is a different question. A torch (flashlight) is necessary for investigating the lava tubes and for the more complex third tube it's essential that the light be sufficiently powerful and, even more important, that be reliable. A walk through all three of the lava tubes will take about three hours.

It's less than a 15-minute walk to the first tube at 750 metres. This cave is about 100 metres long. It's only about 200 metres to the second tube, with two waterfalls just before the entry. The second lava tube is about 300 metres long. Between the second and third tube the trail goes under a stone bridge, the remains of a collapsed lava tube. The third lava tube is longer, darker and more complex. About 100 metres into the tube it divides. The left fork continues for about 300 metres to an exit and the right fork leads to a large cavern, complete with lake and waterfall.

Te Pari

Te Pari means 'cliffs' in Tahitian and it's the name applied to the stretch of the Tahiti Iti coast from Tautira in the north to Vaipoiri Cave in the south. This stretch of practically uninhabited coast is a wild and desolate area 1000 miles from the noise and confusion of Papeete. It is strongly recommended not to visit this coastal region alone as certain parts can be dangerous. There are many archaeological sites scattered in the vegetation along the route and alone you will find some difficult to locate. You can call on the competence and experience of the peninsula guides to recount the legends and clear the clouds of mystery so that your imagination can wander. Since you will often have to wade through water, bring a change of clothes and plastic shoes. A waterproof bag will be very useful to protect your camera equipment. If your guide doesn't provide a mask and fins, bring your own.

From Tautira you usually go directly to the mouth of the Vaiote River, where you find the petroglyphs, by speedboat in about 25 minutes. This saves three hours of dull walking along the coast. The boat is moored over the coral near a small sand motu in the lagoon and the petroglyphs are found facing the motu, 30 metres back from the beach to the right of a banyan tree. On one of these petroglyphs you can distinguish a solar disk with its rays surmounting a pirogue. The second petroglyph illustrates the same motif but with hands around it. According to old people the chiefs of the neighbouring tribes

met here to hold councils of war and to plan attacks on the rival tribes of Teahupoo. The god Ra answered their incantations, and left his imprints on the stones.

A 15-minute walk from here, after you have crossed the Vaiote River and pushed in towards the interior of the island, you discover the Honoura drums (Te Pahu O Honoura). The rocks have cavities, about 20 cm in diameter and with peculiar acoustics so that they resonate when struck with a coconut tree branch. According to legend, the hero Honoura tapped on the first rock (the one with two holes) to warn the inhabitants of Tautira of an attack by their enemies from Teahupoo. On hitting the second rock, which has a large hole and a smaller one to the left, a high-pitched note warned his fiancée of his coming and asked that she wait.

Back on the track, follow the Vaiote for about another quarter of an hour, where you can make out on the left a *pae pae* hidden in a tangle of mapes, *purau*, *hotu* and ferns. This valley, rich in archaeological remains, speaks of an important pre-European population.

Continuing further along the coast to the south, 10 minutes by boat brings you to Vaitomoana Cave, partially invaded by the sea. If you feel like it the guide will lend you a mask and snorkel to collect sea urchins which cling to the bottom of the cliff, five metres below.

Continuing the route south, five minutes by boat or 1½ hours on foot along a ledge overhanging the ocean, brings you to the Devil's Passage, or Vahi Hororaa, 'the place where one must run'. It's a narrow passage on the side of the rock that you must cross over quickly as the waves retreat. You're helped by the ropes attached to the cliff. Just before the passage, the rocky block standing to face the ocean is the stone sentinel which guards the way.

Anaihe Cave is a 20-minute walk from here. Well known to fishers from the Tahiti Iti peninsula, it serves as a shelter during bad weather. They have fitted it out with a fairly basic table and benches of coconut wood and this is a popular place for visitors to picnic.

The coral formations a few metres from the shore make a great snorkelling site.

You can refresh yourself at the waterfall which you'll find not far from here. You emerge in a narrow and slippery horseshoe-shaped passage about 20 metres long, which brings you out five metres above the waves. There are good handholds on the rocks and ropes attached to the sides with pitons help you to reach the other side without difficulty. Your efforts are rewarded by the view of the Queen's Cave, about 10 minutes from here. If you believe the legend, the queen who lived in the Taapeha Valley was accustomed to bathing in the small water hole in the interior of the cave and sitting on the nearby rock to be prepared by her servants. If the sea is calm you can dive in the turquoise water a few metres below. Watch for the returning waves.

The very deep Taapeha Valley is 10 minutes' walk from here. In coming back about 100 metres, where the stream threads its way through the huge stone blocks, you'll find on the right the 'giant *umete* of Taapeha'. A umete is a Tahitian wooden dish or bowl and erosion has given this rock that characteristic shape. This rock makes multiple appearances in legends: it was used to make traditional medications, and it was here that traditional deliveries were performed – its shape follows the body's contours perfectly and new-born children are washed in the stream and coated with *monoi*, tiare flower oil.

The Faaroa refuge is the next stopping point. It's on the banks of the river of the same name which also forms the boundary between the Tautira and Teahupoo districts. If you are on a two-day walk, this is where you spend the night. The walk can be continued the next day to Vaipoiri Cave, where you can go swimming. The return to Tautira is made by boat with a possible picnic stop on Motu Fenua Ino.

Teahupoo to Vaipoiri Cave

It's a long walk to Vaipoiri Cave if you go right around the coast from Tautira, but from Teahupoo it's an easy 2½ hours. The south coast road ends at the footbridge across the Tirahi River at Teahupoo. From here the walk commences along the black-sand beach passing numerous homes in its early stages. Further along the walk cross the Atihiva, Vaitutaepuaa and Vaiarava rivers. The tough two-day walking path directly across the peninsula to Tautira goes up the Vaiarava River, and on the north coast descends down the Vaitepiha River. The walk continues through a swampy stretch with some fine groves of mape trees stretching right down to the coast. You cross the small Taura River and the coastal walk ends at Maraetiria Point, just past the first branch of the Vaipoiri River. The impressive cave with its subterranean lake is a short distance inland.

DIVING

The diving around Tahiti does not have a reputation to compare with other islands in French Polynesia, but Tahiti can offer some agreeable surprises to the diver, whether beginner or experienced. Furthermore the cost of diving is usually less than on other islands.

Dive Centres

There are six dive centres on Tahiti: three to the west of Papeete in Punaauia, one to the east in Arue, one in Vairao on Tahiti Iti, and a boat anchored in the port of Papeete used for diving cruises. Each centre organises two or three daily dives, typically at 9 and 11 am,

and 2 pm. Reservations are imperative, particularly at weekends or during the high season. You will always find a dive instructor who speaks English.

Three of the clubs – Eleuthera Plongée, Ta'i Tua and the Tahiti Yacht Club Diving Centre – offer Tridive, a card which offers you discounted dives at any or all of the centres. Cards are available with 15 points for 16,000 CFP or 30 points for 30,000 CFP and each dive 'costs' three points.

Eleuthera Plongée Eleuthera Plongée (☎ 42-49-29) at the Taina Marina at Punaauia, 400 metres past the Continent Hypermarket, is run by three very energetic people. They offer a wide range of possibilities because their two fast boats give them access to a huge area of the coast from Paea to Arue, where more than 30 dive sites can be found. A dive costs 5000 CFP or a five-dive package is 20,000 CFP, including equipment. Night dives can be made for the same cost if at least two people are interested. The CMAS course costs 27,000 CFP. One of the divemasters is also a PADI instructor and a PADI open-water certification course can be completed for 50,000 CFP.

Twice a month trips are made to Moorea (20 minutes to an hour by boat). It costs 10,000 CFP for two dives. A shark-feeding trip is made on Saturday morning. The centre is open every day and credit cards are accepted.

Tahiti Aquatique Tahiti Aquatique (☎ 42-80-42) is found at the Sofitel Maeva Beach Hotel pontoon, just beyond Faaa airport. This centre is an offshoot of the Beachcomber Parkroyal Hotel operation. You pay 8000 CFP for a beginners' dive, 5000 CFP for a dive or 20,000 CFP for five dives. The divemasters have PADI and CMAS qualifications and you can choose between a PADI open-water certification course (35,000 to 50,000 CFP depending on the number of participants) or CMAS. Unfortunately, Tahiti Aquatique is a centre for all sorts of nautical activities and diving sometimes

seems to be the poor relation. Credit cards are accepted for hotel guests.

Tahiti Charter Island Anchored across from Le Rétro in the centre of town, you can't miss the flamboyant new yacht of Tahiti Charter Island (☎ 77-02-33, 45-07-75 or 45-28-12). The divemasters on this luxurious, air-con boat offer an original product: half or full-day diving cruises to Tahiti, Moorea or Tetiaroa. A half-day, one-dive trip to Moorea is 7000 CFP; a full-day trip with two dives, breakfast and lunch costs 12,000 CFP to Moorea or 16,000 CFP to Tetiaroa. A first dive costs 4000 CFP, regular dives are 3500 CFP or 15,000 CFP for five dives, and night dives are 5000 CFP including a meal. Diving trips to the almost untouched dive sites on the Tahiti Iti peninsula cost 10,000 CFP including two dives, breakfast and lunch. Equipment is provided.

Tahiti Plongée At the water's edge between the Beachcomber and Sofitel Maeva Beach Hotel, beside the defunct Te Puna Bel Air Hotel, Tahiti Plongée (☎ 41-00-62 or 43-62-51) is a French Polynesian institution. The director, Henri Pouliquen, has dedicated his life to diving and has been a pioneer of this activity in the territory. He's also the representative in Polynesia of the Diving Federation of France.

Dives cost 4000 CFP or 19,000 CFP for five dives and every second Wednesday there are night dives for 8000 CFP. You can also have your dive videotaped for 8000 CFP. CMAS certification costs 31,000 CFP and includes seven dives in the lagoon and three in the ocean. You can take all the levels up to instructor certification. Equipment is supplied free of charge but it isn't brand new. Tahiti Plongée has a number of boats including a whaleboat big enough for 25 divers and the centre offers trips to a variety of dive sites suitable for the various levels of divers.

The club is 'très français' in its concept of diving and in its mode of operation. Of course it doesn't turn away PADI divers, but it accepts them with a certain condescension. Of course this is the official office of the

Diving Federation of France so PADI diving courses are not offered. Residents constitute an important part of their clientele, who appreciate the relaxed family atmosphere. Tahiti Plongée is also one of the rare centres which has Tahitians among its employees. It's closed on Sunday afternoon and all day on Monday. Credit cards are accepted.

Tahiti Yacht Club Diving Centre The only east coast dive operator is the Centre de Plongée du Yacht club de Tahiti (☎ 42-23-55 or 42-78-95) at PK 4 in Arue, just east of the centre of Papeete. The yacht club is at the same marina. Coming from Papeete take the small road to the left, right across from the PK 4 marker and 100 metres past the Arue camp.

Pascal Le Cointre, the proprietor, offers very attractive tariffs to CMAS and FFESSM divers who pay 3500 CFP for a single dive or 15,000 CFP for a series of five, including equipment. Divers with PADI or NAUI cards pay 5000/22,500 CFP for one/five dives. Two PADI instructors run PADI open-water certification courses for 45,000 CFP. CMAS certification cost 29,500 CFP. Their dive sites, less than 15 minutes from the centre, are less numerous than those on the west coast but are worth exploring, particularly The Cliffs and the Dolphin Bank. The latter is near Point Venus and is said to have been named after the Samuel Wallis boat, which anchored here over 200 years ago.

Dives take place at 9 am and 2 pm daily, with a supplementary dive at 4 pm on Tuesday and Friday. The centre is closed on Sunday afternoon and all day on Monday. In conjunction with Jet France (see the Tetiaroa section in the Other Leeward Islands chapter) dives are organised on their day trips to Tetiaroa for 15,000 CFP (one dive). Another possibility for a party of five divers is a one-week trip to Takaroa in the Tuamotus (see the Tuamotus chapter for more details).

Tai Tua Plongée Tai Tua (☎ 57-77-93 or 57-77-98), which means 'calling from the

sea', is at the Puunui Marina in Vairao at PK 6 on the Tahiti Iti peninsula. Joël Roussel has original dives to sites rich in gorgon corals and with a more varied marine life than the sites around Tahiti Nui.

The family-like ambience is very convivial and the prices are also good: 3500 CFP for a single dive or 16,000 CFP for five, including equipment, although you must supply your own wet suit. Students pay 3000 and 14,000 CFP respectively. A CMAS certification course costs 21,000 CFP, without insurance. The first weekend of the month a trip is made to the Tautira Pass, noted for its gorgonians. There are trips at 9 am and 2 pm daily, except for Monday.

Dive Sites
From Arue to Punaauia there are at least 20 dive sites in the lagoon and the ocean. The sites described here are just a taste of the multiple possibilities offered to divers.

The Cliffs of Arue This is the best known site on the east coast, in Matavai Bay. The configuration of the site permits three different sorts of dive, suitable for beginners through to experienced divers. On the outside of the reef a plateau of coral emerges at five metres' depth, ideal for beginners and sited above a drop which sinks into the abyss. Less than 100 metres from here, between 10 and 30 metres' depth, two narrow rifts form

---

Diving Young, Diving Old
Tahiti Plongée is particularly proud of its children's diving school, which is unique. If your children are at least eight years old they can discover the underwater world in the company of the divemasters. Using aluminium minitanks specially made for their size, they can make their first dives in less than three metres of water at the site known as the Aquarium. At the opposite end of the scale a grandmother of 80 years made her first dive at the centre in late 1994. ■

indents in this plateau which shelter an abundance of marine life, including a variety of corals, nudibranchs (sea slugs), anemones and crabs, all of which offer great opportunities to underwater photographers.

A little lower it's fish-feeding time, if the divemaster has brought some bread. You will find yourself nose-to-nose with napoleons, as curious as they are voracious, triggerfish, picassos and trumpetfish. It's best to make this exploration in the morning when there are fewer particles in the water.

The Aquarium Inside the lagoon, on the Faaa coast, not far from the western extremity of the Faaa airport runway, the Aquarium is an enchanting place for beginners. In effect it's a partly natural, partly artificial aquarium, the work of Henri Pouliquen and his divemasters (see the Dive Operators section). With the aid of parachutes filled with air they moved hundreds of tonnes of coral which had been gathered together close to the airport runway. In July 1995, using the same technique, the wreckage of a Cessna, which made a forced landing, and the wreck of a schooner joined the coral blocks at seven metres' depth.

This rather varied aquarium is classified as a submarine minireserve by the Territory and has been enjoyed by hundreds of divers. The dozens of species which have made the reserve their home and accompany divers on their exploration include triggerfish, perches, remoras, parrotfish, butterfly fish, puffer fish, damselfish, angel fish, trumpet fish, moray eels, sea urchins, cowries and anemones. It would be easy to go on! Nowhere else in Tahiti will you find such diverse marine life.

There's another aircraft and boat combination near Faaa airport. Just north of the airport and inside the outer reef edge, a Catalina flying boat and the decaying wreckage of an old wooden inter-island cargo boat lie close to each other at a depth of 15 to 20 metres. It's possible to swim into the fuselage of the Catalina and sit in the flight deck but visibility can be poor.

The Spring At the site known as the Spring, facing Fishermans Point in Punaauia on the west coast, a freshwater spring gushes out of the summit of a coral pinnacle, several metres underwater. The site is not far from the Museum of Tahiti & Its Islands, at PK 15. The column of emerging water gives the diver the impression of looking through rippled glass. Many other coral pinnacles around the spring are the home for a dense reef fauna between 15 and 20 metres' depth. Trumpet fish, perches, triggerfish and napoleons are frequently found here and white-tipped reef sharks sometimes appear. On your way to or from the site it's not unusual to see dolphins playing around the boat. Just north is the Saint Étienne drop-off, offshore from Saint Étienne's Church.

Tahiti Iti Dives There are several good dive sites along the south coast of Tahiti Iti, a long way from Papeete. The Vavi is a popular dive on the outer reef, south of the deep Tapuaeraha Pass. The reef drops in a series of steps to more than 50 metres, with very rich sea life and colourful corals.

SURFING

Tahiti may well have been the birthplace of surfing so it's no surprise that surfing has a keen following. Some of the prime surf spots include the Papenoo break at PK 17, just west of Papenoo on the north coast. Closer to Papeete there are several breaks around Arue and Point Venus. South of Papeete there is a popular reef break at Punaauia at PK 15 near the Museum of Tahiti and at Paea around PK 21. Further round at Papara at PK 36 there can be good waves from May to November. Several outlets in Papeete deal in surf equipment and there are a number of board makers on the island.

SAILING & FISHING

The tourist office can supply information on the many boats available for charter, including cruising yachts, catamarans and a number of game-fishing boats. The Mers et Loisirs office (☎ 43-97-99) on the Papeete waterfront can also advise on charters. There are nautical activity centres at the large hotels and at the Arue Yacht Club (☎ 42-78-03).

GOLF

If you've come all the way to Tahiti to play golf, then the Olivier Breaud Golf Course (☎ 57-40-32 or 57-43-41) is the only place to do it. The 18-hole course is at PK 42 on the site of Tahiti's former cotton plantation.

OTHER ACTIVITIES

There are tennis courts at a number of the hotels as well as a number of private tennis clubs. The Hotel Matavai has three squash courts. If you want a gym try the Gymnase Garden Club (☎ 53-49-50) at 95 Ave Georges Clémenceau in Mamao. Horse riding can be arranged through a number of equestrian clubs – the tourist office has details. Tahiti's dramatic mountains provide superb hang-gliding opportunities; contact Tahiti Parapente Excursions (☎ 58-26-12 or 46-60-12).

Moorea

Population: 11,000
Area: 132 sq km
Passes: 12

Mountains that leap almost vertically out of the lagoon, some fine beaches, terrific scuba diving, interesting *maraes*, a number of excellent walks, a pleasantly unhurried pace of life and absurdly easy access from Tahiti combine to make Moorea the second most popular destination in French Polynesia. Subtract the Tahiti visitors who are simply passing through the major island, en route to somewhere else, and Moorea could well be the most popular island. One-third of all the hotel rooms in French Polynesia are in Moorea.

HISTORY

Moorea is the remains of a massive volcano, the northern half of which has been eroded away. Cook's Bay and Opunohu Bay mark the floor of the ancient crater and if you follow the trail from the Opunohu Valley up to the Three Coconut Trees Pass you stand very clearly on the knife-edge of the old crater rim. The island and its mountains feature in ancient Polynesian legends.

The island was once known as Aimeho or Eimeo, but Moorea means 'yellow lizard' and it's speculated that this was the name of one of the ruling families of the island. Marae Umarea at Afareaitu is the oldest marae on the island, dating back to 900 AD, but the Opunohu Valley has the greatest number of maraes and in the pre-European era was heavily populated.

Samuel Wallis, on HMS *Dolphin*, was the first European to sight the island in 1767, followed soon after by Bougainville in 1768 and Cook in 1769. When Cook returned on his second voyage in 1774, Tahiti was preparing for a war with Moorea and it was not until his third voyage in 1777 that Cook visited Moorea. Curiously, he anchored not in Cook's Bay but in Opunohu Bay, which

he belatedly discovered looked even better than his old favourite anchorage at Matavai on Tahiti. The bay certainly looks achingly attractive in the Mel Gibson 1984 remake of *The Bounty*.

Despite being bypassed by the early European visitors, Moorea was the springboard from which the LMS (London Missionary Society) took Christianity to the other islands of French Polynesia. Missionaries arrived at Papetoai, just west of Opunohu Bay, in 1808 and it was established as the site for their Pacific headquarters in 1811. The octagonal church in Papetoai, built between 1822 and 1827, is the oldest surviving European building in the South Pacific.

Afareaitu was the site of the missionaries' South Seas Academy in the 1820s, and the first book to be printed in the South Pacific rolled off their press in 1817. William Ellis, a pioneering missionary, wrote *Polynesian Researches – The Recollections of a Protestant Missionary in the Leeward Islands from 1817 to 1823* about his time in Moorea and Huahine.

Moorea had long been a refuge to which Tahitians on the losing side of power struggles could flee. Pomare I conquered the island in 1790, leaving his son Pomare II in control of Tahiti. In 1808, however, Pomare II had to retreat to Moorea. He settled at Papetoai, befriended the missionaries and, when he mounted his return to power in 1815, he took Christianity with him, and it quickly became dominant. From then on Moorea was subservient to Tahiti. European diseases, weaponry and alcohol had a disastrous effect on the population during the mid-19th century, reducing it to less than 1000 in 1860. A French protectorate was first established in 1843.

Copra and vanilla have been important crops in the past and today Moorea is the pineapple-growing centre of French Polynesia. Although tourism is the island's other major business and continues to grow

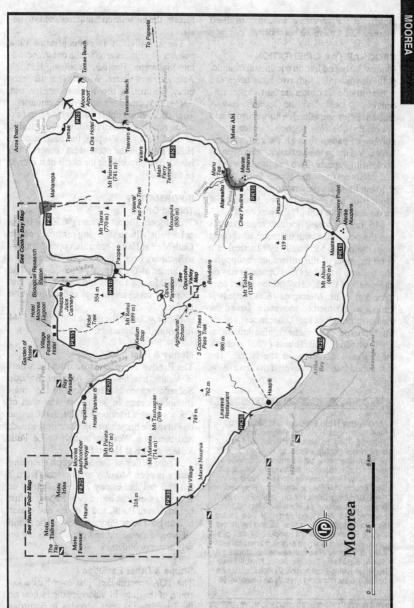

To Papeete

Temae Beach

Moorea Airport PK0

Aroa Point

Lake Temae

Temae

Ia Ora Hotel

Teavaro Teavaro Beach

Mt Fairurani (741 m)

Valare

Maharepa

Vaiare Pass

Teavaro

Vaiare/ Pao Pao Trek

Main Ferry Terminal PK5

Motu Ahi

Manu Tea

Marae Umarea

Taotoi Pass

Temaroto Pass

See Cook's Bay Map PK5

Mt Tearai (770 m)

Mouaputa (830 m)

Atiraeuhu

Chez Pauline PK10

Haumi

Nuupere Point

Marae Nuupere

Paopao

Cook's Bay

Biological Research Station

419 m

Maatea PK15

Teavaroa Pass

554 m

Hotel Moorea Lagoon

Pineapple Juice Cannery PK15

PK10

Opunohu Plantation

See Opunohu Valley Map

Belvedere

Mt Tohiea (1207 m)

Mt Ahutea (480 m)

Village Faimano Hotel

Garden of Roses

Mt Rotui (899 m)

Kellum Stop

Rotui Trek

Agricultural School

Bay Passage

860 m

3 Coconut Trees Pass Trek

PK20

Atiha Bay

Taira Pass

Opunohu Bay

762 m

Haapiti

Avaepue Pass

PK20

Papetoai

Hotel Tipaniér III

749 m

Linareva Restaurant

PK35

Mt Parata (517 m)

Mt Tautuapae (769 m)

Mt Matatea (714 m)

Taotai Pass

Marae Nuurua

Maunanui Pass

See Hauru Point Map PK25

Moorea Beachcomber Parkroyal

Hauru

PK30

318 m

Tiki Village

Animatu Pass

Motu Irioa

Motu Tiahura

The Tiki

Motu Fareone

Taotaroa Pass

Taota Pass

Moorea

0   2.5   5 km

rapidly, it's a very new industry; in 1960 Moorea had a mere 13 hotel beds!

GEOGRAPHY & ORIENTATION

Moorea is shaped like an equilateral triangle, point downwards, with two bites taken out of the top side. The bites are the two magnificent bays, Cook's Bay and Opunohu Bay. A reef encircles the island with a narrow and generally shallow lagoon. There are a number of passes through the reef, particularly at Vaiare on the east coast, where ferries dock from Papeete. Two beautiful *motus* lie just offshore from the Hauru Point tourist strip but there are only two other motus, tiny Motu Irioa just east of the two Hauru Point motus and Motu Ahi off the east coast.

Moorea is magnificently mountainous and the peaks rise with dramatic abruptness from the coast. Mt Rotui (899 metres) is a good example of this rollercoaster topography because it tumbles into Opunohu Bay on one side and Cook's Bay on the other, only three km apart. Mouaputa (830 metres) is known as the pierced mountain, famed for the hole through its top. Other mountains are Mt Mouaroa (880 metres), also known as 'the cathedral', and Toheia (1207 metres), the highest mountain on the island. The untouched interior is covered in dense *mape*

Hiro & the Hole through Mt Mouaputa

One dark night Hiro, the Polynesian God of Thieves, tried to steal Mt Rotui and tow it behind his mighty canoe to Raiatea. It was probably the same canoe which he carelessly rammed into Huahine, splitting the island into two parts. Unfortunately for Hiro, his thieving was spotted by Pai, a legendary Polynesian hero. Climbing Tataa Hill on Tahiti, Pai hurled his mighty spear at Hiro but missed, and created the hole you can still see in Mt Mouaputa today. The spear carried on all the way to Raiatea, where it knocked off part of a peak. Hiro still managed to grab a small hill and carry it back to Raiatea where he plonked it down near Marae Taputapuatea. The hill bears vegetation similar to that on Mt Rotui, and quite unlike the surrounding growth on Raiatea. ∎

forests, the gigantic chestnut trees of Polynesia.

The population is concentrated in a number of villages around the coast, including Maharepa, Paopao, Papetoai, Haapiti, Afareaitu and Vaiare. With its frenetic ferry quay, Vaiare is the busiest centre but Afareaitu is the administrative headquarters. Tourist development is concentrated in two strips, one from Maharepa down the east side of Cook's Bay to Paopao, the other around Hauru Point on the north-west corner of the island. The airport is at the north-east corner of the island.

INFORMATION
Tourist Office

The Moorea Tourist Bureau (☎ 56-29-09) is at Le Petit Village shopping centre, opposite Club Med at Hauru Point. It's open Monday to Saturday from 8 am to 5 pm. There is also a counter at the airport (☎ 56-26-48). The active Moorea tourist business churns out scores of brochures, maps and information leaflets.

Phone ☎ 17 for the police and ☎ 56-13-44 for police headquarters.

Money & Post

The Banque Socredo across from the wharf at Vaiare has an ATM. Another Banque Socredo branch can be found in the small shopping centre in Maharepa (the start of Cook's Bay); a Banque de Tahiti and Banque de Polynésie branch are right across the road; and there's a Westpac branch in Le Petit Village centre at Hauru Point.

A post office at the Maharepa shopping centre is open Monday to Thursday from 7 am to 3 pm and Friday 7 am to 2 pm. The island's other post office is in Papetoia, just before Hauru Point, and it opens and closes half an hour later. Phone boxes can be found all around the island and phonecards are on sale at many outlets.

Shops & Other Facilities

The TOA supermarket, just over half a km south of the quay in Vaiare, is the largest on the island and is open Monday to Saturday from 8 am to 8 pm and Sunday 6 am to noon. There are other supermarkets and smaller shops around the island. There are fish markets in Maharepa and at the Municipal Market in Paopao, where the night's catch goes on sale around 5 to 6 am in the morning. The Municipal Market is open every day from 5 to 8 am.

The shopping centre at Maharepa has a bookshop and newsagency, a variety of other shops and a pâtisserie. Le Petit Village centre at Hauru has the Lav Matic laundrette in Tahiti Parfum. It's open from 9 am to 1 pm and costs 800 CFP for seven kg of washing and another 800 CFP to dry it. Other shops include the Supersonics newsagency.

Medical Services

As usual your hotel can advise if you need medical assistance. The Moorea Hospital (☎ 56-23-23 or 56-24-24) is in Afareaitu. Island doctors include Dr Dominique Baraille (☎ 56-27-07) at PK 27 near Hauru Point, Dr Brigitte Busseuil (☎ 56-26-19) at PK 19 on the north coast and Dr Hervé Paulus (☎ 56-10-19) at Le Petit Village at Hauru Point. Jean-Marc Thurillet (☎ 56-32-44) is a dentist at PK 5.5 in Maharepa. There's a pharmacy (☎ 56-10-51) at PK 6.5 in Maharepa, open every day but only in the mornings on weekends.

AROUND THE ISLAND

It's 60 km right around the island and the circuit can easily be made in a day by bicycle. The PK (*pointe kilométrique*) markers start at 0 at the airport and go round the coast clockwise to Haapiti at PK 24 and anticlockwise to Haapiti at PK 35. The following circuit starts at the airport and proceeds in an anticlockwise direction. As you progress round the island it's worth noting that one reason for Moorea's enduring attractiveness is the absence of electrical power poles, the work of former mayor John Teariki.

Temae (PK 1, 1 km)

This village has long been famed for its dancers. They performed for Tahitian royalty when the Pomares held court at Papetoai, put on a hot version of the sexually charged *lori-lori* for Herman Melville and still appear at tourist dance performances today. The village is well inland from the coast, which is unusual not just for Moorea but almost anywhere in Polynesia.

Maharepa (PK 4 to 5, 4 to 5 km)

The technicolour *pareus*, floating in the breeze like an artist's washing line, announce the start of Maharepa village at the Lili Shop. Opposite the lagoonside Jehovah's Witness church, a road runs directly inland towards the mountains, getting rougher the further it goes. It doesn't lead anywhere in particular.

At PK 5 the turn-of-the-century **Maison Blanche** is a fine example of a *fare vanira*, a plantation house from Moorea's vanilla boom era. Around the island, particularly from the airport to Cook's Bay and around Papetoai, there are a number of these elegant, single-storey houses with verandahs, reminders of the fortunes made from vanilla production. From 1860 to 1960 vanilla, backed up by copra, dominated the economy. The prime years of the vanilla 'boom' were 1910 to 1915 but a vanilla crop disease and the growth of tourism finished off the vanilla business. Today, hardly any vanilla is produced on Moorea. Maison Blanche, just beyond the Bali Hai Hotel, is now a souvenir shop with a typical selection of pareus and Balinese wood carvings.

Around Cook's Bay to Paopao (PK 6 to 9, 6 to 9 km)

Cook's Bay is somewhat of a misnomer since Cook actually anchored in Opunohu Bay, but that's unimportant; it's simply a spectacular stretch of water, especially when there's a tall ship like the *Windsong* or *Club Med II*, anchored in the middle. Cook's Bay is also one of the two tourist centres of Moorea. The tourist activity starts at PK 5 with Maharepa and continues round to PK 9 with the Belvédère turn-off in Paopao. The Cook's Bay shops, restaurants and hotels are not lined up side by side, however. There's simply a handful of them dotted along the lagoonside road.

Cook's Bay also has an interesting art gallery and aquarium. **Galerie van der Heyde** (☎ 56-14-22) has paintings arrayed around the inside wall of the enclosure and a collection of primitive Pacific art inside. The **Tropical Aquarium** (☎ 56-24-00) and the experimental **Black Pearl Farm** are open from 9 am to noon and 2 to 5.30 pm; entry is 500 CFP. The Moorea Pearls Center is open Monday to Saturday at the same site.

At the top of Cook's Bay is the village of **Paopao**, with a shipping dock, a popular market and a variety of shops. The market has a wall mural painted by Moorea-based artist François Ravello. A road turns inland from Paopao, leading to the maraes of the Opunohu Valley, the belvédère lookout and walking tracks across the ridge to Vaiare and up to the Three Coconut Trees Pass.

Catholic Churches (PK 10, 10 km)

Two Catholic churches stand side by side on the west side of Cook's Bay. The dull, modern St Joseph's Church dates from 1979 and has mother-of-pearl inlays in the altar. The adjacent abandoned old church has a fine mural painted by Peter Haymann (1908-82) above the altar depicting Polynesian-featured Joseph, Mary, the Archangel Gabriel and the infant Jesus with the lush and mountainous profile of Moorea as a background.

Biological Research & Pineapple Juice (PK 11, 11 km)

Just before the PK 11 marker, on the bay side of the road, the South Pacific Biological Research Station is operated by the Berkeley campus of the University of California. Funded by grants from the San Francisco jewellery entrepreneur Richard Gump, the station opened in 1987 to conduct marine and terrestrial research. It is not open to the general public.

A short distance inland from the coast road, Distilleries Tahiti-Moorea or Jus de Fruits de Moorea (☎ 56-11-33) has a pineapple juice factory. Juice production starts with a strong man heaving baskets of pineapples on to a conveyor belt, helped by women with very big and very sharp knives whacking both ends off before the pineapples are carried to the pulping machine. Open Monday to Friday from 8 am to 4 pm, there's an exhibition room and a shop labelled, like the best French wineries, '*exposition – degustation – vent*' (exhibition, tastings and sales). Pineapples are the main crop but grapefruit and papaya are also handled here.

Opunohu Bay (PK 14 to 18, 14 to 18 km)

The coast road rounds Mt Rotui and at about PK 14 turns inland along the east side of Opunohu Bay. There is less development than around Cook's Bay and if anything Opunohu Bay is even more spectacularly beautiful. Most of the Polynesian scenes in the most recent *Bounty* movie, the Mel Gibson one, were shot on Opunohu Bay.

The yacht cruising organisation Archipels Croisières is based at PK 17 and a little further along is **Kellum Stop** (☎ 56-18-82) at PK 17.5, almost at the top of the bay. This fine old house has an interesting history. In 1925 the wealthy Medford Kellum visited Tahiti on his 55-metre four-mast *Kaimiloa*. On board his ship were six scientists from the Bishop Museum in Hawaii, including Kenneth Emory on his first trip to Polynesia. Emory spent the next 15 months on the islands making pioneering studies of ancient Polynesian marae.

Medford Kellum fell in love with Moorea, bought 1500 hectares of the Opunohu Valley, and with his wife, Gladys, spent most of the rest of his life on the island. His ownership of the valley facilitated Emory's early archaeological investigations on Moorea. Roger Green's more extensive studies of the valley in the 1960s also owed a debt to the Kellums. The Kellums raised cattle and grew copra and vanilla on their plantation which extended right up to the ridge line at the Three Coconut Trees Pass. The trampled-down barbed wire along the ridge once marked the southern boundary of their plantation. The French Polynesian government bought the plantation in 1962 and it is now the site of the government's agricultural college.

JEAN-BERNARD CARILLET

JEAN-BERNARD CARILLET

TONY WHEELER

TONY WHEELER

JEAN-BERNARD CARILLET

Top Left: Tikis in Marae Arahurahu, Tahiti, Society Islands
Bottom Left: Marae Ahu-o-Mahine, Opunohu Valley, Moorea, Society Islands
Top Right: Vaiote petroglyph, Tahiti Iti, Society Islands
Middle Right: Hanapaaoa, skulls near Moe One tiki, Hiva Oa, Marquesas
Bottom Right: Vaikivi petroglyph, Ua Huka, Marquesas

JEAN-BERNARD CARILLET

JEAN-BERNARD CARILLET

TONY WHEELER

JEAN-BERNARD CARILLET

Top Left: Scraping copra with a *pana*, Takaroa, Tuamotus
Top Right: Copra drier, Hiva Oa, Marquesas
Bottom Left: Ice-cold coconuts, Bora Bora, Society Islands
Bottom Right: Banana drier, Marquesas

The Kellums' daughter Marimari also became an archaeologist and after her education in the US returned to French Polynesia and conducted notable studies in the Marquesas. Today Marimari Kellum conducts personal tours around the gardens of her house, a sweep of land running down to the bay that is dense with local plants and flowers. Highlights include a magnificent banyan tree, huge cauldrons used for boiling down whale blubber and personal mementos like her father's hefty redwood surfboard. A small sign on the mountain side of the road announces 'Kellum Stop'. Cross the road, ring the cowbell hanging by the gate and wander in. Kellum Stop welcomes visitors Tuesday to Saturday, preferably in the mornings, and the stroll round the garden costs just 300 CFP.

At PK 18, right at the top of the bay, a road turns off inland along the Opunohu Valley to the valley maraes, the Belvédère lookout and the walking route to Three Coconut Trees Pass.

Papetoai (PK 22, 22 km)

Established as the Pacific headquarters of the LMS in 1811, it was to Papetoai that Pomare II retreated from Tahiti in 1808. Between 1822 and 1827 the missionaries built an octagonal church at Papetoai; today this is the oldest European building in the South Pacific, although it was rebuilt in the late 19th century. As at many other locations around Polynesia the missionaries deliberately built their church atop an old marae. A single spike-like stone is the sole reminder of the ancient Marae Taputapuatea, dedicated to the god Oro.

Papetoai is a busy little village with a post office and a number of restaurants.

Hauru Point (PK 25 to 30, 25 to 30 km)

The coast road rounds Hauru Point, the north-west corner of the island, between PK 25 and PK 30. This is one of the island's major tourist enclaves but addresses and locations can be a little confusing here as the area is often referred to as Haapiti, since it's in the Haapiti district, even though the village of Haapiti is well to the south. The tourist strip starts with the big Moorea Beachcomber Parkroyal Hotel at about PK 25, quickly followed by the equally sprawling Club Méditerrané, along with a host of smaller establishments, restaurants and shops. Round the point the shops and resorts fade out and Tiki Village at PK 31 marks the end of the strip.

Hauru Point has one of the best beaches on the island, a narrow but sandy stretch which extends for about five km. Finding

---

Four Royal Maraes

Although visitors are most likely to see the maraes of the Opunohu Valley, there are four much more ancient maraes dotted around the coast. These national maraes or *marae arii*, royal maraes, were recorded by the Polynesian historian Teuira Henry and located by the archaeologist Kenneth Emory in the 1920s and '30s.

The oldest of the four, dating from around 900 AD, is Marae Umarea in the east coast village of Afareaitu. Marae Nuupere is a few km south, just beyond the village of Maatea. It is of the same type as Marae Umarea but it's slightly difficult to reach since it's on private property and little remains apart from an impressive heap of coral boulders.

Marae Nuurua is just south of the popular Hauru Point tourist strip and although totally neglected, standing forlornly in a scrap of coconut plantation beside a football field, it is the most evocative and best preserved of the coastal maraes. The fourth and final coastal marae is Taputapuatea, just east of Hauru Point. It was almost completely destroyed by the Christian missionaries who built the octagonal church at Papetoai on the site. A solitary vertical stone outside the church serves to remind that there was an earlier religion on Moorea. Taputapuatea, like the great marae of the same name in Raiatea, was dedicated to the god Oro, a cult which spread from Raiatea in the 18th century, just before European contact quickly overwhelmed the old Polynesian beliefs. ■

your way to the beach is not easy because of the continuous nature of beachside developments. All beaches, however, are public property in French Polynesia and the hotel proprietors along this popular strip do not seem to mind if you walk through their grounds.

Immediately offshore from the point are Motu Tiahura and Motu Fareone, attractive little islets so close to the shore you can easily swim out to them and enjoy fine snorkelling on the way. A little further east is the tiny Motu Irioa. In 1769, when Cook and his party observed the transit of Venus from Point Venus on Tahiti, Joseph Banks, the young scientist on the expedition, came to Moorea and made back-up measurements from this motu.

Marae Nuurua (PK 31.5, 31.5 km)

Marae Nuurua is easy to find. Continue past the Tiki Village Theatre on the lagoon side and then the combined ambulance and fire station on the mountain side. On the lagoon side there's a football field and the marae is right on the water's edge, just past the end of the field.

An impressive wall of coral boulders stands at the water's edge with a trail of tumbled boulders leading back to another cairn of boulders and then a restored three-level structure. This is flanked by twin spike-like upright stones, one of them broken off but with clear petroglyphs, including one of a turtle. Despite neglect and its relatively populated setting, it's a very evocative ruin, overgrown with vegetation, creepers and surrounded by coconut trees. Marae Nuurua was dedicated to the god Taaroa, popular before the Oro cult developed.

The marae marks the start of the *sauvage* (wild) side of Moorea, but the road is sealed and although the traffic is lighter and the population even sparser it doesn't feel that different from other parts of the island.

Haapiti to Atiha Bay (PK 24 to 18, 35 to 41 km)

The largest village on the more lightly populated west coast, **Haapiti** boasts two churches. The small grey-trimmed church in the centre of the village is dwarfed by the huge twin-towered Catholic Église de la Sainte Famille on the mountain side of the road. Built of coral and lime by stone masons who came to Moorea from Easter Island towards the end of the 19th century, the church was once the centre of the island's Catholic mission. Haapiti or Matauvau Pass has a popular surf break (see the Surfing section later in this chapter).

Moorea's lazy west coast atmosphere continues round to **Atiha Bay**, a sleepy fishing village which also attracts some surfers.

Marae Nuupere (PK 14, 45 km)

Nuupere Point is immediately south of **Maatea** village and the marae stands just 100 metres or so south of the point. Drive out to the point and walk along the coast to a small group of holiday homes – if anybody is there ask if you can look at the marae but if not just duck under the fence and proceed. The marae is a massive coastal cairn of coral boulders.

Back on the coast road the route continues through Maatea village and, two km further along, don't blink or you will miss tiny **Haumi** village (PK 12, 47 km).

Afareaitu (PK 10, 49 km)

The government centre of the island, Afareaitu has shops, a hospital, a small hotel, walks to two beautiful waterfalls, a church dating from 1912 and the oldest marae on the island. Chez Pauline is the village's hotel, with a fine collection of ancient stone tikis and other pre-European artefacts. Only about 100 metres south of Chez Pauline is **Marae Umarea**, thought to date from about 900 AD and the oldest marae on the island. Take the road which goes straight to the coast to see the marae, which is a long wall of coral boulders right along the waterfront. Marae Matairea stands inland, up the valley.

Roads turn inland to two waterfalls on the rivers which enter the sea at Afareaitu. See Afareaitu Waterfall Walks in the Walking & Climbing section later this chapter for more details.

Vaiare Ferry Dock (PK 4, 55 km)

The constant arrival and departure of ferry boats and high speed catamarans coming from and going to Papeete, the busy market scene on the wharf and the cars, taxis and *le trucks* shuttling visitors to and from their hotels combine to make the 100 metres or so around the dock area the busiest patch of real estate on Moorea. Vaiare is also the starting point for the interesting walk across the ridge to Paopao and Cook's Bay. See the Surfing section later in this chapter for more details.

Teavaro & Temae Beaches (PK 1 to 0, 58 to 59 km)

The best beaches on the east coast stretch from Teavaro round to the airport. The expensive Sofitel Ia Ora Hotel occupies Teavaro Beach, where there's good snorkelling in the shallow water. The island road climbs away from the coast to the **Toatea Lookout**, high above Teavaro Beach and with great views over to Tahiti. Temae Beach is close to the end of the airport runway, a pleasant stretch of sand with an unfortunate accumulation of garbage. When the swells run from the south, the reef at **Faaupo Point**, at the south end of the runway, can have the most powerful waves in French Polynesia.

A road on the lagoon side of the runway extends around **Temae Lake**, almost to Aroa Point, but the route is cut off by the swampy inlet so it is not possible to rejoin the main coastal road. The lake has lost almost half of its area and two-thirds of its depth over the past century, a process accelerated by the construction of the airport. Salty and semi-stagnant, the isolated lake is one of the rare breeding grounds for the only species of duck found in French Polynesia.

Paopao & Opunohu Valleys

From Moorea's two great bays valleys sweep inland, meeting south of the coastal bulk of Mt Rotui. Today settlements are creeping up the Paopao Valley but the principal activity is still agriculture, with many hectares of pineapple plantations. In the pre-European era the valleys were densely populated and the Opunohu Valley was dotted with maraes, some of which have been restored and maintained. The great marae sites of Titiroa and Afareaito were extensively reconstructed by Yosihiko Sinoto in 1967. The depopulation

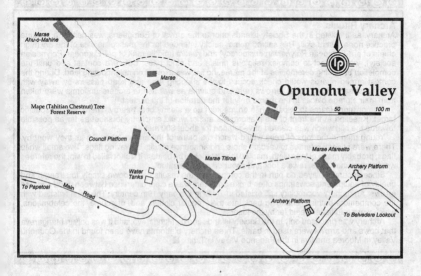

of these central valleys was a result both of the general depopulation of Moorea and the simultaneous decline of the Polynesian religion.

All maraes seem to attract mosquitoes and the Opunohu Valley maraes are no exception. Bring insect repellent or expect to have difficulty withstanding their onslaughts while you read the information boards!

The road leading inland from Paopao and Cook's Bay meets the Opunohu Valley road, just before the agricultural college. From here the road continues inland and up to the marae sites and finally to the Belvédère lookout, on the slopes of Mt Tohiea (1207 metres).

Marae Titiroa & Marae Ahu-o-Mahine Past the agricultural school, the valley road comes to a car parking area beside the huge Marae Titiroa, on the edge of a dense forest of magnificent mape trees. From the marae a walking track leads to the council platform, or *tohua*, and on to two smaller maraes. From there it continues to the Marae Ahu-o-Mahine, a more recent marae of individually

hewn round stones with an imposing three-stepped *ahu* which may have been an even more recent addition towards the end of the 18th century.

Marae Afareaito & the Archery Platforms
A short distance further up the road from Marae Titiroa is Marae Afareaito. Although there is a walking path between the two, it is not easy to follow; the main road is an easier route. The large marae has a small raised terrace ahu and backrests used by the priests.

The marae is flanked by two crescent-shaped archery platforms from which competing archers would shoot their arrows down a cleared range. Archery was strictly a pastime of the nobility and purely a ritual sport; bows and arrows were not used in battle.

The Belvédère
Beyond Marae Afareaito the road continues to climb steeply, winding up to its conclusion at the Belvédère. This lookout offers superb views of Mt Rotui, which splits the two bays, and back to the towering mountains that rise

---

Archery Rituals

Archery, as it existed in the Society Islands prior to the arrival of Europeans, was neither a wartime practice nor a test of skill. This sacred game, strictly intended for the masculine elite of the *arii* (high chiefs of pre-European Polynesian aristocracy) and *raatira* (middle rank of pre-European Polynesian society), was subject to complex religious rituals and strict rules. Before a contest and until the completion of closing ceremonies at the marae, no fire was allowed on neighbouring land. During the contest armed guards would check access to the shooting area and keep passers-by away with crossed spears. Bows (*fana*), arrows (*tea*) and quivers as well as the archers' uniforms were taken from their storage places in the marae only for the duration of the contest.

Two or more teams took part while drums kept up a steady beat nearby. There was no specific target. Kneeling at the front of the platform the archer would simply try to shoot as far as possible towards the hill, which was cleared of vegetation for about 300 metres.

Young men in the tops of trees would watch the paths of the arrows, shouting as they went by. There were several referees to validate shots and announce results by waving flags. Two small white flags, probably made of tapa cloth, marked the distance to be beaten. If a shot failed to win, the referees would lower their flags, raise a foot and shout *ua pau*, 'defeated'.

Since accuracy played no part in the competition, the results came down simply to strength and quality of equipment: bowstrings often broke and there was a clear difference between good and bad arrows. An archery vocabulary still existed in Tahiti in the early 19th century. The ritual finished with the competitors bathing, changing back into their regular clothes and, of course, the celebrations, which were traditionally paid for by the losers.

Archery was practised only in the Society Islands and on Mangareva, and it was only in Mangareva that bows and arrows were used in battle. Three archery platforms have been found in the Opunohu Valley in Moorea and five in the Papenoo Valley in Tahiti. ■

in the centre of the island and once formed the southern rim of the ancient crater.

WALKING & CLIMBING

Moorea's in-your-face mountains offer some fabulous walks which you can easily manage in a morning or afternoon. The catch is that finding the starting points of the walks can be tricky and it's very easy to lose the trails. Painted trail marks fade rapidly in this damp environment and once you've lost the trail you'll soon find yourself floundering around in the jungle, wondering where the path went to.

If you're good at following a trail and have the patience to work out where you've gone wrong, you'll find Moorea's walks amply rewarding. A couple of hours climbing through the jungle will leave you hotter and sweatier than you've ever been at any gym workout but the vegetation is wonderful and the views, when you finally get to the top, can be mind-blowing.

If you're concerned about being lost forever in that enveloping greenness, take a guide. Lots of round-the-island-type trips will take you on short strolls, like the Afareaitu Waterfall walk. Annie Langridge (☎ 56-41-34) of Opunohu will lead you on all the best walks and do it with a sense of humour and a real feel for local culture and life. What's more she speaks excellent English and her prices are very fair. The walk up to the Three Coconut Trees Pass costs 3000 CFP per person, Rotui takes four hours and also costs 3000 CFP per person. The longer walk up Moaputu takes 6½ hours after a 4.30 am start; the cost is 4000 CFP.

Derek Grell of Tefaarahi Adventure Tours (☎ 56-41-24, 56-29-09 or 56-26-48) speaks fluent French and leads walkers to the Three Coconut Trees Pass for 2500 CFP or to the summit of Rotui for 4000 CFP. He'll make these climbs even with just one walker.

Vaiare to Paopao

This interesting and reasonably easy walk takes about two hours, starting from Vaiare and climbing up to the ridge between Mt Tearai (772 metres) and Mt Mouaputa (830

metres) before dropping down into the central valley and emerging at Paopao on Cook's Bay. There are some great views and a good look at the dense vegetation which cloaks the island's steep mountains.

From the ferry terminal at the centre of Vaiare walk south across the first bridge and turn inland along the road beside the Chez Méno store. The road forks and then forks again; take the right fork on both occasions. There may well be a sign pointing to Paopao at the second fork, and on the right side of the road just before the fork is a 70-cm-high, 1.5-metre square stone block with a circular hole in the top. Monoi oil used to be mixed in this receptacle.

Don't take the next turn right but keep following the road, which deteriorates to a muddy track as it passes through plantations of pineapples, taro, papaya and then bananas and climbs up above the south bank of the river. Do not follow the track right to the end, however. If you do you'll find yourself on a walking track which follows the river to an eventual dead end. Look for a walking track which turns sharply off the wider vehicle track just before the track becomes too narrow even for an enthusiastically driven 4WD. Finding the start of the walking track is the most difficult part of this walk. It may be indicated by a red arrow painted on a pole on the opposite (river) side of the vehicle track or you may just have to cast around until you find the red splashes of paint on trees which are the trail markers.

The walking track climbs steeply uphill and can be slippery after rain but once you've found it it's easy to follow and is marked by very regular splashes of red paint on tree trunks. Eventually the track emerges on the ridge between the two peaks with a faded sign announcing: 'Moi, j'aime la nature'. Follow the ridge uphill, south, a short way to a rock with a wonderful view east across the sea to Tahiti and west over the pineapple plantations in the valley below. Towering above is the spectacular peak of Mt Mouaputa, the mountain with the 'hole' through it.

Back on the track the route drops very

steeply but handy vines and creepers make the descent fairly simple. The track passes through a thicket of bamboo and crosses a river before emerging on the flat valley floor and following gravel roads down to the head of the bay. The confusing maze of roads on the valley floor plus the steepness of the trail on this side of the ridge means it is easier to start this walk from Vaiare.

The Three Coconut Trees Pass

The climb to Les Trois Cocotiers is one of the most exhilarating in the Society Islands. It's hard sweaty work but the pay-off is superb views from the ridge separating Mouaroa (880 metres) from Toheia (1207 metres). There are not, however, three coconut trees – two of them were blown down in an early 1980s cyclone. Of course coconut trees don't grow on mountain tops by accident – somebody has to carry a sprouting coconut up there and plant it. Replacement coconut trees have been planted but until they grow the pass is really the One Coconut Tree! If you study the saddle between the two peaks you should be able to spot the single tree, standing proudly above the ridge.

Start by taking the inland road from the top of Opunohu Bay towards the Opunohu Valley maraes and the Belvédère lookout. Shortly after the road from the top of Cook's Bay joins the route, and before you get to the agricultural college, another road turns off to the right. A sign pointing up the valley indicates the way to the 'Vue de Roto Nui et du Marae' while a much smaller and rather obscure pictogram illustrates three coconut trees. Follow the turn-off road a couple of hundred metres to its end and park just before the pig farm.

The walking path continues straight on from the road and drops down to a small stream then climbs up the other side, through ferns, with the ridge and the coconut tree clearly visible to the right. The red trail markers along this part of the trail seem almost superfluous, the pathway is so clear and visible, but you'll soon be very glad of them and wish there were more.

The route takes a sharp turn and drops very steeply down to a wider river. Cross this river but don't go straight up the other side, an easy mistake to make. The path now follows the river, crossing it half a dozen times as it tumbles down through a dark and magnificent mape forest. Eventually the walking trail diverges from the river and heads up the hill. By this time you will probably have lost it once or twice but the route *is* marked. If you're uncertain whether you're still on the correct route, search for those red markers. If you go far without them you're lost.

Higher up the hill the markers seem to fade but bits of plastic tied to branches help and, for a time, as the trail gets steeper it also becomes more distinct and easy to follow. Clearings are the easiest places to get lost; make sure you're on the right trail each time you exit from a clearing. Closer to the top a clearing can cause confusion but there's a red marker on a big, mossy rock off to the right of the clearing. The final climb to the top of the knife-edge ridge is a real root hanger but you emerge from the undergrowth to the first unobstructed views on the way up.

Trodden-down barbed wire along the ridge line shows where a fence once ran along the line, dividing the land to the north and south. Follow the ridge to the right (west) for the best views over the bays divided by Mt Rotui and all the way to Tetiaroa on a clear day. There are equally good views to the south and keen walkers could follow a very steep route down to Haapiti on the south-west coast. Take care since it's little used and can be slippery.

Descending the same way you came, continue to keep an eye out for the route markers. It's even easier to lose them on the way down when you're walking faster and possibly paying less attention.

Rotui by the North Ridge

More than a mere walk, the difficulties make this ascent akin to a real mountain climb. Mt Rotui is oriented north-south, parallel to Opunohu and Cook's bays, which lie on either side. At only 899 metres, the height isn't that spectacular but the panorama over the two bays, which gradually comes into view as you climb, makes the effort worthwhile. Count on a minimum of four hours to make the exhausting climb, and about two hours to come down.

The departure point is near the waterfront Village Faimano hotel at PK 14.5 (see Places to Stay – Cook's Bay to Hauru Point). Theoretically, the walk begins along the path facing Village Faimano but their neighbours are unhappy about tourists who encroach on their property. So from this starting point it is preferable to continue about 100 metres towards Opunohu Bay to the coconut plantation on the mountain side of the road. At the 'propriété privé – tabu' sign you can rejoin the walking path; although this land is indeed private property it does have the advantage of being uninhabited.

It is definitely not a good idea to attempt this walk without a local guide. The route is used infrequently and it's often necessary to wield a machete to cut through the dense vegetation. The route is punctuated by dangerous drops where you need to hang on to the bushes, and on both sides of the ridge there are vertical drops. In case of an injury, a simple sprain for example, you would not be able to descend to get help. Don't start if there has been rain in the past few days and this is not a good walk for anyone who suffers from vertigo. You need to be in good physical condition and, at the risk of being repetitive, there are many passages which are more like rock climbing than walking.

It's vitally important to take plenty of drinking water because, once you're on the ridge, there is no shade. A hat or cap, sunscreen and sunglasses are also necessary. Good walking shoes which are not prone to slipping are highly recommended, as are trousers to protect your legs from scratches.

The first part of the climb, to the *aito* (flame tree) massif, which you can see from the road, is the most testing. If you're forced to leave the path due to wasps' nests it will be necessary to hack a way through the bushes and the guava trees. Just before the aito trees, particularly steep rocky boulders

make the climb very difficult. From this rocky spur the route continues along the crest, unprotected from the sun, through *puarata* and ferns. Great care is needed on this part of the walk because the path is narrow and there are sheer drops on each side. It's like walking up a series of stairways with relatively flat passages followed by steep slopes where you will need to hang on with your hands. The views of Cook's Bay to the left and Opunohu Bay to the right defy all the superlatives, and if it's clear you can distinguish the foothills of Tahiti to the south-east.

At the summit you can see the ancient volcano crater and, to the south, Mt Tohiea (1207 metres) and Mouaputa (830 metres). The descent should be made with the maximum of care. Take particular care at the aito massif level where it is necessary to go round to the right. It's easy to miss the trail among the piles of rocks and there are small and large cliff faces in the vicinity. After this little jaunt you'll understand better why, according to the Maohi legends, Mt Rotui is the place of purgatory for the dead before they ascend to paradise.

Afareaitu Waterfall Walks

Afareaitu has a couple of short waterfall walks. The Putoa and Vaioro rivers both reach the sea at Afareaitu, where a low ridge divides the wider valley behind the village into these two smaller river valleys.

From right in the middle of town, opposite the church and between the Ah Sing store and the Putoa River bridge, a road runs back up the valley. It starts sealed, soon becomes dirt, then gets rougher and narrower until even a 4WD couldn't proceed further. Depending on how far you want to push your wheels, you're left with a 20 to 30-minute walk to the falls. There's a somewhat confusing maze of tracks and footpaths but if you basically head north along the valley, and follow the footprints, you'll get there. The falls fan out as they tumble down a wide rock face, dropping into a pool edged by a wide arc of boulders and stones.

The other waterfall on the Vaioro River is

quite well known and is reached by a very short walk. If you look up the valley you can see the falls from the coast road. The dirt road is just north of the hospital or just south of the Vaioro River bridge. There's a series of speed bumps on the first few hundred metres, before you come to a sign reporting that the road and the falls are on private property, care of the Atna Association, and that you should pay a 200 CFP entry charge. After that the road deteriorates, although your rent-a-car will manage it with care. When the road ends it's only a 10-minute walk along a well tended path to the falls. Obviously the flow varies with the amount of rain but the waterfall can be a beautiful thin wisp, feathering down the rock face to a ferny pool at the bottom.

DIVING

Since the first Moorea dive centre opened in 1984 the activity has become a veritable craze. Moorea's coral reefs are remarkably well preserved and the visibility is often better than 40 metres. The marine life is also much more abundant than around nearby Tahiti. Regular fish feedings, which artificially increase the density of marine life at certain sites, are undoubtedly part of the reason for this phenomenon.

You definitely have a range of possibilities when it comes to exploring the underwater world – there are four dive centres from Cook's Bay to Hauru Point. Although they all go to the same sites they each have their own style and personality. Don't hesitate to knock at different doors and make comparisons. Don't forget that transfers between your hotel and the dive operators may not be included beyond a certain distance. Each centre gives preferential rates to divers staying at the hotels they are associated with. During the busy times, mainly July-August, it is prudent to make reservations several days in advance. The personnel at the four centres speak English because much of their business is with Anglophones. Dives outside the reef for certified divers are generally made at 9 am and 2 pm, while dives within the lagoon for beginners are made at 10.30 am.

The dive centres can be divided into two groups. Bathy's Club and MUST are larger and higher priced operations and both are involved in shark feeding. Scubapiti and Moorea Fun Dive both eschew shark feeding but are also smaller, more relaxed, 'no frills' operations where you might have to carry your own air tanks and shouldn't necessarily expect help in getting geared up.

Dive Centres

Bathy's Club This club (☎ 56-31-44) is based at the Beachcomber Parkroyal and is the deluxe shop window for diving in French Polynesia. Bernard Bégliomini, the proprietor, is well known in the diving world. A pioneer of shark feeding (in 1985), he is the major protagonist of this activity and although a more aggressive female bit him once he has also trained moray eels to take part. Vincent and Michael, the two divemasters, have become expert in the art of teasing grey sharks, lemon sharks and moray eels. Bernard Bégliomini likes to boast of the well known clients he has taken diving, including astronaut Buzz Aldrin.

Bathy's Club is unique in being the only PADI five-star centre in French Polynesia. PADI divers will certainly be welcome here – in any case they make up a large part of the clientele. Bathy's Club even has a PADI-approved qualification, the 'Polynesian Shark Diver'. It's unique to this region and you can qualify for the certificate for 19,900 CFP. At Bathy's Club a single dive costs 5000 CFP, five dives cost 22,500 CFP, beginners' dives are 6900 CFP, night dives are 7500 CFP, certificate courses are 43,500 CFP for a five-lesson CMAS course or 48,000 CFP for a PADI open-water course. They will also video your dive for 12,000 CFP.

Except for a beginner's first dive, rental of a buoyancy compensator, regulator and wet suit are not included in the price; each item costs 500 CFP to rent. The sites are less than 10 minutes by boat from the dive centre. The Tiki, the Taotoi Pass and the Ray Passage are popular with Bathy's Club. The centre provides transfers from places between the Moorea Village and Moorea Lagoon Hotel. It's closed on Monday and credit cards are accepted.

MUST Philippe Molle's Moorea Underwater Scuba-Diving Tahiti (MUST; ☎ 56-17-32 or 56-15-83) is on Cook's Bay, right by Cook's Bay Resort. Molle is the author of numerous publications on the theory and practice of diving. You pay for this expertise: the prices are the same as Bathy's Club, 5000 CFP for a dive, 22,500 for five, 6500 for a beginner's dive. There are rental charges of 300 CFP for a regulator, 400 CFP for a buoyancy compensator and 250 CFP for other equipment, but prices are reduced by half if you opt for

a five-dive programme. There's also an extra 3% added for credit card payments.

Transfers are provided for the hotels on Cook's Bay. If you come from further away with your own transport, you may be offered a 10% discount on the dive costs. Philippe Molle warmly recommends the Cook's Bay Resort, whose guests get a reduced price. CMAS certification costs 34,000 CFP, night dives are 6500 CFP and you can have your dive videotaped for 6000 CFP. PADI divers are welcome. The centre is closed on Monday.

Most of MUST's dives are at the Tiki, the Ray Passage, the Taotoi Pass or the Garden of the Roses. Like Bathy's Club, shark feeding is usually offered on the morning dives. In this field Philippe Molle is a good match for his rival Bernard Bégliomini: he is

---

Shark Feeding

If drift diving through the passes is the major attraction in Rangiroa, then shark feeding, occasionally called *'repas des requins'*, is the number one dive thrill in Moorea. The two older dive centres, pioneers in this field, offer shark-feeding sessions to divers looking for excitement.

The choreography is orchestrated in minute detail. At the quay the divers are equipped while the divemasters load an enormous tuna carcass on the boat, wrapped in a plastic bag. During embarkation and en route to the dive site, the divemaster explains the feeding process and repeats security instructions to the divers. After entering the water the divemaster takes the group down, holding the tuna carcass tightly against his chest.

A myriad of colourful fish immediately converge on the group of divers, attracted by the smell of blood. Perches, surgeonfish and damselfish surround the divemaster, excited by the possibility of a free meal. Fifteen metres below the surface and outside the pass, the divemaster signals to the divers to form an arc several metres around him and to keep down, close to the bottom. The orgy can then begin.

He takes the carcass out of the plastic bag and begins to chop it up meticulously with his knife. The invitees arrive in greater and greater numbers: butterfly fish, parrot fish and many other small fish as well as larger visitors like napoleons. Suddenly, arriving like a torpedo out of the blue, a grey shark (*raira*) jumps the queue and gobbles up a quarter of the tuna. Several minutes later about 15 larger sharks (grey, black-tipped and white-tipped reef sharks) join in, squabbling over the morsels of tuna offered by the divemaster. Silhouetted against the maelstrom of fish, the other divers can barely see him, but before the situation becomes critical he discards the rest of the fish, rejoins the group and they leave the scene. The dive proceeds in quieter circumstances and the feeding frenzy is all over in about a quarter of an hour.

Shark feeding is also practised on some other islands but opinion is not unanimously in favour of the practice; indeed, the two smaller dive centres on Moorea do not offer this type of dive. Various reasons are given: they worry about the security of their clients during the 15 minutes that the divemaster disappears in the mass of fish. Then there's the ecological effects of the practice, as feeding attracts fish to every diver, making it very easy for unscrupulous spear fishers to take fish. As for the local fishing boats, they worry that sharks will devastate their catch. Finally, although there have been no serious accidents as yet, the behaviour of the sharks is unpredictable. Without being paranoid, attracting them so close to the beaches, even though they are still outside the reef, must raise concerns about safety. ∎

said to favour grey sharks, moray eels and napoleons as much as the lemon sharks which come to eat out of his hand.

Moorea Fun Dive Based at the Moorea Lagoon Hotel, this organisation (☎ 56-40-38 or 56-40-74) offers CMAS and PADI courses. It charges 5000 CFP for a lagoon dive (4800 CFP for Moorea Lagoon guests), 22,500 CFP for five dives and 6000 CFP for night dives. CMAS certification (five lessons) costs 31,500 CFP or the PADI open-water course is 45,000 CFP. You can have your dive videotaped for 8000 CFP. Note that beginners' dives are the same price as regular dives, 5000 CFP. Dive costs include all equipment.

This is the only dive centre on Moorea with a female divemaster, Pascale. Unlike other dive centres, transfers are provided from any of the north coast hotels. Divers are offered a preferential tariff if they stay at the Moorea Lagoon. Credit cards are accepted and the centre is open every day.

Scubapiti This club (☎ 56-20-38 or 56-12-67) is at the Les Tipaniers Hotel and has the advantage of lower prices: 4500 CFP for a dive, or 40,500 CFP for 10 dives, equipment included. The cost of a PADI open-water course is exactly the same as a CMAS course, 32,500 CFP. Unfortunately, it costs 5% extra to use a credit card for payment. Transfers are provided within a radius of 10 km. At the time of our visit, Marc Quattrini was the only person running the centre but he will be joined by a female divemaster. The sites visited are the same as the other centres, along with several exploration dive sites (the Taota Canyons and the Matauvau Pass) on the west coast of the island for experienced divers. The centre is open every day.

Dive Sites

There are about 20 dives sites in Moorea but the most popular are along the north coast, easily reached by the four dive operators. They include:

Opunohu Bay There are several popular dives around the entrance to Opunohu Bay. One descends to the remains of the *Kersaint*, which ran on to the reef on its way out of the bay in 1919. The scattered fragments lie at 15 to 25 metres' depth and include the ship's engine. Opunohu also has a fine coral wall dive with a great deal of colourful coral and sponges. You'll encounter schools of fish as well as black-tipped reef sharks.

The Tiki This well known dive site is renowned for the exceptional density of its marine life. Dives are made along the outside of the reef, at the extreme north-west of Moorea, close to Motu Fareone and facing Club Med. The water is exceptionally clear, to the delight of underwater photographers, and there is no current except when a strong swell is running. The combination of these two factors make this dive very safe and it is not necessary to descend to more than 25 metres. As soon as you enter the water, perches, surgeon fish, butterfly fish and other small fish crowd around, and as you descend further napoleons, black-tipped reef sharks and grey sharks approach. Finally, at the bottom, the lemon sharks, feared and fearsome, make their appearance. To assist at a shark feeding at this site is the star turn.

Regular fish feeding over the years has ensured a large population of fish waiting for a free handout. Black-tipped reef sharks, grey reef sharks and lemon sharks from one to three metres are regular visitors and the feeding can be a spectacular sight. Other fish are even more numerous and include tuna and barracuda.

Ray Passage On the west side of Tareu Pass, this dive certainly deserves its name. Flights of leopard rays are regularly seen at this rendezvous, in a channel about 20 metres deep. Because of the west to east current through the pass, visibility can be limited but there's a better chance of seeing the rays. Along the drop-off, at less than six metres' depth, you find the usual panoply of reef life. The site is particularly safe; at the top of the dive the lagoon is less than 1.5 metres deep and because of this it is popular with beginners.

Garden of Roses Entered via the Tareu and Teavarua passes, this spectacular dive is reserved for more experienced divers. The descent through open water reaches a depth of about 50 metres. For once the fish are not the main attraction. Anchored on the ocean side of the reef, the rose coral is displayed like flower petals. Mother nature has compensated for the lack of light by deploying the coral in an outgrowth more than three metres in diameter in order to capture the maximum amount of light. These strange corals make you think of a petrified salad!

Taota Pass This pass south of Hauru Point features a coral wall with a great variety of reef fish, black-tipped reef sharks and grey sharks. Numerous leopard rays are also sometimes encountered. Taota Canyons is a more difficult drift dive from the ocean into the pass. Leopard rays are attracted by the current and there are also colourful coral and reef fish.

Avamotu Pass Just north of Haapiti on the west coast, this small pass offers superb visibility, colourful coral and large numbers of reef fish and moray eels.

Matauvau Pass Further south, so less frequented, the pass to Haapiti village can be a difficult dive due to the strong outgoing current. But the continuous stream of fish compensates. Eagle rays particularly like a strong current, but shoals of red snapper, large napoleons and perches are also seen. The caverns in the pass attract white-tipped reef sharks, grey sharks and sleeping nurse sharks.

SURFING
The break at Haapiti or Matauvau Pass, off the village of Haapiti on the west coast, is consistent and produces, according to visiting surfers, 'a world-class wave'. Surfers can leave their gear at Tubb's Pub. The bar owner runs a water taxi out to the pass; he'll take

you out there and bring you back for 800 CFP round trip. Not only does it save a half-hour paddle but it gives you somewhere safe to leave your gear.

Faaupo Point, by Temae Beach near the airport, can be superb when it breaks with a swell from the south. When conditions are right, which is rare, it's one of the strongest waves in Polynesia and unusual for being a reef break rather than on one of the passes.

HORSE RIDING
Rupe Rupe Ranch (☎ 56-26-52) at PK 2 offers horseback trips to the mountains and valleys or along the beach for both beginners and more experienced riders. Morning and afternoon rides are scheduled and cost 1000 CFP for a 45-minute canter along the beach or 2000 CFP for a longer 1½-hour ride. Tiahura Ranch (☎ 56-28-55) at PK 26 at Hauru Point offers 1½ rides into the mountains Tuesday to Sunday from 9 am and 4.15 pm for 2500 CFP. You can make a *tour de pony* according to their sign.

ORGANISED TOURS
Land Tours
There are numerous island circuit tours which bus you round the coast road and take you up to the central valley marae sites and the Belvédère lookout. Your hotel will tell you about them even before you ask!

Ron's Tours (☎ 56-35-80 or 56-29-09) conduct a variety of adventure tours including 4WD safaris, walks and mountain bike (VTT or *vélo à tout terrain* in French) trips. The morning and afternoon 4WD tours visit maraes, plantations and the interior highlands of Moorea and cost 4000 or 4500 CFP. The morning Mountain Bike Adventure costs 4000 CFP, while walks follow the most popular hiking trails, including the walk to the Three Coconut Trees Pass and the Vaiare to Paopao walk (both 3000 CFP).

Inner Island Safari Tours (☎ 56-20-09) does trips Sunday to Friday at 8.15 am and 1.15 pm. The four-hour 4WD excursions go through the Opunohu Valley, around the island and to the Afareaitu Waterfalls and cost 4500 CFP.

Derek Grell, the American proprietor of Tefaarahi Adventure Tours (☎ 56-41-24, 56-29-09 or 56-26-48), speaks fluent French and has a comprehensive programme for walkers, mountain bikers and 4WD enthusiasts. Tours are taken in a 4WD Land-Rover and you can discover petroglyphs in the mountains for 2500 CFP, explore the Opunohu Valley for 3500 CFP or do both for 4500 CFP on the four-hour complete tour. The mountain bike tour goes around Rotui by the two bays and costs 3000 CFP for the half-day trip with a guide. Children under 12 years of age get a 30% reduction.

Albert Tours (☎ 56-13-53) does a four-hour island circuit from 9 am for 2000 CFP or a three-hour photo safari into the central valleys by 4WD at 9 am and 2 pm for 3500 CFP.

Cruises & Boat Charters

Island boat tours focus on the twin bays (Opunohu and Cook's) and the twin motus (off Hauru Point), with shark feeding as a popular sideline. Moorea Mahana Lagoon Activities (☎ 56-19-19 or 56-20-44, or at the Beachcomber Hotel) do Cook's Bay and Opunohu Bay cruises, sunset cruises and dinner cruises. They also operate the 11.5-metre catamaran *Manu* on half-day and full-day cruises or for charters. From 9 am to 3 pm their semisubmarine operates hourly.

What to Do on Moorea Tours (☎ 56-13-68 at the Club Bali Hai, ☎ 56-13-59 at the Sofitel Ia Ora) does island circuits in a motorised pirogue (3500 CFP), motu and bay tours (2300 CFP), glass-bottom boat trips (2500 CFP), motu picnic trips (4000 CFP) and sunset cruises on Cook's Bay. Albert Tours (☎ 56-13-53) does a two-bay lagoon safari and a trip out to the motus by pirogue. The five-hour trip costs 3500 CFP on Tuesday or 4500 CFP on Thursday, when they also have a barbecue.

There are a variety of boats available for fishing trips, lagoon cruises or other charters. Tea Nui Charters (☎ 56-15-08) is at the Beachcomber Parkroyal Hotel.

Air Tours

Air Moorea (☎ 86-41-41) does flightseeing tours over the island in its small Britten-Norman Islander aircraft. The 30-minute flights from Tahiti operate on Saturday and Sunday at 10 am (costing 6500 CFP per person) and will operate even if only one passenger turns up. Moorea is truly spectacular when seen from above and the flight takes in views of Opunohu and Cook's bays, the motus off Hauru Point, the central mountains and Belvédère lookout. Heli-Pacific (☎ 85-68-00) offers helicopter trips over the island.

PLACES TO STAY

Although there are accommodation places scattered around the island, most places are concentrated in the four km from PK 5 to PK 9 on the east side of Cook's Bay and in the five km from PK 26 to PK 31 around Hauru Point. Both these centres are very spread out; if you're staying at one end and want to eat at the other it's not a case of just wandering a few steps along the road.

Moorea has the best selection of economical (by local standards, of course) accommodation in French Polynesia. There are backpacker centres with camping sites and dormitory facilities, some cheaper hotels and a host of local bungalow complexes which generally include kitchen equipment so you can cook your own food. Note that while most places supply sheets and other bedding, towels are often not provided in the cheapest places. The top-end places and most of the mid-range places accept credit cards; any exceptions are noted.

Cook's Bay

Cook's Bay has one cheaper establishment and a number of mid-range hotels and resorts.

Bottom End *Chez Albert* (☎ & fax 56-12-76), on the mountain side of the road at PK 7 at Cook's Bay, has 18 bungalows in total.

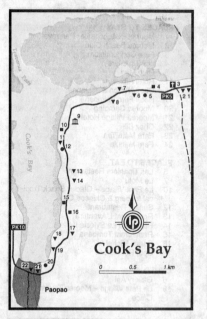

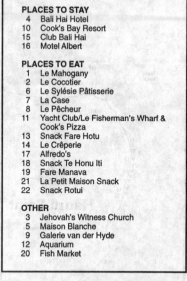

PLACES TO STAY
4	Bali Hai Hotel
10	Cook's Bay Resort
15	Club Bali Hai
16	Motel Albert

PLACES TO EAT
1	Le Mahogany
2	Le Cocotier
6	Le Sylésie Pâtisserie
7	La Case
8	Le Pêcheur
11	Yacht Club/Le Fisherman's Wharf & Cook's Pizza
13	Snack Fare Hotu
14	Le Crêperie
17	Alfredo's
18	Snack Te Honu Iti
19	Fare Manava
21	La Petit Maison Snack
22	Snack Rotui

OTHER
3	Jehovah's Witness Church
5	Maison Blanche
9	Galerie van der Hyde
12	Aquarium
20	Fish Market

Cook's Bay

0   0.5   1 km

Paopao

Ten have two rooms, one with a double bed and the other with two single beds, and cost 7000 CFP for up to five people.

The other eight single-bedroom apartments consist of four with a double bed and four with two double beds. These cost 4000 CFP for one or two people. The rooms are simple but well equipped, with kitchen facilities, attached bathrooms and hot water. Monthly rates are available but credit cards are not accepted.

Middle The *Bali Hai Moorea* (☎ 56-13-59, fax 56-19-22) is just past PK 5, at the start of the hotel and restaurant strip around Cook's Bay. It's one of the longest established tourist hotels in French Polynesia but remains popular with tour groups. The hotel has a well-stocked boutique, a pool, tennis court, a very popular bar, restaurants and a tiny patch of beach. The usual range of island activities are on offer and the island night

dance performance is one of the best on Moorea. The 63 rooms are variable; the 12 cheapest rooms at 9500 CFP are depressing little boxes which are best avoided. There are much more attractive rooms on Moorea at that sort of price. The bungalows are much brighter and more cheerful, starting at 14,000 CFP for the garden and poolside bungalows and costing 24,000 to 27,000 CFP for the over-water bungalows. *Demi-pension* (breakfast and dinner) adds 3900 CFP per person. There's an additional 8% tax on these figures. Bookings can be made through BP 26, Temae, Moorea.

At PK 7 the unusual colonial-looking *Cook's Bay Resort Hotel* (☎ 56-10-50, fax 56-29-18) is a big, two-storey place perched on the edge of Cook's Bay. There's a swimming pool with adjacent snack bar, and a bar and Mexican restaurant reached by an over-water walkway. The associated Fisherman's Wharf restaurant and pizzeria are only a short stroll along the bayside. Snorkelling equipment is available free of charge and outrigger canoe trips are also provided at no

MOOREA

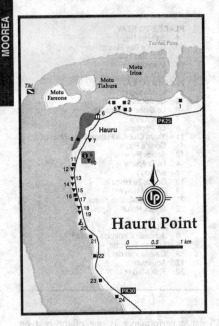

PLACES TO STAY
1 Moorea Beachcomber Parkroyal
2 Moorea Beach Club
3 Fare Condominium
4 Les Tipaniers
8 Club Med
11 Hotel Hibiscus
16 Chez Nelson & Josianne
17 Hotel Fare Vaimoana
20 Moorea Camping
21 Moorea Village Hotel
22 Chez Billy
23 Fare Mato Tea
24 Fare Manuia

PLACES TO EAT
5 Les Tipaniers Restaurant
7 Le Motu
10 Le Petit Village – Glacier Snack/Tropical Iceberg & Chinese Café
12 Sunset Restaurant
13 Restaurant L'Aventura
14 Pâtisserie Le Sylésie II
15 Restaurant Tumoana
18 Snack Michel
19 Spot Restaurant

OTHER
6 Gallery Api
9 Le Petit Village – Moorea Tourist Office

cost. The 76 motel-style rooms are small and simple but they do have telephone, fan or air-conditioning, refrigerator and tea and coffee-making facilities. They cost 8400 CFP fan-cooled or 9900 CFP air-con for one or two people. The hotel is popular with families and interconnecting rooms are available. Family rooms with two double beds are 10,800 CFP. The resort also has 24 separate bungalows with similar facilities. They cost 9600 CFP (garden) or 14,200 CFP (lagoonside). All prices are subject to the 8% government tax, credit cards are accepted and bookings can be made through BP 30, Temae, Moorea. Discounted prices are sometimes available.

Further round the bay at about PK 8 the *Club Bali Hai* (☎ 66-31-49, fax 56-19-22) has 39 rooms and bungalows ranging from 9500 CFP bayview to 18,000 CFP beachfront and 22,500 CFP over water. There's a swimming pool, tennis court, restaurant, a very popular bar and a nice setting right on

the bay. Bookings can be made through BP 8, Temae, Moorea.

Cook's Bay to Hauru Point
Bottom End & Middle At PK 14, right up at the north-east corner of Opunohu Bay, *Village Faimano* (☎ 56-10-20, fax 56-36-47) has six bungalows in a very pleasant beachside setting. Three of the bungalows are 8000 CFP, one of them is 8500 CFP and the two family *fares* are 11,000 CFP. The cheaper ones are very simple units but the more expensive family fares are quite nice, with two rooms and a mezzanine level. The bungalows all have kitchen facilities and attached bathrooms with hot water. The two family fares can accommodate up to six people at no extra cost. Credit cards are not accepted but lower rates can be negotiated for longer stays.

There are several other places between the

two bays. *Chez Nani* (☎ 56-19-99) at PK 14.5 has three fares, each with a single and a double bed, attached bathroom (cold water) and a kitchen. The costs are 6000 CFP (garden) or 7000 CFP (beach) for one or two people and one or two children under 12. Credit cards are not accepted. Close by is *Chez Francine*, (☎ 56-13-24) with a two-bedroom house. Each room has two single beds and attached bathroom with hot water. The room without a kitchenette is 6000 CFP for one or two, while the room with a kitchenette is 7000 CFP.

Two km back at PK 12.5 *Chez Dina* (☎ 56-10-39) is on the mountain side of the road and has three fares, all with kitchenettes and shared cold water bathrooms. They cost 4500 CFP for up to four people and 5000 CFP for up to six. Credit cards are not accepted.

The biggest and most expensive hotel between the Cook's Bay and Hauru Point enclaves is the 40-bungalow *Hotel Moorea Lagoon* (☎ 56-11-55 or 56-14-68, fax 56-26-25) at PK 14, beside the lagoon. The hotel has a small beach, swimming pool, tennis court, bar, restaurant and other facilities. The bungalows cost from 11,000 to 17,000 CFP; the pricier rooms are by the water's edge. Although it is a bit more expensive than other bungalow resorts, the rooms are definitely a higher quality. Bookings can be made through BP 11, Temae, Moorea.

Associated with the popular Les Tipaniers at Hauru Point, *Tipaniers Iti* (☎ 56-12-67, fax 56-29-25) has five very pleasant bungalows with kitchen, sitting area and verandah. The bungalows costs 7500 CFP a night plus the 8% tax and special prices are available for longer stays. A boat will shuttle you over to Hauru Point for 500 CFP return and there's also a free bus service which runs out at 10 am and back at 2 pm and to the Le Tipaniers restaurant at night. There's no beach but the lagoonside setting at PK 21 at the entrance to Opunohu Bay is very attractive and there are terrific views. Guests have free use of Les Tipaniers' facilities, including outrigger canoes and bicycles.

Hauru Point

Hauru Point has every accommodation bracket in French Polynesia. At the bottom end are two of the most popular backpacker locales with camping space, dormitories and cheap rooms. In the middle range are a host of beachside bungalow establishments ranging from cheaper and simpler places to romantic Polynesian fares and larger bungalows catering for family groups. Finally at the top of the range is Club Med and the luxurious Beachcomber Parkroyal.

Bottom End At PK 27, *Chez Nelson & Josianne* (☎ 56-15-18) has very spacious beachfront grounds which straddle a new mid-range development. The kitchen and dining area is neat, comfortable and very well equipped with fridges, burners, tables and chairs. Camping costs 700 CFP on day one, and 500 CFP on subsequent nights. Two dormitory fares each have five very simple little rooms for two which cost 1200 CFP per person on night one, 1000 CFP thereafter. There are five beach cabins, with two single beds, costing 2500 CFP for one or two people on night one, 2200 CFP thereafter. Four fares down one side of the site cost 3000 CFP for one or two people on day one, 2500 CFP on subsequent nights. Finally, three pleasant larger family fares have a double bed and their own kitchen and bathroom. These cost 6000 CFP for one or two people. Credit cards are not accepted.

Moorea Camping (☎ 56-14-47, fax 56-30-22) at PK 27.5 has a pleasant beachside camping area, dormitory facilities and a variety of simple but functional bungalows. There's an equally functional dining house right by the beach with kitchen areas at each end. The beach is good as well; in fact, for budget-minded backpackers, Moorea Camping fits the bill just fine. A tent site costs 800 CFP for night one, 500 CFP on subsequent nights. A dorm bed is 1000 CFP on night one, 800 CFP thereafter. The two dormitory fares are divided up into six small rooms in one and 10 in the other. Simple rooms for one or two people are 3000 CFP on night one, 2000 CFP thereafter. Slightly more luxurious bungalows are 5000 CFP on night one and 4000 CFP thereafter, while bungalows with a mezzanine area and space for three or four people are 6000 CFP on night one and 5000 CFP thereafter. Bathroom facilities with cold water are all shared but you do share them with fewer people in the more expensive rooms. Credit cards are not accepted.

Across the road from the campsite, *Moorea Fare* is operated by Moorea Camping and has a bungalow with a double bed and single bed, a mezzanine loft with two single beds, plus a kitchen and bathroom with hot water. Costs range from 7000 CFP for two people up to 10,000 CFP for five. There's a three-night minimum and credit cards are accepted.

At PK 28 *Chez Billy Ruta* (☎ 56-12-54) has fairly basic bungalows with two single beds and cold-water bathrooms. The seven standard fares are 4000 CFP per person, and the five with kitchenettes are 5000 CFP per person. Credit cards are not accepted.

Middle After the big Beachcomber, the first hotel along the main Hauru Point strip is the *Moorea Beach Club* (☎ 56-15-48, fax 41-09-28), a rather unexciting hotel with 40 identical motel-like rooms arrayed in two-storey blocks. There's a pool, tennis courts and a restaurant. The nightly cost is 12,000 CFP plus 8% tax. Bookings can be made through BP 1017, Papetoai, Moorea. On the same site, *Fare Condominium* (☎ 56-26-69, fax 56-26-22) is a funny name for a bunch of bungalows. There are 43 of them and they're pretty spartan but they do have kitchenettes. The cost is 9500 CFP for one or two people in the garden bungalows or 11,800 CFP in the beach bungalows.

Also at the beginning of the Hauru Point hotel and restaurant strip, *Hotel Les Tipaniers* (☎ 56-12-67, fax 56-29-25) is one of the most pleasant of Moorea's bungalow hotels. The 22 fares are dotted around a flowery garden leading down to the beach and the beachfront restaurant and looking across to the motus. The thatched-roof bungalows have a verandah, a small inside seating area, a bedroom area and a bathroom. The standard bungalows cost 7800/10,000 CFP for singles/doubles. Slightly larger bungalows have an equipped kitchen and couches that fold down into extra beds. As a garden bungalow, these cost 9800 CFP while as a beach bungalow they are 12,500 CFP, all with space for up to four people. Larger bungalows that accommodate up to five or six are 12,500 CFP. These rates are all subject to 8% tax.

Les Tipaniers restaurant has an excellent reputation (see the Places to Eat section). There's a bar and a variety of sporting facilities. It's an easy swim out to the motus, outrigger canoe trips and the use of bicycles are free for guests. Bookings can be made through BP 1002, Papetoai, Moorea

The *Hotel Hibiscus* (☎ 56-12-20, fax 56-20-69) at PK 27 has 29 very functional and slightly spartan thatched-roof bungalows, in a pleasant garden. They all have three beds, an attached bathroom and verandah and some have kitchenettes. They cost 10,000 CFP (garden), 12,000 CFP (beach), plus 8% tax. The beachfront restaurant is quite good and there's a swimming pool. Bookings can be made through BP 1009, Papetoai, Moorea.

Brand new in 1996, *Hotel Fare Vaimoana* (☎ & fax 56-17-14), at PK 27.5 is straddled by Chez Nelson & Josiane. There are 11 bungalows costing from 8000 to 12,000 CFP depending on their location, the more expensive ones being right on the beach, of course.

A little further round the point from Moorea Camping and also right on the beach at about PK 28 is *Moorea Village* (☎ 56-10-02, fax 56-22-11), which is sometimes known as Fare Gendron. It has 48 functional and rather simple bungalows, with and without kitchenettes. The garden bungalows are 8000/ 9000 CFP as singles/doubles or 12,500 CFP with kitchenette. The beachfront bungalows are 10,500/11,500 CFP or 15,000 CFP with kitchenette. All prices are subject to the 8% tax. There's a tennis court, swimming pool, bar and restaurant where breakfast costs 700 CFP (continental) or

1200 CFP (American); demi-pension is 3900 CFP. Bookings can be made through BP 1008, Papetoai, Moorea.

At PK 28.7 *Fare Mato Tea* (☎ 54-14-36) has simple motel-style beach cabins with a big kitchen and dining area and lots of sleeping space so they're perfect for families. Dotted around a wide expanse of lawn, sweeping down to the beach, are eight bungalows. Five of them have a bedroom with one double bed and two sofa-beds in the living room and cost 8500 CFP per day. The other three have two bedrooms, each with a double bed and two convertible sofas and cost 10,500 CFP per day. Bookings can be made at BP 1111, Papetoai, Moorea, but credit cards are not accepted.

Fare Manuia (☎ 56-26-17) has a pleasant stretch of beach at PK 30, towards the end of the Hauru Point strip. There are five bungalows spaced out around the grassy grounds of this family-oriented place. All of them have bathrooms with hot water, kitchen facilities and large verandahs. The two smaller fares have a double bedroom plus two single sofa-beds and cost 8000 CFP for up to four people. The three larger fares have a double bedroom and a mezzanine area with two double mattresses, plus a living room. They cost 10,000 CFP for up to six people in the garden, 12,000 CFP by the beach. There's a washing machine at the site and canoes are available for guests to use. Credit cards are not accepted.

At Tiki Village at PK 31, marking the extreme end of the Hauru Point tourist strip, *Polynesian Bungalows* (☎ 56-30-20 or 56-30-77, fax 56-32-15) have 10 rather jammed-together units for two to five people. The thatched-roof bungalows have bathrooms, a kitchenette and a mezzanine area. For two people the nightly cost is 8000 CFP plus 8% tax; longer-term discounts are available. The Tiki Village theatre complex is between the bungalows and the beach and the whole thing is a bit isolated from the activity of Hauru Point.

Top End The start of the Hauru Point tourist strip is demarcated by the big *Moorea Beachcomber Parkroyal* (☎ 56-19-19, fax 56-18-88), one of the most luxurious and expensive, not to mention biggest, hotels on the island. Lots of time and lavish amounts of money have turned a swathe of swamp into the winner of a PATA (Pacific Asia Travel Association) environmental excellence award. The beach may be artificial and the coral may have started life elsewhere but the end result certainly looks the part.

The Beachcomber has a lavish reception, restaurant and bar area stepping down to a swimming pool and waterfront activities area, while the 151 rooms wind around the artificial lagoon which resulted from dredging the swamp. This is where the hotel's resident dolphins live. Nightly costs range from 28,000 CFP for the basic rooms, 30,000 CFP for the garden bungalows, 34,000 CFP for the beachfront bungalows and up to 38,000 CFP for the over-water bungalows. All prices are subject to 8% tax.

The hotel has bars and restaurants: *Fare Hana* by the pool and the more haute cuisine *Fare Nui*. Breakfast is available for 1650 CFP (continental) or 1950 CFP (American); demi-pension costs 6100 CFP. There are tennis courts, a variety of other sporting facilities, shops, tour booking desks and everything else you'd expect at this sort of hotel. Bookings can be made through BP 1019, Papetoai, Moorea.

The *Club Méditerranée Moorea* (☎ 56-15-00, fax 56-19-51) at Hauru Point opened in 1963 and is still the largest resort in French Polynesia with 350 double rooms. It's a typical Club Med facility with activities intended to keep you running until you drop. On Moorea that includes the usual gamut of island activities including boat trips, diving, horse riding, fishing, island tours and trips to Tetiaroa (Marlon Brando's island). Club Med visitors will almost always have booked their holiday prior to arrival in Tahiti. Typical daily cost, including all meals (with wine and beer) and most sporting activities is around US$220 to US$260 per day per person in a double room, usually with a three-day minimum and a Club Med 'joining fee'.

There is a Club Med office in the Vaima

Centre in Papeete and the address is BP 575, Papeete, Tahiti.

Haapiti

Just north of Haapiti village, at PK 34.5 just past where the PK 24 clockwise markers meet the PK 35 anticlockwise ones, *Residence Linareva* (☎ & fax 56-15-35) has very pleasant bungalows in a well-kept garden by the beach and a respected restaurant. The bungalows are attractively furnished (including a TV), have a terrace area at the front, attached bathrooms and very well equipped kitchen facilities. Garden rooms are 7200/8200 CFP as singles/doubles. The beachfront rooms are 9500/10,500 CFP while the beachfront bungalows are 11,200/12,200 CFP. There are also beachfront suites which have a bedroom and sitting room, accommodate up to four people and cost 15,500 CFP. All of these prices are subject to the 8% tax and reduced rates are available for longer stays. Bicycles, outrigger canoes and snorkelling equipment are all provided free of charge. So long as you don't mind the somewhat isolated location it's a great place to stay.

Afareaitu

All by itself in the village of Afareaitu, five km south of the Vaiare ferry quay and a long way from the tourist activity at Cook's Bay and Hauru Point, *Chez Pauline* (☎ 56-11-26) is one of the most interesting places on the island. It was originally opened by Pauline Teariki's mother in 1918 and for many years was the only hotel on the island. Pauline has been running the hotel since 1947 and although it lacks the comforts of a modern hotel it has a definite charm and offers a real opportunity to sample local life. There are seven rooms, sharing two cold-water bathrooms. Costs are 2500 CFP for one person, 4000 CFP for two or 6000 CFP for four to six people. The restaurant specialises in Tahitian cuisine but you must book ahead (see the Places to Eat section). Credit cards are not accepted.

On the Vaiare side of Afareaitu, *Fare Manu* (☎ 56-29-82) at PK 8.2 is a two-room

house rented at 10,000 CFP per day or by the month. Bookings can be made through BP 34, Afareaitu, Moorea. Credit cards are not accepted.

Temae

Looking across from Temae Beach to Tahiti, the *Sofitel Ia Ora Moorea* (☎ 56-12-90, fax 56-12-91) is just two km south of Moorea's airport. It vies with the Beachcomber Parkroyal for the title of Moorea's most luxurious hotel. Beautifully situated on one of the island's best beaches, the hotel has restaurants, bars, tennis courts and 80 attractive thatched-roof bungalow rooms. They all have ceiling fans, refrigerators, bathrooms with shower and tea/coffee-making equipment on request. The 42 garden bungalows are 21,500 CFP, the 33 beach bungalows are 24,500 CFP, the one suite is 36,500 CFP and the four two-bedroom villas are 48,000 CFP. All rates are subject to 8% tax.

The restaurants include the open-air *La Perouse* and the luxurious over-water *Molokai*. Breakfast is available for 1500 CFP, while demi-pension is 5000 CFP. The hotel includes some excellent shops and boutiques. Bookings can be made through BP 28, Temae, Moorea.

PLACES TO EAT

Like its accommodation, Moorea's dining options are concentrated in Cook's Bay and Hauru Point, with just a smattering of places elsewhere around the island. Although there are more hotel beds at Hauru Point, there are more restaurant tables at Cook's Bay, where you will find the island's best selection of restaurants.

Many of Moorea's bungalow resorts offer kitchen facilities and if you're planning to fix your own food there are small food stores at a number of locations and a large supermarket at Vaiare. See the Information section at the start of this chapter for details.

Cook's Bay

Snack Bars & Cafés *Le Sylésie Pâtisserie* in the Maharepa shopping centre has ice cream for 120 and 220 CFP, pizzas at 650 CFP, burgers at 380 to 420 CFP, and crêpes at 350 to 530 CFP, with fancier ones at higher prices. This is a good place for a coffee and croissants breakfast.

La Crêperie, on the mountain side of the road, is a great place for breakfast or lunch. Continental breakfast costs 600 CFP and omelettes are 400 to 500 CFP, but the crêpes for 400 to 500 CFP or the waffles for 250 to 400 CFP are the house speciality. At lunchtime you could have one of the variety of burgers and chips for 450 to 900 CFP or there are savoury crêpes ranging from a chicken curry filling to ham and cheese. They cost from 500 to 700 CFP and can be followed by more crêpes; there's a big range of sweet ones from 250 to 400 CFP. La Crêperie also has a pleasant verandah from which you can watch the world go by.

Right at the Paopao end of Cook's Bay, where the road turns off inland to the Opunohu Valley and where the river from the valley enters the bay, there are a number of small snack bars including *Snack Fare Hotu*, *La Petite Maison Snack* and *Snack Rotui*.

Restaurants The three larger Cook's Bay hotels, the *Bali Hai*, *Cook's Bay Resort* and *Club Bali Hai*, all have standard restaurant facilities. Come here if you're after a breakfast buffet. The Cook's Bay Resort has *Rusty's Snacks* by the pool and the lagoonside *Tom & Jerry's* Mexican restaurant (☎ 56-10-50) reached by an over-water walkway. It's closed on Thursday.

Starting from the eastern or airport end of the Cook's Bay development, *Le Mahogany Snack Restaurant* (☎ 56-39-73) is a pleasant little place past PK 4 in Maharepa. Starters are 500 to 1200 CFP and main courses 1250 to 1750 CFP. The menu is essentially French but with some Chinese dishes to add variety. You could try a tuna steak with black pepper for 1250 CFP, mahi mahi meunière or grilled for 1250 CFP or swordfish tournedos for 1350 CFP. Wine is 300 CFP for a glass, 1200 CFP for a one-litre carafe and 1700 to 2400 CFP by the bottle.

Le Cocotier (☎ 56-12-10), in Maharepa

village just before the PK 5 marker and the Bali Hai Hotel, is a popular and well-run restaurant. Main courses are in the 1400 to 1600 CFP bracket and include dishes like escalope of tuna in a spicy tomato and onion sauce for 1450 CFP and mahi mahi cooked in foil for 1500 CFP. Starters range from 450 CFP to 1350 CFP, desserts are 450 to 600 CFP. Wine is 200 CFP for a glass, 600 CFP for a half-litre carafe and there is a range of bottles from 1200 to 2900 CFP. It's closed on Sunday.

At *Le Pêcheur* ('the fisherman'; ☎ 56-36-12) it's seafood, hardly surprisingly, which is the speciality. Starters are 700 to 2100 CFP, main courses are 1400 to 2300 CFP and desserts are 500 to 800 CFP. Dishes include shrimps in curry with chutney for 1600 CFP, fresh salmon à la florentine for 2000 CFP or pork steak in beer for 1600 CFP. The restaurant is on the mountain side of the road, between the Bali Hai Hotel and the Cook's Bay Resort and it's closed on Wednesday. Across the road the same team have a new Caribbean/Creole-style restaurant called *La Case* (☎ 56-42-95), with a barbecue, salad bar and Creole specialities.

Just past Cook's Bay Resort and nicely situated right out over the water *Le Fisherman's Wharf* and *Cook's Pizza* (☎ 56-15-56) are closed on Sunday evening and for Monday lunch. Starters range from the usual green salad at 450 CFP up to 1250 CFP. Pasta dishes are 850 to 1050 CFP, small pizzas cost 850 to 1200 CFP while large ones are 1250 to 1750 CFP. Fish and seafood dishes are in the 1200 to 2000 CFP range. Wine is 250 CFP for a glass, 550 CFP for a half-litre, 1100 CFP for a litre and 1920 to 2800 CFP for a bottle.

On the mountain side of the road *Alfredo's* (☎ 56-17-71) is a popular Italian restaurant with an attractive outdoor eating area. Pizza is the house speciality but there are lots of other dishes. Starters range from 650 to 1300 CFP, pasta dishes are 950 to 1400 CFP and pizzas are around 1150 CFP. Main courses are 1400 to 1900 CFP and include freshwater shrimps, tuna, mahi mahi and salmon. You can finish with an excellent dessert and a complete meal for two will cost about 8000

CFP including a bottle of wine. It's closed on Sunday.

Snack Te Honu Iti (☎ 56-19-84), almost at the top of Cook's Bay, is really a restaurant despite its diminutive name. Starters range from 600 to 1200 CFP and main courses cost around 1500 to 2500 CFP. Mahi mahi with mushrooms or salmon grilled with butter cost 1700 CFP. This very popular and often crowded restaurant is closed on Monday evening and all day Tuesday.

Close to the fish market, *Fare Manava* (☎ 56-14-24) has a straightforward Chinese and Tahitian blend of dishes. It's closed on Monday.

Papetoai
There are a number of places to eat in this village, just east of Hauru Point. *Chez Serge – Restaurant Ofai Tere* (☎ 56-13-17) is right by the turn-off to the octagonal church. They do an interesting variety of local dishes, including poisson cru for 850 CFP, and other fish dishes from 1000 to 1400 CFP. There are special Tahitian food nights on Wednesday and Sunday.

Snack Vaitepiha'a and *Restaurant Chez Coco's* (☎ 56-10-03) are also in Papetoai.

Hauru Point
Snack Bars & Cafés In the first small shopping centre coming from the airport, *Le Motu* has pizzas from 800 to 1000 CFP, burgers from 450 to 800 CFP and salads from 650 to 1200 CFP. A salade niçoise is 750 CFP.

Le Petit Village shopping centre has the *Chinese Café* (☎ 56-39-41) and the popular *Tropical Iceberg/Snack Glacier* (☎ 56-29-53), with great pizzas from their wood-fired oven (au feu du bois) for 950 to 1100 CFP (small) or 1350 to 1500 CFP (large). Salads range from 400 CFP for a green salad to 800 CFP for a salade niçoise, burgers are 400 to 450 CFP, omelettes are 300 to 500 CFP and main courses are 1200 to 2000 CFP. There's also good ice cream in this popular and pleasantly breezy establishment. It's closed on Monday.

Near the Hibiscus Hotel, *Pâtisserie Le Sylésie II* is the Hauru Point branch of the popular pâtisserie at Maharepa. It's open for breakfast and lunch until 6 pm except on weekends. There are sandwiches and croissants, crêpes for 300 to 500 CFP and pizzas at 600 CFP.

A few steps further along the strip, *Snack Michel* is a straightforward small café with burgers and similar light meals. It's closed on Tuesday. A bit further along is the *Spot Restaurant*, with snacks and light meals like spaghetti bolognaise for 850 CFP and chicken curry for 950 CFP.

Restaurants The restaurant at the *Beachcomber Parkroyal* (☎ 56-51-10) has big buffet meals including a terrific lunch.

Les Tipaniers Restaurant (☎ 56-12-67) is a moveable feast with a French and Italian style and Tahitian flavour. For breakfast and lunch it operates from the beach, but at dinnertime it shifts up to the main road. At lunchtime you could opt for pizzas (950 to 1050 CFP), pasta dishes (950 to 1050 CFP) or an excellent hamburger (800 CFP). Starters range from 400 to 1500 CFP and include poisson cru at 950 CFP, Pacific salad at 1050 CFP or tuna sashimi at 1500 CFP. Meat or fish main courses are 1600 to 1950 CFP. Desserts are 500 to 650 CFP, wine by the carafe is 250 CFP for a quarter-litre, 500 CFP for a half-litre, 1000 CFP for a litre or there are many bottles from 1300 to 2400 CFP.

The beachfront *Sunset Restaurant* (☎ 56-26-00) at the Hotel Hibiscus has a great location, looking out over the lagoon to the two motus. It turns out a thoroughly professional pizza from 900 CFP or burgers with chips for 800 to 900 CFP. Mahi mahi is cooked with coconut or vanilla for 1500 CFP and grilled tuna is 1200 CFP. There are great-looking desserts including lots of cakes and pies at 400 to 1000 CFP. Wine costs 700 CFP for a half-litre or there are a variety of bottles in the 1400 to 2500 CFP range.

Beside the road *Restaurant L'Aventura* may not look too exciting but the food can be excellent. Starters and salads are in the 400 to 1200 CFP range, fish main courses are 1600 to 2000 CFP while meat main courses are 1700 to 2300 CFP. The restaurant is closed on Monday. *Restaurant Tumoana* further down the strip does grilled food and Chinese specialities.

Haapiti

At PK 34.5 the Linareva Hotel's very French *Le Bateau* (☎ 56-15-35) is a 'floating' restaurant (it sank once) at the end of the pier. There's a very sea-going décor, portholes, nautical pictures and the like. Starters are mainly from 750 to 1250 CFP but go up to 2250 CFP, main courses are 1850 to 2250 CFP. Calamari, jackfish and swordfish all feature on the menu. There are quite a few wines between 1500 and 3300 CFP and up towards the stratosphere from there. The restaurant will pick you up from Hauru Point hotels for 400 CFP. This is the restaurant equivalent of all those over-water rooms.

Right in the village *Tubb's Pub* is on the waterfront and has a small restaurant with cheeseburgers and tunaburgers for 650 CFP.

Afareaitu

Reservations must be made in advance if you want to dine at *Chez Pauline's* (☎ 56-11-26), where Polynesian cuisine is the speciality, from poisson cru to shrimp curry in coconut milk and desserts like papaya in coconut milk.

Vaiare

You won't starve while you wait for your ferry to depart. *Roulottes* (van-style restaurants and set up by the wharf to feed hungry voyagers when boats are coming and going) pop up at various other locations around the island when the mood strikes them.

ENTERTAINMENT
Cold Beers

Although Moorea is a fairly early to bed sort of place, there are some good places for a sunset drink. The *Club Bali Hai's* bar may not be, as it claims, the World's Greatest Bar, but, set right on the water's edge and with Cook's Bay providing stunning scenery, it isn't bad. There's a happy hour on Tuesday and Friday. Round towards Maharepa the *Bali Hai Hotel* is also a good place for a cold

beer and also has a happy hour on Tuesday and Friday.

At Hauru Point *Les Tipaniers* and the *Sunset Restaurant* have popular beachside bars. The Linareva Hotel's *Le Bateau* restaurant is a great place to watch the sunset with a cocktail in hand and it's also right out over the water.

Dance Performances

The *Tiki Theatre Village* (☎ 56-10-86, 56-18-97), just south of Hauru Point at PK 31, has a dance performance on Tuesday, Thursday, Friday and Saturday at 6 pm. The show alone costs 2200 CFP, the show plus dinner is 5800 CFP. Transport to and from your hotel adds another 1000 CFP. The Tiki Village also put on round-the-island tours and the terminally romantic can try a Tahitian wedding – including a tattooing ceremony for the man – before sailing off in a royal canoe for a sunset cruise. Well, Dustin Hoffman did it.

The *Bali Hai Hotel* at Cook's Bay has a Sunday dance and feast and a Wednesday dance performance, rated as one of the best on the island.

Clubs & Discos

Better head back to Papeete if you want real nightlife, although young Tahitians patronise *Chez Tabou* (☎ 56-14-68), opposite the Moorea Lagoon Hotel at PK 14, between the two bays. Round at Hauru Point *Club Med* does let in outside visitors, but you must register at security and buy a string of beads, the universal Club Med currency.

THINGS TO BUY
Souvenirs & Crafts

Lots of places sell *pareus* (sarongs), T-shirts, the Balinese wood carvings which have become worldwide tropical souvenirs and other curios. At the eastern end of the Cook's Bay strip, Maison Blanche has a fairly typical selection. Look for the colourful roadside display of hand-painted pareus at the Lili Shop, between the airport and Cook's Bay.

At Hauru Point Te Anuanua claims to be

Moorea's biggest T-shirt and pareu emporium. A second boutique, called Vanille, is in Le Petit Village shopping centre. Leilani and the Carole Boutique are other pareu and T-shirt specialists at Hauru Point.

Galleries & Art

At Cook's Bay, Galerie van der Hyde displays the Dutch owner's art around the inside wall of the compound. As well, there are Papua New Guinean wood sculptures on the verandah and a shop with jewellery and wood carvings.

Patrice Bredel's Galerie Api (☎ 56-13-57), right on the waterfront by Club Med at Hauru Point, opens from 9.30 am to noon and 2.30 to 5.30 pm. This interesting gallery deals in works by popular resident artists Michèle Dallet and François Ravello and also in 18th and 19th-century Pacific art and prints and in primitive art of the Pacific. Woody's Sculpture (☎ 56-17-73) at PK 24, just before the Hauru Point enclave, has interesting wood carvings. You can be the canvas for some traditional Tahitian art at Poonui Tatoo (☎ 56-37-53), across from Club Med, or at Tattoo at the Chinese Café in Le Petit Village.

On the opposite side of the island there's an interesting art gallery at the Sofitel Ia Ora.

Black Pearls

A number of places around Moorea specialise in Tahitian black pearls. They include pearl specialists in the Beachcomber Parkroyal Hotel, the Sofitel Ia Ora, Club Med and the two pearl shops in Le Petit Village. The Moorea Pearls Centre (☎ 56-30-00) is at the aquarium by Cook's Bay and features an experimental pearl farm. Island Fashions at Cook's Bay (☎ 56-11-06) also deals in black pearls.

GETTING THERE & AWAY

There's less than 20 km of blue Pacific between Tahiti and Moorea and getting from one island to the other is simplicity itself. You can stroll down to the quay in Papeete, hop on one of the high-speed catamaran ferries and be in Moorea in less than half an hour. Or you can go out to the airport, hop on an Air Moorea aircraft and be there in less than 10 minutes. There's so much transport between the two islands that simple arithmetic proves you could totally evacuate Moorea in a couple of days!

Air

Air Moorea (☎ 86-41-41 on Tahiti; 56-10-34 on Moorea) flies from Faaa Airport on Tahiti to Moorea about every half hour from 6 am to 6 pm. There's no need to book – just turn up and if there's a surfeit of passengers they'll just put on more flights. The advertised flight time of 10 minutes is really being conservative. Seven or eight minutes is more like it! The one-way fare is 2700 CFP. Air Moorea also does island flightseeing tours (see the Organised Tours section earlier this chapter for details).

Air Tahiti (☎ 86-42-42 on Tahiti, 56-10-34 on Moorea) also flies to Moorea but chiefly for passengers making onward connections to other islands in the Society group. There's usually only a couple of flights a day. Onward fares are Moorea-Huahine for 11,000 CFP and Moorea-Bora Bora for 16,000 CFP.

Sea

Competition is fierce between Tahiti and Moorea across the 'Sea of the Moon', with two high-speed catamarans and the regular car ferries. First departures in the morning are usually around 6 to 6.30 am, last trips in the afternoon around 4.30 to 5.30 pm.

The car ferries, *Tamarii Moorea VIII* and *VIII H*, take about an hour for the crossing and operate about six times a day, more often on Friday, less often on Sunday. The return fare is 1400/700 CFP for adults/children. A motorcycle costs 1000 CFP or a car 4000 CFP, round trip. The car ferries and the *Tamahine Moorea II B* are operated by Eurl le Prado (☎ 43-76-50 in Tahiti, 56-13-92 in Moorea).

The two high-speed catamaran ferries on the route both operate about six times a day. The 380-passenger *Tamahine Moorea II B* takes less than half an hour, while the 320-

Catamaran Racing

The Australian-built high-speed catamarans positively hurtle back and forth between Tahiti and Moorea. When the new *Tamahine Moorea II B* entered service in late 1995 the operators announced that it could make the crossing in 12 minutes! In fact that's a bit of an exaggeration – it may well be able to do 100 km/h but there are speed limits in the harbours at both ends and quay to quay takes closer to half an hour. Stand outside on the roof deck during a crossing, looking back at the wake from the four waterjet engines, and you'll quickly realise just how fast the thing is.

Not only are the catamarans fast but the operators are also competitive. Taking the *Tamahine Moorea II B* to Papeete early one morning I (Tony) watched as the crew of the *Aremiti* rushed to get going ahead of the new boat. Motorcycles were raced up the ramp, baggage was hurled on board and passengers were chivvied to get up the steps faster. As the final passengers, a mother with a baby, made their way up the ramp, the child was virtually torn from her arms and tossed on board! The activity was just as frenetic on board the *Tamahine Moorea II B*, but it was the *Aremiti* which surged away from the quay first. A few minutes later we were on our way too and a couple of km out from Moorea slipped by the *Aremiti*, conclusively proving just who has the faster boat. ■

passenger *Aremiti* (☎ 42-88-88 in Tahiti, 56-31-10 in Moorea) takes a few minutes longer. Fares on the catamaran for adults/children are 800/400 CFP one way or 1400/700 CFP return. Students pay 800 CFP return, 400 CFP one way. Motorcycles can be taken on the ferry for 500 CFP one way.

Departures from Papeete are from the Moorea ferry quay, just north-east of the tourist office and Vaima Centre. On Moorea the le truck service meets arriving ferries at the quay. There is so much capacity on the route that bookings are really not necessary except perhaps for cars on the car ferry at particularly busy times. Many Tahiti residents treat Moorea as a weekend escape, travelling over to the island on Friday afternoon or Saturday morning and returning on Sunday afternoon.

GETTING AROUND
To/From the Airport & the Wharf

The Cook's Bay hotels are five to nine km from the airport while the Hauru Point establishments are 25 to 30 km away. It's a further five km from the Vaiare wharf. Moorea's taxis are notoriously expensive; from the airport to the Beachcomber Hotel at the very start of Hauru Point will be about 3300 CFP, from the wharf about 3800 CFP, more if you want to go to somewhere further around the point.

A le truck shuttle service meets all the boat

arrivals Monday to Saturday and costs just 200/100 CFP for adults/children to any of the Cook's Bay or Hauru Point Hotels. On Sunday you're stuck. There is no airport bus service although you could catch the North Coast Shuttle service if you time it right (see the following Bus section).

Bus

The GIE Moorea Nui (☎ 56-12-54) bus shuttle operates at 8, 9 and 11 am, 1, 3 and 5 pm on two routes. The North Coast Shuttle goes from the TOA store in Vaiare to Tamae, Maharepa, Paopao, Pihaena, Urufara, Papetoai, Tiahura, Varari and finally the store in Haapiti. The South Coast Shuttle continues around the south coast from Haapiti to the TOA store in Vaiare.

Taxi

Taxis are horribly expensive in Moorea, even by French Polynesian standards. It's not much more expensive to rent a car than to take a taxi from the airport or ferry quay to a hotel at Hauru Point. If you have to take a taxi they can be found at the airport (☎ 56-10-18) from 6 am to 6 pm and at the taxi rank in front of Club Med at Hauru Point (☎ 56-33-10).

Car

Although public transport is much improved, Moorea is still an island where having your own wheels is very useful. There are plenty of rental cars to fill that need. Rental-car operators can be found at the Vaiare boat quay, at the airport, at some of the major hotels and dotted around the Cook's Bay and Hauru Point tourist centres. Discount coupons are often available, usually giving 10% discount on the rates. If you haven't got one (there may well be one on the counter in front of you), just ask for a discount.

Pacificar is at the airport (☎ 56-11-03), at the Vaiare quay (☎ 56-16-02) and at half a dozen other locations, including the main hotels and opposite Club Med at busy Hauru Point. Four and eight-hour rentals are available and daily rental rates start from 5400 CFP for a Fiat Panda. The popular Mega Ranch open vehicles are 6400 CFP per day. Cheaper two and three-day rentals are available.

Europcar is also at the airport (☎ 56-41-08), the Vaiare quay (☎ 56-28-64) and major hotels and opposite Club Med. They also start with Fiat Pandas, at the same 5400 CFP for one day. A variety of larger vehicles are available including Fiat Unos, Fiat Puntos and Fiat Tempras.

Local operator Albert Rental has agencies at Club Bali Hai (☎ 56-19-28), the Bali Hai Hotel (☎ 56-30-58) and Club Med (☎ 56-33-75). Their Fiat Panda rate is 5500 CFP a day.

Petrol stations can be found by the airport, by Le Petit Village shopping centre at Hauru Point, in Paopao and in Vaiare.

Scooter & Bicycle

Pacificar (see Car above) has 50 cc scooters for 2800 CFP for eight hours or 3100 CFP for a day, while 80 cc scooters are 3000 CFP and 3500 CFP respectively. Cheaper two and three-day rentals are available. Europcar and Albert Rental (see Car), have scooters at the same daily rates.

Bicycles are supplied free by many hotels and can be rented from various outlets, including Europcar which has regular bikes at 1000 CFP a day (900 CFP for eight hours) or mountain bikes at 1500 CFP (1200 CFP for eight hours).

Boat

Moorea Jet Tours (☎ 56-22-87) at the Sofitel Ia Ora offers guided jet ski tours of half an hour or one hour plus longer two to three-hour circuits of the island. Jet Ski Rental (☎ 56-12-90) also operates from the Sofitel Ia Ora.

Other Windward Islands

Tahiti and Moorea are the only major islands in the Windward group. However, the group also includes two small high islands and a single atoll. Tetiaroa, north of Tahiti, is the atoll; Maiao, to the west of Moorea, is one of the high islands; uninhabited Mehetia, well to the east of Tahiti, is the other high island.

TETIAROA
Population: 50
Area: 6 sq km
Passes: 1

A dozen or so sandy *motus* dotted around the seven-km diameter, 55-km circumference of a 30-metre-deep lagoon, that is Tetiaroa. It's the postcard-perfect atoll: beautiful beaches, water as clear as fine vodka, a population comprised mainly of migratory birds, and the whole show is owned by Marlon Brando. Nowhere does Tetiaroa rise more than three metres above sea level. In the pre-European period the atoll was known as Teturoa.

The first European known to have visited the atoll was none other than William Bligh, who went there in search of three deserters in January 1789. Later he probably wished he hadn't found them as, embittered by their treatment, they all joined the initial mutineers on the *Bounty*. The island was once a Pomare family playground, an escape from their kingdom on Tahiti. In 1904 the Pomare family presented Dr Williams, Tahiti's only dentist, with the atoll, perhaps as payment for their dental bills. Williams was the British consul for French Polynesia from 1916 to 1935. He turned Tetiaroa into a copra plantation and died on the atoll in 1937. It made its next significant change of ownership in 1965 when Brando, fresh from making *Mutiny on the Bounty*, acquired the island on a 99-year lease and added the airstrip and the low-key hotel on Motu Onetahi.

Motu Rimatiai was the Pomare family residence. There are *marae* ruins on the island and a number of gigantic *tuu* trees.

Motu Tahuna Iti is the nesting island, a bird reserve used by countless migratory sea birds to lay their eggs and hatch their young. Frigates, gannets, petrels, black terns, brown and red-footed boobies and long-tailed tropical birds all nest on Tetiaroa.

Places to Stay
Tetiaroa's hotel, indeed the only habitation, is on Motu Onetahi, where the airport is located. The *Hotel Tetiaroa Village* (☎ 82-63-02 or 82-63-03, fax 85-00-51) has just seven beach bungalows. These Polynesian-style *fares* are very low key and not in prime condition. Tetiaroa is simply a rather expensive back-to-nature experience. A two-day-and-one-night excursion to the island costs 32,000 CFP, leaving at 8.30 am on the first day and returning at 4 pm on the next. Bookings can be made through BP 2418, Papeete, Tahiti.

Getting There & Away
Tetiaroa is 40 km north of Tahiti and is linked

Tetiaroa

by regular 20-minute flights operated by Air Moorea and by a variety of day trips by boat. The round-trip air fare, including lunch at the Hotel Tetiaroa Village and an excursion to the Tahuna Iti bird island, is 22,500 CFP; you leave at 8.30 am and return at 4 pm. A variety of boats shuttle across from Papeete, but, since they are not currently allowed to leave guests overnight, it's strictly a day trip. Furthermore, restrictions have been placed on where they can land, so your visit may be somewhat restricted. In any case the atoll's sole pass is really only accessible to canoes. The Mers et Loisirs office (☎ 43-97-99) on the Papeete waterfront takes bookings on boats ranging from yachts to high-speed catamarans with day-trip prices in the 10,000 to 13,000 CFP range.

MAIAO
Population: 250
Area: 9 sq km
Passes: 2

Maiao comes under the administration of Moorea, 75 km to the east. It consists of a high island, rising to 154 metres at its highest point, and a low motu which wraps around

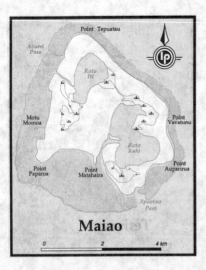

the high island, almost totally enclosing two brackish lakes, Roto Iti and Roto Rahi.

The island was sighted by Samuel Wallis in 1767, a postscript to his 'discovery' of Tahiti, but until 1809, when a pair of LMS missionaries were forced to stop, no Europeans are known to have visited the island. During the late 1920s and early '30s, an Englishman named Eric Trower tried to take over the island so that he could exploit the guano deposits he thought were there. His actions resulted in the islanders developing a strong mistrust of foreign influence, and for many years Europeans and Chinese were forbidden to live on the island. Even today the small population prizes its isolation and has vigorously resisted the construction of an airstrip. The island can only be reached by boat. Avarei Pass on the north-west side has been widened to allow small boats to enter, and Apootoo Pass to the south-east is the only other pass. Day trips to Maiao may be available from Moorea; contact Ron's Tours (☎ 56-35-80 or 56-29-09) for more information.

Some copra is produced on Maiao but the island is famed for the exceptional quality of its pandanus leaves, used for traditional Tahitian roof thatching. Today houses on Maiao are roofed with more prosaic tin. This is not traditional and less picturesque, but it's infinitely better for collecting rainwater on an island where freshwater supplies are scarce.

MEHETIA
Population: 0
Area: 3 sq km
Passes: 0

Geologically the youngest island in the Society group, Mehetia is 100 km east of Tahiti, 1.5 km across and rises steeply from the sea to 435 metres' altitude. The island is totally uninhabited, has no lagoon and landing on the uninviting shoreline is, to say the least, difficult. Only in one place does the rocky shoreline form a small pebbly beach. Yet when Wallis, en route to 'discovering' Tahiti, chanced upon Mehetia in June 1767, the population is said to have been 1500. It seems scarcely possible that the population could have been that large, but the marae ruins confirm that it certainly was populated. The fierce piratical warriors of Anaa in the Tuamotus drove the population of Mehetia

off the island in 1806, but it was used briefly in 1835 as a penal colony. The island has freshwater springs, and coconut and bread-fruit trees and the surrounding waters are rich with fish. Privately owned today, it's occasionally visited from Tahiti to gather copra.

Huahine

Population: 5000
Area: 75 sq km
Passes: 5

Huahine is actually two islands, Huahine Nui (Big Huahine) to the north and Huahine Iti (Little Huahine) to the south. The islands are only barely separated and at low tide you can wade from one to the other, a road bridge spans the narrow gap. A Polynesian legend relates that the split came about when the god Hiro ploughed his mighty canoe into the island, creating Bourayne Bay to the west and Maroe Bay to the east.

Huahine is green, lush and beautiful, just like other Society Islands, but it also has an easy-going atmosphere which entices visitors to kick back and watch the world go by. The port and principal settlement of Fare can take a large slice of the blame as it's the very image of a lazy South Seas port, but it's just big enough to have most of the modern facilities a visitor might require. Huahine has some fine beaches, excellent snorkelling and scuba diving, some popular surfing breaks and, in the village of Maeva, the most extensive complex of pre-European *maraes* in French Polynesia.

HISTORY

Just north of Fare, archaeological excavations conducted at Vaitootia and Faahia revealed some of the earliest traces of settlement in the Society Islands. Display cabinets in the Hotel Bali Hai show some of the items discovered right on the hotel site. Research has revealed that Huahine managed to maintain a degree of independence during the era when the powerful chiefs of Bora Bora were extending their power to the east and west.

In 1769 Cook was the first European to visit Huahine and, although he did not receive a warm welcome, he returned in 1774. In 1777 he visited again, bringing with him Omai, the young Tahitian he had taken back to Britain following his second expedition (see the Two Visitors aside in the Fact about the Islands chapter). Cook had his carpenters build a house for Omai in what is now the town of Fare, but his stay in Britain and his visits to British mansions had given Omai a taste for grandeur and he pronounced it 'too small'.

A group of LMS (London Missionary Society) missionaries moved to Huahine in 1808 to escape the turmoil in Tahiti, but remained for only a year. The group returned in 1818 and *Polynesian Researches*, published in London in 1829 by William Ellis, one of the pioneering LMS missionaries, describes early 19th-century Huahine in great detail.

Huahine sided with Pomare in the struggle against the French which resulted in a number of clashes between 1846 and 1888, when French rule was eventually, and reluctantly, accepted. A monument on the ocean side of the Maeva bridge marks the site of a skirmish in 1846. Although the French kicked the Protestant English missionaries out, the island remains predominantly Protestant.

Pouvanaa a Oopa (1895-1977), who founded the RDPT (Democratic Assembly of Tahitian Populations) in 1949 and took centre stage on the political scene for about 10 years, was born in Huahine.

ORIENTATION

A road follows the coast most of the way around both islands, but on the less densely populated Huahine Iti the road is often unsealed. A series of motus stretches along the east coast of the two islands, while around the north coast is Lake Fauna Nui, which is actually an inlet from the sea. It almost cuts off the motu-like northern peninsula, with the airport, from the rest of Huahine Nui.

Fare, the port and principal town, is on the west coast of Huahine Nui, just 2.5 km south

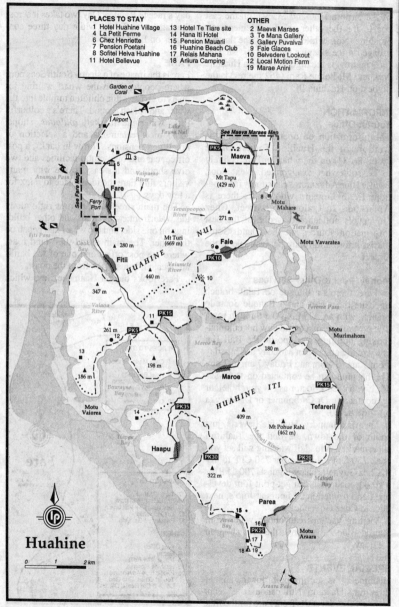

PLACES TO STAY
1 Hotel Huahine Village
4 La Petit Ferme
6 Chez Henriette
7 Pension Poetani
8 Sofitel Heiva Huahine
11 Hotel Bellevue
13 Hotel Te Tiare site
14 Hana Iti Hotel
15 Pension Mauarii
16 Huahine Beach Club
17 Relais Mahana
18 Ariiura Camping

OTHER
2 Maeva Maraes
3 Te Mana Gallery
5 Gallery Puvaivai
9 Faie Glaces
10 Belvedere Lookout
12 Local Motion Farm
19 Marae Anini

Garden of
Coral

Airport

Lake
Fauna Nui

See Maeva Maraes Map

PK5

Maeva

Vaipaano
River

Mt Tapu
(429 m)

Avamoa Pass

Fare

Ferry
Port

Motu
Mahare

Tevaipoopoo
River

Tiare Pass

Fiti Pass

HUAHINE   NUI

271 m

Cook
Bay

Fitii

280 m

Mt Turi
(669 m)

Faie

9
PK10

Motu Vavaratea

347 m

Vaiumete
River

440 m

10

Vaiana
River

Farerea Pass

11   PK15

261 m   PK5

12

Maroe Bay

Motu
Murimahora

13

186 m

198 m

180 m

Motu
Vaiorea

Bourayne
Bay

14   PK35

Maroe

HUAHINE   ITI

PK15

Tefareii

Tiapaa
Bay

Haapu

PK30

409 m

Mt Pohue Rahi
(462 m)

Maheti River

PK20

Mahuti
Bay

322 m

Parea

15

Avea
Bay

16
PK25

17

Motu
Araara

18   19

Huahine

0   1   2 km

Araara Pass

of the airport. Faie and Maeva, on the east coast, are the other main settlements on Huahine Nui, while Haapu is the largest village on the sleepier Huahine Iti. Mt Turi (669 metres) is the highest peak on Huahine Nui, and Mt Pohue Rahi (462 metres) is the highest on Huahine Iti.

INFORMATION
Tourist Office

The information on opening hours in the window of the Huahine Tourist Office (☎ 68-86-34) on the wharf in Fare is likely to be somewhat exaggerated. Next door, Pacific Blue Adventures can supply information; Heidi Lemaire who works there is American. Just along the street, Chez Guynette's noticeboard is one of the best information sources on the island. Some tourist information may be available at the airport.

Money, Post & Other Services

In Fare, there's a Banque de Tahiti branch opposite the wharf and a Banque Socredo branch, with an ATM, on the through road. The post office, in a brand new but colonial-looking building, is opposite the Bali Hai entry road and is open Monday to Thursday from 7 am to 3 pm and Friday 7 am to 2 pm. The hospital can be contacted on ☎ 68-82-48; if you need a doctor ask at your hotel, or try contacting Dr Carbonnier or Dr Motyka on ☎ 68 82 20.

There's a laundry, Huahine Laverie, just south of the town, beyond the Taahitini supermarket. A load of washing will set you back 750 CFP, plus another 750 CFP to dry it. Chez Guynette charges guests 700 CFP for a six-kg load. You can get print film developed and printed in 24 hours at Jojo's, next door to Chez Guynette.

Visiting yachties can obtain water from Pacific Blue Adventures, the dive shop on the quay.

SPECIAL EVENTS

Huahine is the starting point for the annual three-day Hawaiki Nui canoe race. This wonderful event starts from Fare for the first day's race to Raiatea. Day two takes it across the lagoon to Tahaa, while day three concludes on Bora Bora.

FARE

Fare is the image of a sleepy South Seas port, where people sit on the wharf waiting for boats to arrive while children tumble into the water and splash around. There's a colourful little waterside market, *roulottes*, shops, some nice restaurants and a selection of hotels and pensions. Throw in banks, a post office, car and bike-rental facilities and two dive shops and it's easy to see why many visitors find Fare the ideal place to relax for a few days.

The main street of Fare runs right along the waterfront, with shops and other buildings on one side, and the wharf and beach on the other. The main round-the-island road, where the post office and one of the banks are located, is just back from the coast.

Fare looks out on Haamene Bay, which

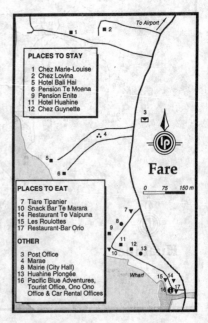

To Airport

PLACES TO STAY

1 Chez Marie-Louise
2 Chez Lovina
5 Hotel Bali Hai
6 Pension Te Moana
9 Pension Enite
11 Hotel Huahine
12 Chez Guynette

Fare

0   75   150 m

PLACES TO EAT

7 Tiare Tipanier
10 Snack Bar Te Marara
14 Restaurant Te Vaipuna
15 Les Roulottes
17 Restaurant-Bar Orio

OTHER

3 Post Office
4 Marae
8 Mairie (City Hall)
13 Huahine Plongée
16 Pacific Blue Adventures, Tourist Office, Ono Ono Office & Car Rental Offices

Wharf

has two passes out to the sea. The northern Avamoa Pass is the main entry point for inter-island shipping. The town only really came into existence with the arrival of the missionaries in 1818, but within a few years it was already a bustling little port. Whalers started to call in at Fare from the 1830s and the French protectorate brought an influx of island merchants and traders. The wooden shops and buildings along the main street came with the Chinese shopkeepers who settled here in the 1920s, but sadly some of Fare's most interesting buildings used to be at the southern end of the street and were destroyed in a fire in 1995.

AROUND HUAHINE NUI

This 60-km circuit of the larger island starts at Fare and goes around the island in a clockwise direction.

Archaeology at the Hotel Bali Hai

The Hotel Bali Hai is only a few minutes walk along the beach north of Fare. The ponds that wind around the Bali Hai's bungalows were a swamp until they were dredged out during the hotel's construction in 1972. When pre-European artefacts were found, archaeologists were notified and Yosihiko Sinoto started work on the site in August 1973.

It is believed that a village was sited here over 1000 years ago. The swampy ground preserved wooden objects including house foundations and constructions, canoe planks and water bailers, and a wide variety of tools, tool handles and weapons. Further excavations took place in 1974 and 1975 and it is estimated that the area was inhabited from around 850 to 1100 AD.

Showcases in the hotel lobby display items found on the site. These include ornaments, canoe anchors, grindstones and pestles, pearl-shell fish hooks, terebra-shell wood chisels, whalebone mallets, pearl shell coconut graters and many stone adze heads. For archaeologists, the most interesting find were *patus*, flattened club-like weapons made of wood or whalebone and used by New Zealand Maoris for striking and thrusting under the ribs. Such weapons had never previously been found outside New Zealand and their discovery here supported theories of migration from Tahiti to New Zealand.

Beside the entrance road to the hotel, the small Marae Tahuea was discovered and restored during the excavations.

Lake Fauna Nui

The shallow expanse of Lake Fauna Nui (also known as Lake Maeva) is referred to as a lake or sometimes as a lagoon, but in fact is an inlet. Nevertheless, the land to the north is in every way – except for its firm connection to the main island – like the motus off the east coast, and indeed is known as Motu Oavarei and Motu Papiti. From Fare the main sealed island road runs along the mountain side of Lake Fauna Nui, but it's also possible to take the unsealed road on the ocean side of the lake and return to the main island by the bridge at Maeva village. At this end the lake narrows down to a channel, extending for three km to Faie Bay.

Maeva Village & Maraes

Prior to European influence Maeva was the seat of royal power on the island and the maraes are still found along the shoreline,

Fish Traps
The V-shaped fish traps on both sides of the Maeva bridge are ancient devices still in everyday use. The principle is simple: the V shape points towards the ocean and the long stone arms are built up to water level. Fish, carried by the outgoing currents or chased by villagers beating the water, enter the wide mouth of the trap and swim towards the narrow point of the V. Once they have crossed the threshold stone, which is slightly raised towards the outside, they are trapped and the trap ends in a round basin about three metres in diameter and a metre deep. They can be kept here until needed or scooped out with a landing net (*toto haipu*). Each enclosure has an owner whose rights to the fish trapped there is always respected. Unfortunately, pollution of Lake Fauna Nui has been a problem in recent years but the fish traps continue to function, just as they have for centuries. ■

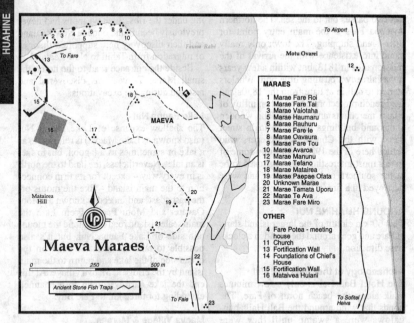

To Airport

To Fare

Fauna Rahi

Motu Ovarei

MAEVA

Matairea
Hill

Maeva Maraes

0   250   500 m

Ancient Stone Fish Traps

To Faie

To Sofitel
Heiva

MARAES

1 Marae Fare Roi
2 Marae Fare Tai
3 Marae Vaiotaha
5 Marae Haumaru
6 Marae Rauhuru
7 Marae Ie
8 Marae Oavaura
9 Marae Fare Tou
10 Marae Avaroa
12 Marae Manunu
17 Marae Tefano
18 Marae Matairea
19 Marae Paepae Ofata
20 Unknown Marae
21 Marae Tamata Uporu
22 Marae Te Ava
23 Marae Fare Miro

OTHER

4 Fare Potea - meeting
house
11 Church
13 Fortification Wall
14 Foundations of Chief's
House
15 Fortification Wall
16 Mataivea Huiarii

scattered among the modern buildings of the village, and up the slopes of Matairea ('Pleasant Wind') Hill. The traditional stone fish traps across the narrow neck of Lake Fauna Nui also survive, some of which remain in everyday use. Excavations and restoration on the site commenced in 1923 and nearly 30 maraes have been located and more than half of them restored, making this the most extensive site in Polynesia. Dr Kenneth P Emory of the Bishop Museum in Honolulu, Hawaii, made the first systematic study of the Huahine maraes in 1925. Major restorations were conducted by Dr Sinoto in 1967 and 1968. He returned in 1979 to launch a five-year series of excavations on the maraes on Matairea Hill. The exceptional density of maraes on the hill has led to a theory that the hillside was entirely inhabited by families of the chiefs and nobility.

Maeva village is about seven km from Fare. There is an information board in front of Fare Potea but otherwise information around the site is very sparse. The Sofitel Heiva produces a useful brochure and map to the site, available from the lobby. The circuit walk along the water's edge and up Matairea Hill can be hot work, so take some drinking water. Mosquitoes show their usual liking for maraes so carry insect repellent as well. And if you've come in a car, you'll find it like a pressure cooker when you get back. Park under the trees across from the school, just on the Fare side of the church.

Fare Potea On the water's edge on the Fare side of Maeva, the Fare Potea is just an empty, thatched-roof *fare*. It looks as if it would make a good museum, but in fact a board in front of the fare has the only explanation on the site. The fare is a 1970s reconstruction (with another major rebuild in 1995) of the original community fare, although it is slightly upstream from the original site. Around the Fare Potea are 10 or more maraes, some of which may date back to the 16th century. Flagstones cover a wide expanse of land along the shoreline.

Matairea Huiarii It is easiest to start the walk at the defence wall on the Fare side of Maeva. It's thought that the wall was built in 1846, when French marines mounted an assault on the Polynesian resistance forces on the island. Look for the trail going uphill; it soon enters dense forest and passes through patches of vanilla plantations then crosses through another fortification wall. This second, older wall was built during the pre-European era, probably as protection against raiding parties from the warlike Bora Bora tribes.

A side path leads off to the big multitiered complex of Matairea Huiarii, or Te Ana, draped up the hillside. This area included maraes, houses, agricultural terraces and other signs of habitation from around 1300 to 1800 plus indications of an early settlement around 900, contemporaneous with the discoveries at the site of the Hotel Bali Hai near Fare.

Marae Tefano The side path winds prettily on through the forest to Marae Tefano, a real Indiana Jones complex with a massive banyan tree overwhelming one end of the *ahu*.

Marae Matairea Rahi Further on, a trail branches off and runs slightly downhill to Marae Matairea Rahi, another multitiered complex. This was the principal marae at Maeva, where the most important island chief sat on his throne at major ceremonies. It was superseded by the Marae Manunu down on the motu below. The other surviving structure is the foundations of a *fare atua* or 'god house', where images of the Polynesian gods were safeguarded, protected by a 24-hour watch.

From here you can catch glimpses of the lagoon, revealing how high you've climbed. A few steps further along is the small Marae Matairea. You can continue down this way, as the trail eventually emerges behind a house in the middle of the village.

Marae Paepae Ofata Retrace your steps to the main trail and continue to the turn-off to Marae Paepae Ofata, a steep climb above the main trail. It's worth the effort: the marae is like a large platform perched on the edge of the hill with fine views down the hillside and across Motu Papiti to the outer lagoon, and down to the mouth of Lake Fauna Nui.

Marae Tamata Uporu Retrace the route to the main path which continues over a second part of Marae Paepae Ofata. The path winds on around the hillside to Marae Tamata Uporu, before dropping steeply down to the road, past mango and other village fruit trees.

Marae Te Ava & Marae Fare Miro The path emerges just south of the lagoonside Marae Te Ava. A short walk east leads to the lagoonside Marae Fare Miro, which has some particularly neat stonework and a fine setting.

Marae Manunu A final marae stands on the motu, across the bridge from the main Maeva complex. The 'Eye of the North' marae is a massive structure stretching 40 metres long by nearly seven metres wide and standing two metres high. The ahu slab at the west end has a faint petroglyph of a turtle.

Marae Manunu replaced Marae Matairea Rahi as the community marae of Huahine Nui; Marae Anini was the community marae of Huahine Iti. The two-stepped ahu platforms at these two maraes are unique in the Leeward Islands. While Marae Anini was dedicated to Oro and Hiro, gods worshipped on other Polynesian islands, Manunu was dedicated first and foremost to Tane, Huahine's own god of war and fish. Oro, however, was also honoured here. Raiti, the last high priest of Huahine, was buried here in 1915. Nearby is a monument to the battle with French forces in 1846.

Faie & the Route Traversière
The coast road turns inland beside Faie Bay to the village of Faie. Huahine's famous blue-eyed eels can be seen in the river immediately downstream of the bridge. The

large eels are quite used to visitors and are happy to be hand fed. Tinned sardines will do just fine although they will eat fresh food!

Just inland from Faie you can pause for an ice cream at Faie Glaces (closed Sunday) before making the steep climb to the Belvédère lookout on the slopes of Mt Turi. From the high point the Route Traversière drops even more steeply to the shores of Maroe Bay. A heavily loaded small rental car can have real difficulty getting up this steep and dusty road.

Local Motion

This local farm grows a wide variety of organically grown tropical fruit and coffee and produces jams, preserves and dried fruit. You can visit the farm and orchards, eat in the restaurant and climb to the lookout, though the 800-metre walk to the 'panoramic view' is not very interesting. Worse, the impossibly steep track is a good example of how not to cut a 4WD track. The entry charge is waived if you buy anything, such as a glass of their excellent fruit juice.

Fitii

Just before completing the Huahine Nui circuit, the road passes through the Fitii district. This is an important agricultural area in

the shadow of Mt Paeo (440 metres) where taro, vanilla and other crops are grown.

AROUND HUAHINE ITI

The smaller and more lightly populated southern island is reached by the bridge which separates the two bays, Maroe and Bourayne. The route circles the island in a clockwise direction.

East Coast

The village of Maroe stands on the south side of Maroe Bay, an area dotted with reminders of the god Hiro's cataclysmic visit to the island. Apart from splitting the island in two with his canoe, you can spot the marks left by his paddle, the imprint of his finger, and even his rocky phallic symbol. The coast road skirts across the mouth of a number of shallow inlets, looking across to Motu Murimahora, before coming to Tefarerii, the 'house of the kings'. This small village was the centre of Huahine's most powerful family a century ago, but today the inhabitants devote their time to fishing and growing watermelons and other produce on the nearby motu.

Marae Anini

Right at the southern tip of Huahine Iti is the important Marae Anini, a community marae echoing the role of Marae Manunu on the larger island. This massive coastal marae was a comparatively recent construction, dedicated to Oro (the god of war) and Hiro (the god of thieves). The Oro cult, with its human sacrifices, was almost a last gasp for the old religion, but it soon collapsed before the growing influence of Christianity. In his recollections of 1818 the pioneer missionary William Ellis reported that the marae's last priest could remember at least 14 human sacrifices.

Despite its beautiful lagoonside setting and its historical importance, the marae area is liberally sprinkled with garbage and many of the marae stones have been disfigured with feeble graffiti. One almost wishes for some modern human sacrifices.

Island Agriculture

Huahine has a busy agricultural workforce with plantations of vanilla, grapefruit, breadfruit and pineapples. On the motus melons and water-melons (pastèque) are grown, many of which are sold in Papeete's market. This market-gardening technique originated on Maupiti but has been taken up successfully on Huahine. Some of the village plantations look remarkably wild and neglected, but don't think for a moment that somebody doesn't own every single plant. Casually gathering fruit, in particular the much prized pineapples, may result in an enraged villager emerging from the undergrowth with a sharp machete. Mangoes are one of the few exceptions: they fall from the trees, rot on the ground and, delicious though they may be, are treated like trash. ∎

West Coast

Some of the best beaches around Huahine are found on the southern peninsula and along its western shore around Auea Bay. There is good snorkelling around the point and towards Motu Araara, and the Araara Pass is also a popular surfing break.

The road comes to a junction where a left turn leads to the village of Haapu. Turning right, the route soon brings you back to the bridge and the completion of the island circuit. Just before the bridge another left turn leads to the remarkable Hana Iti Hotel, a wonderful extravagance or a grand folly, depending on your point of view. The luxury resort is built on land originally owned by singer Julio Iglesias.

DIVING

Huahine has two dive operators, both based in Fare, so dive sites tend to be close to the town. There are several sites around the reef passes off Fare and around the reef to the north of the island.

Dive Operators

Pacific Blue Adventure This operation (☎ 68-87-21) is on the wharf in Fare and usually does two dives a day either in the lagoon or outside the reef. The dive instructors are CMAS and PADI certificated, they offer diving courses and also conduct night dives. A single dive costs 5000 CFP.

Huahine Plongée A recent arrival on the Huahine diving scene, this group (☎ 68-70-68) is operated by the same people as Raiatea Plongée in Raiatea. Like Pacific Blue it does morning and afternoon dives with typical costs of 5000 CFP per dive.

Dive Sites

There are several good dive sites around Huahine, including the following:

Avapeihi Pass The favourite dive site is Avapeihi Pass, just south of the town. It's known locally as Fitii Pass as it leads into the settlement of Fitii, south of Fare. There are several popular sites on this pass, including

Fitii Pass or Fitii Tombant, one of the top dives in French Polynesia. This dive is usually made behind the breaking waves, starting with a 10-metre drop then a gentle 25-metre descent into the pass. The dive plateaus out and you'll see many small and large fish including eagle rays, tuna, barracuda and sharks.

The other main site is on the south side of the pass, where the dive goes down a sheer 30-metre vertical wall. This is a pretty dive with caves, chimneys, yellow coral and many fish caves, including schools of snapper.

Garden of Coral An alternative to the Avapeihi Pass is the Garden of Coral, the sloping reef face just north of the airport. Not so many large fish are encountered here but there are many small fish and some moray eels, as well as some yellow coral.

Yellow Valley South of Cook's Bay and north of Bourayne Point is Yellow Valley, the major site for coral viewing.

WALKING & CLIMBING

The marae walk at Maeva will work up a sweat for most people, but another interesting walk is the three-km or so trail from midway along the road between Fitii and the Bellevue Hotel across to the mountainous Route Traversière, joining that road close to the Belvédère lookout. This pretty trail is shown as a track on the maps but is best for walkers or riders; the Petite Ferme two-day horseback trek takes this route. It's possible to climb Mt Turi (669 metres) from Fare but you'd certainly need a guide.

SNORKELLING

There's good snorkelling at many places around Huahine including right off the beach in the middle of Fare. Just walk straight down to the water from Chez Guynette. Take a short walk north to the Hotel Bali Hai and you'll find more good snorkelling just off the beach. On the east side of the island there's good snorkelling close to the Sofitel Heiva, while on Huahine Iti the southern point, close to the Huahine Beach Club, Relais

Mahana and the Marae Anini, offers more good snorkelling.

You can rent a mask, snorkel and fins from Jojo's, next door to Chez Guynette, for 300 CFP for a half day or 500 CFP for a whole day.

SURFING

Huahine has some of the best and most consistent surf in French Polynesia and attracts a steady stream of international surfers. A little caution is required, however, the local surfers can be very possessive and visitors should make a serious effort to fit in. The best breaks are the two passes into the lagoon by Fare: the Avamoa Pass to the north and the Avapeihi, or Fitii, Pass to the south; the Tiare Pass, south of the Sofitel Heiva on the east coast; and the Araara Pass, by Motu Araara and Marae Anini at the southern point of Huahine Iti.

BOATING

Huahine Lagoon, at the north end of the waterfront main street in Fare, rents out boats and provides you with a map. Masks and snorkels are included, fuel costs extra and the cost is 3000 CFP for two hours, 5000 CFP for four hours or 8000 CFP for eight hours. Jojo's, next door to Chez Guynette, rents surfskis for 500 CFP for two hours.

HORSE RIDING

La Petite Ferme (☎ 68-82-98), between Fare and the airport, offers an interesting variety of horse-riding trips using Marquesan horses which are suitable for both beginners and more experienced riders. For 2800 CFP you can take a one-hour ride along the beach and through the coconut plantations. A 4000 CFP, two-hour ride takes you along the shore of Lake Fauna Nui. Longer excursions include an all-day ride with a picnic lunch for 9000 CFP. Or you can go on a two-day mini-expedition which combines riding on the beach, around Lake Fauana Nui and up into the mountains for a cost of 13,500 CFP, including meals and camping equipment.

ORGANISED TOURS
Island Tours

Huahine Land (☎ 68-89-21) operates 4WD trips at 9 am and 2 pm every day except for Sunday morning. The three-hour trips cost 4000 CFP, go round both islands and visit vanilla, grapefruit, pineapple and breadfruit plantations, the maraes, the Faie eels and other attractions.

Felix Tours (☎ 68-82-26) uses a small minibus for its Monday to Saturday 8.30 am to 12.30 pm island circuit. The trips cost 3500 CFP.

Lagoon Tours

Vaipua Cruises (☎ 68-86-42) does daily cruises from 9.30 am to 4 pm including lunch on a motu for 5000 CFP. Matairea Cruise (☎ 68-89-16) does Monday to Saturday cruises from 10 am to 4 pm. The trip includes a picnic lunch on a motu beach, snorkelling stops and swimming with the rays. The cost is 4000 CFP per person and can be booked through Jojo's in Fare. Moana Tropicale (☎ 68-87-05) has half-day boat tours several times a week for 5500 CFP.

PLACES TO STAY

Most of Huahine's accommodation is concentrated in and around Fare. Two places are further afield on Huahine Nui – the mid-range Hotel Bellevue and the top-end Hotel Sofitel Heiva. On Huahine Iti there are four places right down at the southern point (the economical Ariiura Camping, the interesting Pension Mauarii, plus the middle to top-end Relais Mahana and Huahine Beach Club), while on Bourayne Bay there's the unique (with prices to match) Hana Iti.

Fare

There are three places to stay right in Fare, a couple just south of the town and several north of Fare towards the airport.

Main Street Amusingly dubbed 'Club Bed', *Chez Guynette* (☎ 68-83-75) is one of the most popular backpackers' centres in French Polynesia. It's right on the colourful main street of Fare, only about a minute's walk from the wharf and right across from the beach. Hélène and Alain Guerineau run their pension efficiently and although it's sometimes a narrow line between 'well run' and 'rule bound' they manage to stay on the right side of the border.

A bed in the dormitory at the back of the building costs 1200 CFP per night. The seven simple, but quite comfortable, rooms are named after islands in French Polynesia and cost 3000/3500 CFP for singles/doubles. They have attached bathrooms with cold water, a fan and wire-screened windows that really keep the mosquitoes out. Some of the rooms also have bunk beds so they can accommodate families. Bedding is supplied but you have to provide your own towels. There's an additional charge of 300 CFP per person for one-night stays. Credit cards are accepted and bookings can be made by writing to BP 87, Fare, Huahine. Chez Guynette is often booked out so if you want to be certain of a bed it's wise to phone or write ahead.

There's a communal kitchen and dining area at the back of the building which shuts down precisely at 10 pm. The lights for the kitchen and dormitory area are on a timer! Each guest has their own plastic food container and there is a circulating fridge programme whereby food is periodically moved from one fridge to another, the inevitable forgotten supplies are discarded and the fridge is cleaned. Now that's efficiency! At the front, looking out at the passing scene, there's an open-air café area where breakfast and lunch are served (see Places to Eat) and drinks are available until late in the evening. Just inside the front door, where shoes are left since Chez Guynette is shoe-free, is a very informative noticeboard.

On the corner where Fare's main street turns away from the beach is *Hotel Huahine* (☎ 68-82-69), a large building with a definite 'old South Seas hotel' feel. It's recently had a much-needed refurbishment and is pretty good value with 10 rooms with attached toilet and shower at 2500/3500 CFP for singles/doubles, although that price may be about to rise slightly. There's also a dormi-

tory at 1000 CFP and the hotel has a snack bar, a restaurant and a bar which can get a bit noisy at times. The Hotel Huahine has a reputation as the local surfers' hangout.

Across the road from Hotel Huahine is *Pension Enite* (☎ 68-82-37) with eight rooms with various combinations of single and double beds. The nightly cost is 5500 CFP per person *demi-pension* (breakfast and dinner) and there's a minimum stay of two nights. The fan-cooled rooms share bathrooms and a living room. Food at Enite, served in an open restaurant right by the beach, has an excellent reputation. Bookings can be made by writing to BP 37, Fare, Huahine.

North of Fare

There are half a dozen places between Fare and the airport, two km to the north. Several of them are on the beach, while others are set slightly back.

Pension Te Moana (☎ 68-88-63) has some Pacific style. The six garden bungalows are airy fares with loose coral pebble floors and a comprehensively mosquito-netted main bed on a raised wooden platform. Your bathroom is a separate fare a few steps away. Charming though it is, insects can fly straight through (there's no windows, no netting) so you need to burn coils, wear repellent, retreat behind the mosquito net and not be too concerned about things that buzz in the night. In fact the mosquito population is so well known that staff at the adjacent Hotel Bali Hai will slyly ask how well you slept with all the buzzing. Rooms cost 6500 CFP for one or two people including breakfast.

There's also one family bungalow on the beach. This has a double and two single beds and a double bed on a mezzanine level. There's an equipped kitchen, a TV and nightly cost is 11,000 CFP for up to six people. Te Moana is right on the beach, the same pleasantly sandy stretch as the Hotel Bali Hai. It's only a five or 10-minute walk to Fare along the beach or by road. There's a good restaurant right by the beach. Credit cards are accepted and bookings can be made by writing to BP 195, Fare, Huahine.

Right next to the Te Moana, the long-running *Hotel Bali Hai* (☎ 68-84-77, 68-82-77) has certainly had its ups and downs (it was closed for some time) but currently seems to be on an up. The hotel has a large collection of very comfortable individual bungalows built around a small lake. Dredging these ponds revealed an important archaeological site, and showcases in the lobby area exhibit some of the finds. There's also a reconstructed marae right beside the entrance road.

The nightly cost for one or two people in the bungalows is 12,000 CFP for a garden bungalow, 14,000 CFP for a lake bungalow and 17,000 CFP for a beach bungalow. In addition there are some simple rooms at 9500 CFP. All these costs are subject to 8% tax and there's an additional charge of 2000 CFP for a third person. Demi-pension adds another 3900 CFP per person. The hotel has a swimming pool and tennis court and there's a restaurant overlooking the hotel's excellent stretch of beach. It's only a short stroll along the beach or the road to the centre of Fare. Bookings can be made by writing to BP 2, Fare, Huahine.

Further north are two budget places, both slightly set back from the beach. *Chez Marie-Louise* (☎ 68-81-10) has camping space for 750 CFP per person, small rooms for 2500 CFP for one or two people, small and minimally equipped bungalows for 3000 CFP and two larger bungalows for 5000 CFP. Credit cards are not accepted; write to BP 5, Fare, Huahine, for bookings.

Close by is *Chez Lovina* (☎ 68-88-06, fax 68-82-64) in a quiet location near the surf break. This popular backpackers' centre has camping space at 1000 CFP per person, dorm beds for 1200 CFP (1500 CFP for a single night) and five small garden fares for 3000/4000 CFP for a single/double. Bathroom and kitchen facilities are shared. Then there are four larger family bungalows with attached bathroom which start at 5000/6000 CFP. Two of them have space for eight people and have small kitchen units. Two of them have a double bedroom with a mezzanine area with more bed space plus a living room and kitchen facilities. There are plans to add a small restaurant and bar. Credit cards are not accepted; book by writing to BP 173, Fare, Huahine.

Between here and the airport are two places, one on the beach and one on the road. On the road the friendly and well-run *La Petite Ferme* (☎ 68-82-98) is a popular horse-riding centre that also offers accommodation. There is a small dormitory for six people at 1500 CFP per person including breakfast. There is also a double room costing 1800 CFP per person, again including breakfast. For one-night stays there's an additional charge of 500 CFP per person. A separate bungalow with mezzanine, bathroom and kitchen facilities costs 5000/7500 CFP for one/two people. Lunch is available for 1200 CFP, dinner for 1500 CFP. Write to BP 12, Fare, Huahine, for bookings.

Right on the beach, and closer to the airport, is the new *Hotel Huahine Village* (☎ 68-87-00, fax 68-86-99). The 28 individual bungalows are simple and modern constructions with a double bed, attached bathroom and terrace. The nightly cost is 8000 CFP for a garden bungalow or 10,000 CFP for a beach bungalow, plus 8% tax. Demi-pension costs an additional 4500 CFP per person. Round-trip transfers to and from the airport or the quay in Fare are 600 CFP. Bookings can be made through BP 295, Fare, Huahine.

South of Fare

There are two places just south of Fare. *Pension Poetani* (☎ 68-89-49) is big, clean, empty and completely incongruous looking, like some suburban builder's back-of-an-envelope dream of a mansion in the southern states of America. It's about a km out of town, on the mountain side of the road at the turn-off just past the bridge. A dorm bed costs 1500 CFP, the four standard rooms are 6000 CFP with shared bathroom facilities and the one family room is 8000 CFP with private bathroom. Credit cards are not accepted. The pension is very neat and clean, perhaps because it's hardly been used, and there's a kitchen for guests' use and a lounge area on each floor.

Less than half a km further along the road and on the lagoon side is *Chez Henriette* (☎ 68-83-71). There are six bungalows on the lagoon side, looking across to Fare, and although the setting is not beachlike, there's quite a pleasant garden. The three big bungalows are 6000 CFP for up to four people, and the three smaller ones are 3000 CFP or 4000 CFP for one or two people. The traditional-looking thatched-roof bungalows have attached bathrooms and the larger units have kitchen facilities. Book through BP 73, Fare, Huahine. Credit cards are not accepted.

Elsewhere on Huahine Nui

The *Sofitel Heiva Huahine* (☎ 68-86-86, fax 68-85-25) is at the southern tip of Motu Papiti, the peninsula which starts at the airport as Motu Oavarei and curves around Lake Fauna Nui. It's the biggest hotel on the island and beautifully situated with a sandy beach and shallow water separating it from Motu Mahare. There's good snorkelling close by and a popular surfing break just off the reef edge.

There are 61 well-equipped rooms starting with garden bungalows at 21,000 CFP and moving up through beach and lagoon bungalows to half a dozen of the inevitable over-water bungalows at 60,000 CFP. The 8% government tax is additional. There's a swimming pool, the Manuia Bar, the Omai Restaurant and island night performances. The hotel is somewhat isolated, about eight km from the town of Fare, but it is conveniently close to the Maeva marae sites and commendably produces a useful brochure about the sites.

The *Hotel Bellevue* (☎ 68-82-76 or 68-81-70, fax 68-85-35) is rather a long way from anywhere: five km south of Fare, seven km from the airport and close to the junction where the road down to the Huahine Iti bridge splits off from the road that encircles Huahine Nui. The main building has eight rooms with a double and single bed and attached bathroom (with cold water). These

rooms are 3500/4500 CFP for singles/doubles. In addition there are 15 bungalows with a double bed (with mosquito net), attached bathroom (with hot water) and a terrace. These bungalows cost 6000/7000 CFP and the 8% tax is added to all these rates.

The hotel has a restaurant with good food and a swimming pool. There are great views from a hillside lookout and it's only 300 metres to the sea. A variety of excursions, lagoon and motu trips can be organised and transfers to the airport cost 500 CFP one way. The Bellevue has a pleasant setting and is well run; fans in the rooms would be nice but otherwise they're well equipped. The location is the only real drawback. Bookings can be made by writing to BP 21, Fare, Huahine.

Out at the south-west corner of Huahine Nui, construction of the *Hotel Te Tiare Beach Resort* looks ominously stalled. Let's hope this is not another pipe dream project leaving only ugly scars on the lagoonside when the money and enthusiasm run out. Garden and over-water bungalows were clearly the intention and it was planned to bring guests to the hotel by sea. In fact you can drive to within a couple of hundred metres of the hotel and walk along the beach for the last stretch.

For longer-term visitors there are a number of houses at the end of the road along the north side of Maroe Bay. They accommodate three to six people and cost 12,500 to 25,000 CFP per day, including use of a car and boat. Contact *Jean Rolland* (☎ 82-49-65, fax 85-47-69), PO Box 123, Papeete, Tahiti, for more details.

Huahine Iti

The smaller island offers both the cheapest and most expensive night-time possibilities on the island. Camping at Ariiura Camping can cost you less than US$10 per night while, at the other extreme, meals and a few drinks and a night at Hana Iti can set you back US$1000.

Ariiura Camping (☎ 68 85 20 or 68 83 78) is right on the beach. You can put up your tent for 600 CFP per person, or there are bungalows for 2000 CFP for one or two people. Bungalow camping means a tiny A-frame palm-thatched cabin with a mattress on the floor. It's camping for people who don't have tents. There's a small dining area, fridge and cooker so you can prepare your own meals. Hubert Cecele, the operator, speaks good English and will run you into town for 800 CFP each way or to the airport for 1200 CFP. The local le trucks leave for Fare about 7.30 am and return about 11.30 am. Count on paying about 500 CFP.

The *Huahine Beach Club* (☎ 68-81-46, fax 68-85-86) has eight garden bungalows at 19,000 CFP and nine beach ones at 21,000 CFP, plus 8% tax. It's right on the beach and looks across to Motu Araara, only a short distance offshore. There's a pool, bar, restaurant and other facilities and the hotel has bicycles and scooters to rent for their guests. Bookings can be made through BP 39, Fare, Huahine.

Almost at the southern point of Huahine Iti, the *Relais Mahana* (☎ 68-81-54, fax 68-85-08) is right on one of the best stretches of beach on the island. There are 11 garden bungalows at 15,800 CFP and 11 beach bungalows at 17,800 CFP, plus 8% tax. Meals cost an extra 1200 CFP for breakfast, or a demi-pension package costs an extra 3500 CFP per person. Transfers from the airport or quay at Fare cost 1800 CFP return. There is a swimming pool and a wide variety of sporting equipment, including canoes, sailboards, bicycles, snorkelling gear and tennis equipment, all available free for guests' use. The hotel is run with almost military precision, however, which some visitors find off-putting. Bookings can be made through BP 30, Fare, Huahine, but note that, like Paris in August, the hotel completely closes down from mid-November to mid-December.

Further west towards Haapu is *Pension Mauarii* (☎ & fax 68-86-49) a new feature at the popular beachside Snack Mauarii (see Places to Eat). There's a dormitory where a bed costs 2000 CFP, rooms at 8500/10,000 CFP with breakfast or you can have the very interesting house for 35,000 CFP a day or from 180,000 CFP a week. Meals, of course, are available at the restaurant. There's a two-night minimum stay at this interesting location.

Last, but far from least in the Huahine hotel listings, is the unique *Hana Iti* (☎ 68-85-05 or 68-87-41, fax 68-85-04), a surprising place from start to finish. Merely getting to reception is the first surprise – is there any other super luxury hotel in the world with such an appalling entry road? Relax, your Fiat Uno will survive the two km of mountain punishment even though it may look like a 4WD test track.

Having got there, the next trip starts because the guest carpark and reception is still only halfway down the hill. The guest rooms are scattered down the hillside to the beach, where the lounge, bar, restaurant, activities area and pool, fed by a 20-metre-high waterfall, are sited. You're delivered to your bungalow in a mini-le truck and whenever you want to get down to the restaurant, or back up to reception, you call for a pick up!

When you reach your room you may decide the effort was worthwhile. The rooms range from a millionaire's fantasy tree house to the sort of thing Robinson Crusoe would have put together if he had a bigger budget and access to modern building supplies. There are 15 deluxe rooms at 54,000 CFP and 10 more special rooms at 64,000 CFP. Breakfast is 2200 CFP, breakfast and dinner is 7800 CFP, and breakfast, lunch and dinner costs 10,800 CFP. Reservations can be made by contacting the Hana Iti through BP 185, Fare, Huahine, or BP 718, Papeete, Tahiti.

PLACES TO EAT
Fare

For cheap eats and late eats the wharfside roulottes are Huahine's best bargain. Otherwise plan to eat early, as after 8 pm most places start to close their doors. Roulottes, if you haven't already met them in Papeete, are mobile restaurants – vans with side flaps that fold down to make counters along which their hungry customers sit. It's all out in the open and it's easy to see what looks good. Fish, chicken, burgers, steaks and chips are the order of the day and a meal typically costs around 700 or 800 CFP. Your meal could be followed by crêpes and gaufres (waffles) or a slice of pastèque (watermelon). The roulottes operate from early morning until late at night and if a ship is due in the early hours they'll open up to feed the passengers.

There are a number of places to eat along the main street of Fare. In the pleasant open-air area at the front of *Chez Guynette* you can get breakfast (continental for 480 CFP, American for 780 CFP), light meals and snacks (a croque-monsieur for 350 CFP or their own version of a croque-madame, a croque-vahine – which means with an egg on top – for 450 CFP). The bar operates from 7 am (for early drinkers) to 9 pm, but they don't do evening meals.

At the north end of the main street, *Snack Bar Te Marara* (☎ 68-89-31) is more restaurant than snack bar. It's right on the beach with an interesting blend of dishes from steaks to seafood and is open every day.

Te Vaipuna Restaurant (☎ 68-70-45) is opposite the wharf and has a strong local reputation for its excellent, and reasonably priced, Chinese food. Most dishes are in the 900 to 1400 CFP range, though crab and lobster will take the bill higher. The house wine is available by the half litre for 600 CFP or by the litre for 1200 CFP. Te Vaipuna is open Monday to Saturday for breakfast, lunch and dinner until the commendably late – for Fare that is – hour of 9.30 pm.

At the southern end of the Fare main street, and also right out over the water, *Restaurant-Bar Orio* (☎ 68-83-03) has main courses at 1000 to 1600 CFP and also features Chinese dishes. It's closed on Monday.

Probably the most popular restaurant in Fare is *Tiare Tipanier* (☎ 68-80-52), which manages to combine excellent food with good value for money. It's a good place for lunch with burgers at 400 CFP, pizzas at 800 CFP and omelettes at 350 to 550 CFP. At dinnertime there's an 1800 CFP fixed price menu for a three-course meal plus a glass of wine or a beer. This menu might feature a salad to start with followed by a dish like tuna with green pepper sauce. Other main courses are 950 to 1500 CFP and wine is available by the carafe (950 CFP for the house red), or bottled wines are 1600 to 2200 CFP and up. Tiare Tipanier is open for lunch and dinner, Monday to Saturday.

Just north of Fare along the beach, *Pension Te Moana* (☎ 68-88-63) has a very pleasant little open-air seafront restaurant with meals at 1000 to 1800 CFP. These include grilled steak or wahoo (tazar in French) with Polynesian ginger at 1600 CFP, or with a three-pepper sauce at 1800 CFP. Desserts are 400 to 600 CFP.

If you're preparing your own meals, fruit, vegetables, fish and other fresh supplies are available from the impromptu quayside marketplace. Super Fare Nui, right across from the quay, and Taahitini, just south of the town centre, are well-equipped supermarkets. Bread is baked daily in the bakery at the back of Wing Kong, the store next door to Chez Guynette, and supplied to the other stores.

Around Huahine

Once you've left Fare there aren't too many places to eat if you're touring around the island, apart from at the hotels. An exception is the excellent waterside *Snack Mauarii* (☎ 68-86-49) just west of Parea and Tiva Point on Huahine Iti. Starters are 650 to 1150 CFP while fish courses are 1250 to 1450 CFP. Seafood is the speciality and they're serious about it. Lighter meals at lunchtime might include a 950 CFP fishburger. Wine is available by the glass and bottle.

In the south-west corner of Huahine Nui *Local Motion* (☎ 68-86-58) is a local fruit farm and orchard offering an 'exotic lunch' for 1000 CFP or an 'ocean lunch' for 2500 CFP.

There are small shops around the island at Maeva and Fitii on Huahine Nui, and at Haapu and Parea on Huahine Iti. Just inland from Faie, *Faie Glaces* (☎ 68-87-95) does great home made coconut, pineapple, banana, vanilla and lemon ice cream. It's closed on Sunday.

ENTERTAINMENT

The *Hotel Bali Hai* often has Tahitian dance

nights. Currently they're on Friday nights and you can just turn up and enjoy the performance for the price of a drink. On other evenings there are often local musicians performing in the restaurant. The *Sofitel Heiva Huahine* also has dance performances and there are trips to them from Fare.

THINGS TO BUY

Plenty of places sell souvenirs and local crafts in and around Fare. Right across from the wharf on the single main street, Rima'i Te Niu Taue (☎ 68-85-59) is a friendly, small boutique with pottery, jewellery and colourful pareus. Souvenirs des Îles is right beside it and also has a good selection. A few steps along the street brings you to the bright and energetic Photographe Jojo, where you can not only buy postcards and other souvenirs, but also hire a bicycle and get your film processed in 24 hours. At the end of Fare's main street, next to the Snack Bar Te Marara, is Faahotu Arts Creation, with good-quality local crafts including paintings and pottery.

Two of the island's most interesting shops are just out of Fare, en route to Maeva and the airport. Gallery Puvaivai (☎ 68-70-09) has paintings and hand-painted pareus by the Perrones, a long-term resident couple. A little further along from Fare, right by the airport turn-off, is Te Mana (☎ 68-81-56), with a wide variety of local crafts including jewellery, pottery and clothing. The owner has a special interest in the late American musician Bobby Holcomb, who had a great influence on Polynesian art and music. There are books about him and CDs and tapes of his music.

At Maeva the Boutique Bellais Blanche (68-83-97) specialises in *tifaifai*, the colourful Polynesian appliqué bedspreads or cushions.

GETTING THERE & AWAY

Westbound from Tahiti it's 170 km to Huahine, the first of the Leeward Islands. The twin islands of Raiatea and Tahaa lie a further 35 km to the west.

Air

Air Tahiti (☎ 68-82-65 or 68-82-89) connects with Papeete at least three or four times daily, taking 35 minutes (slightly longer on the connections via Moorea). Onward flights continue to Raiatea and/or Bora Bora. The short hop to Raiatea is scheduled to take just 15 minutes and can take even less. Connections to Maupiti are more complex, usually requiring a change of aircraft at Raiatea or Bora Bora. One-way adult fares to or from Huahine are Bora Bora 6500 CFP, Maupiti 7700 CFP, Moorea 11,000 CFP, Papeete 8800 CFP and Raiatea 4400 CFP. The Air Tahiti office is at the airport.

Sea

The high-speed *Ono-Ono* and the more traditional *Raromatai Ferry* and *Taporo IV* operate to Huahine. The *Ono-Ono* can be booked through the office (☎ 68-85-85) on the quay in the centre of Fare. It takes just 3½ hours to get to Papeete (4300 CFP) or an hour to Raiatea (1600 CFP) with continuations to Tahaa and Bora Bora.

GETTING AROUND
To/From the Airport

You could walk into town from the airport if you were really intent on saving CFP, but pensions and hotels in Fare will arrange taxi transfers for 400 CFP each way.

Le Truck

The extreme shortage of public transport is Huahine's biggest drawback. A le truck belonging to each district shuttles in to Fare early each morning and returns to the various villages late in the morning. So the only way to get anywhere on public transport is to leave Fare on the late-morning return trip and to return to Fare on the early morning trip to town.

Taxi

Pension Enite (☎ 68-82-37) and one or two other operators provide a taxi service but any of the various places to stay will arrange transport to or from the airport.

Car

As usual, Pacificar and Europcar are the two operators in Huahine. Pacificar is cheaper but Europcar (represented by Kake Rent-a-Car) seems to have the most cars – the most Fiat Unos that is. To be more specific, the most white Fiat Unos. In the parking lots of island hotels it can take five minutes to work out which slightly battered white Fiat Uno is yours. Some other cars are available but the Uno is overwhelmingly the number one car on Huahine.

The main Pacificar offices are at the airport (☎ 68-89-39) and at the quay in Fare (☎ 68-81-81). Cost for a Pacificar Fiat Uno is 5900/10,600/14,300 CFP for one/two/ three days. Europcar's main office is by the Bali Hai turn-off (☎ 68-82-59) and there's also an office at the quay in Fare (☎ 68-88-03). Its Fiat Unos are 6500 CFP a day (three door) or 7000 CFP (five door). Both operators have desks at a number of island hotels. You can often get a 10% discount because you are staying at a local *pension*, because you have a coupon from one of the tourist information

papers or simply because you ask for it. There are petrol stations in Fare.

Scooter & Bicycle

Europcar (Kake) rents bicycles from 1000 CFP for four hours to 1800 CFP for a day. It also has scooters from 3500 CFP for four hours to 4500 CFP for a day. Pacificar has scooters from 2200 to 2400 CFP for four hours or from 3100 to 3500 CFP for a day.

Several of the hotels supply bikes for their guests. Huahine Lagoon, at the north end of the waterfront main street in Fare, rents bikes for 1000 CFP a day, and mountain bikes (VTT in French) for 1200 CFP. The hotel plans to take good care of its shiny new (in early 1996) mountain bikes, as lack of maintenance is the main drawback of most island bicycle rental operators. Jojo's, next door to Chez Guynette, rents regular bikes for 500/800 CFP for a half/full day or mountain bikes for 600/1000 CFP half/full day. On Huahine Iti the Relais Mahana provides bicycles for their guests, while the Huahine Beach Club has bicycles, mountain bikes and motor scooters for hire.

Raiatea & Tahaa

Between Huahine and Bora Bora, the twin islands of Raiatea and Tahaa share a common lagoon. Less touristed than their neighbours to the east and west, the islands offer an opportunity to enjoy a more old-fashioned and relaxed Polynesian lifestyle. A narrow three-km channel separates the two islands, but the airport is on Raiatea and most inter-island ships dock at Uturoa, so visitors to either island will usually come to Raiatea first.

Raiatea

Population: 8600
Area: 170 sq km
Passes: 8

Largest of the Leeward islands and outranked in the whole Society group only by Tahiti, Raiatea has no beaches on the main island. This may account for its comparatively untouristed flavour although there are fine beaches on its many motus. Uturoa, the principal town on Raiatea, is the administrative center for the Leeward Islands of the Society group. Often referred to as 'sacred Raiatea', the island had a central role in ancient Polynesian religious beliefs, and Marae Taputapuatea is the largest *marae* in French Polynesia and one of the most important. It's said that any new marae on another island had to incorporate a stone from Marae Taputapuatea. Raiatea also has the only navigable river in French Polynesia, the Faaroa River, which runs into Faaroa Bay. Polynesian oral history relates that it was from this river that the great migration voyages to Hawaii and New Zealand commenced.

HISTORY

Raiatea is the cultural, religious and historic centre of the Society Islands and it was from here that the great Polynesian navigators are said to have continued the voyages to colonise other islands in the Pacific. Even earlier Polynesian legends relate that Raiatea and Tahaa were the first islands to be settled, probably by people from Samoa, far to the north-west. The Samoan island of Savaii was probably the legendary Havaii, or Raiatea Havaiki, which gave the island its name. It is said that Raiatea's first king was the legendary Hiro, and that it was Hiro and his companions who built the great canoes which sailed on to Rarotonga and New Zealand.

Later, Raiatea was a centre for the Oro cult, which was in the process of replacing the earlier Taaroa cult when Europeans turned up and disrupted the entire Polynesian religious pattern. At the time of Cook's first Polynesian visit, Raiatea was probably under Bora Bora's control and the Raiatean chiefs were scattered far and wide. Tupaia, who sailed with Cook from Tahiti on the *Endeavour*, but died in the Dutch East Indies, was one of these exiled Raiateans.

Raiatea today is the most popular yachting base in French Polynesia. This is a fitting role since it was a centre for the great Polynesian-migration voyages, and because Captain Cook, the greatest European Pacific navigator, visited Raiatea so often and at such length. He first came to the island on the *Endeavour* in 1769 when he anchored off Opoa. He returned in 1774 during his second great Pacific voyage and on this occasion took Omai back to Europe. In 1777 he made a prolonged visit before sailing to Hawaii and to his death.

The pioneering English missionary John Williams turned up in Raiatea in 1818 and the island remained under British missionary influence long after Tahiti came under French control. It was from Raiatea that missionaries continued on to Rarotonga in the Cook Islands in 1823 and to Samoa in 1830. The French takeover of Tahiti in 1842 led to

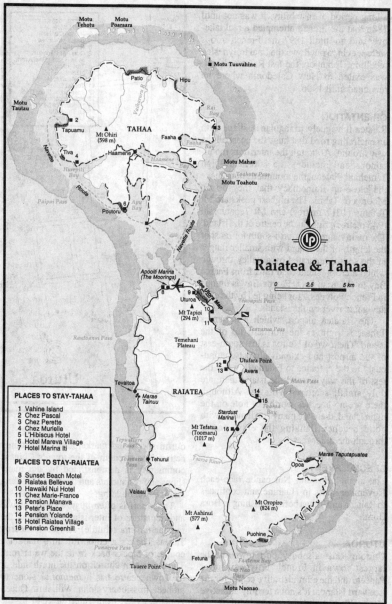

Motu
Tehotu
Motu
Poaraara

1 Motu Tuuvahine

Patio
Hipu

Motu
Tautau

Rai
Bay

2
Tapuamu
Mt Ohiri
(598 m)

TAHAA

3

Faaha

Faaha
Bay

Tiva 4
Haamene

5

Motu Mahae

Haamene

Haamene
Bay

Motu Toahotu

Hurepiti
Bay

Route

Paipai Pass

6

Poutoru

Apu
Bay

7

Navette Route

Apooiti Marina
(The Moorings)

8

9

Uturoa

10

Mt Tapioi
(294 m)

11

Navette

Teavapiti Pass

See Uturoa Map

Temehani
Plateau

Teavanua Pass

Rautoanui Pass

12
13

Utufara Point

Avera

Maire Pass

Tevaitoa

Marae
Tainuu

RAIATEA

14
15

Faaroa
Bay

Tepua Pass

Tepuatire
Pass

Stardust
Marina

16

Mt Tefatua
(Toomaru)
(1017 m)

Faaroa River

Marae Taputapuatea

Opoa

Toomaru
Pass

Tehurui

Vaiaau

Mt Oropiro
(824 m)

Punaeroa Pass

Mt Aahinui
(577 m)

Puohine

Tauere Point

Fetuna

Faatemu Bay

Nau Nau
Pass

Motu Naonao

Raiatea & Tahaa

0   2.5   5 km

PLACES TO STAY-TAHAA

1 Vahine Island
2 Chez Pascal
3 Chez Perette
4 Chez Murielle
5 L'Hibiscus Hotel
6 Hotel Mareva Village
7 Hotel Marina Iti

PLACES TO STAY-RAIATEA

8   Sunset Beach Motel
9   Raiatea Bellevue
10 Hawaiki Nui Hotel
11 Chez Marie-France
12 Pension Manava
13 Peter's Place
14 Pension Yolande
15 Hotel Raiatea Village
16 Pension Greenhill

a long period of instability. It was not until 1888 that the French attempted a real take-over and not until 1897 that French troops were sent in to put down the final Polynesian rebellion. Teraupoo, the last Raiatean chief, was exiled to New Caledonia where he remained until 1906.

ORIENTATION
Raiatea is vaguely triangular in shape with an encircling road that hugs the coast all the way around. Although the interior is mountainous and includes the 800-metre-high Temehani Plateau, the mountains don't have the close-up immediacy that they do on Moorea or Tahiti. The highest peaks are Mt Tefatua (1017 metres) and Mt Tepatuarahi (945 metres), right in the centre of the island. The main range runs north-south for most of the length of the island with smaller ranges in the south, separated by a valley through which a cross-island road runs from Faaroa Bay to Faatemu Bay. Faaroa Bay is unique in French Polynesia for being fed by the only navigable river on the islands.

The Raiatea airport, which also serves Tahaa, is right at the northern tip of the island. The town of Uturoa is just south-east of the airport and extends almost continuously to the entrance to Faaroa Bay, but the rest of the way around the island there are only small, scattered villages. Although there are no beaches worthy of note on the main island, there are many small motus with good beaches flanking the eight passes through the outer reef.

SPECIAL EVENTS
The annual Hawaiki Nui canoe race each November starts in Huahine and continues to Raiatea and Tahaa before finishing in Bora Bora.

UTUROA
Uturoa, Raiatea's busy port town, is the largest town in French Polynesia after Papeete and the administrative centre for the Leeward Islands. It's not a terribly attractive place, although the main street, with its col-

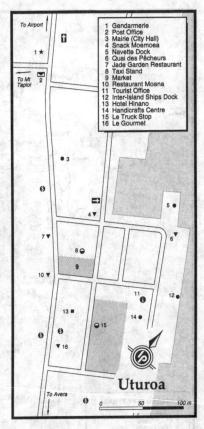

1 Gendarmerie
2 Post Office
3 Mairie (City Hall)
4 Snack Moemoea
5 Navette Dock
6 Quai des Pêcheurs
7 Jade Garden Restaurant
8 Taxi Stand
9 Market
10 Restaurant Moana
11 Tourist Office
12 Inter-Island Ships Dock
13 Hotel Hinano
14 Handicrafts Centre
15 Le Truck Stop
16 Le Gourmet

Uturoa

ourful shops and marketplace, is certainly active. The strength of the town's Chinese community is demonstrated by the many shops and restaurants and the Kuo Min Tang Association building.

The wharf is often busy with the arrival and departure of inter-island boats and the regular *navette* (shuttle) service to nearby Tahaa. There's a colourful little market a couple of blocks back from the waterfront. The Protestant church on the north side of the town centre has a memorial stone to pioneer missionary John Williams. Queen Pomare, exiled from Tahiti in 1844 by the

French takeover, took refuge in Vairahi, now swallowed up by the southward expansion of Uturoa. She remained there for three years before returning to Tahiti.

Uturoa is overlooked by Mt Tapioi, topped by TV-relay masts and offering fine views over the lagoon. See the Activities section for details on climbing the peak.

Information

Tourist Information There is a tourist office near the ferry wharf in town (☎ 66-23-33), with an adjacent small crafts market, and a desk at the airport (☎ 66-23-34). Official opening hours are Monday to Friday, 8 to 11 am; on Tuesday and Thursday the office also opens in the afternoon from 2 to 4 pm.

Money, Post & Other Services There are branches of all four of the French Polynesian banks in Uturoa. Banque Socredo has an ATM at the front of the market building, not in the Banque Socredo building itself. The post office, just north of the centre, is open Monday to Thursday from 7 am to 3 pm; Friday from 7 am to 2 pm, and Saturday from 7.30 to 11.30 am. For the gendarmerie call ☎ 66-31-07, for the police in Uturoa call ☎ 66-38-97.

Doctors in Raiatea are Dr Bataillon (☎ 66-34-55 or 66-25-05), Dr Lazarni (☎ 66-23-01 or 66-38-90) and Dr Repiton (☎ 66-33-89 or 66-30-15). For the hospital call ☎ 66-35-03. There's a pharmacy (☎ 66-34-44) in Uturoa open every day.

AROUND THE ISLAND

There are not a great number of specific 'sights' along the 98-km circuit of Raiatea – it's more an opportunity to enjoy the island's relaxed atmosphere and the splendid views of mountains and motus. Just over half of the circuit is on unsealed roads, or *soupe de coral* (coral soup) as they're known locally. Although they certainly don't require a 4WD, and the Raiatea rental-car companies are totally unconcerned about their little Renaults and Citroëns venturing forth on these roads, some first-world visitors who are used to glass-smooth road surfaces back home have expressed dismay at their confrontations with the odd pot hole.

In the south of the island a short mountain stretch of fine road takes you away from the coast and past an excellent lookout. Adding this road into the itinerary, adding it twice in fact by making the circuit into a figure eight, extends the drive to just 111 km. The following drive starts from Uturoa and goes clockwise, but the bottom half of the figure eight goes anticlockwise. Apart from the two yacht-charter stations at 12.5 km and 106.5 km, there is virtually nowhere along the way to get lunch. You'd be better to bring a picnic if you want to make a day of it, although the drive is an easy morning or afternoon excursion.

Uturoa to the Mountain Turn-Off (0 to 16 km)

From the centre of bustling Uturoa the town blends seamlessly into **Avera**, site of the final battle between the French and local rebels, before turning away from the coast up the long narrow Faaroa Bay. At 12.5 km the road passes **Stardust Marina**, one of the island's two major yacht-charter operations. Soon after you reach the turn-off to the south coast. The **Faaroa River**, the only navigable (albeit barely!) river in French Polynesia, leads inland from the end of the bay.

The Turn-Off to Faatemu Bay (16 to 22.5 km)

From the turn-off the smooth new road climbs effortlessly to the **Belvédère lookout** (26.5 km) with great views down along Faaroa Bay towards the coast and of the surrounding mountains. The road drops down to the coast where the sealed stretch ends.

Faatemu Bay to Marae Taputapuatea (22.5 to 42 km)

Turn left at the coast so that the bottom half of the figure-eight circuit will take you round the coast anticlockwise. The crushed-coral coastal road winds along the coast crossing narrow bridges over many crystal-clear little streams.

In places near the village of **Puohine** (25 km) the road runs on embankments, cutting off shallow ponds used to farm oysters and mussels. There's a long stretch past the village where the steep green mountainsides, falling down towards the coast, are streaked with innumerable waterfalls during the wetter months of the year. Along this part of the road there are many king-size coconut crabs scuttling across the road, and not all of them make it. Just before reaching Raiatea's sacred marae you come to the outskirts of the village of **Opoa** (41 km). A short stretch of sealed road commences right at the marae but it only lasts for two km.

Marae Taputapuatea (42 km)
The most important marae in Polynesia, Marae Taputapuatea looks out to the Te Ava Moa Pass. Dedicated to Oro, the god of war who dominated 18th-century Polynesian religious beliefs, the marae sprawls extensively across Cape Matahira. The marae only dates from the 17th century, when it replaced Marae Vaearai, which was dedicated to Taaroa, the god of creation, and located further inland. Despite its relatively short history, the marae had clearly assumed central importance in the Polynesian religion as any marae constructed on a island had to incorporate one of Taputapuatea's stones.

The main part of the marae is a large flag-stoned platform with a long *ahu* stretching down one side. At the very end of the cape is the smaller Marae Tauraa, a *tapu* (taboo) enclosure with the tall 'stone of investiture'. The lagoonside Marae Hauviri also had an upright stone. The huge double canoes of royal pilgrims used to sail through the Te Ava Moa (or 'sacred') Pass en route to the marae.

Marae Taputapuatea back to Faatemu Bay (42 to 64 km)
The road winds around bays and inlets for 10 more unsealed km before the surface improves along the south side of Faaroa Bay. At 57.5 km you again turn off the coast road

to repeat the short mountain stretch back to the south coast.

Faatemu Bay to Tevaitoa (64 to 95 km)
The road follows the coast, sometimes running over causeways cutting off shallow, stagnant inlets, through the village of **Fetuna** (68 km). Motu Naonao, just across from the Fetuna village, has a pleasant beach and is a popular picnic spot. During WWII when the US military occupied Bora Bora, a landing strip was constructed here. Just before **Vaiaau** (85.5 km), where the sealed road recommences, there may be a small stall by the roadside selling nicely crafted models of paddle and sailing pirogues for 3000 to 3500 CFP. The road continues through **Tehurui** (88.5 km).

Marae Tainuu (95 km)
In the middle of the village of **Tevaitoa** stands the island's oldest Protestant church, an architecturally curious-looking creation but not of great interest were it not built, in one of those examples of Christian respect for other beliefs that warms the heart, smack on top of a magnificent marae. Behind the church the walls of the marae stretch for just over 50 metres with some of the massive upright stones standing over four metres high. At the entrance to the church enclosure, right by the road, there is a circuit of half-buried stones, several of them inscribed with petroglyphs including one with Polynesia's popular turtle motif and another with what looks like a crudely drawn centipede!

Marine-Life Museum (107 km)
From Marae Tainuu to the Apooiti Marina the road continues around the convoluted coast line with more superb views, more waterfalls visible on the hillsides and turn-offs leading to the Temehani Plateau. **Apooiti** was the last centre for fire-walking on Raiatea.

The mega-bucks Moorings Marina, also known as the Apooiti Marina, features shops, a restaurant and bar, a diving centre and, apart from all the yachts of course, a small marine-life museum. The museum, also

Hermit Crabs

Cycling round the coast road late one night I (Tony) was astonished to find a busy traffic of large hermit crabs scuttling across the road, all of them occupying the large brown shells of the giant African snails which have become a pest on a number of islands. Had they evicted the snails from their shells? It's a nice picture, a hermit crab hauling a reluctant snail out of its shell and leaving it shivering in the undergrowth while the crab settles into its new home.

Hermit crabs are common on many islands, ranging from miniature little things to medium-sized snail-shell inhabitants and even larger. Hermit crabs live in shells to protect their fragile carapace. When a hermit crab outgrows its home it has to find a larger shell and make the swift move to its new mansion. Hermit-crab races are a popular activity with children on the beach. Just gather up a collection of crabs, put them down together, draw a large circle around them and wait for them to decide it's all clear, emerge from their shells and scuttle off. First across the outer circle wins. ■

known as the Na Te Ara Museum, includes the not-unexpected diverse range of shells as well as several other examples of Polynesia's marine life, including a wide variety of crabs and a big sea-urchin collection. Nor is Polynesian fauna above sea level ignored. There are some stuffed birds, some of which are already suffering from the threadbare look of tired taxidermy. Polynesia doesn't have much to offer in the four-legged mammal line but the museum does its best with a selection of Polynesian rats.

A second room contains a collection of aquarium tanks featuring local sea life including a beautiful (but deadly) scorpion fish, its ugly sister, the equally nasty stonefish, plus crabs, shrimps, and even a juvenile moray eel. A tank with a message shows what people chuck into the lagoon – cans, bottles and even old shoes. Unfortunately, the environmentally conscious message is somewhat undermined when the museum shop sells shells.

Opening hours are Monday to Saturday from 9 am to noon and 2 to 5 pm; entry is 500 CFP for adults, 250 CFP for children.

From the marina the road passes by the airport and returns to Uturoa, 111 km from the starting point.

DIVING

There's excellent diving within the large Raiatea-Tahaa lagoon and there are two dive operators on Raiatea and one on Tahaa. The Raiatea operators have morning and afternoon dives typically costing 5000 CFP per dive.

Dive Centres

Hemisphere Sub Hemisphere Sub (☎ 66-12-49 or 66-14-19) is at the Apooiti Marina and offers French CMAS-certification courses.

Raiatea Plongée Raiatea Plongée (☎ 66-37-10) is at Chez Marie-France in Uturoa. Many of the guests stay there simply to be close to the dive operation. Guests at the pension get a 1000 CFP discount on the usual dive costs. Patrice Philip is the operator and both CMAS and PADI divers are catered for.

Dive Sites

The size of the lagoon and the numerous passes offer plenty of diving opportunities. There are numerous good dive sites just offshore from Uturoa. Some of the favourite Raiatea and Tahaa dive sites include:

The Octopus Grotto This difficult dive, in the lagoon between Raiatea and Tahaa, is for experienced divers only. The divers venture into a 120-metre-long cave at a depth of 50 metres.

Teavapiti & Teavarua Passes There are two passes just south of the centre of Uturoa. The Teavapiti Pass is the more northerly, between Motu Ofetaro and Motu Taoru. The Teavarua Pass is south of Motu Taoru. There are a number of dives around these passes including the Catalina Wreck, on the northwest side of Motu Taoru. A 1958 landing accident left this Catalina seaplane on the bottom in a depth of just seven metres. Teavapiti Pass itself has very dense marine

RAIATEA

life and this is a favourite spot for hand-feeding sharks. Teavarua Aquarium, on the southern point of Motu Taoru, is another very popular dive site as is the Aquarium Flat, just to the south.

Other Dive Sites Other popular sites include the Japanese Garden, a beginners' dive in only five metres' depth. Visits by huge napoleons have given the Napoleon Cliff its name and the Coral Roses is equally indicative of what you will find. Raiatea and Tahaa have a wide variety of interesting dive sites around the many passes.

WALKING & CLIMBING

Popular walks and climbs around Raiatea include the following:

Mt Tapioi

Between the post office and gendarmerie in Uturoa, just north of the centre, take the road inland towards Mt Tapioi. A short distance along this road a sign indicates 'Mt Tapioi' off to the right, quickly followed by another sign proclaiming (in French): 'private road, bad dogs, no entry', but hey, we can't read French can we?

Several more Tapioi signs confirm this is the right direction as the slightly rough road switchbacks up, but it's nothing your Citroën or Renault won't manage. Unhappily the next 'no' sign means it, a chain across the track, backed up by half a dozen padlocks, underlining the negatives. From here it's a half-hour uphill stroll, passing some surprised cows on the way to the TV masts and superb views of the Raiatea-Tahaa reef, the lagoon, Uturoa and the airport and across to Huahine, Bora Bora and, if you look carefully and the visibility is reasonable, Maupiti; that is to say, from here you can see all the high islands of the Leeward group.

Temehani Plateau

Tracks suitable for 4WD vehicles climb up to the 750-metre Temehani Plateau at the northern end of the island. There are also some interesting walks. The plateau is home to the *tiare apetahi*, a white gardenia

endemic to Raiatea. Further south Mt Tefatua (1017 metres) is the highest point on the island.

HORSE RIDING

Using Marquesan horses, Kaoha Nui (☎ 66-25-46) has a variety of horse-riding trips from 1½ hours for 3000 CFP to all-day excursions for 8000 CFP. Longer two to four-day camping trips can also be arranged. The trips visit plantations, marae sites and the mountainous central parts of the island.

SAILING

Raiatea may not have the beaches and fancy resorts of the other islands but it is the yachting centre of French Polynesia. Three marinas, two of them international yacht-chartering operations, cater to the needs of visiting sailors. The twin islands of Raiatea and Tahaa are not only centrally located in the Leeward group but also provide excellent sailing within their large encircling lagoon. Tahaa in particular appeals to visiting yachties and two of the hotels make a real effort to keep them happy with moorings and other facilities. A recommended one-week sailing itinerary out of Raiatea is:

Day 1:	Raiatea-Tahaa
Day 2:	Tahaa-Huahine
Day 3:	Huahine
Day 4:	Huahine-Tahaa
Day 5:	Tahaa-Bora Bora
Day 6:	Bora Bora
Day 7:	Bora Bora-Tahaa
Day 8:	Tahaa-Raiatea

The boats chartered out of Raiatea range from 11 to 15 metres in length. Many of them are real luxury yachts with a shower and toilet for each cabin. Although most people will be sailing themselves (bareboat charters), skippered cruises can also be arranged and some of the larger boats are only available with the skipper. A wide variety of chartering costs and times are available but there's usually a three-day minimum. Costs climb in the July-August high season, and drop in the January-March low season. The rest of the year, April through June and September through December, is the middle season.

The two marinas with yacht-chartering operations are The Moorings at the Apooiti Marina, just west of the airport and about four km from Uturoa, and Stardust Marina on Faaroa Bay, 12 km south of Uturoa. Both have 20 to 30 yachts available to charter. The third marina is the New Marina ('Nouvelle Marina') between Uturoa and the airport, before the Apooiti Marina.

The Moorings

US-owned The Moorings has operations in Australia, the Caribbean, Florida, Mexico, Turkey, various European locations and in the Pacific in Tonga and French Polynesia. In Raiatea there are 30-odd boats available starting from around US$3200 for a one-week low-season charter of an 11-metre yacht accommodating six people in three double cabins. Costs climb to up to US$10,000 to US$12,000 for larger boats.

The Moorings (☎ 66-35-93 or 66-26-26, fax 66-20-94) can be contacted through BP 165, Uturoa, Raiatea. In the US call ☎ 1-800-535-7289 for information.

Stardust Marina

French-owned Stardust Marina has 350 yachts worldwide at their marinas in the Caribbean, Turkey and in Raiatea in French Polynesia. The 30-odd boats in the Raiatea fleet include the *Stardust 363* (11 metres, accommodation for eight, six in three cabins, two in the saloon), *Stardust 403* (12 metres, accommodation for six in three cabins), *Stardust 443* (13.36 metres, accommodation for six in three cabins), *Stardust 442* (13.8 metres, accommodation for four in two cabins), *Stardust 474-G* (14.2 metres, accommodation for eight in four double cabins), the *Stardust 515* (15.3 metres, accommodation for 10, eight in four cabins plus two in crew quarters), *Stardust 43* (13-metre catamaran, accommodation for 10 in five doubles) and the *Stardust 48* (14.7-metre catamaran, accommodation for 10, eight in four doubles plus two in crew quarters, only available with skipper). Chartering

rates are quoted in French francs but weekly rates range from approximately US$2600 to US$6600 in the low season up to US$3100 to US$8000 in the high season.

Stardust Marina (☎ 66-23-18, fax 66-23-19) can be contacted through BP 331, Uturoa, Raiatea.

BOATING & FISHING

Game-fishing trips can be organised with the *Sakario* (☎ 66-35-54) or the *Te Manu Ata* (☎ 66-32-14). Half-day trips cost 35,000 CFP and full-day trips cost 60,000 CFP. The 51-foot cruising yacht *Bisou Fute* (☎ 65-64-97) is based out of Haamene in Tahaa. The 50-foot fast catamaran *Fai Manu* (☎ 65-62-52) is at Uturoa.

ORGANISED TOURS

Visits to Marae Taputapuatea, tours of the island and expeditions into the highlands are the prime land-based tours. Afloat there are trips up the Faaroa River and boats out to the motus for beaches and snorkelling.

Trips to visit the plantations, valleys and rivers of Raiatea are operated with 4WD vehicles. Raiatea 4x4 (☎ 66-24-16) makes half-day 4WD trips into the backroads of Raiatea for 5000 CFP per person for one or two people, 4000 CFP per person for three or more people. Raiatea Safari Tours (☎ 66-37-10) at Chez Marie-France covers the gamut of standard Raiatea excursions. They make 4WD trips into the back country for 4000 CFP, trips around Raiatea for 7500 CFP and they take the short cruise up the Faaroa River for 2800 CFP. Their boat trips around Tahaa are 4500 CFP or 7500 CFP around Raiatea.

Almost Paradise Tours (☎ 66-23-64) rather proudly announces on its leaflet that tours are 'in English only'. Operated by a long-term American resident, the three-hour minibus trip to Marae Taputapuatea and island plantations costs 3000 CFP.

You can even flightsee over Raiatea on an ultralight flight for 6000 CFP for 20 minutes or 8000 CFP for 30 minutes. Call Jean-Louis (☎ 66-25-73 or 66-35-93) at ULM Polynésie for more information.

RAIATEA

PLACES TO STAY
Raiatea's accommodation is in or close to the main town, Uturoa. The sole exception was the Te Moana Iti, close to Marae Taputapuatea and 35 km from Uuturoa, but this mid-range hotel has closed down. It has been up for sale though and may reopen. The Sunset Beach Motel, north of Uturoa, offers camping facilities.

Uturoa
Uturoa has one hotel right in the centre and several other possibilities a km or so north of the centre and a couple of km south.

The *Hotel Hinano* (☎ 66-13-13, fax 66-14-14) is right in the centre of Uturoa, only 100 metres from the docks. Although it looks drab and dull on the outside, the recently renovated rooms are quite modern and presentable. Staying in the centre of Uturoa, however, is unlikely to appeal to most visitors. All 10 rooms have patios and attached bathrooms and there is a restaurant downstairs. Singles/doubles cost 4350/5350 CFP in the six rooms with ceiling fan, 5350/6350 CFP in the four air-con rooms. Bookings can be made through BP 196, Uturoa, Raiatea.

Right on the water's edge, at PK 2, just south of the centre of Uturoa, the *Hawaiki Nui Hotel* (☎ 66-20-23, fax 66-20-20) has 32 rooms, including nine over-water bungalows. All the rooms and bungalows have attached bathroom and cost 12,000 CFP for the garden rooms, 17,000 CFP for the garden bungalows, 20,000 CFP for the lagoon-front bungalows and 29,000 CFP for the over-water bungalows. These prices are subject to 8% tax. There's a bar, restaurant, shop and swimming pool. Breakfast costs 950 CFP (continental) or 1450 CFP (buffet). Bookings can be made through BP 43, Uturoa, Raiatea and credit cards are accepted.

Half a km further along the road, at about PK 2.5, is Raiatea's budget travellers' favourite, *Chez Marie-France* (☎ 66-37-10, fax 66-26-25). This very well equipped little place has dorm beds, cabin rooms, bungalow rooms, a bar, an excellent restaurant, a swimming pool and rental bikes, and is the centre for all sorts of island activities. It's also the base for Raiatea Plongée. The excellent little restaurant does breakfast at 600 to 1000 CFP.

Dorm beds are 1200 CFP per night, 1500 CFP if you only stay one night. They share toilet and shower facilities with the simple cabin rooms which accommodate one or two people and cost 4000 CFP per night, 4500 CFP if you only stay one night. The four more luxurious cabins have attached bathrooms, TV and a mezzanine level which, in a couple of the cabins, can be used for children. They cost 7000/8000 CFP as singles/doubles, or an extra 1000 CFP if you only stay one night. Bookings can be made through BP 272, Uturoa, Raiatea, and credit cards are accepted. Yachts wanting to moor at Chez Marie-France can contact them on VHF 12.

On the north side of town, heading towards the airport, *Raiatea Bellevue* (☎ 66-15-15) labels itself a bed and breakfast. The three rooms have their own verandahs and cost 2750 CFP per person. There is a swimming pool and transfers from the airport are free. Bookings can be made through BP 98, Uturoa, Raiatea, and credit cards are not accepted.

South of Uturoa
Avera Just beyond the southern fringes of Uturoa, there are three places at Avera, all on the mountain side of the road, close to the PK 6 marker. There are three more places four km further along at PK 10, at the southern end of Avera.

First of the PK 6 threesome is the *Kaoha Nui Ranch* (☎ 66-25-46), which has a main building with four rooms, each with two single beds and shared bathroom facilities for 1500 CFP per person. A separate double room with its own attached bathroom costs 6000/10,000 CFP for one/two people. Kitchen facilities are available. Horse riding is the speciality here (see the Activities section for more details). Bookings can be made through BP 568, Uturoa, Raiatea, and credit cards are not accepted.

Next up is the very friendly *Pension Manava* (☎ 66-28-26) with rooms in a larger building and pleasant small bungalows dotted around the garden. The larger *fare* has two rooms sharing a cold-water bathroom and equipped kitchen. One room will accommodate up to three people, the other up to five and they cost 3500 CFP for two people, and an additional 1000 CFP for each extra person. Two bungalows have attached bathrooms but share a kitchen and cost 4500 CFP for one or two people. The other two bungalows have their own bathroom and kitchen and cost 5500 CFP. There's an additional 500 CFP charge for one-night stops and breakfast is available for an additional 500 or 800 CFP. Free transfers are provided from the airport or ferry quay. Bookings can be made through BP 559, Uturoa, Raiatea, and credit cards are not accepted.

Just beyond Pension Manava, at PK 6.5, is *Peter's Place* (☎ 66-20-01), where you can camp for 700 CFP. There's also a single row of eight spartan rooms, each with two single beds for 1200 CFP per person or 1400 CFP for a one-night stand. There's a shared kitchen area, two showers and toilets, all of it fairly basic. The grassy grounds are on the mountain side of the road and although the whole set up is as simple as it comes, economy-minded backpackers may find it hits the low-priced spot. Credit cards are not accepted.

There are three possibilities right around the PK 10 mark, just before the road turns away from the coast to follow the north side of Faaroa Bay inland. All three are on the lagoon side of the road. *La Rose de Porcelaine* (☎ & fax 66-14-78) has two rooms with mosquito nets, fans and shared cold-water bathroom facilities. The nightly cost is 7000/11,000 CFP including all meals. There's a sailboard and two mountain bikes for guests' use and a variety of tours are on offer. Bookings can be made through BP 453, Uturoa, Raiatea, and credit cards are not accepted.

Pension Yolande (☎ 66-35-28) right on the water, is a large house with four rooms, each with kitchen facilities and a private bathroom. Each room accommodates up to three people, two with a double bed and a single, two with three singles. Although the walls are a bit thin, so noise carries, the pension is clean and well kept. It's run by the cheery Yoland Roopina and the nightly cost of 5000 CFP per person for one or two people, 1000 CFP for each additional person, includes an excellent breakfast. Bookings can be made through BP 298, Uturoa, Raiatea, and credit cards are not accepted.

Hotel Raiatea Village (☎ 66-31-62, fax 66-10-65) is a small resort right on the water's edge. There are 12 bungalows, all with attached bathrooms and kitchens, with singles/doubles at 5000/7000 CFP plus 8% tax. Airport or ferry-quay transfers cost 1000 CFP round trip. Bookings can be made through BP 282, Uturoa, Raiatea, and credit cards are accepted.

Faaroa Bay Right opposite the entry to the Stardust Marina on the north side of Faaroa Bay, 12 km from the centre of Uturoa, is *Pension Greenhill* (☎ 66-37-64), BP 598, Uturoa, Raiatea. A big green letter 'G' on the mailbox on the mountain side of the road is the only identifier. Greenhill is one of the most interesting and idiosyncratic places to stay on the island. From the road the driveway leads steeply uphill to the house, complete with a pleasant garden, pool and spa, looking down on the yacht marina and across Faaroa Bay.

Singles/doubles cost 6500/8000 CFP *demi-pension* and the food is excellent, served family-style at a table on the open verandah area. It's requested that visitors book at least two nights ahead and there is a minimum two-night stay, but both rules may be waived if you come at a quiet time. Enjoying Greenhill is very much a case of getting on with Marie-Isabelle, the charming but definitely strong-minded hostess. If you click with her and follow her rules you'll enjoy your stay, but if you don't you won't! If you book ahead you can be collected from the airport or the quay (1000 CFP round trip). The location is definitely a little isolated, however, so it's nice to have your own wheels. A very definite plus at Greenhill is the free trips thrown in: Faaroa River excursions or picnic visits to a motu are often provided and bicycles are also provided free. Bookings can be made through BP 598, Uturoa, Raiatea, and credit cards are not accepted.

North of Uturoa

The *Sunset Beach Motel* (☎ 66-33-47, fax 66-33-08), at PK 5, is only a km beyond the Apooiti Marina, two km beyond the airport or about five km from the Uturoa town centre. Right on the waterfront, the extensive grounds contain 16 large and comfortable bungalows, all with bathroom, kitchen and TV. Rates are 6500/7500 CFP for one/two people but the units will accommodate up to five. There's a 1000 CFP extra charge per bungalow for one-night stays. Camping space is also available at 1000 CFP per person per night and there are kitchen facilities and bathrooms. Bookings can be made through BP 397, Uturoa, Raiatea, credit cards are accepted and free transfers to and from the airport or the ferry quay in Uturoa are provided.

PLACES TO EAT
Uturoa

Snack Bars & Cafés There are several simple snack bars between the ferry quay and the market, like *Snack Chez Remy*, a good place for a cheap meal and a cold beer. On the waterfront *Snack Moemoea* is a pleasant little café with outdoor tables, cold beer and snacks. It closes soon after 5 pm.

Snack Temehani (☎ 66-37-10) is the bright little restaurant at Raiatea's surprisingly bustling little airport. How many airports have a sign hanging out on the roadside announcing the plat du jour? The special meal of the day costs 800 CFP. It's open for lunch only.

Restaurants Right on the quay, as its name indicates, the *Quai des Pêcheurs* (☎ 66-36-83) is a great place to watch the waterfront activity, whether it's the coming and going of the navette to Tahaa or larger inter-island ships in dock. There's a pleasant outdoor eating area and light meals at lunchtime like chao mein, poisson cru or mahi mahi provençale for 900 CFP. At dinner time mahi mahi, curried, grilled or cooked in foil is 1600 CFP, entrecôte steak is 1800 CFP, and shrimp dishes are 1800 to 2200 CFP.

Le Gourmet (☎ 66-21-51) is right next to the Hinano Hotel and has typical French dishes at 1000 to 1200 CFP. It's closed on Sunday. *Restaurant Michele* (☎ 66-14-66) is right in the Hinano Hotel and offers a mix of Chinese and standard European dishes. It's also closed on Sunday.

Uturoa has two popular Chinese restaurants with very standard Chinese menus. The *Restaurant Moana* (☎ 66-27-49) is closed Sunday lunchtime and all day Monday. The *Jade Garden Restaurant* (☎ 66-34-40) is closed all day Sunday and Monday.

A couple of km south of the town centre *Chez Marie-France* (☎ 66-37-10), the popular budget accommodation centre at PK 2.5, has an excellent restaurant and bar with a three-course dinner at 2500 CFP.

Around the Island

If you're travelling round the island bring a picnic as the only places to get a meal are the two yachting marinas, four km north and 12 km south of Uturoa.

Veranda (☎ 66-10-71) is the popular waterside restaurant at the Stardust Marina at PK 12 on Faaroa Bay. It's closed on Sunday. The *Club House* (☎ 66-11-66) at the Apooiti Marina is the biggest and fanciest restaurant on the island and offers breakfast from 6 am as well as lunch and dinner from its French menu.

ENTERTAINMENT

Both the yacht marina restaurant bars are good places for a cold beer at sunset. The Moana Restaurant metamorphoses into the *Zenith Discothéque* (☎ 66-27-49) later in the evening from Wednesday to Sunday. The *Quai des Pêcheurs* (☎ 66-36-83) restaurant on the Uturoa waterfront also features a disco on Saturday night.

THINGS TO BUY

There is a local handicraft outlet beside the tourist office, a block back from the waterfront. Several shops along the main street of Uturoa sell postcards and other standard souvenirs. Black pearls are available from La Palme d'Or (☎ 66-23-79) in the town centre, while the Anuanua Art Gallery (☎ 66-12-66) is just beyond the post office, towards the airport. The Boutique de l'Aéroport (☎ 66-36-67) at the airport also has standard souvenirs.

GETTING THERE & AWAY

Raiatea is 220 km north-west of Tahiti, 40 km south-east of Bora Bora and separated by a three-km-wide channel from Tahaa.

Air

Air Tahiti (☎ 66-32-50 or 66-30-51) flies to Raiatea at least twice daily from Tahiti, taking 40 minutes direct or slightly longer via Huahine. Onward connections go to Bora Bora direct or via Maupiti. One-way adult fares to or from Raiatea include Bora Bora 5100 CFP, Huahine 4400 CFP, Maupiti 5600 CFP and Papeete 10,100 CFP. The Air Tahiti office is at the airport.

The charter operator Air Alizé (☎ 66-10-00) is based on Raiatea and offers flights between the Leeward Islands.

Sea

To/From Distant Islands Several ships operate regular services from Tahiti through the Leeward Islands, stopping at Raiatea and sometimes Tahaa, en route to Bora Bora. See the Getting Around chapter for more details about the inter-island ferries, in particular the *Ono-Ono* and the *Raromatai Ferry*.

The *Ono-Ono* is the fastest and most frequent of the inter-island services. The *Ono-Ono's* high-speed route through the Society Islands takes just one hour from Huahine to Raiatea at a fare of 1600 CFP and another 1¾ hours on to Bora Bora at a fare of 1600 CFP. The trip is slightly longer on the days it goes via Tahaa. For information call ☎ 45-35-35 in Tahiti or ☎ 66-35-35 in Raiatea.

The *Raromatai Ferry* takes two hours between Huahine and Raiatea or four hours from Raiatea via Tahaa to Bora Bora, includ-

ing an hour in port in Tahaa. A Pullman seat costs 3800 CFP from Papeete or 1000 CFP to or from Huahine or Bora Bora, and cabins are also available. For information call ☎ 43-19-88 in Tahiti.

Get a big enough group together and you can take the Raiatea-Tahaa navette further afield. Phone ☎ 65-67-10 to enquire about 7 am to 5 pm round trips to Bora Bora or Huahine.

To/From Tahaa Tahaa Transport Services (☎ 65-67-10) operates navettes between Uturoa on Raiatea and various stops on Tahaa. The services operate Monday to Friday, although there is no service on Sunday. On Saturday there is no service to Haamene. It takes less than 15 minutes from Uturoa to Apu Marina, the closest stop on Tahaa. The one-way fare is 750 CFP. A smaller eight-seat taxi-boat can be chartered at other times and on Sunday.

	Arrive	Depart
Tapuamu	6.15 am	6.15 am
Tiva	6.25 am	6.25 am
Poutoru	6.35 am	6.35 am
Apu Marina	6.45 am	6.45 am
Uturoa	7.00 am	7.00 am
Haamene	7.30 am	7.30 am
Uturoa	8.00 am	8.15 am
Apu Marina	8.30 am	9.30 am
Uturoa	9.45 am	10.45 am
Poutoru	11.00 am	11.00 am
Tiva	11.10 am	11.10 am
Tapuamu	11.20 am	11.20 am
Haamene	11.30 am	11.30 am
Tiva	11.40 am	11.40 am
Poutoru	11.50 am	11.50 am
Apu Marina	12.00 pm	12.00 pm
Uturoa	12.20 pm	12.30 pm
Haamene	1.00 pm	1.00 pm
Uturoa	1.30 pm	1.30 pm
Apu Marina	1.45 pm	4.30 pm
Uturoa	4.45 pm	5.00 pm
Apu Marina	5.15 pm	5.15 pm
Poutoru	5.25 pm	5.25 pm
Tiva	5.35 pm	5.35 pm
Tapuamu	5.45 pm	–

GETTING AROUND

Hitchhiking appears to be fairly acceptable on Raiatea as a result of the low-key tourism and lack of public transport.

To/From the Airport

There are taxis at the airport but most island accommodation will either pick you up for free or provide airport transfers for 400 to 500 CFP each way. It's only three km from the airport to the centre of Uturoa.

Le Truck

There are *le truck* services to outlying districts during the day but they're not very convenient for sightseeing trips. The colour-coded le trucks run from Uturoa to Opoa near Marea Taputapuatea (blue), Fetuna on the south coast of the island (turquoise) and Vaiaau on the west coast (red). The le truck terminus is centrally located in Uturoa. To most remote locations there is simply one le truck in each direction in the morning and perhaps an outward-bound service from Uturoa, but no return, in the afternoon. Check that there will be a return trip if you don't want to get stuck at your destination. To get to Marae Taputapuatea take the early morning Opoa le truck, from where it's a short walk to the marae.

Taxi

There's a taxi stand by the market (☎ 66-20-60, 66-20-80 or 66-36-74) and taxis can also be found at the airport, but, as usual in French Polynesia, they're very expensive.

Car

Europcar (☎ 66-34-06) is at the airport and also has offices at the Haiwaiki Nui Hotel (☎ 66-20-23) and in Uturoa (☎ 66-35-35). They have Fiat Pandas for 6000 CFP a day, Fait Unos for 7500 CFP a day and scooters and bicycles. Pacificar (☎ 66-11-66) has a desk at the airport (☎ 66-15-59); you can rent a Fiat Panda for 5400 CFP a day, a Citroën AX or Fiat Uno for 5900 CFP or motor scooters for 3100 or 3500 CFP.

Bicycle

Chez Marie-France rents straightforward cruiser-style bikes for 600 CFP for four hours, 1000 CFP for eight hours. The Hawaiki Nui has fancier bikes for their guests while the Pension Greenhill provides free bikes for its guests.

Tahaa

Population: 4000
Area: 90 sq km
Passes: 2

Raiatea may be quiet but Tahaa is even quieter. Like its southern sister, there are no beaches to speak of on the main island and the tourist facilities are even more basic. A coast road encircles most of the island but traffic is very light and there is no public transport. Vanilla cultivation is an important activity but the main tourist attraction is the string of beautiful motus along the northern reef edge. The easily navigable lagoon and safe yacht anchorages make Tahaa's lagoon a favourite for visiting yachties.

HISTORY

Tahaa was once known as Kuporu (or Uporu), a name which pops up in other Polynesian centres, perhaps indicating some great migratory connection. The name may have come from the Samoan island of Upolu, sister island to Savaii, which was probably the Raiatea Hawaiki or Hawaii from where the migration legends emanated. Tahaa lived in the shadow of Raiatea, its larger, stronger and more important neighbour, although it was at times a pawn in struggles between Raiatea and the fierce rulers of Bora Bora.

The first missionaries arrived from neighbouring Raiatea in 1822 and the island came under French control at the same time as Raiatea. Tahaa was once a centre for fire-walking ceremonies, but they are now a rare occurrence.

ORIENTATION

Tahaa is a quiet little place with a 70-km road winding around most of the convoluted coast. The crushed-coral road is in reasonable condition and there are sealed sections through the main towns and where the road leaves the coast and climbs over the hills, particularly the nicely sweeping road up and over the centre from Haamene to Tiva.

The population is concentrated in eight main villages. Tapuamu has the main wharf, Patio is the main town while Haamene is where the roads round the south and north part of the island meet, forming a figure eight. Mt Ohiri (598 metres) is the highest point on the island. Apu Bay to the south, Haamene Bay to the east and Hurepiti Bay to the west are deep inlets offering sheltered anchorages for yachts.

INFORMATION

For information on the island contact the Tahaa Visitors' Bureau (☎ 65-63-00) in Patio.

The one-desk branch of Banque Socredo is in Patio and is open weekdays. There are reasonable-size island shops in Haamene, Tiva, Tapuamu and Patio.

SPECIAL EVENTS

The annual Heiva No Te Pahu Nui O Tahaa stone fishing festival takes place in the last week of October. Events include singing and dancing, agricultural and craft displays, local sporting events (including fruit-carrying races!), fishing contests and canoe races. A fire-walking ceremony is a highlight of the festivities before the final event, the stone fishing festival. Flower-bedecked pirogues fan out across the lagoon and the surface of the water is beaten with stones to herd the fish into an enclosure.

In November Tahaa is the final overnight stop on the Hawaiki Nui canoe race before it concludes in Bora Bora.

AROUND THE ISLAND

The 70-km circuit of the island is quite possible as a bicycle day trip although most of the route is unsealed crushed coral and there are some steep up-and-down sections where the road leaves the coast and climbs over the hills. PK markers start at Haamene and go up clockwise and anticlockwise around the northern half of the island, terminating at Patio.

Starting from the Marina Iti, the first navette stop if you're coming from Raiatea and the best place to rent bicycles, the road sticks to the coast around Apu Bay. At the top of the bay there's a turn-off south to the Mareva Village Hotel and the village of Poutoru, where the road ends. The round-the-island route leaves the coast and climbs up and over to the larger village of **Haamene**. At Haamene the road barely reaches sea level before climbing again, a long sweeping ascent and descent down to pretty Hurepiti Bay and the village of **Tiva**. Bora Bora comes into view as you round the end of the bay, looking surprisingly close beyond the lagoon edge.

Tapuamu is the site of the island's main wharf. From here the chain of motus that fringe the northern coast of the island come into view. **Patio** is the administrative centre of the island, with offices, a post office, a bank, shops, a small artisans' centre and, in a sharp jolt back to reality, a memorial to a Tahaa man killed with the UN in Sarajevo in May 1995. The crazy conflicts in the Balkans seem a long way from this sleepy island.

Beyond Patio more of the 60-odd motus around the north of the island are visible as the road winds along the coast. They include the luxurious resort motu of Vahine Island. The road continues around the coast, past copra plantations, to **Faaha** and Faaha Bay before climbing over a headland and dropping down to Haamene Bay. Alternatively, a rougher track turns off the coast road just beyond Patio and takes a direct route over the hills and down to Haamene.

From the coast road where it meets Haamene Bay, turn east to L'Hibiscus Hotel where the Foundation Hibiscus is dedicated to saving turtles which have become entangled in local fishers' nets. They're transferred to remote Scilly Island (see the Other Leeward Islands chapter), a favourite nesting ground for sea turtles. Smaller turtles are kept in pens beside the hotel's pier until they've grown large enough to be released. Up until early 1996 they had saved nearly 250 endangered turtles.

From L'Hibiscus Hotel the coast road goes

round the north side of the bay to Haamene, then along the south side of the bay and, on the final long stretch back to the starting point, winds in and out of seemingly endless small bays before coming back to the Marina Iti.

DIVING

Tahaa Plongée (☎ 65-61-01), based at the Hotel Marina Iti, is the Tahaa-based dive operator, an offshoot of Raiatea Plongée in Uturoa. See the Raiatea section for dive site information.

WALKING & CLIMBING

You can take the little-used route across the centre of the island from Patio to Haamene but otherwise there's very few trails into the Tahaa interior.

ORGANISED TOURS

The Raiatea hotels offers trips around Tahaa by pirogue with stops at deserted white-sand motus and a vanilla-plantation tour for 4500 CFP.

Alain and Cristina Plantier's Vanilla Tours (☎ 65-62-46) makes 4WD excursions around Tahaa to visit the mountainous interior and the Plantier's own vanilla plantation. The four-hour trip costs 3500 CFP per person from the Plantier's house at the top of Hurepiti Bay, or 4000 CFP if they pick you up from a Tahaa hotel. Yachties can call on VHF 9 and moor outside the house. Tahaa Vanilla Safari Tours (☎ 65-61-06) at L'Hibiscus Hotel visits a pearl farm, a vanilla plantation and the Foundation Hibiscus turtle-protection operation on their Tahaa island tours.

The Hotel Marina Iti (☎ 65-61-01) has a host of Tahaa activities, including fishing trips, pirogue trips around the island, sailing trips and sunset excursions.

PLACES TO STAY

Tahaa's places to stay are dotted around the coast – there's no concentration in a single area. Don't count on them all being open all the time; it would be a drag to come over from Raiatea, make your way to one of them

and then find it wasn't open or the operators had gone off to town for the day. None of the cheaper places to stay has a sign. Where they are in relation to the navette stops also counts, although most places will pick up guests and the more expensive places will come all the way to the airport or dock on Raiatea. Tahaa's accommodation possibilities range from rock bottom to mid-range with one top-end place on a motu.

On the Island

Going round the island from the first regular navette stop, the *Hotel Marina Iti* (☎ 65-61-01, fax 65-63-87, radio VHF 68) on Toamaro Point has its own boat stop, right on the pier to the hotel. This is the busiest place on the island, with a popular restaurant and a regular yachtie clientele. It's right on the waterfront looking across to Raiatea, and the forests of yacht masts at Raiatea's north-coast marinas are clearly visible. There's no beach at the hotel but there are lots of fish off the end of the pier, and it's a good place for a swim.

Accommodation is in five bungalow rooms, which are pleasant with very necessary mosquito nets over the beds, attached bathrooms and handy little verandah areas. The nightly cost is 10,000 CFP. Stroll along the sea wall at night when a good torch (flashlight) will illuminate all sorts of creatures from eels and crabs to colourful scorpion fish.

Meals are served in the restaurant and bar by the pier, and visiting yachties who use the restaurant get free moorings. See the Places to Eat section for more details. The Marina Iti has cars and mountain bikes to rent (see Getting Around). It offers a variety of tours and is the centre for Tahaa Plongée, the island's scuba-diving operator. Bookings can be made through BP 888, Uturoa, Raiatea, and credit cards are accepted.

Right across the bay from the Marina Iti, shouting distance away – and near the next navette stop – the *Hotel Mareva Village* (☎ 65-61-61, fax 65-68-67) is also just 10 minutes across the lagoon from the airport at the northern end of Raiatea. The small development has six prefab bungalows, shipped over from New Zealand and lined up side by side above the water's edge. The units have a kitchen, bathroom and TV and cost 7000 CFP for one or two, or there are family rooms for two adults plus four children for 8000 CFP. Bookings can be made through BP 214, Haamene. Across the road from the rooms and atop the promontory, with fine views across the bay and right across the lagoon to Raiatea, there's a restaurant with varied cuisine and a pleasant open-air dining area.

Continuing round the island the next place is *Chez Murielle*, also known as *Ti'Amahana* (☎ 65-67-29), an unmarked house halfway along Hurepiti Bay, before you get into the village of Tiva, the next navette stop. There are three bungalows, two with a double bed and one with twin beds and a couple of bunk beds. In this very Polynesian-flavoured pension and restaurant, demi-pension is 6500 CFP for one person or 12,000 CFP for two. Credit cards are not accepted.

The final navette stop is at Tapuamu, the island's main dock where inter-island ships like the *Ono-Ono* also make their stops. Continue clockwise along the island road out of Tapuamu after the sealed road ends and crosses the bridge; the first turn inland comes to *Chez Pascal* (☎ 65-60-42), the island's cheapest accommodation possibility. The three very simple, but quite neat and clean, little bungalows have shared toilet and shower facilities and cost 2500 CFP per night or 4500 CFP demi-pension. Credit cards are not accepted.

The PK markers going up from Haamene stop at about PK 25 clockwise in Patio and go down from there back to Haamene. Right at the PK 10 marker, ie 10 km from Haamene, *Chez Perette* (☎ 65-65-78) is a big, white house on the coast side of the road. There are two bungalows with a double bedroom and attached bathroom, while the house has two double bedrooms and a mezzanine dormitory with eight beds, all sharing a bathroom. A mattress in the dorm costs 2500 CFP a day or per person, and the cost in the rooms or bungalows is 8500 CFP demi-pension. Round-trip boat transfers are

provided but once you're there you're pretty well stuck in this rather remote area of Tahaa.

The final island possibility is *L'Hibiscus Hotel* (☎ 65-61-06, fax 65-65-65) on the north side of Haamene Bay. Like the Marina Iti, it's popular with visiting yachties. There are 14 moorings, and the open-air dining area and bar is a busy, active spot. The bar and restaurant extend to an outside area and have a decidedly nautical look. Leo, the all-singing, all-dancing patron, is also the patron of Foundation Hibiscus, dedicated to saving turtles accidentally snagged in local fishing nets.

There are five bungalows, two with shared shower and toilet at 5750 CFP for one or two and three with attached shower and toilet for 7850 CFP. Dinner and breakfast costs an extra 3500 CFP per person; adding lunch as well makes it 5500 CFP. Bookings can be made through BP 184, Haamene, Tahaa, and credit cards are accepted.

Off the Island

Vahine Island (☎ 65-67-38, fax 65-67-70) occupies a motu on the outer reef to the north of Tahaa. This small resort has just nine rooms, three of them over-water bungalows and is the only real beach-type resort on Raiatea or Tahaa. There's a white-sand beach and clear water and, on a much smaller scale, it manages to compete very effectively with the luxury resorts on other islands. The six beach bungalows are 35,000 CFP for one or two people, while the larger over-water bungalows are 45,000 CFP. You can quickly add another 10,000 CFP per person per day for meals but transfers from the airport in Raiatea are included. Bookings can be made through BP 119, Uturoa, Raiatea.

PLACES TO EAT

There aren't many dining possibilities for people making a circuit of the island. It comes down to the stores, the restaurants at the Marina Iti and L'Hibiscus Hotel or the restaurant at Chez Murielle, if it's open when you pass by. At the *Marina Iti* (☎ 65-61-01) the à la carte menu features meals from 1500 to 2600 CFP, the three-course dinner costs

3200 CFP and their speciality, seafood fondue, is also 3200 CFP. On the other side of Apu Bay the *Mareva Village* (☎ 65-61-61) has a restaurant atop the promontory with great views across the lagoon. Chez Murielle's *Restaurant Ti'Amahana* (☎ 65-67-29) is a good choice if it is open. At *L'Hibiscus Hotel* (☎ 65-61-06) casual lunchtime visitors pay 3000 CFP for a substantial three-course meal.

THINGS TO BUY
The Sophie Boutique (☎ 65-65-56) on Haamene Bay has paintings, pottery, *pareus* and local handicrafts.

GETTING THERE & AWAY
There is no airport on Tahaa although the airport on Raiatea is only a few minutes away across the lagoon and the more expensive hotels will pick up their guests from the airport or from the ferry quay at Uturoa on Raiatea.

See the Getting There & Away section in Raiatea for information on the navette service between Raiatea and Tahaa. This local ferry service shuttles back and forth between Uturoa and a variety of stops on Tahaa and costs 750 CFP one way.

Inter-island ships stop at Tapuamu on Tahaa between Raiatea and Bora Bora but not on every voyage. If your trip doesn't stop at Tahaa it's easy enough to debark at Uturoa and take the navette across. The high-speed *Ono-Ono* and the *Raromatai Ferry* are the two most regular ships coming through Tahaa.

GETTING AROUND
There is no public transport on Tahaa and if you're contemplating hitching remember that traffic is very light. The lack of transport is a major drawback; if you don't have your own wheels you're pretty much trapped wherever you're staying.

If you want to explore, the choice comes down to renting a car or mountain bike from the Hotel Marina Iti (☎ 65-61-01). The hotel has three Renault Clios (and remarkably all three of them are sometimes rented out) plus a number of slightly clunky but solid enough mountain bikes. The cars cost 10,000 CFP per day including fuel and 100 free km – it's 70 km around the island so that should just about do it. The bikes cost 1000/1500 CFP a half/full day. If you're reasonably energetic you should be able to circle the island in a day.

Bora Bora

Population: 5000
Area: 38 sq km
Passes: 1

If there's a postcard-perfect island anywhere in the Pacific it's Bora Bora; the soaring volcanic peaks, the lush green colours, the shimmering lagoon, the encircling chain of *motus*, it's all here. Pinned up on the wall this is the tropical-island dream, although close up the reality is not quite so dream-like: the lagoon is in danger of being fished out, the prices are sky high and there are some ugly reminders that not every tourist project comes to glowing fruition.

HISTORY

The huge volcano which created Bora Bora came into existence three to four million years ago. In the pre-European era the island was known as Vavau, perhaps indicating that it was colonised from the Tongan island of the same name. The name Bora Bora means something like 'first born', indicating that this may have been the most important island after 'sacred' Raiatea. The legendary Hiro, said to have been the first king of Raiatea, was also said to have sent his son Ohatatama to rule Bora Bora.

Land pressures, due to the shortage of level ground, helped to create a warlike population that not only squabbled with each other, but also campaigned against other islands in the Society group. Only Huahine managed to resist the warriors of Bora Bora at their most expansive.

Cook was the first European to sight Bora Bora, in 1769, on his first voyage. He paused briefly on the island in 1777 on his last voyage. An LMS missionary station was established on the island in 1820 and, to this day, Bora Bora remains chiefly Protestant. Bora Bora supported Pomare in his push for supreme power over Tahiti, but the French protectorate over Tahiti in 1842 was not extended to Bora Bora, which resisted

French influence until it was annexed in 1888. Bora Bora was the setting for the classic silent movie *Tabu*, shot on Motu Tapu in 1928-29 and one of the few movies to have been made in French Polynesia apart from the three *Bounty* sagas.

Although WWII never got as far south as French Polynesia, it had a major effect on Bora Bora. Soon after the Pearl Harbor bombing on 7 December 1941, the decision was made to establish a US supply base on the island. The supply force left South Carolina in late January 1942, less than two months after Pearl Harbor, with nine ships, 20,000 tons of equipment and nearly 5000 men on board. From early 1942 to mid-1946 Operation Bobcat transformed the island and at its peak up to 6000 men were stationed on Bora Bora. The island was used as a supply base for material en route to the Solomon Islands. The huge runway on Motu Mute is the clearest (and most useful) reminder of those frenetic days. It was completed in 1943 and after a period out of use after the war it was put back into operation in 1951. Until Faaa airport on Tahiti opened in 1961 this was the international airport for French Polynesia, and passengers were transferred from Bora Bora to Tahiti by seaplane. Eight massive seven-inch naval cannons were installed around the island during the war and all except one of them are still in place. The inter-island shipping dock at Farepiti was also an American WWII creation.

GEOGRAPHY

Like the other high islands, Bora Bora was created by volcanic action and it's easy to trace the rim of the ancient volcano. The sea has broken into the crater to form Povai Bay, and Motu Toopua and Motu Tuopua Iti are fragments of the old crater rim, not low-lying sand motus like those on the northern and western edge of the lagoon.

Bora Bora is spectacularly mountainous, rising to Mt Hue (619 metres), Mt Pahia (661

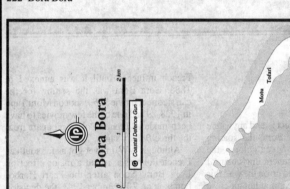

Bora Bora

© Coastal Defence Gun

0   1   2 km

Motu Tofari

Mantas Reef

Fitiiu Point
(Tuivahora Point)

Haamaene Bay

Vairau Bay

Puhia Point

Motu Ome

Motu Muri

Airport

Airport Wharf

Motu Mute

Outurau Point

Taihi Point

Taimoo Bay

249m

Hitiaa Bay

Mt Matahua
(314m)

FAANUI

Mt Hue
(619m)

Bora Bora

Vaitape Bay

Vairupe Bay

Motu Tane

Motu Piroaverahi

West Point Dive

Motu Paahi

Motu Moute

Motu Haapiti
Rahi

Faanui Bay

Tereia Point

Farepiti Point

Vaitape – Airport boat

Motu Tevairoa

Motu Ahuna

Paoeo Point

Teavanui Pass
Entrance

Teavanui Pass

Inter-Island boat

Tapu Dive

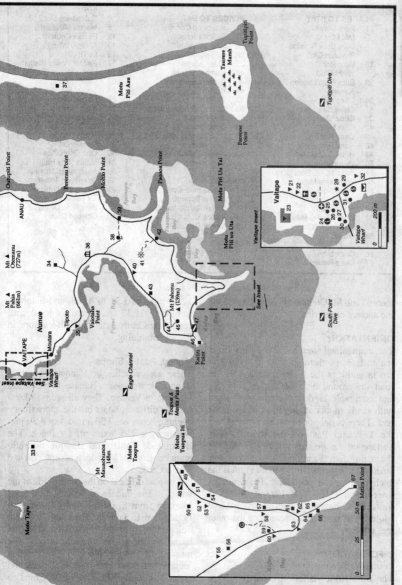

Vaitape Inset

Vaitape

Vaitape Wharf

See Inset

See Vaitape Inset

Tupitipiti Dive

South Point Dive

Eagle Channel

Tooputa & Marita Pass

Matira Point

PLACES TO STAY

1	Fare Corail
2	Mai Moana
4	Bora Bora Condos
9	Revatua Club
15	Bora Bora Yacht Club
33	Bora Bora Lagoon Resort
34	Chez Ato
37	Oasis du Lagon
39	Chez Stellio
42	Club Med
43	Chez Rosina
46	Hotel Bora Bora
49	Hotel Sofitel Marara
50	Vairupe Villas
51	Beach Club Bora Bora
54	Bora Bora Motel
56	Chez Reva
57	Village Pauline
59	Hotel Matira
61	Chez Maeva Masson
64	Pension Claire
65	Moana Beach Parkroyal
66	Chez Nono
67	Chez Robert & Tina

PLACES TO EAT

21	Snack au Cocotier
22	Snack Michel
23	L'Appetisserie
32	Le Vaitape
35	Blue Lagoon
40	Bamboo House Restaurant
44	Bloody Mary's
52	Le Tiare Restaurant
53	La Bounty Restaurant
55	Ben's Place
58	Snack Pauline
60	Matira Restaurant
62	Temanuata
63	Mahana View

MARAES

7	Marae Fare-Opu
10	Marae Taharuu
11	Marae Aehua-tai
14	Marae Marotetini
18	Marae Tianapa

OTHER

3	Hyatt Slums
5	Seaplane Ramp
6	Submarine Dock
8	Marine Museum
12	Faanui Church
13	Farepiti Wharf
16	Le Récif
17	Faanui Power Station
19	Lagoonarium
20	Club Med Slums
24	Tourist Office
25	Handicrafts Centre
26	Alain Gerbault Memorial
27	Air Tahiti Office
28	Police Station
29	Car Rental
30	Ono Ono Office
31	Mairie (City Hall)
36	Abandoned Museum
38	Telephone Tower
41	Belvédère Lookout
45	TV Tower
47	Bora Bora Diving
48	Calypso Diving

metres) and Mt Otemanu (727 metres) along the ancient crater rim.

ORIENTATION

The main island stretches about nine km in length from north to south, and about four km in width at the widest point. A 32-km road runs around the coast. A wide, sheltered and navigable lagoon encircles the island with sandy motus edging most of the outer reef. There is only one pass into the lagoon, the Teavanui Pass on the western side. Vaitape on the western side of the island is the main town. Faanui and Anau are other smaller settlements while Matira Point is the anchor for the tourist enclave. The wharf for inter-island ships is at Farepiti, between Vaitape and Faanui. The airport is on Motu Mute at the northern extremity of the outer reef edge.

INFORMATION

Tourist Office

The Bora Bora Visitors' Bureau (☎ 67-76-36) has an office on the wharf at Vaitape, open Monday to Friday from 7.30 am to 12.30 pm and 1.30 to 4 pm, and Saturday from 8 to 11.30 am. There's a local craft centre, the Centre Artisanal de Bora Bora, in the same building.

Money, Post & Shops

There are branches of Banque de Tahiti, Banque de Polynésie, Banque Socredo and Westpac in Vaitape. They all seem to keep slightly different hours but the approximate opening hours are 7.30 am to 4 or 4.30 pm, with one or 1½ hours off for lunch. The Banque de Tahiti and Banque Socredo branches have ATMs which accept Visa and MasterCard.

The post office is on the Matira side of the wharf in the middle of Vaitape. It's open Monday from 8 am to 3 pm, Tuesday to Friday 7 am to 3 pm and Saturday 7 to 9 am. Telephones are scattered all around the island and phonecards can be bought at a number of shops, hotels and restaurants. Vaitape has a number of supermarkets and general stores like Magasin Nunue, Chin Lee and Établissement Loussan. Visitors staying near Matira Point and preparing their own

TONY WHEELER

TONY WHEELER

TONY WHEELER

TONY WHEELER

Top:	Sunset looking across to Moorea from Tahiti, Society Islands
Middle:	Surfers at Punaauia, Tahiti, Society Islands
Bottom Left:	Lake Vaihiria, Tahiti, Society Islands
Bottom Right:	Papeete Market, Tahiti, Society Islands

JEAN-BERNARD CARILLET

TONY WHEELER

JEAN-BERNARD CARILLET

Top: Opunohu Bay, Moorea, Society Islands
Middle: Pareus, Maharepa, Moorea, Society Islands
Bottom: *Club Med II* in Cook's Bay, Moorea, Society Islands

food can now get supplies at the Tiare Market, just past the point road.

Medical Services
If you need medical assistance enquire at your hotel. There's a medical centre in Vaitape and several doctors in the town: Dr JP Martina (☎ 67-74-43), Dr Juen (☎ 67-70-62) and Dr Azad Roussanaly (☎ 67-77-95). There's a pharmacy in Vaitape open every day although only briefly on Sunday.

Yacht Facilities & Warnings
Visiting yachts are warned to take care while moored in Bora Bora. Always take all valuables and documents with you when leaving the boat. Don't leave things outside: lock clothes, diving equipment and other stealable items away. Lock away dinghies and outboards which have a tendency to sail away at night. At the Yacht Club de Bora Bora moorings cost 2500 CFP per day and showers are 300 CFP, but these charges are waived if you eat at the yacht club.

VAITAPE
Passengers arriving by air are transferred by catamaran from the Motu Mute airport to Vaitape, the island's main settlement. The town has shops, offices, banks, schools and eating places but no places to stay.

At Vaitape wharf, the centre of island activity, stands a monument to Alain Gerbault, the pioneering French yachtsman who made the first nonstop solo crossing of the Atlantic in 1923. Between 1923 and 1929 he circumnavigated the world in his yacht *Firecrest*, visiting Bora Bora in 1926. From 1934 to 1940 he lived on Bora Bora but he died on the island of Timor, just north of Australia, in 1941. His remains were returned to Bora Bora in 1947 and the monument was erected in 1951.

AROUND THE ISLAND
Bora Bora's 32-km coast road hugs the shoreline almost all the way around the island. Except for a short stretch at Fitiiu Point, the road is sealed all the way around. Only at Fitiiu Point and just east of Club Med

The Trashing of Bora Bora
Flattened coconut crabs may be an unhappy sight but even less happy is the trash that disfigures stretches of the coast. The shoreline around Anau village sports a particularly dense scum of soft drink cans and plastic packaging. It's a shame that an island frequently rated the most beautiful in the Pacific fades so badly when examined close up. The local government hardly seems to be setting an example with eyesores like the garbage dump at the end of Fitiiu Point, set up right beside that magical lagoon. Nor do some international businesses operating in the Pacific set a very good example. When Club Med built a new resort on the island they left its predecessor to rot, and Hyatt have had their name attached to a decaying slum for years. ■

at Paoaoa Point does the road rise slightly above sea level. Since it's so level, doing the circuit by bicycle is easy, although doing motor scooters and cars can also be rented. The tour that follows commences at Vaitape and goes anticlockwise around the island.

Along the route there are a number of ancient *maraes* and four WWII gun emplacements. The ground beside many stretches of the coast road is pockmarked with the holes of coconut crabs. The metal sleeves around coconut palms are there to prevent crabs and rats from climbing the trees. At night the crabs are often seen scuttling across the road and their crushed shells tell of unhappy encounters with passing vehicles.

'Museum' & the Overland Road (3 km)
Just south of Vaitape a collection of military junk on the mountain side of the road marks the abortive site of a museum. One of the coastal defence guns from Tereia Point was dragged round here along with a couple of old anchors and assorted other WWII debris.

Just beyond the 'museum', look for the small road opposite the soccer field and the gymnasium which leads to a shortcut across the island. A decorative miniature wooden powerhouse marks the turn-off. The road turns into a steep paved track following the power lines up the hill past the water chlorination plant. At the top, turn left towards the telephone tower or right towards a private house. Just before the house an overgrown footpath turns left down to the village of Anau, just beyond Club Med. Right across the island it's only 10 minutes up and 10 minutes down. Starting from the Anau side, the path commences behind the truck workshop – directly across the road from Chez Stellio.

The top of the hill offers fine views in both directions. To the west you can look out over Vaitape and the lagoon, while far to the east, across the lagoon and beyond the long sand-and-palm line of Motu Piti Aau rise the profiles of Tahaa and Raiatea.

TV-Tower Lookout & Bloody Mary's (5 km)

Beyond the shortcut across the island via the telephone tower, the coast road passes the Bamboo House Restaurant, some shops, the Chez Rosina *pension* and, just before Bloody Mary's, the turn-off to the TV tower. Bora Bora's TV-relay station makes a good lookout over the lagoon at this end of the island. Almost immediately beyond the turn-off is Bloody Mary's, the best known restaurant on the island. A large outrigger canoe marks the site and a long sign catalogues the varied list of 'celebrities' who have dined there.

Matira Beach & the Coastal Defence Guns (6 to 7.5 km)

The luxurious and expensive Hotel Bora Bora at Raititi Point marks the start of this pleasant stretch of beach. Along the road are several boutiques, the popular Ben's Place snack bar and a Chinese restaurant on the beach side of the road at the Hotel Matira.

From the eastern edge of the Hotel Matira property, a walking trail runs up the hill to a battery of coastal defence guns. It's only a 10-minute hike up to the emplacement.

Matira Point (7.5 km)

The Moana Beach Parkroyal Hotel sign points the way to the small road which runs out to Matira Point. Matira Beach extends out along the west side of the point where there are several popular pensions. The annual Hawaiki Nui canoe race in November finishes the final leg, from Raiatea to Bora Bora, right on the beach. On the east side is the classy Moana Beach Parkroyal Hotel with its collection of over-water bungalows branching out over the lagoon.

The point takes its name from the 490-tonne British ship *Mathilda*, wrecked on Moruroa Atoll in the Tuamotus in 1792. The crew managed to get back to Tahiti where they were robbed, but Pomare I offered his protection and punished the thieves. Three of the survivors decided to remain in Tahiti and one of them, a James O'Connor, married Pomare's cousin. The cannons from the ship were salvaged at Moruroa in 1968 and are now on display at the Museum of Tahiti & Its Isles in Tahiti.

Matira Point to Club Med (7.5 to 9 km)

Immediately past the Matira Point turn-off, the Galerie Rosine Temauri-Masson has lithographs by the French artist Jean Masson, who lived and worked here. His widow now takes guests in their home, Chez Maeva Masson, which displays some fine examples of his work.

From Matira Point, the coast road passes a busy little collection of shops, restaurants and hotels, including the popular Village Pauline. The road rounds the point and passes the new Club Med (nine km) on its own bay and with its own Belvédère lookout atop the ridge above the bay. The path to the lookout is accessed by Club Med's private tunnel under the road, but if you go just beyond the Hibiscus shop towards Anau you can see the steps where they emerge from under the road and make your way up to the path.

The road climbs the hill as it passes Club Med and then drops back down to the coast, past the Club Med tennis courts, just before the village of Anau.

Anau (10 to 12 km)

The village of Anau is a rather strung-out

affair along a rather dismal stretch of shoreline. The Chez Stellio campground (10.5 km) is at the start of the village, across the road from a truck workshop. The short, steep pathway to the telephone tower and down to the other side of the island starts from beside the workshop. Just past Chez Stellio is the bureau for the Lagoonarium on Motu Tofari. Trips out and back cost 6000 CFP.

Fitiiu Point Maraes & Guns (15 km)
Fitiiu Point is also known as Tuivahora Point. At this finger-like peninsula, extending out into the lagoon, the road climbs briefly away from the coast. There are several interesting sites along the point but none of them is signposted or maintained, and the authorities seem almost to have gone out of their way to make access difficult.

Just as the road starts to climb, a track peels off and runs down to **Marae Aehua-tai** at the water's edge. There are good views across the bay from the marae site with Mt Otemanu in the background.

Further along the point there's a natural 'marae' and two more **WWII coastal guns**. The walking trail along the ridge starts right behind the first house, at the sharp bend in the road, at the top of the ridge. If there's anybody around you should ask permission to take the trail, but if there's nobody around you can simply go. There is also an alternative route. Simply continue on the road back down to sea level and take the track which turns off to the right and runs along the north side of Fitiiu Point. The track terminates at, of all things, a scenic lagoonside garbage dump! Just before the dump a steep path runs uphill and emerges on the top of the ridge just before the gun site. From the site there are fine views out over the lagoon to the motus.

Backtrack along the ridgetop footpath to **Marae Taharuu**, a natural rock pinnacle locally revered as a marae.

Haamaire & Taimoo Bays (16 to 21 km)
The road beyond Fitiiu Point traverses the most lightly populated stretch of coast around the island as it rounds Haamaire and Taimoo bays. The middle-of-nowhere Revatua Club at 16.5 km on Taimoo Bay is a good place for a lunch or drink stop on a circuit of the island.

Marine Museum (21 km)
The small Musée de la Marine (☎ 67-75-24) has an interesting collection of ship models made by architect Bertrand Darasse. Most of them have a distinct connection with French Polynesia. They include a variety of Polynesian pirogues and other island boats. There are models of the ships of the early European explorers including Cook's *Endeavour* and Durmont d'Urville's *L'Astrolabe* of 1811. This ship, then known as *La Coquille*, visited Bora Bora with d'Urville in 1823. The pioneering French explorer went on to make important discoveries in the Antarctic before his death in the very first French railway disaster, on the Paris-St Germain line in 1842. Of course there's also a model of Bligh's *Bounty* and Alain Gerbault's *Firecrest*.

Entry to the museum is free but a donation is appreciated. Just before the museum there's a small gallery of carvings, *pareus* and other items.

Taihi Point & the Hyatt Slums (22 km)
Another lightly populated stretch of coastline continues to Taihi Point and the Hyatt slums. Just before the point, a steep and often very muddy track climbs up to an old WWII radar station atop Popotei Ridge and on to a lookout above the village of Faanui. See the Walking & Climbing section for more details.

A major hotel project was started at this site but the money ran out close to completion and the whole thing was left to rot. Just beyond the wreckage are the Bora Bora Condos, on stilts above the lagoonside road.

More Wartime Reminders (23 to 26 km)
After the Hyatt slums there are several more reminders of WWII activity. A seaplane ramp and an old ferry jetty pop up around 24 km. At the end of Tereia Point, a rectangular concrete water tank marks the position of

another coastal gun. There's no path: just clamber straight up the hill behind the tank for a couple of minutes. There's only one gun here, as the other was removed to the aborted museum between Vaitape and Matira Point. Finally, there's a small harbour, originally built for submarines but now more likely to shelter visiting yachts.

Marae Fare-Opu (26 km)

Right after the former submarine base and immediately before the Faanui village and speed-limit signs, the Marae Fare-Opu temple is squeezed between the roadside and water's edge. Two of the slabs are clearly marked with turtle petroglyphs. Turtles were sacred to the ancient Polynesians and very similar design can be seen incised into stones at numerous other sites in the Society Islands.

Faanui Bay & Village (27 km)

Faanui Bay was the site of the main US military base during WWII and there is still much evidence of the wartime operations. From the picturesque church at the head of the bay a road runs directly inland. Where the sealed road bends to the right, take the unsealed fork to the left. The road climbs up towards the ridge and you continue to bear left as you encounter more forks. The track often deteriorates into a muddy morass more suitable for mountain bikes than the single-speed Peugeots rented out on Bora Bora. Eventually the track comes to the ridgetop and drops down the other side to Vairau Bay just south of Fitiiu Point.

Marae Taianapa (28 km)

Set well back off the mountain side of the road in private property, this fairly large marae overlooks a small field from the edge of a coconut plantation. It was restored in 1963. You've overshot the access to the temple by about 100 metres if you get as far as the Hiano Beer and Coca Cola depot. Right behind this depot is the Faanui Power Station, a steam generator powered by burning coconut husks.

Marae Marotetini & Farepiti Wharf (29 km)

Inter-island ships dock at Farepiti wharf, at the western end of Faanui Bay. The wharf was built during WWII and is often crowded with visitors arriving or departing.

Walk 100 metres west along the shoreline to Marae Marotetini. This second royal marae on the island is a fine, 50-metre-long shore marae and was restored by Dr Yosihiko Sinoto in 1968. The Bora Bora Yacht Club is just beyond the marae so there are often yachts moored offshore from the point.

Club Med Wreckage & Coastal Guns (30 km)

Along the road from Farepiti Point to Pahua Point, one of the WWII defence guns can be seen silhouetted against the skyline. The road rounds the point and arrives at Bora Bora's second international tourist development slum. In this case it's Club Med which is the guilty party. When one typhoon too many devastated their Bora Bora resort it upped and moved to a better site on the south side of the island, leaving the old resort to rot in the tropical air.

Two coastal defence guns overlook the point. They're a short walk up from the road although, as usual, the route is not indicated in any way. A very circuitous and rather rotten 4WD track leads to the gun site from a turn-off just on the Faanui village side of Farepiti wharf. These guns were placed here to overlook the Teavanui Pass, the shipping route into the lagoon.

DIVING

There are two dive operators on Bora Bora. Both of them dive in the morning and afternoon inside and outside the lagoon. Both of them also operate through the hotels but will often give you a slightly better price if you deal with them directly.

Dive Centres

Calypso Club Claude Sibani's Calypso Club (☎ 67-77-85, fax 67-70-34) has its office opposite the Hotel Beach Club and Sofitel Marara, just beyond Matira Point.

There are three boats, four instructors and three assistants and it offers dives for beginners and PADI open-water courses. They specialise in diving with the manta rays and other rays, shark feeding and drift dives.

Bora Diving Bora Diving (☎ & fax 67-74-83) is on Matira Beach, right beside the Hotel Bora Bora. It has five fully qualified, bilingual instructors with PADI, NAUI and CMAS qualifications. With four boats and more than 60 aluminium dive tanks, it regularly operates morning dives inside and outside the lagoon for certified divers, afternoon dives for all levels from beginners upward and night dives for a minimum of four divers. Singles dives cost 5000 CFP, a package of five dives costs 22,500 CFP and night dives are 6000 CFP. CMAS courses take three days and cost 33,000 CFP. PADI divers who have completed their swimming pool and theory instruction before arriving in French Polynesia can complete the open-water part of the course with Bora Diving.

Dive Sites

There are popular dive sites both inside and outside the lagoon at Bora Bora and, despite the shortage of some species of fish depleted by local overfishing inside the lagoon and Asian longline overfishing outside, there is still a great deal to see. Since there is only one pass, Teavanui Pass, out of the lagoon, it can be a long trip to some of the outer reef dive sites and sites closer to the pass are particularly popular. Some of the interesting dive sites include:

In the Lagoon Manta rays are often seen in the shallow waters of the lagoon, and Calypso Club does a manta-ray dive every day in the waters between Anau village and Motu Piti Aau, an area nicknamed Manta Bay or Mantas Reef. Manta rays are harmless plankton feeders but their impressive size (up to six metres in length and weighing up to two tonnes!) and graceful appearance make them firm favourites with divers. Moray eels and turtles may also be seen on this dive. Manta Ray Channel or Manta Ray

Pit is another lagoon dive site where the magnificent manta rays are regularly encountered. It's just south of Motu Toopua Iti, the smaller island to the south of Motu Toopua. Eagle rays are also encountered in the lagoon, particularly in Eagle Ray Channel between Motu Toopua and the main island.

The Aquarium is a popular diving and snorkelling site between Motu Piti Aau and the inner edge of the outer reef near Tupitipiti Point, immediately offshore from Club Med and just south of their motu beach.

Outside the Reef The Tapu Dive is popular both for its proximity to the Teavanui Pass and for the large numbers of moray eels which are seen. The dive starts at about 25 metres and makes its way up almost to the surface as it approaches the outer edge of the reef, then turns and descends back to the dive boat's anchor line. Moray eels are encountered all along the way and have become so familiar with divers that they often come up and make close-up face-to-mask inspections. The Teavanui Pass Entrance, right at the mouth of the pass, is another popular outer reef dive.

White Valley Dive, also known as Muri Muri, is a curving sandbar off Paharire Point, off Motu Mute, the motu where the airport is located. Larger species, in particular barracuda, are often seen in large shoals here. Outside the reef, Tupitipiti Point, just the other side of the reef from the Aquarium lagoon dive, is an excellent dive site, but the long trip through the Teavanui Pass and round the outer reef discourages the dive operators from using the site. Ditto for the South Point Dive on the outer reef directly south of Matira Point.

WALKING & CLIMBING
Pahia & Otemanu

Bora Bora's three dramatic mountains – Hue (619 metres), Pahia (661 metres) and Otemanu (727 metres) – soar with dramatic abruptness from the lagoon. Pahia was the 'high, forbidding peak' of Rarahu's 'lost island' in *The Marriage of Loti*, and it's possible to climb it although you will probably need a guide to find the route. Ato, at Chez Ato (☎ 67-77-27) near Vaitape, will take you up and down for 3000 CFP per person. It takes about three hours up and two hours down.

It is said that Otemanu has never been climbed because of the unstable nature of the sheer rock walls which lead to the summit, although such a claim seems to be just the sort of thing to inspire somebody to do it! There's an ancient cave burial site high up on the eastern side of the mountain.

If you'd like to ascend the mountains without all that sweaty effort, contact Bora Bora Trekking (☎ 67-72-81) who will take you up and bring you back by helicopter. The trip costs 12,000 CFP and includes three hours on top with a guide who takes you on a walk past the three peaks.

Along the Tracks
The 4WD tracks following the old WWII routes can open up some interesting walking opportunities. Just after Taihi Point, before reaching the hotel wreckage, a track turns off up the ridge. This long 4WD track can be very muddy and cut up, and it's scarcely worth taking a bicycle up. A turn-off leads to a lookout above the Hyatt site and over to the airport but the main track continues, climbing gradually up along the ridge. It eventually ends but a walking track continues to a rocky outcrop which can be easily climbed, by the young or the fit in any case! From the top there are superb views in all directions, including straight down over Faanui with the village church right at your feet. To the west you can see Maupiti, to the north Tupai and to the south-east Tahaa and Raiatea.

SNORKELLING
Overfishing of the lagoon has taken the edge off snorkelling, although the end of Raititi Point, where the Hotel Bora Bora has established a reserve, can be pretty good. Off the southern end of Motu Piti Aau, near Tupiti-piti Point, there is good snorkelling in a shallow area just inside the outer reef edge.

CRUISES & CHARTERS
There are lots of boats based in Bora Bora for trips both inside and outside the lagoon.

The 12-metre catamaran *Taaroa III* (☎ 67-76-67 or 67-74-78) does half-day cruises as 'Bora Bora Fun' (4500 CFP) or operates charters around the lagoon and out to the motus. The 14-metre catamaran *Vehia* (☎ 60-44-05) also does half-day and full-day cruises and charters.

If you need a really big boat, there's the 20-metre *Epicurien II*, big enough for 12 on a day trip or six for trips lasting two or three days. Or there's the *Coup de Cœur*, a comfortable 12-metre sloop for two to four passengers. Either of these boats can be booked through Bora Bora hotels or on ☎ 3698 (Mahina Radio). *Maraamui II* (☎ 67-72-37) is a 19-metre ketch based at Club Med and offering four-day cruises around the Leewards for up to eight people.

Game-fishing trips are made outside the reef with a number of operators. Usually trips are for half a day or all day, the boats range from eight to 11 metres and trips to other islands in the Leeward group can easily be arranged. Contact the *Jessie L* (☎ 67-70-59 or 67-75-22), the *Lady C* (☎ 67-72-12), the *Mokalei* (☎ 60-44-60 or 67-74-93) or the *Te Aratai II* (☎ 67-71-96).

ORGANISED TOURS
Bora Bora has some very popular round-the-lagoon boat tours and round-the-island 4WD tours. Island visitors regularly recommend both.

Island Tours
The American military operations on Bora Bora during WWII left some interesting but often very rough and muddy tracks, ideal for rugged 4WD trips, and exploring these routes has recently become very popular. The cross-island route from Faanui to Vairoa Bay and the long climb up the ridgeline from Taihi Point are the two main routes.

Bora Bora Jeep Safari (☎ 67-70-34) offers a 9.15 am and 2.15 pm Land Rover trip taking in the island's vegetation, history and culture, including ancient maraes and the

---

Feeding Sharks & Stroking Rays

The *repas des requins*, meal time for the sharks, is a popular activity on a number of the islands of French Polynesia, and Bora Bora is no exception. Shark-feeding trips are organised by all and sundry. At certain established spots in the lagoon, the sharks have got used to having a free meal and while visitors snorkel around the action the island's shark experts hand feed them (generally the smaller black-tip variety). Ecologically this is probably not a very sensible activity, but the shark-feeding trips do stick to the smaller sharks found inside the reef. Petting the stingrays has become an equally popular part of a number of island tours. ∎

---

more recent evidence of WWII activity. Similar 4WD tours are offered by Tupuna Mountain Safari (☎ 67-75-06) which also makes morning and afternoon trips. The two-to-three-hour tours cost 4500 CFP.

Lagoon Tours

Trips around the Bora Bora lagoon are very popular and usually include a motu picnic, snorkelling over the reef or with the rays and, the *pièce de résistance*, a session of shark feeding. Visits to shore maraes, walking on the reef and outrigger canoe trips may also be part of the story. The tours typically go from 9 or 10 am to around 4 pm and cost 4500 to 5000 CFP for adults, including lunch.

Lagoon-trip operators include Teremoana Tours (☎ 67-71-38), Moana Adventure Tours (☎ 67-61-41) and Bora Bora Poe Iti Tours (☎ 67-78-21).

PLACES TO STAY

Although places to stay can be found all around the island and on the motus the majority are concentrated along the south side of the island, from the Hotel Bora Bora at Raititi Point (six km from Vaitape) to Club Med on Faaopore Bay (nine km from Vaitape). Despite its justifiably high-priced reputation, Bora Bora does have some budget-priced accommodation. Top-end and

mid-range places all accept credit cards unless otherwise noted, but most of the bottom-end places do not.

Vaitape to Raititi Point

There's nowhere to stay in Vaitape but there are a couple of budget places between Vaitape and Raititi Point.

Turn off the main island coast road just over two km from Vaitape and go inland about half a km to *Chez Ato* (☎ 67-77-27) in a lush green setting on the slope running up to the central mountains. The main accommodation block has five rooms arranged around a central open area. They share shower and toilet facilities and cost 4000 CFP for one or two people. There are also six bungalows, three at 50,000 CFP a month and three at 60,000 CFP a month. Chez Ato has got a bit rough around the edges in recent years but is still good value for Bora Bora and is in a quiet and attractive location.

There's a warm and friendly atmosphere at *Chez Rosina* (☎ 67-70-91), on the mountain side of the road, 4.5 km from Vaitape. Each of the house's four bedrooms has a double bed and attached bathroom and there's a communal living and dining room and an equipped kitchen. The nightly cost is 4500/6500 CFP including breakfast or 6500/10,000 CFP *demi-pension* (dinner and breakfast). Bookings can be made through BP 51, Vaitape, Bora Bora. Credit cards are not accepted.

Around Matira Point

The three km from the Hotel Bora Bora to Club Med is packed with various places to stay from the island's most popular backpackers' centre to several of the island's best known luxury hotels. Beautiful Matira Beach, sweeping round from Raititi Point out to Matira Point, is a prime reason for all this activity. The accommodation possibilities in this area are dealt with by price bracket moving along the road from west to east.

Bottom End Matira Point, the eastern end of the best sweep of beach on the main island, has three budget-priced pensions. The very top-end Moana Beach Parkroyal Hotel occupies the other side of the point, where the beach is not so good.

Just before the Matira Point turn-off is *Chez Reva*, with two rooms at 5000/6000 CFP for singles/doubles. First along the Matira Point road is the very rudimentary *Pension Claire* (☎ 67-60-00), which is as bare bones as it gets in French Polynesia, although, of course, the prices are not like that!

Right next door is *Chez Nono* (☎ 67-71-38, fax 67-74-27), a two-storey house with six rooms at 5000/6000 CFP with shared bathroom facilities and a large kitchen and lounge area downstairs. There are two rooms upstairs with a double bed and two with a single bed, while downstairs the two rooms have a single and a double bed. The rooms are quite comfortable, some with verandahs, although the walls are paper thin. There are also two small bungalows with a double bed at 8000 CFP for one or two people and two larger family bungalows with a single and a double bed at 10,000 CFP. The bungalows have attached bathrooms with hot water. Additional people cost 2000 CFP and children under 12 can stay for 1000 CFP.

Chez Nono is right on the beach and has bicycles for rent. Breakfast is 800 CFP, credit cards are accepted and bookings can be made by writing to BP 282, Vaitape, Bora Bora.

Right down at the end of the point, *Chez Robert & Tina* (☎ 67-72-92) has two houses. The first house has three doubles while the second house has five doubles. There are communal kitchen facilities, shared bathrooms and a lounge area in each house. The nightly cost is 4000/6000 CFP for one/two people, children under 12 are half price and credit cards are accepted.

Village Pauline (☎ 67-72-16, fax 67-78-14) is down near Matira Point and seems to strengthen its position as the island's budget favourite a little more each year. It's efficient, well kept and fairly extensive. The site sprawls across both sides of the road. Accommodation possibilities start with camping on the mountain side of the road where you can pitch your tent on the lawn

for 1600 CFP per person. In the village's neat dorms the nightly cost is 2000 CFP, if you stay at least two nights. A one-night stay will cost 3000 CFP.

Then there are private rooms, back towards the mountain, with nightly costs for one or two people of 6000 CFP or 7000 CFP if it's for just one night. Eight simple beach cabins, also for one or two people, are 5000 CFP or 6000 CFP for a one-night stand. The six private bungalows are more luxurious and have attached bathrooms. The cost is 9000 CFP for one or two, or 12,000 CFP if it's just for one night. Finally, there are larger family bungalows which start at 15,000 CFP for up to three people.

There are good bathroom and shower facilities for the campers and other visitors. The village's own small and economical restaurant, Snack Pauline, is in the middle of the mountainside part of the site. A le truck service meets arriving ferries (500 CFP) and the catamaran from the airport (300 CFP) to transfer visitors to Village Pauline. Bookings can be made by writing to BP 215, Vaitape, Bora Bora. Credit cards are accepted.

Middle Right on Matira Beach, shortly before the Matira Point turn-off, the *Hotel Matira* (☎ 67-78-58 or 67-70-51, fax 67-77-02) has a restaurant on the lagoon side of the road and a collection of 27 simple, thatched-roof bungalows. The bungalows all have attached bathrooms and outside terraces, and some of them also have kitchenettes. The basic 'garden' and 'mountain' bungalows are 12,000 CFP for one or two people. Garden bungalows with kitchenette are 15,200 CFP, the five beach bungalows with kitchenette are 17,000 CFP and the four deluxe beach bungalows, which do not have kitchen facilities, are 26,000 CFP. All these prices are subject to the 8% tax. Breakfast is available for 950 CFP, and demi-pension costs 3500 CFP per person. There's an extra 1000 CFP charge for airport transfers. Bookings can be made by writing to BP 31, Vaitape, Bora Bora.

Right on the water's edge, just beyond the Matira Point turn-off, is *Chez Maeva Masson*

(☎ 67-72-04). This is the very neat home of Rosine Temauri-Masson, the widow of the artist Jean Masson. Staying here is very definitely a stay-in-a-home situation so being able to fit in is imperative. The house is full of Masson's exuberant paintings and the lagoonside setting is a delight. There are two rooms downstairs at 5000/6000 CFP and two upstairs at 4500/5500 CFP. In addition there's an upstairs dorm-style room with four single beds and a bungalow at 6000/7000 CFP. There's an additional charge of 1000 CFP per person for a one-night stay, credit cards are accepted and bookings can be made at BP 33, Vaitape, Bora Bora.

On the mountain side of the road, the new *Vairupe Villas* (☎ 67-62-66, fax 67-62-79) is run by the same people as Village Pauline. The 10 traditional Polynesian-style *fares* have a bedroom, separate living room with TV, kitchen area and outside terrace. The nightly cost is 23,000 CFP.

The *Bora Bora Motel* (☎ 67-78-21, fax 67-77-57) is a smaller, beachfront place with two types of rooms. A large fare is divided into four studios, each with a double bedroom, a bathroom with hot water, a kitchen, a living-and-dining area and an outside terrace. These studios cost 13,000 CFP for one or two people. In addition there are three separate apartments with a sofa bed in the living room. These cost 17,000 CFP for one or two people. There's a good stretch of beach by the site. Bookings can be made through BP 180, Vaitape, Bora Bora. Credit cards are accepted.

The *Beach Club Bora Bora* (☎ 67-71-16, fax 41-09-28) is after the Bora Bora Motel and before the expensive Hotel Sofitel Marara. There are 36 fairly simple rooms at 12,000 and 13,000 CFP plus the 8% tax. Beware of mosquitoes; the rooms are not in the best condition and there's plenty of opportunity for insects to pay a visit. The location is right by the beach and there is a bar and restaurant. Bookings can be made at BP 252, Nunue, Bora Bora.

Top End On Raititi Point, about seven km from Vaitape, *Hotel Bora Bora* (☎ 67-44-60,

fax 60-44-66) has the best location on the island, with terrific views and a good beach. It is now part of the AmanResorts group of hotels, an Indonesian-owned series of super-luxury small hotels which includes the acclaimed Amanpuri in Thailand and Amandari in Bali. It's typical of the AmanResort approach that when it took over the hotel it actually *reduced* the number of rooms.

Built right out on the point, the hotel has a restaurant overlooking the lagoon and a bar and restaurant down towards the beach. The food is excellent, and this is one of the best places to eat on the island. There are 55 bungalows including 15 over the water and eight secluded luxury bungalows with their own swimming pools! And yet there's not a swimming pool for the entire resort itself. Commendably, the rooms don't have the things which lesser places might think necessary, like TV sets and air-conditioning.

Prices start at 39,500 CFP for the standard garden bungalows but even these are very pleasantly designed and equipped with separate bedroom and living room areas and an outside sitting area. Superior bungalows are 49,500 CFP, deluxe and over-water bungalows cost 65,000 CFP, premium over-water bungalows cost 70,000 CFP, the private villas cost 60,000 CFP, or 65,000 and 70,000 CFP with private pool. The 8% government tax goes on top of those figures.

Because the hotel owners have gone to some efforts to protect the fish around the point, this is one of the island's better snorkelling sites. The hotel has a boutique and tour desk, and hires cars, scooters and bicycles. Bookings can be made at BP 1, Nunue, Bora Bora.

On the east side of Matira Point the *Moana Beach Parkroyal* (☎ 60-49-00, fax 60-49-99) is relatively small, with just 41 rooms, but very classy. Costs are 43,300 CFP for the 10 beach bungalows and 59,700 CFP for the 31 over-water bungalows. The latter come complete with the glass coffee tables for lagoon viewing which have become a French Polynesian trademark. There is an 8% government tax to be added to those prices, but for their 35,000 to 50,000 CFP a night guests do get picked up from the airport by private speedboat. There is a bar, two restaurants, no swimming pool and regular dance performances. Bookings can be made through BP 156, Vaitape, Bora Bora.

The *Hotel Sofitel Marara* (☎ 67-70-46, fax 67-74-03) is at the end of Taahina Bay, before the road rounds the next point to Club Med. There are 64 rooms: 32 garden bungalows at 27,000 CFP, 11 beach bungalows at 35,000 CFP and 21 over-water bungalows at 50,000 CFP, all plus 8% tax. There's a beachfront restaurant and bar, a swimming pool, a tennis court and the usual sporting and shopping facilities.

Around the next point from the Sofitel is the 'new' *Club Med Coral Garden* (☎ 42-96-99, 42-16-83) on Faaopore Bay, just before Paoaoa Point. It's big with 150 rooms: 72 garden rooms and 78 beach rooms. The blocks, painted in a variety of pastel shades, are straightforward two-storey affairs but the rooms are simply but very tastefully designed and furnished. There's a swimming pool, two tennis courts, a wide range of other sporting facilities and a private stretch of beach on Motu Piti Aau. The Club Med outrigger canoe shuttles back and forth to the motu beach all day.

It goes without saying that you have to be a Club Med sort of person to enjoy Club Med. If you don't like being social at meal times (the *gentils organisateurs* do not like antisocial types who do not sit where they are told) then you definitely won't enjoy Club Med. And if you don't want to throw yourself into windsurfing, tennis, aerobics, catamaran sailing and a dozen other activities then you certainly won't get your money's worth. Apart from activities like scuba diving, all sporting facilities are included at no extra cost.

Club Med stays are all inclusive apart from pre-dinner and after-dinner drinks, and activities like scuba diving. Meals are all you can eat, usually served buffet-style, and at lunch and dinner the wine and beer are also included. The food is middle of the road – no culinary thrills but generally quite professionally prepared. This particular Club Med usually has a sizeable percentage of Japanese visitors and their enthusiasm when it comes to the evening entertainment almost makes a stay worthwhile no matter what your attitude to Club Med. See the Entertainment section for more details.

Club Med visitors will generally book through a travel agent. Typical per-person daily costs are in the US$220 to US$260 range, including all meals. There's usually a three-day minimum stay requirement. If, however, you've always wanted to try Club Med and you just happen to be in Bora Bora, give them a call. If there's space, casual visitors are taken at 28,600 CFP for one person or 44,000 CFP for two in the garden rooms, 32,500 CFP for one and 50,000 CFP for two in the beachfront rooms. This cost includes three meals, and children under 12 are charged half price. Club Med has an office in the Vaima Centre in Papeete, Tahiti, and bookings can be made by writing to BP 575, Papeete, Tahiti.

The Rest of the Island

Continue right around the island beyond Club Med back to Vaitape and there are four more varied accommodation possibilities.

Not far beyond Club Med is *Chez Stellio* (☎ 67-71-32), with camping space at 1000 CFP, dorm beds at 1500 CFP and rooms at 4500 CFP, all sharing the communal kitchen area. Although the facilities are basic, they're also clean and well kept. It's right on the water's edge but there is no beach along this stretch of coast. Free transport is offered to and from Chez Stellio and there's a very pleasant family atmosphere at this relatively remote location.

The most isolated outpost on the island, the pink and white *Revatua Club* (☎ 67-71-67, fax 67-76-59) is almost exactly opposite Vaitape. Coming from the island's main population centre it's 16 km to the hotel in either direction! The hotel usually picks up its guests directly from the airport. The vaguely colonial-looking establishment has a pleasant bar and restaurant by the lagoon with a long quay reaching out over the water to a saltwater swimming pool.

The 16 fan-cooled rooms are across the road on the mountain side and have attached bathrooms, fairly simple furnishings and private terraces. They cost 8900/10,400 CFP for singles/doubles, plus the inevitable 8% tax. There's also one villa on the lagoon side which has a separate lounge-and-kitchen area and costs 15,600 CFP. Breakfast costs 1000 or 1500 CFP or you can add breakfast and dinner for 3800 CFP (budget) or 4900 CFP (gourmet). There's a small shop, bicycles are available free and there's even a billiard table. Bookings can be made through BP 159, Vaitape, Bora Bora.

The *Bora Bora Condos* (☎ 67-71-33) are 10 km from Vaitape, at the north end of the island beside the decaying remains of the aborted Hyatt Hotel. This is really long-term accommodation because there is nowhere to eat here. The hillside bungalows on stilts cost 12,000 CFP a day or 140,000 CFP a month, the over-water ones are 15,000 CFP a day or 185,000 CFP a month. The bungalows are like a small house and have two bedrooms, a living room, dining room, kitchen and outside terrace. Bookings can be made through BP 98, Vaitape, Bora Bora, but credit cards are not accepted.

Only three km from Vaitape, almost completing the island circuit, the *Bora Bora Yacht Club* (☎ 67-70-69 or 67-71-50) has two garden bungalows with room for up to four people at 9000 CFP and three over-water bungalows for 10,000 CFP. The yacht club's waterfront restaurant and bar is justifiably popular and is a good place for a meal. Bookings can be made by writing to BP 17, Vaitape, Bora Bora.

Of course the yacht club also has moorings, laundry and washing facilities for visiting yachties. It has also had sea turtles penned up near its wharf which is not commendable. See Yacht Facilities & Warnings in the introductory Information section for more details.

On the Motus

Fare Corail (☎ 67-74-50) is on Motu Tane,

very close to the airport motu at the northern end of the lagoon. There's a fine beach and good swimming around the motu. The house was built by French polar explorer Paul-Émile Victor and, since his death in 1995, has been run by his widow. There is a double bedroom, living-and-dining room, equipped kitchen and bathroom with hot water. The cost for one or two people is 20,000 CFP, there is a minimum three-night stay and round-trip transfers cost 2000 CFP. Bookings can be made through BP 77, Vaitape, Bora Bora, and credit card are not accepted.

Also at this end of the lagoon is the *Mai Moana* (☎ 67-70-69 or 67-71-50) on Motu Haapiti Rahi. There are three fares, each with a double bedroom and bathroom with hot water. Costs are 32,000 CFP per day for up to three people including breakfast. Other meals are available: lunch costs 1200 CFP, dinner 3200 CFP. Bookings can be made through BP 164, Vaitape, Bora Bora and credit cards are accepted.

The *Oasis du Lagon* (☎ 67-73-38) is on Motu Piti Aau on the east side of the lagoon. There are five fares, all with bathroom, kitchen facilities and living area but with sleeping accommodation ranging from one bedroom in the smallest fare to three bedrooms and a mezzanine area in the largest 'villa' fare. Costs start at 15,000 CFP for two in the smallest fare, 20,000 CFP for four in the larger two-room fares and 30,000 to 35,000 CFP in the larger ones that can accommodate six to 10 people. Its pleasantly sited in a lagoonside coconut plantation, and transfers can be arranged directly from the airport for 2000 CFP round trip (minimum three people) or from the Sofitel Marara on the main island. Bookings can be made through BP 249, Vaitape, Bora Bora, but credit cards are not accepted.

The island's newest super-luxury resort has had a chequered history. The *Bora Bora Lagoon Resort* (☎ 60-40-00, fax 60-40-01) is on Motu Toopua, looking across the lagoon to Vaitape and across the Teavanui Pass, the only real entry into the lagoon. The resort has 80 rooms, including 30 beachfront units at 52,000 CFP and 30 over-water units at 69,000 CFP. For this cost you get almost every luxury in the book and the resort has a swimming pool, tennis courts, gymnasium, boutiques, two restaurants and three bars. Three meals will add another 12,000 CFP per person per day. Between the resort and the main island a shuttle boat operates every half hour to an hour (8.30 am to 11.30 pm from the resort, 8.35 am to 11.45 pm from the base just north of the centre of Vaitape).

PLACES TO EAT

It may be a popular tourist spot but Bora Bora still goes to bed early – most restaurants firmly shut the door at 9 pm. A number of the pricier restaurants, including Bloody Mary's, the Bamboo House and L'Espadon at the Revatua Club, offer a free transfer service, collecting you from and returning you to your hotel.

Vaitape

There are no real restaurant possibilities in Vaitape but there are a number of good places for breakfast, a snack or a cheap meal. *L'Appetisserie* (☎ 67-78-88) is a very pleasant little open-air snack bar and pâtisserie in the Commercial Centre near the quay. It's not the cheapest place for breakfast or a snack but it's certainly the most sophisticated. You can start the day with a 100 CFP croissant or a 120 CFP pain aux raisins, and at lunchtime quiche, a pizza slice or a croque-monsieur cost 350 CFP or the plat du jour is 1100 CFP. The ice creams are great at any time of the day for 120 to 200 CFP. L'Appetisserie is open every day.

Right across from the post office *Le Vaitape* (☎ 67-75-43) is a cheap café with some baked goods, light snacks and cold beer. On the northern side of town *Snack Michel* (☎ 67-71-43) is open for breakfast and lunch, Monday to Friday, and for dinner on Sunday. It may even be open on Saturday. It's a cheerful and neat little open-air place with tables and benches outside and a variety of meals and daily specials at 700 to 900 CFP, or sandwiches and casse croûtes from 100 CFP. At this end of town *Snack au Cocotier* (☎ 67-74-18) is also good value.

Vaitape to the Hotel Bora Bora

There are several interesting places to eat along the six km from Vaitape to the start of Matira Beach at Raititi Point. The *Blue Lagoon* (☎ 67-63-11) is right on the water just over a km from Vaitape with a nice verandah out front. It's closed on Thursday.

The *Bamboo House Restaurant* (☎ 67-76-24) is about 3.5 km from Vaitape towards Matira Point. This pleasant and well-run restaurant turns out a variety of lunchtime pastas at 1000 to 1600 CFP, excellent burgers and chips at 700 to 900 CFP or a Caesar salad for 900 CFP. At dinner time starters are 950 to 1500 CFP, the pasta dishes at 1350 to 1900 CFP include a superior prawn fettuccine, fish dishes are 2300 to 2600 CFP and include mahi mahi provençale for 2300 CFP or freshwater shrimps in green pepper with ravioli for 2500 CFP, meat courses are 2300 to 2800 CFP and desserts are 600 to 800 CFP. There's also a good winelist.

Bloody Mary's (☎ 67-72-86), five km from Vaitape or a km before the Hotel Bora Bora, is the island's best known restaurant and one of the best known in the Pacific. It's very pricey and inordinately proud of the list of celebrities who have dined there. The décor is planned to look island-like, with a sandy floor, coconut-tree-stump chairs and a thatched roof.

Bloody Mary's is open for lunch from Monday to Saturday and dinner every night. Pizzas are the lunchtime speciality at 750 CFP for a plain one, 850 CFP with up to three toppings, a green salad is 500 CFP and a pitcher of Hinano beer is 750 CFP. At dinner you choose your seafood and the chef grills it for you; one variety of fish costs 2500 CFP, two varieties 2600 CFP, fish plus lobster takes the cost to 3500 CFP, lobster alone is 4000 CFP, chicken or steak is 2300 CFP or a vegetarian dish is 1600 CFP. Desserts are 350 to 500 CFP. A glass of draught beer is 300 CFP, a bottle of wine adds 2500 to 5000 CFP and all up dinner for two could easily cost 12,000 to 15,000 CFP.

Matira Point

There are no places to eat right on Matira

Point, apart from at the places to stay, but there's a good selection on both sides of the point. In addition, the opening of the Tiare Market, beside Le Tiare Restaurant, means that if you're preparing your own food at Village Pauline or one of the pensions you no longer need to trek into Vaitape to get supplies.

Cheap Eats Several local snack bars dot this stretch of coast. They tend to be open some days, closed others – it's a matter of luck. The one immediately beyond the Matira Restaurant is particularly good.

Along the beach road from the Hotel Bora Bora to Matira Point is *Ben's Place*, a popular little open-air café with a straightforward menu. It's slightly pricey but this is a pleasant place to eat. Pizza costs from 1000 CFP, spaghetti is 1250 CFP, lasagne is 1900 CFP, Mexican dishes like fajitas are 1400 CFP and dishes like tuna, mahi mahi or steak with salad and chips are 1900 CFP. It's open for lunch and a reasonably early dinner, Friday to Wednesday, and closed Thursday.

Snack Pauline, in the inland part of the popular Village Pauline, is a handy little snack bar in a nice garden setting with straightforward food like grilled tuna for 950 CFP, chicken for 800 CFP or steak for 1100 CFP, all with chips.

Restaurants The Hotel Bora Bora and the Sofitel Marara bracket Matira Point, while the Moana Beach Parkroyal is right on the point. All three offer high-quality dining possibilities.

The Hotel Bora Bora's *Matira Terrace* (☎ 60-44-60) in particular offers excellent food in a romantic open-air setting looking out over the point. Breakfast on the terrace costs 1800 to 2200 CFP. At dinnertime soups are 600 to 700 CFP, starters are 1000 to 1750 CFP, meat main courses are 2450 to 3550 CFP, fish main courses 2300 to 3650 CFP, desserts 800 to 850 CFP. You could try grilled wahoo medallions with ginger and grapefruit or sautéed curried shrimps with coconut milk. Mahi mahi, tuna steaks and parrotfish also feature on the menu. There's

also a set meal at 5000 CFP. Wines start from around 1600 to 1800 CFP, but if you want to spend 49,500 CFP they do have Château Latour 1985. Champagne is 7500 to 28,000 CFP a bottle.

Less expensive restaurants dot the 2.5 km from the Hotel Bora Bora to the Sofitel Marara, starting with the Chinese *Matira Restaurant* (☎ 67-70-51), right on the beach at the Hotel Matira and just before the Matira Point turn-off. The standard Chinese dishes are mainly in the 1100-to-1400 CFP bracket, the food is quite good and the setting, right on the beach overlooking the water, is very attractive.

Two more very pleasant places stand either side of the Matira Point turn-off. Just before the turn-off is *Mahana View* (☎ 67-76-23), perched right on the beach with just a handful of tables. Starters range from 600 CFP (green salad) to 1500 CFP (shrimps), main courses are 900 to 1500 CFP (including chicken curry or grilled chicken breast at the bottom of that range, or pepper steak or the fish of the day at the top). Pasta dishes and Chinese dishes at around 900 CFP are also on offer and wine by the glass costs 350 CFP. Immediately beyond the turn-off is *Temanuata* (☎ 67-75-61), with a garden setting and starters, including a very good salade niçoise, at 600 to 1200 CFP and main courses at 1300 to 1500 CFP. Chinese dishes are also featured. They will only accept cash – credit cards are not accepted.

Continue past Village Pauline to *La Bounty Restaurant* (☎ 67-70-43), a popular place with starters at 750 to 900 CFP, fish dishes at 1300 to 1500 CFP, meat dishes at 1100 to 1500 CFP, pizza at 1000 to 1400 CFP and pasta dishes at 850 to 1200 CFP. It's open for lunch and from 6.30 to 9.30 pm for dinner. Almost next door, *Le Tiare Restaurant* (☎ 67-61-39) has starters at 850 to 1050 CFP, fish main courses at 1000 to 1650 CFP, meat main courses at 1100 to 1700 CFP and desserts at 450 to 750 CFP.

Matira Point to Vaitape
From Matira Point right round to Vaitape, moving in an anticlockwise direction, there

are only a couple of places to eat, apart from local shops and snack bars. Either makes a good dinner excursion, if you have transport, or a good place for a lunch stop during a circuit of the island.

At the Revatua Club (☎ 67-71-67), the lunchtime *Snack Le Totara* and evening *L'Espadon Restaurant* both do excellent food. At lunch you could opt for an excellent hamburger for 450 CFP, omelettes for 400 to 600 CFP, a pizza for 500 CFP, a Caesar salad for 980 CFP, a salade niçoise for 1200 CFP or the day's special for 1200 CFP. The Revatua Club is 16 km from Vaitape in either direction, and nine km from Matira Point. At night the restaurant offers starters from 550 CFP (green salad) to 2800 CFP (lobster), fish main courses at 1800 to 2400 CFP, meat main courses at 1400 to 2600 CFP and desserts at 300 to 550 CFP. You'll be collected and returned to your hotel if you phone ahead and book.

The alternative is the *Bora Bora Yacht Club* (☎ 67-70-69 or 67-71-50) with a very nice setting by the water, a cool and breezy bar and an open-air eating area. Starters include a 750 CFP green salad or a 950 CFP Caesar salad. Main dishes are 2100 to 3100 CFP, lobster is 4050 CFP and there are dishes like tuna steak with mustard sauce, mahi mahi with basil, prawns in coconut milk curry or spaghetti bolognaise, all at 2300 CFP. Burgers are 1100 to 1200 CFP, a club sandwich is 1000 CFP, chips are 400 CFP – it's certainly not cheap but the setting is great and the seafood is particularly good.

ENTERTAINMENT
Cold Beers
The fancy hotels – the *Hotel Bora Bora*, the *Moana Beach Parkroyal* and the *Sofitel Marara* – will all provide a good cold beer in an attractive lagoonside setting. Several of the roadside snack bars cater to a local clientele and come sunset will often have someone strumming on a guitar as another round of cans or bottles are passed out. The one right at the dock at Farepiti is a good example, as is the one by the road between the Marae Fare-Opu and the Faanui Church.

Probably the most evocatively Pacific place on the island would be the waterside bar of the *Bora Bora Yacht Club*, just past the Farepiti dock towards Vaitape. Sitting and watching the yachts at anchor and the motus on the lagoon edge is just perfect. On the opposite side of the island, *Laurents Bar* at the Revatua Club also has a great waterside setting. Or try the *Blue Lagoon*, just outside Vaitape towards Matira Point. Finally, *Bloody Mary's* is the all-hours expats' hangout.

Tahitian Dancing & Other Entertainment
There are regular dance performances at the *Sofitel Marara*, where the performance area has a nice beachfront location and the dancers are excellent. The *Moana Beach Parkroyal* has performances twice a week, four times in the high season. At both locales you only need buy a drink to enjoy the show.

At *Club Med* buying 1800 CFP worth of drink beads will get you in for the show after 9 pm, or for 4500 CFP (children 3000 CFP) you can have dinner; another 500 CFP makes it dinner and show. In typical Club Med style, the show is part Club Med staff and part Club Med guests. The large Japanese contingent

in Bora Bora can make for an over-the-top evening – they really let their hair down.

Le Récif, north of Vaitape towards Faanui, is the only real local disco: noisy, dark and lots of drinking until all hours. Everybody lets loose at the annual party after the finish of the three-day Hawaiki Nui canoe race in November. There's dancing, drinking and music until the early hours for 1000 CFP entry or 3000 CFP if you include dinner. Bora Bora also has one of the best Bastille Day celebrations in French Polynesia on 14 July.

THINGS TO BUY

Vaitape has T-shirts and pareus and other souvenirs in shops like Boutique Pakalola (☎ 67-71-82) and some real local crafts in the Centre Artisanal de Bora Bora in the same building as the tourist office. Other craft stores are uniformly dotted around the island. Making the circuit in an anticlockwise direction there's the Boutique Gauguin (☎ 67-76-67) and then the Honeymoon Boutique (☎ 67-78-19) by the Bamboo House Restaurant. The Chez Alain & Linda Galerie d'Art (☎ 67-70-32) is on the lagoon side, close to the turn-off to the cross-island road via the telephone tower. They have clothes and original art.

Moana Arts (☎ 67-70-33), on the lagoon side just before the Hotel Bora Bora at Raititi Point, has clothing and cards, while on the mountain side the Paofai Shop sells post cards, books and drinks. The Hotel Bora Bora has its own shop with up-market resort clothes and swimwear and some interesting paintings and other crafts.

Beyond Raititi Point is Martine Creations (☎ 67-70-69), a small shop which specialises in hand-dyed T-shirts. Immediately beyond the Matira Point turn-off is Galeries Rosine Temauri-Masson (☎ 67-72-04) with a variety of crafts plus prints of works by the late Jean Masson. More mundane shopping can be accomplished at the Tiare Market (☎ 67-61-38), a small supplies store which can save the trip into Vaitape. There's quite a selection of shops along this stretch including La Boutique (☎ 67-70-43) by La Bounty

restaurant and Matira Pearl & Fashions (☎ 67-79-14) with Tahitian black pearls. Just past Club Med is Boutique Hibiscus (☎ 67-72-43) with gifts, souvenirs and bicycles to rent.

GETTING THERE & AWAY

Bora Bora is 270 km north-west of Tahiti, only 15 km north-west of Tahaa.

Air

Air Tahiti (☎ 67-70-35 or 67-70-85) connects Bora Bora four to six times daily with Papeete, sometimes direct in about 45 minutes, other times via Moorea, Huahine, Raiatea or some combination of those islands. There are onward connections to Maupiti. One-way adult fares to or from Bora Bora are Huahine 6500 CFP, Maupiti 5300 CFP, Moorea 16,000 CFP, Papeete 12,400 CFP and Raiatea 5100 CFP. Flying into Bora Bora, the left side of the aircraft offers the best views.

Bora Bora offers the only connections to the Tuamotus apart from via Papeete, with flights to Rangiroa (one hour and 20 minutes, 20,700 CFP) with an onward connection to Manihi. Flights operate to Rangiroa three times a week but in the reverse direction only once a week.

The Air Tahiti office is on the wharf at Vaitape and is open Monday to Friday from 7.30 to 11.30 am and 1.30 to 4.30 pm, and Saturday from 8 to 11 am.

Heli-Inter Polynésie (☎ & fax 67-62-59) does helicopter tours over the island for 6000 to 24,000 CFP, or will get you to Tupai in nine minutes, Maupiti in 18 minutes or Huahine in 24 minutes.

Sea

Inter-island boats dock at the Farepiti wharf, three km from Vaitape.

The high speed *Ono-Ono* (☎ 67-78-00 on Bora Bora, 45-35-35 on Tahiti) zips out to Bora Bora three times a week from Tahiti, taking six to seven hours for the trip with stops en route at Huahine, Raiatea and, on some days, Tahaa. The fares to Bora Bora are 5800 CFP from Tahiti, 2800 CFP from

Huahine, 1600 CFP from Raiatea and 1200 CFP from Tahaa.

The more traditional *Raromatai Ferry* (☎ 43-19-88 on Tahiti) takes 17 hours on its overnight journey from Tahiti two or three times week. It takes 226 seated passengers and 75 in cabins. The one-way fare from Tahiti is 3800 CFP with a seat, 6000 CFP in a cabin for four or 17,000 CFP in a cabin for two. Inter-island fares are 1000 CFP and all meals are extra. The *Taporo IV* runs to a similar schedule. See the Yacht Facilities & Warnings section earlier in this chapter for that information.

GETTING AROUND
To/From the Airport
The airport is on Motu Mute at the northern edge of the lagoon and free transfers are made to and from the Vaitape wharf on two large catamaran ferries. Some hotels transfer their visitors directly to and from the airport, others pick them up at the wharf.

Le Truck
Although there's no really regular le truck service there often seems to be one going somewhere at the appropriate times, particularly for flight and boat departures. Big hotels usually transfer their guests and there's a service specially for the Matira Point pensions and Village Pauline. It charges 300 CFP as far as Village Pauline or 500 CFP to detour down Matira Point, which is only a short walk so you may want to ask to be dropped off at the junction. From the Farepiti wharf the cost to Village Pauline is 500 CFP

Car, Scooter & Bicycle
Pacificar doesn't operate on Bora Bora, but Europcar, operating as Bora Bora Rent-a-Car (☎ 67-70-15 or 67-70-03, fax 67-79-95), is represented at the major hotels and has its main office directly opposite the wharf at Vaitape. It's open from 8 am to 6 pm daily. Vehicles can be rented for two, four, eight and 24-hour periods. It rents Fiat Pandas, Fiat Unos, Peugeot 106s and Renault Twingos from 7000 to 8000 CFP a day. Note that rentals only cover driving on the circle island road. If you want to try taking a regular car over the internal 4WD tracks it's your own lookout! Europcar also has scooters at 5000 or 5500 CFP a day. Europcar offers a free pick-up service for up to 10 km from Vaitape. Other local rental operators include Fredo Rent-a-Car (☎ 67-70-31, fax 67-62-07) in Vaitape.

Unfortunately, most of the bicycles on hire on the island are Peugeot village bikes, fine for cruising the coast route but for Bora Bora's back roads you really need a good mountain bike. A number of accommodation places (from cheap pensions to the Hotel Bora Bora) have bikes to rent as does Europcar in Vaitape. Village Pauline, for example, charges 900 CFP for the morning or afternoon or 1300 CFP all day. Hibiscus, just beyond Club Med, has bikes for 600 CFP for four hours, 800 CFP for six hours or 1000 CFP for eights hours. Europcar is more expensive at 1500 CFP for eight hours.

Boat & Jet Ski
Small outboard-powered boats can be rented from the Bora Bora Yacht Club for 5500/9000 CFP for a half/full day, plus fuel. You can hire jet skis from Heremiti Jet Tours (☎ 67-77-70) and Matira Jet Tour (☎ 67-62-73), which conduct jet ski tours as well as rent the craft. See the section on Cruises & Charters for more information.

Population: 1000
Area: 11 sq km
Passes: 1

The smallest and most isolated of the Society high islands, Maupiti is a miniature version of Bora Bora. Like its beautiful big sister, just 40 km to the east, Maupiti has impressive soaring rocky peaks with slopes tumbling down to the lagoon, cloaked in the waving green of coconut plantations. Like Bora Bora there's a shimmering, shallow lagoon edged by a string of *motus* flaunting luxuriously white-sand beaches. The difference is size: it's 32 km round Bora Bora's coastal road, just 10 km round Maupiti's.

Maupiti is like Bora Bora once was – it's more authentically Polynesian and much more low key, perhaps too low key for some tastes. Bora Bora may have too many tourists and too much tourist hype, but Maupiti doesn't have a restaurant or even a bar. In fact it's not unknown for the island shops to run right out of beer, enforcing an unplanned dry spell until the next supply ship turns up. Although TV has taken its toll on village life, the homes still have a traditional touch, often with the family tombs right in the front yard.

HISTORY

Like Raiatea, the island of Maupiti has enjoyed great cultural significance and the chiefs from other islands used to come to Maupiti for ceremonial purposes. Archaeological investigations on Motu Paeao, at the northern end of the lagoon, revealed fish hooks and other items dating back to around 850 AD. Their similarity to objects discovered in New Zealand has played a part in the theories on Polynesian migration. This is one of the oldest archaeological sites in the Society Island. The islanders crafted a unique mortar-and-pestle design (*penu*), examples of which have been discovered on

other islands in Polynesia – the island's black basaltic rock was particularly prized.

The European discovery of Maupiti is credited to the Dutch explorer Roggeveen in 1722, nearly half a century before Wallis, Bougainville and Cook made their important landfalls on Tahiti. Early in the 19th century the island came under the influence of Bora Bora, but the arrival of European missionaries brought another power struggle, eventually ending with Protestantism as the major religion. Later in the century another struggle blew up with Bora Bora over control of the remote Scilly atoll. French influence first touched the island during this period but the missionaries and the local chiefs continued to wield power until after WWII.

Maupiti has managed to remain remarkably untouched by mass tourism. The tricky pass, site of a number of shipwrecks over the years, is frequently suggested as one of the reasons for the lack of tourist development, but it's just as likely to be because the Maupitians simply aren't too keen on being overrun. Growing watermelons on the motus is a major source of income for the islanders. Copra production, heavily subsidised by the government, remains important, but recently much energy has gone into producing pearl oysters on the atoll of Mopelia. These are sold to Tuamotans to be transported back for pearl production on those islands.

ORIENTATION

Maupiti is very easy to come to terms with. There's one road which encircles the island, only deviating from the coastline for a short stretch where it climbs over the ridgeline running down to Tereia Point. On the east coast of the island the string of houses along the road technically constitutes two villages, Farauru to the north and Vaiea to the south, but it's impossible to discern where one stops and the other begins. The main shipping wharf is at the south-east corner of the island,

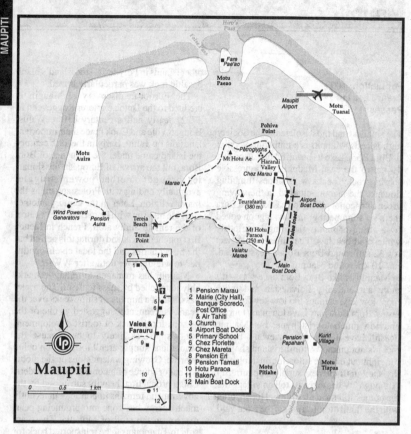

Maupiti

1 Pension Marau
2 Mairie (City Hall),
   Banque Socredo,
   Post Office
   & Air Tahiti
3 Church
4 Airport Boat Dock
5 Primary School
6 Chez Floriette
7 Chez Mareta
8 Pension Eri
9 Pension Tamati
10 Hotu Paraoa
11 Bakery
12 Main Boat Dock

directly across from the Onoiau Pass. The small airport wharf is halfway up the east side of the island, just south of the church.

Inland the terrain climbs steeply to the 380-metre summit of Mt Teurafaatui, or Nuupure, but the most conspicuous feature is the sharp ridgeline running north-south, overlooking the village. The high island mass is encircled by a wide but very shallow lagoon. The motus which fringe the lagoon equal the main island's area and villagers grow watermelons on plots on the two large motus. The airport is on Motu Tuanai. At the southern end of the lagoon, Motu Tiapaa and Motu Pitiahe, two smaller motus, flank Maupiti's single pass.

INFORMATION

The church in the middle of the village is the most notable landmark. Immediately south is the primary school with the airport wharf. Just to the north is the *mairie* (town hall), post office, Air Tahiti office and Banque Socredo office, all together in one neat little group. The post office is open from 7.30 am to 12.30 pm on weekdays, and until 3 pm on Tuesday. The bank is only open when a

Watermelons
Growing watermelons (pastèque in French) on the motus is a Maupiti speciality which has spread to other Society Islands, particularly Huahine. The process is laborious since the motu soil is not very fertile and trenches must be dug and filled with soil brought from the main island. Stones cover the planted seeds to retain the humidity and the growing melons must be regularly watered and treated with fertiliser. The delicious melons find a ready market on Tahiti. ■

representative comes to the island, so don't plan to change money.

The mairie and the church may be centres of village life on the island but in the evening the basketball and volleyball courts, just south of the school, are likely to be where you'll find Maupiti's young people.

AROUND THE ISLAND

It's just under 10 km right round the island, including the little side trip to Tereia Beach, so it's easy to walk it in a couple of hours. The road, paved only for a km or so through the village, sticks resolutely to the coastline and to sea level, except for the short stretch where it doubles back and climbs the saddle of the ridge running down to Tereia Point. The neat village houses, brightened with hibiscus, are strung along the road and often have breadfruit trees shading the family tombs which front many of the houses. The following tour starts in the village and proceeds around the island in an anticlockwise direction.

Petroglyphs

Leave the village past the football field at the northern end, round the point and pass the church basketball court. You're now in the Haranae Valley and, just before Tahiti Yacht Charter on the mountain side and a curious little house built out on the lagoon, is a track heading inland. Follow it to where it ends at a small pumping station about 200 metres inland. From here follow the rocky riverbed, which may have water in it during the wet season. After only 100 metres you'll find boulders in the stream cut with petroglyphs. The biggest and most impressive is a turtle image on a flat boulder just to the right of the stream. If you follow the rocky riverbed further inland for a few hundred metres it leads to a ruined *marae*.

West Coast Maraes

The west coast, from Pohiva Point to Puoroo and Tereia points, is dotted with coastal maraes. Some of them can be clearly discerned, but it's thought that at one time there were as many as 60 maraes along this stretch of coast, probably marking the boundaries of family landholdings.

Tereia Beach

Lying between Tereia and Puoroo points, at the western end of the island, Tereia Beach is the finest on the island for white sand and swimming. It's easy to walk right across the lagoon to Motu Auira, particularly at low tide. Beware of rays lying in the sand although they usually shoot away when they sense your approach.

Continuing around the island, the coast road climbs up over the low ridgeline running down to the point, then drops down to Atipiti Bay on the south side of the island.

Vaiahu Marae

Just north-west of the main wharf is the area known as Tefarearii, the 'house of the kings'. The island's nobility once lived here and Maupiti's most important marae is a large coastal site with a wide expanse of paving-like stones and a rectangular 'fish box' used for ceremonial purposes to ensure successful fishing. Made of coral blocks the box has four stones representing four different kinds of fish.

Just beyond the marae a sheer rock face rises up beside the road, overlooking the shipping quay at the south-east corner of the island. Traces of a fortified *pa* have been discerned atop this imposing outcrop.

THE MOTUS

Picnic trips are regularly arranged to the motus by the village *pensions* or it's easy to organise your own. Motu Paeao, at the northern end of the lagoon, was the site for the important archaeological discovery of a series of burial sites over 1000 years old. There are marae sites on Motu Tiapaa and Motu Auira.

From the west coast road on the main island you can see the surreal sight on Motu Auira of a series of tall towers carrying huge propellers. Although they look very similar to the 'wind farm' power generators being experimented with in Europe and the USA, these were, in fact, intended to pump water. The idea seems to have failed, however, as they are no longer working.

Motu Paeao has the False Pass on its west side and the Te Area or 'Hiro's Pass' on the east side. An island legend relates that Hiro tried to create this pass under the cover of night, using his mighty canoe to plough through the reef. He had already neatly chopped the island of Huahine in two by exactly the same method. Unfortunately for Hiro, an island warrior discovered his plan and hid nearby with his well-trained rooster. At a signal from the warrior the cock crowed and Hiro, thinking dawn was about to break, sailed away.

ACTIVITIES

Phone August (☎ 67-81-84) for walking and other land-based activities or Richard (☎ 67-80-62) for activities on the water.

Walking & Climbing

Above the Village Although it doesn't take you to the highest point on the island, the short climb to the ridge above Vaiea and Farauru gives excellent views over the lagoon and straight down to the village, right beneath your feet. A spectacularly rocky ridge parallels the village road. From the village look up to the final rocky pillar, ending right at the south-eastern corner of the island, directly above the main dock. At the north end of the pillar is a clump of coconut palms. Just north of the clump is a single palm, then a small saddle, then another clump of palms marking the southern end of the next rocky pillar. In less than an hour (30 minutes if you're fit and in a hurry) you can be up there.

Walk past Pension Eri, heading south towards the main dock, and you'll see a very clear driveway-like track heading inland. After about 100 metres, where the track turns left, veer right and start climbing straight up the hillside. The trail can be faint at times but it's generally quite easy to follow. About halfway up, about 100 metres above sea level, there's a small rock strip to clamber over, but apart from this it's almost all walk rather than climb. You're soon rewarded with the first views back over the village – the church already toy-like below. The trail, now much clearer, bends off south and ascends the slope to arrive at the saddle between the two rocky outcrops.

You can now follow the trail north or south. The southern extension takes you to the clump of palms from where you can look down on the dock and the southern end of the village. The northern extension and a bit of clambering will take you to the northern end of the imposing rocky outcrop towering directly above the main part of the village. Going further in either direction will involve real climbing. From the top you can see Bora Bora to the east and beyond to Raiatea and Tahaa. If it's clear you may be able to spot low-lying Tupai to the north of Bora Bora.

Climbing Mt Teurafaatiu It's a superb climb to the summit of Mt Teurafaatiu (380 metres), also known as Mt Nuupere, the highest point on the island. Allow three hours for the round trip and bring plenty of drinking water, or a good knife for opening coconuts. The walk starts from the high point where the road crosses the ridge above Tereia Point. From the apex of the corner the walking track starts straight up the ridge which it follows most of the way to the peak. At times it can be indistinct but it generally sticks firmly to the ridgeline so it's no problem finding your way.

At first there are views over the northern

lagoon, and higher up a short detour offers views to the south. Eventually the track hits the steep outcrop of the peak and traverses around to the south side, with some short stretches requiring real climbing. As you approach the top there are wonderful views over the northern lagoon, the three motus at the northern edge of the lagoon and the airport runway, jutting out into the lagoon, far below. This would be a fine spot to watch an Air Tahiti flight arrive.

The rocky summit offers a 360° perspective but you can drop down into the saddle and climb up again to the actual high point, with even better views to the north and of the long, rocky ridge running down to the main island's south-east corner. A final small summit stands directly above the village.

Snorkelling

There are no scuba-diving operators on Maupiti but there is good snorkelling and lots of fish in the Onoiau Pass, the only navigable pass into the lagoon.

PLACES TO STAY

There are no 'hotels' on Maupiti – everything is family-style although the motu resorts are probably a little less unplanned. The choice divides neatly into the village (where there are half a dozen very informal little pensions) or the motus (where there are four small-scale resorts). Because there are no places to eat apart from the places you stay, most Maupiti visitors opt for *demi-pension*, which

means a room plus breakfast and dinner. You can fend for yourself for lunch. Children under 12 years of age are usually charged half price.

Only one of the motu resorts takes credit cards, otherwise everything must be paid for in cash. Remember that there are no regular banking facilities on the island so bring sufficient money. Hot water is not on the menu at any of these places, so be prepared for cold showers.

In the Village

Officially it may be subdivided, but in practise the island's single real village is just one long main street, the only bit of paved road on the island. It stretches for a bit over a km and visitors will arrive at the old dock at the northern end (if they come by air and transfer from the airport motu) or the new dock at the southern end (if they come by sea). None of the village pensions has any sort of identifying sign, but if you've not made prior arrangements they're easy enough to find. If you don't spot them, any village kid will point them out. South of the airport dock Chez Floriette and Chez Mareta are side by side, just south of the primary school and both backing on to the well-used basketball court. *Chez Mareta* (☎ 67-80-25) has a peaked blue roof and tends to be a bit shabby. There are two rooms, each with a double bed, sharing a bathroom, living room and kitchen. Nightly costs are 1000 CFP per person (room only) or 3000 CFP (demi-pension).

Sharks & Rays

You expect to see fish when you're snorkelling or diving but shark spotting on foot and ray spotting from the air are more unusual. Walking along the water's edge on the outer side of Motu Auira, I (Tony) spotted the unmistakeable fin of a black-tipped reef shark. Lazily cruising the shallow waters, the shark was generally in water only shin deep. So I strolled in after it and for a couple of hundred metres followed it from rock pool to rock pool. When it started to get away from me I cut back to the shore, ran along the beach and walked back into the water ahead of it. Quietly following interesting wildlife on dry land is one thing but how often do you get to stalk a shark, on foot?

Crossing the shallow, sand-bottomed Maupiti lagoon, rays often dart away from your boat, or you may spot them quietly basking on the bottom. A few days later I was flying back into Maupiti, on a roundabout route from Bora Bora to Raiatea. As we banked down over the lagoon the black rays stood out against the white sand like large-print exclamation marks on a huge sheet of white paper. ■

The popular and well-run *Chez Floriette* (☎ 67-80-85) has four bedrooms, two with a double and a single bed, two with just a double bed. The bathroom, living room and equipped kitchen are shared. Nightly cost is 4500 CFP per person demi-pension.

Continue south to *Pension Eri* (☎ 67-81-29), also on the lagoon side of the road. This well-run pension is slightly unusual in that the family lives across the road in another house and bring breakfast and dinner over to their guests, but apart from that you're pretty much left to your own devices. There are four bedrooms, each with a double bed, sharing bathrooms, kitchen and living room. Demi-pension costs 4500 CFP per person.

A short walk further south and on the mountain side of the road is *Pension Tamati* (☎ 67-80-10), a dismal-looking two-storey building with a verandah. Unfortunately, this first impression is correct – it's just as gloomy and depressing inside this 'grande maison' and visitors don't give glowing reports. Treat this pension as an emergency backup if everything else is full. It is big: there are nine rooms in total, six with a double and a single bed, and three with just a double. Demi-pension costs 3300 CFP per person.

Pension Marau (☎ 67-81-19) is in the opposite direction, north of the mairie and post office and up above the road on the mountain side. There are three rooms, each with a double bed and, as usual, sharing living and dining areas and bathroom. The nightly demi-pension cost is 5000 CFP per person.

On the Motus

Three of the motus have places to stay. They're generally more expensive than the village pensions although they're equally small scale. In exchange for the low-key bustle of village life, motu-dwellers get beach and water activities. Transfers to the main island are easily arranged. Although these places are much like small resorts, the range of facilities and activities is very limited. Don't expect swimming pools, water-sports equipment or diving trips.

On the east side of Motu Auira is *Pension Auira* (☎ & fax 67-80-26), on the water's edge looking across to Tereia Beach on the main island. At low tide you can wade across to the mainland, as the deepest water is about waist high. There are three 'beach' bungalows at 6000 CFP demi-pension per person and three 'garden' bungalows at 5000 CFP. The beach bungalows are each slightly different; one of them has a mezzanine level and a small entry room so it's ideal for visitors with children. All the bungalows have attached toilets and showers but the garden bungalows are as basic as it gets and the extra 1000 CFP for the beach versions is probably well spent.

Children aged from three to 12 pay half price, lunch adds another 2000 CFP to your bill and transfers from the airport are 2000 CFP per person. This is the only place on Maupiti which takes credit cards. Write to PO Box 2, Vaiea, Maupiti, if you want to book.

Motu Paeao at the northern edge of the lagoon separates the larger Auira and Tuanai motus. On the western edge of the motu, the small *Fare Pae'ao* (☎ & fax 67-81-01), also known as Chez Janine, has just three self-contained bungalows, each with a verandah looking over the water. There's a pleasant restaurant area, also looking out on the False Pass and the menu even features wine by the carafe for 1000 CFP. The bungalows cost 6000 CFP for one or two people; demi-pension adds 3000 CFP per person, full board adds 5000 CFP. Children under 12 are half price and airport transfers are 1000 CFP. Write to PO Box 33, Vaiea, if you want to make a booking.

There are two places on Motu Tiapaa, on the east side of Maupiti's sole pass. At the northern end of the motu is *Pension Papahani* (☎ 67-81-58), right on the beach beside the pass. It's also known as Pension Vilna. A beachfront *fare* has four very simple double rooms and separate toilet and shower facilities. Nightly demi-pension cost is 5000 CFP per person, an extra 1000 CFP if you want lunch. Back from the beach are two slightly more luxurious, and slightly more expensive, separate bungalows. Attached bathrooms may be added to these at some time in the future. Round-trip airport transfers are 1000 CFP per person. Write to PO Box 1, Vaiea, for bookings.

Further south and on the ocean side of the motu is *Kuriri Village* (no phone, fax 67-82-00) which is the only place on Maupiti aiming much above the basic accommodation bracket. There are four bungalows, one of them above the kitchen-and-dining area, each showing some individual flair in design. Each has its own separate bathroom building, again with some individuality in design like internal gardens or open-air showers. The food here is mainly home made and has a good reputation but, of course, prices are commensurately higher than anything else on the island. The nightly cost with all meals is 10,000 CFP per person, including airport transfers. You can also include daily activities, ranging from mountain climbing on the main island to whale watching in October.

Despite the higher costs, hot water is still not on the programme, nor are credit cards accepted. Bring plenty of cash. Run by proprietors Gérard and Evy Bede, this is one of the few places in Maupiti where English is understood. The views across the reef edge to Bora Bora are superb.

PLACES TO EAT

There are none! Apart from wherever you're staying, the only eating possibilities are the sandwiches which some of the village stores sell in the morning. There's a bakery just beyond the main dock and adjacent to the electricity generating house. Get there before 7 am as the day's baking is quickly sold out, and the doors shut soon after. The stores sell basic foodstuffs, including canned goods, the ubiquitous minute noodles and soft drinks. Only a couple of them, including one right at the northern outskirts, are licensed to sell beer.

Watermelons are grown on the motus, breadfruit and coconuts grow everywhere, bananas are common and mangoes are so prolific they fall on the ground and rot, but pineapples are relatively rare. The mains water supply is a relatively recent arrival on Maupiti, and in 1996 work was still progressing on finding adequate supplies as the island's water table tends to be easily contaminated by seawater.

ENTERTAINMENT

Bring some good novels, as Maupiti doesn't even have a bar if you're a hankering for a cold Hinano at sunset. The nearest thing to a real bar is the table and adjacent cooler set up right at the back of Pension Tamati, the big and rather shabby two-storey building towards the southern end of the village.

GETTING THERE & AWAY

Maupiti is 320 km east of Tahiti, and just 40 km east of Bora Bora.

Air

Air Tahiti (☎ 67-80-20 or 67-81-24) operates flights to Maupiti from Papeete about four times a week, via Raiatea and/or Bora Bora. One-way adult fares from Maupiti are Bora Bora 5300 CFP, Huahine 7700 CFP, Papeete 12,700 CFP and Raiatea 5600 CFP. The Air Tahiti office is beside the mairie and post office in the village.

If you're on a flight passing by Bora Bora, the right side of the aircraft offers the best views of that fabled island en route to Maupiti or the left side flying from Maupiti. If, however, you are flying in via Bora Bora, the best views of that island will be from the left side westbound and from the right side eastbound.

Sea

Onoiau Pass, at the southern end of the lagoon, is the only entry point to the Maupiti lagoon and strong currents and a tricky sand bar means the narrow pass can only be navigated by smaller ships. Great care is required when entering the lagoon and ships must often wait for the appropriate tidal conditions. Several small ships do operate to Maupiti including the *Te Aratai* and the *Maupiti To'u Aia*, usually bringing supplies from Raiatea. The trip takes about six hours

A Ship in Port

The arrival of a ship in Maupiti is a major event. Late one afternoon the small *Maupiti To'u Aia* zipped in through the pass, bustled importantly up to the quay and was fallen upon by what looked like half the population of the island. The other half sat down to watch the frenetic activity. Is there a Polynesian dockers' union? If so they were on holiday as everybody seemed to pitch in and most goods appeared to go straight into the hands of their owners. A batch of bicycles were handed down off the stern while 3000-odd bottles of beer in cases of 20s went from hand to hand and into the back of a pick-up. An equal or even greater supply of soft drink followed a parallel route. Drums of fuel were rolled off the ship, across the dock and straight into waiting dinghies. Furniture was carried off on strong shoulders. The working party was about equally divided between male and female, but in between this confusing melee children ran back and forth while overhead the ship's crane nonchalantly swung bags of cement, bundles of water pipes, stacks of roofing iron and pallets of cement blocks. An hour or two later the activity was over and the docks were deserted once again. ∎

and costs from 1000 CFP. Schedules can get knocked around during the June to August period when the south-east *maaramu* blows.

The island-owned *Maupiti To'u Aia* also does regular trips to Mopelia atoll, far to the west. Pearl oysters are raised on Mopelia and sold to Tuamotans for pearl production. See the Other Leeward Islands chapter for more information on visiting Mopelia.

GETTING AROUND
To/From the Airport

If you've booked accommodation you'll probably be met at the airport on Motu Tuanai – a necessity if you're staying on one of the motus. The village pensions will probably meet their guests as well; not everybody on Maupiti has a car but nearly everybody has a dinghy with an outboard motor. If you're not met, there's a boat which takes the Air Tahiti staff and any hangers-on back to the main island, after the flight has departed. The one-way fare for the 15-minute trip is 400 CFP (children 200 CFP). The Air Tahiti boat also goes out to the airport motu for departing flights. Boat departure times are posted at the Air Tahiti office.

Around the Motus

It's relatively simple to arrange a boat out to the motus from the village since virtually every house has a boat. Many of the village pensions organise a weekly motu picnic trip for a minimal cost. It's equally simple to get across the main island from the motus. Fare Pae'ao, on Motu Paeao, for example, will transfer you to the village for 500 CFP per person round trip.

Around the Island

Walk. Village pensions may offer island tours or loan bicycles to their guests but otherwise the only public transport is the school bus. No problem – you can walk right around the island in two hours.

Other Leeward Islands

There are four other Leeward Islands in the Society group, all of them atolls and three of them far to the west of the high islands of the Leeward group. Immediately north of Bora Bora is Tupai, very much under Bora Bora's influence. The other three islands come under Maputi's aegis. Wallis, the first European to come upon Tahiti, sighted Mopelia and Scilly in 1767 as he continued west, but he did not pause to investigate them further. Mopelia is the only one of these Leeward atolls with a pass for ships to enter its lagoon. All four atolls are important breeding grounds for green turtles, which lay their eggs on the beaches from November each year.

TUPAI

Ancient Polynesian beliefs held that the souls of the dead had to pass through Tupai on their way to the afterworld. Also known as Motu Iti, the 11-sq-km atoll is only 16 km north of Bora Bora and has a double lagoon. An outer reef encompasses a narrow lagoon

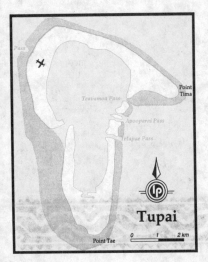

inside which is the circular atoll. Cloaked in coconut palms, the atoll motus are treated as a Bora Bora copra plantation. In the 1860s a Canadian produced coconut oil on the island using a steam engine. There is an airstrip on the island but no pass big enough to allow ships to enter the lagoon.

MOPELIA

It's 160 km south-west of Maupiti to Mopelia (also known as Maupihaa), an atoll treated very much as a Maupiti possession. The atoll is roughly circular, with a diameter of about eight km and an area of about four sq km. Wallis was the first European to sight the island, following his visit to Tahiti in 1767. In 1917 the German raider *Seeadler* (Sea Eagle) was wrecked on Mopelia when it paused for repairs. In search of a replacement, the ship's commander, Count Felix von Luckner, sailed off to Fiji in the ship's lifeboat but was captured on Wakaya Island. One of the *Seeadler's* cannons can be seen in Bougainville Park in the centre of Papeete. Von Luckner's account of his Pacific adventure, *The Sea Devil*, became a postwar best seller.

The atoll has a population of almost 100 people, stationed there purely to harvest pearl oysters which are brought back to Maupiti and then sold to pearl farmers. They, in turn, fly them back to the Tuamotus where they are implanted with seed pearls. A small oyster will fetch 100 CFP, larger ones up to 500 or 600 CFP. The isolated island is also noted for its many bird species and abundant turtles.

The atoll's tricky pass is just wide enough for small ships to enter the lagoon and the *Maupiti To'u Aia* ship sails from Maupiti to Mopelia every two weeks. The overnight trip is followed by two days on the island. There is no formal accommodation on Mopelia so potential visitors must arrange to stay with one of the residents. This is usually organised through a friend or relation on

Maupiti. The options are to stay two days, while the ship is in port, or two weeks, until the next visit. Yachts occasionally call into Mopelia – the only atoll in the Society Islands with a navigable pass.

SCILLY

Like Mopelia, the even more remote Scilly atoll (also known as Manuae) is home to green turtles and oysters. Manuae is about 60 km north-west of Mopelia and is covered in coconut palms. Although the atoll is about 15 km in diameter, it has a land area of only about four sq km. In 1855, the three-mast *Julie Ann* was wrecked on the atoll and the crew and passengers, including 24 women and children, were marooned there for two months until they managed to build a small boat and sail to Raiatea.

BELLINGHAUSEN

Bellinghausen (also known as Motu One) was 'discovered' in 1824 by the Russian explorer of that name. He also visited Antarctic on three occasions between 1819 and 1821. Four low-lying islands, with a total area of about three sq km, encircle the reef but there is no entrance to the lagoon.

The Tuamotus

HISTORY

The Tuamotus

Scattered in a wide arc to the west of Tahiti and the Society Islands and to the south of the Marquesas, the Tuamotus stretch for over 1000 km. The closest islands are about 300 km from Tahiti, the most distant over 1500 km away. With one exception, the islands are classic coral atolls, some of them little more than reefs barely breaking the water's surface, others long circular chains of islands and *motus* encircling massive lagoons.

The archipelago comprises about 80 atolls, 30 of which have narrow passes into a central lagoon. The group's population is about 12,000, scattered over 45 inhabited islands ranging from those with a mere handful of often transient occupants to Rangiroa, with its two large villages and total population of 1800. The largest Tuamotu population is, however, made up of the French armed forces and nuclear-testing employees on Moruroa. The total land area of the Tuamotus is only about 700 sq km and apart from one island there's hardly a square metre which rises more than a few metres above sea level. The narrow chains of low-lying motus which make up the islands encircle around 6000 sq km of sheltered lagoons, more than 1000 sq km in the vast Rangiroa lagoon alone.

HISTORY

European explorers first chanced upon the Tuamotus in 1521, when Portuguese explorer Ferdinand Magellan, heading across the unknown Pacific towards the Philippines, chanced upon Pukapuka. An isolated outlier, well to the east of the dense mass of islands and reefs that make up the central part of the Tuamotus, Pukapuka gives no hint of the sheer number of islands in the chain – French explorer Louis-Antoine de Bougainville was, however, all too aware of the peril they presented to unwary navigators when he dubbed the islands the 'dangerous archipelago'.

It's thought that the Tuamotus were settled much later than the high islands of the Society group and Marquesas. Conflicts in those groups probably led to the first settlements in the archipelago around the 14th century. The people of the chain were known as the Paumotus and the islands were divided into loose groupings of antagonistic islands. At the western end of the archipelago, Rangiroa and other nearby islands including

Forming an Atoll

It's generally assumed that all the islands of French Polynesia are formed by volcanic action; the low-lying Tuamotu atolls are simply further along in their development than the high islands of the Society group. High islands are formed by an erupting volcano rising above sea level. The volcano becomes dormant and gradually erodes away over the eons. A fringing coral reef grows up around the island and a lagoon forms between this protective reef and the central island.

Bora Bora is a fine example of this development; the sea has already broken into what was once a huge volcano crater (*caldera*) and a wide lagoon has been formed. Eventually the central island erodes away completely but the outer reef islands survive, continually supplanted by the growth of fresh coral. Even rising sea levels can be coped with if the growth of coral is faster than the change in depth.

The Tuamotus are classic coral atolls. Some of them are little more than enclosed reefs with shallow channels called *hoa*, which carry water in and out of the lagoon with tidal changes. Many others are near-continuous strings of islands with narrow passes offering seaways into the sheltered lagoons. The one exception is the 80-metre-high island of Makatea, the only example of a raised atoll in French Polynesia. The word *makatea* is the scientific description of an upthrust reef – a coral atoll which has been raised high above the waterline by geological disturbances. ■

Makatea, Mataiva, Tikehau, Arutua, Apataki and Kaukura were part of the Mikiroa association. East of Rangiroa, Manihi, Ahe, Takaroa and Takapoto were part of the Vahitu group, while to the south the Matahoa group included Anaa, Fakarava and other atolls. European rule over the scattered settlements came with Christian missionaries in the 1850s. They established copra plantations from the 1870s and were also responsible for the introduction of pearl diving. Today Catholic and Mormon missions vie for the atoll population and many villages boast fine churches from both sects.

For over 50 years, from 1908 until 1966, phosphate mining on the island of Makatea, south-west of Rangiroa towards Tahiti, was the principal export activity not only for the Tuamotus but for all of French Polynesia, but this was an unusual exception to the slow pace of life in the whole island group. The relatively isolated culture of these islands made them a fertile ground for studies by Honolulu's Bishop Museum during the late 1920s and early '30s but the islands remained remote and little known until after WW II. The population of the islands was always small but began to decline dramatically in recent decades as copra production fell away and plastics killed off the mother-of-pearl business.

It was not until the 1970s, when airstrips were built on many of the islands, that the population decline was slowed and the group's economic prospects began to brighten. Regular flights from Tahiti brought tourists to the archipelago, attracted by the postcard beauty of the atolls and the superb snorkelling and diving in the lagoons. The flights back to Tahiti carried not only suntanned tourists but loads of fresh reef fish for the busy markets of Papeete. At the same time pearl farms began to produce the black pearls which have become synonymous with French Polynesia.

Unhappily the 1970s brought another far less congenial employment prospect to the Tuamotus when the Centre d'expérimentations du Pacifique (Centre for Nuclear Experiments, in the Pacific) euphemistically referred to as the 'Pacific Experiment Centre', took over the central atoll of Hao and began to test French nuclear weapons on the western atolls of Moruroa and Fangataufa. The early '80s also

---

Ciguatera: When 'Poisson' Means Poison

Ciguatera is the name of a disease endemic in all coral seas, and French Polynesia is seriously affected.

This type of food poisoning occurs after eating normally edible fish contaminated with a micro-organism. Named *Gambierdiscus toxicus* after the Gambier archipelago where it was first identified in 1977, the micro-organism lives in seaweed growing on dead coral. It is the causal agent of ciguatera and fishes which have absorbed it become carriers. This micro-alga has two cilia which enable it to move around. Normally present in only small quantities in the reef environment, it proliferates when the coral biotope suffers natural attacks (cyclones, changes in salinity, temperature or oxygen content of the water) or attacks inflicted by humans (pollution, coastal development). The coral dies and the seaweed develops on its surface. The *Gambierdiscus toxicus* proliferates and secretes ciguatoxin, which invades every level of the food chain, from herbivorous fish which graze on the coral to the final consumer: humans.

The first symptoms appear two to 20 hours after eating the contaminated fish. Digestive upsets, itching (which has earned it the name of 'scratch' in Polynesia), stinging or pins and needles, a slow heartbeat, and sensory and neurological disorders are characteristic signs. No fatalities have yet been officially recorded.

Although Polynesians sometimes resort to *raau* (traditional medicine), it is essential to see a doctor. Treatment is purely symptomatic.

Since there is no means of detection nor any specific treatment for this disease, you have to rely on prevention. In a region reported to be infected with ciguatera, check with the inhabitants of the atoll, who know from experience which species are prone to carry the disease and the places where they are to be found. As a general rule, snapper, grouper, black surgeonfish and perch are best avoided. ■

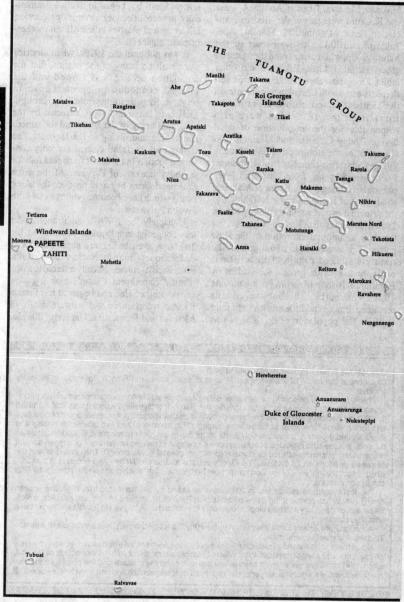

THE TUAMOTUS

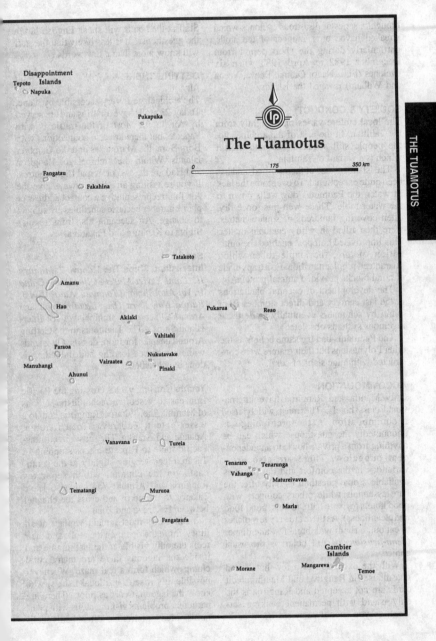

Disappointment Islands

Tepoto

Napuka

Pukapuka

The Tuamotus

0   175   350 km

Fangatau

Fakahina

Tatakoto

Amanu

Hao

Akiaki

Vahitahi

Paraoa

Manuhangi

Vairaatea

Nukutavake

Pinaki

Ahunui

Pukarua

Reao

Vanavana

Tureia

Tenararo   Tenarunga

Vahanga

Matureivavao

Tematangi

Muruoa

Maria

Fangataufa

Gambier Islands

Morane

Mangareva

Temoe

brought a series of disastrous cyclones which wreaked havoc on a number of the atolls, particularly during the short period from December 1982 to April 1983 when six cyclones (Lisa, Nano, Orama, Reeva, Veena and William) ravaged the islands.

SOCIETY & CONDUCT

The local culture varies only slightly from the Tahitian. In the east of the archipelago, the people still speak a Paumotu dialect which is a variant of Tahitian.

The islanders' use of their limited land has been quite exceptional. To overcome the lack of water, the Paumotus dug wells down to the water table. These well-pits, once dry, often covering hundreds of square metres, were then filled in with vegetable matter. This improvised compost enabled the cultivation of *taro*, the staple tuber which guaranteed regular nutrition. Fish traps made of coral blocks provided animal protein.

The development of coconut plantations in the last century and direct supplies from Tahiti by schooners eventually made these ingenious systems obsolete.

The Paumotus had the same beliefs as the other Polynesians but their maraes were constructed with huge slabs of coral.

ACCOMMODATION

Only Manihi and Rangiroa have international-class hotels. The most widely used accommodation in the archipelago is undoubtedly the guesthouse which can be anything from a private house to an independent bungalow. There are also great variations in the comfort and the facilities available. Some guesthouses only offer the bare essentials while others compete with good hotels (private bath, towels, good food and cleanliness). As there are very few places to eat out, a room with breakfast and dinner (*demi-pension*) or full board is the usual choice.

With the exception of a few hotels and guesthouses in Rangiroa and Manihi, credit cards are not accepted and Rangiroa is the only island with permanent banking services, so you should carry sufficient cash.

Staff at the hotels will speak English but in the guesthouses it is less likely that the staff will know more than a few words.

GETTING THERE & AWAY
Air

The archipelago is very accessible by plane. Today, 23 atolls have airstrips and are served by Air Tahiti. Most of the traffic is with Papeete, but there are also connections with Bora Bora, the Marquesas and the Gambier Islands. Within the archipelago, Rangiroa and Hao are the two principal flight centres. If you're visiting an island, always give the Air Tahiti representative a contact address or phone number because schedules are subject to change. Air Oceania also runs regular flights to Kaukura and Fakarava.

Sea

Inter-Island Ships The *Manava 2, Manava III, Saint Xavier Maris Stella, Dory, Cobia II, Vai-Aito, Tamarii Tuamotu, Auura'Nui 3, Rairoa Nui, Kura Ora, Kauaroa Nui* and *Aranui* all serve the archipelago; see Inter-Island Ships – The Tuamotus in the Getting Around chapter for more details. On islands without wharves loading and unloading is done by whaleboat.

Yachts Cruising yachts crossing the Pacific from east to west often anchor in the lagoons of Manihi, Ahe, Takaroa, Rangiroa and, to a lesser extent, Fakarava, Toau, Arutua, Apataki and Aratika. The most direct trans-Pacific route to Papeete means stopping in Takaroa then verging slightly to the south-east, via the channel which separates Rangiroa and Arutua. You can also leave Takaroa to the north and cross the channel between Fakarava and Toau.

Yacht crews must remain vigilant at all times. From the open sea the atolls and their reefs are only visible at the last minute and inside the lagoons there are many coral clumps which form a real maze. Whenever possible, it's wise to use local fishers, who know the lagoon, to act as pilots. There are particular problems visiting atolls with pearl farms. Many platforms, often badly indi-

Top: Bora Bora, Society Islands
Middle: Faanui Church, Bora Bora, Society Islands
Bottom: Matira Bay, Bora Bora, Society Islands

TONY WHEELER

TONY WHEELER

JEAN-BERNARD CARILLET

JEAN-BERNARD CARILLET

Top Left: Summit of Mt Taita, Tubuai, Australs
Top Right: A motor scooter load of baguettes, Rurutu, Australs
Bottom Left: Takapoto, Tuamotus
Bottom Right: Mataiva, Tuamotus

cated by buoys, dot the lagoons. In Takaroa, a sign at the edge of the pass states that anchorage in the lagoon is forbidden, but you can ask the locals to guide you to a safe anchorage. Entering and leaving the lagoons through the passes can also be dangerous. It's wise to avoid the strong tidal currents and wait for calm water.

You'll need to obtain authorisation to visit the islands south and east of Anaa, which are part of the French nuclear-testing zone. Sailing westward, enquire at the *gendarmeries* in the Marquesas Islands.

GETTING AROUND

The road networks on the Tuamotu Islands are often just crushed coral or sand tracks, perhaps just a few km long, linking the village to the airport or to the areas where copra is produced. On some islands the airport will be close to the village, on others it may be on a motu on the opposite side of the lagoon. If you have booked accommodation, your hosts will come and meet you but transfers are not necessarily free. If there is a charge it will depend on the distance travelled and the means of transport. Hitching, by car or boat, is possible as many islanders go to the airports for arrivals and departures.

It's usually easy to get across the lagoons by local outboard-powered boats. On atolls with relatively long tracks there may be a handful of cars but traffic is usually nonexistent. Bicycles and scooters are often used in the villages and some guesthouses rent them out or they can be hired from islanders.

Rangiroa

Population: 1800
Lagoon Area: 1640 sq km
Passes: 3

Rangiroa (from Rairoa, literally 'long sky') is the second-biggest atoll in the world, out-ranked only by the Kwajalein atoll in Micronesia. 'Rangi', as it is usually called, measures 75 km from east to west and 25 km from north to south. The pear-shaped coral ring could contain the whole island of Tahiti. From the edge of the lagoon, it is impossible to see the opposite bank. In fact 'lagoon' seems a rather feeble word to describe the immense marine spread, encircled in the reef crown – 'internal sea' would be more appropriate.

Rangiroa, 350 km north-east of Tahiti, is also the most populated atoll in the Tuamotu archipelago, except for those where there are military bases. In two decades, it has established itself as the most famous tourist destination in the Tuamotus. Its reputation is based on diving and the abundant possibilities for excursions offered by the idyllic lagoon. Apart from tourism, fishing and pearl production have provided additional activities for the inhabitants.

Rangiroa is also an important link for air and sea communication, located at the mid-point between Tahiti, in the Society Islands, and the Marquesas.

HISTORY

Rangiroa atoll has more than 10% of the total population of the Tuamotus. It must have been even more populated in the past; maraes and some cultivation pits reveal evidence of many population centres spread around the whole atoll at Tereia, Fenuaroa, Otepipi, Tevaro, Avatoru and Tiputa.

Historically, Rangiroa has had to contend with two types of threat: pirates from the Anaa atoll in the south-east and devastating cyclones. Faced with the extortions of the pirates, the Rangiroa inhabitants sought refuge close to the Taeoo Motu (now the Blue Lagoon) on the south-west side of the atoll. As for the climatic disasters, a cataclysm, probably a tsunami, is said to have destroyed the human settlements in the west of the atoll in 1560.

Two centuries later, the population was settled mainly in the vicinity of the three passes, Tivaru, Avatoru and Tiputa. Rangiroa established strong relations with the other atolls of the northern Tuamotu Islands. This good fortune did not last long, for the Anaa warriors pillaged the atoll again at the end of

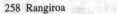

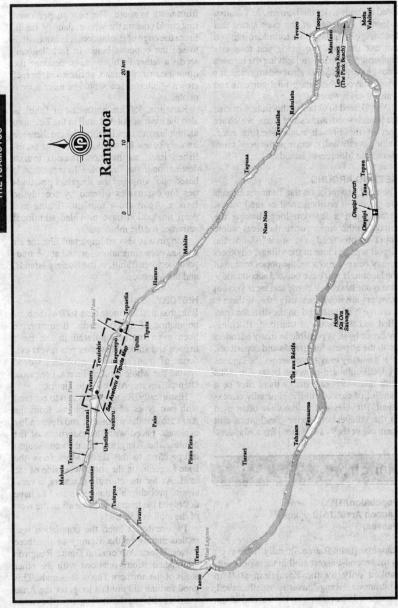

Toopae

Teraro

Manfano

Motu
Vahituri

Les Sables Roses
(The Pink Beach)

Rahuiatu

Tevaioihe

Tapuaa

Tepau

Taua

Otepipi Church

Otepipi

Nao Nao

Mahitu

Hararu

Tepaetia

Tiputa Pass

Tiputa

Keporepo

Tevaiohe

Hotel
Kia Ora
Sauvage

L'île aux Récifs

Avaturu

See Avatoru & Tiputa Map

Avatoru

Anatoru Pass

Faurumai

Paio

Utuhioe

Fenuaroa

Tehaare

Teumearou

Mahuta

Maherehonae

Pirau Pirau

Tiarari

Tutepua

Tivaru

Tivaru Pass

Tereia

Blue Lagoon

Taeo

Rangiroa

0   10   20 km

the 1770s and destroyed the public buildings. The survivors were forced into exile on Tikehau or Tahiti, where the Pomares gave them protection. They were able to return to Rangiroa in 1821 and repopulated the atoll.

Although discovered by the Dutchman Le Maire on 18 April 1616, Rangiroa saw the first Europeans settlers only in 1851: Christian missionaries who introduced coconut cultivation. Copra production enjoyed constant development until overtaken by fishing. Refrigeration facilities have been built, but direct dispatch by plane to the markets in Papeete is still a significant practice. Before plastic buttons replaced mother-of-pearl, pearl-oyster cultivation also flourished in Rangiroa. Today it has been replaced by cultured-pearl production. The opening of the airport in 1965 boosted the development of tourism, a leading activity since the 1980s.

ORIENTATION

The atoll's coral belt is no more than 200 to 300 metres wide but the long circuit of islands, motus and *hoa* (channels) stretches for more than 200 km, oriented on a northwest/south-east axis. The lagoon opens to the ocean via three passes: Tivaru to the west and Avatoru and Tiputa to the north. The Tivaru Pass is narrow and shallow while the Avatoru and Tiputa passes are each more than 200 metres wide. About 10 km separates the Avatoru and Tiputa passes.

Rangiroa has two villages, Avatoru and Tiputa, situated on the edge of the passes. Avatoru is to the west of a string of islets, separated by a number of hoa which are usually dry, except when inundated by high tides. At the east end, the Tiputa Pass opens, beyond which you see the village of the same name. Twice a day the tides carry water to and from the lagoon through these passes, creating strong currents and attracting abundant marine life.

Hotels and other essential tourist facilities are scattered along the 10-km-long Avatoru string of islets. There is only a handful of guesthouses in Tiputa. A few people live on a motu south of the lagoon, in the vicinity of the Kia Ora Sauvage, an annexe of the Kia Ora Village Hotel.

INFORMATION
Money

Rangiroa has branches of the Banque de Tahiti and Banque Socredo. Both have an agency in Avatoru and Tiputa, but take turns to serve the two villages on designated days.

In Avatoru, the busy Banque de Tahiti (☎ 96-85-52) is situated between the small supermarket, close to the Catholic church and the town hall. It is open Monday, Wednesday and Friday from 8 to 11.30 am and 1.30 to 4 pm, and Thursday from 1.30 to 4 pm. Tourists mistakenly think that it is the only bank in Rangiroa. In fact, the Banque Socredo (☎ 96-85-63), with no distinguishing sign, is housed in the town hall building. It operates on Monday, Tuesday, Thursday and Friday from 8 to 10.30 am, and on Wednesday from 8.30 to 10.30 am and 1.30 to 4 pm. You can exchange currency and withdraw cash with your credit card at either bank.

In Tiputa, you won't be stranded either. The Banque de Tahiti has no phone but operates from the town hall on Tuesday from 1.30 pm to 4 pm, and Thursday from 8 to 11.30 am. Banque Socredo (☎ 96-75-57), also in the town hall, is open Monday and Thursday, 1.30 to 4 pm. At Tiputa you can change currency, but you can't withdraw cash with your credit card.

Post & Telecommunications

In Avatoru, the post office is open Monday to Thursday from 7 am to 3 pm, and Friday from 7 am to 2 pm. In Tiputa, it operates Monday to Thursday from 7 am to 1 pm, and Friday from 7 am to noon. There are card-only telephone booths in Avatoru (next to the post office, at the airport, in front of the secondary school, and at the wharf in front of the Chez Glorine guesthouse) and in Tiputa (in front of the Maihiti shop).

Medical Services

The medical centre in Avatoru (☎ 96-03-75)

is two km east of the village. There is a hospital in Tiputa.

AVATORU

This village on the western end of the string of islets, on the edge of the pass and beside the lagoon, is organised around the town hall annexe. The Catholic church, 100 metres away, seems a precarious sentinel at the edge of the pass, while the Mormon church rises a little further off. There are a few small businesses and shops in the village.

EVAAM (l'Établissement pour la Valorisation des activités aquacoles et maritimes), a fishing and research centre, has a sub-branch in Avatoru, a few km east of the village and a stone's throw from the Chez Beatrice snack bar. Its staff of 12 specialises in cultured-pearl production research and manages the cold room for the fishers. Le Centre des métiers de la nacre et de la perliculture, on the ocean side of the island a little more than two km east of the village, trains young Polynesians in pearl-grafting.

Rangiroa College, which, together with Hoa College forms the main secondary

teaching centre in the Tuamotu archipelago, is about 3.5 km east of the village and has more than 400 students from the northern Tuamotu islands.

TIPUTA

Tiputa is in striking contrast to Avatoru. Huddled on the edge of the pass and the lagoon, it offers the visitor a more intimate atmosphere and a better preserved setting, away from the rather more intrusive tourism of Avatoru. There are fewer *popaa* (foreigners) here and it is easier to meet the locals. Tiputa is the administrative centre and is the main town for Rangiroa, Makatea, Tikehau and Mataiva. It has a gendarmerie with authority over several atolls. As for teaching, the village has the CETAD (Centre d'études des techniques adaptées au développement) which trains young people for catering and hotel jobs.

In the middle of the village there is an immaculately white Catholic church. In the same street, set back slightly, you can make out a discreet Marian altar (a shrine to the Virgin Mary), decorated with mother-of-pearl. There is a small Sanito temple for a

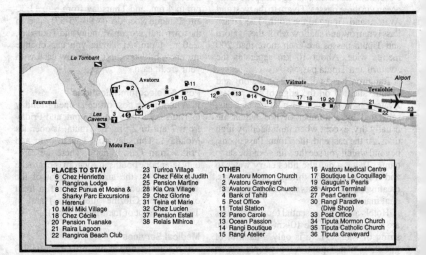

PLACES TO STAY		OTHER	
6 Chez Henriette	23 Turiroa Village	1 Avatoru Mormon Church	16 Avatoru Medical Centre
7 Rangiroa Lodge	24 Chez Félix et Judith	2 Avatoru Graveyard	17 Boutique Le Coquillage
8 Chez Punua et Moana &	25 Pension Martine	3 Avatoru Catholic Church	19 Gauguin's Pearls
Sharky Parc Excursions	28 Kia Ora Village	4 Bank of Tahiti	26 Airport Terminal
9 Herenui	29 Chez Glorine	5 Post Office	27 Pearl Centre
10 Miki Miki Village	31 Teina et Marie	11 Total Station	30 Rangi Paradive
18 Chez Cécile	32 Chez Lucien	12 Pareo Carole	(Dive Shop)
20 Pension Tuanake	37 Pension Estall	13 Ocean Passion	33 Post Office
21 Raira Lagoon	38 Relais Mihiroa	14 Rangi Boutique	34 Tiputa Mormon Church
22 Rangiroa Beach Club		15 Rangi Atelier	35 Tiputa Catholic Church
			36 Tiputa Graveyard

Fish Farms

Easily recognisable by their posts, which pierce the surface of the water in channels or lagoons, fish farms are a familiar part of the landscape on many of the Tuamotu atolls.

These enclosures enable the fishers to regulate the numbers of fish taken according to the consumption needs of the inhabitants, the arrival of the schooners or the availability of air freight.

The establishment of a fish farm takes into account the currents, where the fish usually pass by and the layout of the sea bed. Generally, they are set up near channels or inside the reef ring, in two to four metres of water. Their method of operation is simple: two collecting branches arranged in a V shape (*rauroa*) and open at varying angles lead to a rounded chamber (*aua*). The aua is in turn connected by a narrower entrance to a secondary hoop net (*tipua*), placed at the side. The fish which enter this maze are unable to turn back. The fishers simply have to harpoon them or catch them in a hoop net. The passages, made of wire netting fixed to metal or kahaia wood posts, require constant maintenance. Formerly, piled-up blocks of coral were used to fulfil the same functions. ■

dissident branch of the Mormons almost opposite the town hall.

AROUND THE LAGOON

The huge Rangiroa atoll contains sights well worth a day's excursion by boat. Most are on the opposite side of the lagoon from Avatoru, which takes at least an hour to cross. Enquire at one of the tourist agencies mentioned in the Organised Tours section later in this chapter.

These tours rely on the state of the lagoon and weather conditions. In the event of *maraamu* (south-east wind), they may be cancelled. A minimum number of participants is required. Take along some plastic sandals, sunscreen, sunglasses, a swimsuit and a change of clothes.

The Blue Lagoon

One of Rangiora's most popular tourist spots, the Blue Lagoon is one hour away by boat on the western edge of the atoll, close to the Taeoo Motu. A string of motu and coral

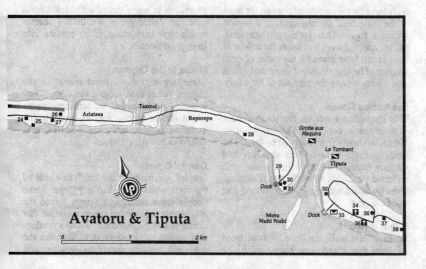

Avatoru & Tiputa

THE TUAMOTUS

Black Pearl, Jewel of the Tuamotus

The trump card of the Polynesian economy, the black pearl, or *poe rava*, is the result of natural phenomena and complex human intervention. The main centres of production are on the Tuamotus and the Gambiers. Manihi, Takapoto, Takaroa, Arutua, Makemo and Mangareva are the best known. Their lagoons, studded with pearl farms standing on piles, look like lakeside towns. The size of the operation varies from one or two people to more than 80 people for the industrial sites. The source of this activity is an oyster (*Pinctada margaritifera*), found in abundance in Polynesian lagoons.

The shells of these bivalves were used in ancient times to make ceremonial jewellery, fish hooks and lures. Last century, they were much sought after by the European button industry. In the 1960s, overexploitation of natural beds and the decline of the button industry sounded the death knell for this activity. The culture of oysters for pearl production took over, initially in Manihi.

The formation of a pearl results from the accidental or artificial introduction of a foreign body inside the oyster. In response to this intrusion, the epithelial cells of the mantle, the animal's secretory organ, produce nacreous material to isolate the foreign body. In this way, the nucleus is gradually covered in nacre (mother-of-pearl). If the foreign body is introduced by natural means (a grain of sand or coral, for example), the result is an extremely rare natural pearl, known as a fine pearl.

The pearl farmer must reproduce this natural mechanism. Firstly, the oysters are methodically reared. At certain times of the year, they release sexual substances which are fertilised in the water. After swimming around for several weeks, the young oysters (seed oysters) attach themselves to the coral. The pearl farmer catches the seed oysters in artificial collectors sunk in the lagoon and then attaches them to underwater rearing lines.

The first stage consists of sacrificing a perfectly healthy oyster, known as the donor oyster, and this happens when the oysters reach maturity. A fragment of its mantle is removed and divided into about 50 minute particles, the grafts. The second stage is the grafting proper. The recipient oyster is fixed to a support and held open with forceps. Using a scalpel, the grafter firstly incises the back of the gonad (reproductive organ) and inserts the graft. He then introduces a perfectly spherical bead (the nucleus), about six mm in diameter, into the gonad so that it is in contact with the graft. The operation takes just a few seconds. The graft cells then develop around the nucleus to form the pearl sack which, once closed, secretes the nacreous material. The grafted oysters are placed inside keepnets (metal baskets) and lowered back into the lagoon suspended from strings. They are then regularly inspected and cleaned.

---

reefs have formed a natural pool on the edge of the main reef, thereby creating a lagoon within a lagoon. Its sparkling white sand, ruffled coconut trees and water the colour of lapis-lazuli have earned it the name of Blue Lagoon. The lagoon is not deep and offers safe diving among the myriads of little fish.

Les Sables Roses

This magnificent site on the south-eastern edge of the lagoon, near Vahituri Motu, is 1½ to two hours from Avatoru by boat. The sands contain Foraminifera deposits and various coral residues which glow with reflected pink light when the sun is shining. The crystalline water invites swimming and snorkelling.

L'Île aux Récifs

South of the atoll, an hour by boat from Avatoru, this island, also known as Ai Ai Motu, lies in water dotted with raised coral outcrops called *feo* – weathered shapes which have been chiselled by erosion into strange silhouettes.

Motus in the Lagoon

There are a few scattered motus in the lagoon, rather than around the edge. They include Paio Motu and are bird sanctuaries which shelter nesting species found in the Tuamotu islands including noddies, sea-swallows and frigate birds.

Otepipi Church

Otepipi is a motu on the south-east side of the atoll which once had a village. Some people say a contagious illness forced the inhabitants to leave but others maintain that cyclones and the demands of copra production caused the inhabitants to abandon the area and regroup closer to Avatoru and

Layer upon layer, the mother-of-pearl thickens around the nucleus at the rate of one mm a year. Eighteen months later, the first harvest is gathered. A second implantation may be made with a second nucleus to obtain a second, larger (15 to 20 mm) pearl 15 months later.

Grafting entails risks inherent to all surgical operations: of 100 grafted oysters, 25 to 30 do not survive the shock of the operation and another 25 to 30 reject the nucleus. When the time comes to harvest them, only five of the remaining 40 (just 2%) are perfect pearls. When a second graft is performed, the rejection rate drops to less than 10%.

Until recently, the only grafters were Japanese. They were virtual superstars who had to be retained at great expense, but they are gradually being replaced by Polynesians who have discovered the alleged 'secret' of the technique. A centre for the pearl shell and pearl culture professions has been established on Rangiroa and provides training for future pearl farmers. Nonetheless, the act of grafting is still partly veiled in mystery.

The pearls are mainly used for jewellery in rings and pendants. Several factors determine their value: the diameter (from 8.5 to 18 mm); shape (whether it's round, ie perfectly spherical; ringed, ie with visible rings; baroque ie asymmetrical; or pear-shaped); quality (absence of flaws or marks) and colour. 'Black pearl' is in fact an inaccurate term. The pearl produced by *Pinctada margaritifera* covers a wide range of colours from pearly white to black, including deep purple, champagne and grey. The orient (the pearl's iridescent reflection) and lustre (mirror effect) also enter into the equation. Jewellers generally classify pearls by using two letters followed by a figure: a pearl classed as RB 12 is perfectly round (R), has a few pits or surface flaws, a correct orient (B) and measures 12 mm in diameter.

Less well known, the Japanese terms *keshi* and *mabe* are two other products of pearl culture. Keshi is pure mother-of-pearl, a pearl without a nucleus. In some cases the nucleus is rejected but the secreting graft continues to produce mother-of-pearl. The resultant pearl varies from two to eight mm in diameter and is often baroque in shape. The pearl farmer does not discover it until harvesting. They are used to make earrings or bracelets. Mabe, by contrast, is the result of deliberate manipulation. The technician sticks a plastic mould on the inner surface of the shell. The mould is gradually covered in layers of mother-of-pearl. After a few months, the mother-of-pearl is cut off with a diamond disk and the mould is removed. The result is a pure, hollow mabe. It is then filled with epoxy resin and a small mother-of-pearl plate is welded on to form the base. Mabe is highly valued in the jewellery trade for making pendants, brooches, earrings or cufflinks. ■

THE TUAMOTUS

Tiputa. Today, only a church remains but religious retreats and pilgrimages are still made to the church periodically.

PEARL FARMS

Rangiroa has three pearl farms. Two of them are on the Avatoru string of islets and are open to visitors.

Gauguin's Pearl (☎ 96-05-39), 800 metres east of the airport and on the lagoon side, is part of the Jean-Pierre Fourcade empire. There are tours, in English or French, up to three times daily, including a demonstration of grafting. Direct purchases can be made.

Another farm, of more modest dimensions, belongs to the Tetua family who owns the Martine guesthouse (see Places to Stay – Middle). Mr Tetua looks after the grafting while Corinne, who is French and in charge of marketing, will take you around the farm

and answer your questions. Direct sales take place at the shop, opposite the guesthouse.

DIVING

In the last 10 years Rangiroa has established itself as one of the best centres for diving in the Pacific, offering all the ingredients of a diver's Shangri-la.

Dive Centres

Yves Lefèvre, director of the Rai Manta club dive centre founded in 1985, has contributed to the success of this activity in the Tuamotu archipelago. Two other centres have since been set up, one in 1992 and the other in 1995. The three centres, all on the Avatoru string of islets, are relentless competitors, though they have made tacit agreements with guesthouses, hotels and other tourist businesses to 'channel' customers.

Equally competent and professional, each

of the three centres has its own distinct style. As with the guesthouses, it is best to form your own opinion by visiting each centre. This competitive drive to attract customers has led to overstatements which offer ever more sensations. The race to deeper and deeper diving is a far from commendable and has led to several accidents. Indeed, divers used to be taken to a depth of 50 metres, sometimes twice in the course of the same day. Things now seem to have reverted to healthier practices.

You should book your dive one or two days ahead, particularly in July and August. The three centres offer free transfer to your guesthouse or hotel. Most instructors speak enough English to cater to English speakers. PADI divers will always find at least one instructor with PADI certification to welcome them. The three centres operate the same dives. They are usually made between 8 am and 2 pm, but the exact timing depends on tidal times, currents, swell and wind conditions. All three centres accept credit cards.

Raie Manta Club The head office of this club (☎ 96-84-80, fax 96-85-60) is at the entrance of the village of Avatoru, on the lagoon side, between the Herenui and Rangiroa Lodge guesthouses. The centre also has an annexe near the Tiputa Pass, next to the Teina et Marie guesthouse. This centre, the first one in Rangiroa, has an excellent reputation which extends beyond French

Polynesia. Yves Lefèvre and his team invite you to experience the currents in the passes of Tiputa and Avatoru for 5000 CFP per dive or 45,000 CFP for 10 dives, including equipment. The first dives which, take place in front of the club or on Nuhi Nuhi Motu, cost the same as a single dive. A day excursion to Les Failles, which includes two dives and a picnic, costs CFP 18,000. The Raie Manta Club benefits from an exclusive arrangement with the Kia Ora Village.

Paradive Paradive (☎ 96-05-55, fax 96-05-50) is at the end of the string of islets, next to the Chez Glorine guesthouse and 30 metres from the wharf. Bernard Blanc and his team (with one woman instructor) offer their expertise for the cost of 5500 CFP for a first dive, 5000 CFP for a single dive, 23,500 CFP for five dives and 45,000 CFP for 10 dives, including equipment. Paradive also offers CMAS and PADI training: expect to pay 35,000 CFP for the CMAS certificate or the PADI open-water certificate. Allow 15,000 CFP, picnic not included, for a day excursion to Les Failles.

The Six Passengers The most recent arrival in Rangiroa, the Six Passengers (☎ & fax 96-02-60) is on the edge of the lagoon, 500 metres east of Kia Ora Village. Frederic Aragones has sought to provide conviviality, simplicity and a relaxed style. The small bamboo *fare* which houses the centre is very friendly. You must lay out 5500 CFP for a first dive, 5000 CFP for an exploratory dive and 45,000 CFP for 10 dives, including equipment. The excursion to Les Failles, including two dives and a picnic, costs 14,000 CFP. All dives are shot on video by someone from Ciao Rangiroa (☎ 96-04-14) and you can watch the film at the centre on your return or buy a copy of the video for 10,000 CFP.

Dive Sites
In reality, there are not many sites regularly used in Rangiroa – 10 at the most. What makes diving here so exceptional is the pass currents and the density of the deep-sea

Shark Mealtime?

Diving at Rangiroa is famous for encounters with sharks. Lots of them. My (Tony's) second dive there started at a spot called Shark Point, and if ever a name was well chosen it was this one. We jumped out of the dive boat, dropped straight to the bottom and all around us, in every direction, were sharks. Wall to wall sharks. In fact, symmetrically arranged against the deep-blue backdrop, they looked remarkably like shark wallpaper. Nothing to worry about: these were white-tip reef sharks, a nonbiting variety so it's said, and after getting our wide-eyeful of sharks we set off to drift with the current through the Tiputa Pass between two of Rangiora's islands. Our instructor led the way with three Japanese divers and myself following, but we hadn't left the shark meeting point far behind when we heard the instructor yell (not an easy task underwater) and turned around to find one much larger shark following us intently. Was this to be a new variation of the *repas des requins* (shark feeding) which seems to be so popular in French Polynesia? When we all turned to face it, the monster shyly turned away, but as soon as we resumed our drift it swung back to have another look at us. This little dance was repeated several times before it eventually decided to look for something more bite-sized. ■

marine life, particularly the abundance of sharks. But don't expect rich coral formations – the 1982-1983 cyclones were devastating and the deposits swept along by the currents deter coral development.

The configuration of the atoll and the tidal flows create particular diving conditions; Rangiroa is a centre for drift dives which may be better suited to more experienced divers. Everything is regulated by the tide and the current. As the tide rises and falls powerful currents move through the lagoon particularly around its openings (particularly its two passes) to the ocean.

Enormous volumes of water surge into the atoll passes, forming bottlenecks and creating violent currents of nearly six knots. For the diver, these are unforgettable moments; in an incoming current, all you do is immerse yourself in the ocean and let yourself be carried away, accompanied by a procession of fish, through the pass into the lagoon where the effects of the current dissipate. This sensation of being propelled or sucked in is indescribable. For about 10 minutes, divers feel as though they are gliding and flying through the depths of the pass.

When the tide is going out, dives are never made in the pass itself, but outside the reef, along the reef rim and away from the current. In fact, the conditions are riskier since the current is heading for the open sea. Moreover, if the swell or the wind is going in the opposite direction to the current, a phenomenon called *mascaret* is produced at the exit to the pass. The area becomes turbulent with whirlpools and full of suspended particles which make it difficult to see, rendering the site extremely dangerous.

Transport to the sites that are less than 10 minutes away is done by zodiac. The entry procedure is rather daunting: the divers put their equipment on and, at a signal from the instructor, topple backwards into the blue. Because it is impossible to anchor, the pilot remains on the zodiac at the surface and follows the progression of the dive by tracking the bubbles. At the end of the dive, the instructor inflates an inflatable buoy and pulls it, signalling the exact position of the group to the zodiac pilot who comes to collect the divers. To get on board they take off their equipment in the water, lean on the zodiac and heave themselves onto the boat.

Such conditions mean that this type of diving is best suited to more experienced divers, although there are also opportunities for beginners.

Avatoru Pass Four or five different dives can be done in this pass, west of the Avatoru string of islets, where the average depth is about 15 to 20 metres. 'Avatoru' which means 'three passes', is aptly named, as the main pass is divided into two arms by Fara Motu, in the south. In the western channel, called *petite passe* and less than 15 metres deep, there is a lagoon and reef fauna, next to the coral formations. The pointe Papiro, the southern continuation of the petite passe, is ideal for snorkelling. The coral colonies and reef fauna less than five metres under the surface, making this site safe and attractive.

Les Cavernes Between the Avatoru wharf and the eastern side of Fara Motu, Les Cavernes is the name given to a series of crevices sheltering a multitude of fish. Mahuta, south-east of the pass and Fara Motu, is an intermediary zone between the lagoon and the ocean, full of lagoon fish as well as deep-sea species.

The most spectacular dives take place on the external sides, to the right and left of the pass, along the outer rim of the reef. This is where all the manta rays, grey shark, jack, tuna, barracuda and surgeonfish usually converge. The divers follow the outer rim of the reef at 20 to 25 metres' depth until they reach the level of the pass. They then let the current carry them into the lagoon where the zodiac picks them up. It is not unheard of to be escorted into the pass by a few manta rays.

Tiputa Pass This pass lies between the Avatoru string of islets and Tiputa village, 10 km east of the Avatoru Pass. For thousands of divers this represents diving par excellence. Such notoriety results from a large concentration of open-sea species and a particularly strong current. There are dolphins, grey sharks (*raira*), white-pointers (*tapete*), hammerhead sharks (*tamataroa*) and, between November and February, napoleons, barracudas, manta rays and leopard rays. Tiputa is an exceptional submarine plateau.

Some instructors have seen gatherings of several hundred grey sharks outside the pass, but this is a very rare occurrence. However, you will often find yourself face to face with dozens of dogfish. This pass is rougher than the Avatoru channel. With the incoming current, the masses of ocean water which fill the lagoon don't encounter any obstacles

except for Nuhi Nuhi Motu in the south, a narrow little islet which offers little resistance. Tiputa also has open-sea marine life, present in greater numbers and easier to observe than in the Avatoru Pass.

Grotte aux Requins (Shark Cave) This is the most sensational dive in Rangiroa. The entry is particularly impressive, taking place at the edge of the reef drop-off, on the left exit of the pass, in the middle of the ocean, with an incoming current. The descent is made in water of an intense cobalt-blue colour to a depth of 30 metres where you can see rock formations. Only a few metres under the surface you can already see a few inquisitive sharks. However, be careful not to linger, in case you drift and miss the cave 35 metres down.

The cave is in fact an overhanging rock where a line of divers can shelter from the current and watch the predators from a safe distance. A wealth of surgeonfish, mullets, *nasons* and napoleons gravitate around the group of divers. In the background, facing the pass, you'll see a group of grey sharks. The divers then join the pass entrance further to the south and let themselves be swept into the lagoon by the current.

La Vallée Certainly, the topography of the pass has the appearance of a valley. The submarine plateau, which is very wide at the ocean mouth of the channel, narrows at the east and west rims on either side of it, and rises towards the lagoon to the south.

There are a couple of choices: you can explore all the way to the Grotte aux Requins and continue into the pass, or dive directly to a depth of 50 metres. This second option is only available to seasoned divers. Such a deep descent is justified by the presence of hammerhead sharks which remain in the depths and can generally be seen between November and February. The depth reduces progressively, reaching 20 metres at the southern exit of the pass. The current makes the formation of coral impossible and the pass bed looks like an eroded slab. Finally back in the lagoon, divers can swim among small fish.

Le Tombant & l'Éolienne On the ocean side, to the right of the pass exit, Le Tombant and l'Éolienne offer relatively equivalent dives. Free of currents, they are very safe and perfectly suited to the less experienced diver. Le Tombant is immediately after the curve of the channel, while l'Éolienne is a little further east. The dives can be made in either incoming or outgoing currents. Depending on the diver's level of experience, they take place along the outer reef, with depths varying from 15 to 45 metres. Surgeonfish, jacks, grey sharks, barracuda and leopard rays can be seen here. Hammerhead sharks roam the deeper waters between 40 to 55 metres at certain times. Dolphins also appear from time to time.

Rangiroa is not the prerogative of licensed divers only: Nuhi Nuhi Motu, called the Aquarium, south of the Tiputa Pass, at the lagoon entrance, is a favourite place for first dives. In just three metres of water, you can safely take your first steps in the underwater world, surrounded by a multitude of colourful and inquisitive reef fish.

Les Failles This site is not comparable with the others. It is a more conventional dive, to the south-west of the atoll, 1½ hours away from Avatoru by boat. The dive takes place along the outer reef, which is between 10 and 30 metres deep. What makes this exploration interesting are the numerous crevices, tunnels and rifts, all covered in multi-coloured corals. Underwater photographers will love the translucent water and the light reflected on the underwater cliff.

ORGANISED TOURS
Cruises
Archipels Croisières, based in Moorea (see Cruises in the Getting Around chapter) has an 18-metre catamaran based in Rangiroa. Cruises in the Rangiroa atoll are organised regularly either for three days (Saturday to

Monday, 71,000 CFP) or four days (Tuesday to Friday, 95,000 CFP). Costs are per person, including all meals. They depart from Rangiroa and visit the atoll's main sites of interest and include fishing and snorkelling.

On request and in association with the Raie Manta Club (see Dive Centres), there are diving cruises from Rangiroa or Fakarava, for a six-day minimum. Enquire at the Raie Manta Club or at the head office of Archipels Croisières.

The Paradive dive centre will also help you discover the underwater depths of Manihi, Tikehau, Toau or Fakarava on board *Papa Jo*, a 17-metre ketch.

Other Tours
Several small tourist agencies offer excursions to various places on the lagoon. You can enquire directly at the agencies or your guesthouse hosts will do it for you free of charge. The day tours usually include a picnic or a barbecue, and a minimum of four participants will generally be required. The prices quoted are per person.

Les Croisières Bleues (☎ 96-86-01) organises excursions to the Blue Lagoon (5500 CFP), the Sables Roses (8500 CFP) and the Île aux Récifs (5500 CFP). Punua Tamaehu (from the Chez Punua et Moana guesthouse), is the manager of Sharky Parc Excursions (☎ 96-84-73). He arranges two outings a day to discover rays, moray eels and small sharks which are kept in a natural pool.

The company Parasail (☎ 96-04-96) offers you 15 minutes of parasailing, 60 metres above the lagoon, for 5000 CFP.

Atoll Excursions (☎ 96-02-88) works primarily with Kia Ora Village Hotel, but accepts other customers. On board the *Heikura Iti*, he will take you to the Blue Lagoon or the Île aux Récifs for 6500 CFP or to the Sables Roses for 8500 CFP. You can also go fishing (four people maximum) for 7500 CFP per hour.

Tane Tamaehu, from Chez Henriette, owns Tetiare Excursions (☎ 96-85-85 or 96-84-68). He specialises in tours to the Blue Lagoon, for which he charges 5500 CFP.

With Matahi Tepa (☎ 96-84-48), you can

THE TUAMOTUS

savour the underwater sights aboard a glass-bottom boat. A tour of Nuhi Nuhi Motu, south of Tiputa Pass, takes 1½ hours and costs 1700 CFP.

The Kia Ora Village Hotel offers more expensive excursions than the other agencies: 9000 CFP to the Blue Lagoon, 9000 CFP to the Île aux Récifs, 12,000 CFP to the Sables Roses, 1800 CFP for the glass-bottom boat tour, 5000 CFP for parasailing and 2000 CFP to go long-line fishing. The hotel has three boats: *Tukute*, *Parata* and Ava. Aboard *Te Onoono* (☎ 96-85-61), whose owner works exclusively with the Kia Ora Village, you can go around Avatoru Island for three hours, via the two passes, for 4000 CFP. A snorkelling stop is made at one of them. The boat is occasionally escorted by dolphins.

Alban, Cécile's husband (from the Chez Cécile guesthouse), knows the atoll and its history very well and organises tours to Otepipi for 6000 CFP.

PLACES TO STAY

Whether you choose to spend the night in a tent, a family guesthouse or a luxurious over-water bungalow, the choice in Rangiroa is vast. Guesthouses and hotels are dotted over a distance of 10 km from the village of Avatoru in the west to the village of Tiputa, beyond the Tiputa Pass, in the east. On the other hand, the prices do not vary much: apart from the luxury hotels, most guesthouses charge relatively similar prices. To be on the safe side, it's wise to book in but once you are there you can change to another place if you prefer. Prices quoted are per person per day and transfers to and from the airport are included, unless otherwise indicated.

Almost all the places to stay organise tours, either directly or through tour agencies.

PLACES TO STAY – BOTTOM END
Avatoru

Hotels and guesthouses are on the edge of the lagoon, on the Avatoru string of islets. Bungalows usually accommodate two people, but a mattress or single bed can be added.

Chez Henriette (☎ 96-84-68, Avatoru,

Rangiroa), in the Avatoru village next to the Daniel shop and close to the marina, has four bungalows with bathroom (cold water only) for 5000 CFP demi-pension, or 6000 CFP full board.

A little further along the ocean side, you will notice a fare next to an independence flag. This is the kingdom of the Tamaehu, which owns the guesthouse *Chez Punua et Moana* (☎ 96-84-73; BP 54 Avatoru, Rangiroa), directly opposite, on the lagoon side. Their two bungalows with shared bathroom are 4000/5000 CFP, half/full board. The Tamaehu used to rent out a bungalow in Teavatia Motu, but have now replaced this with an excursion to the Green Lagoon for 3000 CFP per person, picnic included. Punua has made a name for himself as a boat builder, which he still does occasionally. He is also the person behind the slickly named Sharky Parc Excursions (see Organised Tours).

Nearby, the *Herenui* guesthouse (☎ 96-84-71; BP 31 Avatoru, Rangiroa) is next to the Raie Manta Club. Its five bungalows, only three of which are rented out, have cold-water bathrooms and are available for 5000/6000 CFP half/full board.

Rangiroa Lodge (☎ 96-82-13; Avatoru, Rangiroa), also next to the Raie Manta Club, is a favourite spot for divers, and Jacques and Rofina Ly are famous for their warm welcome. A bed in a six-bed dormitory costs 1500 CFP, and a bed in one of the four independent rooms in the same fare is 2000 CFP (meals not included). They're equipped with mosquito nets and shared bathroom (cold water). Add 200 CFP for rental of a fan. Breakfast is 500 CFP and lunch and dinner are 1500 CFP each, but the owners prefer you to cook your own meals in the kitchen.

The *Hinanui* guesthouse (☎ 96-84-61; BP 16 Avatoru, Rangiroa) is 200 metres further on and has two comfortable bungalows with mezzanines that can accommodate four people and a bungalow for two with bathroom (cold water) for 3000 CFP (bed only), 5500/6500 CFP half/full board per person. A fourth bungalow is being added as well as a fare restaurant. The owners' house is opposite, on the ocean side. Mme Bizien prides herself on serving French, Spanish and Chinese meals, and even her own couscous. Credit cards are accepted.

Chez Nanua (☎ 96-83-88; BP 54, Avatoru, Rangiroa) is set back from the Pareo Carole shop and will suit the traveller on a tight budget since it is the cheapest address in Rangiroa. Nanua Tamaehu and his wife, Marie, offer a six-bed dormitory, a great family fare with a mezzanine and bathroom (cold water) and four small bungalows with shared bathroom. It will cost you 3000 CFP per person, full board in the dormitory: 3500 CFP for the small bungalow and 4500 CFP for the big fare. The dorm is not very clean and the iron roof is only partly water-proof. The last resort for the insolvent traveller is to set up a tent next to the bungalows for 1000 CFP per person, 2000 CFP with the three meals. The simple meals are taken with the family.

Chez Cécile (☎ 96-05-06; BP 98, Avatoru, Rangiroa), is halfway between the airport and the village and is famous for Cécile's superb cooking. The meals are succulent and generous, based mostly on local specialities and taken under a *fare potee*. The two bungalows for two to three people and the bungalow with a mezzanine for five people are comfortable and clean; with bathroom and mosquito net, they cost 5000/6000 CFP half/full board. Cécile's English is OK and credit cards are accepted.

The newest guesthouse in Rangiroa, *Turiroa Village* (☎ & fax 96-04-27; BP 26, Avatoru, Rangiroa), is just west of the airport. The four bungalows for four people, with mezzanine, bathroom (cold water) and fan, are all fitted. Half/full board costs 5000/6000 CFP and longer term rates are available.

Chez Martine (☎ 96-02-51 or 96-02-53; BP 68, Avatoru, Rangiroa), about 600 metres west of the airport, is entitled to be very proud of its Polynesian cooking. Everyone will find something to enjoy among the vanilla fish, tartare de thon (tuna tartare), crêpes flambées aux fruits, etc. The dining room looks directly out on the lagoon. The

six bungalows with bathroom (cold water) and a fan, accommodating two to four people each, are impeccably clean and cost 5000/6000 CFP half/full board. The Tetua also has a pearl farm. Credit cards are accepted.

Next door, *Chez Félix et Judith* (☎ 96-04-41, BP 18, Avatoru, Rangiroa) has four bungalows that can accommodate two to four people, with bathroom (cold water). The dining room is spacious, but a little impersonal. Half/full board costs 4500/5500 CFP. Félix Tetua has important political responsibilities in the Tahoeraa Huiraatira, Gaston Flosse's party.

In contrast to its counterparts, the *Tuamotel* (☎ 96-02-88 or 96-03-34, fax 96-02-90; BP 29, Avatoru, Rangiroa) offers room-only accommodation. It's well hidden behind the coconut plantation, east of the Avatoru string of islets and right next to the Six Passengers dive centre. It is a large and comfortable family bungalow with mezzanine and costs 4500 CFP per person per day. The price decreases according to the length of stay, for instance, it costs 6500 CFP per day for two people for a one-week stay. Transfers from the airport are not included and cost 500 CFP per person.

The *Teina et Marie* guesthouse (☎ 96-03-94, fax 96-84-44; BP 36, Avatoru, Rangiroa), at the end of the Avatoru string of islets, on the edge of the Tiputa Pass (access through the track that crosses the coconut plantation, on the left, about 200 metres before the Paradive dive centre), is a great success among divers. It is only a few dozen metres' walk to Paradive or to the Raie Manta Club annexe. The food is delicious and generous and meals are taken in a large fare opposite the lagoon. There are seven comfortable bungalows (with bathrooms) of varied sizes, accommodating one to five people. The per-person cost is 5000/6000 CFP half/full board.

Lovers of fine food will enjoy Glorine's cooking, the owner of the *Chez Glorine* guesthouse (☎ 96-04-05 or 96-03-58; fax 96-03-58, call first) on the end of the Avatoru string of islets, next to the wharf and the

Paradive dive centre. She has made a name as a fine cordon bleu chef and her mahi-mahi or parrotfish, prepared in a host of ways, are always marvellously tasty. Glorine has her taro delivered from Tubuai, where she was born, and will garnish your plate with taro chips and uru (breadfruit). Her pancakes and famous banana cake have long tempted visitors. The meals are taken in a fare potee, on the edge of the lagoon. She has three two-person bungalows and three family bungalows with bathroom (cold water). They're well looked after and cost 5000/6000 CFP half/full board. Glorine charges 800 CFP per family for transfers to the airport. Credit cards are accepted but cash is preferred.

Tiputa

Chez Lucien (☎ 96-73-55; BP 69, Tiputa, Rangiroa), on the edge of the pass, on the lagoon side, is a well-maintained guesthouse that is certain to please. For 4000/6000 CFP half/full board, there are three spacious bungalows available, one accommodating as many as seven people, with a mezzanine and bathroom (cold water). Transfers to the airport are 500 CFP return per person. The generous meals are served in a covered dining room on the edge of the lagoon. If you stay for a minimum of three nights, Lucien will take you for a free picnic on a motu.

At the village exit, in a coconut plantation next to the ocean, the *Pension Estall* (☎ 96-73-16 or 96-74-16; BP15, Tiputa, Rangiroa) belongs to the mayor, Ronald Estall, as does the Tiputa shop. He obviously prefers to invest his energies in his political and business activities, for the guesthouse is poorly looked after. The four bungalows and the big main house for 11 people are advertised for 3500/5000 CFP half/full board. Transfers are not included.

PLACES TO STAY – MIDDLE

Avatoru

The *Miki Miki Village* (☎ 96-83-83, fax 43-99-63 in Papeete; BP 5, Avatoru, Rangiroa) has succeeded Rangiroa Village. The nine fan-cooled bungalows, entirely renovated

with bathroom (hot water), for two to four people cost 6000 CFP per person including breakfast, or 8000 CFP demi-pension. Couples pay 12,000/14,000 CFP. The restaurant-bar has a balcony overhanging the lagoon. The hotel organises its own tours, including the Blue Lagoon (6000 CFP) or the Sables Roses or the Île aux Récifs (9000 CFP). Credit cards are accepted.

Pension Tuanake (☎ 96-03-29, fax 96-04-45, BP 21, Avatoru, Rangiroa), two seconds away from Gauguin's Pearl, almost halfway between the airport and the village, has two small and two large bungalows with room for three or six people, with bathroom (cold water) and fan and is extremely clean. Per person costs start at 6000/8000 CFP for half/full board in the smaller bungalows and decrease as you pack more people in. The food here has a good reputation. Credit cards are accepted.

The *Raira Lagoon* (☎ 96-04-23, fax 96-05-86; BP 87 Avatoru, Rangiroa), 4.5 km east of the village and 1.5 km west of the airport, has seven individual bungalows for two people, one bungalow for three, and two twin bungalows for a family, with bathroom (cold water) and fan. All are comfortable, well maintained and marvellously clean. For two people the per person costs are 7000/9000 CFP for half/full board. You will have to pay an extra 4000 CFP if you are alone. Add 800 CFP for the transfers to the airport. The restaurant balcony faces the lagoon and the French chef serves fine cuisine, specialising in fish dishes. Credit cards are accepted.

The décor of the 11 bungalows at the *Rangiroa Beach Club* (☎ 96-03-34 or 43-08-29; fax 96-02-90 or 41-09-28 in Papeete; BP 17, Avatoru, Rangiroa), 150 metres from the Raira lagoon, is attractive, with cane furniture, bath (hot water) and fan. This hotel belongs to the THR group, which also owns the Tahiti Country Club in Punaaui and the Moorea Beach Club and concentrates on group tours. You might get a bungalow if you negotiate with the manager; allow 10,000 to 15,000 CFP per room. The Rangiroa Beach Club organises its own excursions, including the Blue Lagoon (6500 CFP), the Sables Roses (9500 CFP) and the Île aux Récifs (6500 CFP). Credit cards are accepted.

Tiputa

The *Relais Mihiroa* (☎ 96-72-14, fax 96-75-13; BP 51 Tiputa, Rangiroa) would be the favoured destination of any traveller seeking a Robinson Crusoe-type of holiday. Honeyed beaches, coconut palms bending in the trade winds – this is an idyllic place. However, the Relais Mirihoa is about four km east of the village, on the edge of the lagoon. You must therefore be prepared to pay transport costs: 1500 CFP per person for a transfer to the airport, and 400 CFP per car trip to the Tiputa wharf. Alternatively, you can hire a bicycle for 500 CFP.

Costs are 6000/7500 CFP half/full board to spend heavenly days in one of the four bungalows with bathroom (cold water), fan and cane furniture. You can borrow flippers and masks to explore the coral formations close to the shore. Meals are served on the terrace of a fare, facing the lagoon. Although the food is OK, it's no match for the variety and generosity of the best guesthouses in Avatoru, and drinks are extremely expensive: a bottle of mineral water costs 300 CFP.

The proprietors, who have their own boat and organise excursions. They charge 7500 CFP per person to the Blue Lagoon and 8500 CFP to the Sables Roses. Credit cards are accepted.

PLACES TO STAY – TOP END

The supreme symbol of luxury hotels in the Tuamotu Islands, the *Kia Ora Village Hotel* (☎ 96-03-84, fax 96-04-93; BP 1, Tiputa, Rangiroa) has 45 dream bungalows dotted in a magnificent coconut plantation on the edge of the lagoon, 2.5 km east of the airport. Everything is beautifully set out in this tropical Eden. The annexe of 10 over-water bungalows is reached by a wooden bridge over the lagoon. The 10 beach bungalows and the five suites are on the beach. All the ingredients of luxury are provided: hot water, fan, fine wood or cane furniture, meticulous décor, terraces and the most

beautiful white-sand beach in the atoll. Not to mention the restaurant-bar on stilts (see Places to Eat) and a complete programme of activities, ranging from scuba diving to excursions on the lagoon (see Organised Tours) as well as tennis and windsurfing.

This temple of luxury comes at a price: 32,000 CFP for a beach bungalow or a suite and 49,000 CFP for an over-water bungalow for two people. For a third person, allow an extra 4500 CFP and add 8% tax. You will have to spend another 5300 CFP per person for breakfast and dinner or 7800 CFP for full board. Credit cards are accepted and there are money-changing facilities for hotel patrons.

PLACES TO STAY – OTHER MOTUS

Sara Nantz, an American living in Rangiroa, owner of *Village Sans Souci* (☎ 96-83 72), used to have a uniquely novel offer: nine bungalows (with shared bathroom) on Mahuta Motu, about nine km west of Avatoru Pass and completely cut off from the world. Full-board cost 7500 CFP per person (three-night minimum), and airport transfers were 16,000 CFP per couple. Unfortunately, this business did not attract the number of customers it required and it was up for sale as this book was being written. Once you are there, enquire whether this guesthouse will eventually reopen.

The Kia Ora Village Hotel (see Places to Stay – top end) has an annexe on Avearahi Motu, south of the lagoon, about an hour away by boat, called Kia Ora Sauvage. The setting of this motu will delight you. The five fare, typical of this area, are rented for 24,000 CFP(for two), to which you must add 8% for tax, compulsory full board (7000 CFP per person) and the boat transfer (7500 CFP return). There is a two-night minimum stay.

PLACES TO EAT

Eating in Rangiroa offers a range of possibilities for all tastes and budgets. There are grocery stores and snack bars or guesthouse and hotel restaurants.

Shops & Snack Bars

Avatoru has a few well-stocked supermarkets, all in the village. The same is true of Tiputa, where you can buy provisions in Tiputa and Maihiti. You can enjoy coconut-bread and firifiri (doughnuts) at the pâtisserie Afaro (☎ 96-04-91), on the ocean side less than 1.5 km east of Avatoru Village and run by a Frenchman. Orders must be placed the day before and it's closed on Monday.

Each village has a few snack bars where you can eat in or take away. There's also a bar at the airport which opens before every flight. The *Chez Béatrice* snack bar (☎ 96-04-12), about five km east of Avatoru, on the lagoon side and opposite the cultured pearl school is a little more formal. The décor is stark but the place is impeccably clean and the food is OK. It provides an opportunity to eat Chinese food: a vegetable omelette is 980 CFP, maa tinito (pork and red kidney beans) is 750 CFP and baby goat curry is 1200 CFP. A Hinano beer costs 290 CFP. It's open daily from 11 am to 10 pm.

In Tiputa, an unusual destination for lunch is the restaurant of the CETAD technical school. The students prepare and serve the food and there is a fixed menu for 1000 CFP which might feature quiche lorraine, fish with bananas, poulet basquaise or tarte. You can get a boat transfer from the wharf next to the Chez Glorine guesthouse, on the east end of the Avatoru string of islets, near the pass. Lunch is available only on Tuesday and Thursday and booking is imperative on ☎ 96-72-96 or ☎ 96-02-68 at the weekend.

Another cheap eatery in Tiputa is the small kiosk opposite the CETAD. If you have a solid stomach, try the fish-cakes (maoa) for 100 CFP. More wisely, order kebabs (100 CFP), chicken and chips (500 CFP) or poulet Saladruce (Russian chicken salad) for 500 CFP.

Guesthouse Restaurants

The full-board formula, chosen by the majority of travellers in the Tuamotu archipelago, is a bit constrictive in Rangiroa. You can enjoy more variety by choosing demi-pension and having lunch or dinner in different places.

Some guesthouses are renowned for their excellent cooking and accept nonresident customers, provided they have places available and you have booked in advance. This is true for *Chez Glorine*, *Chez Martine*, *Raira Lagon*, *Teina et Marie*, *Relais Mihiroa* and *Chez Lucien*. Allow between 1500 and 2500 CFP for a meal, not including drinks. There is a set menu.

Hotel Restaurants

It is also worth exploring hotel restaurants with à la carte menus (see Places to Stay). The cuisine at the *Rangiroa Beach Club* offers a great range of meat, fish and poultry dishes at moderate prices. The chicken grilled in lime, for instance, costs only 1200 CFP. Excellent cocktails, such as maitai, are served at the bar.

The cuisine at *Kia Ora Village Hotel* is, of course, high class. In a setting full of charm, the chef at the over-water restaurant-bar offers a wide and appetising menu of Polynesian and French dishes. The prices vary from 1100 to 2300 CFP per dish. Dinner costs 3800 CFP and there is a choice of three entrees and three main courses, one or two of which will invariably be fresh fish. Twice a week there is a sumptuous buffet with barbecued and grilled meat and fish from the lagoon. A Polynesian dance show follows. Allow about 800 CFP for the cocktails served at the bar.

Miki Miki Village turns into a food-bar at lunchtime, with a 2200 CFP menu regardless of the specialities offered. The restaurant looks out over the lagoon. Aperitifs and cocktails cost 500 and 600 CFP respectively.

THINGS TO BUY

A few shops around Avatoru sell souvenirs, postcards, hand-painted *pareus*, film and a few local handicrafts. Go shopping at Pareo Carole, about 1.5 km east of the village, close to the Nanua guesthouse, at Ocean Passion. Or, 300 metres further on there's Rangi Boutique, about 2.2 km east of the village (next to Rangi Atelier). Another good place is Le

Coquillage, 300 metres after the Chez Béatrice snack bar.

If you wish to buy pearls, contact the owners of the pearl farms direct (see the earlier section on Pearl Farms). There is also a modest jewellery shop at the entrance to the village. Pearls can also be bought from a couple of college teachers who sell them directly from their house, about 800 metres past the airport on the lagoon side.

GETTING THERE & AWAY
Air
The airport is about 5.5 km east of Avatoru village. The office of the Air Tahiti representative (☎ 96-03-41 or 96-05-03) is inside the air terminal fare building. It is open Monday to Thursday from 8 am to noon and from 1 to 4.30 pm. On Friday it opens from 8 am to noon and from 1 to 5.50 pm; on Saturday, Sunday and public holidays, it varies according to flights.

Rangiroa is connected to the Tahiti, Bora Bora and the Marquesas. There are a few daily flights between Rangiroa and Papeete, which take 70 minutes. Rangiroa is also a centre for access to other Tuamotu atolls like Tikehau, Manihi, Kaukura, Fakarava, Faaite and Apataki. From the Windward Islands, there is a direct flight from Bora Bora to Rangiroa on Wednesday, Friday and Sunday, with a continuation to Manihi on Friday, and a Rangiroa-Bora Bora flight from Manihi on Friday. Manihi is serviced by the Papeete-Rangiroa-Manihi-Nuku Hiva flights on Saturday, Papeete-Rangiroa-Napuka (alternating with Puka Puka)-Atuona on Wednesday and Atuona-Napuka (alternating with Puka Puka)-Rangiroa-Papeete on Friday.

The Rangiroa-Papeete flight costs 13,600 CFP one way; Rangiroa-Tikehau, Rangiroa-Kaukura and Rangiroa-Fakarava cost 4400 CFP; Rangiroa-Manihi costs 8800 CFP; Rangiroa-Bora Bora costs 20,700 CFP; and Rangiroa-Nuku Hiva or Atuona cost 24,500 CFP.

Sea
Dory, Manava 2, Vai-Aito, Saint Xavier Maris Stella and *Rairoa Nui* serve Rangiroa.

They load and unload freight at the wharf in Avatoru Pass and the wharf close to the guesthouse Chez Glorine on the other end of the motu string, as well as the Tiputa wharf next to the town hall.

The *Aranui*, on the way back from the Marquesas, also stops at Rangiroa for half a day, anchoring in the lagoon, opposite the Kia Ora Village Hotel, the last stop before Papeete. For more information see Inter-Island Ships – The Tuamotus in the Getting Around chapter.

GETTING AROUND
A sealed road that runs almost in a straight line links Avatoru village at the western end of the string of islets to Tiputa Pass at the eastern extremity, some 10 km apart. There is no regular service crossing the pass to from the Avatoru islets to Tiputa village. However, there are often speedboats travelling between the wharf east of the Avatoru islets, next to Chez Glorine, and the Tiputa landing platform. You will have no difficulty getting aboard.

To/From the Airport
The airport is 5.5 km east of Avatoru village. If you have booked accommodation, your hosts will be there to welcome you. Transfers are not automatically included in the accommodation price.

Car, Scooter & Bicycle
Rangi Location (☎ 96-84-92), part of the Europcar group, is 2.2 km east of the village on the lagoon side, and hires out Mokes (small jeep-like open cars) for 6000 CFP for four hours or 7000 CFP for eight hours, scooters for 3000 CFP for eight hours or bicycles for 500 CFP for eight hours.

Pareo Carole (☎ 96-82-45), close to Chez Nanua and about 800 metres east of the village, offers bicycles for 500/1000 CFP for a half/full day and scooters for 3000/4000 for a half/full day CFP. Kia Ora Village also rents out bicycles for 400/800 CFP for a half/full day and scooters for 3500/4800 CFP for a half/full day. Some guesthouses also offer bicycles to their customers for equivalent prices.

Organised Tours

For boat excursions on the lagoon see the preceding Organised Tours section.

Northern Tuamotu Atolls

Though Rangiroa is the main tourist destination in the Tuamotu archipelago, other atolls in the north of the archipelago are also well equipped for tourism.

The northern group comprises Makatea, south-west of Rangiroa, Tikehau and Mataiva in the west and Manihi and Ahe in the north-east. Only Tikehau, Mataiva and Manihi have airports and tourist accommodation. Ahe is visited mainly by yachts.

Further to the east, Takaroa and Takapoto, accessible by plane, also have accommodation facilities. The atolls to the east of Rangiroa, Aratua and Kaukura, are less well known. Further to the south-east, the giant Fakarava competes in size with Rangiroa. Anaa is a small atoll further south.

MAKATEA
Population: 40
Surface Area: 30 sq km

Flying between Papeete and Rangiroa, the pilot might draw your attention to the raised atoll of Makatea, 210 km north-east of Tahiti. The only high island in the Tuamotus, Makatea is a bean-shaped plateau with precipitous cliffs 80 metres high forming its outer edge. These cliffs are in fact a former barrier-reef and the plateau was once the basin of the former lagoon where vast amounts of phosphate accumulated. It is thought that the atoll may have emerged as an indirect consequence of the uplifting of Tahiti.

The original history of Makatea, discovered by the Dutch navigator Roggeveen in 1722, is intimately linked to the exploitation of phosphate, the presence of which was noted at the end of the 19th century. The CFPO (Compagnie française des phosphates d'Océanie) was created in 1908 to exploit the deposit on a grand scale. Infrastructure appeared from nowhere: industrial equipment (including a rail network), houses, schools, a cinema, places of worship and shops. Until the beginning of the 1950s, labour came largely from Asia.

With more than 3071 inhabitants in 1962, Makatea was the most populated island of the Tuamotu archipelago. Vaitepaua mushroomed like a boom town in a gold rush. The only difficulties were the shallow waters and the absence of a lagoon, forcing the mineral ships to anchor some distance away from the harbour. The transfers were made by barge until 1954, when a 100-metre metal jetty was built.

Makatea phosphate became the core of the French Polynesian economy. From 12,000 tonnes in 1911, the extraction rate rose to 251,000 tonnes in 1929 and 400,000 tonnes in 1960, a record year. Until WWII, exports were mainly to Japan, New Zealand and Australia. From 1956, phosphate became the most valuable export, ahead of copra and vanilla.

The depletion of reserves in 1966 brought this industrial epic to an end. Nearly 11 million tonnes of phosphate had been torn from the island. In the space of a few weeks, the workers packed everything up and Vaitepaua became a ghost town. Today only a few people live in Moumu, making their living from copra production and the sale of *kaveu* (coconut crab) to passing tuna boats.

The cessation of mining in Makatea had little impact, however three years earlier, the CEP (Centre d'expérimentation du Pacifique) had been established in Moruroa, and Fangataufa and Polynesia had entered the nuclear age.

TIKEHAU
Population: 312 inhabitants
Lagoon Area: 461.2 sq km
Passes: 1

Tikehau, just 14 km west of Rangiroa, was discovered on 25 April 1816 by the Russian

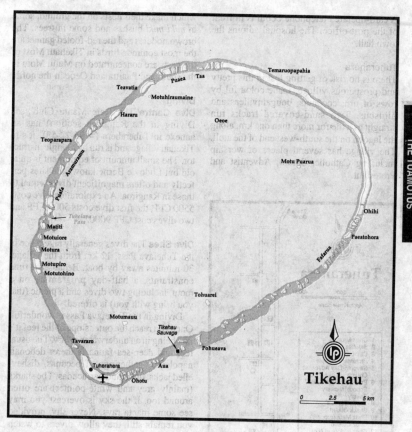

Puaea
Taa
Temaruopapahia
Teavatia
Motuhiraumaine
Hararu
Oeoe
Teoparapara
Motu Puarua
Alamumumu
Puafa
Ohihi
Tuheiava Pass
Paeatohora
Matiti
Motuiore
Motura
Fafarua
Motupiro
Motutohino
Tohuarei
Motumauu
Tikehau
Sauvage
Tavararo
Pohueava
Tuherahera
Aua
Ohotu

Tikehau

0   2.5   5 km

navigator Kotzebue. The atoll forms a ring, slightly oval-shaped, which is 26 km on its longest diameter. It's cut by only one pass, Tuheiava in the west, and by more than 100 hoa. Dotting the lagoon are a number of motus which provide nesting-grounds for birds. Tikehau has been the subject of detailed research into reef and lagoon environments, conducted by ORSTOM, the French oceanographic research organisation.

The inhabitants are grouped in the village of Tuherahera, in the south-west of the atoll. Their livelihood is fishing, as the variety and quantity of fish is exceptional. Frequent connections by plane and boat to Tahiti allow the transport of fresh fish to the markets of Papeete. The enchanting landscape of the motu and the quietness of Tuherahera mean that more and more Tahitians are choosing Tikehau as their holiday destination.

Information
There is no bank in Tikehau. The post office is open Monday, Wednesday and Friday from 7.30 to 9.30 am, and Tuesday and Thursday from 7.30 to 11.30 am. The post office has fax facilities and sells phonecards.

A card-operated telephone booth is in front of the post office. The hospital adjoins the town hall.

Tuherahera

There is no risk of getting lost in this pretty and prosperous village, made colourful by rows of uru, coconuts, bougainvilleas and hibiscus. Two sand-covered tracks run straight as a die for more than one km, along the lagoon on the south-west end of the atoll. The village has several places of worship including Catholic, Sanito, Adventist and Protestant.

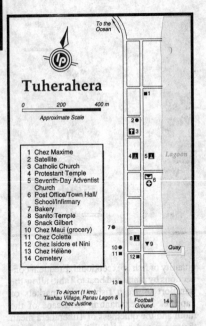

To the Ocean

Tuherahera

0   200   400 m

Approximate Scale

1 Chez Maxime
2 Satellite
3 Catholic Church
4 Protestant Temple
5 Seventh-Day Adventist Church
6 Post Office/Town Hall/School/Infirmary
7 Bakery
8 Sanito Temple
9 Snack Gilbert
10 Chez Maui (grocery)
11 Chez Colette
12 Chez Isidore et Nini
13 Chez Hélène
14 Cemetery

Lagoon

Quay

To Airport (1 km), Tikehau Village, Panau Lagon & Chez Justine

Football Ground

Fish Parks

There are numerous fish parks close to the Tuheiava Pass.

Îles aux Oiseaux

On the lagoon, the scattered motus are inhabited by several species of birds, some of which make their nests on the ground, some in miki miki bushes and some in trees. The brown noddies and the red-footed gannet are the most common birds in Tikehau. Most of the nests are concentrated on Mauu Motu in the south and Puarua and Oeoe in the north.

Diving

Dive Centre The Raie Manta Club (see Diving in the Rangiroa section) has an annexe in Tuherahera (☎ 96-22-53). It's in Tikehau village and is run by a single instructor. The small amount of equipment is quite old but Ludovic Berne knows the sites perfectly and offers magnificent dives, equal to those in Rangiroa. An exploration dive costs 5500 CFP, the first dive costs 5000 CFP and two dives cost CFP 9000.

Dive Sites The dives generally take place in the Tuheiava Pass, 12 km from the village, 30 minutes away by boat. Because of time constraints, a half-day programme on a motu, including two dives and a picnic (that you bring with you) is offered.

Diving in the Tuheiava Pass is wonderful. Once you reach the outer slope of the reef it's like being in an underwater aviary. The usual reef and deep-sea fauna is there: debonair napoleons, gatherings of becunas, dishevelled jacks, tunas and barracudas. The sharks (mainly grey and white-pointer) are often around too. If the sky is overcast you may see some manta rays. Never shy, provided you remain still, they allow divers to watch their nonchalant and graceful dance.

Most of this takes place between the surface and a depth of 30 metres. Finally, you'll be carried by the current into the lagoon and a coral garden. In scarcely a few metres of water, under a rock overhang, you can often see a tight group of white-pointer lagoon sharks. Protected in this improvised 'nursery', they enjoy a breather without moving too much.

Places to Stay

Accommodation in Tikehau is unlikely to disappoint you. There are a few superior guesthouses which charge moderate prices and offer comparable services. You may choose between a bungalow and a room. Four are in the village and three are close to the airport, less than 1.5 km from Turaherera. Prices quoted are per person per day and include transfers to the airport.

North of the village, close to the lagoon, the *Chez Maxime* guesthouse (☎ 96-22-38) offers four rooms for two people and one room for four people. These are quite satisfactory, with shared bathroom (cold water), and cost 3500/4500 CFP for half/full board. The food is fairly ordinary, comprising mostly lagoon fish and rice or vegetables. It is a pity that all the mosquitoes in the village seem to head for this guesthouse.

The *Chez Isidore et Nini* guesthouse (☎ 96-22-38), near the village entrance coming from the airport, belongs to the same family as Chez Maxime and charges the same prices: 3500/4500 CFP for half/full board. There are three spartan and impersonal bedrooms for two people, with shared bathroom. The food is nothing special, but the garden is beautiful with uru, bougainvillea, kava, lemon, hibiscus and coconut trees all around the house.

Also in the village, *Chez Colette* (☎ 96-22-47) about 100 metres from Chez Isidore et Nini, right next to the grocer's shop Chez Maui, is well kept and brilliantly clean. The Huri family offers five rooms for two people, one with bath (cold water), for 3000/5000 CFP half/full board. There is an equipped kitchen, but if you don't want to cook meals are served in a comfortable outdoor dining room.

For comfort and service, the *Pension Hélène* (☎ 96-22-52), at the village entrance on the left track coming from the airport, is hard to beat. For 3500/4500 CFP half/full board, Hélène, the post-office agent, offers two rooms for two or three people, shared bathroom (cold water) and a fan. It is immaculate. Hélène also offers a night in a small chalet on a private motu for 1500 CFP per person.

Situated 600 metres from the village and 400 metres on the left coming from the airport, *Tikehau Village* (☎ 96-22-86),

managed by Caroline and Paea Tefaiao, is an attractive place. Its seven bungalows for two to four people, with bathroom (cold water) and fan, are built on the edge of an enchanting beach. Rays and sharks come up to the water's edge to beg a few morsels from the tourists. To spend a few happy days in this picture-postcard landscape will cost you 5500/6700 CFP half/full board. Meals, based on local specialities, are served in a large fare potee which also has a bar.

Tikehau Sauvage is also run by the Tefaiao couple. It is a set of four bungalows with shared shower on Ahumiti Motu, about three hours north-east by boat. The prices are the same as at Tikehau Village.

On the edge of the lagoon, 1.2 km from the village entrance and 250 metres on the right coming from the airport, *Panau Lagon* (☎ 96-22-34, 96-22-99) has five comfortable bungalows for two people and one bungalow for four people with bathroom (cold shower) and mosquito nets. Prices are 4000/5500 CFP for half/full board, and credit cards are accepted.

Chez Justine (☎ 96-22-88 or 96-22-37), on the edge of the lagoon, 1.5 km from the village entrance and 500 metres on the right coming from the airport, is in the most isolated location. Needless to say, it will suit those souls in search of peace and solitude. Relaxing in one of the five clean and friendly bungalows (one is a family bungalow) with bathroom (cold water), will cost 4500/5000 CFP half/full board.

Places to Eat

Apart from the guesthouses, there are not many places to eat. The *Chez Maui* shop is a multiservice grocery and on some days of the week you will find coconut cakes in the only bakery in the village.

The only exception in this deprived area is *Snack Gilbert*, next to a huge breadfruit tree on the lagoon side, opposite the small Sanito temple. It is more like a food stall than a food bar and the menu is purely hypothetical since everything relies on deliveries. Allow 600 CFP for a plate of chao men, maa tinito (pork and kidney beans) or fish with rice. The hours vary with the weather forecast and the owner's moods.

Getting There & Away

Air The airport is little more than a km from the village entrance which is to the east. The Air Tahiti representative can be reached on ☎ 96-62-66. Air Tahiti has four weekly flights between Papeete and Tikehau: Wednesday and Friday (Papeete-Rangiroa-Tikehau-Papeete), Saturday (Papeete-Tikehau-Rangiroa-Papeete) and Sunday (Papeete-Mataiva-Tikehau-Papeete), by ATR 42. The Papeete-Tikehau fare is 13,600 CFP, the Tikehau-Rangiroa fare is 4400 CFP.

Sea The *Rairoa Nui*, *Manava 2*, *Saint Xavier Maris Stella*, *Dory* and *Vai-Aito* all stop in Tikehau and tie up at the wharf on the lagoon side (see Inter-Island Ships – The Tuamotus in the Getting Around chapter).

Getting Around

A 10-km track goes around the motu on which Tuherahera is situated and passes by the airport. Your hosts can hire or lend you bicycles. The Tikehau Village guesthouse has several bicycles in good working order.

To visit the fish parks and the Île aux Oiseaux, consult your hosts directly, since nearly all of them have boats. Allow 3000 CFP to 4000 CFP for an excursion to the Île aux Oiseaux, 2000 CFP for a picnic on a motu, and 3000 CFP for a visit to the fish parks in the pass.

MATAIVA
Population: 200
Lagoon Area: 25 sq km
Passes: 1

The first European to land on Mataiva, at the north-west end of the Tuamotu archipelago, was Bellinghausen in 1820. There is a great risk that its appearance will change dramatically in the years to come as there are plans to mine the lagoon substratum which contains about 70 separate phosphate deposits, succeeding Makatea, which closed in 1966. The accessible part is estimated to contain 12 million tonnes, enough for 10 to 15 years of mining. Such large-scale industrial activity

---

From Coconut to Copra

Copra is found everywhere in the Tuamotus and Marquesas, and you can recognise it by the unmistakable, rancid smell it gives off in the coconut plantations, on the rack dryers or in the warehouses near the wharves.

Copra (which comes from the Tamil word *kopparah*) is the dry residue of the white substance lining the inside of the coconut. Rich in vegetable fat (palmitin), it is regularly collected by schooners and taken to Papeete. Crushed, heated, pressed and refined in oil, it is then sold to the food and cosmetics industries.

Copra production is relatively recent. Introduced by the missionaries towards the end of the 1860s, it has continued to develop and is still an essential economic activity on numerous islands and atolls in Polynesia.

The copra producers go outside the village to the coconut plantations, and gather the coconuts fallen on the ground. Their basic tools include a machete and a *pana*, an implement with a short handle and a curved, narrow metal blade. The coconuts are split with a blow from the machete. The half nuts are then turned over and left in the sun for a few days.

The second operation consists of scooping out the coconut: using a pana, the copra producer separates the dried kernel from the shell with a quick, vigorous twisting action. The shavings collected are then placed on copra dryers, like raised racks topped with a movable roof to protect them from rain, until completely desiccated.

They are then packed in hessian bags, weighed and put away in a hangar until the schooner arrives to collect them. The copra producer is paid directly by the inspector at the time of weighing, or by the supercargo when loading the ship, at a rate of 80 or 60 CFP per kg, depending on the quality. ∎

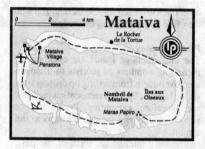

Mataiva

Le Rocher
de la Tortue

Mataiva
Village
Pensions

Nombril de
Mataiva

Îles aux
Oiseaux

Marae Papiro

in such a restricted space will automatically aggravate ecological problems.

Pahua, the village, is divided in two by a pass that is just a few metres wide and no deeper than 1.5 metres. At the same level as the reef, this pass only allows light boats to get through. A bridge spans the pass and links the two parts of the village. Nine hoa, thin trickles of water, provide small links between the lagoon and the ocean. Mataiva (literally 'nine eyes') is named after these channels.

The structure of the Mataiva lagoon gives it a very special appearance: the coral constructions at the surface of the water create dividing walls of 50 to 300 metres which form about 70 basins of a maximum depth of 10 metres. Seen from a plane, the play of light on this underwater tessellation forms a mosaic of green.

Information
There is no bank on the atoll. Paeua has two shops and a post office, south of the bridge. The post office is open Monday to Thursday from 7.30 to 11.30 am, and on Friday from 7.30 to 11 am. It has a fax service and sells phonecards. There are card-operated telephone booths opposite the post office and at the airport.

Pahua
For the 200 inhabitants of this peaceful village the phosphate-mining project is like a sword of Damocles. Their hostility is palpable. 'To matou roto, to matou ora' ('our environment is our life'), is written on two

boards, close to the south end of the bridge. For the time being, most of the inhabitants live off fishing and copra production.

Le Rocher de la Tortue
Called Ofai Tau Noa or 'the rock of the turtle' by the inhabitants of the atoll, this rock is a remnant of a former uplifted coral reef (feo), with the shape of a splayed mushroom. It gave rise to the cloud legend: if a cloud of the same shape as the rock appears above the pass, weather changes can be predicted and turtles will come to the surface. It will then be time to hunt them.

To get there, take the track which starts at the bridge on the northern side of the pass and follow it for 4.7 km. Then take the secondary track on the left, which crosses the coconut plantation to the ocean.

Beaches
In the south of the atoll, along the edge of the lagoon, there are many fine beaches. Take your mask and fins along.

Marae Papiro
Mataiva has a well-kept marae on the edge of a hoa, about 14 km from the village, south-east of the atoll at the end of the track. In the centre of this marae, you can clearly see the lithic-stone seat from which, according to the legend, the giant Tu guarded the pass against invasion. In case of attack from enemy tribes, he needed to take no more than three steps to push the assailants off the island and crush them. Tu is one of the gods in the Tahitian pantheon. It is also the name of a fierce warrior king from Anaa atoll, an ancestor of the Pomares, who conquered the surrounding atolls as far as Fakarava. This throne is surrounded by rectangular maraes and bordered by little blocks of coral limestone driven into the ground. In the centre of each marae, two larger stones stand on their sides.

Île aux Oiseaux
A propitious place for nesting, east of the lagoon, this crescent-shaped coral tongue (Island of Birds) covered in small shrubs is

a favourite place for *oio* (noddies), *tara* (sea-swallows) and *uaau* (red-footed gannets).

Nombril de Mataiva

According to legend, a rock on the surface of the lagoon, next to Île aux Oiseaux, called Mataiva Papa (the navel, or belly button, of Mataiva), is the place where King Tu (see Marae Papiro) first set foot. Tradition has it that a foreigner reaching Mataiva should put a foot on this rock.

Fish Parks

Don't miss accompanying the fishers on their way to trap fish in one of the numerous parks spread out in the lagoon and the pass. A first fisher, wearing a mask, jumps into the water carrying fencing wire that is closed at one end in the form of a hoop net, while the other fisher splashes the surface. The frightened fish rush into the trap. All the fishers have to do is empty them into the boat and repeat the same routine. The few big fish who escape the trap are harpooned. Sorted out, scaled and gutted, they are sold in the village for around 500 CFP per kg. Balistes, mullets, parrotfish and jackfish are all part of this bounteous catch.

If you get a chance to accompany Orirau and Jean, fishermen who work for the guesthouse Mataiva Village (see Places to Stay), they will show you the technique used to skin the famous moon-fish, and how to remove the poisonous part inside the intestines.

Shipwreck

Stuck right in the middle of the coconut plantation, this rusted wreck, of which only a part of the bow remains, is a symbol of nature's violence. According to the elders, this ship sank in the 1906 cyclone and then was carried to the coconut plantation by cyclones in later years.

To get there, follow the track for about three km, then take the secondary track which turns right towards the ocean. After 450 metres, you will come to a fork, from where you can catch a glimpse of the ocean. Don't head towards the ocean, but follow the other track to the left for 250 metres. You will then find yourself facing the wreck.

Places to Stay

The inhabitants of Pahua are counting on increasing numbers of tourists to dissuade the government from setting up drilling sites on the lagoon. The accommodation facilities are, therefore, expanding. Prices are per person per day and include transfers to the airport.

The only guesthouse north of the pass, near the lagoon and 150 metres from the bridge, is *Mataiva Village* (☎ 96-32-33), run by Edgar Tetua. Six two-person bungalows are on the edge of the pass. They cost 4000/6000 CFP half/full board. They're clean, comfortable and have cold-water bathroom facilities. Meals are served in a large dining room on stilts. Inside is a Greenpeace poster with the inscription 'No te Pararura'a O Te A'au', calling for protection of the environment. As a point of honour, Edgar insists on serving succulent crayfish. The mosquitoes, however, are abundant.

A rival guesthouse, also full of charm and personality, *Mataiva Cool* (☎ 96-32-53), south of the bridge, on the edge of the pass, is run by Mme Huri. She has two bungalows for three people and two more for two people, each with a bathroom (cold water) and a fan, for the sum of 6000 CFP. Your eye will inevitably be drawn to the little wooden constructions behind the bungalows, looking like kennels on stilts or kids' tree-houses. They comprise seven fares that can each accommodate one or two people, with two shared bathrooms. For 5000 CFP you can stay in one of these authentic huts. A few tables and chairs on the edge of the pass make for an improvised terrace.

Until the beginning of 1996, these were the only two guesthouses catering for travellers but three new guesthouses were about to be opened: one in the village and two outside the village, in the coconut plantation. The prices had not then been fixed, but are likely to be somewhere between 5000 and 6000 CFP. *Pension Natua* (☎ 96-32-34) on the south side of the pass, opposite the Sanito temple, offers three bungalows for two people with bathroom. Two other bungalows are also planned, south of the atoll. The Natua family owns several fish parks, one in the pass which they will certainly take you to see. The *Heiata Village* (☎ 96-32-43) belongs to Moana and Violette Richmond, the owners of the shop on the south side of the pass, in the two-storey yellow building. About four km south of the village, three bungalows (with bathroom) for two people, on a white-sand beach, a few metres from the coconut trees and the lagoon, will enchant the leisurely visitor. The *Ava Hei Pension* (☎ 96-32-58), also in the coconut plantation area on the edge of the lagoon, about one km beyond the former guesthouse, is practically on the threshold of paradise. On the edge of the beach three bungalows built in the local style (a *niau* roof and crushed-coral floor), with bathroom and fan; they are only available with demi-pension. A fare restaurant and a fare potee for a bar complete the scene.

Places to Eat
For meals you'll have to rely on what's provided in the guesthouses. The two little shops south of the pass sell only a few tins and basic food. The one 50 metres before the Sanito temple, opposite the pass, is run by Damien Deligny, the president of the Ia Ora Mataiva (Save Mataiva) Association.

Getting There & Away
Mataiva is 350 km north-east of Tahiti and 100 km west of Rangiroa.

Air The airport and the Air Tahiti office (☎ 96-32-48) are less than 500 metres from the village, on the south side. It's open Monday from 8 am to noon; Tuesday from 8 to 11.30 am; Friday from 8 to 9 am and 10 am to 2 pm; and Sunday from 9 to 10 am and 1 to 4 pm. Edgar Tetua, owner of Mataiva Village, is the Air Tahiti representative.

Mataiva is serviced by a twice-weekly direct flight from Papeete that costs CFP 13,000. On Friday, the ATR 42 of Air Tahiti does a Papeete-Mataiva-Rangiroa-Papeete round trip, while on Sunday the route it follows is Papeete-Mataiva-Tikehau-Papeete. Mataiva-Rangiroa or Mataiva-Tikehau costs CFP 4400.

Sea Mataiva is on the route of the *Manava 2*, *Saint Xavier Maris Stella* and *Vai-Aito* schooners. See the Inter-Island Ships – The Tuamotus in the Getting Around chapter for more information.

Getting Around
A track goes almost all the way around the island, in the middle of the coconut plantation. To the north, the track finishes at Marae Papiro, about 14 km away. To the south, allow about 10 km to the end. Cycling is an excellent way of getting around. The Mataiva Village and Mataiva Cool guesthouses, rent out bicycles for 1000 CFP per day. Cars can be rented for 1500 to 2000 CFP with a driver. Enquire at the guesthouses.

All the guesthouses have motor boats and will suggest a visit to the Île aux Oiseaux, the fish parks and the Nombril de Mataiva. Allow 2000 CFP for the day, including a picnic and the visit.

MANIHI
Population: 430
Lagoon Area: 192 sq km
Passes: 1

Some 175 km north-east of Rangiroa, Manihi has acquired an international reputation in the field of pearl production. The big names in this business, Bréaud, Paul Yu and SPM chose to set up here and the lagoon is now scattered with large-scale family and industrial pearl production farms.

Shaped like an ellipsis, the atoll is 28 km long and eight km wide, with only one opening, the Tairapa Pass in the south-west. The exhilarating beauty of the lagoon and the riches of its underwater world were quickly recognised and an international hotel was built in 1977. Tourism and pearl production have created many jobs and provide work for most of the inhabitants, while fishing and

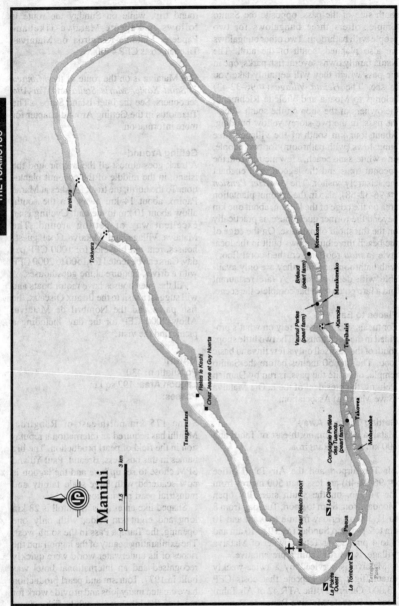

copra production provide a supplementary income.

Manihi is also a pioneer in the field of infrastructure. After Rangiroa, the second airstrip in the archipelago was built in the south-west of the atoll in 1969. A cyclone in February 1993 destroyed 70% of it but was rebuilt and raised in order to avoid a similar disaster. A few relics of old maraes still exist on the reef circuit. The Tokivera and Farekura maraes are in the north of the atoll and Marae Kamoka is in the south.

Information

There is no bank on the atoll. The post office is in Paeua village, on the first floor of a white administration building opposite the marina. It is open Monday and Thursday from 7.30 am to 3 pm, Tuesday and Wednesday from 7.30 am to 1 pm and Friday from 7.30 am to noon. There are card-operated telephone booths on the ground floor of the building, at the airport and at the hotel Manihi Pearl Beach Resort. The hospital is in the building next door.

Paeua

This charmless, almost neglected village is in striking contrast to villages on other atolls and will not entice you to stay. The pace of life is set to the rhythm of work in the pearl farms where most of the inhabitants are employed. Paeua has four places of worship: Sanito, Mormon, Protestant and Catholic.

Pearl Farms

The first pearl farm was set up in Manihi in 1968 and the atoll has steadily established itself as a principal centre for black pearls in the South Pacific. The number of active stations is estimated at 30 to 40. For travellers, visiting a pearl farm is a must. The best idea is to visit to a small family farm and a larger industrial farm. Avoid December and January, when the grafting is interrupted by the mother-of-pearl reproduction period. The farm staff are often on leave at this time.

The Manihi Pearl Beach Resort (see Places to Stay) is the main organiser of pearl farm visits. Three times a week guided tours

organised by the Compagnie Perlière des Tuamotu are combined with a picnic and an excursion to the village for 6500 CFP. You can also contact the farms directly; it is less common, but will save you a sizeable sum of money. Bear in mind though, that a pearl farm is a company, not a tourist site. You must phone beforehand to make an appointment.

Direct buying is possible most of the time but, contrary to popular belief, the most beautiful pearls aren't always found where they are produced. Pearls are quickly sent to Papeete, where they are put in jewellers' windows, but prices are, on average, 30% cheaper than in Papeete and abroad. The Manihi Pearl Beach Resort has a specialist jewellery shop.

The pearl farms mentioned here are only suggestions. As you get to know the people in the village, you will be invited to visit other farms.

A visit to the biggest farm in Manihi, Bréaud (☎ 96-43-41) on Korakoru Motu in the central-south part of the atoll, is absolutely fascinating. It is a hive of activity, employing more than 80 people (grafters, divers, assistants, technicians, cooks, accountants, etc). Many employees live on the farm itself. Francis Haoatai, the main grafter, will let you inside the grafting house if you get on his good side. To visit, ring first and speak to the manager Lise Bréaud.

Although they work hand in hand with the Manihi Pearl Beach Resort, the Compagnie Perlière des Tuamotu (CPDT; the Tuamotu Pearl Company), run by the Bouche family (☎ 43-43-68 in Papeete), accepts individual visits. The third-largest farm on the atoll, it employs 10 or so people and is on Takovea Motu, about five km east of the village. In particular, it specialises in *mabe*. Tours in English can be arranged, direct purchases can be made and credit cards are accepted.

Vaunui Perles is a family farm operated by the Buniets (☎ 96-42-89), on Marakorako Motu, less than three km west of the Bréaud farm. Vaiana does the grafting and Edmond ensures that everything runs smoothly. Edmond will talk about his job with endless enthusiasm, in English if necessary. You'll know everything about pearls and all his secrets by the time you leave his farm. The Buniet family specialise in mabe. Direct sales of pearls and mabe are available and credit cards are accepted.

The Meurisse, owners of Relais Le Keshi (see Places to Stay) have a small farm which they will be happy to show you. Direct sales are available. Pat Lancelle's small farm (☎ 96-42-19) also accepts individual visitors. English speakers should get in touch with Richard Steger (☎ 43-31-19), who manages Pai Moana Pearls farm, a thriving business in Papeete. He employs a Japanese and an Australian grafter. Contact him in Papeete beforehand to arrange a visit.

In the village, you may meet Petero Tupana, well known in the pearl-production world and was the first Polynesian to break the Japanese monopoly in pearl grafting. Others have followed in his footsteps and he is now an itinerant grafter, capitalising on his talents by working in various farms on the atoll.

Diving

There is superb marine life inside the lagoon and around Tairapa Pass, south-west of the atoll.

Dive Centre Manihi boasts one of the best dive centres in Polynesia. Manihi Blue Nui (☎ 96-42-17, fax 96-42-72) is led by Gilles Pétré and his multilingual team of instructors. Situated within Manihi Pearl Beach Resort, it is as immaculate and luxurious as the hotel. The buildings are brand new and the equipment is faultless. PADI divers will feel at home in this centre. You will be charged 6500 CFP for a first dive, 5500 CFP for a dive, 25,000 CFP for five dives and 45,000 CFP for 10, equipment included. You can buy a video of your exploits for 8000 CFP. CMAS and PADI training can also be arranged. Credit cards are accepted.

Dive Sites The main diving sites are less than 10 minutes away from the centre, close to the Tairapa Pass.

Le Tombant West of the pass, on the ocean side, Le Tombant is an outstanding dive. The boat anchors in shallow water, where first dives take place in barely three metres of water. A few fin strokes on and the reef drops sharply into an abyss. The dive consists in going along the length of the outer reef, to various depths, depending on the diver's ability. Grey sharks, napoleons, jackfish, groupers, perches and loaches are the hosts of this area. In the spawning season, generally July, impressive processions of groupers gather in the pass to reproduce. Their marbled brown and white colours will enchant underwater photographers. Returning to the shallow waters where the boat is anchored, you often find yourself face to face with a cloud of *poissons bagnards* (literally, prison fish), easily recognisable with their black stripes.

For experienced divers, the dive will continue to Tairapa Pass, which is 70 metres wide and 20 metres deep. The highlight of the show consists in crossing the mouth of the pass in the current, clinging on to bits of coral at the bottom. All you have to do then is look up to enjoy the most exquisite sight: shoals of barracuda and troupes of nasons which have adopted the habit of swimming against the current to stay in the same place. Suspended between the two streams, they wait open-mouthed, ready to gulp down any supplies carried by the current. When the current is incoming, you may let yourself be carried into the channel, to the lagoon.

Le Cirque Inside the lagoon and close to the pass, there is an entanglement of pinnacles down to a depth of 20 metres, teeming with multicoloured fish. This place is also where eagle rays come to satisfy their hunger. Slow-moving napoleons and black-tipped reef sharks can also be seen passing through.

La Pointe Ouest The West Point refers to the south-west end of the crown of the reef. The water is so clear that visibility may be up to 60 metres. Multiple coral formations flourish on the outer slope of the reef.

Places to Stay

Reasonably priced accommodation is difficult to find in Manihi and the facilities are scattered all over the atoll. New accommodation facilities are planned, however.

Places to Stay – bottom end

Marguerite Fareea (☎ 96-43-03) used to have bungalows on Tupihairi Motu, but they were destroyed in the 1993 cyclones. There are plans rebuild them and reopen the guesthouse in 1997.

In Paeua, *Manahune Village* (no phone) is a large building with a niau roof, easily spotted on the ocean shore near the school and the satellite dish. You should only choose this place as a last resort. It has a big room overlooking the ocean and four rooms with shared bathroom. They are basic, cell-like, expensive at 6000 CFP and generally rented out to casual pearl workers. The owners seem to have no wish to accommodate tourists and prefer running the bar in the big room, where young people congregate on Friday nights.

The last resort in the village is the *Pension Teiva* (no phone). Unfortunately, it is no more inviting than Manahune Village, and the friendly Madame Teanau Teiva seems to have trouble keeping the five wooden fares minimally clean. She charges 3500/5000 CFP per person, half/full board. This is exorbitant if you consider the dilapidated state things are in: faulty, even dangerous, electrical installations, ramshackle doors and windows and broken plumbing (you wash at the tap outside). Meals are invariably fish and rice served with soy sauce.

Places to Stay – middle

The Meurisse family run the *Relais Le Keshi* (☎ & fax 96-43-13), on Taugaraufara Motu, about nine km north-west of the airport. There are eight impeccable bungalows with bathroom (cold water), four of them over the water, for two to four people, set in very relaxing surroundings. Meals are served in a large tiled room near the beach. The food, which is very ordinary, reflects the impersonal décor of the dining room. You will have

to spend 8800/9800 CFP for a bungalow on the beach (half/full board) and 10,800/11,800 CFP for a bungalow on stilts, transfers to the airport included. The Keshi has a small swimming pool that is not always operational; it's better to take a dip in the nearby lagoon.

Excursions and picnics are organised on request. Allow 800 CFP for a visit to the village and a boat ride on the pass and 4000 CFP for a picnic day. You can borrow fins and masks. There is no charge for laundry and Visa cards are accepted.

About 500 metres south-west of Keshi, on Taugaraufara Motu at the edge of the lagoon, *Jeanne et Guy Huerta* (☎ 96-42-90, fax 96-42-91) have two bungalows. Each bungalow is in perfect condition and can accommodate a family of four. The cost is 8000 CFP per day, including transfers to the airport. This is an appealing choice, but you have to do your own shopping and cooking as meals are not provided.

Places to Stay – top end

Two minutes from the airport, south-west of the lagoon, *Manihi Pearl Beach Resort* (☎ 96-42-73 or 43-16-10 in Papeete, fax 96-42-72), formerly known as Kaina Village, is now part of the Air Tahiti group. The airline completely renovated and extended the resort in 1995. The 30 units (soon to become 36), including eight beach bungalows and 22 over-water bungalows (14 luxury class), provide tough competition for the most prestigious hotels in the archipelago. There's a bath with hot water in each unit.

The whole development is harmoniously integrated with the idyllic natural setting: airy coconut groves, white-sand beaches, a sea-water swimming pool and the magnificent lagoon. The Poe Rava Restaurant has a beachfront terrace. The bar, with its own terrace, directly overlooks the pool, the lagoon and the beach. It will cost you the trifling sum of 23,000/31,000/46,000 CFP for a beach bungalow/over-water bungalow/luxury over-water bungalow. They accommodate up to three people but the 8% tax is not included. Breakfast and dinner add

5950 CFP per person per day. Lunches are à la carte. Organised activities include long-line fishing, snorkelling or visits to a pearl farm and the village. Credit cards are accepted.

Places to Eat

Apart from the guesthouses and hotels, there are hardly any other eateries. In Paeua, the self-service *Jean-Marie*, near the marina, has good supplies but the shop closes at 5 pm in order to limit alcohol sales. The house of Petero Tupana, the pearl grafter, has a tiny grocery. The bakery is in a street parallel to the lagoon, near the Protestant church.

Try lunch at the *Manihi Pearl Beach Resort* where the French chef prepares excellent and elaborate dishes in a delightful setting. You will be able to choose from a selection of entrees between 800 and 2000 CFP, main courses (including baby goat meat) between 1300 and 2200 CFP and desserts for about 900 CFP.

Getting There & Away

Air The office of Turai Faura, the Air Tahiti representative (☎ 96-43-34 or 96-42-71 on flight days), is located in Jean Marie's supermarket in Paeua. There are Papeete-Rangiroa-Manihi-Rangiroa-Papeete round-trip flights on Tuesday, Wednesday, Friday, Saturday and Sunday. Papeete-Manihi costs CFP 17,000, Rangiroa-Manihi costs CFP 8800. On Wednesday, Friday and Sunday, there is a Bora Bora-Rangiroa-Manihi service (changing planes in Rangiroa) for 23,000 CFP. The Manihi-Rangiroa-Bora Bora flight is on Friday. On Saturday, there is a Manihi-Nuku Hiva (Marquesas) flight for 24,500 CFP.

Sea *Manava 2*, *Saint Xavier Maris Stella* and *Vai-Aito* service Manihi. Loading and unloading takes place at the Paeua wharf in the pass.

Getting Around

The only track links Taugaraufara to the airport and is about nine km long. To rent a bicycle, enquire at the Manihi Pearl Beach Resort. Allow 500 CFP per day.

To/From the Airport The airport is at the south-west end of the atoll, two minutes away from Manihi Pearl Beach Resort. This hotel, Relais Le Keshi and the Chez Jeanne et Guy Huerta guesthouse handle the transfers. To get to the village you have no choice but to hitch a boat ride from the wharf right next to the airport fare.

Sea To get to the dive centre from the village, you can use the Manihi Pearl Beach Resort staff shuttle, which generally leaves the Paeua marina at about 6 am and returns around 4 pm. Ask in the village. The Keshi charges 800 CFP per person, on a two-person basis, for transfers to the village and the dive centre.

To get to the Bréaud pearl farm, board the shuttle that transports the farm workers. It leaves the Paeua marina around 6.30 am. Check the times, because the schedule is not in the least official. The same principle applies to get to the CPDT (the Tuamotu Pearl Company): keep a look out at the marina for the workers who go by launch early in the morning.

If you wish to visit Edmond Buniet's farm, you can try to take the Bréaud farm shuttle and ask to get off at the Edmond Buniet wharf. This means that you depend on the pilot agreeing to take you and you have to wait for the return shuttle, unless the owner brings you back to the village in his own boat. You can also ask Lai or Frederic Teiva, both of whom own boats and are well known in the village. Negotiate a price with them.

AHE
Population: 161
Lagoon Area: 170 sq km
Passes: 1

Situated 15 km west of Manihi, Ahe was 'discovered' by the Englishman Wilkes in 1839. The atoll is 20 km long by 10 km wide and is entered by the Tiareroa (or Reianui) Pass in the west. The village of Tenukupara is on the south-west side. Cultured-pearl production is beginning to develop. Ahe is well known to yachties who often pull in when sailing from the Marquesan islands.

Getting There & Away

Ahe doesn't have an airport but the current project to construct one should help to open up the island and develop tourism. The *Saint Xavier Maris Stella*, *Manava 2* and *ai-Aito* service Ahe.

TAKAROA

Population: 396
Lagoon Area: 113 sq km
Passes: 1

First seen by European eyes on 15 April 1616 by Le Maire, Takaroa atoll (literally, 'long chin') and its close neighbour, Takapoto, form an inseparable pair. Conservative

marine maps have persisted in calling them the Roi Georges Islands, ever since Byron's visit in June 1765.

Takaroa is, with Manihi and Tepoto, one of the northernmost island in the Tuamotu archipelago. The rectangular atoll is 27 km long by six km wide and has only one pass, Teauonae, in the south-west. The only village, Teavaroa, was built on the edge of the pass. Takaroa's most singular feature is that it is a Mormon bastion, which contrasts with the traditional religious characteristics of the Tuamotu archipelago. The population is 90% Mormon and alcohol is prohibited. The inhabitants live off cultured-pearl production and, to a lesser extent, copra production and fishing.

Information

For tourist information you can ask Angelina Bonno, the mayor. There is no bank in Takaroa. The post office, near the bridge at the end of the village and next to the hospital,

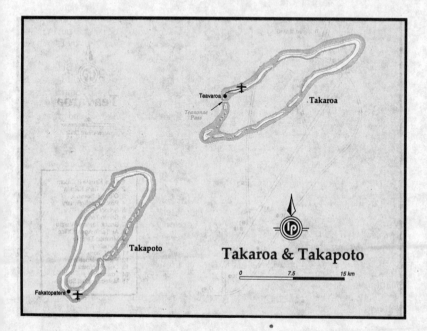

Takaroa & Takapoto

0   7.5   15 km

is open Monday, Wednesday and Thursday from 7 am to 3 pm, and Tuesday and Friday from 7 am to noon. Fax facilities and phonecards are available. There's a card-operated public telephone in front of the town hall and a first-aid room beside the post office.

Teavaroa

Sleepy quietness emanates from this village, which time seems to have passed by. Life takes a gently monotonous course, punctuated by fishing, copra production and work at the pearl farms. In the evening, young Paumotus gather near the pass and fish with long wooden rods to the sound of *kaina* music. There is no danger of losing your way: you will inevitably see the Mormon church with its red steeple, built in 1891. A weather bureau, the biggest in northern Tuamotu, is located near the town hall.

A totally unexpected minidisco, Tiare Kahaia, is next to the village exit, near the road to the airport. It looks more like a ballroom and an orchestra occasionally plays kaina music here on Friday. If no band arrives, a sound system produces high decibels of local music. Admission is 500 CFP for men or 300 CFP for women. Because of local religious beliefs in the village, no alcohol is served here.

A few metres away, at the end of the main airstrip, is a stone construction, probably an old lighthouse.

Maraes

There are two maraes close to the village, but they have been neglected and all you can see is a shapeless mass of fallen rock, covered in miki miki bushes. The first one is beside the bungalow belonging to the Temanaha family, next to the north-east end of the airstrip, on the edge of the lagoon.

The second marae is hidden under some bushes, about 500 metres from the bridge at

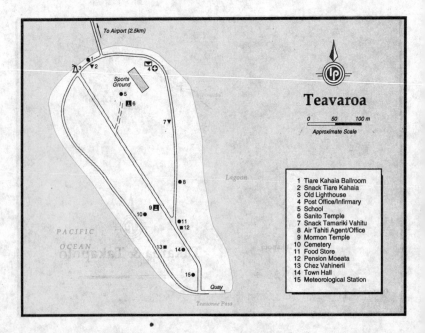

Teavaroa

0   50   100 m
Approximate Scale

1 Tiare Kahaia Ballroom
2 Snack Tiare Kahaia
3 Old Lighthouse
4 Post Office/Infirmary
5 School
6 Sanito Temple
7 Snack Tamariki Vahitu
8 Air Tahiti Agent/Office
9 Mormon Temple
10 Cemetery
11 Food Store
12 Pension Moeata
13 Chez Vahinerii
14 Town Hall
15 Meteorological Station

To Airport (2.5km)

Sports Ground

Lagoon

PACIFIC

OCEAN

Quay

Teavonae Pass

the village exit, just on the left of the track towards the airport. Walk beyond the white house, which is also the bakery, for 200 metres and you'll see the marae is hidden on your left.

Shipwreck

The imposing wreck of a four-mast vessel, which ran into the coral reef at the beginning of the century, is an indication of how difficult sailing is in the Tuamotus and of how violent the cyclones are. The rusted hull of the ship is now tastefully covered in graffiti. From the airport fare, it is six km along the track, going in the opposite direction from the village.

Pearl Farms

There are three big farms on Takaroa – Paul Yu, Giot and Vaimeareva – but almost all Teavaroa inhabitants have a family farm. Your hosts will probably be delighted to show you round their grafting house on stilts at the edge of the lagoon. This is the case with the Puaroo family (from Pension Moeata) and Hiriata Tehina, whose guesthouse bears her name. The farm of the Temanaha family (from the Chez Vahinerii) is directly in front of the bungalow available for rent near the airport. Also ask Nicolas at the weather bureau. English speakers should contact the Puaroo family, who employ an American grafter in their farm. Pearls may be purchased.

Another option is to visit Fernand Faura (☎ 98-22-47), who can provide complete explanations, in French or English, about grafting and mother-of-pearl work. Well-known to passing yacht owners, who anchor right in front of his property, he runs a small family business about 300 metres beyond the village exit. He taught himself grafting, excelled at it and now trains young Paumotus to do the same. To get there, take the second path on the right after the bridge, at the village exit. You will see his house and farm on the edge of the lagoon in the distance.

Diving

Together with the Pension Poe Rangi (see

Places to Stay), the dive centre of the Tahiti Yacht Club can dispatch an instructor to show you the underwater depths of Takaroa (five people minimum). For more details, enquire at the dive centre of the Tahiti Yacht Club in Papeete.

Places to Stay

There are guesthouses in the village or bungalows near the airport. The Temanaha family, who own the guesthouse *Chez Vahinerii* (no phone), will rent one of their impeccably clean bedrooms for 3000 CFP per day for one or two people, with shared bathroom. Their house is opposite the Mormon church. Meals are extra: 800 CFP for breakfast, 1200 CFP for lunch and 1500 CFP for dinner.

The permanent bungalow, with TV, bathroom and kitchenette, is in pristine condition and right on the edge of the lagoon. Coming from the airport, it is 800 metres on the left, opposite their pearl farm. This dreamlike setting costs 5000 to 6000 CFP for two to three people per day, meals not included. The coral plates surfacing from the water near the shore will delight snorkelling enthusiasts.

The simple but clean *Pension Moeata* (☎ 98-22-73) has three rooms for two to four people, with a shared bathroom next to the house. The shower has not worked for a long time and you will have to make do with a water tank to perform your ablutions but a small terrace adds charm to the house. A room only costs 3000 CFP but add 500/700/700 CFP per person for breakfast/lunch/dinner. The food leaves a great deal to be desired, however. The guesthouse is one or two steps from the shop and the Mormon church.

David Huti, from the *Tamariki Vahitu* food bar/shop (☎ 98-22-32), charges 3000 CFP for a mattress in an attic above the food bar. In place of a bathroom, there is a single tap on the floor below. He also rents out a much more comfortable bungalow near the airport for 4500 CFP.

The *Pension Hiriata Tehina* (no phone) has a bungalow with a mezzanine floor, about 400 metres beyond the village exit in the direction of the airport, on the right at the edge of the lagoon. The bungalow is no longer attractive, despite the mezzanine and bathroom (cold water) since it needs a good clean (and some paint) to recover its former lustre. Full board is an expensive 7000 CFP per person.

Opened in early 1996, the *Pension Poe Rangi* (☎ 98-23-65, fax 98-22-65), literally 'Heaven's Pearl', is run by Jean Parker, who works at the weather bureau. It is the only guesthouse on the other side of the pass, and is 10 minutes by boat from the village. A bungalow with a kitchenette for four people and a bungalow for two people, with bathroom, are available for 6000 CFP per person per day (full board), including airport transfers. Meals are served in the fare potee restaurant-bar.

Places to Eat

Takaroa is not the place for gourmets, although the guesthouses provide simple and unpretentious food. Don't forget that Takaroa is a Mormon domain, so you won't find any alcohol. Basic food and tinned sup-plies can be found in the only village shop, run by Manfred Ennemoser, an Austrian. His shop is next to Pension Moeata, opposite the Mormon church.

The two village snack bars are, in fact, plywood stalls, where a few weary sandwiches sit next to ageing pastries. The *Snack Tiare Kahaia*, opposite the Tiare Kahaia ballroom close to the bridge at the end of the village, offers chow mein for 800 CFP, omelettes for 700 CFP, poisson cru for 600 CFP and maa tinito for 700 CFP; there are only one or two dishes available and they must be ordered. The *Tamariki Vahitu* snack bar, a little beyond the post office towards the pass, is a sad sight.

Getting There & Away

Takaroa is 575 km north-east of Papeete and less than 100 km east of Manihi.

Air The airport is 2.5 km north-east of the village. The office of the Air Tahiti representative is in the village and is open Monday from 8 to 11 am and 1 to 3.30 pm, Thursday from 9.20 to 11 am and 1 to 4 pm, and Saturday from 9.30 to 11 am and 1 to 4 pm.

Air Tahiti has thrice-weekly flights connecting Papeete, Takaroa and Takapoto. On Monday and Saturday, the ATR 42 has a Papeete-Takaroa-Takapoto-Papeete service; and on Thursday it operates a Papeete-Takapoto-Takaroa-Papeete service. The Papeete-Takaroa flight costs 18,000 CFP, and Takapoto-Takaroa is 4400 CFP. The Papeete-Takaroa flight takes one hour and 35 minutes.

Sea *Manava 2*, *Saint Xavier Maris Stella* and *Tamarii Tuamotu* service the atoll. They draw up to the wharf in the pass.

Getting Around

The only track in the village goes from the village to Paul Yu's pearl farm through the airport – in all about 10 km. Your hosts will arrange picnics on the lagoon motu for 2500 to 3500 CFP per person. To rent a bicycle, ask at the Pension Vahinerii.

TAKAPOTO
Population: 450
Lagoon Area: 102 sq km
Passes: 0

Takapoto atoll (literally, 'short chin') is nine km south of Takaroa and was 'discovered' on 14 April 1616 by the Dutchman Le Maire. It's 20 km long and six km across at its widest point and doesn't have a pass. On a scientific level, this atoll is one of the best known in the Tuamotu. Since 1974 it has been closely examined within the multidisciplinary studies of the UNESCO MAB (Man & Biosphere) programme.

The second pearl farm in the Tuamotus was built on this atoll in the late 1960s. As this activity flourished at the beginning of the '70s, the shore mushroomed with the characteristic cottages on stilts. Apart from pearl production, the protected lagoon has maintained its traditional collection of young oysters. It is studded with coral pinnacles where the *Pinctada margaritifera* grow. In 1985, 600,000 young oysters took to the underwater platforms in Manihi. Copra production and fishing are a further source of income for the inhabitants.

Information
There is no bank service on the atoll. The post office, next to the town hall, is open Monday, Wednesday and Thursday from 7.30 am to 3 pm. Fax facilities and phonecards are available and there is a card-only telephone in front of the town hall. The community clinic is also next to the post office.

When they arrive in Takapoto, tourists on the *Aranui* are welcomed by Louis Faarii (☎ 98-65-57), who lives about 300 metres in front of the Pension Mere, seven km northeast of the village. He speaks English.

Fakatopatere
The appearance of this little village, southeast of the atoll and next to the airport, is quite surprising because it spreads across the entire width of the reef crown, and its streets – in fact, sand tracks – create a criss-cross pattern, with a Catholic church in the middle.

There is an EVAAM agency in Fakatopatere, an organisation whose purpose is to develop and promote aquaculture and maritime activities.

Pearl Farms
To see the whole process of pearl production you'll have to make an appointment with the cultured pearl producers. However, almost all guesthouse proprietors own a pearl farm and will suggest that you visit theirs. This is the case for Clotilde Vaitiare, Pimati Toti, Terai Mehahea and Cathy Ruamotu, among others. You can buy pearls directly from these producers.

Walter Toti, the owner of the Snack Agnès, has a brother, Sydney, who owns a farm on a motu, isolated from the village. English-speaking tourists are welcome.

The Roura Black Pearls International farm, owned by Pension Mere, has a not-inconsiderable advantage: it is located right in front of the bungalow which they rent to tourists. The owner, Georges Roura, will happily escort you through the areas of mabe, pearl and *keshi* production. His numerous trips around the world have given him a good grasp of English.

Beaches
Numerous white-sand beaches border the lagoon shore, which is easily accessible by a track. In the village itself, there is a small beach close to Pimati Toti's house. During their stop-over in Takapoto, *Aranui* tourists usually picnic on a beach, two km east of the village. Follow the track through the coconut grove until you come to the white building on the left, less than five km from the village. Walk on for 700 metres and turn off at the path on the left which crosses the coconut grove towards the lagoon.

Marae Takai
This archaeological site is worth the long walk. It consists of three small maraes surrounded by vertical coral slabs. According to Walter Toti, the owner of the land, it could be a funeral site containing bones. Northwest of Fakatopatere, the marae is well

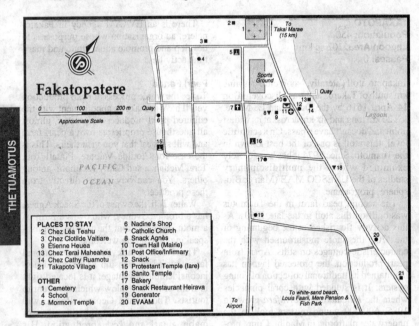

Fakatopatere

PACIFIC OCEAN

0   100   200 m
Approximate Scale

To Takai Marae (15 km)

Quay

Sports Ground

Quay

Lagoon

To white-sand beach, Louis Faarii, Mere Pension & Fish Park

To Airport

PLACES TO STAY
2 Chez Léa Teahu
3 Chez Clotilde Vaitiare
9 Étienne Heuea
13 Chez Terai Maheahea
14 Chez Cathy Ruamotu
21 Takapoto Village

OTHER
1 Cemetery
4 School
5 Mormon Temple

6 Nadine's Shop
7 Catholic Church
8 Snack Agnès
10 Town Hall (Mairie)
11 Post Office/Infirmary
12 Snack
15 Protestant Temple (fare)
16 Sanito Temple
17 Bakery
18 Snack Restaurant Heirava
19 Generator
20 EVAAM

hidden behind bushy vegetation. Follow the track which goes past the cemetery at the village exit for 15 km. You will see a hoa, spanned by a stone bridge. Cross this bridge and immediately on the right, walk 60 m along the hoa towards the lagoon. Turn left for about 30 metres, clearing your way through *kahaiai*, miki miki bushes and coconut trees and you will come upon the three maraes in a little clearing.

The walk to Marae Takai will take you through magnificent and beautifully maintained coconut plantations. The lagoon shore is festooned with pearl farms and white-sand beaches.

Fish Parks
Follow the north-east track to the end, about nine km, to Teavatika, a fish park built of coral blocks in a hoa. This traditional public park is a rare example of its kind. It contains a large number of multicoloured fish.

Places to Stay
You need to choose carefully in Takapoto. The old guesthouses are in decline, while some more comfortable new places are just beginning to see the light of day.

Next to the wharf on the lagoon side, opposite the town hall and away from the road, are two guesthouses standing side by side. The first, *Chez Terai Maheahea* (☎ 98-65-14), is the green one near the copra barn. Do not expect any comfort, or privacy. A room for two people, with a mattress on the floor, is 3000/5000 CFP half/full board. To wash, you will have to manage with a can filled with water.

Next door, is Cathy Ruamotu's house (☎ 98-64-19, at her parents'). Cathy, who is very friendly and speaks good English, rather neglects her present guesthouse. She is planning to build a luxury over-water bungalow next to her pearl farm, in a quiet place away from the village.

If you choose to stay at *Chez Clotilde*

Vaitiare (☎ 98-64-71), not far from Chez Léa Teahu, north-west of the village, halfway between the lagoon and the ocean, the bill will be 4000/6000 CFP per person for half/full board. The house let by Clotilde, better known as Opeta, has three rooms with shared bath, a kitchen and a lounge. The prices are high for what you get: simple setting, faulty water conveyance (the shower has been replaced by a water barrel) and food no better than at the local school canteen. Moreover, mosquitoes seem to like the place. Keep your ears pricked, though, since the Vaitiare are planning to build some bungalows close to the EVAAM.

Chez Léa Teahu (no phone), at the village exit, near the cemetery, has a sinister atmosphere. The three rooms on offer are as dilapidated as the bathroom fittings: the toilet is outside and the shower is no more than a water can. And the mosquitoes haunt the place. Furthermore, the prices are astronomical: 5000 CFP full board per person per day, and 30,000 CFP for a month's rent.

Étienne Heuea (☎ 96-65-09 or 98-65-18 at the Snack Agnès) has a chalet with a mezzanine floor, entirely fitted out, opposite the snack shop, available for CFP 4000 per person per day. It is often rented out to government officials.

A very beautiful guesthouse opened in December 1995, on the edge of the lagoon on a small beach of white sand, south-west of the village, 100 metres from the village. The *Takapoto Village* (☎ 98-65-44) is run by the Toti couple. Mr Toti is also mayor of Takapoto and he has a thorough knowledge of the history of the Tuamotus and can tell you frightening stories about the raids of the Anaa warriors. There are two types of accommodation: a very comfortable bungalow for two people on the edge of the lagoon, with bath (cold water), just in front of the Toti house, for 7500 CFP per person, full board; or an immaculate room for two in the main house, with shared bath, for 5000 CFP per person, full board. In both cases, an excursion, with a picnic on a motu is included. Meals are taken on the bungalow terrace or inside the house.

Along the same lines, but about seven km north-east of the village, the *Pension Mere* (☎ & fax 98-65-05, GSM 77-09-19) is peaceful and quiet. Facing the lagoon and the inevitable pearl farm, Georges and Mere Roura rent out a comfortable bungalow, with an outside bathroom, for two people for 5000 CFP. Breakfast and transfers to the airport are included.

Places to Eat

Apart from the guesthouses, eateries are scarce. The *Nadine* shop, near the wharf on the ocean side, is relatively well supplied. On the other side of the village, opposite the town hall, a tiny stall sells very basic supplies. A small bakery (no sign), open for several hours early in the morning, is set up near the Sanito temple.

The only viable snack bar is *Snack Agnès*, a little off the road behind the town hall. On order, you may have breakfast (coffee, bread, butter and jam) for 150 CFP, steak and chips for 700 CFP, or even the traditional poisson cru for 650 CFP. The bar is open every day but Sunday. Walter Toti, the owner, is a descendant of the Anaa royal family and of *tahua* (sorcerer) lineage. Fiercely independent, he will tell you about the corruption going on in this Polynesian political backwater. He'll also tell you legends, including those about the two giants from the Marquesas who were determined to devour the Takapoto inhabitants. To defend themselves, the Takapotos made a poison from fish extracts and gave it to the giants to drink. After drinking it the giants collapsed – one in the lagoon and one in the ocean. According to the legend, this explains the presence of long clumps of coral in the lagoon. To be more prosaic, the clumps are in fact cob-shaped corals, found in abundance in Takapoto.

Getting There & Away

Takapoto is 560 km north-east of Papeete and less than 100 km east of Manihi.

Air The airport is just a stone's throw from the village. The Air Tahiti representative

THE TUAMOTUS

(☎ 98-65-79) is on duty at the airport Monday to Thursday from 8 to 11 am, as well as an hour before each flight. Air Tahiti has three weekly flights, connecting Papeete, Takaroa and Takapoto. On Monday and Saturday, the ATR 42 does a Papeete-Takaroa-Takapoto-Papeete round trip. On Thursday, it does the same round trip in the other direction. The Papeete-Takaroa leg costs 18,800 CFP and Takapoto-Takaroa costs CFP 4400. The Papeete-Takapoto flight takes 1½ hours.

Sea *Tamarii Tuamotu*, *Saint Xavier Maris Stella* and *Manava 2* serve Takapoto. *Taporo IV* and *Aranui*, on their way to the Marquesas Islands, also stop there (see Inter-Island Ships – The Tuamotus in the Getting Around chapter). The transfers by whale boat take place at the landing stage next to the Nadine shop.

Getting Around

There are two tracks from the village. The first one goes in a north-easterly direction for about nine km, to the fish park made of coral blocks. The other goes in a north-westerly direction.

The ideal way to discover the atoll is by scooter or bicycle. For a scooter, ask Walter Toti at Snack Agnès or Terai Maheahea at her guesthouse. Allow 1500 to 2000 CFP for a day. Pimati Toti, from the Takapoto Village guesthouse, and Terai Maheahea, offer bicycles for 500 CFP a day.

Most guesthouses organise picnics on deserted motus, reached by speedboat. Allow 2000 CFP per person.

ARUTUA
Population: 300
Lagoon Area: 570 sq km
Passes: 1

This almost circular atoll is nearly 25 km in diameter. The lagoon waters meet the ocean through the small Porofai Pass in the east, near the village of Rautini. The village is on a motu south of the airport, half an hour away by boat.

The village, which was devastated by cyclones in 1983, has been entirely rebuilt. The lagoon has a reputation for being rich in fish and crayfish. Fishing, cultured-pearl and copra production are the main economic activities on the atoll.

Places to Stay

Arutua has one guesthouse in Rautini, the *Pension Pikui* (☎ 96-52-34). The owners rent out two rooms for two people and a lounge for three people, with shared bathroom (cold water) for 5000 CFP per person, full board. They also have a house with two bedrooms and three bungalows on Motu Mutukiore, a few km from the village, for the same price.

Getting There & Away

Arutua is about 375 km north-east of Tahiti. To the west, only 30 km separates it from the eastern extremity of Rangiroa.

Air Getting to Rautini from the airport, at the west of Tenihinihi Motu, takes half an hour by boat. Transfers to the airport cost 1000 CFP return, per person. On Wednesday, Friday and Sunday, Air Tahiti operates a Papeete-Arutua-Rangiroa-Papeete service, and a Dornier-Rangiroa flight with an ATR 42 returning to Papeete. It costs 14,000 CFP for the Papeete-Arutua flight, which takes 1 hour 20 minutes. The Arutua-Rangiroa flight costs 4400 CFP.

Sea *Saint Xavier Maris Stella*, *Manava 2*, *Dory* and *Cobia II* service Arutua (see Inter-Island Ships – The Tuamotus in the Getting Around chapter).

KAUKURA
Population: 300
Lagoon Area: 546 sq km
Passes: 1

Kaukura was first reached by Europeans on 28 May 1722 by the Dutchman Roggeveen, who also 'discovered' Easter Island. Oval shaped and measuring 50 km by 14 km at its widest point, there is only one pass into the lagoon. Fishing is the atoll's main activity.

Kaukura, together with Tikehau, is the biggest provider of fish to the Papeete markets from the Tuamotus. Transport is by schooner and plane. The inhabitants live in Raitahiti village, on the north-west side of the lagoon.

Places to Stay

Pension Rekareka (☎ 96-62-40 or 96-62-39) run by Claire Parker in Raitahiti is a multi-storey house with six two-person rooms with shared bathroom for 5000 CFP per person per day, full board. There are also four bungalows for two people with shared bathroom on Tahunapona Motu, 15 minutes by boat from the village. Transfers from the airport are included. Excursions to various motus and on the lagoon can be organised.

Getting There & Away

Kaukura atoll is 55 km south-east of Rangiroa and 340 km north-east of Tahiti.

Air The airport is two km from the village. Kaukura is served by Air Oceania and Air Tahiti. Air Oceania (☎ 82-10-47, GSM 77-01-27, fax 82-10-34) is a charter company based in Faaa airport and has a Papeete-Kaukura-Papeete flight on Wednesday for CFP 13,500 per person, one way. Air Tahiti flies Papeete-Rangiroa-Kaukura-Papeete, on Monday and Friday. Papeete-Kaukura costs CFP 14,000 one way (one hour 40 minutes), Rangiroa-Kaukura costs 4400 CFP.

Sea *Saint Xavier Maris Stella*, *Manava 2*, *Vai-Aito*, *Cobia II* and *Dory* have stop-overs at Kaukura (see Inter-Island Ships – The Tuamotus in the Getting Around chapter for more information).

FAKARAVA

Population: 250
Lagoon Area: 1121 sq km
Passes: 2

Fakarava is the second-largest atoll in the Tuamotus. Roughly rectangular in shape, its lagoon is 60 km long and 25 km wide. The lagoon waters merge with the ocean through

Garuae Pass in the north and Tumakohua Pass in the south. The opening of a permanent airstrip in February 1995, near the northern pass, has helped to open up the atoll. Most of the population is gathered in Rotoava village at the north-eastern end, four km east of the airport. A handful of inhabitants also live in Tetmanu village, on the edge of the southern pass. On the eastern edge, an uninterrupted reef strip stretches for 40 km. The western side, on the other hand, has a few scattered islets. Copra and cultured-pearl production and fishing in the numerous fish parks around Rotoava are the island's main industries.

Diving

This is fast becoming the major tourist attraction in Fakarava. In February 1996 the Spiro Dive Centre Rotoava (☎ 43-07-50, fax 43-07-54; BP 330002, Paea, Tahiti) run by Marc-Antoine Baudart opened near Rotoava, next to Kiritia Village. The equipment is in pristine condition, right down to solar cells for recharging batteries. You pay 5500 CFP per dive although there's a 10% discount after the fifth dive. Remote dives, in the Tunakohua Pass or next to Toau atoll, are an extra 2000 CFP.

Diving in Fakarava is mainly for experienced divers. The sites are totally untouched and the gigantic Garuae Pass, more than 800 metres wide, is the meeting place for all sorts of deep-sea marine life, including hammerheads, grey sharks, tiger sharks, manta rays, dolphins, barracudas and *carangues* – making the Avatoru and Tiputa passes in Rangiroa seem like timid little playgrounds in comparison.

In July, marbled groupers gather in massive shoals in the pass to reproduce. The lagoon is about 40 metres deep, the pass is 16 metres deep, and the reef slopes down for about 600 metres. The numerous motus, as well as the southern pass and the neighbouring atoll of Toau, are also preserved sites which can be explored. It's also possible to visit a family pearl farm, followed by a dive in the farm in the breeding zone, where the precious bivalves live.

Places to Stay

A km south of the village, *Kiritia Village* (☎ 98-42-37), run by Marceline Kachler, has eight bungalows for two people, with shared bathroom, on the edge of the lagoon. It costs 5500 CFP per person per day, full board, transfers from the airport included. Poisson cru in coconut milk and grilled mahi-mahi will satisfy the most ferocious appetites. Kiritia Village is the divers' regular residence (the dive centre is next door). Picnics on the motu can be arranged. Marceline Kachler also owns a pearl farm which she will gladly show you.

At the other end of the atoll, on the edge of Tumakohua Pass, those in search of a complete change of scenery will be delighted by *Tetamanu Village* (☎ 43-92-40, fax 42-77-70; BP 9364, Motu Uta, Tahiti) run by Sané Richmond, a shipowner in Tahiti. For 10,000 CFP per person per day or 65,000 CFP per week, full board, transfers from the

airport included, you can stay here in one of four bungalows for two people with shared bathroom. It's right on the edge of the pass and meals are served in an over-water restaurant. This price includes a programme of activities. A trawler with three cabins conducts excursions on the lagoon and, on request, to the neighbouring atolls of Toau, Kauehi and Raraka.

Getting There & Away

The atoll is 488 km east-north-east of Tahiti and south-east of Rangiroa.

Air The airport is about four km from the village, going west towards the pass. Air Oceania (☎ 82-10-47, GSM 77-01-27, fax 85-52-12) has a regular Papeete-Fakarava-Papeete flight every Wednesday aboard a nine-seater Cessna or a five-seater Aero Commander for 14,000 CFP one way. Divers get a special price: 13,000 CFP one way.

Air Tahiti services Fakarava for 14,700 CFP: on Monday, the ATR 42 flies Papeete-Fakarava-Rangiroa-Papeete, on Friday it flies Papeete-Rangiroa, connecting with the Dornier service for Rangiroa-Fakarava-Papeete. If you have stayed at Rangiroa and wish to go to Fakarava it costs 4400 CFP.

Sea *Saint Xavier Maris Stella*, *Vai-Aito* and *Manava 2* serve Fakarava. *Auura'Nui 3*, whose owner is Sané Richmond, the owner of Tetamanu Village, stops at Tetamanu.

Getting Around

From Rotoava, a track goes to the south-west of the atoll for about 40 km. Marceline Kachler, from Kiritia Village (see Places to Stay) rents out bicycles for 500 CFP per day. For a car allow 3000 CFP rental per day. Boat excursions are arranged by both guesthouses.

ANAA

Population: 425
Lagoon Area: 184 sq km
Passes: 0

Compared to the giant Fakarava, 150 km north, Anaa atoll, oriented on a north-west/south-east axis, is small. It's just 28 km long and five km wide, made up of 11 islets scattered on the reef circumference, and it doesn't have a pass. Anaa, which used to be densely populated, became known for the ferocity of its inhabitants who extended their domination over the northern part of the archipelago, pillaging the atolls they conquered.

Cyclones have cost Anaa dearly. Tukuhora village, razed by a tidal wave in 1906 which left 100 people dead, was entirely devastated again in the 1982-1983 cyclonic season. The inhabitants live off fishing and copra production.

Places to Stay

The *Te Hoa Nui* guesthouse (☎ 98-32-78), 300 metres from the airport, is run by the Gatata family. They have two bungalows for two people, with bathroom (cold water) which cost 3500/5000 CFP half/full board per person. Picnics on the motu and speedboat excursions can be arranged on request.

Another possibility is the *Te Maui Nui* guesthouse (☎ 98-32-64 or 98-32-75, ask for Adele Maro), which is also close to the airport and the lagoon. Two bungalows for two people, one with bathroom (cold water) cost 3500/4500 CFP per person, full board. A two-bedroom house is also available for 3500 CFP per person, full board. Excursions and picnics are organised for guests.

Getting There & Away

Anaa is 450 km away from Papeete, in the east.

Air Anaa is serviced once a week, usually on Monday, from Papeete. Air Tahiti flies Papeete-Anaa-Makemo-Papeete one week, and Papeete-Makemo-Anaa-Papeete the other week. The Papeete-Anaa flight takes one hour and 10 minutes and costs 15,000 CFP. The Anaa-Makemo trip takes 45 minutes and costs 7700 CFP.

Sea Anaa is on the route of *Auura'Nui 4* and *Kura Ora*.

South & East Tuamotus

If not for the presence of the nuclear-testing operations, the infamous Centre d'expérimentation du Pacifique (CEP), this totally isolated region would have remained forgotten. CEP activities have made some of these atolls sadly famous.

Hao is the regional centre where cultured-pearl production, fishing and copra production are the major industries. The smallest atolls in the archipelago are in this region; some, like Tikei, Nukutavake, Pinaki or Akiaki, are barely five sq km. In this marginal world tourists facilities are rare, and so are visitors.

RAROIA
Population: 831 (including Taenga, Katiu and Makemo)
Lagoon Area: 440 sq km
Passes: 1

'Discovered' on 12 July 1820 by Bellinghausen, Raroia is east of the central Tuamotus, eight km south-west of its nearest neighbour, Takume. The lagoon meets the ocean through only one pass, in the west.

It was on the southern part of the reef that the *Kon Tiki* ran aground in 1947, putting an end to one of the greatest sea epics. Thor Heyerdahl and his unfortunate companions (including the ethnologist Bengt Danielsson) had embarked on a mad enterprise 101 days earlier: to sail aboard a balsa and bamboo raft – a replica of the crafts used by Incas on Lake Titicaca and the Peruvian coast – to Mangareva in the Gambier Islands. The purpose of this expedition was to prove that Polynesia had been populated by the Incas.

The adventure was unsuccessful. The raft drifted much more to the north than the route they had first predicted. Moreover, botanists, linguists and archaeologists have all invalidated the thesis of the American Indian origin of the Polynesians.

THE TUAMOTUS

Getting There & Away

Raroia is served by the *Auura'Nui 3*, *Kura Ora* and *Tamarii Tuamotu*.

PUKA PUKA

Population: 195
Lagoon Area: 16 sq km

Described by Magellan in 1521 and by the Dutchman Le Maire in 1616, who gave it the name of Houden Eiland (the Island of Dogs), this atoll, at the easternmost boundary of the Tuamotus, has a lagoon in the process of filling in and drying up. Puka Puka was the first land seen by the *Kon Tiki* adventurers on 30 July 1947.

The Air Tahiti Dornier stops over briefly every week on its way to Atuona (Marquesas), one week on its way, one week on its way back. The schooners *Auura'Nui 3* and *Kura Ora* also serve the atoll.

NUKUTAVAKE

Population: 142
Lagoon Area: 5.5 sq km
Passes: 0

Situated 1125 km south-east of Tahiti, Nukutavake is the only inhabited atoll where the lagoon has been entirely filled in by sand and limestone particles from the external reef. It is entirely covered by a coconut plantation. Enquire first at La Police de l'Air et des Frontières in Papeete about obtaining authorisations.

Places to Stay

This atoll has one guesthouse, the *Pension Afou* (☎ 98-72-53), in the village of Tavananui, on the seashore, one km from the airport. Three bungalows with shared bathroom are available; allow 6500 CFP full board per person and 1500 CFP for transfers to the airport. Fishing trips and boat rides around the island can be organised by your hosts.

Getting There & Away

Air Air Tahiti serves Nukutavake via Hao (change of plane), arriving on Monday and

returning on Tuesday. Allow 35,600 CFP one way. Papeete-Nukutavake (via Hao) and 8600 CFP for Hao-Nukutavake.

Sea Only the schooner *Manava III* serves Nukutavake.

HAO

Population: 1000
Lagoon Area: 609 sq km
Passes: 1

The Spaniard Quiros was the first European to set foot on this atoll in the centre of the Tuamotus in 1606. With only one pass and measuring nearly 60 km in length, it has seen great demographic growth since the 1960s as an administration and transit centre for the CEP nuclear-testing organisation and the installations of the CEA (Commissariat à l'énérgie atomique). It has state-of-the-art infrastructure, including a 3300-metre runway that can handle the military transport planes carrying highly sensitive material destined for Moruroa, 500 km south. When atmospheric tests were conducted, there were up to 5000 people busy on the atoll. With the switch to underground testing, most of the military staff were moved to Moruroa and Fangataufa.

Hao is also a regional centre and the centre for air traffic to the southern Tuamotus and Gambier Islands. It has a college and a medical centre and most inhabitants earn their living from cultured-pearl production in Otepa, a village on the north-east.

Enquire first at the La Police de l'Air et des Frontières in Papeete about getting authorisation to visit.

Places to Stay

In Otepa you can stay at the *Chez Amelie* guesthouse (☎ 97-03-42, fax 97-02-41). Amélie Danzer, the Air Tahiti representative, has at her disposal one to two rooms for two to three people, with hot water and TV for 5500 CFP. A mezzanine level with two double beds is also available for 3500 CFP per person. Weekly prices are negotiable and transfers to the airport are included. Meals are not, however; allow 1500 to 3000 CFP per day per person.

Getting There & Away

Air Air Tahiti has a twice-monthly Papeete-Hao-Mangareva (Gambiers) flight on Monday, returning to Papeete on Tuesday. The Papeete-Hao-Papeete service operates four times a month. The Papeete-Hao flight takes two hours and 20 minutes costs and 26,300 CFP. Hao is also connected to Fangataufa, Fakahina, Tatakoto, Tureia, Vahitahi, Nukutavake, Pukarua and Reao. Enquire at Air Tahiti about flight schedules.

Sea The *Auura'Nui 3*, the *Kura Ora* and the *Manava III* service Hao (see Inter-Island Ships – The Tuamotus in the Getting Around chapter).

MORUROA
Population: 3500
Lagoon Area: 324 sq km
Passes: 1

Often mistakenly spelt 'Mururoa', this atoll, 1250 km south-east of Tahiti, will forever be synonymous with nuclear tests (see the French Nuclear Testing aside in the Facts about the Islands). 'Discovered' in 1792 by the Englishman Weatherhead, it is 28 km long and 11 km wide and opens to the ocean through only one pass.

The atoll was selected because of its isolation from any inhabited zone and the possibility it offered to set up the necessary infrastructure for the tests. It is equipped with ultra-modern electricity production installations, a desalinisation factory and an airport which handles large transport planes. Restaurants, cinemas, sports grounds, an internal radio and TV channel are for the use of the mainly male military staff. The atoll was legally ceded to the French state in 1964. With the final tests completed, jurisdiction should now be given back to the French Polynesian government. For the time being, access is strictly forbidden. The Greenpeace crews have discovered that through bitter experience.

FANGATAUFA
Population: 300
Lagoon Area: 67 sq km
Passes: 0

Forty km south of Moruroa, this atoll which doesn't have a pass, has suffered the same fate as Moruroa.

THE TUAMOTUS

Are not, however, allow 1300 to 5000 CFP per day per person.

Getting There & Away

Air Air Tahiti has a twice monthly flight from Mangareva (Gambiers), arriving on Monday, returning in Papeete on Tuesday.

See also Tuamotus Getting There & Away and Getting Around — How to Get There and Get Away.

MOHOTA
Population: 300
Lagoon Area: 46 km
Passes: 1

FAKATURA
Population: 200
Lagoon Area: 67 sq km
Passes: 0

Forty km south of Mohota, this atoll which doesn't have a pass, has suffered the same fate as Marutea.

The Marquesas

The Marquesas

Te Henua Enana ('Land of Men') is the Marquesans' name for their archipelago; the term 'Marquesas' was introduced by the Spanish.

Four thousand km south of Hawaii, 500 km from the closest of the Tuamotu atolls and 1400 km north-east of Papeete, this is the most northerly archipelago of French Polynesia. The Marquesas' 15 islands, only six of which are inhabited, share a geographical isolation. Even within the archipelago, which stretches diagonally about 350 km from north-west to south-east, distance is the rule. The islands tend to be divided into two groups: northern and southern.

These unprotected blocks of lava rise abruptly from the surrounding vastness of the Pacific Ocean. Ragged and distorted, their rugged contours were formed by the erosion caused by sea and wind. Unlike the high Society Islands, these islands have no sheltering reefs or lagoons to soften the assault of the waves. As a result, necks, needles and peaks towering to more than 1000 metres stand side by side with high plateaus bordered by steep cliffs. This sharp relief is ridged with deep valleys covered with luxuriant tropical vegetation. Partly sunken calderas have formed vast amphitheatres, and it is in these more sheltered areas that the Marquesans chose to build their homes. These are the bewitching islands of legend, boasting a wealth of archaeological remains, many of which are still to be catalogued.

The archipelago is not affected by cyclones, and temperatures are slightly higher than those in Papeete. Rainfall is very variable, but is generally evenly spread throughout the year, with greatest precipitation between June and August. Torrential downpours are often followed by lengthy droughts. Temperatures vary and can be vastly different between one valley and another.

The islands' flora and fauna differ little from those of the other archipelagos. The *nono*, a minute black or white fly with a painful bite, is endemic. The islands are also home to wild horses and goats, introduced by Europeans.

The six inhabited islands have a total of about 7500 inhabitants. The high birth rate helps compensate for the large number of Marquesans who leave for Papeete. The agricultural sector, in particular the cultivation of copra, is by far the biggest source of income. The public service (health, education, administrative services) is also an important source of employment. Notoriously underdeveloped until the early 1980s, the Marquesas are beginning to catch up with technology. Projects aimed at reducing the islands' isolation and dependence on Tahiti are currently being carried out, including the

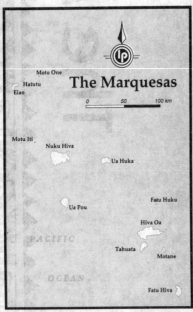

Haakakai O Te Henua Enana: the Legend of the Land of Men

This creation legend is one of the most important Marquesan myths. At the dawn of humanity, two deities, Oatea and Atuana, ruled over the vastness of the ocean. One day, Atuana expressed the wish to live in a house. Oatea, her husband, didn't know what to do. He decided to draw upon the divine powers within him and promised Atuana that the house would be built by dawn the following day.

He then devoted himself to incantations and chose a site for the future house on the ocean. He commenced by putting up two posts, and exclaimed, 'This is Ua Pou!'. He then took a roof beam and placed it on the two posts. After tying it with coconut-fibre ropes, he cried, 'This is Hiva Oa!'. He continued his assembly work. When fitting the rafters he said, 'This is Nuku Hiva!'. He then made the roof of the house from nine coconut palms and cried, 'This is Fatu Hiva!'. To bury the leftover vegetation which was strewn over the ground, he dug a hole.

Atuana saw the glimmer of dawn on the horizon. 'This is Tahuata!' Oatea shouted. And when Atuana added impatiently, 'I can hear the morning bird song!', Oatea replied, 'This is Motane!'. He quickly threw the scraps into the hole and said, 'This is Ua Huka!' With his last breath, as he felt his divine powers leaving him with the sunrise, he murmured, 'This is Eiao!'.

This creation myth likens the birth of the archipelago to the construction of a *hae* (house). It relates only to those islands which were inhabited long ago; today, Motane and Eiao are no longer inhabited. ■

development of fishing and agricultural resources, construction of new schools, improvement of inter-island transport and roads, and promotion of tourism.

HISTORY
Pre-European Period

The Marquesas were amongst the first islands to be settled by the Polynesians during their great South Pacific migrations, being settled after Melanesia, Tonga and Samoa. The Marquesas served as a dispersal point for the whole Polynesian triangle, from Hawaii to Easter Island and New Zealand. The exact date of the islands' initial colonisation, however, has not been established. Estimates vary from prehistory to between 300 and 600 BC.

This initial period of settlement is characterised by the people's affirmation of an original identity. Witness to this are the numerous archaeological remains which have survived to modern times, including *tohuas*, meaes, *pae paes* and *tikis* – wood, stone and bone sculptures.

European Contact

The Marquesas' isolation was broken in July 1595, when the Spanish navigator Alvaro de Mendaña y Neira arrived in sight of Fatu Hiva by pure chance. The expedition had left Peru a month earlier with the aim of discovering the hypothetical Terra Australis Incognita, a land which was believed to abound in gold and spices. This initial, unexpected contact ended in the death of several islanders. Mendaña's fleet then sailed along past Motane and Hiva Oa, and anchored for around 10 days in Vaitahu Bay on Tahuata.

Mendaña christened these four islands Las Marquesas de Mendoza in honour of the viceroy of Peru, García Hurtado de Mendoza, marquis of Cañete, who had supported him in his endeavour. Finding neither gold nor spices, the ships returned to sea.

In April 1774, Captain Cook lingered for four days on Tahuata during his second great voyage. He managed to form a more cordial relationship with the islanders than did his European predecessors. Ingraham, the US commander of the *Hope*, came upon the northern group of the Marquesas in April 1791, arriving slightly ahead of the Frenchman Etienne Marchand, captain of the merchant vessel *Le Solide*, who took on fresh supplies on Tahuata and then landed on Ua Pou in June 1791.

A Russian geographical and commercial mission took Admiral Krusenstern to Nuku Hiva in 1804. Aboard the vessel were men of science and artists who published their observations when they returned to Europe.

From the early 19th century onwards, sea traffic increased in this area of the Pacific. A triangular trading route was established between the Marquesas, China and Australia, and it was during this time that the islands' precious sandalwood trees were plundered. This was also the period of the whalers, for which the Marquesas acted as a base for taking on fresh supplies. On board one of the vessels was the writer Herman Melville.

In 1813 Nuku Hiva was requisitioned by the American Captain Porter as a US naval base during the conflicts between the USA and Britain. The US presence was short-lived, however, since Porter's territorial designs were not supported by his government.

Annexation by France

French interest in the region grew as a means of countering English expansion in the Pacific. After an initial reconnaissance voyage in 1838, Rear Admiral Abel Dupetit-Thouars took possession of Tahuata on 1 May 1842 in the name of King Louis-Philippe. The Marquesan chieftains, who didn't realise the ramifications of the act, did not oppose this transfer of sovereignty. Only Iotete, a chieftain from Tahuata, rebelled some months later, but his opposition was in vain.

The Marquesas were quickly marginalised in favour of Papeete for geographical, economic and strategic reasons. Only the Catholic missionaries, who had been active since their arrival on Tahuata in 1838, persevered. Their evangelising endeavours were more fruitful than those of their Protestant rivals from the LMS (London Missionary Society), who had been on the island since 1825, and Catholicism became firmly entrenched in the Marquesas.

Upon contact with Western influences, the foundations of Marquesan society collapsed. The crews of the whalers brought alcohol, firearms and syphilis, while the colonial administration and missionaries paid little attention to the ancestral values of the Marquesan people. The stunning decline in population reflects the steady process of disintegration: from an estimated 18,000 in 1842, the population fell to 5264 in 1887 and 2096 in 1926.

Recent History

Thanks to the efforts of Louis Rollin, the doctor appointed to the Marquesas from 1923 to 1930, the decline in population was stemmed. Vaccinations and assistance for new arrivals also helped boost the population.

This century, the experiences of the French-men Paul Gauguin and Jacques Brel on the islands drew world attention to the Marquesas. More recently, the development of transport and telecommunications infrastructures are helping to lessen the archipelago's isolation.

SOCIETY & CONDUCT

Many aspects of Marquesan culture are unique, and have survived both time and outside influences.

Traditional Marquesan Society

The original inhabitants' cannibalism was long concealed because of the repugnance it aroused in Westerners. Warriors captured or killed in combat were automatically used as propitiatory victims, as only chieftains or warriors could blend with the *mana* (spirit) of the enemy. The practice was officially outlawed in 1867.

Socially, each clan (*huaka*) occupied a valley, which it considered to be its *henua* (territory) and which was jealously defended. Conflicts between the valleys' inhabitants were frequent and bloody.

As in the other archipelagos, the community was stratified by the apportionment of tasks. A chieftain (*toa*) or chieftainess (*hakaiki*) wielded authority and ensured that prohibitions (*tapu*) were observed. The high priests (*taua*), who were endowed with a powerful mana, acted as intermediaries between the tribe and the gods. The warrior chief, adorned with cockerel feathers and mother-of-pearl, was entrusted with leading the soldiers.

The remainder of the population were the *meie*, among whom the most notable were the *tuhuna*, experts in activities such as tattooing, sculpture and architecture. Marquesan tattooing was particularly fine and each victory in battle was celebrated with a new tattoo.

Marquesan sculpture was well developed, combining monumental forms and sculptural rendering. Plaiting and the manufacture of items from esparto grass were also advanced, and clothing was made from beaten bark (*tapa*).

However, little is known of Marquesan narratives, song and dance.

Marquesan Culture Today

Marquesan culture has been conserved largely due to the efforts of the Motu Haka association. Established in 1978 on Ua Pou,

the group promotes Marquesan language and heritage through activities such as the Marquesas Islands Festival. Sculpture and tattooing have been revitalised, artisans are setting up their own businesses and a sculpture school has been established in Taiohae. Exhibition and sales centres can be found in many villages, displaying a range of island crafts.

The restoration of archaeological sites by international and local experts has also boosted recognition of the islands' unique culture, and each new discovery reveals a little more of the overall picture. Small museums have been established to display examples of the archipelago's heritage.

The Marquesan language, long threatened with extinction, is again being taught and spoken.

ACCOMMODATION

There are several good hotels on Nuku Hiva

THE MARQUESAS

The Marquesas Islands Festival: Symbol of Cultural Revival

The Marquesas Islands Festival (Matava'a o te Henua Enata), which was held for the fourth time on Ua Pou between 17 and 20 December 1995, is proof of the vitality of Marquesan culture. The event was the creation of Toti Teikiehuupoko, a Hakahau (Ua Pou) school teacher who laid the foundations of the Motu Haka association (or 'gathering') in 1978, with the aim of safeguarding and promoting Marquesan culture by introducing the teaching of the Marquesan language in the archipelago's schools. Initially just a discussion group, the association took a decisive step in 1985 when, in the wake of the Pacific Arts Festival in Tahiti, the idea to similarly organise demonstrations of dancing, singing, traditional sports, cuisine and arts and crafts took hold.

The first Matava'a was held on Ua Pou in May 1987. Greater awareness, larger delegations, smoother organisation and a well-defined theme ('the birth of the Marquesas Islands') guaranteed the success of the second festival, which was held on Nuku Hiva in June 1989. This festival made the restoration of the Piki Vehine site at Taiohae possible. In December 1991, it was the turn of Hiva Oa to host the third festival. For the occasion, archaeological sites at Atuona, Puamau and Taaoa underwent restoration work and a museum was opened at Atuona.

Due to lack of finances, the fourth festival, which was initially planned for 1993, was postponed to December 1995, the year of the 400th anniversary of the arrival of the first Europeans in the southern group of the Marquesas. More than a thousand people flocked there in their festival costumes, and the theme of the event was Te Mevaha (the Migrations). Sculpture competitions using *keetu* (red tuff), wood (rose wood, *tou*) and *poa* (coconut palm) or *paeore* (pandanus) weaving were organised around this theme. Archaeological sites were cleared and restored, and each delegation was invited to demonstrate their culinary skill, particularly in the preparation of *kaaku*. The best storytellers from each island told Marquesan legends, engaging in oratorical contests with miming and various vocal sound effects. A large *vaka* (dugout canoe) was built, and a Marquesan song competition and the performance of a Haka Manu (bird dance) by each delegation were also held.

This festival is in no way designed to satisfy passing tourists' thirst for the exotic. While admission is free, these events are aimed primarily at Marquesans themselves. The purpose is to reactivate their collective memory and to increase the standing of ancestral practices.

Be patient: the curtain rises on the fifth festival in December 1999 in Taiohae. ■

and Hiva Oa, and the tourism boom expected in the wake of the extension of Nuku Hiva airport should see an increase in facilities.

Almost all the villages on the islands have several guesthouses, although prices and standards vary. Most can organise excursions, and unless otherwise stated, accommodation rates are per person, per day.

GETTING THERE & AWAY
Air

Nuku Hiva, Hiva Oa, Ua Huka and Ua Pou all have airports, however, only Hiva Oa and Nuku Hiva can accommodate Air Tahiti's ATR 42s. Nuku Hiva airport (Nuku Ataha) is currently being extended to handle the faster ATR 72 aircraft, while the secondary airfields of Ua Pou and Ua Huka are served by a 19-seater Dornier once a week.

The Marquesas are linked with Papeete, Rangiroa, Manihi, Puka Puka and Napuka. The exorbitant fares between Papeete and the Marquesas have long impaired tourism opportunities on the archipelago, but the introduction of more attractive fares in January 1996 has finally made the Marquesas accessible to most travellers. The prices quoted in this chapter are full fare.

Flight time is about three and a half hours direct from Tahiti; the more powerful ATR 72s will take only three hours. Make yourself known to the Air Tahiti representatives on each island in case of timetable changes, and don't forget that the Marquesas are half an hour ahead of Papeete.

Sea

Inter-Island Ships The *Taporo IV*, *Tamarii Tuamoto* and *Aranui* serve Taiohae, Hakahau and Atuona. The islands' other bays, which lack suitable quays, are served by whalers. These ships are known locally as schooners or tramps, but they are in fact cargo boats and freighters (see Inter-Island Ships in the Getting Around chapter).

Pleasure Boats The Marquesas are popular stopping-off points for round-the-world sailors who, blown by the trade winds from the North American continent, sail towards the south-west Pacific. Easily spotted from dozens of km away, the Marquesas are a haven for sailors, with numerous sheltered bays with safe mooring and plenty of opportunities for taking on supplies. In the high season, between March and September, there can be up to 30 sailing boats in the harbours of Taiohae (Nuku Hiva) or Tahauku (Hiva Oa).

Sailors must ensure that their first landing place is on one of the islands with a police station: Nuku Hiva (Taiohae), Hiva Oa (Atuona) or Ua Pou (Hakahau), and they must register each time they land. Some sailors arrive at Fatu Hiva first, and then tack close to the wind as far as Hiva Oa. This is risky, however, as the *mutoi* (representative of the authorities) on Fatu Hiva will forewarn the authorities at Atuona, and the vessel runs the risk of a fine. Sailors should be aware that all vessels in the area remain under the surveillance of the authorities, because of concerns about drug and arms trafficking.

Marquesas International Airport: Mad Hope or Reality?

The international airport project at Terre Déserte in the island of Nuku Hiva (which was triumphantly announced in November 1995 by the president of the Territory, Gaston Flosse) still causes much ink to flow. Whether it's a case of media and political bluff or a realistic prospect, it's hard to tell.

The project involves lengthening the current runway by 500 metres to accommodate medium-size planes. The estimated cost, however, is between US$50 and US$70 million.

The project has raised great hope among Marquesans, as the economic benefits are believed to be considerable. Apart from the direct spin-offs for local employment and tourism, the transportation of fresh fish from the airport to markets in the USA and Japan would boost the archipelago's fishing industry.

But the Marquesans are cautious in their optimism; too many unfulfilled promises in the past have made them wary. The one definite sign of progress is the arrival of Air Tahiti's ATR 72s, expected in 1996-97. ■

Anchorages On Nuku Hiva, in addition to Taiohae harbour, there are excellent anchorages in Hakatea and Hakaui bays in the south-west, Hatiheu and Anaho in the north-east and Taipivai in the east. Rose Corser, the American owner of the Keikahanui Inn (see Places to Stay in Nuku Hiva), is the person to talk to about laundry and poste restante facilities in Taiohae.

On Ua Huka, magnificent Haavei Bay is a haven of tranquillity. You can also stop off in Vaipaee or Hane harbours.

There is a marina on Ua Pou at Hakahau Cove. The Pukuéé restaurant/guesthouse (see Places to Stay in Ua Pou) acts as the agent for poste restante and laundry. The island's other anchorages are all on the west coast at Hakamaii, Hakahetau and Vaiehu. In Hakahetau, ask for Etienne Hokaupoko, the polyglot *tavana* (mayor).

On Hiva Oa, Tahauku Inlet is sheltered and has a marina (moor near to the nautical club). In the north-west of the island, it is possible to put in at Hanapaaoa (ask for Shan Aniel) or at Hanamenu.

Tahuata has several idyllic inlets, notably Hanahevane, Hanamoenoa and Hapatoni.

On Fatu Hiva, the legendary Bay of Virgins (Hanavave) is a world-famous port of call.

GETTING AROUND

Getting around the Marquesas is difficult, whether by sea or land. The valleys are isolated from each other, making it virtually impossible to do island tours by road, and only the main towns or villages have sealed roads. Some villages have no landing stage and the sea is often rough, making beaching difficult.

The introduction of helicopter shuttles within the northern and southern groups has improved inter-island transport, which was previously only possible by Air Tahiti or according to the whims of passing boats.

Helicopter

Based at Taiohae (Nuku Hiva), the Héli Inter Marquises company provided its first regular services in the northern group in August 1994. From Taiohae, an Ecureuil flies to Ua Huka and Ua Pou in a few minutes. Links are also made with the villages of Nuku Hiva to connect with Air Tahiti. A subsidiary base was established at Atuona (Hiva Oa) in January 1996 to serve the southern group (Hiva Oa, Tahuata and Fatu Hiva).

While practical, this method of transport is costly. As inter-island shuttle services are generally weekly or fortnightly, book a few days or even a few weeks in advance, especially if there are several of you.

4WD

The 4WD is the most common means of transport and is best suited to handle the rugged contours of these islands. With two exceptions (Atuona and Taiohae), they are hired with the services of a driver. Self-drive rental has been abandoned because most visitors are not used to such deplorable road conditions and inevitably damage the vehicles.

Enforced passenger status may seem restricting at first, but it has its advantages. You will soon notice that driving in such conditions is exhausting and dangerous, and as a result, the drivers drive with infinite caution at an average of 10 to 15 km/h. In addition, they know the whole population and can introduce you to local communities, as well as guiding you to difficult-to-find locations.

Rental is charged at a flat rate per vehicle. If you are travelling alone, try to join up with a group or ask your hotel about its excursion programme. Bookings for 4WD tours are essential, and although guesthouses or hotels will make bookings on your behalf, it may prove wiser to meet the hirers face to face.

Excursions often take a full day, and as it will be much more comfortable if there are only three or four other passengers travelling with you, it's a good idea to find out in advance how many passengers have booked.

Horse Riding

Horses are an integral part of the Marquesan landscape. Originally from Chile, they were introduced by Dupetit-Thouars, who gave

THE MARQUESAS

them to Chief Iotete (Tahuata) in 1842. Horse riding is an excellent way of getting to know the valleys and taking in the islands' imposing scenery. Each island has hire facilities, with or without the services of a guide. Ua Huka has the greatest number of horses; they are a pony-thoroughbred mix, and are renowned for their sense of balance.

Hitching

Although uncommon due to the small volume of traffic, hitching is possible. Position yourself at the edge of the road or approach 4WD or commercial vehicle owners directly outside premises such as shops, the post office or town hall. Alternatively, you can try your luck with the valley dwellers, who come into the main towns on a regular basis.

Boat

Bonitiers, Speedboats & Schooners
Speedboats and *bonitiers* (old whaleboats, from the term 'Boston whalers') are faster than 4WD and can reach all the valleys. Hire charges are made at a flat rate and include the compulsory services of a driver. If you are travelling alone, enquire at hotels, guesthouses or boat owners to find out about their trip schedules, and in this way you will share the costs.

The capacity of the boats varies. Bonitiers, for example, are larger than speedboats and can take up to 15 people. Tahuata and Fatu Hiva have a communal bonitier which runs a regular ferry service to Hiva Oa.

Boat hitching is possible if you are lucky. Ask the boat owners in the marinas if they will take you on board. Amateur sailors will probably agree to take you from one island to another.

Another possibility is to hitch a ride with doctors doing their rounds by boat. They regularly do a one-day round of the remote valleys by speedboat or 4WD. Try to join the team.

The movements of the *Kaoha Nui*, a fairly large vessel which provides inter-island transport for sports tournaments, religious celebrations or school outings, are totally unpredictable. If it should happen to moor at the island where you are staying, jump on.

Lastly, the schooners which pass at more or less regular intervals may let you make a few short hops. Ask about arrival dates of the *Aranui*, *Tamarii Tuamotu* or *Taporo IV*.

Cruises

Archipels Croisières and Omati Marquises offer cruises around the Marquesas (see Cruises in the Nuku Hiva and Hiva Oa sections, and the introductory Getting Around chapter).

The Northern Group

The northern group consists of three main inhabited islands – Nuku Hiva, Ua Huka and Ua Pou – and the deserted islets further to the north – Motu Iti (Hatu Iti), Eiao, Hatutu (Hatutaa), Motu One (Sand Island) and the Clark Bank.

NUKU HIVA

Population: 2100
Area: 340 sq km
Highest Point: 1224 metres (Mt Tekao)

The main island of the northern group, and the largest in the archipelago, Nuku Hiva (the 'rafters' in the Marquesas Islands legend) is the administrative and economic capital of the Marquesas, and outshines its traditional rival in the southern group, Hiva Oa.

Nuku Hiva has the largest population but one of the smallest population densities. Settlement is concentrated in Taiohae on the south coast, Hatiheu on the north coast and Taipivai on the east. Hamlets such as Anaho, Hooumi, Aakapa and Pua are home to only a handful of inhabitants.

Nuku Hiva was formed from two volcanoes, stacked one on top of the other, which gave rise to two concentric calderas. The top of the main caldera forms a jagged framework which surrounds the Toovii plateau. To the south of this plateau, the broken-mouthed caldera of the

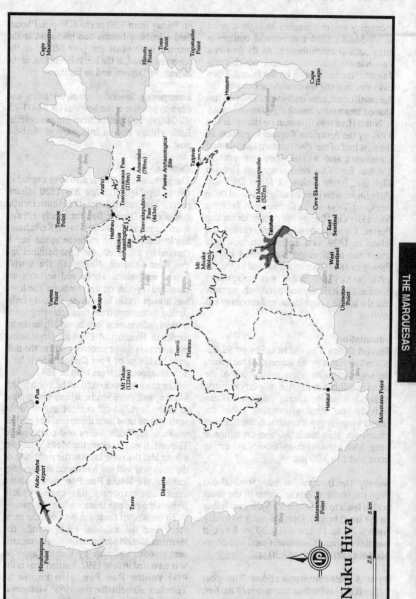

Nuku Hiva

Cape Maatautua

Hinutu Point

Teea Point

Topatuoho Point

Cape Tikapo

Hooumi

Controller Bay

Anaho

Teavaimaoaoa Pass (218m)

Mt Amotako (789m)

Paeke Archaeological Site

Taipivai

Temoe Point

Hatiheu

Teavaitapuhiva Pass (443m)

Hikokua Archaeological Site

Cave Ekamako

East Sentinel

Taiohae

West Sentinel

Vaetea Point

Aakapa

Ahuii Falls

Mt Moukopaoho (527m)

Taiohae Bay

Uhutotao Point

Pua

Mt Tekao (1224m)

Mt Muake (864m)

Toovii Plateau

Vaipo Waterfall

Hakaui Bay

Nuku Ataha Airport

Déserte

Hakaui

Motuanano Point

Terre

Hinahaapapa Point

Mataeteiko Point

Marquisienne Bay

N

0   2.5   5 km

THE MARQUESAS

THE MARQUESAS

secondary volcano reaches its highest point at Mt Muake (864 metres) and outlines a huge natural amphitheatre. At its foot is a vast natural harbour, around which curls Taiohae, the main town on the island. Deep bays cut into the south and east coasts. On the north coast, erosion by wind and rain has shaped impressive basalt aiguilles (needles).

Nuku Hiva was first seen by Europeans in 1791 by the American Captain Ingraham. In the first half of the 19th century, sandalwood merchants and whalers put into port in Taiohae Bay. One such sailor was Herman Melville, future author of *Moby Dick* and *Billy Budd*, who jumped ship and spent three weeks at Taipivai. A fortress was built on Nuku Hiva in 1813 by the American captain Porter. Catholic missionaries reached the island in 1839, and the religion took hold when the archipelago was seized by the French in 1842. During the second half of the 19th century the island was ravaged by disease, and it is only comparatively recently that the island's population and economy has revived.

Information

Tourist Office The tourist office (☎ 92-02-20) in Taiohae is by the marina, set back from the seafront, in an office at the back of the stone building housing the property registry. Deborah Kimitete speaks English and can provide you with information about the island's tourist opportunities. Some free brochures are also available, and the office is open Monday to Friday from 7.30 am to noon and 1 to 3.30 pm.

Money The Banque Socredo (☎ 92-03-63) is on the seafront, on the corner of the street which leads to Frenchmen's Valley and close to the small bridge. Open Monday to Friday from 7.30 to 11 am and 1.30 to 4 pm, it handles exchange and credit card withdrawals. Last exchange is at 3.30 pm.

Post & Telecommunications The post office (OPT) is on the eastern side of the bay, opposite the police station. It is open Monday to Thursday from 8 am to 3 pm and on Friday from 7.30 am to 4.30 pm. Phonecard telephone booths can be found at the marina, in front of the post office, at the schooner wharf, at the Keikahanui Inn, at the airport, in Taipivai and in Hatiheu.

Emergency Several doctors, surgeons and dentists practise at the hospital (☎ 92-03-75, 92-04-79), 100 metres from the post office. Each village has an infirmary or first-aid post.

Taiohae

The economic and administrative capital of the archipelago, Taiohae has 1620 inhabitants. The town hugs the semicircular contours of Taiohae Bay for nearly 3.5 km, from the marina in the east to the Keikahanui Inn in the west. The entrance to the bay is flanked by two islets, the East Sentinel and the West Sentinel. Nearly all the town's hotels, restaurants, shops and services are clustered together on the seashore. The town hall houses Radio Marquises, the only radio station to transmit from the archipelago, and a local information centre which includes works in French and English. Dominating the marina is the promontory where the military buildings of **Fort Collet**, which have now disappeared, were built in 1842.

The town is overlooked to the north by Mt Muake, and three roads, which correspond to the valleys, go off at right angles to the seafront and head in its direction. The middle road crosses Pakiu Valley and continues to Taipivai. If you go along the Meau Valley for a little less than one km, on the right side of the road you will see a restored archaeological site, the **Mauia Pae Pae**, over which a small contemporary tiki keeps watch. Behind the pae pae there's a banyan tree.

To the west of the town, between the cemetery and the nautical club, stands the **Herman Melville memorial**. This magnificent wooden sculpture by Kahee Taupotini was unveiled in July 1992. Further east is the **Piki Vehine Pae Pae**, also known as Temehea. Rebuilt for the 1989 Marquesas Islands Festival, it is decorated with several impressive tikis made by the island's sculptors and by artisans from Easter Island. The influence of the latter can clearly be seen as some statues are reminiscent of the *moai* of Easter Island. The daring and varied designs attest to the vitality of contemporary Marquesan art.

A hundred metres or so further east again stands a stone cross at a crossroad, marking the vicinity of the Catholic mission. Take the road which turns left to **Notre-Dame Cathedral of the Marquesas Islands** built on the Tohua Mauia, a sacred place venerated by the ancient Marquesans. The entry porch is flanked by two pinnacles and leads to a

paved esplanade which adjoins the church building. Carved into a tree is a statue of Monsignor Dordillon, bishop of the Marquesas from 1848 to 1888, who was given the land by the traditional Moana chieftain to build a school there; the cathedral was built alongside in 1977. The stone used in the construction of the church comes from the six inhabited islands: on the east façade are the red *keetu* of Hiva Oa and white sandstone of Nuku Hiva; on the north side, stone from Ua Pou; on the west, stone from Ua Huka and Fatu Hiva; and on the south, pumice stone from Tahuata. The square in

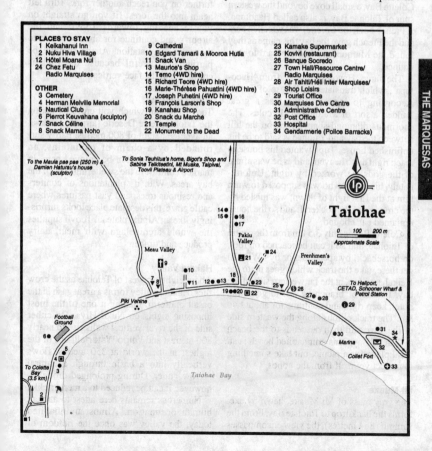

PLACES TO STAY
1 Keikahanui Inn
2 Nuku Hiva Village
12 Hôtel Moana Nui
24 Chez Fetu
   Radio Marquises

OTHER
3 Cemetery
4 Herman Melville Memorial
5 Nautical Club
6 Pierrot Keuvahana (sculptor)
7 Snack Céline
8 Snack Mama Noho

9 Cathedral
10 Edgard Tamarii & Mooroa Hutia
11 Snack Van
13 Maurice's Shop
14 Temo (4WD hire)
15 Richard Teore (4WD hire)
16 Marie-Thérèse Pahuatini (4WD hire)
17 Joseph Puhetini (4WD hire)
18 François Larson's Shop
19 Kanahau Shop
20 Snack du Marché
21 Temple
22 Monument to the Dead

23 Kamake Supermarket
25 Kovivi (restaurant)
26 Banque Socredo
27 Town Hall/Resource Centre/
   Radio Marquises
28 Air Tahiti/Héli Inter Marquises/
   Shop Loisirs
29 Tourist Office
30 Marquises Dive Centre
31 Administrative Centre
32 Post Office
33 Hospital
34 Gendarmerie (Police Barracks)

THE MARQUESAS

front is made from phonolite slabs from Ua Pou. The various carvings, such as the cross, the bishop's throne and the tabernacle, are striking testimony to the local sculptors' talent.

On the seafront, opposite the Kamake supermarket, is the **Monument to the Dead**, an obelisk which bears a commemorative plaque in honour of Etienne Marchand. This is a popular area for Sunday pastimes such as *petanque* and bingo, shaded by the surrounding mango trees.

Colette Bay

Colette Bay, a small cove beyond the western spur of Taiohae Bay, is also called Haaotupa. A French boat, the *Colette*, was wrecked here and the French gave the bay this name as they found the Marquesan word too hard to pronounce.

The name 'Haaotupa' comes from 'Haeotupa', which translates as 'house of Tupa'. According to legend, Tupa was a great builder, a sort of Marquesan Hercules. The enormous diamond-shaped rock on the hill between the bay and Taiohae is said to be his unfinished house. Tupa wanted his house to reach right up to heaven, and as he was afraid of the gods, he worked by night. Unfortunately, his sister, who was supposed to warn him at the first light of dawn, was misled by the crowing of the cockerel, and so the house remained earthbound.

Colette Bay is only 3.5 km from the centre of Taiohae, and so it can be reached on foot, on horseback, by speedboat or by 4WD. To get there, take the track which goes up to the Keikahanui Inn, at the far western side of the bay. Instead of branching left to go to the hotel, keep right and continue for about two km. The track climbs along the western side of the cove and then descends to the beach at Colette Bay. This uninhabited beach is an ideal place for a picnic, but take something to protect yourself from the nonos.

Mt Muake

The grey mass of Mt Muake, hewn by axe, forms the backdrop to Taiohae Bay. From the summit (864 metres), the view encompasses

Taiohae harbour and Ua Pou to the south, part of Contrôleur Bay to the east, and the ridge of the main crater to the north. Muake is used as a takeoff site for hang-gliders, and it is also quite common to see tropicbirds wheeling around this magnificent space.

Muake can be reached on foot or by 4WD along a picturesque track which takes you through tropical vegetation to conifers and resinous trees near the summit. From the seafront at Taiohae, by François Larson's shop, take the road which goes up towards Pakiu Valley. Continue just under seven km to the first fork, go left, and some four km further on you reach another fork. Turn left again into the forest (if you go straight on you're heading towards Toovii and the airport), and continue for about two km to the radio relay station. At the summit, be particularly careful because the rock is crumbly and the face vertical.

Toovii Plateau

Toovii Plateau, which you cross by taking the Taiohae-Terre Déserte (airport) track, at an average height of 800 metres. Partly surrounded by a chain of mountains, an welcome coolness can be enjoyed here, in marked contrast to the sweltering heat of the bay areas. With its plantations of conifers and resinous trees, and vast pastures where cattle graze, this desolate place looks surprisingly like an Alpine plateau. Toovii supplies the whole archipelago with meat, dairy produce and timber.

Hakaui Valley

About eight km west of Taiohae as the crow flies, Hakaui Valley forms a great gash in the basalt platform, making it one of the most imposing sights on Nuku Hiva. On either side of the river vertical walls rise to nearly 800 metres, and **Vaipo Waterfall**, one of the highest in the world at 350 metres, flows vertically into a basin through a natural narrow gutter. During prolonged droughts, however, it can be reduced to a mere trickle.

Numerous remains here attest to ancient human occupation. Almost uninhabited today, the valley was once the fiefdom of

King Te Moana and Queen Vackehu. A paved road, which was an ancient royal way, goes up the valley following the river, and concealed in the cliff faces are funerary caves containing the remains of chieftains placed in mortuary canoes.

From Taiohae, the valley can be reached by speedboat (about 20 minutes), on foot or on horseback by a 12-km bridleway. Take a picnic, some plastic sandals, a swimming costume, mosquito repellent and waterproof bags for your camera. From the bay where the boat anchors, allow two hours to reach the waterfall on foot. The path, which is not particularly difficult except for a few fords, follows the course of the river and includes stretches of the ancient royal way. Kapok and breadfruit trees, pandanus and coconut palms make the walk quite picturesque, and the occasional pae pae, tohua and tikis can be spotted under the tangle of vegetation. The path becomes steeper as it nears the waterfall basin, making its inviting natural swimming pool all the more welcome.

Hatiheu

In the north of the island, 12 km from Taipivai and 28 km from Taiohae, this village is full of charm, to which the Scottish writer Robert Louis Stevenson succumbed. The town's focal point is the wooden church, with its yellow façade and two biscuit-coloured symmetrical steeples. To the rear, the cemetery encroaches on the hill behind the church. The seafront, which is planted with lawns and coconut palms, is decorated with tikis, the recent work of local sculptors, and to the west, the silhouette of the basalt peaks looks rather like a baroque fortified castle. On one of the peaks, at a height of 300 metres, is a white Virgin, erected in 1872.

The tiny town hall on the seafront houses a small **museum** with a collection of traditional Marquesan artefacts. Yvonne Katupa, the mayor of the village, actively promotes Marquesan cultural heritage, and it was at her instigation that the tikis along the seafront were sculpted and the numerous archaeological remains in the area were restored.

The **Hikokua Tohua** archaeological site is the most notable in the area. As you come from Taipivai, it's about one km from the Chez Yvonne guesthouse, along a small track suitable for vehicles. Ask at the guesthouse for Alphonse Puhetini (also known as Rua) to accompany you, as he has worked with the archaeologists in this valley. Formerly the site of festivities and human sacrifices, the site is still occasionally used for traditional dancing, and ancient sculptures coexist with recent works. Most eye-catching is the phallic-shaped fertility tiki at the left of the entrance to the site. Another of the tikis is double sided: on one side is a human face and on the other a tortoise.

From Taipivai, follow the main road inland towards the west. The track quickly becomes rocky and in poor condition, but the steep ascent to Teavaitapuhiva Pass (443 metres), 7.5 km from Taipivai, provides impressive views over Hatiheu Bay and the Teuakueenui and Mahuiki falls. Four km further on, just before Hatiheu, some meaes are concealed beneath the plant cover.

Taipivai

The ancient fiefdom of the Taipi tribes, Taipivai lies 16 km north-east of Taiohae. The town carpets the floor of a river valley, and its single street follows the river's course for nearly two km. At the eastern end of the village the river rushes into Contrôleur Bay.

The majority of Taipivai's inhabitants are farmers, and the village is filled with the subtle perfume of vanilla, the cultivation of which is well suited to this fertile alluvial plain. Many of the locals grow this precious orchid, and pods can be purchased by passing visitors when stocks are available. Try asking Monsieur Tava, whose blue house is on the Hooumi road, set back on the left after the school (take the little road on the left); Edmond Ah Scha, who lives in the bamboo house just alongside; or Monsieur Teikitohe, who lives in a beige house on the left below the Hatiheu road, about one km from the bridge. The pods cost 1000 to 1500 CFP for 100 grams. The production of copra is another important activity in Taipivai.

In the early 19th century, the inhabitants of Taipivai distinguished themselves by fiercely resisting the incursions of the American Captain Porter, who tried to annex the island in 1813. His soldiers used cannons to massacre the population.

Literature has also made Taipivai well known. In July 1842, the American whaler *Acushnet* put in at Taiohae, and on board was a sailor named Herman Melville, who jumped ship. He reached Taipivai Valley and was taken in by the Taipi people, whose life he shared for three weeks. He gathered a wealth of information about their way of life, and his unusual experiences were later related in *Taïpi*, a highly successful novel which was published in 1846.

The place where the writer is supposed to have lived is marked with a sign reading 'Cité Melville'; it's about 4.5 km from the bridge in the centre of Taipivai, on the left-hand side of the Hatiheu road.

Allow 1½ hours by 4WD to reach Taipivai from Taiohae; take the road at right angles to the seafront in front of François Larson's shop.

Paeke Archaeological Site This site features two well-maintained meaes, flanked by a set of brick-coloured tikis. Massive and squat, with well-developed lower limbs, they radiate a forbidding power which makes them look like petrified Cerberuses. The meae further up the hill has a pit into which human remains were thrown.

To get to the site from the little bridge in the centre of Taipivai, take the road for Hatiheu (uphill) for about 1.5 km until you leave the village. Then follow the path which passes the blue house on the right and goes up through the coconut plantation. It's a 20 or 30-minute steep walk uphill, so take some mosquito repellent, a hat and sunscreen.

Hooumi
Once inhabited by the fierce Teavaaki, this charming hamlet, surrounded by luxuriant vegetation, is about four km east of Taipivai. The track from Taipivai goes through the village, which features a row of pae paes, on which houses have now been built, and the ubiquitous copra-drying sheds. The village also has a picturesque small timber church, its doors and windows outlined in blue giving it the appearance of a dolls' house. The track was initially a cliff-top road, and it affords marvellous views over Contrôleur Bay and ends at a stunning white-sand beach opposite one of the two inlets of Contrôleur Bay. Unfortunately, the beach is plagued by nonos and mosquitoes.

Anaho
In 1888, Robert Louis Stevenson moored in Anaho Bay while he was cruising the Pacific on his sailing boat the *Casco*. The setting inspired him to write pages and pages of words eulogising the unsettling beauty of the place.

A few families live in this peaceful hamlet which has been untouched by time. The long white-sand beach, sadly infested with nonos, stretches for nearly a km, and the bay, with its north-south orientation and surrounding ring of mountains, is perfectly sheltered from the wind and the swell, contrasting sharply with the coves on the other islands. The only coral reef on the Marquesas has formed here, creating a lagoon-like effect. The shore is edged by copra-drying sheds, a magnificent coconut plantation and a tiny chapel.

Anaho can be reached by speedboat from Hatiheu in less than 10 minutes or on foot along a picturesque track. Take walking shoes, water and mosquito repellent. At the crossroad 100 metres east of the Hinakonui restaurant, take the tar-sealed track which goes up to the right. About 500 metres further on there's a small clearing, and if you have a vehicle it's best to leave it here. The start of the path is on the left, beyond the little bridge, 100 metres uphill from the white house built on a pae pae. It's about a 30 to 45-minute walk to reach Anaho Beach. At Teavaimaoaoa Pass (218 metres) there's an unbroken view over Anaho Bay, and the descent, right through the middle of a huge coconut plantation, is quite steep.

THE MARQUESAS

Aakapa

On the opposite side of the island from Taiohae, on the north coast, this village is in a superb natural setting characterised by peaks forming a sharp-edged wall. Aakapa can be reached by the path from Hatiheu or by speedboat.

Arts & Crafts

Several important names in sculpture work on Nuku Hiva, and in many cases you can go directly to their homes to place an order; prices are negotiable directly with the artisan.

In Taiohae, you can visit Pierrot Keuvahana (☎ 92-06-14), behind the football ground, who works in *tou* and *miro* wood and makes a wide variety of objects. You can buy clubs or spears from Edgar Tamarii (☎ 92-01-67) or from Mooroa Hutia, who lives nearby. Their workshop is about 100 metres behind the snack van on the seafront. The best known sculptor is Damien Haturau (☎ 92-05-56), who lives in Meau Valley, 300 metres from the Mauia pae in the large house set back from the road. Professor of sculpture at the CETAD technical school in the east of Taiohae, among his most beautiful works are the statues in the cathedral and the Virgin with Child at Vaitahu's church, on Tahuata. You can also see his work at the CETAD.

Taipivai has two renowned sculptors, Edmond Ah Scha and Firifiri (the latter's beige house with green door frames is 300 metres from the church, on the Hatiheu track).

Diving

Until recently, scuba diving was done only off the Society Islands and the Tuamotus. A diving centre opened in Taiohae in 1992, with a secondary base established in February 1996 on Hiva Oa, and the sport is becoming increasingly popular in the Marquesas.

Diving in this region is unique, as the islands' topography is totally different from that found in the other archipelagos. The Marquesas have no coral reefs (other than that off Anaho), peaceful lagoons or crystal-line waters. The water is thick with plankton and rich in alluvium, and visibility is restricted (generally 10 to 20 metres). The cliffs are hollowed with numerous cavities which afford outstanding cave dives. These oxygen-filled waters are home to a variety of creatures: dolphins, hammerhead sharks, whip-tailed stingrays, manta and leopard rays, tazars, tuna, barracuda, lobsters, sea urchins and white-tip sharks are among the species most often found. Owing to the small amount of fishing activity in the archipelago, the creatures come close to the surface, but you will not meet with any grey sharks.

Dive Centre Xavier Curvat, known as Pipapo, is the owner of the *Marquesas Dive Centre* (☎ 92-00-88 or 92-05-13, fax 92-00-88) on Taiohae's marina quay. This former underwater hunter is very familiar with the nearby depths.

The cost of an exploratory or first dive is 4500 CFP. After the second dive, the price goes down to 4000 CFP, including equipment. There are one or two trips per day, and bookings are essential. Full-day trips to Anaho can be arranged and there are diving trips to Ua Pou once a week. It is also possible to arrange one-week diving stays with reduced-rate accommodation at Hôtel Moana Nui or Nuku Hiva Village.

Dive Sites There are around 20 sites on the south and west coasts of Nuku Hiva, about 30 minutes away in the *Makuita*, the dive centre's open-sea launch. Most of the dives are from rocky overhangs or in underwater cavities. With the exception of the cave dives, which are more suited to experienced divers, the dives are accessible to all, although it may take a while to get used to the swell and the relative cloudiness of the water.

Marquesan waters are unpredictable: the same site may provide an exceptional dive one day and be disappointing the next. Trips are also subject to the vicissitudes of the weather, particularly the swell which can make travelling to the sites, manoeuvring and getting into the water dangerous. Not to mention the possible sea sickness!

At the entrance to Taiohae Bay, on the east side, the **Hammerhead Sentinel** did not get its name for nothing, as it's common to see hammerhead sharks 10 to 40 metres down, sporting curious wavy outgrowths near their mouths known as scallops. Manta rays, leopard rays, sea urchins and moray eels are also the privileged inhabitants of this place.

Ekamako Cave, to the east of Taiohae Bay, has an underwater cavity less than 15 metres below the surface. About 10 metres wide, the cave plunges more than 100 metres into the cliff, and is not recommended for the claustrophobic. There's a legend that a large shark called Ekamako, devourer of children, made the cave its home, but in reality the cavern's main attraction is the whip-tailed stingrays. Despite their fearsome spines, they are not dangerous, although it's best to keep well away from them. The instructor will point out masses of fallen rocks where enormous lobsters lurk, almost mesmerised by the light of the divers' torches, and the entrance to the cave is beautifully backlit with cobalt blue.

In another class, but just as exciting, is the dive known as **Tikapo**, from the name of the cape on the south-east tip of Nuku Hiva. Opposite this point jutting right out to sea, a rock called Te Oho Te Kea rises from the ocean, and around it, between 10 and 45 metres, swim abundant and varied sea creatures, including tazars, sharks, leopard rays, barracuda and perch. This trip only operates when the sea is calm.

Point Motumano is a rocky overhang above a sand plateau in the south-west of the island, noted for its passing manta rays and sharks.

On the west of the island, **Point Matateteiko** is a rocky hillock surrounded by waters rich with manta and leopard rays and sharks. Scalloped hammerhead sharks often swim around in the vicinity.

Parapente
Upe O Te Henua Enana is the Marquesas' only parapente club. The Taiohae area lends itself perfectly to parapente, and the club, which has 40-odd members, was launched in Taiohae in 1992.

A takeoff platform for the experienced is on the summit of Mt Muake, near the radio relay station. From the top of the completely vertical cliff, the enthusiasts launch themselves directly into the void, with the gripping spectacle of the valley and Taiohae Bay beneath their feet. Beginners can take their first steps on the infinitely more reassuring slopes on the hills above the town.

You can join these would-be Icaruses by taking out temporary membership (1500 CFP), valid for three months, which will enable you to hire a parapente for 3000 CFP per flight. When booking, novices can be initiated into the art by taking a one-week course led by a qualified instructor from Tahiti. It costs 22,500 CFP for instruction and 11,600 CFP for the licence and insurance costs. The club is planning to purchase a two-person parapente which will make it possible to offer first-time flights. For all information, call Arai (☎ 92-05-23) or Roland (☎ 92-05-30).

Horse Riding
From Taiohae, it is easy to reach Colette Bay on horseback; the best rides are in the north of the island, particularly between Hatiheu and Aakapa. See Getting Around for details.

Organised Tours
Pua Excursions, run by Monsieur Taupotini (☎ 92-02-94, fax 92-01-35, BP 99 Taiohae, Nuku Hiva), who works at the airport snack bar, offers guided tours (with an English-speaking guide) taking three to five days, departing from Nuku Hiva. The itinerary includes Toovii, Taiohae, Taipivai, Hatiheu and Anaho (three days) and Hakaui (five days). The price, which decreases with the number of persons, does not include transport from Papeete nor accommodation and meals. It costs 73,200/ 56,600/49,800 CFP per person on a basis of two/three/four participants for the three-day tour, or 81,500/ 62,500/52,000 CFP respectively for the five-day tour.

Cruises Archipels Croisières, based at Moorea (see Cruises in the Getting Around chapter), offers a Marquesas Discovery trip lasting one week and leaving from Nuku Hiva or Hiva Oa two or three times a month. This tour of the Marquesas aboard a deluxe catamaran concentrates on the main archaeological sites, and includes Nuku Hiva (Anaho, Hatiheu), Ua Huka (Haavei, Vaipaee), Hiva Oa (Puamau, Atuona, Taaoa), Fatu Hiva (Hanavave, Omoa) and Tahuata (Hanamoenoa). It costs 185,000 CFP per person full board, and departs from Nuku Hiva.

For divers, a special dive cruise has been developed in association with the Marquesas Dive Centre. Scheduled to operate about once every two months, it includes 11 dives at unspoilt sites at Anaho, Hatiheu, Point Matateteiko and in the uninhabited islets of the north: Eiao, Motu One and Hatutu. It costs 220,000 CFP per person full board for the week, departing from Nuku Hiva and includes equipment.

Scenic Helicopter Flights Héli Inter Marquises (see Getting There & Away later in this section) operates scenic flights over the island for five people. The cost of 14,500 CFP per person is certainly not within all budgets, but this 20-minute airborne jaunt is worth every CFP, although the sky must be perfectly clear.

A brief commentary is given (in French), and the pilot, Daniel Pelleau, really knows his subject. The tours take in Hakaui Valley, where the waterfall can clearly be seen, Toovii Plateau, Taipivai and Contrôleur Bay, Aakapa, Hatiheu, Anaho and Haatuatua.

Places to Stay
From guesthouses to good-quality hotels and traditional bungalows, Nuku Hiva has various accommodation options distributed around the island.

Taiohae In the bottom-end category the only option worth noting is *Chez Fetu* (☎ 92-03-66; BP 22, Taiohae, Nuku Hiva). Fetu, whose real name is Cyprien Peterano, has a fully equipped bungalow for three people with

bathroom, as well as four rooms in a large house with shared bathroom (cold water). The bare rooms are almost monastic, and cost 2000 CFP plus 500 CFP for breakfast. A huge well-equipped kitchen, clean and tiled, is available to travellers.

Ideally situated right in the centre of Taiohae on the seafront, the more upmarket *Hôtel Moana Nui* (☎ 92-03-30, fax 92-00-02; BP 9 Taiohae, Nuku Hiva) is run by Charles Nombaerts. The seven spotless rooms with bathroom (hot water) cost 4000/4500 CFP single/double with breakfast, 6500/9500 CFP half board and 9500/13,000 CFP full board. Ask for room No 1 or No 2 which directly overlook the seafront. Meals are served in the restaurant on the ground floor, and credit cards are accepted.

At the western end of Taiohae Bay, near the beach, the *Nuku Hiva Village* (☎ 92-01-94, fax 92-05-94; BP 82, Taiohae, Nuku Hiva) is the rising star of Taiohae's hotel industry. Rather than a standard hotel, it is a group of 15 sparkling-clean traditional *fares*. Sleeping two to three people, they are equipped with a bathroom (hot water) and fan, and cost 6500/7500/8500 CFP for one/two/three people, plus 8% tax; add 3500/4700 CFP for half/full board. Meals are served in the large restaurant *fare*, and credit cards are accepted.

Rose Corser and her husband sailed to Taiohae from America in 1979, and now consider themselves locals. Rose runs the *Keikahanui Inn* (☎ 92-03-82, fax 92-00-74; BP 21, Taiohae, Nuku Hiva), named after a fierce warrior of Hatiheu. This hotel is at the far west of Taiohae Bay and is often visited by Rose's yachting compatriots. There are several types of comfortable accommodation, overlooking the bay: four bungalows for three people (8500/12,000/14,000 CFP for one/two/three people per day), two split-level bungalows (5000/7000 CFP for one/two people), and two fully equipped houses for up to four people for 12,000 CFP (one shower) and 15,000 CFP (two showers). The bungalows have private bathroom (hot water) and mosquito nets. Add the 8% tax to the prices quoted; add 3500/5800 CFP per person for half/full board. Credit cards are accepted.

Anaho *Chez Rosemarie Foucaud* (☎ 92-01-46) can pride itself on being the cheapest guesthouse on the island, but comfort is restricted to the bare minimum. The four rooms are austere and timeworn, and the bathroom consists of one tap. Only the prices are heavenly: 500 CFP a night, 250 CFP breakfast and 500 to 1000 CFP a meal. Coming on foot from Hatiheu, go down to the beach (note the enormous tamanu tree, the copra-drying shed and the hut as landmarks), and take the road which goes up opposite the drying shed as far as the yellow house. Rosemarie Foucaud's house is about 400 metres south of Vaianui guesthouse (see below), near to the path which goes to Hatiheu.

The tranquillity of a coconut plantation, the magical setting of Anaho Bay, the sea just a few metres away, friendly owners – this is all it takes for the *André et Juliette Vaianui* (no telephone, call Yvonne Katupa at Hatiheu on ☎ 92-02-97) guesthouse to make you feel years younger. There are three clean rooms for three people with shared bathroom (cold water) and equipped kitchen, as well as two family bungalows with a rather more basic standard of comfort (no bathroom or electricity). B&B costs 2000 CFP, and lunch and dinner are 1500 CFP each. Juliette practises the art of good food Marquesan style, with dishes such as banana *poe*, *poisson cru* (raw fish), rice with coconut milk, roast leg of lamb and octopus curry. On request, and for at least eight people, the Vaianuis will organise a Marquesan oven (2000 CFP per person). Meals are served in the large dining room or on a table beside the beach.

Coming on foot by the path from Hatiheu, go down to the beach and then walk northwards for a few hundred metres; the guesthouse is the last house on the beach.

Terre Déserte The *Moetai Village* (☎ 92-04-91) is certainly the most unusually located tourist accommodation on the Marquesas. About 10 minutes' walk from the island's airport, and more than 30 km from Taiohae, five permanent bungalows for three people perch on a hill. They are equipped with bathroom (cold water) and are available for rent at 6000 CFP full board. Although very well kept, it is hard to imagine how this establishment, in such an austere and remote setting, could ever attract a living soul. Most of the customers are stranded tourists, transit passengers and Air Tahiti crews; the place has been totally booked out to accommodate the airport workers while the runway is being extended. To get to the bungalows, take the track just behind the Air Tahiti counter at the airport.

Taipivai *Chez Martine Haiti* (☎ 92-01-19, fax 92-05-34; BP 60, Taiohae, Nuku Hiva) is on the riverside, 400 metres after the church, going towards Contrôleur Bay. The guesthouse has two charming bungalows for two to four people with bathroom (cold water), costing 2000 CFP per person with breakfast. Opposite, above the owners' residence, is a four-bedroom house with shared bathroom and equipped kitchen, also available for 2000 CFP a night with breakfast; add 2000 CFP per meal. The Haitis also have a small adjoining grocer's shop.

Hatiheu Hatiheu has an excellent guesthouse, *Chez Yvonne* (☎ 92-02-97; BP 199, Taiohae, Nuku Hiva). The Katupa family has five welcoming but small local-style bungalows for two people with bathroom (cold water), facing the seafront and at the entrance to the village as you come from Taipivai. They cost 2500/4800 CFP per person/couple a night with breakfast; meals are served in the Hinakonui restaurant a little further on. Yvonne Katupa, your host, is the mayor of Hatiheu, and she (or her son, Maurice) offers excursions departing from Hatiheu. Travellers' cheques are accepted.

Places to Eat
The gourmet traveller can make a gastronomic tour of the island, thanks to the presence of some very good food outlets.

Taiohae For a cheap bite to eat, head for the *Snack du Marché* on the seafront. The poisson cru or sashimi cost 500 to 800 CFP, and it's generally open from 8 am to 9 pm.

Also on the seafront, 200 metres west of the Moana Nui hotel, the permanently stationed *snack van* offers a dish of the day for 700 CFP (chow mein, goat) at lunchtime, as well as snacks for 350 to 700 CFP. It's also open during the evening. *Snack Mama Noho* is set back on the mountainside near the river, and on Sunday afternoon, on the seafront near the Monument to the Dead, a few stands sell kebabs and drinks.

Hidden by vegetation, the *Kovivi* (☎ 92-03-85) restaurant enjoys an excellent reputation, and you are sure to meet the owners, Marcelline, the Air Tahiti representative, and Monsieur Aumaitre, an employee at the Banque Socredo. The Marquesan chef is called Jean-Michel. At lunchtime, the dish of the day costs 1000 CFP, and a carafe of wine is 500 CFP. In the evening allow 3000 CFP for a full meal when Marcelline takes charge of the kitchen. The restaurant is open Monday to Friday from 11 am to 2 pm and in the evening on demand; bookings are recommended.

The restaurant at the *Hôtel Moana Nui* offers traditional cuisine in a pleasant setting, and under the shady terrace, facing the seafront, you can sip an aperitif for 500 CFP. As a starter, salads are available from 500 CFP, but those with bigger appetites will opt for the generously proportioned sashimi at 1000 CFP. Meat and fish dishes range from 1000 to 1600 CFP. The restaurant is open every day at lunchtime and in the evening; credit cards accepted.

At the *Nuku Hiva Village*, the local décor, with tikis carved on the support posts, goes hand in hand with a delicately interpreted local cuisine. Food lovers will particularly enjoy the salad and fresh sashimi starters (700 to 1500 CFP). The meat dishes are also tasty, especially the traditional entrecôte (1350 CFP), and the bulky Nuku Burger (950 CFP, with fish and chips) will satisfy an empty stomach. The Nuku Hiva Cup at 650 CFP (fresh fruit salad with vanilla ice cream)

is also worth a mention. There's a good winelist, and the menu is written in English; service, however, can be slow. The restaurant is open every day at lunchtime and in the evening. Happy hour is from 6 to 7 pm, and there's sometimes live music. Credit cards are accepted.

The cuisine at the *Keikahanui Inn* restaurant is also worth trying, and it too has traditional décor. It charges 1000 to 1600 CFP for main meals, 450 CFP for dessert and 400 CFP for a drink of punch. A *kaikai enana* (traditional Marquesan meal) is organised once a month on Sunday, and a local band enlivens the atmosphere on Friday. Happy hour (or two) is from 4 to 6 pm, and the restaurant is open every day at lunchtime and in the evening. Booking is recommended and credit cards are accepted.

Terre Déserte Even if you can't stay at the *Moetai Village*, you can still get a full meal there for 2000 CFP. In the airport itself, a snack bar offers a few light meals (750 CFP for the fish in coconut milk) and drinks at moderate prices.

Taipivai The *Martine Haiti* guesthouse also has a restaurant, which serves Marquesan specialities such as goat, pork, lobster or fish. Meals cost 2000 CFP, and bookings are essential.

Hatiheu The *Hinakonui* restaurant at the Chez Yvonne guesthouse has a deservedly good reputation. Its magnificent terrace with traditional *niau* (woven fibre) roof opens directly onto the seafront. In this temple of Marquesan good food Yvonne and her team concoct varied and generously sized dishes priced at 800 CFP for a plate of poisson cru to 2500 CFP for a full meal. Prawn fritters, pork with sweet potatoes and lobster feature among the house specialities. The bar is a good place to relax and bookings are essential.

Self Catering In Taiohae, *Kamake, François Larson's* and *Maurice's* are centrally located shops which sell everything from food to hardware, open Monday to Saturday from 7.30 to 11.30 am and 2.30 to 5.30 pm, and on Sunday morning after mass. Kamake also serves as a bakery from 5.30 am (entry at the side).

Bigot's shop, in Pakiu Valley, about 700 metres from the seafront, by a small bridge to the left of the road, offers the same products and accepts credit cards. *Snack Céline*, on the seafront in Taiohae, is a small grocery shop.

Things to Buy

In Taiohae, some curios and *pareus* are on sale at the Kanahau Shop and Shop Loisirs (which also sells photographic supplies).

Getting There & Away

Nuku Hiva's position as the hub of the Marquesas will be reinforced with the opening of the runway extension in 1997.

Air The Air Tahiti office (☎ 92-03-41) is on the eastern side of the cove, on the seafront. Marcelline, the company's representative, speaks good English and is on duty Monday to Friday from 8 am to noon and 2 to 5 pm, and on Saturday from 8 am to noon. These opening hours are somewhat theoretical as she is also on duty at the Nuku Ataha airport (☎ 92-01-45) on days when there is a flight.

There are five flights a week between Papeete and Nuku Hiva, some of which stop at Atuona or the Tuamotus. On Monday and Wednesday, the ATR 42 does a Papeete-Atuona-Nuku Hiva-Papeete loop; on Thursday the flight flies direct Papeete-Nuku Hiva-Papeete; on Saturday the loop is in the Papeete-Rangiroa-Manihi-Nuku Hiva-Papeete direction; and on Sunday in the Papeete-Nuku Hiva-Atuona-Papeete direction. The direct Papeete-Marquesas flight takes 3½ hours. On Thursday, a Dornier connects with the ATR 42 to pick up passengers for Ua Huka, Ua Pou and Atuona. The Papeete-Nuku Hiva fare is 35,900 CFP, Nuku Hiva-Ua Huka and Nuku Hiva-Ua Pou cost 5100 CFP and Nuku Hiva-Atuona costs 8800 CFP.

Helicopter The Héli Inter Marquises agency (☎ & fax 92-02-17) is adjacent to the Air Tahiti office at Taiohae, and opens Monday to Friday from 7.30 am to noon and 12.30 to 4 pm (3 pm closing on Friday). The heliport, at the east end of Taiohae Bay, overhangs the schooner wharf.

The helicopter provides regular shuttle services to the other islands in the northern group of the Marquesas. Taiohae-Hakahau (Ua Pou)-Taiohae is scheduled for Wednesday at 9 am and costs 12,000 CFP per person one way; flight time is 15 minutes. The Taiohae-Vaipaee (Ua Huka)-Taiohae service is provided every second Thursday (15 minutes flying time) at 9 am and costs 14,500 CFP.

Private Bonitiers In Taiohae, Xavier Curvat at the dive centre operates a weekly Taiohae-Hakahau-Taiohae ferry service, generally on Friday, leaving at 7 am and returning around 4 pm. It costs 4000 CFP for a single and 6000 CFP for a same-day return. The crossing takes one hour 40 minutes, longer if the sea is rough. Bookings are essential, and chartering is possible for a fee of 45,000 CFP (up to 15 people).

Laurent (Teiki) Falchetto's bonitier (☎ 92-05-78), also at Taiohae, can be chartered for Ua Pou for 45,000 CFP (six to eight people) and for Ua Huka for 50,000 CFP. The owner of the bonitier *Dina* (☎ 92-04-78) hires his boat on the same terms.

Inter-Island Ships The *Aranui*, *Taporo IV* and *Tamarii Tuamotu* serve Nuku Hiva and berth at Taiohae quay at the eastern end of the bay. In addition to Taiohae, the *Aranui* also goes to Taipivai and Hatiheu. See Inter-Island Ships in the introductory Getting Around chapter.

Getting Around

A network of roads links the airport, Taiohae, Taipivai, Hooumi, Hatiheu and Aakapa.

To/From the Airport The track linking Taiohae to Nuku Ataha airport at Terre Déserte in the north-west of the island passes close to Mt Muake and crosses Toovii

Top Left: Gathering fish in a fish park, Mataiva, Tuamotus
Top Right: Catholic Church, Tiputa, Rangiroa, Tuamotus
Bottom: Marae Papiro, Mataiva, Tuamotus

Crabs

On many coconut trees in French Polynesia you'll notice a band of metal foil around the trunk. What's it there for? Simple – to keep coconut crabs from scaling the tree and stealing the coconuts.

It's a wonderful image – a Herculean coconut crab scuttling sideways up the trunk, tearing a coconut off with its mighty claw, hurling it down to the ground and swiftly descending to tear the husk off and consume the meat. However, it's not strictly true. Crabs are not great tree climbers and powerful though that fearsome claw is, it's not really up to ripping coconuts from trees nor for tearing coconut husks off. If a coconut has broken open a coconut crab is only too happy to eat, but breaking a coconut open itself is a slow process taking a large crab several weeks.

Coconut crabs are found on many islands in Polynesia and are a familiar sight prancing across the coast road between the coconut trees and lagoon. They're big crabs, weighing two kg or more if they live to a ripe enough old age. Unfortunately, coconut crabs have one big enemy – cars. Big claws and a hard shell are no protection against a car's wheels. Worse, the unfortunate coconut crab freezes as soon as you shine a light on it. Full-moon nights, when the crabs leave their safe hideaway holes and head down to the lagoon to mate, are particularly disastrous. A drive around the coast road on Moorea, where there are clearly dense populations of coconut crabs on some stretches, will provide a steady crunch-crunch-crunch sound effect no matter how carefully you proceed and how studiously you try to avoid crabs standing stock still in the middle of the road. They're the road kill of the Pacific. ■

Coconut crab

Slightly dead coconut crab

Very dead coconut crab

Hermit crabs and their tracks

Photographs by Tony Wheeler

Plateau. It takes about two hours to reach the airport along this bumpy, winding track, longer if it has rained and the ground is muddy – and it's only 18 km! Paving this important cross-country road should be a priority.

Approved 4WD taxis which carry four to six people generally wait for each flight. It is nevertheless wise to book, either through your hotel or guesthouse, or directly by contacting the following taxi drivers: Richard Teore (☎ 92-00-91 or 92-01-44 at Nuku Ataha), Joseph Puhetini (☎ 92-03-47), Sonia Teuhitua (☎ 92-02-22), Marie-Thérèse Pahuatini (☎ 92-04-68), Temo (☎ 92-04-13) or Jeanne Ah Scha (☎ 92-01-84). The airport-to-Taiohae run costs 3500 CFP by day or 5000 CFP at night per person (except with Sonia, who charges 3000 by day).

Héli Inter Marquises (see Getting There & Away above) has a ticket office at the airport. It provides a helicopter-shuttle service connecting with each Air Tahiti flight, costing 6900 CFP per person (eight minutes). Before each flight, the helicopter flies Taiohae-Taipivai-Hatiheu-Aakapa-Terre Déserte, and it flies the same route in reverse after picking passengers up at the airport. If you want to be flown to the airport, ring Héli Inter Marquises in advance so that they'll know to stop at your village.

4WD At Taiohae, in Pakiu Valley, four 4WD hirers live a few yards from each other, just a few hundred metres from the temple: Richard Teore, Temo, Marie-Thérèse Pahuatini who speaks English and Joseph Puhetini. In Meau Valley, Sonia Teuhitua (☎ 92-02-22) speaks a little English and lives behind the bridge which leads to Bigot's shop. Jeanne Ah Scha (☎ 92-01-84) lives behind the Moana Nui (ask Charles Nombaerts to show you the way). It costs 3000 to 5000 CFP for the trip to Muake, 8000 to 12,000 CFP for Taipivai, 15,000 CFP for Hatiheu and 20,000 to 25,000 CFP for Aakapa.

Car You can hire a Suzuki (two people) from Charles Nombaerts, owner of the Hôtel Moana Nui. It will cost you 8000 CFP for 24 hours, including insurance and unlimited km. There is a petrol station on the schooner wharf.

In Taipivai, ask for Henri Pata (☎ 92-01-36), and in Hatiheu, ask Yvonne Katupa at the Chez Yvonne guesthouse.

Horse Riding Sabine Teikiteetini (☎ 92-05-68), a fire fighter at Taiohae, and her father Louis, have 14 horses equipped with leather saddles. Numerous options are available, including rides to Taipivai (6000 CFP per person), Hakaui (7000 CFP per person), Hatiheu (three days with one rest day, 18 000 CFP return per person with guide) or Taiohae and the surrounding area (3500/5000 CFP per person for half/full day). Prices are the same with or without the services of a guide, and the Teikiteetinis prefer to hire their horses to experienced riders rather than beginners. Book at least one day in advance. The Teikiteetini residence is in Pakiu Valley, about 700 metres from the seafront, opposite the small bridge leading to Bigot's shop.

In Hatiheu, ask Yvonne Katupa at the Chez Yvonne guesthouse, who charges 2000/4000 CFP for a half/full day, without the services of a guide.

Speedboat To see the island by speedboat, call the owner of the *Dina* (☎ 92-04-78), Iti Teremiti (☎ 92-00-57), Léonard Hokaupoko (☎ 92-00-16) or Francis Falchetto (☎ 92-01-51). Speedboats take four to six people, and cost around 12,000 CFP (flat rate) to visit such places as Hakaui Bay and the Vaipo Waterfall.

Through Yvonne Katupa at Chez Yvonne, it costs 5000 CFP to make the Hatiheu-Anaho crossing.

UA HUKA
Population: 539
Area: 83 sq km
Highest Point: 855 metres (Mt Hitikau)

Ua Huka (the 'leftover scraps' in the Marquesas Islands legend), 'discovered' in 1791 by the American captain Ingraham, lies 50

Ua Huka

0   5   10 km

km east of Nuku Hiva and 56 km north-east of Ua Pou. Ua Huka's topography is quite different from these nearby islands, yet it rarely features in the traditional itinerary of travellers, who tend to concentrate on its two neighbours.

The island consists of two stacked volcanoes. The caldera of the main volcano forms an amphitheatre facing south-west to south-east, while the secondary volcano occupies the south-eastern part of the large caldera. Vaikivi Plateau, covered with impenetrable clumps of vegetation, occupies the northern edge of the island, while the island's three villages – Vaipaee, Hane and Hokatu – nestle around the edges of steep-sided valleys on the south coast.

Ua Huka has less luxuriant vegetation than its sister islands, and has almost desert-like plains in the south. The desolate scenery is accentuated by the free-ranging herds of horses and goats, and near the coast, a few islets are home to thousands of birds who find them an ideal nesting site.

The island boasts archaeological treasures such as the Hane tikis and the Vaikivi petroglyphs, and the Marquesas' first museum devoted entirely to archaeology was estab-

lished in Vaipaee. Each of the three villages has craft exhibition-and-sales centres, and, surprisingly perhaps, a first-rate arboretum is the pride of the island.

Information

There is no bank on Ua Huka. The post office is in Vaipaee, next to the museum (open Monday to Friday from 7.30 to 11.30 am and from 1 to 2.30 pm, and every time the *Aranui* calls in), and each village has phonecard telephone booths. There is also an infirmary or first-aid post in all three villages.

Vaipaee

The island's main town is at the end of a very deep narrow inlet measuring about one km. It is rightly named Invisible Bay. When the *Aranui* comes in, it manoeuvres in a space the size of a pocket handkerchief and ties up to the rock face with hawsers.

Vaipaee is divided into two sections. The traditional village stretches along the valley, while a housing development is a few km away, going towards Hane.

Museum The museum is in the centre of Vaipaee, on the left of the main street, with your back to the sea. The museum was opened in 1987, largely due to the endeavours of Mayor Léon Lichtlé. Its size may be modest, but it has great symbolic value for the heritage-proud Marquesans.

The museum is housed in a group of buildings which also house the town hall, a craft centre and the post office. On the esplanade in front of the museum is a commemorative plaque dedicated to Captain Étienne Marchand who landed on the northern group of the Marquesas in June 1791. The museum (admission free) includes evidence of the ancient way of life, tikis, finely carved sculptures, a variety of jewellery and period photos. There are also scale reproductions of ancient sites and objects such as paddles and clubs.

Arboretum This botanic garden was created in 1974, again due to the initiatives of Léon Lichtlé, and is well worth visiting. It is halfway between Vaipaee and Hane, and includes dozens of species from around the world. New varieties are introduced each year and 130 species of citrus have been planted. There is a striking contrast between this wealth of plants and the relative aridity of the island. The fact that so many species have adapted to the dry Marquesan soil opens up great possibilities for local agriculture. The species best adapted to the climate are used for reforestation where the vegetation has been destroyed by wild goats and horses.

Unfortunately, signs are either totally lacking or scarcely legible; ask one of the gardeners to show you around.

Hane

The first Polynesian settlement on the Marquesas was established at this site, tucked away in a bay protected on the east by the Motu Hane, an impressive islet shaped like a sugarloaf. The local personality is sculptor Joseph Vaatete, whose workshop can be seen near some roughly hewn blocks of rock, 200 metres from the beach.

The white house on the seafront houses the craft centre and a small **marine museum** which opened in 1995 and contains some traditional dugout canoes. Ask for the key from Joseph Vaatete or Richard Teikihuavanaka, who lives in the first house in the small street which branches left from the Hokatu road.

Meiaute Archaeological Site Less than 30 minutes' walk from the village, this site is one of the major attractions on Ua Huka. It includes three red-tuff tikis more than a metre in height which watch over a group of stone structures, pae paes and meaes, which have not yet been restored and are partly hidden from view by the vegetation. Two of these tikis, squat and massive with finely formed features, have very projecting ears, unlike most of their fellows.

To get there, follow the track from the Auberge Hitikau (see Places to Stay) at the edge of the village for about 200 metres, heading in the direction of the mountain. At the crossroad, go straight on and continue on past the last house, which is blue-green in colour, on the left-hand side of the track. After about 20 minutes you will come in sight of a hill covered in mango trees, 30 metres after a sharp bend on your right. Climb this small steep hill until you reach the pae paes. A little higher up, in a clearing, you will find the tikis.

To avoid getting lost, ask one of the children living in the blue-green house on the edge of the village to accompany you.

Hokatu

This peaceful village lies about three km east of Hane in a sheltered bay. The main street leads to the craft fare and the black-pebble beach.

Footstep Cave

Tupapau (ghosts) are said to haunt this cave, slightly west of Point Tekeho, between Vaipaee and Haavei Bay.

According to legend, a fisherman from the island took refuge in the cave during a storm. When he awoke the following morning, he was alarmed to note large footprints on the sand around him. A few days later, when the rising tide should have washed them away, the footprints were still there. Today, people swear that they are still there, and we did indeed see footsteps and the word '*kaoha*' ('hello') written in the sand – work of the village youngsters, no doubt.

The cave can be reached at low tide when there is not much swell. If you visit with a guide, the boat will stop about 30 metres from the crevice and you will have to swim to the edge, taking care not to be swept onto the reefs by the undertow. Take plastic sandals and ask your guide to bring a torch.

Îles aux Oiseaux

Thousands of sooty terns (*kaveka*) have taken up residence on the islands of **Hemeni** and **Teuaua**, near the south-west point of Ua Huka. They lay thousands of eggs every day, which the islands' inhabitants regularly gather.

Access to Hemeni is prohibited in order to protect the species. Teuaua, the neighbouring islet, is accessible by speedboat, but the only means of (rather perilous) access is via a small ledge which juts out two metres above the surface of the water. The boat isn't able to come in too close because of the risk of being swept onto the rock face by the swell. Your guide will jump into the water and then throw you a rope which is permanently fixed to the rock so that you can jump onto the ledge – mere child's play if you are a champion gymnast. If not, you run the risk of missing the rocky ledge, falling in the water or tearing your hands on the rough surface of the basalt. Your troubles are not over, however, as you then have to climb six metres or so up to the top of the rock, clambering up the rope.

Final test: the smell emanating from the thousands of birds which are sitting on the ground all around you. You will have to put up with the nauseating stench while your guide gathers the eggs, which are whitish and speckled with brown or black marks. Not all of the eggs are fit for eating, and only an expert eye can spot which ones are suitable. The kaveka become infuriated as their eggs are plundered, and their cry is deafening. The more reckless among them are bold enough to swoop over your head, and you will soon be reliving a scene from Hitchcock's *The Birds*.

If, despite all this, the experience still attracts you, go armed with a hat, a pair of trousers and a pair of sneakers.

Beaches

Accessible by speedboat or 4WD, **Manihina Beach**, between Vaipaee and the airfield, is fringed with fine white sand. There are excellent opportunities for snorkelling, as the beach is sheltered by a bay. **Hatuana Beach** is in the west of the island; there are petroglyphs nearby. **Haavei Beach** is a beautiful inlet which belongs to the Lichtlé family. Ask the owners, who live on the coconut plantation, for permission before you plunge in.

Motu Papa

This island picnic spot is just offshore from the airfield, between Vaipaee and Hane. It is a large block of volcanic rock which, at low tide, reveals a fairly wide rocky ledge where you can sit. As the speedboat cannot come alongside, you have to swim about 50 metres to the edge of the rock. Food and various items of equipment are loaded in a large floating bin, and all you have to do is swim with it to the rock.

The rock attracts abundant marine life, including mullet, parrotfish and surgeonfish. In the crevices of the ledge hide pencil urchins which you can see without going underwater.

Take a swimming costume, some sunscreen (there are few shady spots) and plastic sandals as the rock is very slippery.

Vaikivi Petroglyphs

This little-visited archaeological site on Vaikivi Plateau is worth the detour, if only for the walk (or horse ride for part of the way) it offers. A guide is essential as the site is concealed under an impenetrable tangle of vegetation, and it is difficult to get your bearings.

Heading out from Vaipaee or Hane the walk takes about three hours. From Hane, follow the main road to the edge of the village, towards the mountain, and take the track which branches left before the last house. A little further on you will join a small path, and from here you will have to climb along the caldera of the old volcano to the summit, which is a tortuous ascent along a steep path that takes one to 1½ hours. On reaching the clearing at the pass, you are rewarded with an unimpeded view over scalloped Hane Bay. In clear weather, you can see Fatu Huku to the south-east.

The track continues on inland and begins to gently descend, as the thick vegetation gives way to tree ferns. The contrast with the coastal scenery is striking. After about 30 to 45 minutes, you have to branch left and hack your way through a forest of pandanus and other vegetation. Just over half an hour later, you will finally reach the well-restored petroglyphs carved in a grey stone. They feature an octopus and a human face, and a little further up on the right, a pae pae is sheltered by an enormous banyan. More petroglyphs can be seen on the rock nearby, representing a dugout canoe, a face and some geometric patterns.

Take good shoes and sufficient food and water. The services of a guide will cost you 4000 to 5000 CFP. Ask Maurice Rootuehine (see Places to Stay) at Hokatu or Léonard Teatiu or Napoléon at Vaipaee town hall. There are plans to make a proper path.

Arts & Crafts

Arts and crafts are given more prominence on Ua Huka than anywhere else in the Marquesas. Goods are displayed at a craft centre in each of the three villages, and Hokatu has two craft fares, the men's and the women's, near the beach, almost opposite each other.

In Hane, visit Joseph Vaatete (☎ 92-60-74), the well-known stone sculptor.

Horse Riding

Horses thrive on Ua Huka, and the possible itineraries are many and varied, including a ride across Vaikivi Plateau, from Vaipaee to Haavei or Hane, or Hane to Hokatu. The most popular route is to ride from Vaipaee to Hane, passing the arboretum, airfield and wind-swept arid plateaus before reaching the cliff road, which plunges down towards Hane. If the weather cooperates, this ride will certainly be one of the highlights of your stay on the Marquesas (see also Getting Around).

Places to Stay

Vaipaee Alexis Scallamera, owner of the *Chez Alexis Scallamera* guesthouse (☎ 92-60-19 or 92-61-16), has three doubles and two singles with shared bathroom (cold water) for the modest sum of 1500 CFP a night per person or 4500 CFP full board, including transfer to the airfield. The fully equipped kitchen can be utilised. Choose the rooms upstairs, as the ones underneath look like monks' cells. The house, which is blue, is beside the main road, on the right as you

come from the quay, 150 metres before the museum and just before the track which turns to the left.

Another option at Vaipaee is the *Chez Christelle* guesthouse (☎ 92-61-08 or 92-60-04), run by the Air Tahiti representative, Marie-Louise Fournier, and her daughter Christelle. If you stay here you won't have to pay for the transfer to the airfield. It costs 1500 CFP per person for B&B and 1200 CFP per meal. The four rooms with shared bathroom (cold water) are sparkling clean, and Mme Fournier prepares excellent and generously sized Marquesan dishes which feature lobster as the main ingredient.

Hane Hane has a guesthouse which doubles as a very good restaurant, the *Auberge Hitikau* (☎ 92-60-68), run by Céline Fournier. Adjoining the restaurant, the four simple but clean double rooms with shared bathroom (cold water) cost 2500 CFP for one person and 4000 CFP for a couple, including breakfast. Avoid the room without a window. Meals cost 2000 CFP and transfer to the airfield by car is 3000 CFP. To get to the guesthouse, go up the main street towards the mountain, and the Auberge is 300 metres past the church on the right, on the large ranch-like property.

Hokatu The *Chez Maurice et Delphine* guesthouse (☎ & fax 92-60-55), the first house on the left as you enter the village from Hane has three double rooms with shared bathroom (cold water), which are clean and welcoming. One of the rooms has a fan. From the terrace, you can enjoy a beautiful view over the village and the bay, and the prices won't make a hole in your wallet: 1000 CFP per person B&B and 1000 CFP per meal. The transfer to the airfield costs 2000 CFP each way by car (up to five people). If you stay with the Rootuehines for several days, you will have the chance to try a lavish Marquesan oven: pork and fish are wrapped in aluminium foil, placed in an oven hollowed out of the ground, covered with earth and baked. They are eaten the next day. Maurice is also one of the best sculptors on the island: the huge adze on the wall of the lounge is the most vivid proof of his talent.

Haavei Haavei Bay, about five km west of Vaipaee, belongs to the Lichtlé family. A new track makes it accessible by 4WD. The *Chez Joseph Lichtlé* guesthouse (☎ 92-60-72) is run by the mayor of Ua Huka's father, near a very pretty beach. You will have the choice of two bungalows with bathroom (cold water); one large, three-bedroom house with a shared bathroom; and another solar-powered, two-bedroom house with shared bathroom. Joseph Lichtlé, a fine chef, features local specialities on his menu, and charges 5500 CFP a day full board, including transfers to the airfield.

Places to Eat
Choice is restricted on Ua Huka, but fortunately the food offered by the guesthouses is good. Try to sample the succulent kaveka-egg omelette, the indisputable speciality of the island. Instead of yellow, the omelette is orange in colour.

The only true restaurant is the *Auberge Hitikau* in Hane. Local specialities have pride of place: goat, pork or fish in coconut milk, kaveka-egg omelettes and delicious cakes. Tourists from the *Aranui* stop there when they come to the island, and the establishment is taken over by feverish activity which contrasts with the place's usual pace. It costs 2000 CFP for a full set meal, excluding drinks, and bookings are essential.

Getting There & Away
Air The airfield, which was closed for four years, reopened in 1995. Marie-Louise Fournier, owner of the Chez Christelle guesthouse, is the Air Tahiti representative (☎ 92-60-85 or 92-61-08) in Vaipaee. On Thursday, she is on duty at the airfield (☎ 92-60-44).

The island is served every Thursday by a 20-seater Dornier which runs a Nuku Hiva-Ua Huka-Huku Hiva loop, and connects with the ATR 42 which provides the Papeete-

Nuku Hiva link. It costs 37,800 CFP for the flight from Papeete to Ua Huka via Nuku Hiva and 5100 CFP for the Nuku Hiva to Ua Huka leg.

Helicopter Héli Inter Marquises has a weekly Taiohae-Vaipaee-Taiohae shuttle service every second Thursday at 9 am, costing 14,500 CFP a single trip. Flight time is 15 minutes.

Private Bonitiers & Speedboats In Hokatu, Maurice Rootuehine (see Places to Stay) and Paul Teatiu (☎ 92-60-88) have speedboats and on request can do the Ua Huka-Ua Pou or Ua Huka-Nuku Hiva crossings. It costs 50,000 CFP for Nuku Hiva and 55,000 CFP for Ua Pou.

Inter-Island Ships The *Aranui*, *Taporo IV* and *Tamarii Tuamotu* serve Ua Huka (see Inter-Island Ships in the introductory Getting Around chapter).

Getting Around
A 13-km track links Vaipaee to Hokatu via Hane. Since 1995, Haavei has also been accessible by the track from Vaipaee.

To/From the Airport For the transfer costs charged by the guesthouses, see Places to Stay above.

4WD In Vaipaee, contact Alexis Scallamera at the guesthouse of the same name, Christian Lichtlé (☎ 92-60-87) or Jean-Baptiste Brown (☎ 92-60-23). In Haavei, the Lichtlé's also have a 4WD. In Hane, contact Céline Fournier at the Auberge Hitikau, and in Hokatu, Maurice Rootuehine at Chez Maurice et Delphine guesthouse. A full day's hire with driver will cost you 10,000 CFP, a little less with Maurice Rootuehine (7000 CFP).

Horse Riding If you stay at Joseph Lichtlé's at Haavei, your host will make horses available to you, free of charge as a rule. In Vaipaee, contact the Fournier family at the Chez Christelle guesthouse, Jean-Baptiste

Brown (☎ 92-60-23) or Edmond Lichtlé (☎ 92-60-87). In Hane, ask Céline Fournier at the Auberge Hitikau, and in Hokatu, the owners of the Chez Maurice et Delphine guesthouse will act as agents.

It costs 5000 CFP for a ride with the services of a guide. Wooden saddles are still quite commonly used, but fortunately padding is provided to relieve the relative discomfort.

Bonitiers Contact the Fournier family in Vaipaee, Céline Fournier in Hokatu and Maurice Rootuehine in Hokatu. The bonitier hire comes to about 10,000 CFP a day.

UA POU
Area: 125 sq km
Population: 2000
Highest Point: 1203 metres (Mt Oave)

Lying 45 km south of Nuku Hiva, Ua Pou was the site of an ancient settlement, estimated to have been established around 150 BC. Frenchman Etienne Marchand landed on the island in June 1791 and claimed it on behalf of France. In fact, the American Ingraham, captain of the *Hope*, had already noted its existence two months earlier in April 1791.

Ua Pou (the 'pillars' in the Marquesas Islands legend) is geologically the youngest island in the archipelago. Its sharp contours and pointy pinnacles, often shrouded by cloud cover, accentuate the island's mystery.

Hakahau, the island's main settlement, is home to most of the population. A few villages nestled in the steep-sided valleys are dotted along the east and west coasts.

Ua Pou is noted for its culture and arts. It was the birthplace of the Motu Haka association and the revival of Marquesan identity. It is also a breeding ground for talent: singing star Rataro, the Kanahau Trio musical group and most of the well-known Marquesan dance groups are from Ua Pou. Ua Pou's wood and stone sculptors have also brought fame to the island.

Fascinating archaeological remains can be seen in the Hakamoui and Hohoi valleys.

Information
Tourist Office There is no tourist office on Ua Pou. You can, however, contact Tina Klima, the Air Tahiti representative (see Getting There & Away), who is well informed and speaks English. You can contact the Motu Haka association on ☎ 92-53-21.

Money The Banque Socredo (☎ 92-53-63) is housed in one wing of the Hakahau town hall. You can carry out exchange transactions (currency and travellers' cheques) and withdraw currency on presentation of a credit card. The bank is open Monday to Thursday from 7.30 to 11 am and 1.30 to 4 pm and on Friday from 7.30 am to 2.30 pm.

Post & Telecommunications The post office is in Hakahau, open Monday to Thursday from 7.30 to 11.30 am and 1.30 pm to 4.30 pm and on Friday from 7.30 am to 11.30 am and noon to 2 pm. You will find phonecard telephone booths beside the post office, on the quay and opposite the Air Tahiti office.

Emergency In Hakahau, a small medical centre with a doctor and dentist is in the south of the village, halfway between the church and the museum. Every village has an infirmary or first-aid post.

Hakahau
The staging of the Marquesas Islands Festival here in December 1995 gave a lift to this small town, which tends to live in the shadow of powerful Taiohae to the north.

The town's houses are spread along the four almost-parallel north-south-oriented sealed streets. The CETAD (technical school) and the secondary school, decorated with frescoes representing tikis, face the black-sand beach which is often frequented by young surfers fresh from school. A little further west, the market livens up each Sunday after mass.

Inaugurated for the 1995 festival, Hakahau's **museum** faces the esplanade where

THE MARQUESAS

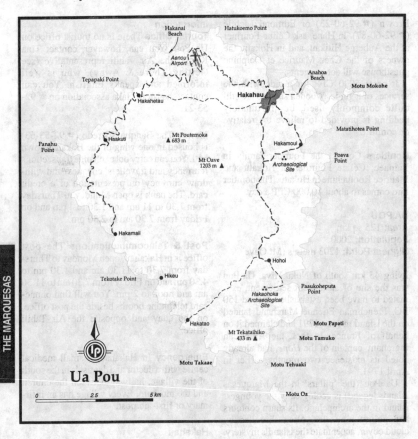

Ua Pou

0   2.5   5 km

Map labels:
Hakanai Beach
Hatukoemo Point
Aenou Airport
Anahoa Beach
Motu Mokohe
Hakahau
Tepapaki Point
Hakahetau
Matatihotea Point
Panahu Point
Haakuti
Mt Poutemoka ▲ 683 m
Hakamoui
Poava Point
Mt Oave 1203 m ▲
Archaeological Site
Hakamaii
Hohoi
Tekotake Point
Hikeu
Paaukoheputa Point
Hakaohoka Archaeological Site
Hakatao
Mt Tekataihiko 433 m ▲
Motu Papati
Motu Tamuko
Motu Takaae
Motu Tehuaki
Motu Oa

the demonstrations were staged. Just as in Vaipaee's museum (Ua Huka), the inhabitants were encouraged to lend objects representative of Marquesan material culture to be displayed. Admission is free.

The recent stone-and-timber **Catholic church** in the south of the village, on the Hohoi road, houses some noteworthy sculptures by local artisans. The monumental pulpit representing the bows of a boat balancing on a net full of miraculous fish is particularly interesting, and behind the altar rises a large, finely shaped statue of Christ and, further back, a Virgin with Child.

As part of the festival, a team from the archaeological department of the Tahiti & Islands Museum travelled to Hakahau to restore the **Tenei pae pae** right in the middle of the village. A nearby inscription reads: 'On the night of the full moon, this pae pae or *upe* was built by Prince Teikitaiuau, descendant of the Atipapa royal family of Hakamoui'.

Admirably restored, this site is representative of the characteristic structure of traditional dwellings, namely a platform consisting of massive blocks of stone supporting a shelter of plant material.

Anahoa Beach

Twenty-five minutes' walk east of Hakahau, this idyllic beach fringes Anahoa Cove and contrasts with the wildness of the neighbouring volcanic scenery. It is regularly treated with insecticides and is free of nonos. It is advisable to go there on foot or horseback to enjoy the panoramic view going down towards the bay. To get there from the quay in Hakahau, follow the direction shown on the sign for 'Restaurant Pukuéé', continue past the restaurant, and after about a 10-minute uphill walk, you reach a pass from which you get an incomparable view over Hakahau Bay and its peaks.

There is a variation on this walk. At the pass, take the right fork and climb up quite steeply for five to 10 minutes until you reach a small flight of steps leading to the cross which you can see from the quay. The view is magnificent: in addition to the jagged profile of Nuku Hiva visible to the north, you can also see blue Anahoa Bay and its white border of sand to the east. In clear weather, you can see Ua Huka to the north-east.

Hakamoui Valley Archaeological Sites

This valley, also known as the 'Valley of the Kings', is now deserted. Formerly inhabited by the dominant Atipapa tribe from which the island's chieftain came, it was one of the main centres of population on the island. Interest in Hakamoui has revived thanks to the Marquesas Islands Festival in December 1995.

The valley is easily accessible from Hakahau. Follow the road to Hohoi for about three km and take the left fork which descends eastwards towards the ocean. One km further on, on the right and set back from the track, is a pae pae which was used as the platform for a recent dwelling but now lies abandoned. You can see a bas-relief which stands out quite clearly and hollowed-out carvings, one on the north side and the other on a stone slab placed edgeways on the east side, both slightly hidden by vegetation. Both are representations of human features with round staring eyes and disproportionate rectangular mouths. Not far away is a well-preserved tiki, slightly leaning to the left. This site, called Mataautea, was restricted to the chief of the Atipapa tribe who reigned over the whole island.

Two hundred metres further on, on the right in an enclosed field, you can see the imposing Temenaha pae pae, built by Chief Puheputoka. This site was completely cleared for the festival. If you get up onto the platform, you will see a series of carvings in relief on the stone.

If you continue on for just over one km, you will reach a pretty coconut plantation fringing a black pebble-and-sand beach.

Hakaohoka Archaeological Site

Hakaohoka Valley, in the south-east of the island, opens onto Hohoi Bay. From the pebbly shore the site goes back more than two km inland. Shaped by legends and mysteries, it has been studied by archaeologist Pierre Ottino of the French oceanographic research institute ORSTOM, who has revealed the geographic, territorial and social unity of this until-recently populated area.

According to an age-old legend told by Jacques Dordillon, who owns the land, Heato, the last king of Ua Pou, wanted to marry the daughter of the chief of the Kaavahopeoa tribe who had taken up residence in Hakaohoka Valley. He was given a categorical refusal. Mad with rage, the king enjoined his warriors to capture the girl and massacre the Kaavahopeoa. The latter fled aboard huge bamboo rafts which they built in one night with the aid of the gods. At dawn, when the aggressors were preparing to start the attack, the fugitives were already in sight of Tahuata. Encountering hostility from the inhabitants of this island, they were unable to land and continued as far as Napuka (in the Tuamotus), which became their adopted home.

More prosaically, it is known that this valley became totally deserted in the 1860s as the result of a smallpox epidemic, and the dwellings became ossified. Along the main river, for a stretch of 70 metres on either side of the river bed, stand stone structures, remains of ancient human occupation of the valley consisting of pae paes, paving and low walls. You can start your visit with Chief Hamipohue's pae pae which is easily recognisable as it has a corrugated-iron roof above it, designed to protect the platform from run-off water and the sun. At one end, you can see the Chief's back rest. At right angles to the terrace are some blocks of tuff on which geometric shapes (people, lizards) are roughly carved. The whole area is full of more pae paes, tohuas and meaes. The ghostly silhouette of the banyans, the islands' sacred trees, reinforces the mystical atmosphere of the place.

Hakaohoka site, accessible by the track, is 13 km from Hakahau. At Hohoi, go down to the pebbly beach and follow it to the end along the track bordered with miro and tou trees. After the first fisher's shelter, you will see a sign with a map of the site, drawn by Pierre Ottino. Take the track which goes up and walk for 15 minutes until you arrive in sight of the pae paes which appear on the right, under the plant cover. At Hohoi, don't forget to give 1000 CFP to the custodian, Willy Hikutini, who can also act as your guide. This money is used to finance the upkeep of the track and restoration of the site.

Hohoi

This picturesque little village in the south-east of the island is accessible from Hakahau. The 12-km track passes numerous types of vegetation, including pistachio, guava, pandanus, acacia and mango. The luxuriance of the vegetation contrasts strikingly with the aridity of the plateaus in the north-west of the island, and there are good views over the sea.

Time seems to stand still in Hohoi. You may pass a few inhabitants returning to the village, leading horses labouring under the burden of bunches of bananas or bags of coconuts. As you enter the village, 100 metres before the house with the blue roof (town hall) on the left, you will spot two pae paes. The curious shape of the church is also noteworthy, as it looks like a pagoda.

On the beach there are a few straw fisher's

huts. It's here that the famous flowering pebbles for which Hohoi is known can be found. They are pieces of phonolite which have crystallised to form amber-coloured flower shapes; this volcanic rock makes a pronounced tone when struck.

Hakanai Bay

Below the track leading to Hakahetau, shortly after Aneou airfield and 11 km from Hakahau, this sheltered bay is a popular picnic spot. It has been nicknamed Shark Beach due to the many dogfish seen in the cove.

Hakahetau

This charming village, noted for its red church tower, was the residence of Monsignor Le Cleac'h, known for his translation of the Bible into Marquesan. Hakahetau's inhabitants live off copra production, fishing, and arts and crafts.

A 15-km track snakes between the bare plateaus of the island's north-west, and along the section between Hakahau and Aneou airfield, you will see wild horses and goats on either side of the road. In the background, due south, the slender profile of Mt Oave (1203 meters) appears, while in the north you can make out the contours of Nuku Hiva.

Hakamaii

This one-street village is only accessible by boat – a difficult manoeuvre at times, as visitors have to reach the shore by tiny dugout canoe. The person paddling has to catch a wave at just the right moment so that the dugout is gently propelled rather than dumped onto the shore.

The façade of the town's stone church, facing the ocean, has unusual yellow, blue and red painted wooden panels which replicate stained-glass windows. Seen from the ocean, the illusion is almost perfect.

There's a path along the river at the far end of the village; take some mosquito repellent.

Haakuti

The tiny village of Haakuti is the terminus of the 22-km track from Hakahau (which will be extended to Hakatao one day). The one street, on a steep incline, links the stone church, built on a pae pae at the top of the village, with the tiny sea-swept quay some 600 metres below. At nightfall, don't miss the return of the fishers. Good-sized bonito and tuna form a large part of the catch.

Hakatao

This minute village, in the south-west of the island, is the most remote on the whole island. It is only accessible by boat.

Motu Oa

South of the island, this motu is home to colonies of thousands of sea birds.

Arts & Crafts

Many of the region's most respected artisans come from Ua Pou. When we visited, the construction of a craft fare inspired by the one at Vaipaee on Ua Huka had almost been completed. Designed to function as a central distribution point for the island's artefacts, it is a stone's throw from the quay.

There is nothing to stop you from paying one of the sculptors an impromptu visit. In Hakahau, Alfred Hatuuku, one of the sculptors who carved the pulpit in the Catholic church, demonstrates his remarkable skill and eye for minute detail. His house and workshop are 100 metres before Snack Vehine, coming from the seafront.

In the Akas family (☎ 92-53-90), sculpture is a family business. William, the son, has a huge repertoire: small tikis, jewellery boxes, jewellery, tortoises, lizards and little tou or miro-wood saddles. Coming from the seafront, you will see his workshop just before Snack Guéranger. Just across the road, Aimé Kohumoetini (☎ 92-51-86) fashions jewellery and jewellery boxes.

Eugène Hapipi (☎ 92-53-28 at his sister's house, next door) makes equally good necklaces from cattle bones, tou wood, volcanic rock or the flowering pebbles from Hohoi. His grandmother makes pandanus hats.

Marcel Bruneau (☎ 92-50-02), known as Maté, lives in the south of the village. He makes carvings from volcanic rock, basalt, tuff and wood, and *popoi* or *raau* (medicine) pestles are one of his specialities.

In Hakahetau, sculptor Apataroma Hikutini's fare (☎ 92-51-56) reveals his skills: the terrace door panel is finely carved and the support pillars are made with pebbled flowers. His wife makes the Marquesan *monoi* (coconut oil and sandalwood powder), *peue* (braids) and woven niau hats. To get there from the quay, facing the sea, go left for about 100 metres.

In the same village, stone carver Tony Tereino (☎ 92-51-68) also runs a shop, at the entrance to the village, on the left as you come from Hakahau.

If you'd like a more permanent memento of your stay on the Marquesas, go and see tattoo artist Siméon Huuti in Hakamaii. He uses a patched-up old electric razor to which he fits needles. Talk to him first and ask him what kind of needles he uses and make sure you take your own. (See HIV/AIDS in the Health section of the Facts for the Visitor about the risks of unclean tattooing equipment.) Siméon Huuti lives in the lower part of the village, in a house built on a pae pae, set back from the road.

In Hakamaii, José Kaiha (☎ 92-50-07) lives in the *fare* with the carved posts in the lower part of the village, near the town hall. Tikis and clubs are his most common sculptural works.

In Hohoi, Uri Ah Lo's double dugout canoe was exhibited in Taiohae (Nuku Hiva). In addition to the typical tikis and spears, he can make a small dugout canoe from mango or banyan wood in a week. His house, painted blue, is on the right as you go down towards the beach.

Horse Riding

For details see Getting Around.

Places to Stay

Ua Pou's guesthouses are well distributed throughout the island.

Hakahau Well known to the yachties who anchor in the bay below are Hélène and Doudou, who run the *Restaurant-Pension*

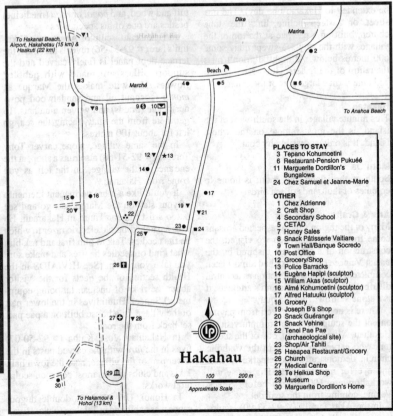

To Hakanai Beach,
Airport, Hakahetau (15 km) &
Haakuti (22 km)

Dike

Marina

Beach

Marché

To Anahoa Beach

Hakahau

0   100   200 m
Approximate Scale

To Hakamoui &
Hohoi (13 km)

PLACES TO STAY
3 Tepano Kohumoetini
6 Restaurant-Pension Pukuéé
11 Marguerite Dordillon's
    Bungalows
24 Chez Samuel et Jeanne-Marie

OTHER
1 Chez Adrienne
2 Craft Shop
4 Secondary School
5 CETAD
7 Honey Sales
8 Snack Pâtisserie Vaitiare
9 Town Hall/Banque Socredo
10 Post Office
12 Grocery/Shop
13 Police Barracks
14 Eugène Hapipi (sculptor)
15 William Akas (sculptor)
16 Aimé Kohumoetini (sculptor)
17 Alfred Hatuuku (sculptor)
18 Grocery
19 Joseph B's Shop
20 Snack Guéranger
21 Snack Vehine
22 Tenei Pae Pae
    (archaeological site)
23 Shop/Air Tahiti
25 Haeapea Restaurant/Grocery
26 Church
27 Medical Centre
28 Te Heikua Shop
29 Museum
30 Marguerite Dordillon's Home

Pukuéé (☎ & fax 92-50-83), ideally located away from the rest of the town. For 3000 CFP per person B&B, you can take up quarters in one of the four impeccable rooms which sleep two to four people and have shared bathroom (cold water).

You can rent one of the two fully equipped fares (kitchen, bathroom) owned by Marguerite Dordillon (☎ 92-53-15) for 2000/3000 CFP a night for singles/doubles. Telephone Marguerite or go straight to her main residence in the south of Hakahau, about 400 metres west of the museum.

Near to Snack Vehine, 500 metres from the seafront, the *Chez Samuel et Jeanne-Marie* guesthouse (☎ 92-53-16) has three simple, clean rooms for two or three people with shared bathroom (hot water). The price is 2000 CFP per person per day, dropping to 1500 CFP on the third day. You can cook for yourself or have your meals at Snack Vehine, run by the owners' daughter-in-law.

Towards the western arm of Hakahau Bay, *Tepano Kohumoetini* (no phone, address BP 61, Hakahau) rents out four clean and well-kept double rooms with shared bathroom (cold water) for 2000 CFP per person per day, including breakfast.

Hakahetau You simply must see the *Pension Vaekehu* (☎ 92-51-03; BP 89, Hakahetau), facing the telephone booth in the centre of the village, next to a pae pae. The chatty owner, Étienne Hokaupoko, a retired school teacher, is an active champion of Marquesan culture and a member of the Motu Haka association. He knows all the legends of Henua Enana, and has an excellent command of English. His three double rooms with shared bathroom cost 2000 CFP per person, and meals, taken with the family, cost 600 CFP each. You will get the chance to try kaikai enana, a typical Marquesan dish based on *uru* (a local plant) and *fei* (bananas). Étienne can make a canoe for you to splash around in the bay in for 2000 CFP.

Also in Hakahetau, you can stay with sculptor Apataroma Hikutini (☎ 92-51-56; see the preceeding Arts & Crafts entry), who has three single or double rooms with shared bathroom for 1000 CFP per person. At 300 CFP for breakfast and 500 CFP for lunch or dinner, it's one of the cheapest full-board deals in Polynesia.

Tony Tereino (☎ 92-51-68), owner of the blue-green shop on the left as you enter the village from Hakahau, plans to build some bungalows. Ask him for more information.

Haakuti This village undoubtedly has the most surprising guesthouse on Ua Pou. Mau Komuetini (☎ 92-53-47) rents out a small yellow fare for four people at 2000 CFP per person per day. It has a bathroom and kitchenette, and is 450 metres from the quay on the left as you go up towards the church. Pinned to the wall in the main room, where you'd expect to see pictures or carvings, you will see photos of a body builder with 'Monsieur Tahiti 86' and 'Monsieur Marquises 87' written underneath in big letters. This is Rimo, Mau's son. His mother can prepare meals for 500 CFP.

Hakamaii Agnès Huuti, nicknamed Pootu ('the beautiful'), offers board and lodging; her house overlooks the church, near the seafront. She has two basic double rooms with shared bathroom for 1000 CFP per person per day, a price which beats all competition. For 500 CFP, Pootu will serve you a typical Marquesan meal (popoi, tuna in coconut milk) on the terrace facing the ocean. To book, leave a message with the duty telephone operator in the village (☎ 92-52-53).

Hohoi If you enjoy Marquesan music, stay at the *Pension Puanea* (☎ 92-50-16 or 92-51-47 in Hakahau) in Hohoi. It is run by Isidore Kohumoetini, singing star of the group Kanahau Trio, and if you give him sufficient notice, Isidore and his group will put on a musical performance for you. These privileges will make up for the spartan standard of the three large rooms and the outside bathroom facilities, priced at 1500/2500 CFP for half/full board per person per day. His wife prepares typical Marquesan dishes such as goat and shrimps in coconut milk, fei and uru. For 1500 CFP, Isidore can act as your guide to Hohoi and the site in Hakaohoka. To get to his house, use the house with the blue roof on the left as you enter the village as a landmark; 50 metres further on, follow the first track which goes up to the right.

Places to Eat

On Ua Pou, the only real eating places are in Hakahau. In the other villages, you can go to a guesthouse or make do with a few provisions from the shops and grocers.

In Hakahau, you can stock up at *Joseph B's* shop opposite Snack Vehine, at one of the two grocers in the same street as the police station or at the Te Heikua shop, opposite the medical centre. On the western side of the bay, Father Gilbert sells honey.

Snack Guéranger, in the south-west of the village, is more of a grocer's but it also sells a few reasonably priced takeaway snacks.

If you are dying for a pastry, go to the *Snack-Pâtisserie Vaitiare*, run by a former legionnaire. Steak and chips and drinks are also available.

At the *Restaurant Haeapea* (☎ 92-51-77), also known as Chez Rosalie, you will often find the doors closed, as it only opens when the tourists from the *Aranui* arrive. If you are lucky enough to be in town then, don't hesitate to join in their feast. It costs 2500 CFP for a full Marquesan meal.

You can eat cheaply at *Snack Vehine* (☎ 92-53-21), opposite Joseph B's shop. Hamburger and chips cost 500 CFP, and steak and chips 800 CFP; on request only, you can have a full set menu for 2000 CFP. You can have a beer there for 250 CFP or a punch for 800 CFP. It's open Monday to Saturday.

The owners of the *Restaurant-Pension Pukuéé* (see Places to Stay) do quite a lot for Marquesan cuisine. Hélène, who is from Ua Huka, excels at cooking lobsters and shrimps, and doesn't skimp on quantity. It costs 2000 CFP for a full meal, or 3000 CFP with lobster and shrimps. The covered terrace restaurant looks out over the seafront and the quay.

The relaxed family atmosphere, rather than the food, is notable at the *Chez Adrienne* snack bar, on the western side of Hakahau Bay, below the road to the airfield. If you arrive unexpectedly at a meal time, Adrienne offers a dish for the token price of 500 CFP; if ordered in advance, a more elaborate meal costs 2000 CFP.

Getting There & Away

Air The Air Tahiti office (☎ 92-53-41) is in Hakahau, inside the shop hidden behind the clump of bougainvillea, opposite the Samuel et Jeanne-Marie guesthouse. It's open Monday and Tuesday from 9 am to noon, Wednesday from 2 to 4 pm and Friday from 9 am to noon and 3 to 4 pm. On Thursday, Tina Klima is on duty at Aneou airfield (☎ 92-51-08). She is very helpful and will do all she can to sort out any booking problems you may have.

The island is served every Thursday by a 20-seater Dornier which does the Nuku Hiva-Ua Pou-Nuku Hiva run. It connects with the ATR 42 which makes the Papeete-

Nuku Hiva link. It costs 37,800 CFP for the Papeete-Ua Pou via Nuku Hiva flight, 5100 CFP for Nuku Hiva-Ua Pou.

The shape of Aneou airfield, built in the middle of a steep-sided valley, is unique: its whole extent slopes down into a curve at its southern end, just like a slide. The sensation on takeoff or landing is quite unforgettable! Check-in at the tiny fare is not without its excitement either: because of the maximum authorised load, passengers have to step onto scales to be weighed with their baggage.

Helicopter Héli Inter Marquises has a weekly Taiohae-Hakahau-Taiohae shuttle service every Wednesday at 9 am for 12,000 CFP a single trip. Flight time is 15 minutes.

Private Bonitiers In Hakahau, contact Joseph Tamarii (☎ 92-52-14). He charges 40,000 CFP to charter his bonitier (for up to 10 people) for Taiohae, and the Hakahau communal bonitier (☎ 92-53-17 or 92-53-22) can also be hired at this rate. Manu Guéranger (☎ 92-51-49), at the snack bar of the same name, charges 45,000 CFP for the same service.

Inter-Island Ships The *Aranui*, *Taporo IV* and *Tamarii Tuamotu* serve Ua Pou. These ships berth at Hakahau. Hakahetau also features on the *Aranui's* itinerary (see Inter-Island Ships in the introductory Getting Around chapter).

Getting Around

On the east cost, a track connects Hakahau with Hohoi (13 km), while on the west coast, Hakahau is connected to Hakahetau (15 km) and Haakuti (22 km). There is a plan to extend the track as far as Hakamaii, which is at present only accessible by speedboat.

To/From the Airport The airfield is at Aneou, about 10 km west of Hakahau, on the Hakahetau track. Your hosts will come to collect you if you have booked accommodation; it costs 500 to 1000 CFP per person for the transfer.

4WD In Hakahau, Patricia Guéranger (☎ 92-51-49), at Snack Guéranger, will drive you to Hakamoui and Hohoi on the east coast or Hakahetau and Haakuti on the west coast for 10,000 CFP. Also contact Rudla Klima (☎ 92-53-86 or 92-50-90), who offers the same rates. If you are so pressed for time that you wish to visit both coasts on the same day, negotiate the rate to 15,000 CFP.

In Hakahetau, get in touch with Étienne Hokaupoko, who charges 4000 CFP for the excursion to Haakuti and 8000 CFP for the trip to Hakahau (with the addition of Hohoi for an extra 7000 CFP). If you hire his services for at least three days you can negotiate a better rate. Apataroma Hikutini charges 14,000 CFP a day (see Places to Stay).

Horse Riding In Hakahau, Albert Kohumoetini (☎ 92-52-28) has two horses which he hires at 5000/10,000 CFP a day per person with/without the services of a guide; ask to speak to Albert's son. Francis Aka (☎ 92-51-83) has three horses (one leather saddle, two wooden ones) hired for 800/2500/5000 CFP an hour/half day/full day (no guide).

In Hakahetau, contact Tony Tereino (see Arts & Crafts) or Étienne Hokaupoko (see Places to Stay). It will cost 4000/5000 CFP a day per person with/without the services of a guide.

Speedboat Prices vary considerably from one hirer to another. In Hakahau, Manu Guéranger (☎ 92-51-49) charges 20,000 CFP to charter his boat to Hakamaii or Hakatao and 35,000 CFP for around the island. Joseph Tamarii's (☎ 92-52-14) services are less expensive at 15,000 CFP for Hakatao. Alain Alho's (☎ 92-52-80) rates are even better: 8000 CFP for Haakuti, 10,000 CFP for Hakamaii, 12,000 CFP for Hakatao and 25,000 CFP for round the island.

In Haakuti contact Martine Pautu (☎ 92-51-89), who runs the blue shop past the Protestant church. It costs 8000 CFP for the transfer to Hakahau.

In Hakamaii, contact Jules and Charles Tissot or José Kautai. The transfer to Hakahau generally costs 8000 CFP.

UNINHABITED ISLANDS OF THE NORTHERN GROUP

Hatu Iti, Eiao, Hatutu, Motu One and the Clark Bank lie to the north of Nuku Hiva. Their waters are occasionally frequented by fishing boats, and Eiao was almost chosen for the recent French nuclear tests.

The Southern Group

The southern group comprises three inhabited islands – Hiva Oa, Tahuata and Fatu Hiva – as well as the four deserted islands of Motane (Mohotani), Fatu Huku, Terihi and Thomasset Rock.

HIVA OA
Area: 320 sq km
Population: 1671
Highest Point: 1276 metres (Mt Temetiu)

Formerly the administrative capital of the Marquesas, Hiva Oa (the 'roof beam' in the Marquesas Islands legend), in the south-east of the archipelago, is now overshadowed by its powerful rival in the northern group, Nuku Hiva. However, it maintains its pre-eminence within the southern group.

Hiva Oa was first seen by Europeans on July 1595 by the Spanish navigator Mendaña. He contented himself with sailing along its coast, and christened it Dominica because it was a Sunday.

Stretching 40 km west to east and about 10 km north to south, this hook-shaped island's distorted relief is evidence of former volcanic activity. A ridge stretching forms a spine across the length of the island, and has an average height of 800 metres. Steep ridges at right angles to this backbone separate each valley, making access difficult.

The slopes of Mt Temetiu and Mt Feani (both over 1100 metres) form a vast amphitheatre, at the base of which is Atuona, the island's capital. Atuona proudly cultivates the memory of its two distinguished

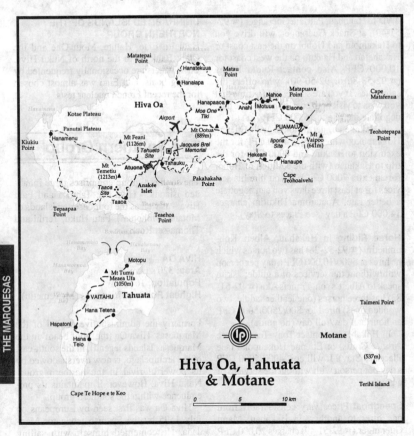

Hiva Oa, Tahuata & Motane

guests: the painter Paul Gauguin and the Belgian singer-poet Jacques Brel, who both chose this small town as the last stopping place on their wanderings.

On the north-east coast, Puamau, ringed by mountains more than 700 metres high, has the most important archaeological remains discovered to date on the Marquesas. The site at Taaoa, in the south-west, is also an archaeological treasure. The lush valleys of Hanaiapa, Hanapaaoa and Nahoe in the north, where the pace of life is set by the schooners, safeguard the traditional Marquesan way of life.

Information

Tourist Office The Atuona Tourist Board (☎ & fax 92-75-10; BP 62, Atuona, Hiva Oa) is housed in the craft fare behind the museum, in the centre of the village. You will be welcomed there by Laura Bonno, who is well informed about the island's places of interest. Some brochures and leaflets are available. Fans of Jacques Brel can have a look at the *Quarterly Review of the Brel Foundation*.

The Tourist Board is open Monday to Friday from 7.30 to 11.30 am and on Saturday from 8.30 to 11.30 am.

Money The Banque Socredo (☎ 92-73-54) is next to the Air Tahiti office, right in the centre of Atuona. You can change currency and travellers' cheques, and make credit card withdrawals. The bank is open Monday to Friday from 7.30 to 11.30 am and 1.30 to 4 pm.

Post & Telecommunications In Atuona, the post office is next to the town hall, 50 metres east of the police station. It's open Monday to Friday from 7.30 to 11.30 am and 1.30 to 4.30 pm (3.30 pm on Friday) and Saturday from 7.30 to 8.30 am. It has a fax service and sells phonecards.

Phonecard telephone booths are in front of the post office and near the school in Atuona, and at the harbour in Tahauku. There is another post office in Puamau. Some villages have phonecard telephone booths; if not, a telephone service can be provided by a private individual.

Emergency In Atuona, the hospital (☎ 92-

73-75) and the dental centre (☎ 92-73-58) are behind the town hall buildings. There is an infirmary or first-aid post in each village.

Laundry Contact Brigitte Chastel (☎ 92-71-27), who speaks French and English.

Atuona

This trim and tidy small town of 1300 inhabitants has the antiquated air of a tropical sub-prefecture, but Jacques Brel (1929-78), who lived there from 1975 to 1978, would no doubt be surprised to see the gleaming 4WD or opulent American commercial vehicles driving through it today. The singer's shadow still hovers over the town, and the museum and the Calvaire cemetery where he is buried are great places of pilgrimage for his fans.

Atuona is at the north of Taaoa Bay, at the mouth of the Vaioa River, and stretches back up the valley for about 1.5 km. Three main sealed roads pass through the town, and most

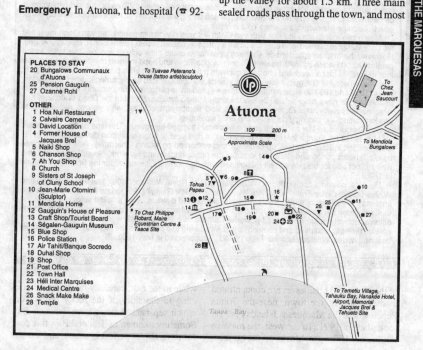

PLACES TO STAY
20 Bungalows Communaux d'Atuona
25 Pension Gauguin
27 Ozanne Rohi

OTHER
1 Hoa Nui Restaurant
2 Calvaire Cemetery
3 David Location
4 Former House of Jacques Brel
5 Naiki Shop
6 Chanson Shop
7 Ah You Shop
8 Church
9 Sisters of St Joseph of Cluny School
10 Jean-Marie Otomimi (Sculptor)
11 Mendiola Home
12 Gauguin's House of Pleasure
13 Craft Shop/Tourist Board
14 Ségalen-Gauguin Museum
15 Blue Shop
16 Police Station
17 Air Tahiti/Banque Socredo
18 Duhal Shop
19 Shop
21 Post Office
22 Town Hall
23 Héli Inter Marquises
24 Medical Centre
26 Snack Make Make
28 Temple

To Tuavae Peterano's house (tattoo artist/sculptor)

To Chez Jean Saucourt

Atuona

0   100   200 m
Approximate Scale

To Mendiola Bungalows

Tohua Pepeu

To Chez Philippe Robard, Maire Equestrian Centre & Taaoa Site

To Temetiu Village, Tahauku Bay, Hanakee Hotel, Airport, Memorial Jacques Brel & Tehueto Site

Taaoa Bay

THE MARQUESAS

Gauguin: the Wild & the Primitive

If one thing is responsible for Polynesia's enduring reputation as a paradise lost, it is the evocative paintings of Paul Gauguin.

Born in 1848, Gauguin did not begin to paint until he was in his mid-20s. After a childhood spent in Peru, he prepared for naval college, joined up as an officer cadet and from 1868 to 1871 roamed the seas. He then worked as a stockbroker in Paris and began to paint his first landscapes, one of which was shown at the Salon Art Exhibition in 1876. Having come to the notice of Camille Pissarro, he exhibited with the Impressionists in 1879. Gauguin then gained the friendship of Edgar Degas, who supported him by buying his pictures. The collapse of the stock market in 1882 put an end to Gauguin's business career and, leaving his wife and children, he devoted himself exclusively to painting. The following years were particularly difficult, and condemned to solitude by poverty, he took refuge in a small town in Finistère named Pont-Aven, went on a voyage to Martinique – his first contact with the tropics – and then returned to Paris, where he met Vincent van Gogh.

Gauguin's second stay in Pont-Aven in 1888 was artistically decisive, as he sought to discover the sources of his own creativity. Influenced by Japanese prints, he adopted a new, simplified style, characterised by large flat areas of colour with clearly defined outlines: 'Pure colour, everything must be sacrificed to it!'. *Vision after the Sermon*, painted during the summer of 1888, embodied a style that was to become the central influence on the Nabis.

After a two-month stay in Arles with van Gogh – it was during this period that van Gogh mutilated his ear – Gauguin painted, one after the other, a series of masterpieces (*Yellow Christ*, *Beautiful Angel*). However, the man who had made so many departures could think only of escape. In a letter to the painter Odilon Redon in 1890, he wrote: 'I am going to Tahiti and hope to finish my life there. I consider that my art...is just a seed and I hope to cultivate it there for myself, in its primitive and wild state.' In Mataiea, where the Gauguin museum now stands, he concentrated on capturing images of daily life, and in 1892 and 1893 he experienced an intensely productive period, painting pictures which he named in Tahitian: *Te nave nave fenua* (Delicious Land), *Manao tupapau* (Spirit of the Dead Watching) and *Arearea* (Amusements). Exuberant settings and flamboyant colours, with yellow, red and blue predominating, increasingly pervaded the artist's painting.

But Gauguin sold few canvases and he was again trapped by poverty. The time had come to leave and he sailed for France in 1893. In November of that year, a large exhibition devoted solely to his work opened in Paris. He took up ceramics and embarked on writing a narrative, *Noa Noa*, inspired by his Tahitian period and designed to make the public understand his work. Nevertheless, the time was still not ripe for his talent to be recognised and, disappointed, he set off for the South Seas again in 1895.

His most powerful compositions, *Te arii vahine* (The Royal Woman, 1896), *Nevermore* (1897) and *Where Do We Come From? What Are We? Where Are We Going?* (1897), date from this second and final stay in Polynesia, which was marked by illness and distress. After a failed suicide attempt, he took refuge on the island of Hiva Oa in the Marquesas, where he defended the inhabitants against the colonial administration and the all-powerful Catholic mission. Although weakened, he did not stop writing, drawing, sculpting and painting, and it was during this period that he produced one of his most beautiful nudes, entitled *Barbaric Tales* (1902). Gauguin died in May 1903. ■

---

of the shops and businesses are concentrated in the centre of the town, near the Tohua Pepeu where the Marquesas Islands Festival took place in 1991. To the west, the massive outline of Mt Temetiu blocks off the horizon, while to the east, carefully maintained houses cling to the sides of the rocky promontory which separates Atuona from Tahauku Bay. Sometimes known as Traitors' Bay, this cove forms an almost perfect U-shape, and attracts sailing boats from the world over. It also serves as a landing stage for the schooners. Beneath Atuona is a black-sand beach, whose rollers are a surfer's delight, fringes the bay. To the south-west stands the lookout post of Anakéé Islet.

Most of the town's working population is employed in tertiary industries, particularly local administration, at the hospital, in schools, at the SMA ('Adapted Military Service') garrison or in small businesses. The medical and administrative services are housed together in attractively decorated traditional-style buildings in the east of the town. In the town centre, the Catholic church is next to the Sisters of Saint Joseph of Cluny school, founded in 1843. It is now one of the most important boarding schools in French Polynesia.

Ségalen-Gauguin Museum This museum (☎ 92-73-77), in the centre of Atuona, next to the Tohua Pepeu, houses a permanent exhibition of drawings, photographs, watercolours, letters and souvenirs of the painter Paul Gauguin and his friend and admirer, the writer-physician Victor Ségalen, who landed at Atuona in August 1903. Rather than revealing the life and work of Gauguin or Ségalen, it presents Polynesian art and culture through the testimonies and contributions of the two artists. The exhibition is built around several themes, including 'Gauguin and Ségalen in Search of the Polynesian Memory', 'Marquesan Motifs', 'Music and Dance', 'Death, Nightmare and Tupapau' and 'Tattooing'. There are plans to expand the collection of Marquesan artefacts.

The museum, built in 1992, was established by a handful of energetic volunteers, who also built a faithful replica of the painter's hut adjacent to the museum. Gauguin christened his hut the 'House of Pleasure' and the name was carved on a lintel. The replica, like the original, is made from woven bamboo, pandanus and niau, and its main façade is decorated with copies of carved wooden panels fashioned by Gauguin depicting outlines of Polynesian nudes and erotic scenes.

Gauguin came to the Marquesas to draw on traditional decorative motifs and to revive his creative inspiration. Called Koke by the Marquesans, with whom he was on good terms, Gauguin joined the local population in opposing the administration and the Church. Looking unfavourably upon the harmful influence of the artist, the Church forbade its parishioners to visit the artist, whose home was the scene of many drunken revelries. Gauguin was subject to a fair amount of harassment by officials, but nevertheless he managed to produce several masterpieces.

The museum's opening hours are Monday to Friday from 7.30 to 11.30 am and Saturday from 8.30 to 11.30 am. Admission costs 300 CFP for adults, 100 CFP for children over 10. Books and videos are on sale. Nearby is an arts and crafts fare and *Jojo*, Jacques Brel's private plane in which he used to fly to Papeete.

Jacques Brel Memorial This memorial to the Belgian singer was erected in 1993 by the tourist office at the very place where the artist wished to build his house. The site, a narrow tongue of land accessible by track, is magnificent and wild.

The memorial is a black-marble plaque set into a large rock. Beside a portrait of the artist is his famous line: 'Do you want me to tell you, moaning is not acceptable...on the Marquesas'. The desolate setting and the symbolism of the site create a poignant atmosphere.

To get there, there are two possible routes on foot (don't attempt them by 4WD). From the Tahauku snack bar, follow the track which goes up to the airfield. After about one km, you will reach the small access road to the Hotel Hanakéé which goes off to the left. Do not take this, but use it as a landmark and go straight on for 400 metres. You will then see a track on your left leading to a private property. Go up here, past the front of the house (beware of the dogs!), and continue on for 300 metres. You will then come out at a small piece of open ground overlooking the Hotel Hanakéé. The path leading to the

The Minstrel's Last Song

A fighter against hypocrisy and proudly iconoclastic, Belgian-born singer songwriter Jacques Brel derided the flaws in our society, and left us masterpieces such as 'In the Port of Amsterdam', 'The Flat Country' and 'The Bigots'.

Wishing to escape media pressure, he set out to sail around the world aboard the *Askoy*, his private ketch. He was accompanied by his female companion, Madly, from Guadeloupe. In November 1975 they arrived at Atuona, and seduced by the serenity of the place, Brel never left. In 1976, he set up home with Madly in a small house on the hillside above the village. He equipped himself with *Jojo*, a Beechcraft aeroplane in which he travelled between the islands in the northern group and as far as Papeete.

Jacques Brel and Madly became involved in village life and were well liked by the local population. From time to time, the artist would perform medical evacuations to Papeete in his plane.

Greatly weakened by cancer, Jacques Brel took his last bow in October 1978 at the age of 48. His last song, 'The Marquesas', resounds as a vibrant homage to this generous country which managed to soothe the blues of his soul. At Calvaire cemetery, where he rests near Paulo, as he called Gauguin, his tomb is lovingly decorated with flowers. ∎

memorial is straight in front of you; it is a two-km walk uphill to the hillside memorial.

Another possibility, which is considerably longer, is to follow the track leading to the airfield, and 300 metres before the Rural Development Department buildings, turn left and go down the track for about 2.5 km.

Calvaire Cemetery Jacques Brel and Paul Gauguin were laid to rest a few dozen metres from each other in the small Calvaire cemetery. Outstandingly well maintained, filled with flowers and arranged on a terrace on the hill, it dominates Atuona Bay.

Jacques Brel's grave is in the lower part of the cemetery, near the access steps on the left. The gravestone, partly hidden by vegetation, is adorned with a medallion depicting the artist with his female companion, Madly.

Two rows further up, at the right-hand edge of the cemetery, is Gauguin's tomb, formed from blocks of red tuff. A stone at the front is simply inscribed with the words 'Paul Gauguin, 1903', while at the rear a

replica of the statue *Oviri* ('wild') stands guard: it depicts a woman with a disturbing, enigmatic face, holding a wolf cub in her hand. Gauguin identified with the violent symbolism of this statue and chose it for his last resting place. Just to the side, a frangipani tree scatters the tomb with white petals and provides some welcome shade.

To get there, take the road which goes up to the right next to the police station. After 200 metres you'll see Jacques Brel's house on the left by the first bend. Continue on for another 400 metres until you reach a fork in the road: follow the direction indicated on the sign until you reach the cemetery 100 metres further on. It's about a 10 to 15-minute walk.

Tehueto Petroglyphs

The Tehueto site is in the Faakua Valley, near Atuona, and features stylised, horizontal human figures, their arms in the air, which have been carved into an enormous basalt block.

From Atuona, take the road towards Tahauku Bay and by the Tahauku snack bar go 100 metres along the unsealed road leading to the airport. You will then see a secondary track and the sign for the Tehueto Historic Site on the left. After going about 1.5 km along this track, you will reach a branching crossroad. Take the left fork, and the petroglyphs are 800 metres from there, in a clearing.

The track is narrow, little used and includes a small ford. Park in front of the Tahauku snack bar and continue your journey on foot.

Taaoa Archaeological Site

This site (also known as Tohua Upeke), seven km south-west of Atuona, has more than 1000 stone platforms, or pae paes. It has been partially restored; the remainder lies buried under twining vegetation, banyans and coconut palms.

Firstly, you will find yourself facing a vast tohua built on several levels. Continue on for 100 metres under the covering of banyans, and on the right-hand side of the site you will see a well-preserved tiki more than a metre in height, sitting on a platform. From a distance, it looks like a plain block of basalt, but as you get closer you can clearly pick out the contours of the eyes and mouth.

To get to the site from the Atuona police station, follow the sealed road as far as the Banque Socredo, turn right and continue on for about seven km. The cliff-top track affords exceptional views over Atuona and its black-sand beach, Anakéé Islet and Taaoa Bay. When you come within sight of Taaoa village, turn right at the telephone booth at the entrance to the village, 200 metres before the stone church, and go up this secondary track for 1.4 km, accessible by 4WD. You will then reach a clearing, and the tohua is set back on the left.

Puamau

Puamau is a 2½-hour drive from Atuona, in the north-east of the island. The village occupies a coastal plain, bordered by a vast ring of mountains, and the elegant seafront is lined with ironwood trees and a black-sand beach. To enjoy the view over the whole bay, follow the track to the Iipona archaeological site and continue as far as the pass.

Iipona Archaeological Site

Discovered by archaeologists last century, the Iipona (or Oipona) site is one of the most important testimonies to pre-contact Marquesan civilisation. Under the leadership of French archaeologists Pierre and Marie-Noëlle Ottino, the site was extensively restored for the third Marquesas Islands Festival in 1991.

Iipona is an exceptional collection of impressive and varied paving, platforms and stone sculptures. It is a religious sanctuary (meae) arranged on two large main terraces covering 5000 sq metres, and banyans, breadfruit trees, coconut palms, mangoes and papayas form a shady fringe.

The area's topography played a key role in the meae's establishment and layout. Orientated along a north-south axis, the site is bordered on the west by Toea peak, a remarkable grey mass which pierces the tangle of vegetation. To the east, the meae is bounded by Ahonu stream, which curves slightly westwards upstream. Between the peak and the stream, the sloping site measures 120 metres in width and 150 metres in length.

At the end of the 19th century, the German ethnographer Karl von den Steinen learnt of the traditions associated with the site from the inhabitants of Puamau. It is said that the valley was inhabited by the Naiki tribe, led by three nobles. During a battle against the tribes in the neighbouring valleys, the nobles captured and sacrificed a Hanapaaoa chieftain. To avenge his death, allied clans joined forces against the Naiki and drove them out of Puamau. The victors transformed the residence of the three nobles into a meae, with two large terraces. They are then thought to have erected the large tikis. Archaeologists date these events to the 18th century.

The site's main attraction is the five monumental tikis which stand in the central and rear part of the site. As you advance towards the first platform, your attention will be caught by the reclining tiki, or Maki Taua Pepe. This exceptional sculpture in grey tuff represents a woman lying on her stomach, her head stretched out and her arms pointing to the sky. Her distorted features and unusual pose have led experts to suppose that she represents a woman giving birth.

A few metres further on is the Manuiotaa tiki, also made from grey tuff. This figure is in complete contrast to the others: less massive, its proportions are harmonious and balanced. The hands are clearly recognisable, as is its female sex.

By climbing up the platform at the back and heading towards the right, you can see Takaii, the site's emblematic tiki, named after a warrior chief renowned for his strength. Fashioned from keetu (the island's characteristic red volcanic tuff) and measuring 2.67 metres above the soil, it is the largest tiki in French Polynesia. It is the archetype of strength, balance and beauty.

The Te Tovae E Noho tiki is set to the left of Takaii, on a lower platform. Less finely worked than the other tikis, its upper torso is hard to make out and the trunk seems to have been omitted. Further back stands the Fau Poe tiki, carved in keetu. Measuring about 1.80 metres, it is sitting with its legs stretched out. Experts believe it to be Takaii's wife.

When the site was restored, the statues were restored to their upright positions by gantry cranes and hoists. Scattered remains such as small tiki heads have been placed on stones or blocks of wood around the site, but, regrettably, thefts have occurred. It has been established that the statues were sculpted from stone from Toea peak, pebbles from the beach and blocks of volcanic tuff extracted from a quarry about 700 metres away.

To gain access to the site from Puamau, follow the track which is at right angles to the seafront, next to the football ground, and continue on for about 1.5 km. You will need to give 200 CFP to Madam Kahau who maintains and guards the site.

Hanapaaoa

This tiny village of 40 inhabitants on the north coast of the island is well off the beaten tourist track and is the place to enjoy traditional Marquesan life. Far from the 'bustle' of Atuona, Hanapaaoa's pace of life is set by fishing, goat hunting and copra production.

The area surrounding Hanapaaoa has a wild beauty. The secondary track which links Hanapaaoa to Anahi and Nahoe a few km to the east winds through valleys covered in guava, pistachio, mango, lemon, mandarin and orange trees. The track, which is partly a cliff road, also affords superb views over Fatu Huku and the north coast. Wild goats abound, scarcely frightened away by your approach, and dozens of pae paes are covered by the vegetation, evidence of a once larger human presence.

South-east of Hanapaaoa, about a quarter of an hour's walk away, stands one of the strangest tikis on the Marquesas, the **Moe One tiki**, about one metre in height. The statue's head is adorned with a carved crown of flowers. According to legend, the inhabitants used to take the tiki down to the beach every year, where they bathed it and coated it with monoi. It is believed to be endowed with a strong mana. Nearby, some human bones and a conch shell (*pu*) are concealed at the foot of an enormous banyan. The sacred character of this place is almost palpable. It is almost impossible to find this tiki on your own; ask some of the village children to take you there.

To get to Hanapaaoa from Atuona, allow a two-hour journey by 4WD. The track accessible to motor vehicles passes the airfield and shortly after it forks into two: the first fork goes to Hanaiapa, and the second leads to Hanapaaoa. Arm yourself with a map and/or guide, and ask at the Atuona Tourist Board for further information. From Hanapaaoa to Anahi and Nahoe, the track is narrow, winding and steeply sloping and great care is needed to prevent your vehicle veering off the road and into the ocean.

Hanaiapa

It is not difficult to succumb to the charm of

this flower-bedecked village in the north of the island, accessible by track from Atuona and Puamau. It stretches for more than one km along a single street which follows the course of the Teheitahi River. Traditional copra-drying sheds are scattered here and there.

In the centre of the village, opposite the reconstructed Marquesan hut, a remarkably well maintained pae pae has pride of place. One of its pavements has three cup-shaped structures, which are thought to have been designed to contain the substances used in tattooing. At the back of the pae pae, slabs of the island's red keetu indicate that the site was the habitation of a chieftain or priest.

Arts & Crafts

Hiva Oa may have fewer artisans than the other islands in the archipelago, but they are just as talented. Rather than going to the craft fare next to the museum, which is not particularly well stocked, go directly to the artisans' homes.

Tuarae Peterano (☎ 92-75-16), a tattoo artist/sculptor well known to the American yachties, can offer you finely worked tikis of tou or miro, spears, ukuleles and carved pigs' teeth and cattle bones. The tattooing, with a razor, is best avoided until he gets a more suitable implement. His house is on the edge of the road which goes along the Vaioa River, 50 metres on the right after the sign saying 'Piste cavalière de Hanamenu' (Hanamenu bridleway) and a 10-minute walk from the Hoa Nui restaurant in Atuona.

Jean-Marie Otomimi's Atuona house (no phone) is an Aladdin's cave. This sculptor, who has taken over from his father, has tikis (from 5000 CFP), ukuleles (from 15,000 CFP), hair clips and bracelets. He carried out the carving on the thrones and stools in the Catholic church. His wife plaits keikaha, the filaments from coconut fibre, to make cords which, when attached to disks of coconut, make original ladies' belts (10,000 CFP). Take the road which goes up to the Pension Gauguin and continue for about 100 metres until you reach a blue sign saying 'Sculpture

traditionnelle sur bois' (traditional wood carving).

Deep-Sea Fishing

Ozanne Rohi can take you fishing for tuna, mahi mahi, marlin or tazar aboard his bonitier for 15,000 CFP a day (flat rate), tackle included. André Teissier, owner of the Pension Gauguin, offers fishing trips for larger numbers for 50,000 CFP (flat rate) a day, all inclusive (see Places to Stay for addresses). Also contact Médéric Kaimuko (see Getting There & Away).

Horse Riding

Some old bridleways cross the western part of the island from Taaoa to Hanamenu, following the coast for some of the way. The route between Atuona and Hanamenu is also possible; allow two days for the round trip (see Getting Around for more details).

Diving

At the time of writing, a subsidiary base of the Marquesas Dive Centre in Nuku Hiva, the Gauguini, had just opened. Phone the centre in Nuku Hiva for details on ☎ 92-00-88 or 92-05-13.

Organised Tours

Cruises OMATI Marquises (☎ & fax 92-75-20; BP 106, Atuona, Hiva Oa) offers customised cruises departing from Hiva Oa aboard a 14-metre luxury catamaran anchored at Tahauku, equipped with three double cabins. The rate per 24 hours with full board varies according to the number of passengers: from 56,000 CFP for two people to 68,000 CFP for six; excursions on land and scuba diving are extra. For a half day (to Tahuata for example), it costs a flat rate of 48,000 CFP.

Archipels Croisières has a one-week 'Marquesas Discovery' programme departing from Nuku Hiva or Hiva Oa on certain dates (see the Cruises section under Nuku Hiva and the introductory Getting Around chapter).

Places to Stay

Accommodation is mainly concentrated in Atuona and its surrounding area, with the exception of one guesthouse in Puamau.

Atuona The atmosphere and prices are attractive at *Chez Philippe Robard* (☎ 92-74-73; BP 46 Atuona, Hiva Oa), a very original rural home four km from Atuona on the left verge of the track leading to Taaoa. Philippe Robard arrived in Hiva Oa by sailing boat in 1979 and has never left. An ecologist, he lives almost self-sufficiently with his family, producing honey, vegetables, citrus and other fruit; he also makes his own bread and roasts his own coffee. The block, on the cliff facing Taaoa Bay, affords an incomparable view, but the lack of comfort in the 'bungalow' which is rented out at 800 CFP per person per night will quickly bring you back down to earth. It is in fact a hut made from bits and pieces with plywood boards, corrugated iron, foam mattresses, a few electric bulbs and a hose pipe for a shower.

In comparison, the *Bungalows Communaux d'Atuona* (☎ 92-73-32 at the town hall, Monday to Friday from 7.30 to 11.30 am and 1.30 to 4.30 pm, fax 92-73-95; ask for Madame Terme) seem luxurious. Next to the administrative centre, ideally situated in the centre of Atuona, seven fully equipped bungalows with bathroom (cold water) are available for rent. The rate for a large bungalow (two bedrooms, four people) is 2500 CFP a night per couple; a small one is 2500/3000 CFP for singles/doubles. Booking is recommended.

Moving up a scale or two, *Jacques Mendiola* (☎ 92-73-88; BP 60, Atuona, Hiva Oa) has two superb bungalows for two to three people in the Atuona hills. Very well fitted out, equipped with bathroom with water heater, they are particularly popular with local administrative staff, such as teachers, who hire them by the month or year. They offer a view like no other over Tahauku Bay, and cost 3000 CFP a day or 50,000 CFP a month. To get to the owners' residence, take the road which goes up to the Pension Gauguin, continue for about 100 metres and take the first road on the right. The Mendiolas' house is on the left-hand corner.

Chez Jean Saucourt (☎ 92-74-34) has two double chalet-style bungalows with bathroom (hot water), fan and mosquito net, costing 3500 CFP a day per bungalow. As at the previously mentioned guesthouse, the owners prefer to rent by the month, or if necessary by the week. Teachers, public servants and SMA military personnel will be competing with you. If you stay for three weeks, the fourth is free. The bungalows are on the hillside in the east of Atuona, looking out over Taaoa Bay, the town and Anakéé Islet. To get there, take the road which goes up towards the Calvaire cemetery. Ignore the fork leading to the cemetery and go on for about 50 metres until you reach a branching crossroad. Take the left branch and continue for 250 metres, until you reach the end of the cul de sac, and you will come out right at the Saucourts' house.

Also in the east of Atuona and on the hillside is *Ozanne Rohi* (☎ 92-73-43), with two simple but clean double rooms with shared bathroom (cold water) and fan for 3000/5000 CFP per person for half/full board. Meals, which are based on Marquesan specialities and fish, are eaten with the family under a *fare potee* in front of the house, from where there is an outstanding view over the black-sand beach below. Ozanne can also offer you two fares in Hanamenu, in the north-west of the island, which he rents out at 4000 CFP per person full board; add 15,000 CFP to hire the boat (flat rate). Each *fare* is equipped with running water (cold). To reach the guesthouse, take the road which goes up to the Pension Gauguin, walk on for about 100 metres and take the first road on the right. Continue for 150 metres, and the Rohis' house is set back on the left, partly concealed behind an enormous avocado tree.

A very popular address with travellers is the *Pension Gauguin* (☎ & fax 92-73-51; BP 34, Atuona, Hiva Oa), in the east of Atuona Bay, a stone's throw from the Make Make snack bar, overlooking the road leading to

Tahauku port. Nestling in luxuriant vegetation, this elegant two-storey building comprises six spotlessly clean rooms with shared bathroom (hot water). A spacious terrace opens onto the bay, and the food served there is stimulating and varied. It will cost you 5500/7500 CFP per person per day for half/full board, 10,000 CFP a couple half board. André Teissier, the master of the house, organises numerous excursions to Hiva Oa and Tahuata.

In the same category, but on the Tahauku Bay side, a 20-minute walk from Atuona, the *Temetiu Village* (☎ & fax 92-73-02; BP 52, Atuona), also known as Chez Gaby, is the other popular choice for travellers. You will be warmly welcomed and Gaby's wife has a good command of English. The two double bungalows and the large family bungalow for five people with bathroom (hot water) are faultless and are available at 5500/10,000 CFP half board per person/couple. The bungalows look directly over Tahauku Bay and the view is magnificent; meals are served on the restaurant terrace. Gaby can also offer excursions to Tahuata.

To get there from the centre of Atuona, follow the road to Tahuaku Bay for a little over one km and take the first road on the left after the SMA building (where the French flag flies). The road goes up for about 400 metres to the guesthouse. Credit cards are accepted.

The ultimate in accommodation on the Marquesas is indisputably the *Hotel Hanakéé* (☎ 92-71-62, fax 92-72-51; BP 57, Atuona, Hiva Oa), perched on the hillside in Tahauku Bay, above the schooner quay. Six comfortable, clean chalets offer an unforgettable view down over the bay, and are equipped with a mezzanine, bathroom (hot water), TV with video recorder, refrigerator and washing machine. The chalets can each accommodate up to five people, and a bar/restaurant adds the finishing touch. It is difficult to sort out the confusing official prices ('18,000 CFP a single/double' and '12,840/19,260 CFP a single/double', tax and breakfast included) and the advertised prices, which are sometimes lower than the

official prices, according to how the owner feels on the day. For this reason, ask for exact prices including tax. Half/full board are 2800/5500 CFP per person.

From the centre of Atuona, follow the road towards the port. At the Tahauku snack bar, take the track on the left leading to the airfield and continue on for one km. The hotel is on the left, at the top of a small access road (follow the sign). Credit cards are accepted.

Puamau The *Pension Bernard Heitaa* (☎ 92-72-27) has two bare but clean double rooms with shared bathroom (hot water), available for 4000/7000 CFP a person/couple half board. Add 1800 CFP for lunch. Bernard Heitaa, known as Vohi, is the *tavana* (mayor) of Puamau and took part in restoring the archaeological site in 1991.

To get there, follow the road which is at right angles to the track along the seafront, beside the football ground, for 700 metres. The house is on the corner of the road which branches off to the right.

Hanapaaoa Shan and Odette Aniel (☎ 92-72-07) intend to build some bungalows on a block they own, on a promontory west of Hanapaaoa. It's worth keeping an eye on the outcome of this plan, as the place is exceptionally wild.

Places to Eat

In Atuona, you will find well-stocked food shops such as *Naiki, Ah You* and *Chanson* and the famous blue colonial-style shop whose customers included Gauguin and later Brel. Ah You and Chanson also act as bakeries from 6 am. At the airfield, a small snack bar opens before each flight, and there are two small grocers shops in Puamau.

Atuona On school days (in the morning) and on Sunday morning after mass, a caravan takes up position near the Tohua Pepeu and sells sandwiches (100 CFP), banana or coconut turnovers (60 CFP) and chocolate cakes (100 CFP).

One hundred metres from the administrative centre, on the mountain side, the owner of *Snack Make Make* (☎ 92-74-26) sells nice snacks at very reasonable prices. The inevitable poisson cru in coconut milk is 850 CFP, the lemon chicken is 900 CFP and the shrimps, vegetables or curry are 1200 CFP. The grilled tazar, freshly caught and priced at 950 CFP, is tasty. You can eat there or take it away. Sandwiches are on sale at 150 CFP, but a bottle of mineral water is an exorbitant 300 CFP. It's open from 7 am to 6 pm as a rule, but hours are variable. Evening meals are available on request.

In Tahauku Bay, stop at *Snack Tahauku* (☎ 92-75-06). The owner serves leg of goat and chips for 900 CFP, tuna meuniere for 800 CFP or entrecôte with Roquefort for 1400 CFP. Opening hours are flexible, but generally from 10.30 am to some time in the evening. The snack bar is two km from the centre of Atuona, at the intersection of the track leading to the airport and the road continuing to the schooner quay.

On the way to Taaoa, five km from Atuona on the left-hand side of the road, the French-run *Snack Bar Maire* (☎ 92-74-55) is a refreshing place to stop. According to what is in stock, they offer poisson cru in coconut milk for 500 CFP, green papaya chicken in coconut milk for 700 CFP and Réunion Island dishes for around 1000 CFP. A beer costs 350 CFP.

The *Hoa Nui* restaurant (☎ 92-73-63), to the left of the road which goes along the Vaioa River, in the north of the village, specialises in Marquesan cuisine. The poisson cru in coconut milk goes well with the lobsters and prawns, and the atmosphere heats up several degrees when the tourists from the *Aranui* feast there when passing through. A full meal costs 2200 CFP without wine, and a single dish is about 1000 CFP. It's open every day at lunchtime and in the evening on request only.

On the terrace of the restaurant at the *Temetiu Village* (see Places to Stay), you can have lunch or dinner while viewing Tahauku and Taaoa bays. Prices are quite acceptable: for the 1500 CFP full meal (2000 CFP with lobster) you can enjoy local specialities such as poisson cru or goat in coconut milk. The restaurant is open every day at lunchtime and in the evening. Bookings are essential and credit cards are accepted.

Another tasty but more expensive possibility is the restaurant at the Hotel Hanakéé (see Places to Stay). It costs 500 to 900 CFP for a salad, 1400 CFP for local fish or 500 CFP for a baked papaya. Credit cards are accepted.

Puamau Tourists staying in Atuona who spend the day at Puamau tend to have lunch at Bernard Heitaa's (see Places to Stay). The set menu based on Marquesan specialities (uru, poe, poisson cru, goat or beef in coconut milk, wild pig) costs 1800 CFP.

Getting There & Away
Air The Air Tahiti office in Atuona (☎ 92-71-14, 92-72-31 at the airfield) is next to the Banque Socredo, opposite the Tohua Pepeu, in the centre of the village. It's open Monday to Friday from 8.30 to 11.30 am and 1.30 to 4.30 pm.

Atuona has connections to Papeete, Nuku Hiva, Rangiroa, Napuka and Puka Puka. On Tuesday and Wednesday, the Air Tahiti ATR 42 does the Papeete-Atuona-Nuku Hiva-Papeete loop, and on Sunday Papeete-Nuku Hiva-Atuona-Papeete. The Papeete-Rangiroa-Napuka (alternating with Puka Puka)-Atuona link is provided on Wednesday, returning to Papeete on Friday. On Thursday there are two flights: Atuona-Nuku Hiva and Nuku Hiva-Atuona. For Ua Pou and Ua Huka, you must change at Nuku Hiva.

The Papeete-Atuona crossing costs 37,800 CFP, Rangiroa-Atuona is 24,500 CFP, Nuku Hiva-Atuona costs 8800 CFP and Napuka or Puka Puka-Atuona is 17,500 CFP.

Helicopter Héli Inter Marquises (☎ & fax 92-72-17) has a heliport in Tahauku Bay. The agency, open Monday to Friday from 7.30 am to noon and 12.30 to 4 pm, is in Atuona's administrative centre, behind the post office.

An Atuona-Omoa (Fatu Hiva)-Atuona shuttle service is provided every second Tuesday to connect with the Air Tahiti flight

THE MARQUESAS

from Papeete. A single trip costs 37,500 CFP, and flight time is 26 minutes. An Atuona-Vaitahu (Tahuata)-Atuona shuttle service operates every Thursday at 8 am and costs 6900 CFP a single trip (seven minutes).

Bonitier/Catamaran The Tahuata communal bonitier connects Vaitahu with Atuona, and the communal catamaran also goes from Fatu Hiva Omoa to Atuona.

Private Bonitiers Ozanne Rohi, André Teissier from the Pension Gauguin and Médéric Kaimuko (☎ 92-74-48; 200 metres behind the Banque Socredo, towards the beach) have bonitiers which can be chartered. It costs 20,000 to 25,000 CFP for Atuona-Vaitahu/Hapatoni (Tahuata)-Atuona, 15,000 CFP for Atuona-Motopu (Tahuata)-Atuona, 55,000 CFP for Atuona-Hanavave (Fatu Hiva)-Atuona.

Inter-Island Ships The *Aranui*, *Taporo IV* and *Tamarii Tuamotu* all stop at Hiva Oa. The *Aranui* serves Atuona, Puamau, Hanaiapa and, occasionally, Hanapaaoa (see Inter-Island Ships in the introductory Getting Around chapter).

Getting Around
To/From the Airport The airfield is 13 km from Atuona. If you have booked your accommodation, your host will come and collect you for 1500 to 1800 CFP; the journey takes about 25 minutes.

By helicopter, it costs 2900 CFP a single trip from Atuona (2½ minutes); the helicopter operates on Tuesday, Wednesday, Thursday and Sunday to connect with Air Tahiti flights.

Helicopter An Atuona-Puamau-Atuona loop is provided every Friday at 8 am for 8900 CFP a single trip.

4WD Excursions by 4WD cost 8000 CFP to Taaoa, 12,000 CFP to Hanaiapa, 15,000 to 20,000 CFP to Hanapaaoa and 15,000 to 20,000 CFP to Puamau (flat rates).

Contact André Teissier of the Pension

Gauguin, Gaby Heitaa of the Temetiu Village guesthouse, Serge Lecordier of the Hotel Hanakéé, Ozanne Rohi (see Places to Stay for their addresses) or Ida Clark (☎ 92-71-33). In Puamau, ask for Etienne Heitaa (☎ 92-75-28).

Car The only exception to the seemingly fixed rule of hiring with a driver is offered by David Location (☎ 92-72-87), who lives in a small street a stone's throw from the shops Chanson, Ah You and Naiki. He has four Suzukis for hire at 10,000 CFP a day, with unlimited km and insurance included. A 20,000 CFP deposit is required and petrol is charged at 145 CFP per litre. He will pick you up at the airfield, and you can also negotiate an hourly or half-day rate.

Horse Riding The Maire equestrian centre, run by the owners of the snack bar of the same name (see Places to Eat) on the Taaoa track, offers horse rides in the Taaoa area (archaeological site and beach) for 5000 CFP for two hours and rides to Hanamenu (rate negotiable).

In Puamau, contact Etienne Heitaa (☎ 92-75-28) who rents horses for 3000 CFP a half day. With the services of a guide, it costs an extra 3000 CFP (up to six people).

Private Bonitiers All the valleys are accessible by bonitier. To charter one, refer to see Private Bonitiers under Getting There & Away above.

TAHUATA
Population: 633
Area: 70 sq km
Highest Point: 1050 metres (Mt Tumu Meae Ufa)

Separated from Hiva Oa by the Bordelais Canal, Tahuata ('dawn' in the Marquesas Islands legend) is the smallest inhabited island in the archipelago. Orientated along a north-south ridgeline, it has numerous inlets, two of which shelter the island's main villages, Hapatoni and Vaitahu.

Vaitahu Bay was the scene of several

important episodes in the history of the Marquesas. In July 1595 the Spanish navigator Mendaña dropped anchor, naming the bay Madre de Dios and the island Santa Cristina. In 1774, Cook visited the bay and named it Resolution Bay. In 1791, the Frenchman Etienne Marchand lay anchor nearby, off Hapatoni to the south.

The pastors of the LMS and the Picpus fathers established a foothold in Vaitahu between 1797 and 1838, and the island became a bridgehead for the evangelisation of the Marquesas.

The year 1842 was a turning point in the islands' history: Dupetit-Thouars forced his former ally Chief Iotete from Tahuata sign the treaty of annexation by France. Realising that he had just been duped, Iotete later opposed the transfer, but his rebellion was crushed by the French. It was also during this period that the island's reserves of sandalwood were plundered.

Tahuata lives in the shadow of its powerful neighbour, Hiva Oa, and its economy is based on copra production and arts and crafts. Several commemorative monuments attest to the island's tumultuous past and are well worth visiting; its dreamlike scenery is another good reason to come.

Information

For tourist information, contact the town hall (☎ 92-92-19) in Vaitahu.

There is no bank on Tahuata. The post office (open from 7.30 to 11.30 am Monday to Friday) is in Vaitahu, as is the infirmary and phonecard telephone booth.

Vaitahu

This tiny village, built against the steep slopes of the central ridge, retains a few vestiges of its stormy past.

On the seafront stands a modest **memorial** topped by a rusty anchor. It recalls the first meeting marked by the seal of friendship between Admiral Dupetit-Thouars and Chief Iotete on 4 August 1838. It was unveiled in November 1988 to commemorate the 150th anniversary of their meeting.

Next to the post office, you can read an **epitaph** to Halley, a French lieutenant commander who perished at Tahuata on 17 September 1842 during the revolt by Iotete and his warriors.

On the hill which dominates the village to the south are a few remains of a building known as the **French Fort**. The stone walls, which are several metres high, are built with lime, but the building is in an advanced state of decay.

The monumental stone **Catholic church**, which towers opposite the seafront, was financed by the Vatican and opened with great pomp and ceremony on 22 August 1988. It recalls the importance of Tahuata in the evangelisation of the archipelago: the first mass on Marquesan soil was celebrated here by the Spanish in 1595, and in 1838 the Brothers of the order of the Sacred Heart of Picpus arrived here on Dupetit-Thouars' *Venus*. The church's interior has beautiful stained-glass windows with dazzling colours which diffuse an atmospheric halo above the altar. Outside, have a look at the imposing wooden statue which dominates the entrance. This *Virgin with Child*, nearly four metres in height, was made by Damien Haturau of Nuku Hiva and is a masterpiece of Marquesan art. It breaks with the traditional representation of the Virgin and Child and originally combines Marquesan culture and Catholic archetypes: the Child Jesus is not curled up in his mother's lap but is held out in both hands, an attitude reminiscent of the posture of the tikis; he is also holding an uru as an offering, a symbol of the Marquesas.

There is a small Polynesian art and history **museum** housed in the town hall, on the seafront. It has a collection of objects characteristic of the island, and admission is free.

Vaitahu is a good place to have a wander. Characteristic copra-drying sheds are dotted here and there, and brightly coloured traditional *vaka* (outrigger canoes) are lined up on the shore. Beside the town hall is a reconstructed Marquesan hut (*hae*) with finely carved posts.

Hapatoni

Hapatoni curves around a wide bay, and is

accessible from Vaitahu by boat in less than 15 minutes or by the bridleway.

The **royal road** is the village's main attraction. Built on a dike on the orders of Queen Vaekehu II in the 19th century, this paved road, lined with hundred-year-old tamanu trees, extends along the shore. On the seafront, a **memorial** commemorates the peaceful visit of Etienne Marchand.

Hapatoni has a meae on the hillside but it is yet to be restored.

Motopu

Motopu has a few dozen inhabitants, and is accessible by the vehicle track which crosses the island's interior.

Hanamoenoa Bay

This enchanting bay is a favourite anchorage for pleasure boats between March and August.

Arts & Crafts

Three top-rate Marquesan sculptors work in Vaitahu: Edwin and Félix Fii (☎ 92-93-04) and Teiki Barsinas (☎ 92-92-67). They exhibit their products in the Marquesan hut near the town hall when the *Aranui* passes through. The hut's support posts, carved with tikis, are the work of Teiki Barsinas.

The sculptors' workshop is a couple of metres from the Pension Barsinas. Walk for about 200 metres up the street which runs along the shore and turn left at the second small bridge; there is a copra-drying shed in front of their house. They sell paddles and bowls made from tou, sandalwood or miro, earrings or hooks made from cattle bone and even daggers of swordfish bone. They are also tattoo artists.

Ronald Teiefitu exhibits his work in the second house on the left coming from the quay. He specialises in women's jewellery (bracelets, brooches and necklaces) carved with Marquesan designs.

In Hapatoni contact Liliane Teikipupuni, who presides over the Mahakatauheipani Cultural & Craft Association, named after a former queen of the valley. She will take you to the craft fare where you can purchase carved animals (lizards, tortoises etc), adzes, wicker-

work and plaited articles, bottles of monoi or paintings on pareus. Prices are negotiable.

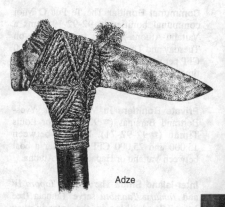

Adze

Horse Riding

The track which joins Vaitahu and Motopu in the north-east, a distance of about 17 km, is an ideal place for riders.

Places to Stay & Eat

You will have to make do with the austere décor of the three rooms in the *Pension Barsinas* (☎ 92-92-26), a split-level house with a shared bathroom (cold water) and kitchen in Vaitahu; a terrace looks out over the street. The price for room only is 1500 CFP per person per day, and meals cost 2000 CFP (except breakfast, which is 500 CFP). You can cook for yourself if you buy supplies at the grocer's shop adjacent to the guest-house. To get there, continue for about 250 metres along the main street at right angles to the seafront, towards the mountain. The guesthouse and the grocer's shop are about 30 metres after the second small bridge, on the left.

Getting There & Away

Tahuata is not served by aircraft, other than helicopter, as it has no landing strip.

Helicopter Héli Inter Marquises has an Atuona-Vaitahu-Atuona shuttle service every Thursday at 8 am for the price of 6900 CFP a single trip.

Communal Bonitier The Te Pua O Mioi communal bonitier (☎ 92-92-19) runs a Vaitahu-Atuona-Vaitahu ferry service on Tuesday and Thursday for the price of 1000 CFP per passenger per journey; the crossing time is about one hour. It departs at about 6.30 am and usually returns at around noon.

Private Bonitiers In Vaitahu, ask Yves-Bertrand Barsinas (☎ 92-92-40) or Louis Timau (☎ 92-92-71). It costs between 15,000 and 25,000 CFP to charter a boat between Vaitahu or Hapatoni and Atuona.

Inter-Island Ships The *Aranui*, *Taporo IV* and *Tamarii Tuamotu* serve Tahuata (see Inter-Island Ships in the introductory Getting Around chapter).

Getting Around

4WD A 17-km track accessible to 4WD vehicles crosses the island's interior to link Vaitahu with Motopu. It costs 15,000 CFP for one day's hire with driver. Contact Louis Timau (☎ 92-92-71), Yves-Bertrand Barsinas (☎ 92-92-40) or Philippe Tetahiotupa.

Horse Riding Simon Timau, known as Kiki, in Vaitahu has several horses (wooden saddles only). His house is just behind the small yellow temple, near the seafront and the quay. It costs 3000 CFP per person for the Vaitahu-Hanahevane-Motopu and return ride, with a guide.

Speedboat Hapatoni is less than 15 minutes away by speedboat from Vaitahu.

In Vaitahu, contact Célestin Teikipupuni (☎ 92-92-13), Yves-Bertrand Barsinas (☎ 92-92-40), Louis Timau (☎ 92-92-71), Donatiano Hikutini or Nicolas Barsinas. In Hapatoni, ask Liliane Teikipupuni or Frédéric Timau. It costs between 3000 and 5000 CFP to hire the boat between Vaitahu and Hapatoni return, and 7000 to 10,000 CFP between Vaitahu and Hanahevane.

FATU HIVA
Population: 497
Area: 80 sq km
Highest Point: 960 metres (Mt Tauaouoho)

Fatu Hiva (the 'roof' in the Marquesas Islands legend) is indisputably the island of superlatives: the most remote, the furthest south, the wettest, the lushest and the most authentic. It was also the first in the archipelago to be seen by the Spanish navigator Mendaña, on 21 July 1595. He christened it Santa Magdalena after the saint whose day it was.

About 75 km south of Hiva Oa, Fatu Hiva consists of two craters, forming arcs open to the west. Between the flanks of the calderas are two valleys, in which nestle the only villages on the island: Hanavave in the north and Omoa in the south, five km apart as the crow flies.

With no landing strip and only poorly serviced by the bonitiers, Fatu Hiva is a

Fatu Hiva

virtually intact, semi-wild paradise. Thanks to its plentiful rainfall, mango, banana, grapefruit, breadfruit, orange and lemon trees thrive on the steep slopes of the island. Thor Heyerdahl, of *Kon Tiki* fame, used his 1½-year stay on the island as the basis for his evocatively titled work *Fatu Hiva, the Return to Nature*.

The jagged relief of the island has created some curiously shaped outcrops. The phallic protuberances of Hanavave Bay caused it to be named Baie des Verges (Bay of Penises). Outraged, the missionaries hastened to add a redeeming 'i' to make the name Baie des Vierges (Bay of Virgins). At sunset, the bay is drenched in purple and the surrounding peaks give off bronze reflections, forming an entrancing spectacle which has intoxicated hundreds of amateur sailors.

Fatu Hiva prides itself on its top-quality art and crafts, whose reputation has spread far beyond the Marquesas.

Information

There is a post office in Omoa, and an infirmary or first-aid post in both villages. There is no bank on the island.

Omoa

In the south of the island, Omoa is dominated by the church with the red roof, white façade and slender spire. Facing the shore, which is partly obscured by a string of multicoloured canoes, the football ground forms a vast seaside esplanade.

Ask someone to take you to the giant **petroglyph** at the edge of the village, near the river: it's an enormous fish carved on a block of rock.

Hanavave

The village is set on the seashore, at the mouth of a steep-sided valley leading onto the beautiful **Bay of Virgins**. Near the shore, the town's sombre small white church with the blue door contrasts with the church in Omoa.

Arts & Crafts

Arts and crafts are the island's major activity,

and Fatu Hiva prides itself on being the only island in French Polynesia to have perpetuated the manufacture of tapa according to ancestral methods. Practically all the women make it, and the villages resound with the sound of uru or mulberry bark being beaten into shape. Guesthouse owners, such as Cécile Gilmore or Norma Ropati, are well known for their work.

In addition to tapa, you will find carved coconuts – small marvels of creativity in which Charles Seigel in Omoa is one of the experts. There are also some wonderful wood carvings. In Omoa, Joseph Pavaouau is one of the last stone sculptors.

Umu hei is a speciality of Fatu Hiva. This is an assortment of gently fragrant plant material such as *ylang-ylang*, vanilla, pieces of pineapple covered in sandalwood powder and various other fruits and plants. It is all held together with a plant fibre, which you can then use to perfume a room or tie in your hair.

You will have no difficulty in finding the artisans, either at their homes or at the craft centre in each of the two villages. In Hanavave, contact the craft centre president, Edwige Pavaouau (☎ 92-80-48), for further details.

Don't imagine that you can buy the artists' work for a few coppers. To give you an idea, a tapa measuring about 1.5 metres depicting a standing Marquesan warrior is priced at around 30,000 CFP; a plaited hat, 8000 CFP; and a carved coconut, 15,000 to 20,000 CFP.

Walking & Horse Riding

A classic activity is to walk or ride to the Bay of Virgins from Omoa along the island's only existing track. On foot it's a three to four-hour walk with no particular difficulties except the climb to the pass separating the two valleys. You must take good shoes and sufficient water. You can also do this trip on horseback or by 4WD if the ground is not muddy (see Getting Around for details).

Places to Stay & Eat

Apart from the guesthouses, eating options

on Fatu Hiva are limited to a few small grocers' shops.

In Omoa, the *Chez Albertine* guesthouse (☎ 92-80-58) has two rooms with shared bathroom (cold water) available for 5500 CFP per person full board. Marquesan specialities have pride of place on the menu.

The *Chez Norma Ropati* guesthouse (☎ 92-80-13) is near to the beach in a separate house. The six double rooms with shared bathroom (hot water) cost 1500 CFP a night per person or 5000 CFP full board. You will be served fortifying traditional Marquesan dishes based on fei bananas, goat in coconut milk and poisson cru. The guesthouse restaurant costs 1500 CFP for a full meal; bookings essential.

Chez Cécile Gilmore (☎ 92-80-54), towards the rear of the village, has two double rooms with shared bathroom (hot water) as well as a fully equipped two-bedroom bungalow with bathroom (hot water planned). It costs 3500/5000 CFP per person half/full board.

The owners of *Chez Marie-Claire Ehueinana* (☎ 92-80-75 or call the town hall on ☎ 92-80-23 and ask for Henri, Marie-Claire's husband) offer two double rooms with shared bathroom (cold water) and kitchen for 3000/5000 CFP for room only/full board per person.

You could also ask Jean Bouyer (☎ 92-80-14), who intends to build some fully equipped bungalows, and Lionel Cantois (☎ 92-80-80), who is planning to build three or four bungalows.

In Hanavave, contact Edwige Pavaouau (☎ 92-80-48), the president of the town's craft centre, whose uncle, Kimitete Kamia (no phone), offers two rooms for 1500/3000 CFP a night room only/full board per person.

Getting There & Away

It was previously only possible to get to Fatu Hiva by the communal bonitier or schooner. The bonitier has now been replaced by a catamaran and, since January 1996, infrequent but regular shuttle flights are provided by helicopter from Hiva Oa.

Helicopter Héli Inter Marquises has an Atuona-Omoa-Atuona shuttle service every second Tuesday to connect with the Air Tahiti flight from Papeete, for 37,500 CFP a single trip.

Communal Catamaran The *Auona II*, which can take 30 passengers, operates the ferry service between Omoa and Atuona (there and back in the same day) every Tuesday for 3000 CFP per trip per person. Allow two to three hours for the crossing, depending on sea conditions.

Private Bonitiers See the Getting There & Away section under Hiva Oa for details of owners of bonitiers who offer the Hiva Oa-Fatu Hiva crossing.

Inter-Island Ships The *Aranui*, *Tamarii Tuamotu* and *Taporo IV* serve Fatu Hiva (see Inter-Island Ships in the Getting Around chapter).

Getting Around

The only road, of beaten earth, is 17 km long and links Hanavave with Omoa. As it is impassable in wet weather, journeys between villages are often undertaken by canoe.

4WD In Omoa, ask Bernard Tehevini (☎ 92-80-41), Joseph Tetuanui (☎ 92-80-09) or Roger Kamia (☎ 92-80-07). It costs 7000 to 8000 CFP a day with driver.

Horse Riding Roberto Maraetaata (☎ 92-80-23 at the town hall) has two horses with leather saddles which he hires out at 5000 CFP a day without the services of a guide. Give him several days' notice.

Motorised Canoe On Fatu Hiva, speedboats have not yet ousted the traditional outrigger canoes which take three to four people. The only concession to modern times are their low-powered outboard motors.

In Omoa, contact Cécile Gilmore (see Places to Stay), who charges 4000 CFP, or Stellio Tehevini (☎ 92-80-79), who charges

Fish park, Mataiva, Tuamotus

Left: Marquesan Tapa
Top: View of the northern coastline, Nuku Hiva, Marquesas
Middle: Woodcarvers, Marquesas
Bottom: Gauguin's tomb, Hiva Oa, Marquesas

3000 CFP a journey. In Hanavave, it will cost 3000 CFP with Jacques Tevenino (☎ 92-80-71) or 5000 CFP with Daniel Pavaouau (☎ 92-80-60).

UNINHABITED ISLETS OF THE SOUTHERN GROUP

The uninhabited island of Motane (Mohotani) lies south-east of Hiva Oa and east of Tahuata. With an area of 15 sq km, and a peak height of 527 metres, it is now home to only wild goats, but it was once the site of human occupation. The islet Terihi is south of Motane.

Fatu Huku is to the north of Hiva Oa, and Thomasset Rock lies east of Fatu Hiva. The waters of Fatu Huku and Motane are occasionally frequented by fishing vessels.

THE MARQUESAS

1000 GFP ... boundary. In Haulover it will cost ...
2000 GFP with Jacques. Travelling (c. 92.8m ...
Tb to ... 5000 GFP with Daniel Paveura ...
692 40 00 ...

UNINHABITED ISLETS OF THE
SOUTHERN GROUP

The uninhabited islands of Motane (Mohotane) lying the south east of Hiva Oa and to ...

... Reef with an area of 12 sq.km. and a peak ... height of 520 metres, is grown from to only ... wild goats, but it was once the site of human occupation. The islet Terihi is south of Motane.

Fatu Huku, to the north of Hiva Oa and Thomasset Rock, the east of Fatu Hiva ... rocks of Thole Hole and Motane are ... nnally frequented by fishing vessels.

The Australs

HISTORY

The Australs

Well to the south of Tahiti and the Society Islands, the Austral group runs north-west to south-east and is effectively an extension of the same range of submerged peaks that make up the southern Cook Islands. Rurutu is a *makatea* island (see the following aside), like Atiu and Mangaia in the Cook group. There are five inhabited islands in the Australs: in sequence they are Rimatara, Rurutu, Tubuai, Raivavae and remote Rapa. In addition there are two uninhabited islands: Maria Island at the north-western end of the chain and the Marotiri Rocks, also known as the Bass Rocks, at the south-eastern end. The chain extends 1300 km from end to end.

The islands lie along the Tropic of Capricorn and it's regularly remarked that the climate is much cooler than on the Society Islands, although only Rapa is really far enough south to qualify as temperate. Nevertheless, the islands are not lush and fecund like the Society Islands, their appearance is altogether more spartan. The population of the entire Austral group is just over 6000.

The Australs are remarkably varied and their features of interest include limestone caverns and ancient *maraes* on Rurutu, reminders of the powerful artwork and massive stone *tikis* of Raivavae and the hilltop fortresses or *pas* of Rapa.

HISTORY
The Australs were the last of the Polynesian islands to be settled, and it is believed the first arrivals came from Tahiti between 1000 and 1300 AD. European sightings of the whole chain were a long and drawn-out affair. Cook first saw Rurutu in 1769,

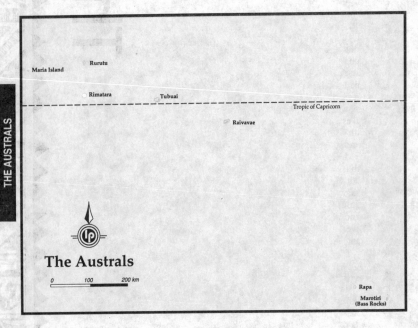

The Australs

0   100   200 km

Austral Arts
Despite their isolation, the islands developed some of the most vibrant and powerful art forms in Polynesia, including the giant stone tikis of Raivavae and the woodcarvings of Rurutu. Unfortunately, with the coming of the missionaries these native arts were totally wiped out and there is virtually nothing to be seen today. Even the largest and most impressive of the Raivavae tikis are now at the Gauguin Museum in Tahiti, rather than on their home island. Rurutu is still a centre for the production of wonderful cane and basketwork.

Both islands specialised in particular forms of wood carving. Delicately carved fly whisks were produced on Rurutu, while ceremonial paddles, ladles and bowls came from Raivavae. No one is quite sure what the paddles were used for as they were too frail to paddle a canoe. A few intricately carved examples of these items have survived in museums, but the missionaries contrived to destroy all examples of Austral statuary. ■

Gayangos and Varela found Raivavae in 1775, Cook was back to make the first landing on Tubuai in 1777 and Vancouver 'found' remote Rapa in 1791. But it was not until Captain Samuel Pinder Henry chanced upon Rimatara in 1811 that the last of the islands came to European attention.

Apart from a colourful chapter in the *Bounty* saga, when the mutineers unsuccessfully tried to establish themselves on Tubuai, contact with Europeans and the Western world was remarkably limited until earlier this century. It was not until 1889 that the French established a protectorate over all the islands, and it was in 1900 and 1901 that the last of them were formally annexed. This long period during which English missionaries, or more frequently their native representatives, held sway has ensured that the Protestant religion remains strong to this day.

GETTING THERE & AWAY

Two of the islands, Rurutu and Tubuai, are about 600 km south of Tahiti and can be easily visited by the regular Air Tahiti flights.

Rimatara and Raivavae can be fairly easily reached by ship, but getting to Rapa, over 1000 km south of Tahiti, takes real effort.

Air

Air Tahiti flies Papeete-Rurutu-Tubuai-Papeete twice a week and Papeete-Tubuai-Rurutu-Papeete once a week. The two Austral Islands can be included in the Society Islands plus Australs air pass (50,500/26,200 CFP for adults/children), making a visit to the two remote islands a reasonable possibility. Weekend packages to Rurutu are also offered by Air Tahiti from time to time, and cost 37,000 CFP, including, for example, air fares, two nights' accommodation, meals and an island tour for example. One-way Papeete-Rurutu fares are 17,700 CFP, Papeete-Tubuai costs 19,800 CFP and Rurutu-Tubuai costs 8300 CFP.

Sea

Local demand can vary the schedule, but the 60-metre *Tuhaa Pae II* operates from Tahiti down the Rimatara-Rurutu-Tubuai-Raivavae chain about twice a month and continues on to Rapa once every two months. The schedule is often very unreliable. Very occasionally a pause is made at the Maria Islands. See the table on page 358 for deck-class and cabin-class fares.

Meals will add a couple of thousand CFP for each day at sea. Contact the Société Anonyme d'Économie Mixte de Navigation des Australes (☎ 42-93-67, fax 42-06-09),

Austral Agriculture
Taro is the principal food staple on the Australs. The root plant is grown like rice in irrigated marsh-like fields. The tuber is boiled then pounded to produce *poipoi*, which is remarkably flavourless and usually eaten sweetened with honey or a fruit purée. Left to ferment for a few days, the poipoi develops a better flavour. Tapioca and sweet potatoes also grow well in the Australs, along with familiar temperate-region vegetables and coffee. ■

THE AUSTRALS

Tuhaa Pae II Fares
One-way fares on the *Tuhaa Pae II* are as follows:

From:	To: Rimatara	Rururu	Tubuai	Raivavae	Rapa
Papeete					
deck class:	3681 CFP	3681 CFP	3681 CFP	5305 CFP	7254 CFP
cabin class:	6442 CFP	6442 CFP	6442 CFP	9284 CFP	12,694 CFP
Rimatara					
deck class:	–	1299 CFP	1732 CFP	2491 CFP	5305 CFP
cabin class:	–	2274 CFP	3031 CFP	4358 CFP	9284 CFP
Rururu					
deck class:	1299 CFP	–	1732 CFP	2491 CFP	5305 CFP
cabin class:	2274 CFP	–	3031 CFP	4358 CFP	9284 CFP
Tubuai					
deck class:	1732 CFP	1732 CFP	–	1732 CFP	2491 CFP
cabin class:	3031 CFP	3031 CFP	–	3031 CFP	4358 CFP
Raivavae					
deck class:	2491 CFP	2491 CFP	1732 CFP	–	2491 CFP
cabin class:	4358 CFP	4358 CFP	3031 CFP	–	4358 CFP
Rapa					
deck class:	5305 CFP	5305 CFP	2491 CFP	2491 CFP	–
cabin class:	9284 CFP	9284 CFP	4358 CFP	4358 CFP	–

BP 1890, Papeete, Tahiti for more information about services.

Rururu

Population: 2000
Area: 36 sq km
Passes: 1

Rururu has a high plateau with great views from the hilltops, limestone caverns dotted around the coast and some ancient maraes. The island is fringed by a continuous reef but it's rarely more than a stone's throw from the shoreline. Occasionally there are small pools between the shore and reef edge, but there's no lagoon as such. So even where there's a good beach, and there are some, particularly south of Arei Point

and at the southern end of the island, there's little opportunity to swim.

Apart from the roads shown on the map, there is a network of minor tracks winding into the island's dense patchwork of plantations.

HISTORY
Cook sailed by Rururu in 1769 during his first great voyage, but the Rurutuans' hostile reception prevented him from landing. Joseph Banks noted the high quality of their canoes and weapons. There was little contact with Europeans until well into the 19th century when LMS missionaries sent native teachers to establish a mission. Christianity quickly took hold, but as on so many other islands in Polynesia, European diseases arrived at much the same time as European religion and the result was usually disastrous.

Airport Terminal Scenes

Arrivals at Rurutu can be a wonderful, heart-warming scene. The little open-sided airport terminal can be absolutely packed with islanders farewelling departees or greeting arrivals. That does not mean a kiss on both cheeks and loud hellos and goodbyes, for in Rurutu flowers are needed, and lots of them. Hours before the flight, a contingent of women set to work in the terminal building making flower *leis*, ready to sell to anybody who hasn't had the time to make their own. As a result the terminal is like a tightly packed flower shop, the heady fragrance of tropical flowers is almost overpowering and passengers stagger to their plane or to the collection of beat-up 4WDs in the airport carpark, submerged in high collars of flowers. At the next stop the aircraft aisles will be carpeted with flower petals.

Things are a little more restrained in Tubuai, but there's still a distinctly different flavour to our modern, hurried and untrusting world. Departing from Tubuai early one morning, three friends from another island *pension* turned up driving the car belonging to their pension owner.

'Where is she?' I asked.

'Oh, she didn't feel like getting up so early,' they replied.

'Just take the car and leave it at the airport, I'll come out and get it later on,' they were told.

Has that ever happened to you when you stayed in a hotel or motel anywhere in our frenetic modern world? ■

Rurutu has the most extensive marae site in the Australs, but unfortunately, it is not well maintained. Although there are no longer any woodcarvers on Rurutu, the statue of the Rurutu ancestor god A'a is one of the most important Polynesian works of art on display in London – the pioneering missionary John Williams took it home.

ORIENTATION & INFORMATION

Rurutu is about 10 km long and averages about five km wide. The population is concentrated in three main villages on the coast. Moerai is the largest village with the island's one dock for ocean-going ships, a post office, branch of Banque Socredo and several shops. It's about four km from the airport. A sealed road runs about a third of the way round the island linking the airport with Moerai and Hauti (also spelt Auti). Another sealed road climbs over the centre of the island to link Moerai with Avera, the third village.

AROUND THE ISLAND

It's 36 km around Rurutu, about the same distance as around Bora Bora. Pedalling yourself around Rurutu is, however, a whole different story because the road does not stick faithfully to the coast. Four times it

drops down right to the coast, then climbs away, rising past the 100-metre level on three occasions and once reaching nearly 200 metres. Keep these altitude changes in mind before you blithely set off to cycle round the island. Nevertheless, it's an interesting ride and worth the effort. The road runs through a wide variety of plantations, passes beautiful stretches of coast and skirts rocky headlands. It's a very quiet route, particularly on the southern half of the island where you'll probably see as many people on horseback as in cars and 4WDs.

Moerai

The main town of the island is about four km south-east of the airport. Tauraatua Pass, the

Stone Lifting

In January each year the Amoraa Ofae stone-lifting competition takes place with preliminary bouts in each village and the finals in a clearing beside the Hauti-Toataratara Point road where the official stones are kept. During preliminary attempts the stone is greased with oil to make lifting it even more difficult! Male contestants must try to lift a 130-kg stone; the female equivalent is 90 kg after the original 110-kg stone was dropped and broken. ■

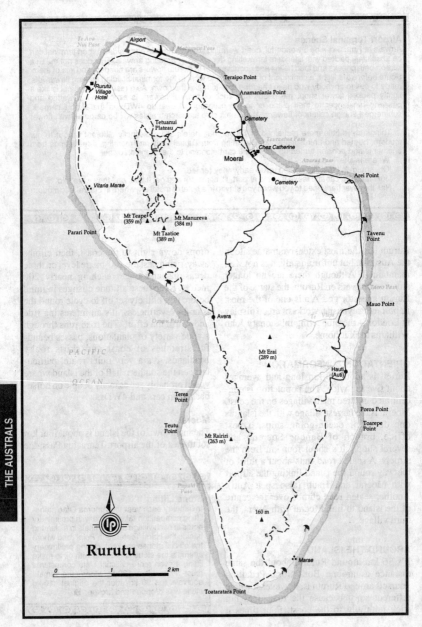

Rurutu

0 — 1 — 2 km

Éric de Bisschop, Navigator & Opportunist

Born in Lille, in the north of France, in 1891, Éric de Bisschop came to fame several times during the 20th century. A lieutenant in the French navy during WWI, he turned up in Lebanon in the 1920s trying to use military vessels for personal commercial purposes, and this resulted in his dismissal from the navy. He was then free to offer his services to the Chinese army in Shanghai and this enabled him to set up a shipping company that specialised in dealing in antique pottery using his first junk, the *Fou Po*. When this sank, he took the *Fou Po II* and sailed to Hawaii, where he was again shipwrecked.

In the late 1930s Éric de Bisschop set off aboard the double canoe *Kaimiloa* – a sort of cruise catamaran with junk's sails – on what was to be a trip halfway around the world. He arrived at Cannes in the south of France having rounded the Cape of Good Hope. Even today, the people of Cannes still remember his arrival in port!

During WWII, he was appointed French Consul in Honolulu by Vichy and was imprisoned by the Americans as soon as he arrived in Hawaii, then released. Once the war was over, he became administrator on Rururu, thanks to yet another political about-face.

In 1947, Thor Heyerdahl's *Kon Tiki* expedition annoyed de Bisschop so much that he decided to prove that it was possible to make the same journey, by the same means, but in the opposite direction. He set out from Polynesia in 1956 aboard the *Tahiti Nui*, a raft with junk's sails, and reached the coast of Chile, where he was washed up together with his crew, including Francis Cowan (now an expert on Polynesian boats) among others. In 1958, in Chile, Éric de Bisschop built a new raft, the *Tahiti Nui II*, and set off for Polynesia. During the voyage the raft soaked up water and gradually began to sink, but this was no problem: in the middle of the Pacific Ocean they dismantled the large raft and made a smaller one from its parts! This became the *Tahiti Nui III*, which was a bit like a trimaran. But alas, when they tried to land on an island, the vessel was crushed on the reef. Éric de Bisschop met his end this way, on a peculiar boat. ■

only pass suitable for ocean-going ships, leads directly into the town's small artificial harbour. The picturesque little Protestant church, just back from the harbour, dates from 1865-72. Éric de Bisschop, the island's most famous resident, was a French Thor Heyerdahl, dedicated to perilous voyages in unsuitable craft. He's remembered solely by his simple gravestone, which states that he was 'born in Lille (France), died at Rakahana (Cook)' (Ici repose Éric de Bisschop, né à Lille (France), décédé à Rakahana (Cook)). His grave is in the second cemetery, towards the mountainside, off the main road to the south of the village centre.

Moerai to Hauti

The solid concrete road continues from Moerai along the coast to Arei Point, one of Rururu's impressive elevated reef cliffs. Just before the point a short path leads up to a large cliff-face cavern, complete with stalactites and stalagmites. There are other similar caverns around the coast and the island has some other interesting cave systems waiting to be discovered.

From the point the road runs directly south along the coast until it reaches the Te Vaipa River, running into the sea beside Mauo Point, another rocky cliff face. Here the road climbs inland and skirts around the point before dropping down to Hauti, the second of the island's three villages.

Hauti to Avera

Almost immediately out of Hauti the concrete road surface ends and the dirt road climbs, drops back almost to sea level then climbs again to over 100 metres before dropping steeply down to the coast near the southern tip of the island, Toataratara Point. This road runs along the ancient lagoon bottom, before it was thrust up above sea level. The east coast of the island, about half a km east of the road, ends in steep cliffs, dropping 50 metres into the sea. This was once the ancient reef.

Where the road turns right just before the coast, take a short diversion to the left and look for a small tin shed on the ocean side of the road. Nearby in the field is the small **Poreopi Marae**, with the spike-like vertical

THE AUSTRALS

Makatea

Rurutu is the Austral island geologically most like the southern Cook Islands because it is a textbook example of *makatea*. At some time in the past, a sudden upthrust raised the whole island above sea level and converted the fringing reef into a coastal cliff. The sheer, rocky cliff faces around much of the island were once the outer face of the island's coral reef. The valley, along which the road south from Hauti to Toataratara Point runs, was once the lagoon between the island and its outer reef. That reef is now the ridgeline falling sheer into the sea along the south-east coast of the island. As on the makatea islands of the Cooks, Rurutu is riddled with limestone caverns, another reminder of the cataclysmic upheaval which raised what were once underwater caves to their new location. ∎

stones characteristic of Austral maraes. A series of beautiful little beaches run to the east of the point. As everywhere around the island, however, there are just shallow pools between the shoreline and the outer reef.

Clinging to the coast the road rounds the point and heads north, passing a curious small garden beside the road. Leaving the coast the road climbs steeply, passing through pine forests and then, at the 190-metre-high point, a coffee plantation. Then it's down again with superb views over the coast and, to the north, over Avera, the third village, to the three peaks of Teape, Taatioe and Manureva. The concrete road surface recommences in Avera and runs over the central pass to Moerai, but continuing on the island circuit route it soon goes back to dirt.

Avera to Moerai

The road climbs round the edge of the headland then drops down to the coast again just beyond Parari Point. In the space between two houses, hidden from the road by a hedge and back among the coconut trees is the remains of the **Vitaria Marae**, the marae of the last Rurutu royal family. It's said that at one time the marae stretched for a km and it's still an extensive site with many of those

spike-like vertical stones. Nearby is the huge **Teanaeo Grotto**. The coast road continues past the Rurutu Village Hotel, finds the concrete surface again and skirts the airport runway before rounding one more impressive sheer cliff face, at Anamaniana Point, and arriving back at Moerai.

WALKING

It's easy to climb the three highest peaks, arrayed along a ridgeline looking down on Avera. Starting from just beyond the Moerai end of the airport runway or from Moerai itself, the routes soon meet and climb steadily to the 200-metre Tetuanui Plateau, a fertile highland plantation area with everything from pineapples to taro. A network of tracks criss-cross the plateau, including a central one leading to some water reservoirs. Tracks to the left or the right will take you towards the summits and the easiest plan is simply to aim for Mt Manureva, distinguished by the small TV-relay station at the top. The mountains are not cloaked in dense vegetation, like Society Island peaks, so finding a route is no problem. A narrow foot trail leaves the larger track to head straight up the ridgeline to the top of Mt Manureva (384 metres) with views over both Moerai and Avera. Follow the ridgeline a short distance to Taatioe (389 metres) and down to Teape (359 metres), with good views of the north-west coast. From there it's easy to make your way back down to the main track.

PLACES TO STAY & EAT

Rurutu offers just two regular places to stay, but neither accepts credit cards.

Chez Catherine or *Pension Catherine* (☎ & fax 94-02-43) is right in the centre of Moerai, the main village on the island. This friendly and well-run place has 10 simple rooms, all with attached bathrooms. Five rooms have double beds, five have two singles, and all have an extra couch-style bed which could be used for a child. Nightly costs are 3000/5000 CFP, or with demi-pension 5500/10,000 CFP.

Chez Catherine's small restaurant offers breakfast for 500 CFP, lunch or dinner for

2000 CFP and a variety of main courses for 1000 to 1800 CFP, including grilled mahi mahi for 1500 CFP or steak and chips for 1000 CFP.

The *Rurutu Village Hotel* (☎ 94-03-92) is not in one of the villages but right on the beach on the north-west coast, about one km or so round from the airport. The hotel was badly hit by the January 1995 cyclone which struck the west coast of the island, but it has undergone major rebuilding. There are seven coral-block bungalows, each with two single beds, bathroom with solar-heated water and a verandah. There's a large fare building housing the restaurant, lounge area, bar and swimming pool. Once upon a time there was even a tennis court but it's now used as a pig pen! It's a comfortable enough place with singles/doubles at 3500/4000 CFP plus breakfast for 500 CFP and lunch or dinner at 2500 CFP. You won't go hungry, as the servings are substantial.

The only other eating possibilities on the island are the village shops, particularly in Moerai.

THINGS TO BUY

You can see hats being made at Artisanat Aerepau, near the waterfront in Moerai, but the best place to see hats and other traditional basketry work is the amazing display at the airport. *Peue* (mats), baskets, bags and other work are displayed but it's the huge selection of hats which dominates. Men's hats have a higher top and narrower rim, while women's hats are flatter on top and have a wider rim. Cheaper hats cost 700 to 1000 CFP there are many mid-range ones at 1500 to 2000 CFP, but the really fine hats, kept in glass showcases, are 10,000 CFP and more. For this work a special pandanus known as *paeore* is grown on shaded hillsides. The pandanus used for hats is bleached.

Brilliantly coloured *tifaifai* patchwork blankets are also produced on Rurutu.

GETTING THERE & AWAY

Rurutu is about 600 km south of Tahiti and is the most accessible of the Austral Islands.

Air

Air Tahiti flies a Papeete-Rurutu-Tubuai-Papeete route twice a week and a Papeete-Tubuai-Rurutu-Papeete route once a week. See the introductory Getting There & Away section for more details. The Air Tahiti office (☎ 94-03-57) is at the airport.

Sea

The *Tuhaa Pae II* sails from Papeete to Rurutu and the other Austral Islands every two weeks. Ships dock at Moerai, entering the harbour through the Tauraatua Pass.

GETTING AROUND

The airport is about four km from the main village of Moerai, where the dock is situated. If you book accommodation you'll be picked up at the airport. Either place to stay will offer round-the-island tours at around 4000 to 4500 CFP per person. The Rurutu Village Hotel has a couple of cruiser-style bikes for their guests' use, while Chez Catherine has three cars for rent for 3500/6000 CFP a half/full day.

Tubuai

Population: 1800
Area: 45 sq km
Passes: 4

It's the largest of the Austral Islands and administrative centre for the group, but Tubuai doesn't have the interesting geology, varied geography or ancient maraes of Rurutu. Virtually the only thing unusual about Tubuai is that, unlike other Polynesian islands, the outrigger canoes have their outrigger on the right. The *Bounty* mutineers did try, unsuccessfully, to establish themselves on Tubuai, as a remote centre far from the long reach of British naval justice, but there's barely any trace left of that visit.

HISTORY

Captain Cook landed at Tubuai in 1777 en route to Tahiti on his third voyage. Some

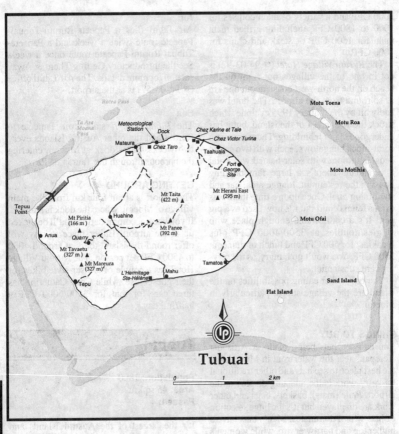

Tubuai

0   1   2 km

theories hold that the island was only settled a few generations earlier, but the locals were certainly fiercely protective of their island, as the *Bounty* mutineers discovered when they attempted to settle there in 1789. Ships bound for Australia started to stop on Tubuai early in the 19th century and the LMS despatched native teachers to the island in 1822.

At about this time European diseases started to afflict the island and in just the few years to 1828 the population was reported to have plummeted from 3000 to less than 300. It was to fall still further before it began to recover. When Pomare II visited the Australs

in 1819 the island chiefs ceded power to him, so when Tahiti came under France's wing in 1842 Tubuai followed. The island was formally annexed by France in 1880.

ORIENTATION & INFORMATION

Tubuai has a remarkably uninflected coast. Compared to islands in the Society group, with their dramatic peninsulas and bays, the coast of Tubuai is rather boring. There are two mountain ranges sloping down to flat plains to the sea and separated by an equally low-lying central region. Mt Taita (422 metres) is the highest point on the island. The island is surrounded by a wide but very shallow lagoon with an outer reef and a handful of motus.

The 25-km coast road only wanders any distance from the water's edge as it passes the airport. A cross-island road (the Route Traversiére) bisects the island but even that doesn't rise very far above sea level. The two mountain ridges stand at each end of the island with a low saddle between them. Most of the island is fringed by beach but the wide lagoon is very shallow. A handful of motus, popular for beach excursions, dot the eastern end of the outer reef.

Mataura, about four km from the airport, is the main village and has a post office, a branch of the Banque Socredo (open Monday to Friday from 7.30 to 11.30 am and 1.30 to 4 pm) and a couple of reasonably sized stores. A few smaller stores are dotted round the island.

AROUND THE ISLAND

Tubuai does not have a great deal of interest – one quick circuit of the island and you've pretty much done it. From the centre of Mataura, proceeding clockwise, the 25-km coast road runs past the Météo France meteorological station, the shipping wharf and through Taahuaia, the island's second village. Just past the village, on the inland side, an empty patch of green is the site of

the *Bounty* mutineers' Fort George. There's no sign or any other memorial to the site's history, but if you look closely you may think you can make out the faint depression marking the foundations of two sides of the stockade.

The three larger motus are visible at the edge of the lagoon as you round the long, even curve of the island's east end. The third village of Mahu marks the southern end of the Route Traversière (the cross-island route), and at the end of the village Nöel Ilari's self-made tomb stands in front of his home. Born in 1897, Ilari was a larger-than-life Frenchman who married a Tubuaian woman and became president of the French Polynesian Territorial Assembly in 1954. However, his squabbles with the French government led to a self-inflicted exile in Tubuai for which he never forgave the government and the inscription recounts his indignation. Convinced his death was imminent, Ilari constructed the tomb in the 1970s, then lived until 1985! His pension, L'Hermitage-Ste Hélène, takes its name from Napoleon's place of exile on the remote South Atlantic island of Sainte Hélène.

From Mahu the road makes a sharp right turn at the island's south-west corner, another sharp right at the airport and quickly ends up back in Mataura. The best beaches and swimming are along this stretch; the

The Bounty

After Bligh was shoved on to a longboat in the Tonga islands on 28 April 1789, the *Bounty* mutineers high-tailed it back to the delights of Tahiti, but Fletcher Christian realised all too clearly that paradise was not going to last forever. Sooner, rather than later, the British Navy was going to start wondering what had happened to the *Bounty* and come looking for it. Even worse, if Bligh should survive and make it back to Britain he'd tell the navy precisely what had happened to the *Bounty*. What was needed was a hideaway much more remote than Tahiti, somewhere right on the edge of the known map – Tubuai, for instance.

So, less than a month later, on 24 May, Christian and his band sailed the *Bounty* to Tubuai, intending to make this their new home. Unfortunately for them, the Tubuaians recognised a bad lot when they saw them and strenuously opposed their landing. After only a week the *Bounty* sailed back to Tahiti, but a month later they were back for a second try. Again their arrival was met with furious resistance and, barricaded in Fort George, just east of the village of Taahuaia, the mutineers held out from 9 July until 15 September before Christian sailed back to Tahiti then set off again, heading to the east and right off the map. See the Facts about the Islands chapter for the full story of the mutiny and its aftermath. It's said that more than 60 Tubuaians died in the conflict with the mutineers. ∎

beach at the Ta Ara Moana Pass, just west of Mataura, is excellent and the water is deep. The Mormons have made a major onslaught on Tubuai and their modern, functional churches, each with a floodlit basketball court, are sprinkled all around the island's coast road.

WALKING

It's an easy climb to the summit of Mt Taita. From the Route Traversière, a track runs east along the ridgeline towards the peaks. The turn-off is just north of the very clear road west to the quarry on the western range. The track switchbacks up through pine plantations until it rounds the top of Mt Panee (392 metres), topped by the small hut of the TV-relay station. From here the 4WD track continues along the ridgeline until it finally terminates and a much more attractive walking path takes over. This pushes through small thickets and patches of fern until you eventually arrive at the tumble of boulders which tops Mt Taita (422 metres). It's a bit of a scramble over the moss-covered boulders to reach the summit but you're rewarded with superb views. It's quite the most picturesque spot on Tubuai, and there's lots of graffiti to confirm that you're not the first to enjoy it.

PLACES TO STAY & EAT

At some places to stay in Tubuai, kitchen facilities are provided and the catering is left up to you. There's a small supermarket and one other reasonable size store in Mataura plus a scattering of smaller stores around the island. However, the choice of goods will be wider and the prices lower in Tahiti, so you may want to bring supplies with you. Come prepared for mosquitoes as well. Nowhere on Tubuai can you use credit cards.

Chez Taro (☎ 95-04-76 and leave a message) is beyond the centre east of Mataura towards the wharf, right before the meteorological station. There are two houses, each with a double and a single bed plus bathroom and kitchen facilities for 3000 CFP per person per day, or 40,000 CFP per month. Meals are available if requested.

Continue another three km towards Taahuaia, the next village along, to *Chez Victor Turina* (also known as *Manu Patia*; ☎ 95-03-27) beside a store just before you get in to the main part of the village. Here there is one house with two apartments, each with a living room, kitchen and bathroom with hot water. One has two bedrooms, each with a double and two single beds. The other has just one double bedroom. This very friendly and well-kept place charges 2500 CFP per person per day. Monthly costs are 55,000 CFP for a complete apartment. Excellent meals are available: dinner costs 1000 CFP and is superb, better than you'll get in many well-known Papeete restaurants! Write to PO Box 7, Mataura, Tubuai, for bookings.

About 100 metres before Victor Turina is *Chez Karine et Tale* (☎ 95-04-52 or 95-04-76) with one really delightful small house complete with bedroom, living room, equipped kitchen and even a verandah. Daily costs are 5000/7500 CFP for one/two people. Write to BP 34, Mataura, Tubuai, for bookings.

In Mahu village, on the south side of the island about seven km from the airport, *L'Hermitage Ste-Hélène* (☎ 95-04-79) is operated by the widow of the colourful Nöel Ilari. There are three bungalows, each with a bedroom with a double bed and a second double bed in the living-room area. There's an equipped kitchen and bathroom facilities and daily costs are 4000 CFP per person or 50,000 CFP per month for a complete house. Meals are up to you. Write to BP 79, Mataura, Tubuai, for bookings.

If these three are full, several other pension possibilities in Mataura and Taahuaia villages will pop up.

GETTING THERE & AWAY

Tubuai is 600 km directly south of Tahiti and about midway between Rurutu to the north-west and Raivavae to the south-east.

Air

Air Tahiti flies a twice-weekly Papeete-Rurutu-Tubuai-Papeete route and Papeete-

Tubuai-Rurutu-Papeete once a week. See the introductory Getting There & Away section for more details. The Air Tahiti office (☎ 95-04-76) is at the airport.

Sea

The *Tuhaa Pae II* comes to Tubuai every two weeks on its route from Papeete to the Australs. The wide pass at the north-west side of the reef leads directly to the quay at Mataura. There are two smaller passes into the lagoon.

GETTING AROUND

The island pensions will collect their guests from the airport or dock if you book ahead. Chez Taro charges 1000 CFP per person for airport transfers, the L'Hermitage charges 3000 CFP for round-trip transfers for up to eight people.

There's no regular public transport but Manu Patia and L'Hermitage both have bikes for rent (1000 CFP a day at L'Hermitage) and Manu Patia also has a car available. It's quite easy to rent a motor scooter – just ask at your pension. Bernard Le Guilloux (☎ 95-06-01) in Mataura has cars, scooters and bikes for rent. The 25-km island-circuit road will probably be sealed all the way round by the time this book is in print, and work is proceeding on the cross-island road.

Other Austral Islands

While Rurutu and Tubuai can be reached by air, the other islands in the group – three high islands and two uninhabited atolls – can only be reached by sea. Visitors are very few. Moving down the chain from the north-west, these less frequented islands start with uninhabited Maria Island.

MARIA ISLAND

Furthest north-west of the Austral chain, uninhabited Maria Island is an atoll with four motus on a triangular-shaped reef. The atoll is about 200 km north-west of Rimatara and about 400 km east of the Cook Islands. The name comes from the whaler *Maria*, whose

crew sighted the island in 1824, although it's also known as Hull Island. The *Tuhaa Pae II* makes occasional stops at Maria Island and visitors from Rurutu and Rimatara come here from time to time to harvest copra. The low-lying island has a very shallow lagoon but there is abundant birdlife.

RIMATARA
Population: 1000
Area: 8 sq km
Passes: 1

The tiny island of Rimatara is a rough circle four km in diameter, rising to 83-metre Mt Uahu (or Vahu) in the centre. Spaced around this low mountain are the three villages of Anapoto, Amaru and Mutuaura, linked by a road running some distance inland from the coast. Like Rurutu, the island is circled by a fringing reef, and the narrow Hiava Pass lets small boats in to land on the beach in front of Amaru or Anapoto. The waterfront cemetery is the first sight visitors get on landing at Amaru. Traditionally, arriving visitors must pass through the smoke of a purifying fire as they step ashore.

The island is the most densely populated

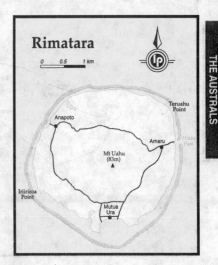

of the Australs. Pandanus work and shell necklaces plus the plantations support the islanders who have even preserved their own distinct dialect.

History

Rimatara was the last of the Australs to be 'discovered' when Captain Samuel Pinder Henry spotted it in 1811. The first native missionary teachers were dropped on the island in 1821 and within two years it was reported that the entire population of 300 had been converted.

Places to Stay

There are two pensions in Mutuaura village. *Chez Paulette* (☎ 94-42-27) has a two-bedroom house with a double bed in each bedroom, plus bathroom, equipped kitchen and living room. The nightly cost is 2000 CFP per person or the whole house is yours

for 60,000 CFP a month. *Chez Rita Hutia* (☎ 94-43-00) is similar in style but with three rather than two bedrooms. Again, it's 2000 CFP per person per day or 70,000 CFP a month for the whole house. You've got to fend for yourself on Rimatara so bring supplies.

Getting There & Away

Rimatara is about 600 km south-west of Tahiti, and about 150 km west of Rurutu. Only small boats can enter the island pass so goods are transferred to shore on whaleboats which land right on the beach.

RAIVAVAE
Population: 1200
Area: 16 sq km

Proclaimed as one of the most beautiful islands in the Pacific, Raivavae is encircled by a motu-dotted reef. The island has five

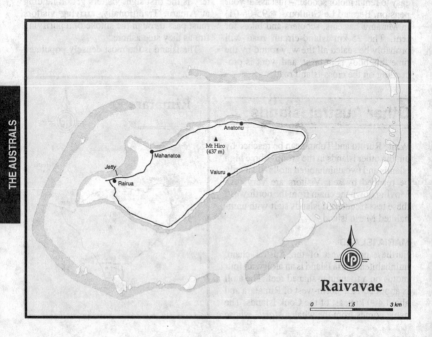

Raivavae

0   1.5   3 km

villages and a mountainous interior rising to Mt Hiro (437 metres). Rairua is the site of the island's main shipping quay but Mahanatoa is the largest of the villages.

History

Raivavae was noted for the massive stone tikis which once stood in the island maraes, but the principal marae, near Rairua, only has one great tiki left today. Its relations stand in the gardens of the Gauguin Museum in Tahiti, but the island's sole remaining tiki is a powerful figure emanating great *mana* (supernatural power). The Raivavae islanders also made unusual sculpted drums, which have also become museum pieces.

Captain Thomas Gayangos of Spain was the European to come upon Raivavae when he stopped there in 1775, sailing south from Tahiti to pick up the westerlies to carry him to Peru. Like Tubuai, the island was ceded to Pomare II of Tahiti in 1819 and thus became a French protectorate in 1842 and annexed by France in 1880.

At the time of the first European contact, Raivavae was a crowded island with around 3000 inhabitants, who had a highly developed social order and a reputation as unparalleled seafarers. It's said they regularly visited the Society Islands and even voyaged as far as New Zealand. Then in 1826 the same European fever which had devastated Tubuai reached Raivavae and almost killed the entire population. Only just over 100 people survived but the island's cultural and seafaring traditions were totally wiped out. Today very little fishing is done around Raivavae and agriculture is the main activity. The cool climate and fertile soil are perfect for growing cabbage, carrots and potatoes as well as more tropical crops such as coffee and oranges.

Places to Stay

Chez Annie Flores (☎ 95-43-28) in Rairua village, where the boats dock, has two rooms, each with a double bed. There are bathroom facilities and an equipped kitchen for a daily cost of 2000 CFP per person. The house can be rented for 35,000 CFP per month.

Getting There & Away

Raivavae is about 650 km south-east of Tahiti and about 200 km further south-east from Tubuai. There is no airport but the ship *Tuhaa Pae II* comes by about twice a month.

RAPA
Population: 500
Area: 22 sq km

Rapa is the most remote and isolated island of French Polynesia – even its nearest inhabited neighbour in the Australs, Raivavae, is 500 km distant. This far south there are no coral reefs, no coconut palms and temperatures as low as 5°C have been recorded in winter.

There are soaring and jagged-edged peaks, six of them reaching over 400 metres, the highest being Mt Perahu (650 metres). The island is the remains of a gigantic volcano cone, with the east side of the cone breached so that the ancient crater is now the wide expanse of Huarei Bay. Numerous other bays indent the convoluted coastline.

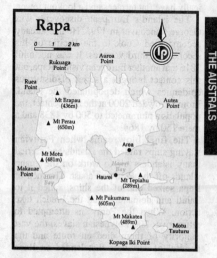

Rapa

0   1   2 km

Auroa Point

Rukuaga Point

Ruea Point

Mt Erapau (436m) ▲

Autea Point

Mt Perau (650m) ▲

Area ●

Mt Motu (481m) ▲

Makauae Point

Hiri Bay

Haurei Bay

Haurei ● Mt Tepiahu (289m) ▲

Mt Pukumaru (605m) ▲

Mt Makatea (489m) ▲

Motu Tauturu

Kopaga Iki Point

THE AUSTRALS

The island is also known as Rapa Iti (Little Rapa) to distinguish it from Rapa Nui (Big Rapa), the Polynesian name for Easter Island. The population is concentrated in the villages of Huarei and Area, on opposite sides of Huarei Bay and linked only by boat since there is no road around the bay. At its peak there were about a dozen villages scattered across the island.

History

Rapa was once densely populated and divided into warring kingdoms whose mountain-top forts, or *pas*, were closely related to those of the warrior Maoris of New Zealand. It is believed that land pressures, due to overpopulation, were the cause of this perpetual warfare.

Morongo Uta, between Huarei and Hiri bays, is the best preserved of these ancient fortresses and was restored by Norwegian archaeologists in the 1950s. The great pa has terraces separated by deep moats around the central fortress, which has a perimeter of over 300 metres and is overlooked by a double-pyramid watchtower. Other pas can be found along the mountain ridge or at the passes from one valley to another. They typically have flat terraces and a lookout tower.

The island's European discoverer was George Vancouver in 1791. He had already accompanied Cook to the Pacific on his second and third voyages. It was not until 1816 that another European visited Rapa, but this contact brought a series of disastrous epidemics which depopulated the island. From a crowded 2000 at the first contact, the population plummeted to 500 by 1838 and a mere 150 by 1864.

The final blow came when Peruvian slaving ships raided the islands and carried many islanders off to work on the guano islands off the Peruvian coast. The men of Rapa seized one of the ships, sailed it to Tahiti and demanded that the French take action. When the Peruvians attempted to return over 300 Polynesian slaves, the vast majority of them died en route and the handful of survivors that landed on Rapa brought a terrible smallpox epidemic to the island.

When steamships began to operate across the Pacific, a coaling station was established on Rapa for ships crossing the Pacific to Australia and New Zealand. It was an attempt to combat this English influence that led the French to annex Rapa.

Today the islanders almost prize their isolation. Taro is the principal crop but there is also fishing and the island is noted for its abundant goat population. Crops include a variety of vegetables, excellent oranges and some fine coffee.

Information

Rapa is in the French military zone and special permission is required for stays of more than a few days. To obtain this you are supposed to contact the *mairie* (town hall) in Rapa with details of your name, nationality, age and profession, and ask for a certificate of *hébergement* (lodging). With this in hand you can apply to the Subdivision Administration des Îles Australes (☎ 46-86-86), BP 115, Papeete, Tahiti, for official permission to stay on the island. To phone Rapa from Tahiti dial ☎ 10 and ask for the Rapa post office (l'OPT de Rapa).

Places to Stay & Eat

There is no regular accommodation on Rapa, but you can write to Mr Lionel Watanabe, Société Anonyme d'Économie Mixte de Navigation des Australes, PO Box 1890, Papeete, Tahiti, to enquire about a place to stay. SAEM is the operator of the ship to Rapa and the other Austral Islands. Alternatively, you can try contacting the Mairie de Rapa, the island's town hall, to ask about accommodation with a family. *Chez Faraire* in Ahurei is one family-run pension that takes guests.

Getting There & Away

Rapa is over 1000 km south-east of Tahiti and nearly 500 km beyond Raivavae, its nearest inhabited neighbour. The *Tuhaa Pae II* visits Rapa every couple of months, so for visitors who don't bring their own yacht, the choice is between the day or two which the ship stays in port and the two months (or more!) until the next arrival.

MAROTIRI

Also known as Bass Rocks, the nine unin-habited rocky spires of Marotiri rise from the sea about 70 km south-east of Rapa. Although even landing on the rocks is diffi-cult, the largest one has a saddle between its two pinnacles and this saddle is defended by a miniature pa!

THE AUSTRALS

The Gambiers

The Gambiers

Population: 600
Area: 27 sq km
Passes: 3

The most remote of the French Polynesian island groups, the Gambier archipelago lies at the extreme south-east end of the long arc of the Tuamotus. On the map they would appear to be just another of the many Tuamotu atolls, but in fact they are high islands and quite distinct from the neighbouring group. The islands consist of a complex of high islands within an encircling reef plus Timoe (or Temoe), a separate island to the south-east. Mangareva, which means 'floating mountain' in Polynesian, is the largest within the group and the only properly populated island. It was the centre for the obsessive missionary activities of Father Honoré Laval between 1834 and 1871, and the islands are almost a monument to his single-minded fervour.

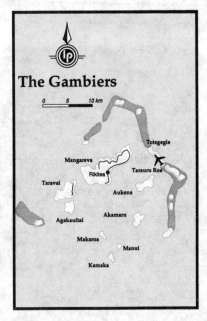

HISTORY

The islands were populated in three waves around the 10th to the 13th century and there is much speculation that this may have been an important stopping point on the Polynesian migration routes to New Zealand or Easter Island. Although the islands have such strong links with French Catholicism, the group was actually named in 1797 by James Wilson, captain of the *Duff*, who brought the pioneering LMS missionaries to Tahiti in that year. He named the archipelago after Gambier, an English admiral who had supported the mission's activities, and the islands' highest mountain is named after his ship. It wasn't until 1826, however, that FW Beechey, another Englishman, set the first European foot on the islands and make contact made with the islands' inhabitants. The islands soon became an important port for ships to replenish their supplies and trade for the abundant mother-of-pearl from the lagoon.

The first Catholic mission in Polynesia, the Sacred Heart Congregation, was established here in 1834 and quickly converted the entire population. Father Honoré Laval, leader of the mission, and his assistant François Caret became virtual rulers of the Gambier Islands. Until persistent complaints about his behaviour led to his exile to Tahiti in 1871, Laval had run the islands like his own personal fiefdom.

Laval transformed the islands, building wide roads, a massive cathedral, nine churches and chapels, monuments, lookout towers, wharves and a whole range of buildings including a prison. Unfortunately, at the same time, the people of the Gambier Islands simply died out. When Laval arrived the population may have been 5000 to 6000, spread across the four main islands, but it quickly went into a free fall. In 1887, when the first official census was conducted, the population was only 463 and even today it is only just over 600, almost all of the inhabitants live on one island.

It's an open question how responsible Laval was for this disaster. The view that's most sympathetic towards Laval is that European diseases, imported by whalers and trading ships, caused the annihilation of the population and culture, and that Laval was merely an observer. The opposite view is that Laval was a single-minded bigot who wiped out the native culture of the islands and then worked the islanders to death constructing a collection of absurdly over-ambitious monuments to his beliefs. Laval's own memoirs recount with delight the destruction of the idols and symbols of the old religion along with the undeniable adventures of that time. Robert Lee Eskridge's *Manga Reva, the Forgotten Islands* tells the story of the missionary period.

Remarkably, Laval and Caret found time, soon after their arrival in the Gambier Islands, to pop over to Tahiti to attempt to carry Catholicism to that bastion of Protestant missionary activity. Their subsequent clash with Queen Pomare IV and the English missionaries was the excuse for the French takeover of Tahiti. Although France established a protectorate over the islands in 1844, they continued as a semi-independent entity and were not formally annexed until 1881.

Today Mangareva is more or less self-sufficient from raising livestock and growing fruit, root crops and a little coffee. The Gambier Islands are also an important centre for the production of black pearls.

Gaston Flosse, the Territorial Assembly president, was born in the villages Rikitea on Mangareva.

GEOGRAPHY

The wide polygon-shaped lagoon is protected by a 90-km coral barrier. There are 25 motus dotted along the reef around its north-

ern half, but the reef edge is partly submerged and dangerously difficult to see around the southern half. There are three passes into the lagoon, the two major ones being on the north-west and south-west side.

Within the lagoon there are 10 volcanic high islands but, apart from a handful of people, only Mangareva, the largest of them, is populated. Mangareva is eight km long but only 1.5 km across at its widest point. The highest points are Mt Duff (441 metres) and Mt Mokoto (423 metres). The three other larger islands are Aukena, Akamaru and Taravai. The airport is on the largest motu, Motu Totegegie, on the north-east side of the lagoon. About 50 km south-east is the small island of Timoe.

INFORMATION

Not only are the Gambier Islands a long way from Tahiti, but getting there requires passing through the sensitive French nuclear-testing zone in the southern Tuamotus, so special permission to visit is required from the Subdivision des Îles Tuamotu-Gambier (☎ 46-86-86, fax 43-64-71), Rue des Poilus-Tahitiens, Papeete. You can write to them at BP 34, Papeete, Tahiti.

Well to the south, the islands have a relatively mild climate and in winter it can actually get cool. The Gambier Islands are one hour ahead of Tahiti.

MANGAREVA

In the dry season the grass-covered hills of Mangareva can take on a sombre brown appearance, but Rikitea, the sole village on the island, is a green, pleasant and quiet little place. At the upper part of the town stands the **Cathedral of St Michael**, the ultimate symbol of Laval's single-minded obsession. The cathedral can accommodate 2000 people – several times the population of the island! It was built on the site of Mangareva's great marae which, when it was visited by Moerenhout, the French consul in Tahiti, just before Laval arrived, featured a coral-decorated *ahu* and an adjacent 30-metre royal house with a roof supported by decorated columns. The cathedral, which has twin blue-trimmed towers, is 54 metres long and was built between 1839 and 1848. The altar is decorated with mother-of-pearl and the woodwork is also inlaid with pearl shell.

Various other Laval constructions stand in the village, including the coastal watchtowers and the turret which are all that remain of the 'palace' Laval built for the island's last king. The king, Maputeao, changed his name to Gregoria Stanislas for Laval and has a memorial in **St Peter's Cemetery**. The island's **Rouru Convent** once had 60 Mangarevan nuns.

OTHER ISLANDS

When the missionaries arrived, all the major islands in the group were populated and **Taravai** had a population of 2000. Today only a handful of people live on the island and the 1868 **Church of St Gabriel**, with its conch-shell decoration, is deserted. There are other buildings in **Agokono**, the all-but-empty village on the island. **Aukena** also has reminders of the missionary period, including the 1839 **Church of St Raphaël** and the hexagonal **lookout tower**, still used as a landmark, on the south-west tip of the island. Akamaru was the island where Laval first arrived and his 1841 **Our Lady of Peace Church** still stands on the utterly deserted island. Occasional groups come over from Mangareva to maintain the church or to pick oranges in season.

TIMOE

The remote island of Timoe, 50 km south-east, has a marae with some Marquesan features leading to theories that canoes from the Marquesas may have paused here en route to Easter Island. Even this remote and tiny island was populated until 1838 when the missionaries shifted the people to Mangareva. Bishop Museum archaeologist Kenneth Emory carried out investigations here and on Mangareva in 1934, and in that

same year James Norman Hall, coauthor of the *Mutiny on the Bounty*, was shipwrecked on the island.

PLACES TO STAY & EAT

It's wise to contact the *mairie* in Rikitea to check on the availability of accommodation.

Chez Pierre et Mariette Paemara (☎ 97-82-87) is just 100 metres from the docks in Mangareva. It has a house with three bedrooms, living room, bathroom (cold water) and kitchen. The daily cost with all meals is 7000 CFP per person, or 50,000 CFP for eight days.

Chez Terii et Hélène Paemara (☎ 97-82-80) offers similar facilities at a similar price in a two-bedroom house. Island tours are easily arranged but credit cards are not accepted. There are various other families in Rikitea who will take guests.

GETTING THERE & AWAY

The Gambier archipelago is about 1700 km south-east of Tahiti.

Air

Air Tahiti has three flights a month to Mangareva. With a half-hour stop at Hao, the flight takes about five hours and costs 34,400 CFP one way. Depending on scheduling, it's possible to stay overnight since some flights arrive on one afternoon and leave the next morning. Otherwise it will be necessary to stay at least one or two weeks.

Sea

The 48-metre *Manava II* does a monthly 20-day voyage through some of the more remote islands of the Tuamotus, en route to Mangareva. Contact the Société Compagnies de Développement Maritime des Tuamotu (☎ 43-32-65, fax 41-31-65), BP 1291, Papeete, Tahiti, for details. Their office is on Motu Uta.

Glossary

ahimaa – underground oven used for cooking traditional Polynesian food

ahu – altar in a marae; in Tahiti the *ahu* was generally pyramid shaped

aito – ironwood

alizs – winds from the east in the tropics

anuhe – fern

arii – the high chiefs of the ancient Polynesian aristocracy

arioi – priest caste or religious society of the pre-European Society Islands

atoll – tropical low island created by coral rising up above sea level and gradually eroding away; the postcard atolls consist of a chain of small islands and reef enclosing a lagoon

atua – collective term for Polynesian gods

barrier reef – coral reef forming a barrier between the shoreline and the open sea but separated from the land by a lagoon

belvédère – lookout

bonitier – whaleboat used for fishing but also for transferring passengers and cargo from ship to shore on islands that have no wharf or quay

breadfruit – a starchy staple food of Polynesia which grows as a football-sized fruit on a breadfruit tree; *uru* in Tahitian or *arbre pain* in French

CEP – Centre d'expérimentation du Pacifique; euphemism for the French nuclear-testing programme

CETAD – Centre d'études de Techniques Adaptés au Développement: technical and vocation college

CFP – Cour de Franc Pacifique; currency in French Polynesia

ciguatera – mysterious malady caused by eating infected reef fish

CMAS – Confédération Mondiale des Activités Subaquatiques: the Francophone equivalent of PADI

copra – dried coconut meat, a traditional Polynesian product used to make an oil

coral – animal of the coelenterate group which, given the right conditions of water clarity, depth and temperature, grows to form a coral reef

croque-madame – toasted ham and cheese sandwich with a fried egg on top, known as *croque-vahine* in French Polynesia

croque-monsieur – toasted ham and cheese sandwich

cyclone – tropical storm rotating around a low-pressure 'eye'; a cyclone is known as a typhoon in the Pacific, and as a hurricane in the Caribbean

demi-pension – half board (bed, breakfast and lunch or dinner), see also *pension complète*

demis – Tahitian-European half castes

DOM-TOM – Départements et Territoires d'Outre-Mer; French overseas departments and territories

emergence – geologic activity which pushes land up above sea level to become an island

EVAAM – Établissement pour la Valorisation des activités aquacoles et maritimes: marine-research organisation

fare – traditional Polynesian house

fare atua – house for the gods on a marae, actually a small chest in the form of a statue

fare potee – chief's house or community meeting place

fare tamoa – dining house

fare taoto – bedroom

fare tupapau – shelters where dead bodies were laid out to decompose in pre-European Polynesia

fare tutu – kitchen

fringing reef – coral reef found immediately alongside the shoreline, not separated from the shore by a lagoon as with a *barrier reef*

gendarmerie – police station

goélette – French for schooner; inter-island cargo or freighter ships are commonly referred to as *goélettes* even though the age of sailing ships has long disappeared

guyot – volcanic island which has been worn down and disappeared below sea level

heiva – festival

herminette – adze, traditional Polynesian tool used by sculptors

high island – an island created by volcanic action or a geological upheaval, unlike the low islands which are created by the growth and erosion of coral or by the complete wearing away of a high island

himenes – Tahitian-language hymns

Hiro – god of thieves who features in many Polynesian legends

hoa – shallow channel across the outer reef of an atoll; these normally only carry water into or out of the central lagoon at unusually high tides or when large swells are running, as opposed to passes which carry water all the time

hoe – ceremonial canoe paddle

honu – turtle

kaina – Polynesian person as opposed to a *popaa*, or person of European descent.

kava – traditional mildly intoxicating drink produced from the root of *piper methysticum*, the pepper plant

kaveu – coconut crab

keshi – Japanese term for pearl formed from pure *nacre*, without a nucleus which has been expelled from the oyster

Koke – Polynesian name for Gauguin

lagoon – the calmer waters enclosed by a reef; the lagoon may be an enclosed area encircled by an outer barrier reef with or without reef islands known as *motus* (like Rangiroa and Tetiaroa) or it may have a high island within the lagoon (like Bora Bora and Tahiti)

lagoon side – on islands with a distinct coast road, locations are often given as 'lagoon side' or *'mountain side'*

LDS – Mormons, followers of the Church of Jesus Christ of the Latter-Day Saints.

leeward – on the downwind side, sheltered from the prevailing winds

le truck – main form of public transport in French Polynesia; trucks with bench seats along each side which operate a bus-like service

LMS – London Missionary Society, pioneering Protestant missionary organisation in Polynesia

maa tahiti – Tahitian or Polynesian food

maa tinito – Chinese food

mabe – another by-product of cultured-pearl production

mahi – fermented breadfruit

mahi mahi – dolphin fish, one of the most popular eating fish in French Polynesia and no relation to the dolphin, which is a mammal

mahu – transvestite or female impersonator

maiore – breadfruit tree

makatea – a coral island which has been thrust up above sea level by some geological disturbance; Rurutu in the Australs and, of course, Makatea in the Tuamotus are good examples

mana – spiritual power

manahune – the peasant class or common people of pre-European Polynesia

mao – shark, *requin* in French

Maohi – Tahitian Polynesians; the word is similar to the word 'Maori'

mape – Polynesian 'chestnut' tree, a massive tree found in the Society Islands which produces an edible nut

maraamu – south-east tradewinds which blow from June to August

marae – traditional Polynesian temple generally constructed with an *ahu* at one end

marae arii – important 'national' maraes

marae tupuna – ancestor or family marae

marara – flying fish

maroura – feather belt worn by a chief as a symbol of his dynasty

meae – Marquesan word for marae

Melanesia – islands of the western Pacific including Papua New Guinea, the Solomons, Vanuatu, New Caledonia and Fiji; the *mela* in the name comes from the Greek word 'melas', meaning black, and relates to the dark skins of the peoples of the region

Micronesia – islands of the north-west Pacific including the Mariana, Caroline, Marshall and Kiribati groups, and Nauru; the peoples of Micronesia are more like the Polynesians than the Melanesians; the *micro* in the name signifies the many small islands of the region

monoi – oil made from coconut oil and perfumed with the *tiare* flower

motu – a coral islet; the small islets along the outer reef of an atoll or on a reef around a high island are generally referred to as motus

mountain side – see *lagoon side*

nacre – iridescent substance secreted by pearl oysters to form the inner layer of the shell and, by extension, the shell of a pearl oyster

naissain – larva of an oyster

navette – shuttle boat

-nesia – the islands of the Pacific are divided into three regions: Melanesia, Micronesia and Polynesia; in each case the *nesia* in the name comes from the Greek word *nesos*, meaning island

noanoa – a good smell; Tahitian word which has been adopted for all forms of perfume

nohu – poisonous stonefish or scorpionfish

nono – very annoying small gnats found on some beaches and particularly in the Marquesas

nucleus – small sphere made from shells found in the Mississippi River in the USA which is introduced into the gonads of the pearl oyster to produce a cultured pearl

ono ono – barracuda

Oro – god of war; the cult which was superseding the Taaroa cult when the first Europeans arrived

oromatua – ghosts

ORSTOM – Office de Recherches Scientifiques et Techniques d'Outre Mer; oceanographic-research organisation

PADI – Professional Association of Dive Instructors; the number one international scuba-diving qualification

pae pae – paved floor of pre-European house or a meeting platform

pahi tamai – double-hulled canoe with paddles, used for long voyages but particularly used for war in pre-European Polynesia

pandanus – palm tree with aerial roots; the leaves are used for weaving hats, mats and bags

pareu – sarong-like traditional attire

pass – channel through the outer reef of an atoll or the barrier reef around a high island which allows passage into the lagoon; compare with *hoa*

Paumoto – alternative name for Tuamotu Islands or for people from the Tuamotus

pension – boarding house

pension complète – full board (bed and all meals), see also *demi-pension*

pétanque – also known as *boules*; French game where metal balls are thrown to land as near as possible to a target ball

peue – mats

pirogue – outrigger canoe

PK – *pointe kilométrique*, distance markers found along the roads of some of the islands of French Polynesia

plat du jour – literally, plate of the day, daily special

Polynesia – islands of the central and south-eastern Pacific including French Polynesia, Tonga and the Cook Islands; the *poly* in the name signifies the many islands

popaa – Europeans, westerners

raatira – the middle rank of pre-European Polynesian society, above the lower class but below the *arii*

rae rae – another word for *mahus*, sometimes applied to mahus when they are homosexual rather than just cross-dressers

requin – shark; see *mao*

roulotte – a van turned into a mobile diner with flaps lowered on each side to become the counters, stools set up outside for the customers and staff inside to prepare food

seamount – underwater volcano which rises more than 1000 metres above the ocean floor but does not break the surface to become an island; see *guyot*

seaward – the side of an atoll island or motu which faces the sea rather than the lagoon

sennit – string or material woven from coconut husk fibre

Taaroa – supreme Polynesian god prior to the European arrival, although at that time a shift was taking place to the worship of *Oro*, the god of war

tabu – see *tapu*

tahua – priests of the ancient Polynesian religion

tamure – hip-jiggling version of traditional Polynesian dance

tane – man

tapa – bark-cloth beaten thin; this was the traditional clothing worn by the people of pre-European Polynesia and much of the Pacific

tapu – sacred or forbidden area; the English word 'taboo' comes from *tapu* or *tabu*

taramea – crown-of-thorns starfish which consumes coral

taro – root vegetable which is a Polynesian staple food

tatau – Tahitian word for tattoo; although tattoos were also known in Japan, it was in Tahiti that sailors first discovered them and adopted the word into European vocabularies

tiare – fragrant flower which has become symbolic of Tahiti

tifaifai – colourful appliquéd or patchwork material used as bedspreads or cushion covers

tii – Society Islands term for the Marquesan word *tiki*

tiki – human-like sculptures usually made of wood or stone, and sometimes standing more than two metres high, which were once found on many *maraes*

timorodee – dance by young girls which surprised early explorers for its erotic explicitness

Tinito – Tahitian for Chinese

tipairua – traditional double-hulled canoe with sails, probably of the type used for the long migration voyages

tiputa – *tapa* poncho, traditional attire in pre-European Polynesia

tiurai – 'July' in Tahitian, the major festival of July

tohua – meeting place or a place for a festival gathering in pre-European Polynesia

tuf – volcanic rock of Polynesia

tupapau – spirit ghosts of the ancient Polynesian religion, still much feared

Tute – Polynesian name for Captain Cook

umara – sweet potato

umete – traditional Tahitian wooden dish or bowl

unu – vertical poles or planks dedicated to gods in a *marae*

upaupa – erotic dance by a couple which intrigued early explorers and outraged early missionaries

uru – breadfruit tree

vaa – Tahitian word for outrigger canoe or pirogue in French

vaa motu – outrigger canoe with a sail

vahine – Polynesian woman

vanira – vanilla

VTT or vélo à tout terrain – mountain bike

windward – the side of an island which faces the prevailing winds; the opposite of *leeward*

Index

TEXT

Map references are in **bold** type

Aakapa 315
accommodation 69
activities 67-8, 146-55, 171,
    195-6, 228-30, 244-5, 343,
    see also individual entries
Afareaitu 158, 162
Afareaitu Waterfall 167-8
Agokono 376
Aguilla 16, 142
Ahe 274, 286-7
AIDS 62-3
air travel 75-80, **83**
    to/from Australia & New
        Zealand 77
    to/from Europe 78-80
    to/from Japan & Asia 78
    to/from other Pacific Islands 75
    to/from South America 78
    to/from the USA & Canada
        75-7
    within French Polynesia 82, 83,
        84, 85-6
Anaa 279, 296-7
Anaho 314
Anahoa Beach 329
Anaihe Cave 150
Anau 224, 226-7

Apu Bay 217
Arahoho Blowhole 130, 132
Aranui, the 90, 93
Aratua 274
archery 164
Archipels Croisières 93
architecture 35
arts & crafts 34-5, 315, 331,
    343, 349, 351
Arutua 294
Atiha Bay 162
Atipapa 329
Atiu 356
ATMs, *see* money
atolls 24
Atuona 337-40, **337**
Auea Bay 195
Australs 24, 356-71, **356**
    getting there & away 357-8
    history 356-7, 358-9, 363-4,
        367, 368, 369-70
    activities 366
Avatoru 259, 260, **260-1**
Avera 207, 362

banks 44-5
Banks, Sir Joseph 18, 51, 162,
    358
bargaining, *see* money

Bass Rocks 371
Bay of Virgins 351
Beaglehole, JC 51
Bell, Gavin 53
Bellinghausen (Motu One) 250,
    278, 297, 335
Bisschop, Éric de 361
Black Pearl Farm 160
black pearls 74, 160, 182, 262-3,
    283
Bligh, Captain William 17-19,
    20, 51, 132, 185, 227, 365
Blue Lagoon 261-2
boating 196
Boboa, Vasco Núñez de 11
Boenechea, Captain Don
    Domingo de 16, 142
books 51-6
    art & culture 52
    European arrival 51
    guidebooks 53-6
    natural history 52-3
    travel health guides 58
    travel literature 52
Bora Bora 221-40, **222-3**
    activities 228-30
    entertainment 238-9
    geography 221
    getting around 240

US $1 = 93 CFP

U5+1= 43C49

LONELY PLANET JOURNEYS

JOURNEYS is a unique collection of travellers' tales – published by the company that understands travel better than anyone else. It is a series for anyone who has ever experienced – or dreamed of – the magical moment when they encountered a strange culture or saw a place for the first time. They are tales to read while you're planning a trip, while you're on the road or while you're in an armchair, in front of a fire.

JOURNEYS books will catch the spirit of a place, illuminate a culture, recount a crazy adventure, or introduce a fascinating way of life. They will always entertain, and always enrich the experience of travel.

FULL CIRCLE
A South American Journey
Luis Sepúlveda
Translated by Chris Andrews

Full Circle invites us to accompany Chilean writer Luis Sepúlveda on 'a journey without a fixed itinerary'. Extravagant characters and extraordinary situations are memorably evoked: gauchos organising a tournament of lies, a scheming heiress on the lookout for a husband, a pilot with a corpse on board his plane . . . Part autobiography, part travel memoir, *Full Circle* brings us the distinctive voice of one of South America's most compelling writers.

THE GATES OF DAMASCUS
Lieve Joris
Translated by Sam Garrett

This best-selling book is a beautifully drawn portrait of day-to-day life in modern Syria. Through her intimate contact with local people, Lieve Joris draws us into the fascinating world that lies behind the gates of Damascus.

ISLANDS IN THE CLOUDS
Travels in the Highlands of New Guinea
Isabella Tree

This is the fascinating account of a journey to the remote and beautiful Highlands of Papua New Guinea and Irian Jaya. The author travels with a PNG Highlander who introduces her to his intriguing and complex world. *Islands in the Clouds* is a thoughtful, moving book, full of insights into a region that is rarely noticed by the rest of the world.

LOST JAPAN
Alex Kerr

Lost Japan draws on the author's personal experiences of Japan over a period of 30 years. Alex Kerr takes his readers on a backstage tour: friendships with Kabuki actors, buying and selling art, studying calligraphy, exploring rarely visited temples and shrines . . . The Japanese edition of this book was awarded the 1994 Shincho Gakugei Literature Prize for the best work of non-fiction.

SEAN & DAVID'S LONG DRIVE
Sean Condon

Sean and David are young townies who have rarely strayed beyond city limits. One day, for no good reason, they set out to discover their homeland, and what follows is a wildly entertaining adventure that covers half of Australia. Sean Condon has written a hilarious, offbeat road book that mixes sharp insights with deadpan humour and outright lies.

SHOPPING FOR BUDDHAS
Jeff Greenwald

Shopping for Buddhas is Jeff Greenwald's story of his obsessive search for the perfect Buddha statue. In the backstreets of Kathmandu, he discovers more than he bargained for . . . and his souvenir-hunting turns into an ironic metaphor for the clash between spiritual riches and material greed. Politics, religion and serious shopping collide in this witty account of an enlightening visit to Nepal.

LONELY PLANET TRAVEL ATLASES

Lonely Planet has long been famous for the number and quality of its guidebook maps. Now we've gone one step further and in conjunction with Steinhart Katzir Publishers produced a handy companion series: Lonely Planet travel atlases – maps of a country produced in book form.

Unlike other maps, which look good but lead travellers astray, our travel atlases have been researched on the road by Lonely Planet's experienced team of writers. All details are carefully checked to ensure the atlas corresponds with the equivalent Lonely Planet guidebook.

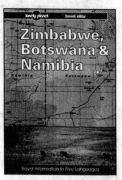

The handy atlas format means no holes, wrinkles, torn sections or constant folding and unfolding. These atlases can survive long periods on the road, unlike cumbersome fold-out maps. The comprehensive index ensures easy reference.

- full-colour throughout
- maps researched and checked by Lonely Planet authors
- place names correspond with Lonely Planet guidebooks
  – no confusing spelling differences
- legend and travelling information in English, French, German, Japanese and Spanish
- size: 230 x 160 mm

Available now:
Chile; Egypt; India & Bangladesh; Israel & the Palestinian Territories; Jordan, Syria & Lebanon; Laos; Thailand; Vietnam; Zimbabwe, Botswana & Namibia

---

LONELY PLANET TV SERIES & VIDEOS

Lonely Planet travel guides have been brought to life on television screens around the world. Like our guides, the programmes are based on the joy of independent travel, and look honestly at some of the most exciting, picturesque and frustrating places in the world. Each show is presented by one of three travellers from Australia, England or the USA and combines an innovative mixture of video, Super-8 film, atmospheric soundscapes and original music.

Videos of each episode – containing additional footage not shown on television – are available from good book and video shops, but the availability of individual videos varies with regional screening schedules.

Video destinations include: Alaska; Australia (Southeast); Brazil; Ecuador & the Galápagos Islands; Indonesia; Israel & the Sinai Desert; Japan; La Ruta Maya (Yucatán, Guatemala & Belize); Morocco; North India (Varanasi to the Himalaya); Pacific Islands; Vietnam; Zimbabwe, Botswana & Namibia.

Coming soon: The Arctic (Norway & Finland); Baja California; Chile & Easter Island; China (Southeast); Costa Rica; East Africa (Tanzania & Zanzibar); Great Barrier Reef (Australia); Jamaica; Papua New Guinea; the Rockies (USA); Syria & Jordan; Turkey.

The Lonely Planet TV series is produced by:
Pilot Productions
Duke of Sussex Studios
44 Uxbridge St
London W8 7TG UK

Lonely Planet videos are distributed by:
IVN Communications Inc
2246 Camino Ramon
California 94583, USA

107 Power Road, Chiswick
London W4 5PL UK

Music from the TV series is available on CD & cassette.
For ordering information contact your nearest Lonely Planet office.

PLANET TALK

Lonely Planet's FREE quarterly newsletter

We love hearing from you and think you'd like to hear from us.

When...is the right time to see reindeer in Finland?
Where...can you hear the best palm-wine music in Ghana?
How...do you get from Asunción to Areguá by steam train?
What...is the best way to see India?

For the answer to these and many other questions read PLANET TALK.

Every issue is packed with up-to-date travel news and advice including:

* a letter from Lonely Planet co-founders Tony and Maureen Wheeler
* go behind the scenes on the road with a Lonely Planet author
* feature article on an important and topical travel issue
* a selection of recent letters from travellers
* details on forthcoming Lonely Planet promotions
* complete list of Lonely Planet products

To join our mailing list contact any Lonely Planet office.

Also available: Lonely Planet T-shirts. 100% heavyweight cotton.

LONELY PLANET ONLINE

Get the latest travel information before you leave or while you're on the road

Whether you've just begun planning your next trip, or you're chasing down specific info on currency regulations or visa requirements, check out the Lonely Planet World Wide Web site for up-to-the-minute travel information.

As well as travel profiles of your favourite destinations (including interactive maps and full-colour photos), you'll find current reports from our army of researchers and other travellers, updates on health and visas, travel advisories, and the ecological and political issues you need to be aware of as you travel.

There's an online travellers' forum (the Thorn Tree) where you can share your experiences of life on the road, meet travel companions and ask other travellers for their recommendations and advice. We also have plenty of links to other Web sites useful to independent travellers.

With tens of thousands of visitors a month, the Lonely Planet Web site is one of the most popular on the Internet and has won a number of awards including GNN's Best of the Net travel award.

http://www.lonelyplanet.com

LONELY PLANET PRODUCTS

Lonely Planet is known worldwide for publishing practical, reliable and no-nonsense travel information in our guides and on our web site. The Lonely Planet list covers just about every accessible part of the world. Currently there are eight series: *travel guides*, *shoestring guides*, *walking guides*, *city guides*, *phrasebooks*, *audio packs*, *travel atlases* and *Journeys* – a unique collection of travellers' tales.

EUROPE

Austria • Baltic States & Kaliningrad • Baltic States phrasebook • Britain • Central Europe on a shoestring • Central Europe phrasebook • Czech & Slovak Republics • Denmark • Dublin city guide • Eastern Europe on a shoestring • Eastern Europe phrasebook • Finland • France • Greece • Greek phrasebook • Hungary • Iceland, Greenland & the Faroe Islands • Ireland • Italy • Mediterranean Europe on a shoestring • Mediterranean Europe phrasebook • Paris city guide • Poland • Prague city guide • Russia, Ukraine & Belarus • Russian phrasebook • Scandinavian & Baltic Europe on a shoestring • Scandinavian Europe phrasebook • Slovenia • St Petersburg city guide • Switzerland • Trekking in Greece • Trekking in Spain • Ukrainian phrasebook • Vienna city guide • Walking in Switzerland • Western Europe on a shoestring • Western Europe phrasebook

NORTH AMERICA

Alaska • Backpacking in Alaska • Baja California• California & Nevada • Canada • Hawaii • Honolulu city guide • Los Angeles city guide • Mexico • Miami city guide • New England • New Orleans city guide • Pacific Northwest USA • Rocky Mountain States • San Francisco city guide • Southwest USA • USA phrasebook

CENTRAL AMERICA & THE CARIBBEAN

Central America on a shoestring • Costa Rica • Cuba • Eastern Caribbean • Guatemala, Belize & Yucatán: La Ruta Maya • Jamaica

SOUTH AMERICA

Argentina, Uruguay & Paraguay • Bolivia • Brazil • Brazilian phrasebook • Buenos Aires city guide • Chile & Easter Island • Chile & Easter Island travel atlas • Colombia • Ecuador & the Galápagos Islands • Latin American Spanish phrasebook • Peru • Quechua phrasebook • Rio de Janeiro city guide • South America on a shoestring • Trekking in the Patagonian Andes • Venezuela

Travel Literature: Full Circle: A South American Journey

ANTARCTICA

Antarctica

ISLANDS OF THE INDIAN OCEAN

Madagascar & Comoros • Maldives & Islands of the East Indian Ocean • Mauritius, Réunion & Seychelles

AFRICA

Arabic (Moroccan) phrasebook • Africa on a shoestring • Cape Town city guide • Central Africa • East Africa • Egypt • Egypt travel atlas• Ethiopian (Amharic) phrasebook • Kenya • Morocco • North Africa • South Africa, Lesotho & Swaziland • Swahili phrasebook • Trekking in East Africa • West Africa • Zimbabwe, Botswana & Namibia • Zimbabwe, Botswana & Namibia travel atlas

MAIL ORDER

Lonely Planet products are distributed worldwide. They are also available by mail order from Lonely Planet, so if you have difficulty finding a title please write to us. North American and South American residents should write to Embarcadero West, 155 Filbert St, Suite 251, Oakland CA 94607, USA; European and African residents should write to 10 Barley Mow Passage, Chiswick, London W4 4PH; and residents of other countries to PO Box 617, Hawthorn, Victoria 3122, Australia.

NORTH-EAST ASIA

Beijing city guide • Cantonese phrasebook • China • Hong Kong, Macau & Canton • Hong Kong city guide • Japan • Japanese phrasebook • Japanese audio pack • Korea • Korean phrasebook • Mandarin phrasebook • Mongolia • Mongolian phrasebook • North-East Asia on a shoestring • Seoul city guide • Taiwan • Tibet • Tibet phrasebook • Tokyo city guide

Travel Literature: Lost Japan

MIDDLE EAST & CENTRAL ASIA

Arab Gulf States • Arabic (Egyptian) phrasebook • Central Asia • Iran• Israel & the Palestinian Territories• Israel & the Palestinian Territories travel atlas • Jordan & Syria • Jordan, Syria & Lebanon travel atlas • Middle East • Turkey • Turkish phrasebook • Trekking in Turkey • Yemen

Travel Literature: The Gates of Damascus

ALSO AVAILABLE:

Travel with Children • Traveller's Tales

INDIAN SUBCONTINENT

Bangladesh• Bengali phrasebook• Delhi city guide • Hindi/Urdu phrasebook • India • India & Bangladesh travel atlas • Indian Himalaya • Karakoram Highway • Nepal • Nepali phrasebook • Pakistan • Sri Lanka • Sri Lanka phrasebook • Trekking in the Indian Himalaya • Trekking in the Karakoram & Hindukush • Trekking in the Nepal Himalaya

Travel Literature: Shopping for Buddhas

SOUTH-EAST ASIA

Bali & Lombok • Bangkok city guide • Burmese phrasebook • Cambodia • Ho Chi Minh city guide • Indonesia • Indonesian phrasebook • Indonesian audio pack • Jakarta city guide • Java • Laos • Lao phrasebook • Laos travel atlas • Malay phrasebook • Malaysia, Singapore & Brunei • Myanmar (Burma) • Philippines • Pilipino phrasebook • Singapore city guide • South-East Asia on a shoestring • Thailand • Thailand travel atlas • Thai phrasebook • Thai audio pack • Thai Hill Tribes phrasebook • Vietnam • Vietnamese phrasebook • Vietnam travel atlas

AUSTRALIA & THE PACIFIC

Australia • Australian phrasebook • Bushwalking in Australia• Bushwalking in Papua New Guinea • Fiji • Fijian phrasebook • Islands of Australia's Great Barrier Reef • Melbourne city guide • Micronesia • New Caledonia • New South Wales & the ACT • New Zealand • Northern Territory • Outback Australia • Papua New Guinea • Papua New Guinea phrasebook • Queensland • Rarotonga & the Cook Islands • Samoa • Solomon Islands • South Australia • Sydney city guide • Tahiti & French Polynesia • Tasmania • Tonga • Tramping in New Zealand • Vanuatu • Victoria • Western Australia

Travel Literature: Islands in the Clouds • Sean & David's Long Drive

THE LONELY PLANET STORY

Lonely Planet published its first book in 1973 in response to the numerous 'How did you do it?' questions Maureen and Tony Wheeler were asked after driving, bussing, hitching, sailing and railing their way from England to Australia.

Written at a kitchen table and hand collated, trimmed and stapled, *Across Asia on the Cheap* became an instant local bestseller, inspiring thoughts of another book.

Eighteen months in South-East Asia resulted in their second guide, *South-East Asia on a shoestring*, which they put together in a backstreet Chinese hotel in Singapore in 1975. The 'yellow bible', as it quickly became known to backpackers around the world, soon became *the* guide to the region. It has sold well over half a million copies and is now in its 8th edition, still retaining its familiar yellow cover.

Today there are over 180 titles, including travel guides, walking guides, language kits & phrasebooks, travel atlases and travel literature. The company is one of the largest travel publishers in the world. Although Lonely Planet initially specialised in guides to Asia, we now cover most regions of the world, including the Pacific, North America, South America, Africa, the Middle East and Europe.

The emphasis continues to be on travel for independent travellers. Tony and Maureen still travel for several months of each year and play an active part in the writing, updating and quality control of Lonely Planet's guides.

They have been joined by over 70 authors and 170 staff at our offices in Melbourne (Australia), Oakland (USA), London (UK) and Paris (France). Travellers themselves also make a valuable contribution to the guides through the feedback we receive in thousands of letters each year.

The people at Lonely Planet strongly believe that travellers can make a positive contribution to the countries they visit, both through their appreciation of the countries' culture, wildlife and natural features, and through the money they spend. In addition, the company makes a direct contribution to the countries and regions it covers. Since 1986 a percentage of the income from each book has been donated to ventures such as famine relief in Africa; aid projects in India; agricultural projects in Central America; Greenpeace's efforts to halt French nuclear testing in the Pacific; and Amnesty International.

'I hope we send the people out with the right attitude about travel. You realise when you travel that there are so many different perspectives about the world, so we hope these books will make people more interested in what they see. These are guidebooks, but you can't really guide people. All you can do is point them in the right direction.'
— Tony Wheeler

LONELY PLANET PUBLICATIONS

Australia
PO Box 617, Hawthorn 3122, Victoria
tel: (03) 9819 1877 fax: (03) 9819 6459
e-mail: talk2us@lonelyplanet.com.au

USA
Embarcadero West, 155 Filbert St, Suite 251,
Oakland, CA 94607
tel: (510) 893 8555 TOLL FREE: 800 275-8555
fax: (510) 893 8563
e-mail: info@lonelyplanet.com

UK
10 Barley Mow Passage, Chiswick,
London W4 4PH
tel: (0181) 742 3161 fax: (0181) 742 2772
e-mail: 100413.3551@compuserve.com

France:
71 bis rue du Cardinal Lemoine, 75005 Paris
tel: 1 44 32 06 20 fax: 1 46 34 72 55
e-mail: 100560.415@compuserve.com

World Wide Web: http://www.lonelyplanet.com